contents

Delays and hold-ups

Call AA Roadwatch

or listen to local radio

to avoid delays on

your journey.

Despite ever-increasing levels of traffic, motorways are still the quickest means of getting from A to B. Nevertheless, a hold-up on a motorway can easily delay your journey for several hours. There are a number of ways of gleaning information about the stretches of motorway to avoid: by phone, radio and newspaper.

AA Roadwatch

This service provides up-to-the-minute information on traffic conditions, roadworks and the weather for the whole country. See page VI for numbers to call.

Radio

Frequent radio bulletins are issued by both the BBC and independent local radio stations about road and weather conditions, and likely hold-ups. By tuning into the local radio stations you can avoid delays and prepare to make changes to your route. However, local radio does not yet cover the entire country.

Daily checks

Carry out regular checks to make sure that you

and your car arrive safely.

Before you start every journey you should always ensure that:

- You check the dashboard warning lights before and after starting the engine
- There are no unusual noises once the engine is running
- All the lights are both clean and working
- The windscreen and all other windows are clean
- You have sufficient fuel for your journey

Weekly checks

Before you set out on a journey you should also ensure that:

- The engine oil level is correct, looking for obvious signs of leakage
- The coolant level is correct, checking the anti-freeze before the onset of winter
- The battery connections and terminals are clean and free from corrosion
- The brake (and clutch, if hydraulic) fluid is correct
- The tyres, including the spare, are properly inflated and not damaged
- The tyres are changed if the tread falls below 2mm
- The fan-belt is not worn or damaged, and that the tension is correct
- The windscreen wipers are clean and that the screen wash reservoir is full

Fit to drive

Are you fit to drive?

Food, tiredness, drink

and medicine all affect

your driving.

Many accidents are caused by one or more of the drivers involved being unfit to drive when the accident occurred. The most obvious reason for such accidents is alcohol; even the smallest quantity can affect driving. The only safe advice is: if you drive, don't drink – if you drink, don't drive. However, alcohol is just one of a number of factors that can make someone unfit to drive.

Tiredness

Some people become tired sooner than others, but the following are guidelines which you should aim to keep: for every three hours on the road, take 20 minutes rest; if possible, share the driving; limit yourself to a maximum of eight hours behind the wheel in any one day; and try to avoid driving at times when you would normally be asleep or resting. You should also avoid driving after hard exercise, a large meal and, of course, after consuming alcohol. Other factors which can contribute to tiredness are temperature inside the car and medication; a stuffy atmosphere – and some drugs – can induce drowsiness. If you are on medication, check with your doctor whether you should be driving at all. One final point: not driving during peak hours keeps delays to a minimum, reduces frustration and minimises journey time.

Driving abroad

Always ensure you know the specific legal requirements and road signs before you set out – and make sure your car conforms to such requirements. If you take an overnight ferry crossing you will probably be tired the next morning; do not set yourself too long a drive after arriving on the Continent. When you begin driving again after taking a break be especially careful to keep on the correct side of the road.

AA

MOTORIST'S ATLAS
BRITAIN

18th edition September 1995
17th edition September 1994
Reprinted January 1995
16th edition September 1993
Reprinted February 1994
15th edition September 1992
Reprinted November 1992
Reprinted March 1993
14th edition September 1991
13th edition September 1990
12th edition October 1989
11th edition October 1988
10th edition October 1987
9th edition October 1986
Reprinted March 1987
8th edition October 1985
7th edition October 1984
Reprinted May 1985
6th edition March 1984
5th edition January 1983
4th edition October 1981
3rd edition January 1981
2nd edition January 1980
1st edition April 1979

Revised version of atlas formerly known as *The Complete Atlas of Britain.*

Published by AA Publishing (a trading name of Automobile Association Developments Limited, whose registered office is Norfolk House, Priestley Road, Basingstoke, Hampshire RG24 9NY. Registered number 1878835).

Mapping produced by the Cartographic Department of The Automobile Association. This atlas has been compiled and produced from the Automaps database utilising electronic and computer technology.

ISBN 0 7495 1147 8

A CIP catalogue record for this book is available from the British Library.

Printed by Jarrolds and Sons Ltd, Norwich.

The contents of this atlas are believed to be correct at the time of printing. Nevertheless, the publishers cannot be held responsible for any errors or omissions, or for changes in the details given. They would welcome information to help keep this atlas up to date; please write to the Cartographic Editor, Publishing Division, The Automobile Association, Norfolk House, Priestley Road, Basingstoke, Hampshire RG24 9NY.

Information on National Parks provided by the Countryside Commission for England and the Countryside Council for Wales.
Information on National Scenic Areas in Scotland provided by the Scottish Natural Heritage.
Information on Forest Parks provided by the Forestry Commission.
The RSPB sites shown are a selection chosen by the Royal Society for the Protection of Birds.
National Trust properties shown are those open to the public as indicated in the handbooks of the National Trusts of England, Wales and Northern Ireland, and Scotland.

journey planning

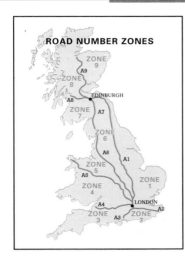

ROAD NUMBER ZONES

How to get there

Special route-planning maps on pages VI-XI enable you to devise a basic route before referring to the main pages of the atlas for greater detail.

Road classification

London is the hub for the spokes of roads numbered A1 to A6, Edinburgh the hub for A7, A8 and A9. Beginning with the A1, running north from London, the roads radiate clockwise from the capital: A2 runs roughly east, the A3 west, and so forth. The system has made the numbering of other roads very simple. Generally, the lower the subsequent number, the closer the road's starting point to London (or Edinburgh).

using the national grid

One of the unique features of AA mapping is the use of the National Grid System.

The National Grid

The National Grid covers Britain with an imaginary network of squares, using blue vertical lines called eastings and horizontal lines called northings. On the atlas pages these lines are numbered along the bottom and on the left-hand side.

The index

Each entry in the index is followed by a page number, two letters denoting an area on the map and a 4-figure grid reference. You will not need to use the two letters for simple navigation, but they come in useful if you want to use your map in relation to the rest of the country and other map series.

Quick reference

For quick reference, the four figures of the grid reference in the index are arranged so that the 1st and 3rd are in a bolder type than the 2nd and 4th. The 1st figure shows the number along the bottom of the grid, and the 3rd figure, the number up the left-hand side. These will indicate the square in which you will find the place name.

Pinpoint accuracy

However, to pinpoint a place more accurately you will also need to use the 2nd and 4th numbers. The second will tell you how many imaginary tenths along the bottom line to go from the first number, and the 4th will tell you how many tenths to go up from the third number. Where these two lines intersect, you will find your place name. For example: Skegness 51TF5663. Skegness is located on page 51 within grid square 56 in National Grid square TF. Its exact location is 5663.

Skegness **51**TF**5663**

Skegness is located on page **51**

within grid square **56**

in National Grid square TF

Its exact location is **5663**

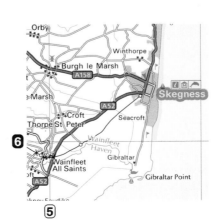

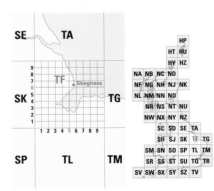

route planner

Planning your route

The route-planning maps on the following pages show principal routes throughout the country and pinpoint the major towns and cities. Detailed routes can be worked out from the maps in the main atlas section of this book. You may find it useful to make a note of road numbers and route directions. You are advised to avoid driving through towns and built-up areas whenever possible, even if such routes appear to be more direct on the map. Delays caused by traffic lights, one-way systems and other road-users will almost certainly be encountered in such areas.

The length of the journey is a fundamental consideration when planning a route. The mileage chart on the inside back cover gives the distances between main towns and can be used to make a rough calculation of the total journey length. The time needed for the journey can then be estimated.

Motorway	
Primary route dual carriageway	
Primary route single carriageway	
Other A roads	

```
0         10        20        30 miles
0    10   20   30   40   50 km
```

SCALE approx 1:1,400,000

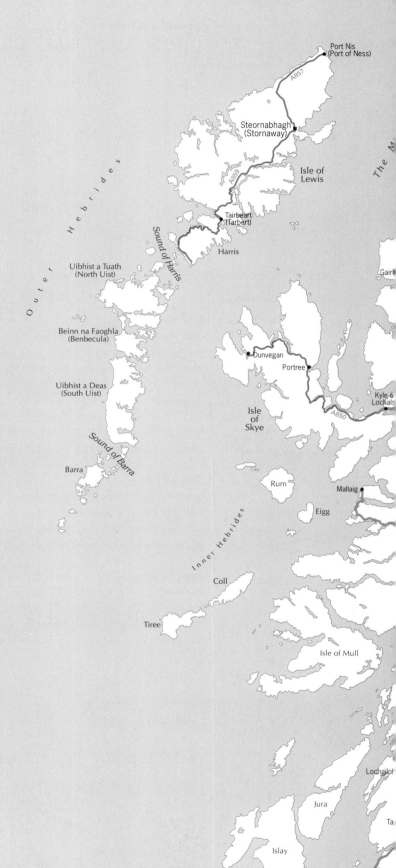

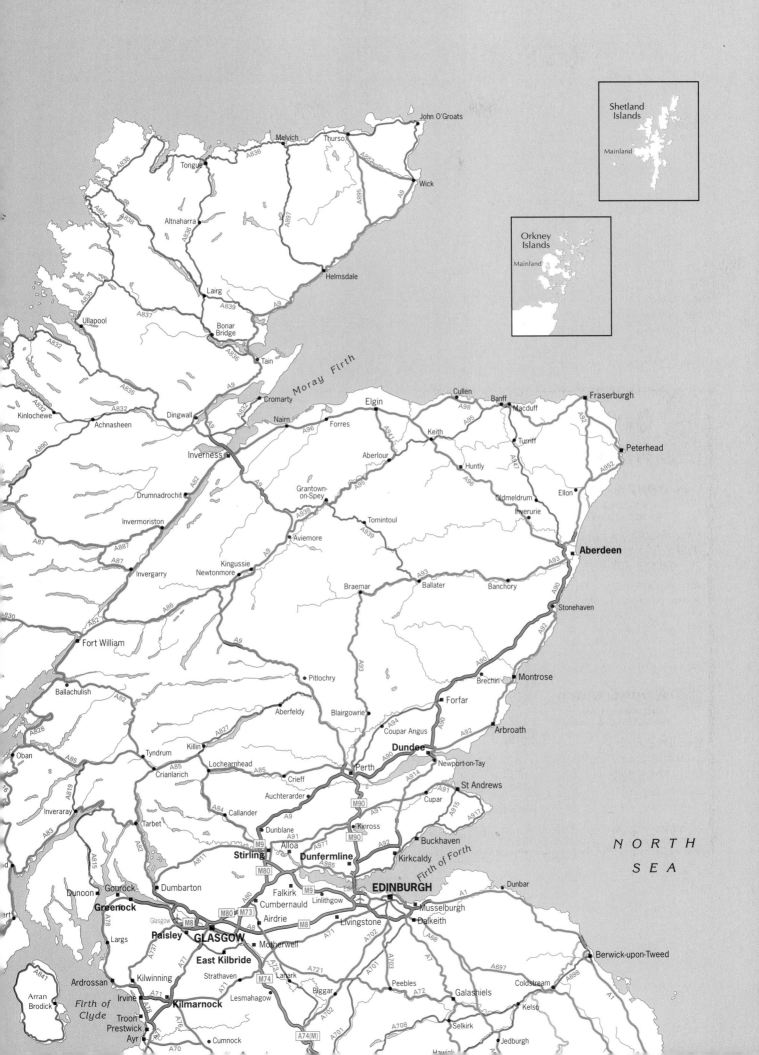

NORTH SEA

Ashlington

Whitley Bay
Tynemouth
South Shields
NEWCASTLE UPON TYNE
sforth
shead
Stanley
Jarrow
Sunderland
hester-le-
Street
Durham
A1(M)
Spennymoor
Hartlepool
nd
Stockton-
on-Tees
Middlesbrough
Darlington
Scotch
Corner
Whitby
Northallerton
Scalby
Scarborough
Thirsk
Pickering
Filey
Ripon
Malton
Bridlington
Harrogate
Driffield
Otley
York
Wetherby
Market
Weighton
Beverley
ngley
Shipley
LEEDS
Selby
HULL
Hessle
ghouse
Goole
Barton-upon-
Humber
Dewsbury
Pontefract
Immingham
ersfield
Wakefield
Thorne
Scunthorpe
Grimsby
Barnsley
Doncaster
Brigg
Cleethorpes
Rotherham
Bawtry
Gainsborough
SHEFFIELD
Market
Rasen
Louth
Dronfield
Worksop
Mablethorpe
Staveley
Chesterfield
Lincoln
Horncastle
akewell
Skegness
Matlock
Alfreton
Mansfield
NT
Ashbourne
Ilkeston
Newark-
on-Trent
The
Wash
Sheringham
Cromer
DERBY
NOTTINGHAM
Sleaford
Boston
Hunstanton
North Walsham
Long Eaton
Grantham
King's
Lynn
Fakenham
Burton upon
Trent
Loughborough
Melton
Mowbray
Spalding
East
Dereham
Norwich
Caister-on-Sea
Ashby-de-
la-Zouch
ichfield
Bourne
Wisbech
Swaffham
Great Yarmouth
Tamworth
LEICESTER
Oakham
Stamford
Downham
Market
March
Attleborough
Lowestoft
Hinckley
Wigston
Peterborough
Bungay
Beccles
Nuneaton
Market
Harborough
Chatteris
Diss
MINGHAM
Corby
Kettering
Ely
Thetford
Southwold
COVENTRY
Huntingdon
Bury St Edmunds
Leamington Spa

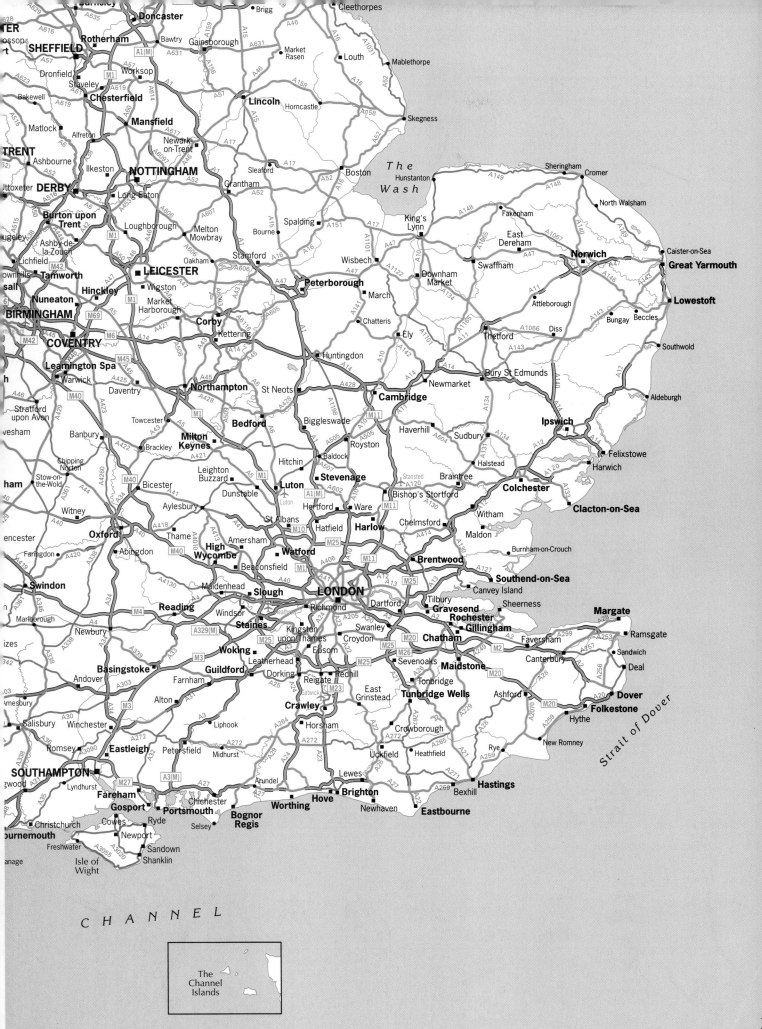

Classes of signs

A consistent and comprehensive set of road signs provides information and warning to the motorist.

These are based on an internationally agreed system, with variations specific to Britain. Signs which give orders and prohibitions are usually circular, and if the background is blue, their instructions are compulsory. Triangular signs carry warning messages and rectangular signs give information.

There are three shapes of road signs: triangles, circles and rectangles. Red triangles warn. Red circles prohibit.

Blue circles give positive instruction. Blue rectangles give general information. Green rectangles are used for direction signs on primary routes.

Junctions and roundabouts

Warning signs lead up to a junction or roundabout and provide information about the nature of the junction.

Warning signs will probably be followed by a give way or stop sign. The road markings at a stop sign consist of solid white lines identifying the farthest point to which you may drive. It is obligatory to stop and look to see that it is possible to enter the major road in safety. The give way sign has different road markings – a pair of white dashed lines – and drivers are required to delay joining the main road until it is safe to do so. If the main road is clear, there is no obligation to stop completely.

| *Countdown markers approaching a major junction* | *Crossroads* | *Side road* | *T-junction* | *Staggered junction* |

| *Stop sign* | *Give way* | *No vehicles* | *Distance to STOP sign* | *Distance to GIVE WAY sign* | *Roundabout* | *Mini-roundabout, give way to vehicles from the right* | *Advance warning of no through road* | *No through road* |

The road ahead

Advance warning of how the road ahead is laid out helps a driver plan his/her approach.

The information given is generally precise about which side of the road is affected or which direction the road will take. The triangular signs give warnings, the circular signs must be obeyed.

| *Bend to left* | *Double bend, first to left* | *Bend to right* | *Double bend, first to right* | *Road hump or series of road humps ahead* | *Worded warning sign* | *Dual carriageway ends* | *Axle weight limit (in tonnes)* | *Steep incline* | *No vehicles over height shown* |

| *No goods vehicles over maximum gross weight shown (in tonnes)* | *Steep decline* | *Sharp deviation* | *Traffic merging with equal priority from left* | *Road narrows on left* | *Traffic merging with equal priority from right* | *Road narrows on right* | *Road narrows on both sides* |

road signs

Hazards ahead

The signs warning of hazards ahead should never be ignored, and provide valuable information about what is round the next corner or just ahead.

| *Pedestrian crossing ahead* | *Hospital ahead with accident and emergency facilities* | *Slippery road* | *Cattle grid* | *Road works ahead* | *Children* | *Wild animals* | *Wild horses* | *Cattle* | *Other danger* |

| *Uneven road* | *Traffic signals ahead* | *Children going to or from school* | *Stop at sign* | *School crossing patrol ahead* | *School crossing patrol; vehicles must stop* |

| *Hump-backed bridge* | *Opening or swing bridge* | *Risk of falling rocks* | *Quayside or river bank* | *Overhead electric cable* |

Traffic behaviour

Information about the way traffic should be organised is given in a series of specific signs.

These signs govern the speed and general approach at any situation. They are signs which must be obeyed.

| *No stopping (clearway)* | *National speed limits apply* | *No U-turns* | *Give priority to vehicles from opposite direction* | *No overtaking* | *Motor vehicles prohibited except for access* | *No entry for vehicles* | *Two-way traffic* | *No right turn* | *No left turn* |

| *Turn left ahead* | | *Turn left* | *Pass either side to reach same destination* | *Ahead only* | *Keep left* |

Level crossings

There are several different types of level crossing. Many have barriers which may cross half or all of the road.

Level crossings may be worked automatically by the approach of the train or they may be operated by an attendant. When flashing lights and bell signals are in operation you should not pass. If you are already crossing when the amber lights flash and the bells start, keep crossing.

| *Level crossing without gate or barrier* | *Level crossing with gate or barrier* | *Level crossing without gate or barrier* | *Countdown markers* | *Alternate flashing lights means YOU MUST STOP* |

M1 London–Leeds

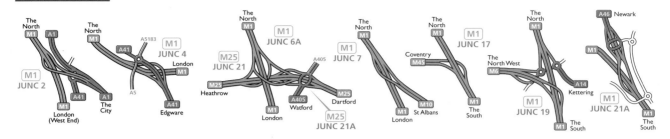

M1 London–Leeds   M2 Rochester–Faversham   M3 Sunbury–Southampton

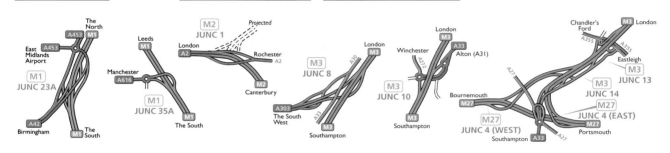

M4 London–South Wales   M5 Birmingham–Exeter

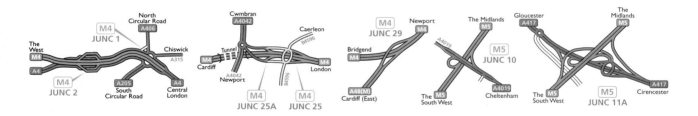

M5 Birmingham–Exeter   M6 Rugby–Carlisle

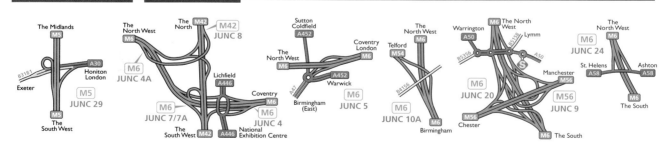

M6 Rugby–Carlisle   M8 Edinburgh–Bishopton

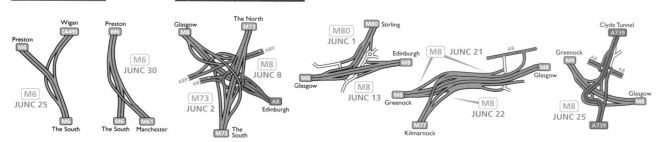

motorways – restricted junctions

Diagrams of selected motorway junctions which have entry and exit restrictions

M8 Edinburgh–Bishopton   M9 Edinburgh–Dunblane   M11 London–Cambridge

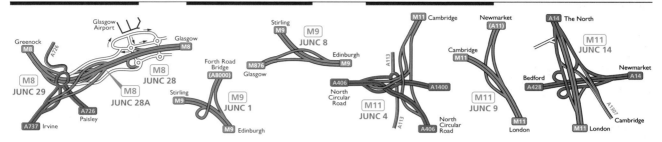

M20 Swanley–Folkestone   M25 London Orbital   M27 Cadnam–Portsmouth M40 London–Birmingham

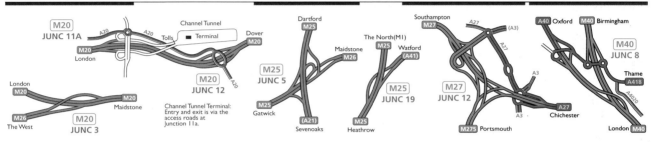

M42 Bromsgrove–Measham   M56 North Cheshire Motorway   M62 Liverpool–Humberside

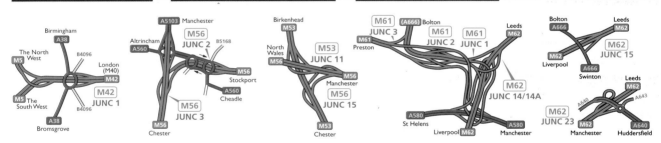

M63 Greater Manchester   M73 East of Glasgow M74 Glasgow–Gretna

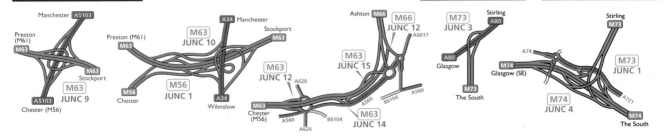

M74, A74(M) Glasgow–Gretna M80 Glasgow–Stirling M90 Forth Road Bridge–Perth A1(M) Scotch Corner–Tyneside

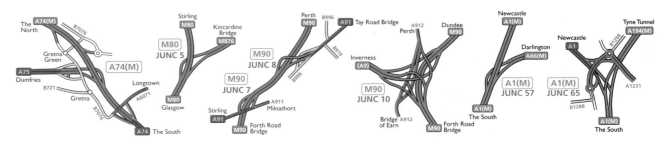

XV

The distances between towns on the mileage chart are given to the nearest mile, and are measured along the normal AA recommended routes. It should be noted that AA recommended routes do not necessarily follow the shortest distance between places but are based on the quickest travelling time, making maximum use of motorways.

Example: Norwich – Preston = 235 miles

Mileage chart (distances in miles, read from the diagonal town label)

Town	Distances to preceding towns (in chart order)
Aberdeen	
Aberystwyth	470
Barnstaple	606 222
Birmingham	433 123 178
Brighton	608 290 202 170
Bristol	516 132 100 88 169
Cambridge	464 215 267 98 120 171
Cardiff	536 118 137 108 205 48 205
Carlisle	234 236 372 199 374 282 259 302
Carmarthen	520 50 199 169 266 109 266 68 286
Colchester	516 289 292 171 112 195 48 231 310 292
Dorchester	598 214 94 170 117 62 180 129 364 191 208
Dover	589 325 272 208 81 206 124 241 401 303 116 201
Edinburgh	125 335 471 298 474 381 336 401 99 385 388 463 461
Exeter	589 206 55 161 172 83 250 121 355 182 275 55 244 454
Fort William	157 446 582 409 585 492 469 512 210 496 520 574 611 133 566
Glasgow	148 334 469 296 472 379 356 399 97 383 408 461 499 46 454 102
Gloucester	481 110 126 53 155 36 150 65 247 127 171 118 192 346 110 458 344
Guildford	566 227 174 128 44 106 91 142 331 203 103 98 97 431 147 542 428 101
Hereford	484 79 143 56 187 53 153 58 250 86 203 135 224 349 127 461 347 31 133
Holyhead	462 105 341 168 344 251 260 228 156 334 333 370 327 325 439 325 216 301 156
Hull	360 228 322 141 282 232 140 252 171 313 191 314 264 232 306 382 268 197 240 201 220
Inverness	106 496 632 459 634 542 519 561 259 545 570 624 661 157 616 65 174 507 592 510 487 431
Kendal	281 190 326 153 328 236 253 256 47 239 319 318 355 146 310 258 144 201 286 204 181 165 307
Leeds	328 174 302 121 262 212 148 231 123 223 199 294 272 200 286 333 220 177 220 180 165 60 302 133
Lincoln	389 199 274 88 215 185 94 204 183 266 146 262 219 261 259 394 280 150 172 153 205 48 443 177 73
Liverpool	360 111 274 101 277 184 193 204 126 167 267 266 303 225 258 336 223 149 234 119 102 129 386 79 74 141
Maidstone	550 286 233 169 66 167 85 202 382 264 77 162 41 422 205 573 459 153 58 185 330 225 622 316 234 180 264
Manchester	355 131 261 89 264 172 161 191 121 181 212 253 291 220 246 331 218 137 222 140 122 99 380 74 44 85 252
Middlesbrough	275 244 359 178 320 269 200 289 94 294 252 351 325 147 344 280 191 235 278 238 235 89 307 83 64 125 145 286 115
Newcastle upon Tyne	236 277 392 211 352 302 233 322 59 326 284 384 357 108 378 240 153 267 310 270 268 145 267 92 97 157 177 318 147 39
Northampton	483 172 211 55 132 115 54 162 249 223 119 155 348 509 155 459 346 79 90 111 217 153 509 267 63 201 138 107 217 310 342
Norwich	488 277 329 159 169 233 63 266 283 328 59 242 173 360 313 493 380 212 161 215 305 151 543 277 173 103 241 134 185 224 257 116
Nottingham	394 160 235 54 195 145 87 165 189 226 138 227 218 266 219 399 286 110 153 113 174 93 449 149 74 36 108 179 71 130 163 66 119
Oxford	505 159 170 68 109 74 100 109 271 171 124 115 146 370 154 482 368 48 67 80 239 190 531 225 171 128 173 107 160 228 260 43 143 103
Penzance	699 316 109 271 283 361 485 292 385 166 356 564 109 676 562 219 258 237 433 415 725 419 395 368 367 355 452 484 305 422 328 264 315 329 130
Perth	86 384 520 347 522 430 381 449 147 433 433 512 549 42 504 103 62 395 480 398 375 277 114 195 245 306 273 510 268 191 153 396 405 311 420 613
Peterborough	435 205 264 87 158 158 38 194 230 255 89 206 162 307 248 440 327 140 116 143 225 111 490 224 120 50 108 123 132 171 204 43 77 58 86 358 352
Plymouth	631 247 61 203 215 125 292 162 397 224 317 98 287 496 45 607 494 151 190 168 365 346 657 351 327 299 299 248 286 384 416 236 354 256 195 85 545 289
Portsmouth	591 245 161 153 49 97 135 160 356 221 148 75 141 456 133 567 453 119 47 151 324 285 616 310 265 217 258 213 310 342 150 246 322 354 134 95 291 227 354 268
Preston	324 147 283 110 285 193 211 213 89 196 276 275 312 189 267 300 186 138 243 161 138 123 349 43 68 135 36 273 32 107 139 160 235 107 183 376 237 182 308 268
Salisbury	551 186 117 123 85 54 139 101 317 162 166 40 159 416 90 527 414 74 62 106 285 254 576 270 235 192 218 120 206 292 324 107 201 167 63 201 464 164 133 43 227
Sheffield	364 167 272 91 233 183 123 202 171 264 174 264 256 236 257 381 268 148 191 151 158 66 431 125 36 47 80 217 38 100 132 103 147 44 141 366 281 94 298 235 83 205
Shrewsbury	415 74 221 48 224 131 140 110 181 112 214 213 251 280 205 391 278 97 142 52 104 163 441 134 125 66 212 70 189 221 98 202 86 121 315 329 130 246 207 91 166 114
Southampton	572 226 140 134 63 76 131 141 337 202 158 54 152 437 112 548 434 100 49 132 305 291 597 291 237 213 239 113 227 294 327 110 193 170 66 223 485 157 155 21 248 23 207 187
Stoke-on-Trent	389 115 221 48 224 131 140 151 155 213 214 213 251 258 254 206 366 252 97 182 100 123 130 415 109 93 92 57 212 45 163 196 98 174 121 315 303 102 246 207 66 166 53 38 188
Stranraer	240 344 479 307 482 389 366 409 186 85 355 440 186 509 122 464 350 84 355 335 279 466 228 202 164 356 391 297 380 573 154 337 505 465 197 424 278 288 446 263
Taunton	557 174 50 129 154 52 219 89 323 150 224 422 35 534 420 77 446 358 335 279 272 583 272 185 291 272 585 230 291 233 470 228 202 164 356 391 297 380 573 154 337 505 465 197 424 278 288 446 263
York	321 200 315 134 276 226 157 245 116 250 208 307 281 131 300 326 213 191 238 194 191 38 376 90 24 81 101 242 71 50 90 146 181 87 184 409 238 127 341 278 95 248 56 145 250 119 224 267
LONDON	548 238 216 120 59 120 60 155 314 217 62 129 78 413 200 524 411 103 30 135 282 188 574 268 199 142 216 39 203 255 288 68 115 131 56 310 462 86 241 75 225 88 168 163 80 163 421 168 212

map symbols

motoring information

Motorway with number		Vehicle ferry – Great Britain	
Motorway junction with and without number		Vehicle ferry – Continental	
Motorway junction with limited access		Hovercraft ferry	
Motorway service area		Airport	
Motorway and junction under construction		Heliport	
Primary route single/dual carriageway		Railway line/in tunnel	
Primary route service area		Railway station and level crossing	
Primary route destination		Tourist railway	
Other A road single/dual carriageway		AA Shop	
B road single/dual carriageway		AA telephone	
Unclassified road single/dual carriageway		BT telephone in isolated places	
Roundabout		Urban area/village	
Interchange		Spot height in metres	
Narrow primary, other A or B road with passing places (Scotland)		River, canal, lake	
Road under construction		Sandy beach	
Road tunnel		County/regional boundary	
Steep gradient (arrows point downhill)		National boundary	
Road toll		Page overlap and number	
Distance in miles between symbols			

tourist information

Tourist Information Centre		Roman antiquity	
Tourist Information Centre (seasonal)		Prehistoric monument	
Abbey, cathedral or priory		Battle site with year	
Ruined abbey, cathedral or priory		Steam centre (railway)	
Castle		Cave	
Historic house		Windmill	
Museum or art gallery		Golf course	
Industrial interest		County cricket ground	
Garden		Rugby Union national ground	
Arboretum		International athletics ground	
Country park		Horse racing	
Agricultural showground		Show jumping/ equestrian circuit	
Theme park		Motor racing circuit	
Zoo		Coastal launching site	
Wildlife collection – mammals		Ski slope – natural	
Wildlife collection – birds		Ski slope – artificial	
Aquarium		National Trust property	
Nature reserve		National Trust property Scotland	
RSPB site		Other places of interest	
Forest drive		Boxed symbols indicate attractions within urban areas	
National trail		National Park (England & Wales)	
Viewpoint		National Scenic Area (Scotland)	
Picnic site		Forest Park	
Hill-fort		Heritage Coast	

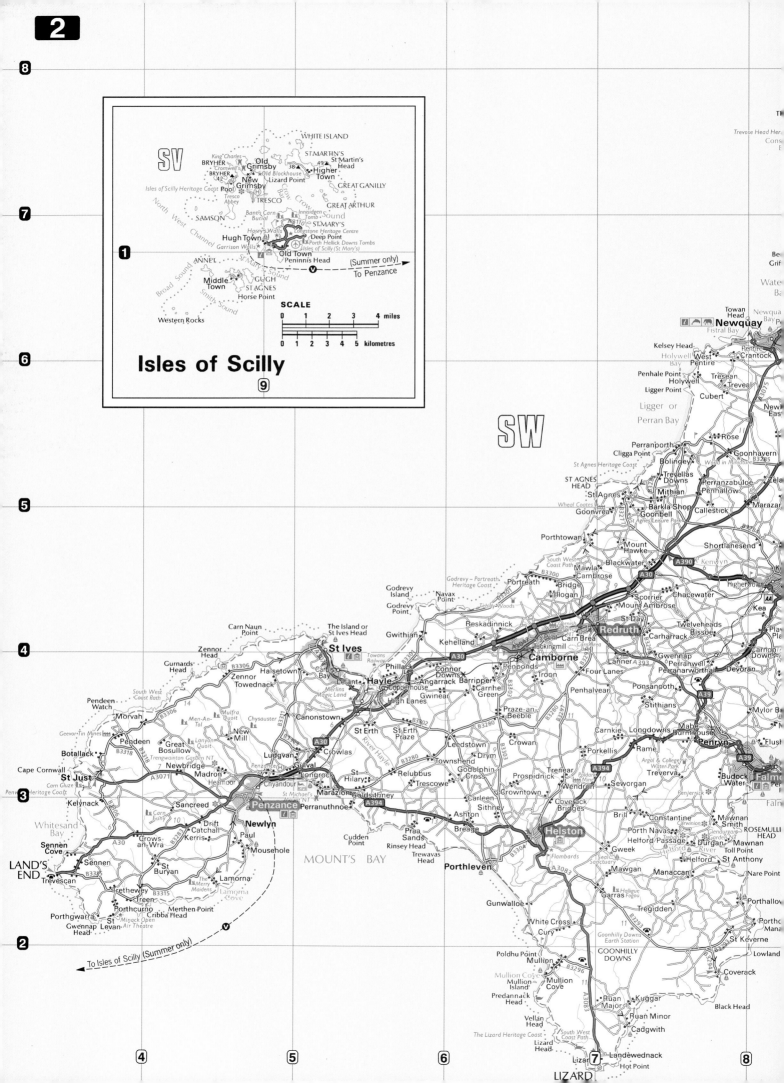

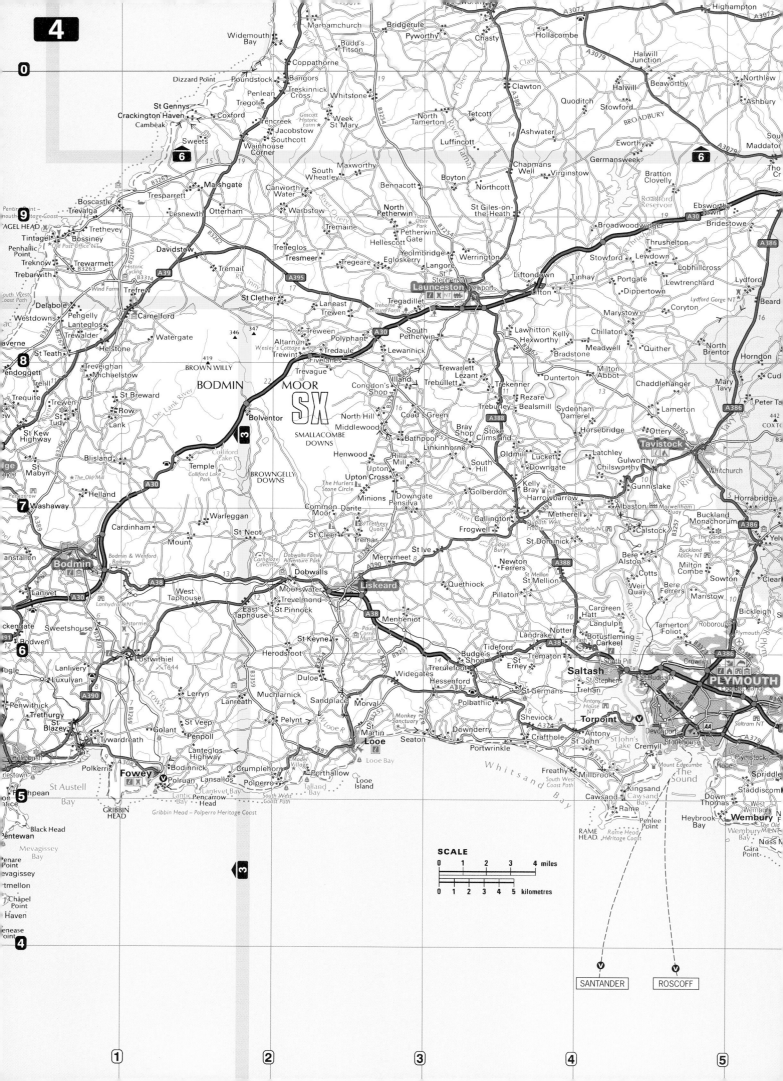

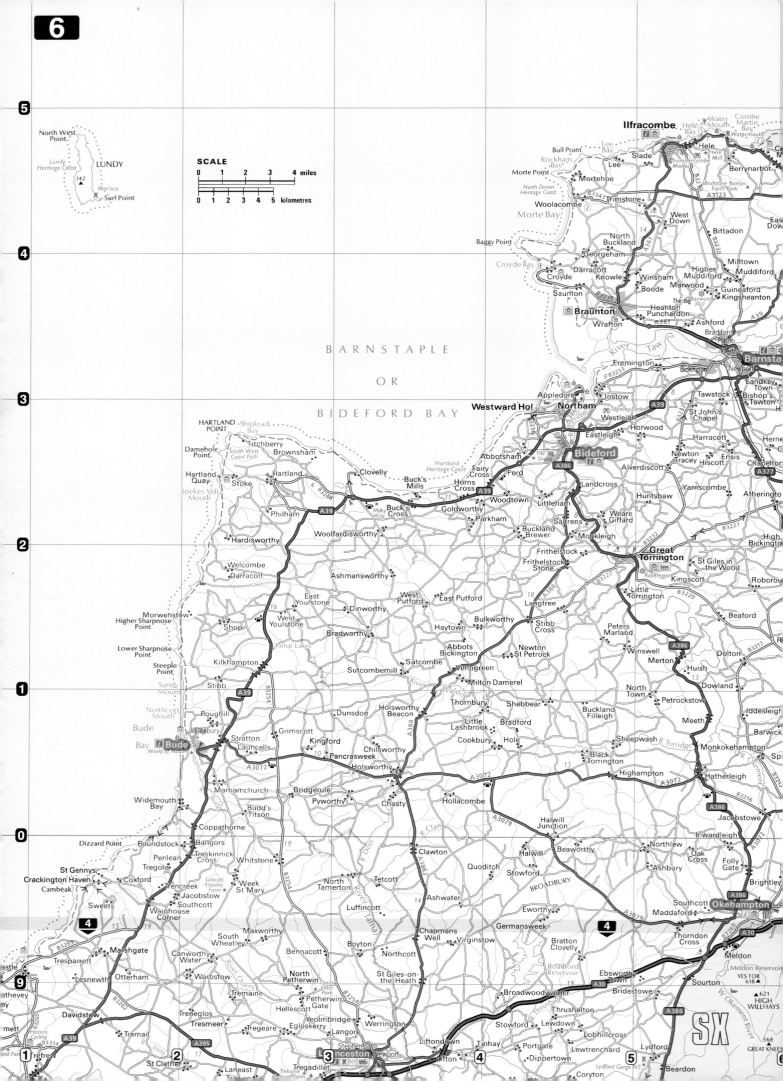

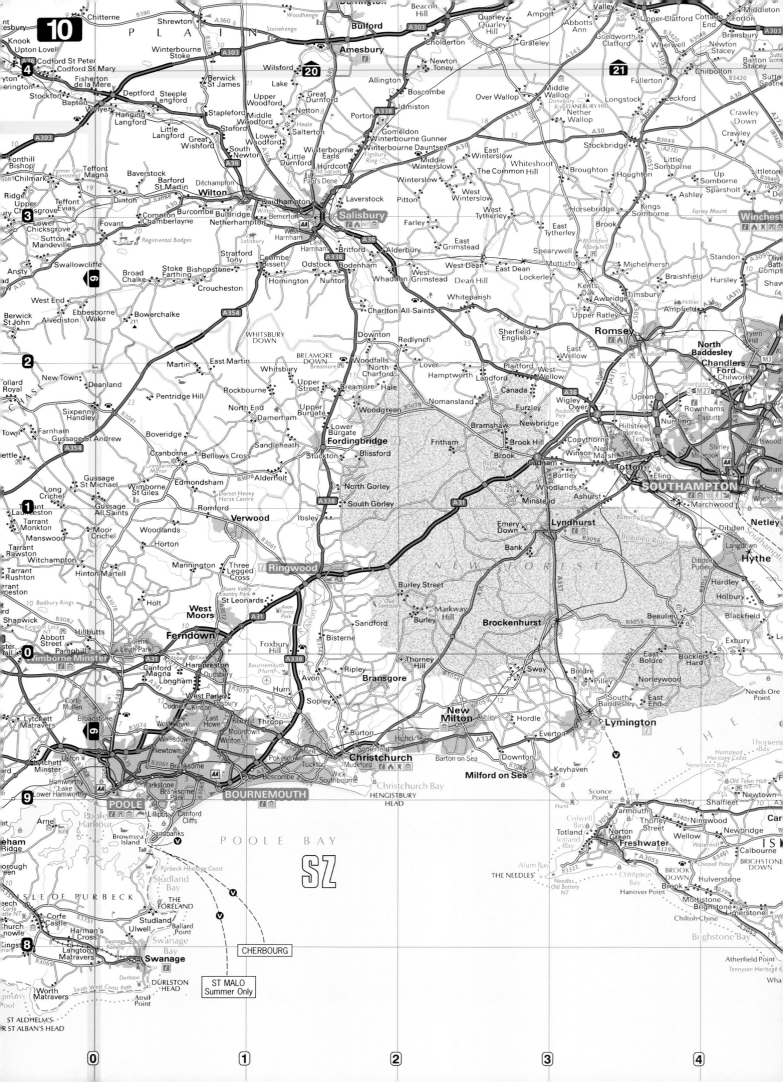

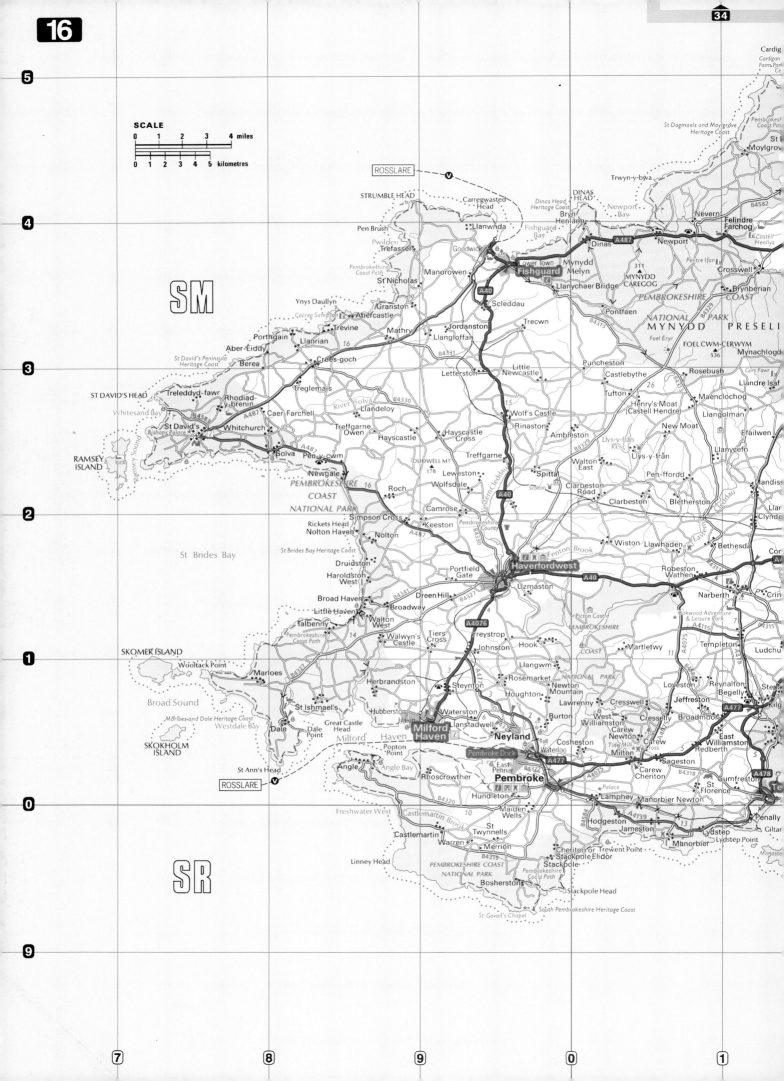

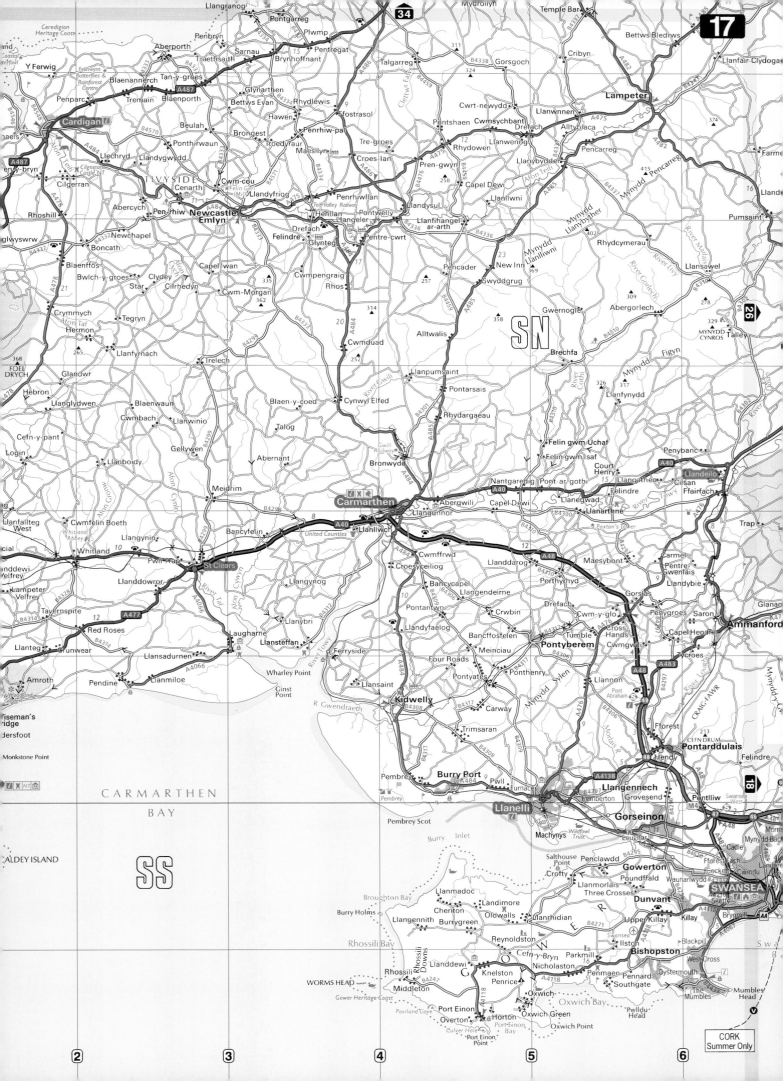

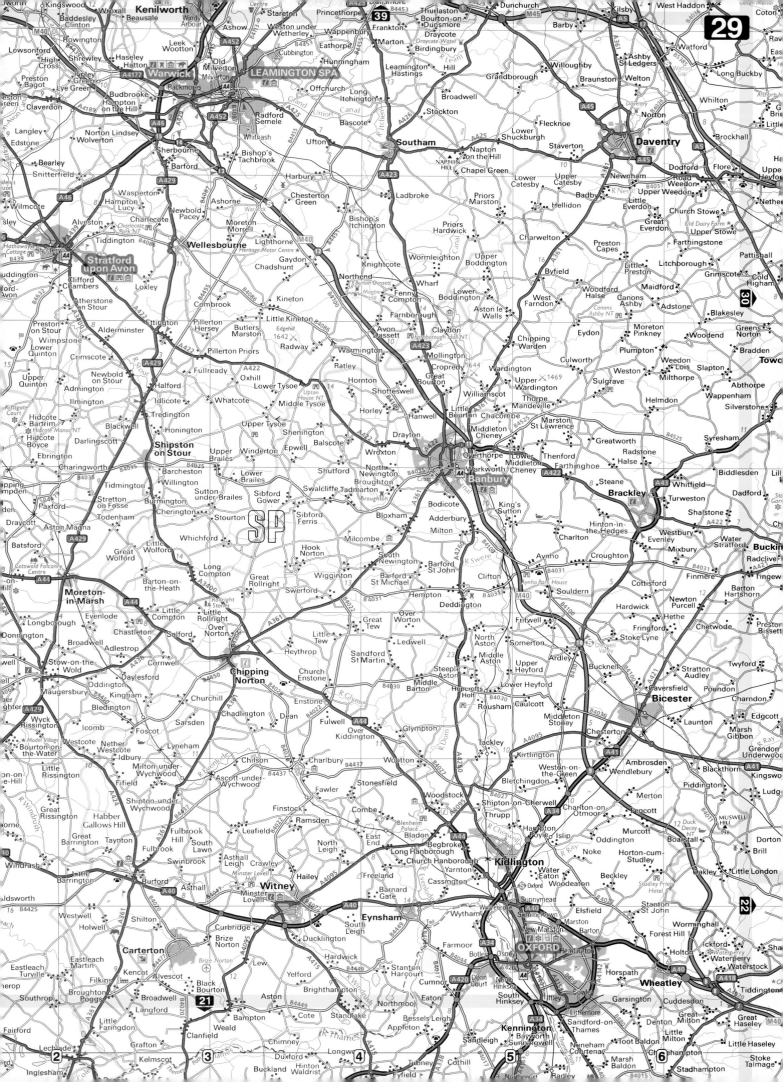

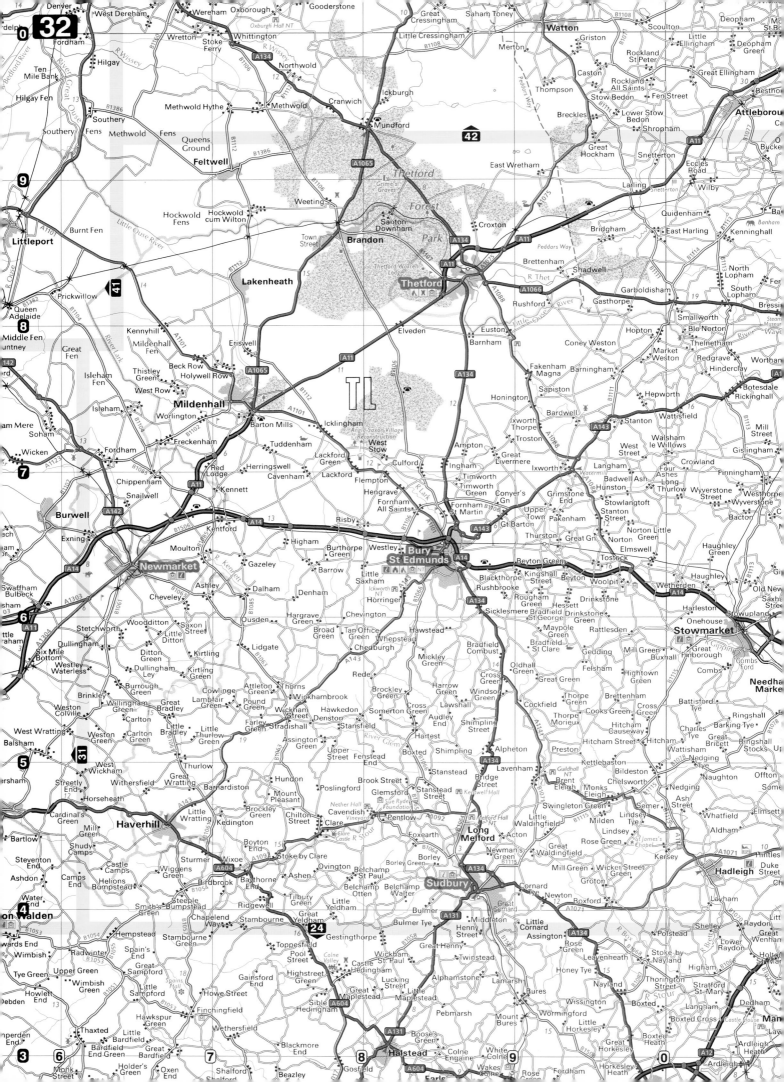

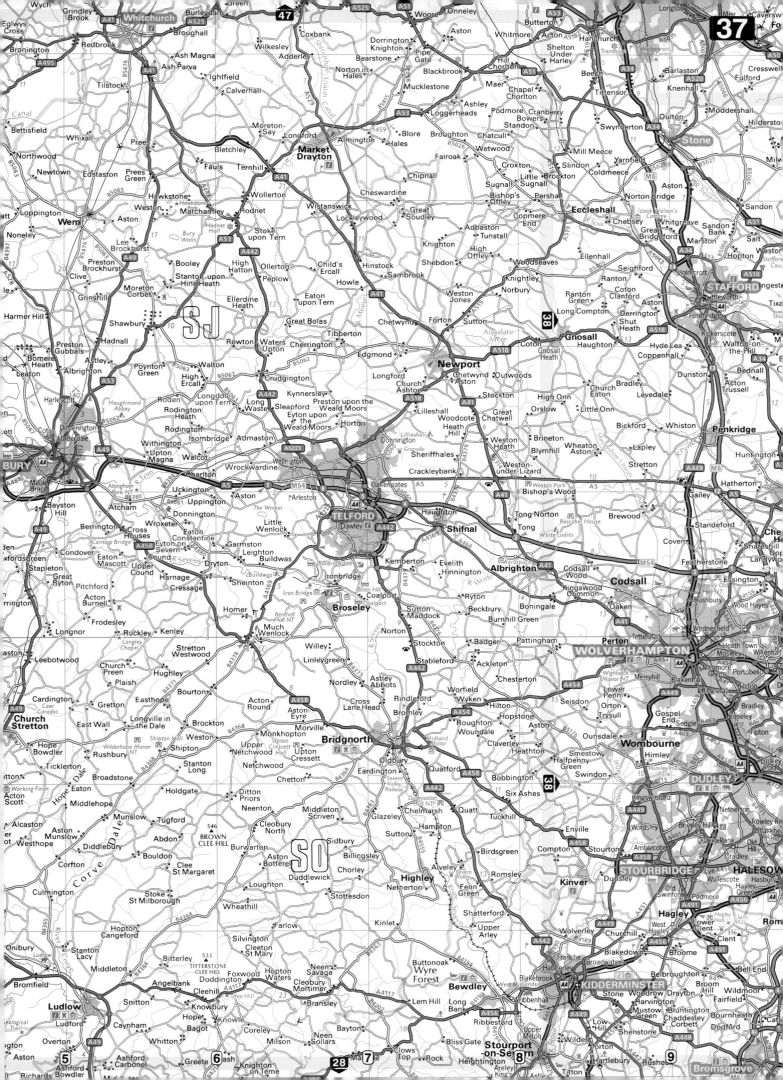

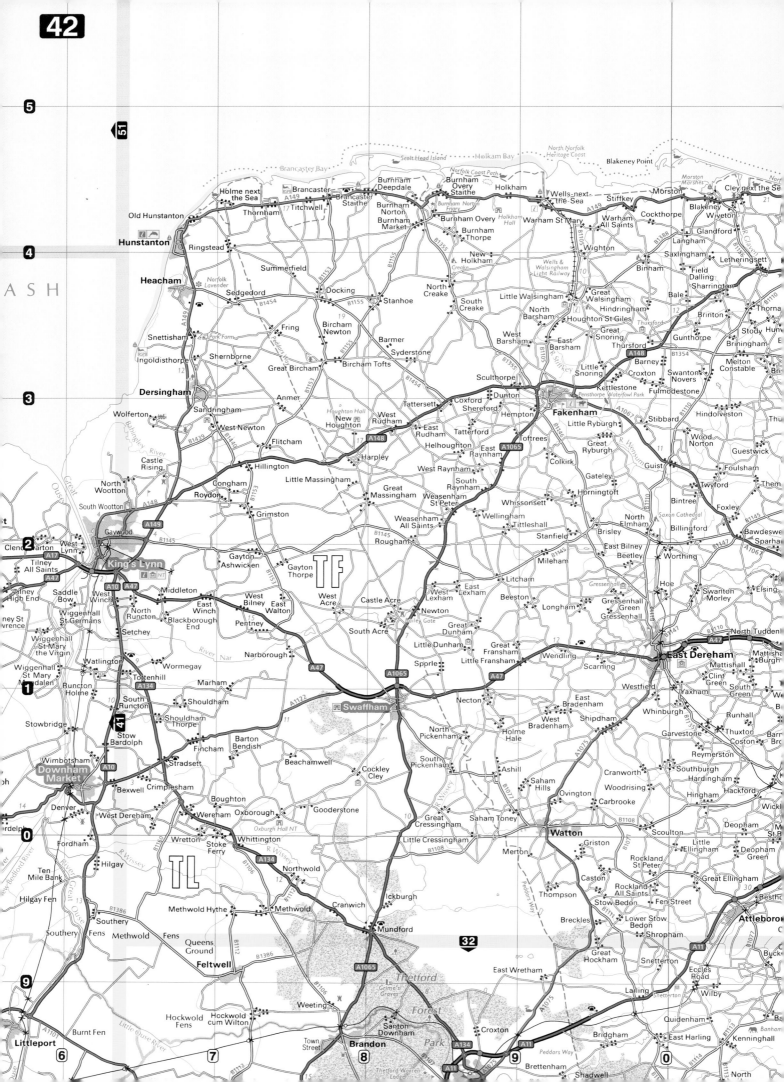

SCALE

0 1 2 3 4 miles

0 1 2 3 4 5 kilometres

Sheringham West Runton East Runton
Weybourne
Cromer
Kelling Upper Sheringham Beeston Regis Overstrand
Bodham Aylmerton Sidestrand
West Beckham East Beckham Felbrigg Northrepps Trimingham
Gresham Crossdale Street
Baconsthorpe Metton Southrepps Gimingham
Hempstead Susted Hanworth Roughton Mundesley
Plumstead Thurgarton Lower Street Paston
Edgefield Green Matlaske Aldborough Thorpe Market Trunch Knapton Bacton
Little Barningham Wickmere Bradfield Edingthorpe Walcott
Saxthorpe Erpingham Suffield Antingham Happisburgh
Calthorpe Colby Swafield Witton Ridlington Whimpwell Green
Itteringham Banningham North Walsham Edingthorpe Green Happisburgh Common
Ingworth Felmingham Meeting House Hill Honing Lessingham Hempstead
Blickling Tuttington Briggate East Ruston Ingham Corner
Aylsham Burgh next Aylsham Stalham Ingham Waxham
Marsham Swanton Abbot Worstead Dilham Calthorpe Street Sea Palling
Oxnead Smallburgh Hickling
Brampton Lamas Tunstead Sutton Hickling Green Horsey
Buxton Market Street Wood Street
Buxton Heath Stratton Strawless Neatishead Catfield
Hevingham Irstead Potter Heigham Winterton-on-Sea
Horstead Coltishall Ludham Bastwick Martham
Hainford Belaugh Hoveton Repps
Frettenham Wroxham Upper Street Hemsby
Alderford Felthorpe St Helena Horning Upper Street Thurne Rollesby Ormesby St Michael Scratby
Newton St Faith Woodbastwick Clippesby Burgh St Margaret California
Morton Attlebridge Crostwick Ranworth Pilson Green Ormesby St Margaret
Weston Longville Horsford Horsham Spixworth Rackheath Salhouse Cargate Billockby Thrigby Filby Mautby Caister-on-Sea
Ringland St Faith Panxworth South Walsham Upton West End West Caister
Taverham Drayton Catton New Rackheath Little Plumstead Burlingham Green Stokesby Runham
Costessey Thorpe End Great Plumstead Hemblington North Burlingham Acle
Marlingford New Costessey Helsdon Witton Lingwood Moulton St Mary Damgate THE BROADS GREAT YARMOUTH
Bawburgh Colney Thorpe St Andrew Blofield Beighton Tunstall Southtown
NORWICH Brundall Strumpshaw Halvergate Burgh Castle Gorleston on Sea
Hethersett Eaton Postwick South Burlingham Berney Arms Bradwell
Keswick Trowse Newton Kirby Bedon Buckenham Freethorpe
Cringleford Caister St Edmund Surlingham Wickhampton Belton
Wymondham Little Melton Arminghall Bramerton Hassingham Freethorpe Common
Ketteringham Dunston Framingham Pigot Rockland St Mary Cantley Reedham Fritton
Swardeston Upper Stoke Framingham Earl Claxton Limpenhoe Hopton on Sea
East Carleton Stoke Holy Cross Yelverton Carlton St Peter Langley Street Hardley Street
Mulbarton Howe Poringland Bergh Apton Thurton Chedgrave Norton Subcourse St Olaves Somerleyton Corton
Bracon Ash Shotesham Brooke Loddon Thorpe Herringfleet Blundeston
Swainsthorpe Hawe's Green Hales Haddiscoe
Silfield Wreningham Newton Flotman Kirstead Green Mundham Thurlton Ravingham
Spooner Row Saxlingham Thorpe Seething Ravingham Wheatacre Oulton
Ashwellthorpe Hapton Saxlingham Nethergate Thwaite St Mary Kirby Cane Maypole Green Toft Monks Aldeby Burgh St Peter Oulton Broad
Fundenhall Tacolneston Saxlingham Green Woodton Stockton Gillingham LOWESTOFT
Tasburgh Hempnall Hedenham Broome Geldeston Worlingham BECCLES Kirkley
Bunwell Street Forncett St Mary Upper Tasburgh Topcroft Ellingham Kirby Row Barnby Pakefield
Forncett End Tharston Hempnall Green Topcroft Street Ditchingham Shipmeadow North Cove Carlton Colville
Aslacton Morningthorpe St Michael Bungay Mettingham Barsham
Great Moulton Long Stratton Shelton Denton Ringsfield Mutford Gisleham
New Buckenham High Green Hardwick Earsham Ilketshall St Andrew Ringsfield Corner Hulver Street Kessingland
Tibenham Tivetshall St Margaret Colegate End Alburgh Flixton Ilketshall St Margaret Rushmere Henstead
Tivetshall St Mary Pulham Market Homersfield Redenhall St Margaret South Elmham Sotterley Benacre
Gissing Pulham St Mary Starston Wortwell St Cross St Michael Shadingfield Benacre Ness

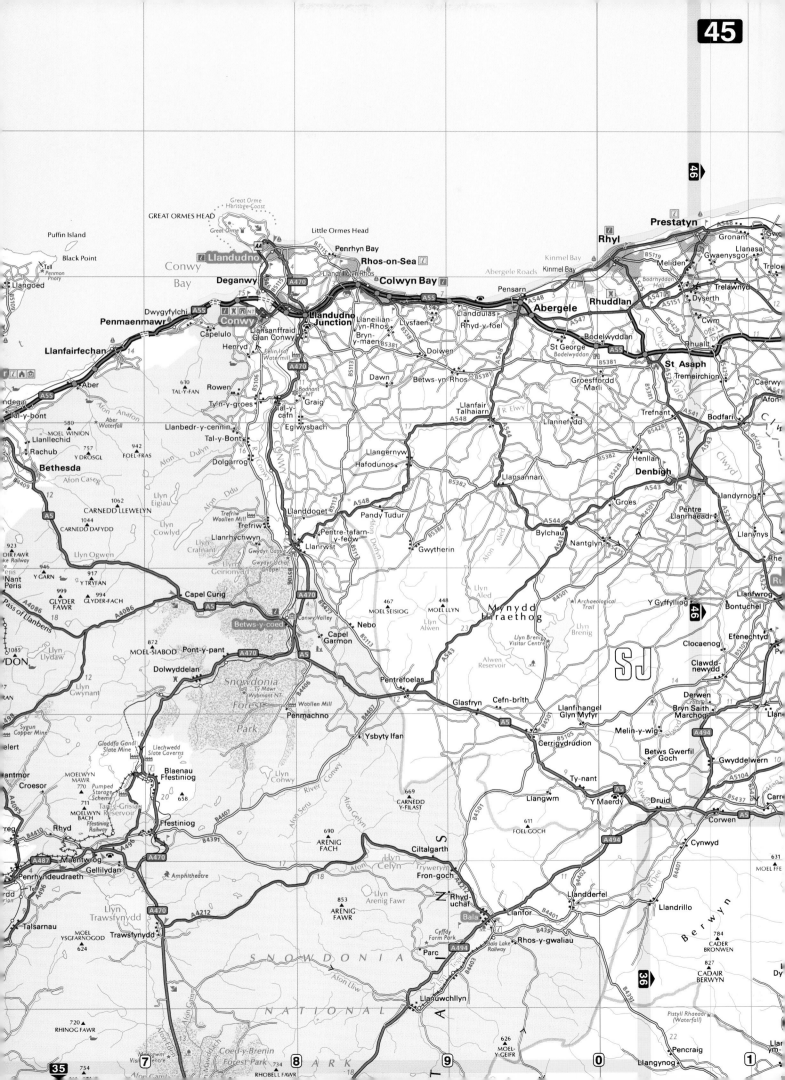

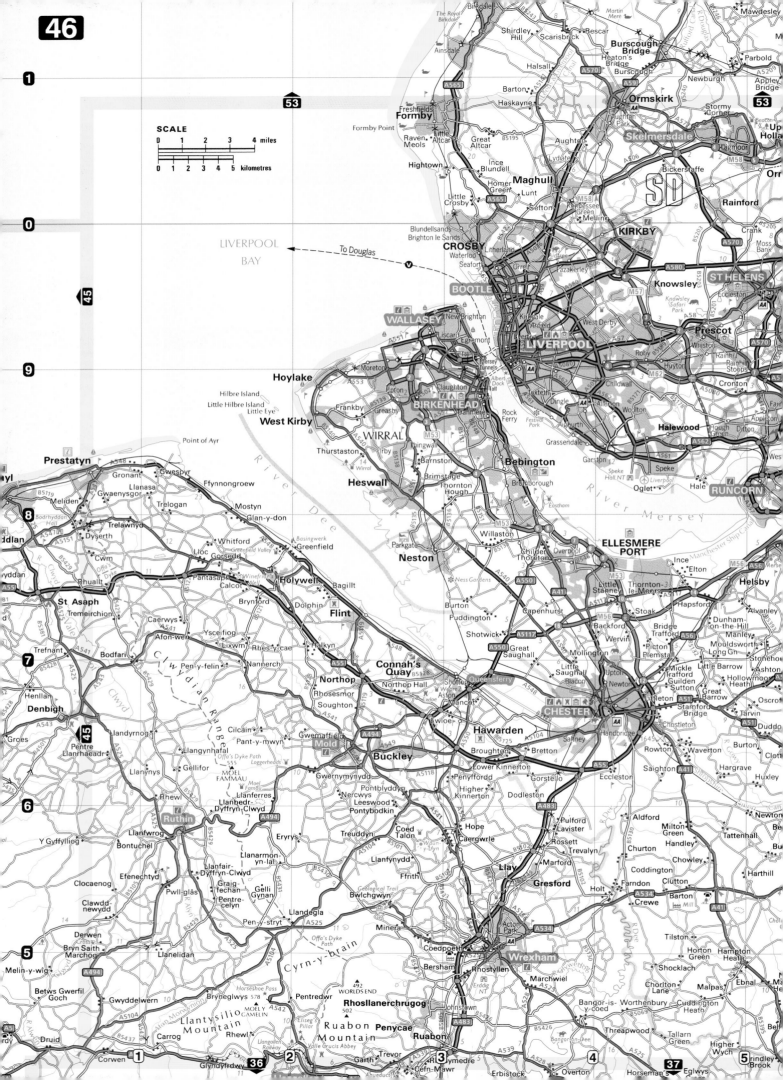

Isle of Man

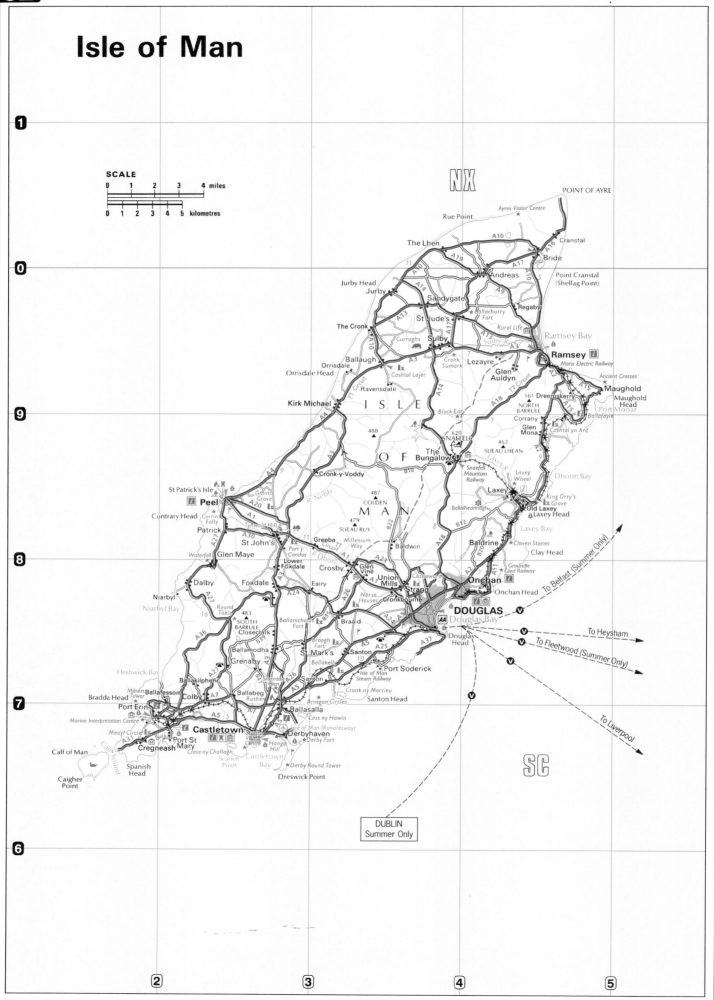

SCALE

0   1   2   3   4 miles

0 1 2 3 4 5 kilometres

NX

POINT OF AYRE

Ayres Visitor Centre

Rue Point

The Lhen

A10

Cranstal

A16

Bride

A17

Andreas

Point Cranstal
(Shellag Point)

Jurby Head

A10

A19

A9

Jurby

A14

Sandygate

Regaby

St Jude's

A13

Ballachurry Fort

The Cronk

A17

Rural Life

A3

Sulby

A10

Curraghs

Sulby R.

A3

Ramsey Bay

Ballaugh

A3

Cronk Sumark

Lezayre

A18

Ramsey

Orrisdale

Cashtal Lajer

Glen Auldyn

Manx Electric Railway

Orrisdale Head

Ravensdale

A14

561 Dreemskerry

Maughold

Kirk Michael

ISLE

Block Eary

NORTH BARRULE

Corrany

Maughold Head

A18

Cashtal yn Ard

Port Mooar

488

620 SNAEFELL

462 SLIEAU LHEAN

Glen Mona

Ballafayle

OF

The Bungalow

Snaefell Mountain Railway

Dhoon Bay

Cronk-y-Voddy

B10

Laxey Wheel

M A N

487 COLDEN

B22

Ballalheannagh

King Orry's Grave

Laxey

St Patrick's Isle

Grants Grave

A20

R. Neb

479 SLIEAU RUY

Old Laxey

Peel

Laxey Head

Contrary Head

Corrins Folly

Tynwald Hill

11

Greeba

Millenium Way

A18

B12

Laxey Bay

Patrick

A1

A30

St John's

Baldwin

Waterfall

Glen Maye

Port y Candas

Lower Foxdale

Crosby

A23

Glen Vine

Groudle Glen Railway

To Belfast (Summer Only)

Union Mills

Clay Head

Onchan

Dalby

Foxdale

Eairy

A26

Norse Houses

Strang

Onchan Head

Niarbyl

A27

A24

Cronkbourne

DOUGLAS

Niarbyl Bay

Round Table

483 SOUTH BARRULE

Braaid

A25

AA Douglas Bay

To Heysham

Closeclark

Ballanicholas Fort

St Mark's

Santon

Isle of Man Steam Railway

Douglas Head

To Fleetwood (Summer Only)

Fleshwick Bay

Ballamodha

Brough Fort

Ballakelly

Port Soderick

Grenaby

Ballabeg

Santon

Cronk ny Merriu

Santon Head

To Liverpool

Bradda Head

Milners Tower

Ballafesson

Colby

A7

Ballasalla

Arragon Circles

Cass ny Hawin

Port Erin

Marine Interpretation Centre

A5

Isle of Man (Ronaldsway)

SC

Meayl Circle

Castletown

Derbyhaven

Derby Fort

Calf of Man

Cregneash

Port St Mary

Close ny Chollagh

Hango Hill

Derby Round Tower

Spanish Head

Scarlett Point

Castletown Bay

Caigher Point

Dreswick Point

DUBLIN
Summer Only

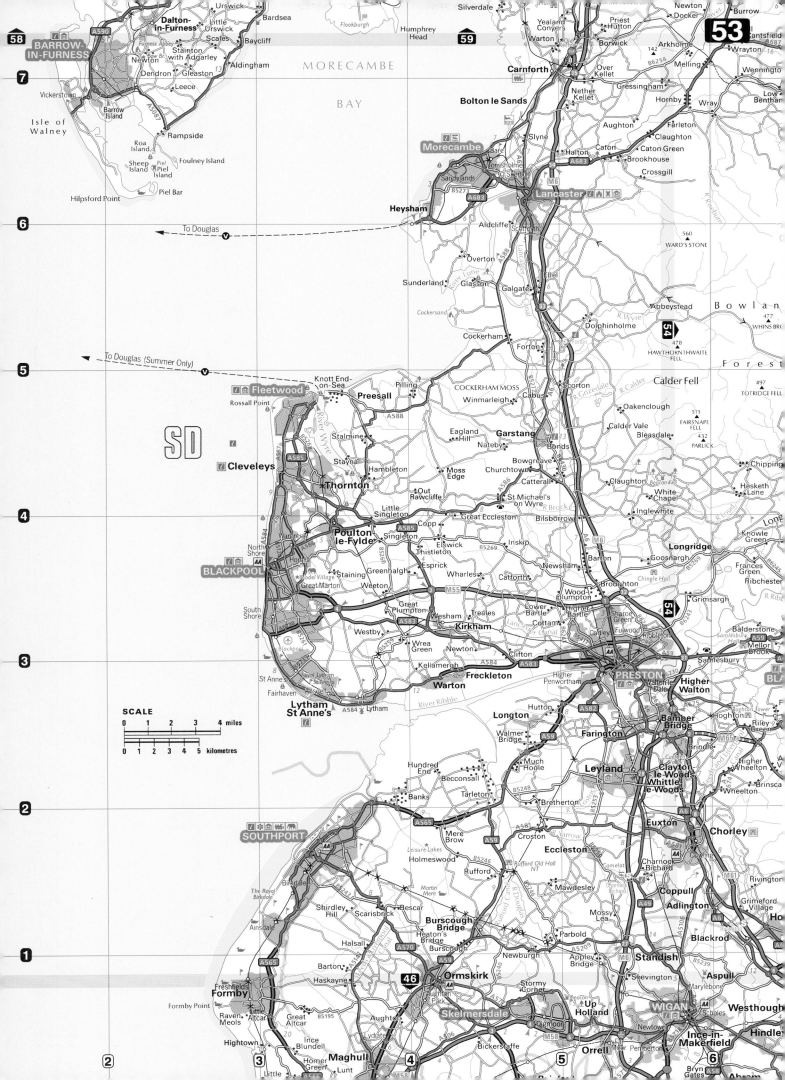

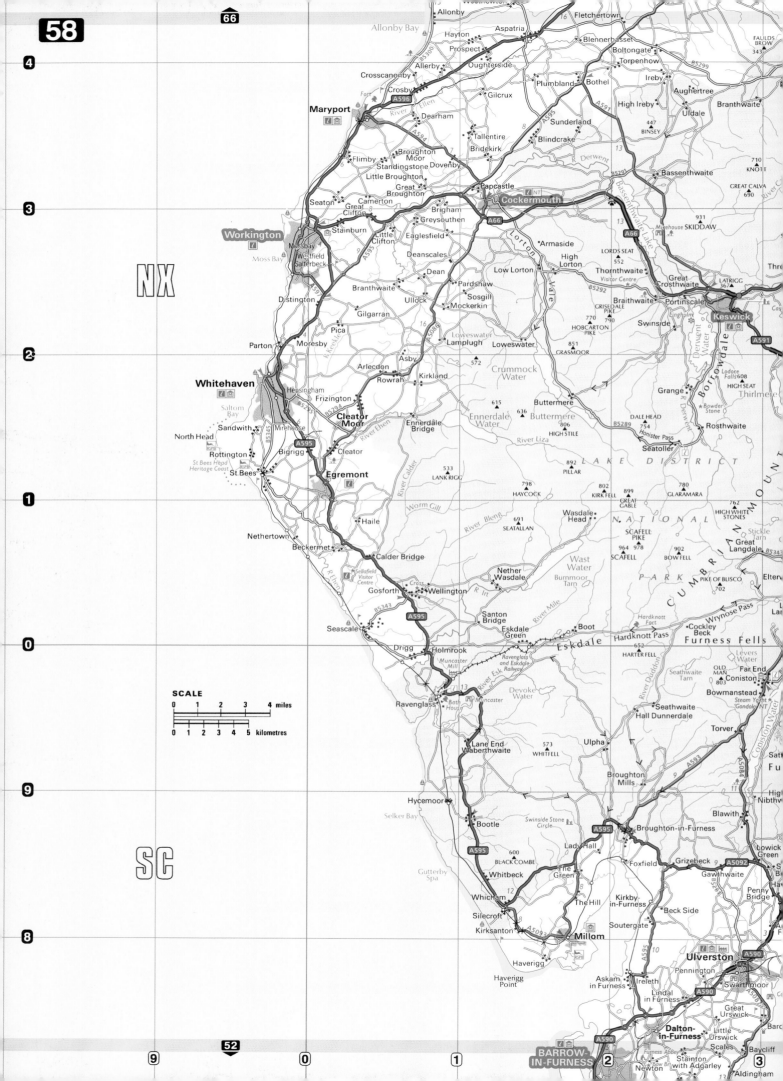

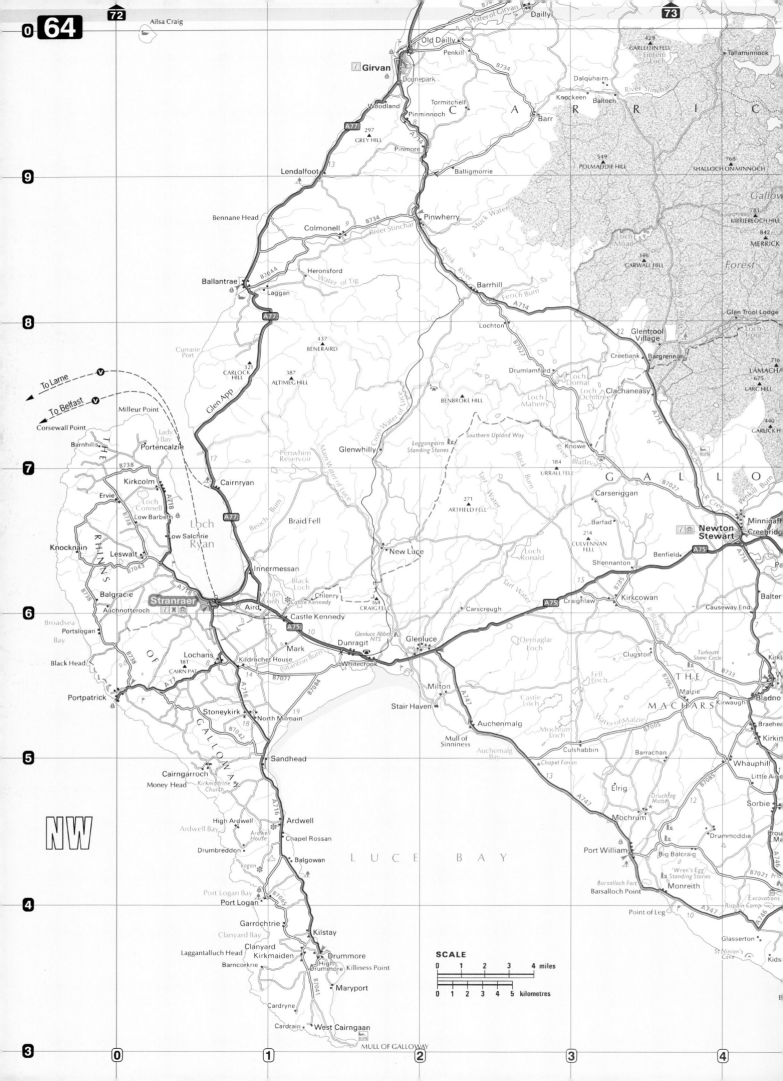

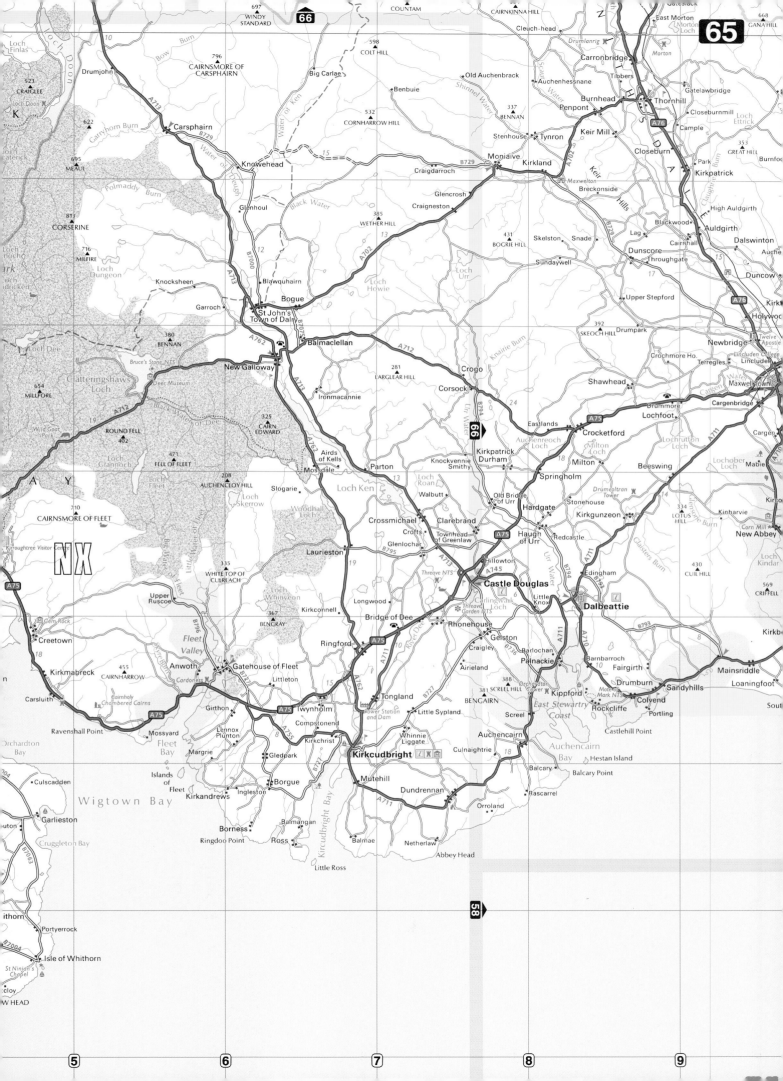

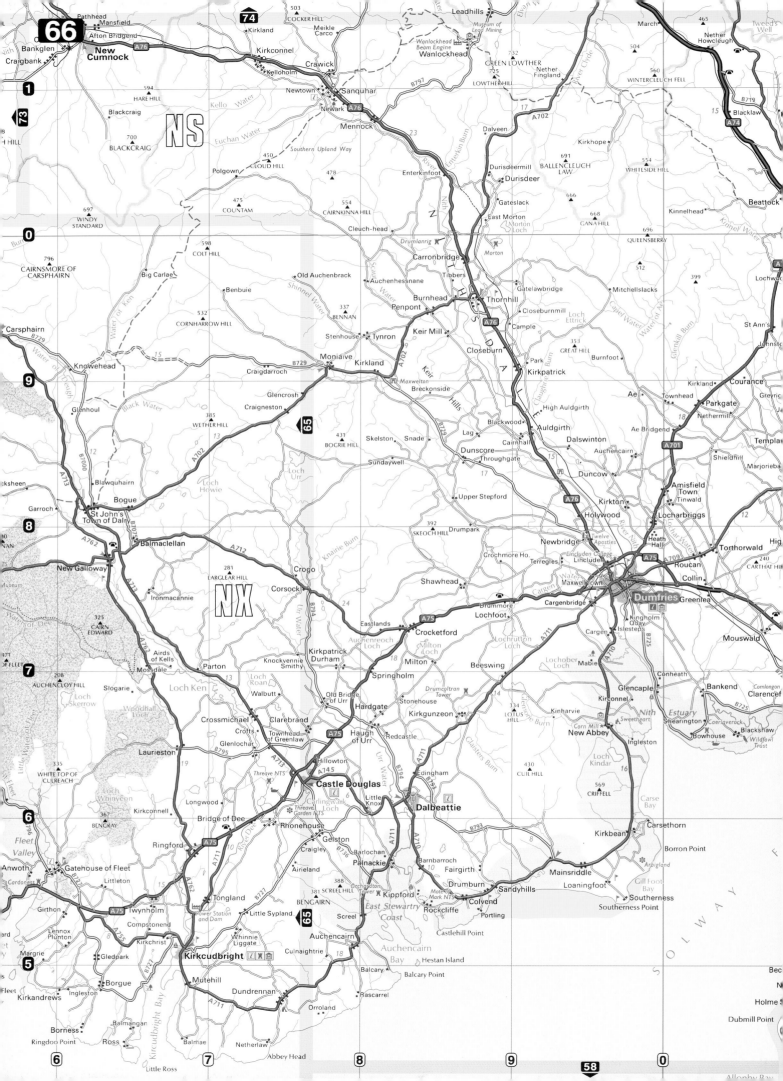

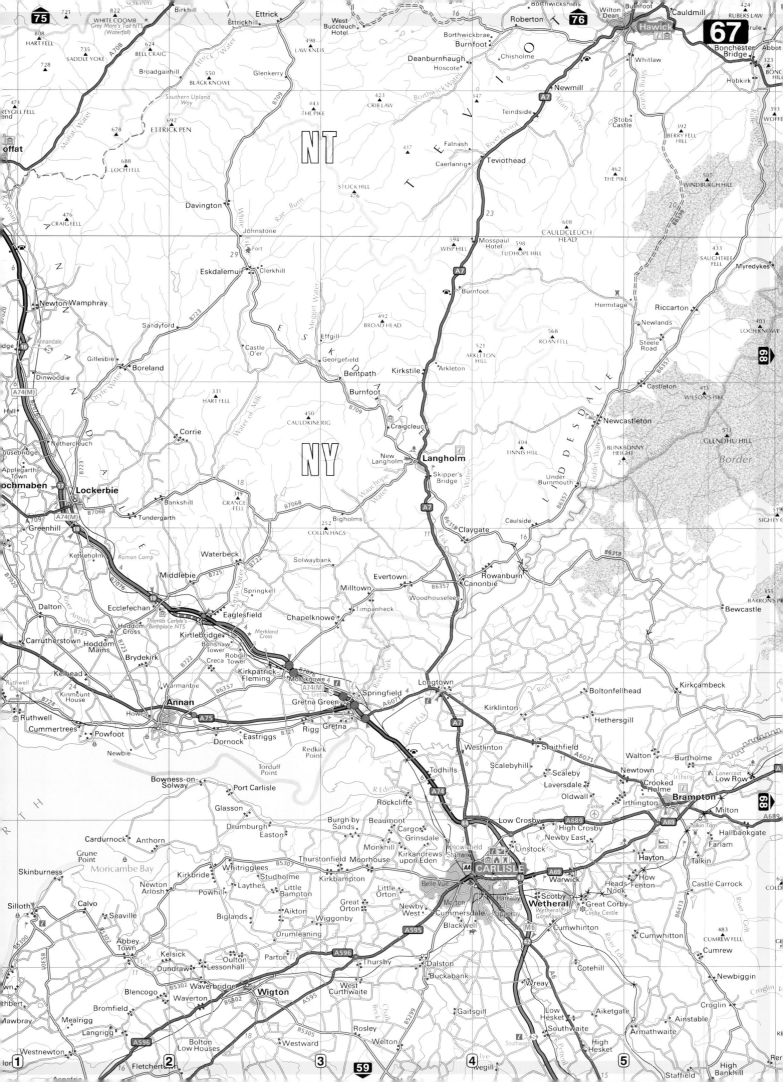

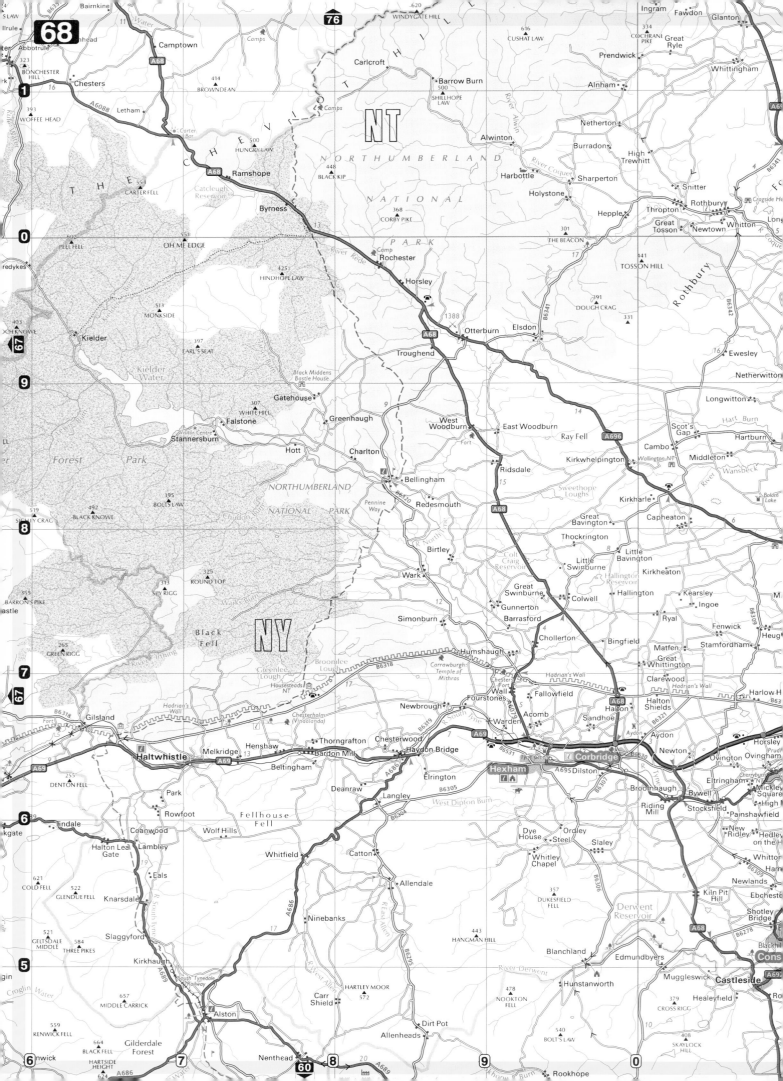

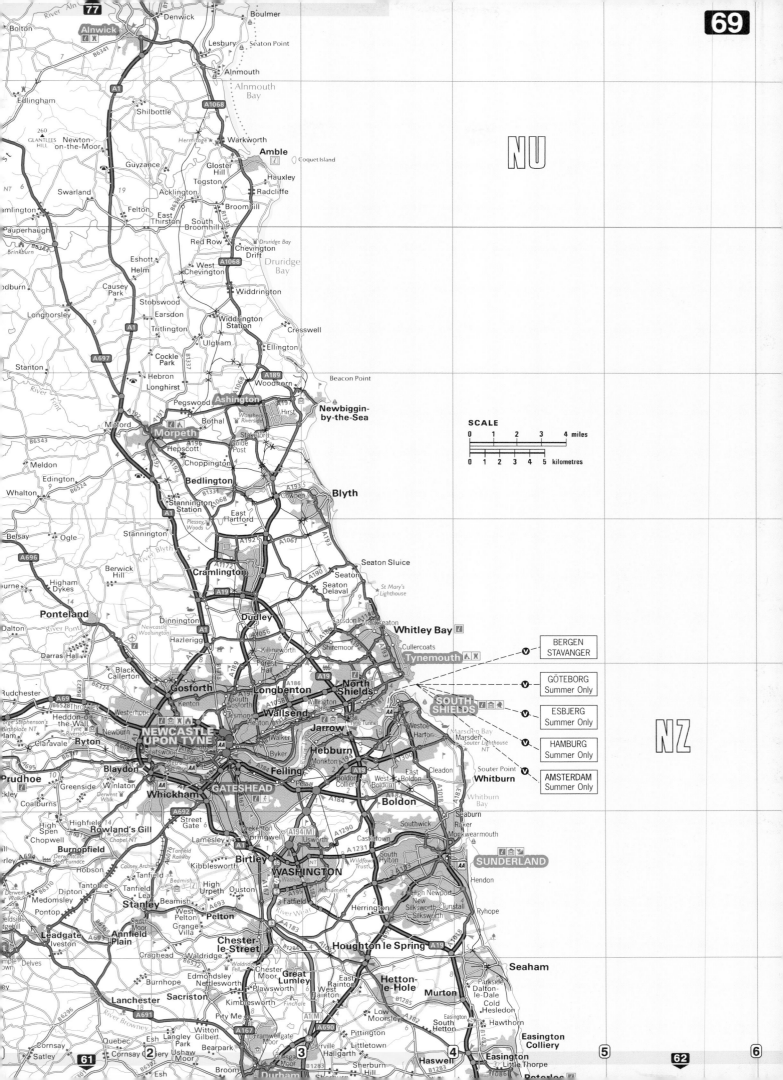

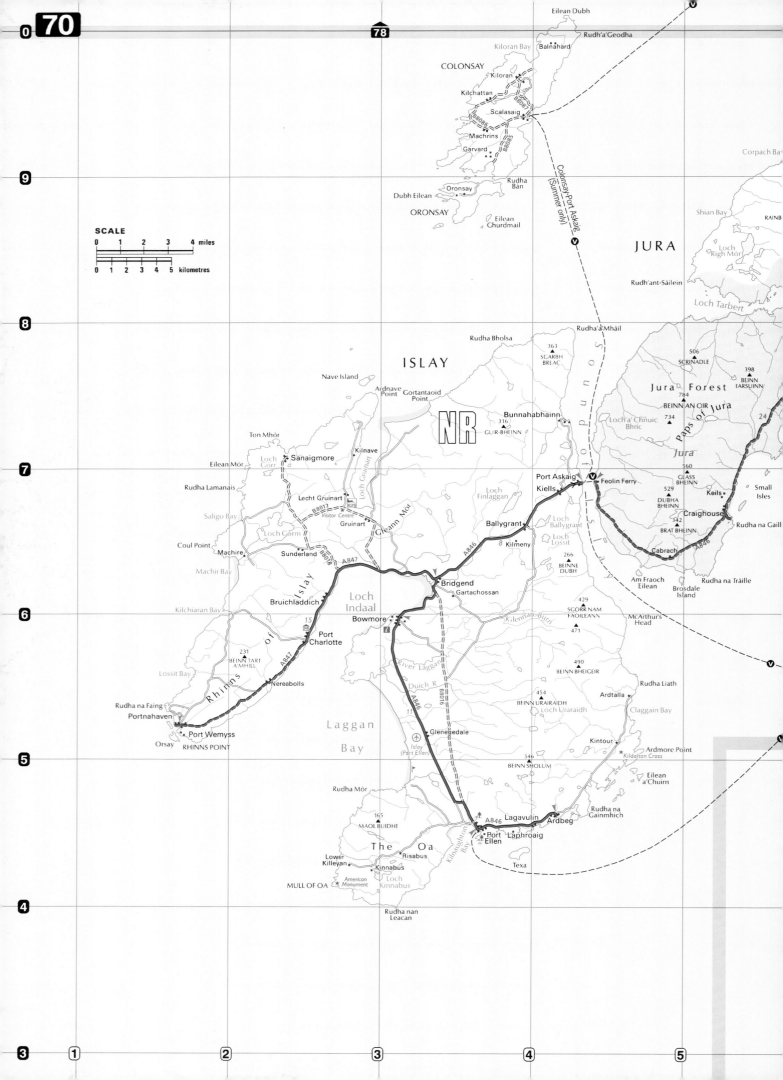

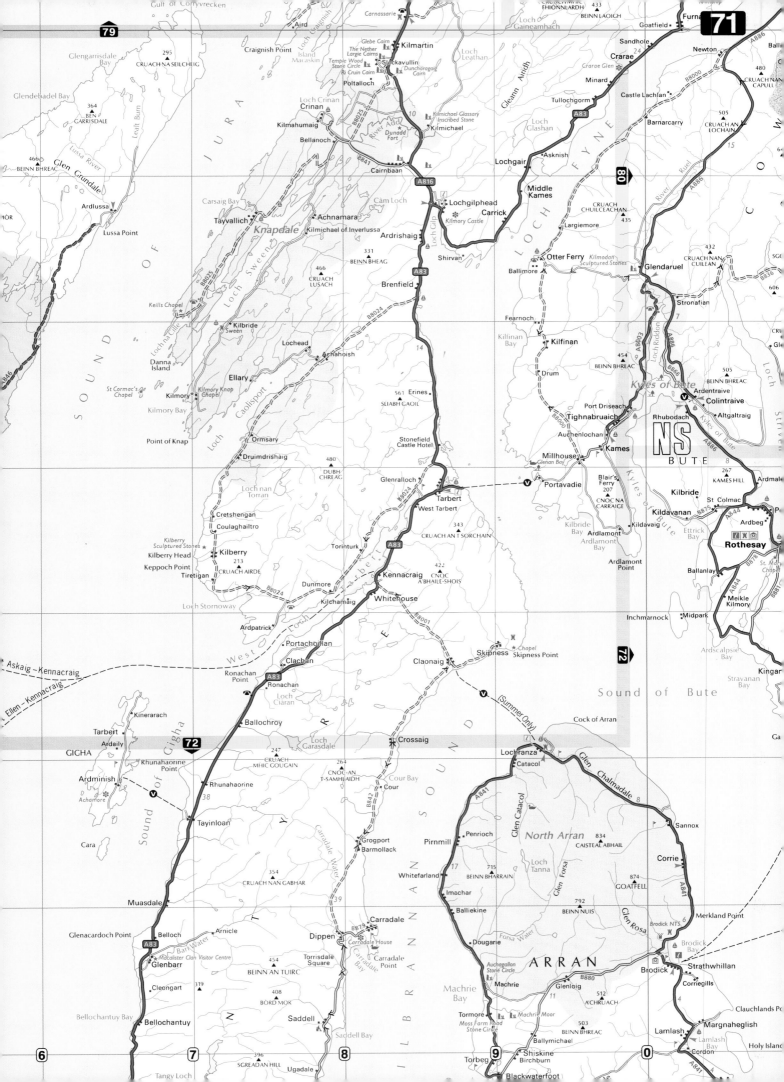

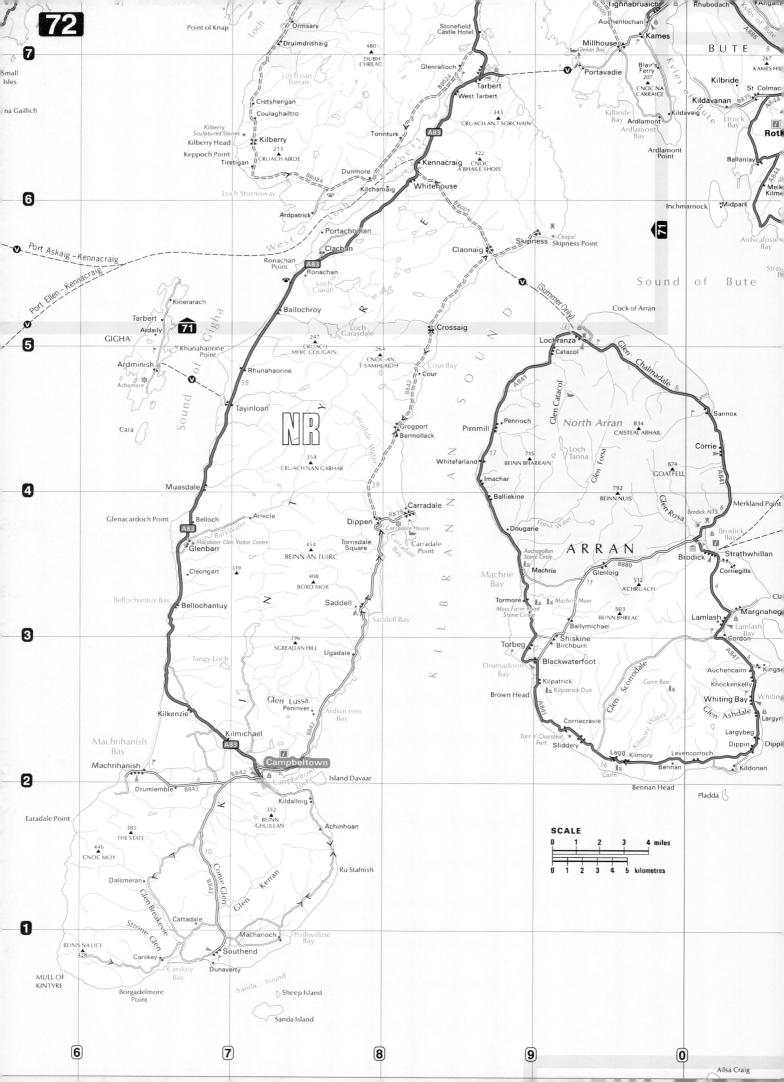

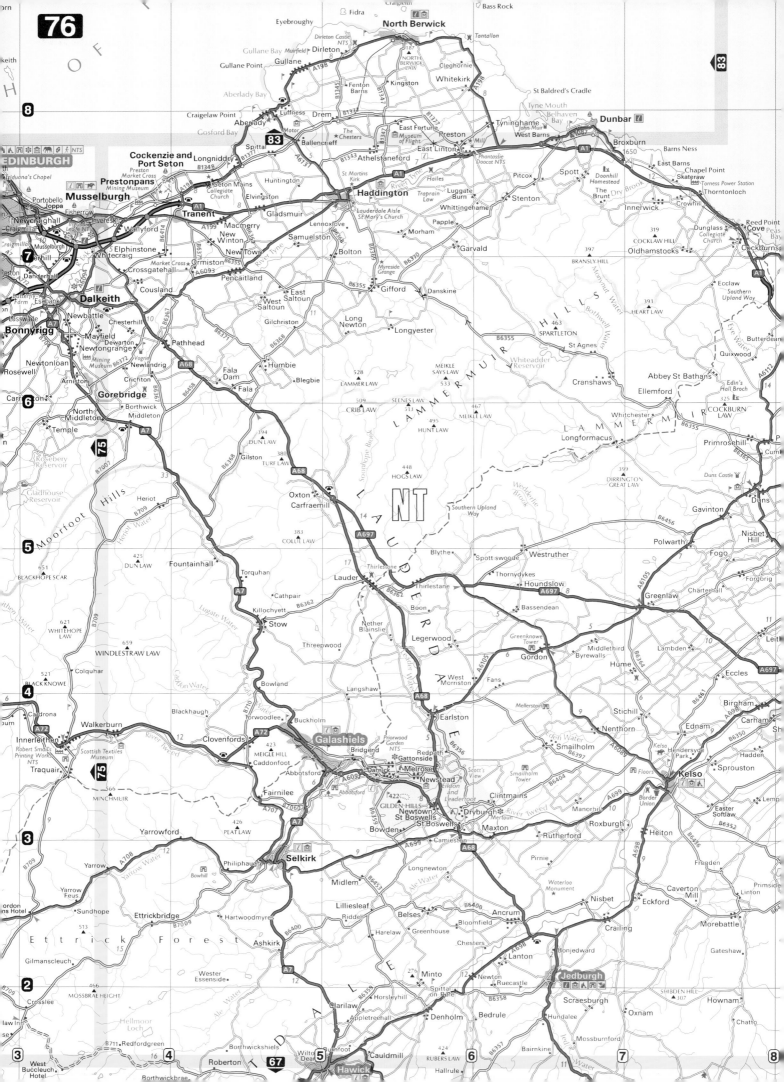

SCALE

0 1 2 3 4 miles

0 1 2 3 4 5 kilometres

ccar Point   Fast Castle Head

196
BROWN RIG

ST ABB'S HEAD

shouse

St Abbs

Coldingham   Coldingham Bay

21   Houndwood

22

Heugh Head   Cairncross   **Eyemouth**

262
HORSELEY HILL   Reston   Ayton   Burnmouth
B6438   A1

Auchencrow

Marygold

law   Lamberton   Marshall Meadows Bay

Chirnside   B6355   North Northumberland
Heritage Coast

Edrom   15   A1   NU
urch   Chirnsidebridge   Foulden   Tithe Barn   1333
Broadhaugh   Edington   Whiteadder   A6105
anderston   Allanton   Hutton   Water

Blackadder Water   Barracks   ✉ Berwick-upon-Tweed
Paxton   Town Ramparts
Blackadder   B6460   Sunwick   B6461   Tweedmouth   Spittal

lair's   Whitsome   Hilton   Fishwick   A698
ll   13
Huds Head
Scremerston

12   Horndean   Murton   A698
Ladykirk   Thornton

B6437   B6470   Norham   Cheswick
Swinton   Upsettlington   Ladykirk   River Tweed   CAUSEWAY
Ho.   Ancroft   FLOODED   HOLY ISLAND
Simprim   A1   AT HIGH TIDE
6   Shellacres   Haggerston   Holy   Lindisfarne Castle NT
A6112   Beal   Island   Castle Point
Hirsel   River Till   Duddo   Bowsden   Lindisfarne   Guile Point
oldstream   15   Priory
Lennel   Donaldson's   Lowick   East   Fenwick   North Northumberland
Cornhill-on-   Lodge   Etal   Kyloe   Heritage Coast
Tweed   Heatherslaw   B6353   Buckton   Inner   FARNE
Light Railway   Heatherslaw   Staple   Sound   ISLANDS
Wark   Mill   The Lady   Sound
West   Crookham   Waterford Hall   St Cuthbert's   Budle   Bamburgh
Learmouth   Branxton   Ford   Cave NT   Bay
East   1513   Belford   B1342   B1340
Learmouth   14   B1341   M
pressen   A697   Fenton   B6349
B6396   Howtel   Milfield   Lucker   Seahouses
Downham   Thornington   Nesbit   North
Mindrum   B6352   Doddington   Sunderland
Mill   Pawston   Kilham   Lanton   River Till   B6348   Beadnell
Mindrum   14   Coupland   Warenford   Swinhoe
Shotton   R Glen   Yeavering   B6525   A1   B1340
Kirknewton   B6351   Akeld   B6348   Newstead   Chathill   Beadnell Bay
Kirk Yetholm   Hethpool   Wooler   Chatton   Ellingham   Preston   Tughall
Town   Ros Castle NT   Newton-by-the-Sea
Yetholm   Newtown   Christon   Brunton
NORTHUMBERLAND   Chillingham   267   Bank   Embleton
525   CATERAN HILL   North   Embleton
Pennine   PRESTON HILL   Charlton   Bay
Way   Falloden   Dunstanburgh
564   NATIONAL   PARK   Ilderton   Old Bewick   Ditchburn   South   Rock   Castle NT
Mowhaugh   816   Charlton   Dunstan   Craster
THE CHEVIOT   New   Eglingham   Rennington   Stamford   Howick
567   Bewick   Beanley   B6346   B1339   Hall
DUNMOOR HILL   Hartside   16   River Breamish   17   Howick
620   Branton   Cullernose Point
WINDYGATE HILL   Ingram   Powburn   River Aln   B1340   Longhoughton
68   9   Fawdon   0   Glanton   1   69   2   Denwick   3   Boulmer
616   334

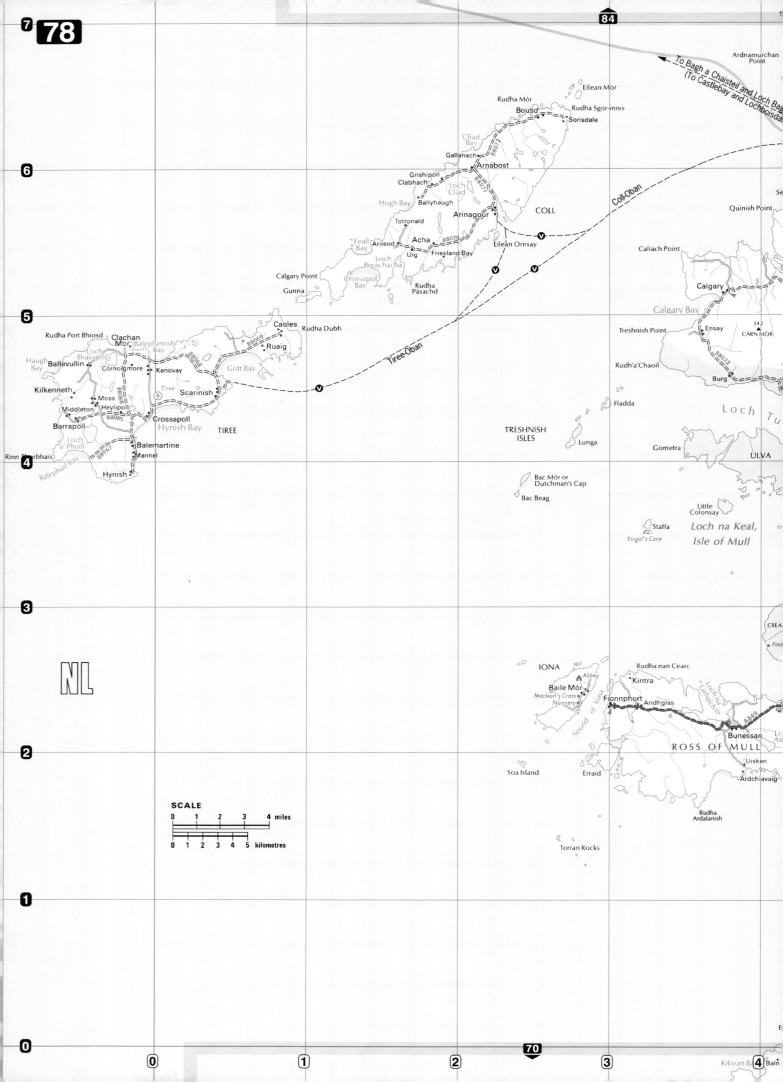

Ardnamurchan
Point

To Bagh a Chaisteil and Loch Bag
(To Castlebay and Lochboisda

Eilean Mòr

Rudha Mòr

Bousd   Rudha Sgor-innis

Sorisdale

Cliad
Bay   B8071

6   Gallanach

Grishipoll   Arnabost

Clabhach   Loch
Cliad   COLL   Quinish Point

Hogh Bay   Ballyhaugh   B8071   Coll-Oban

Totronald   Arinagour   Caliach Point

Feall   Acha   B8070   V   Calgary
Bay   Arileod   Calgary

Uig   Friesland Bay   Eilean Ornsay   Calgary Bay

Calgary Point   V   Treshnish Point   Ensay   342
5   CÀRN MÒR

Gunna   Crossapol   V   Rudh'a'Chaoil

Bay   Rudha   Burg
Pàsachd

Caoles   Rudha Dubh   Tiree-Oban   Loch Tu

Rudha Port Bhiosd   Clachan   B8069   Ruaig
Mòr Balephetrish
Haugh   Ballevullin   Bay   Kenovay   B8068   Gott Bay   Fladda
Bay   Cornaigmore   Tiree   V

Kilkenneth   Moss   Scarinish   TRESHNISH   Gometra   ULVA
Middleton   Heylipoll   ISLES
4   B8065   Crossapoll   Lunga
Barrapoll   Hynish Bay   TIREE
Loch   Bac Mòr or
Rinn Thorbhais a' Phuill B8067 Balemartine   Dutchman's Cap
Mannel   Bac Beag   Little
Balephuil Bay   Colonsay
Hynish
Staffa   Loch na Keal,
Fingal's Cave   Isle of Mull

3   CREA

Foss

Rudha nan Cearc

IONA   Abbey

Baile Mòr   Kintra   Loch na
Maclean's Cross   Bhathaich
Nunnery   Fionnphort   Aridhglas   B8049   Bal
NL   Bunessan

2   ROSS OF MULL

Uisken

Soa Island   Erraid   Ardchiavaig

Rudha
Ardalanish

Torran Rocks

1

SCALE
0   1   2   3   4 miles

0 1 2 3 4 5 kilometres

0   Kiloran Ba Bal

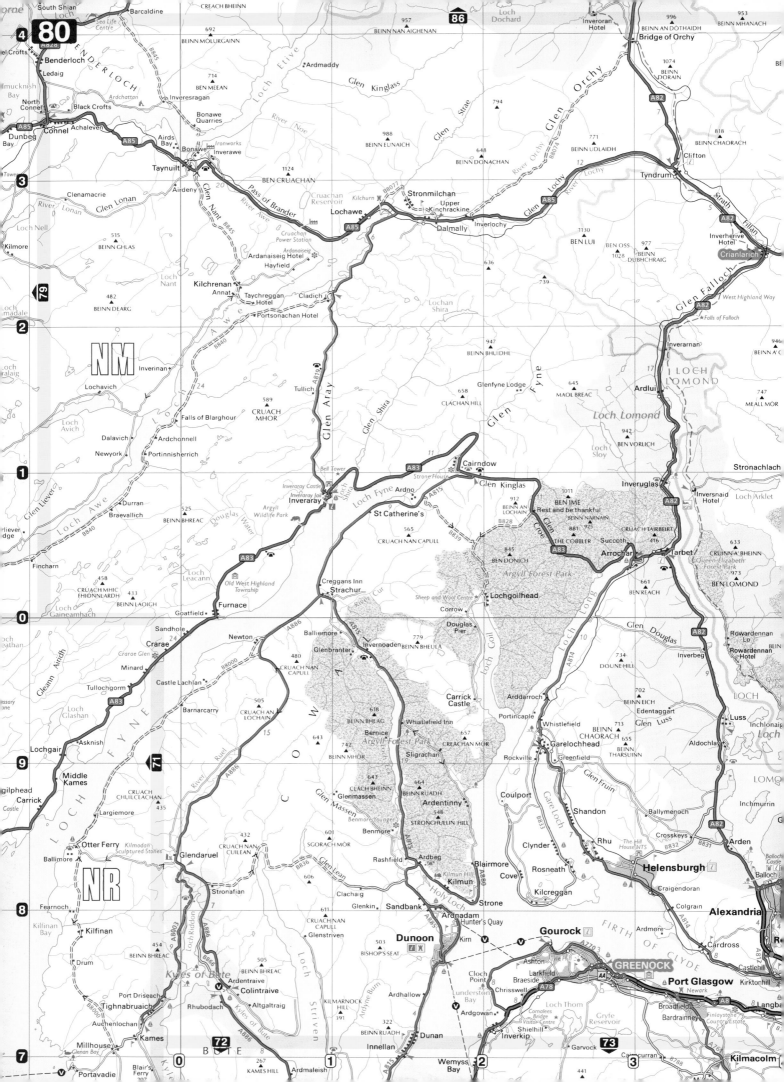

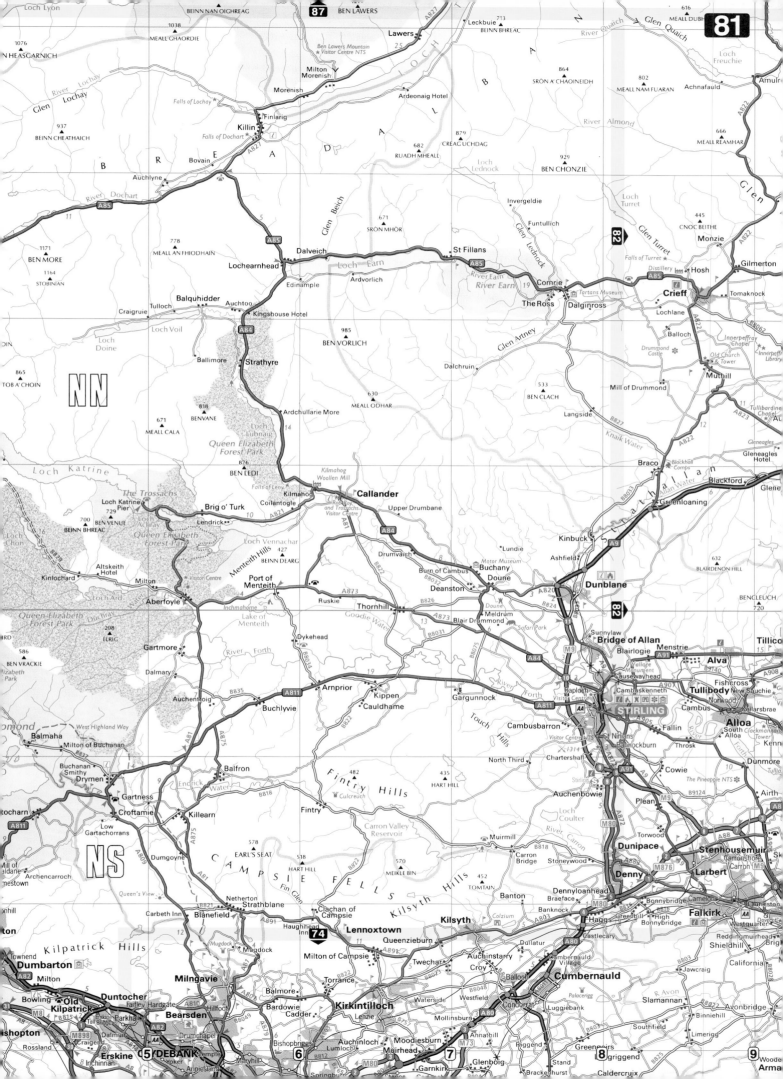

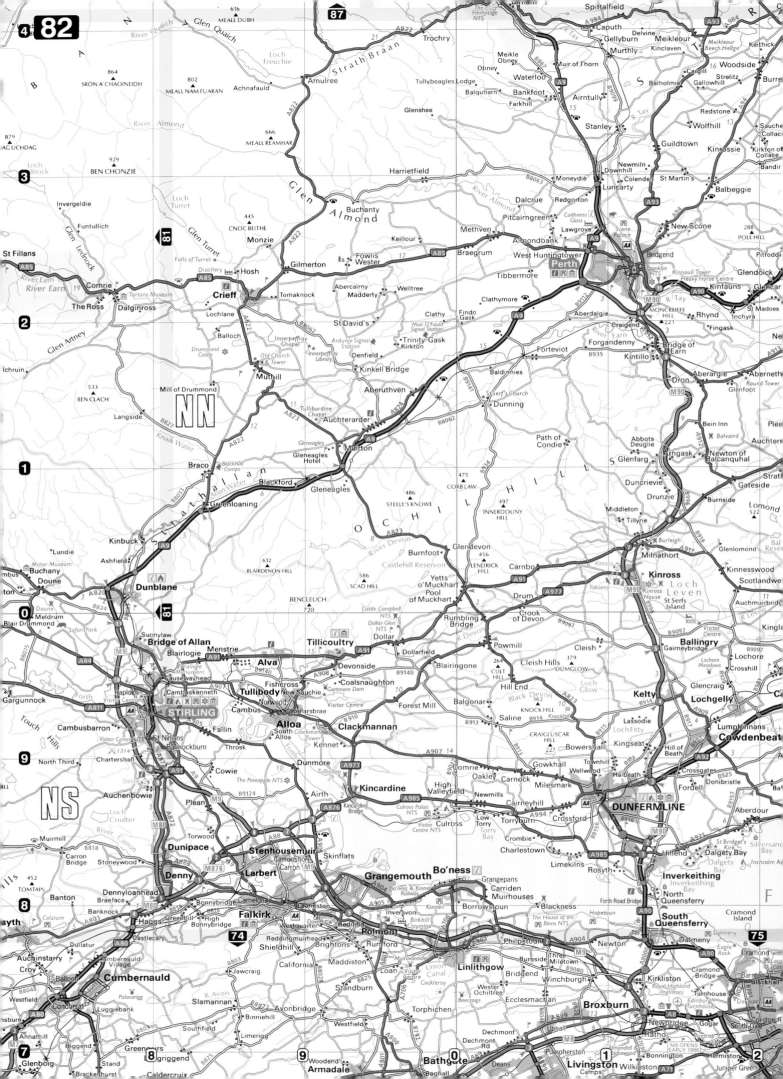

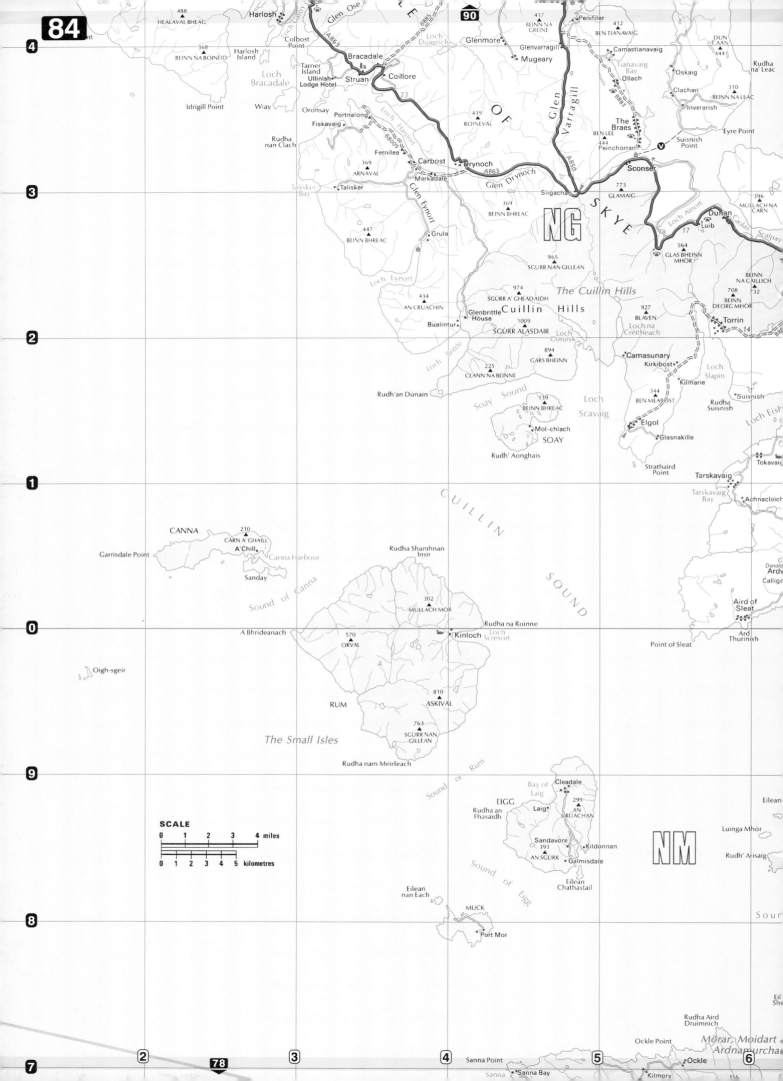

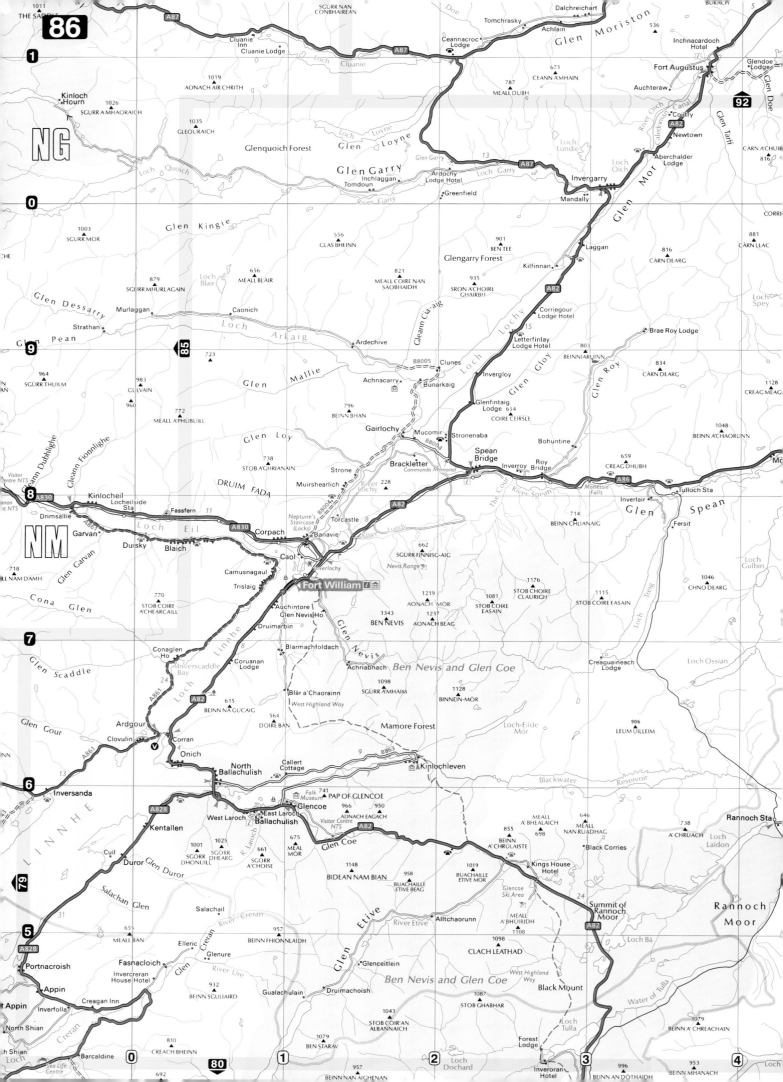

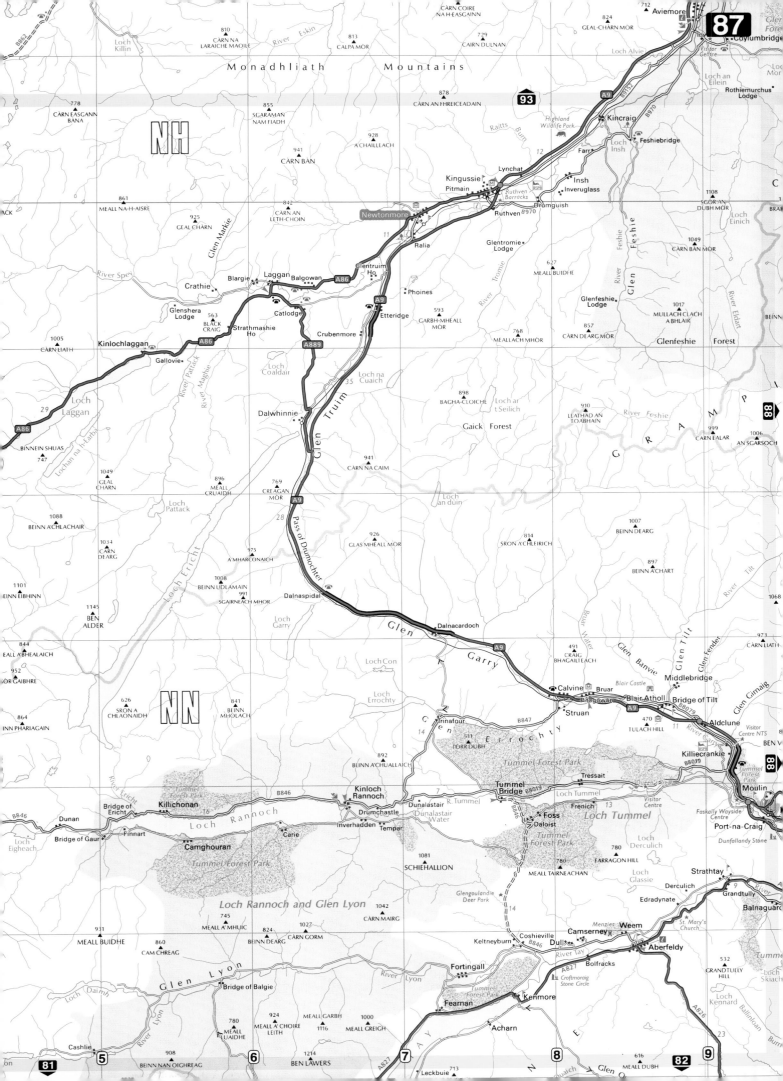

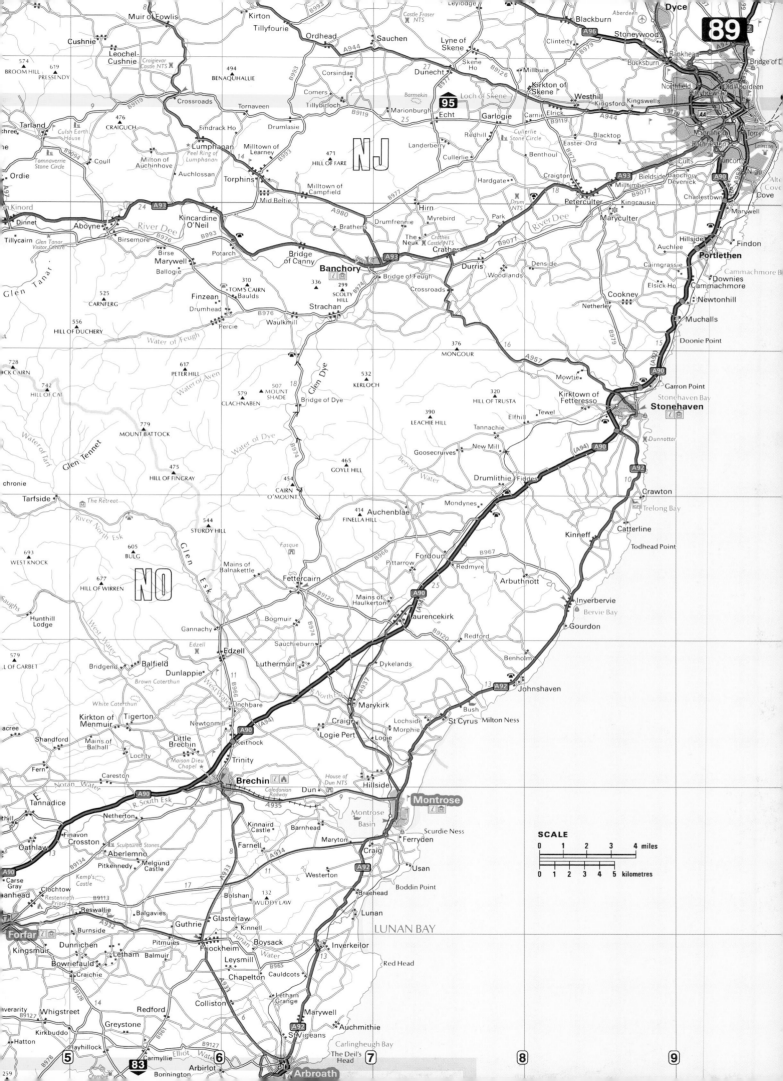

1

0

9

8

7

6

5

102

102

To Tairbeart
(To Tarbert)

To Loch nam Madadh
(To Lochmaddy)

Fladda-chùain

Eilean
Trodday

Duntulm   North
Duntulm

Kilmaluag

Lùb
Score

Museum of
Island Life

Poldorais

Eilean
Flodigarry

Borneskitaig   Flodigarry

Kilmuir
Heribusta

542

Staffin
Bay

Staffin
Island

Kilvaxter

Balgown

MEAL NA
SUIREAMACH

Digg

Brogaig

Linicro

464

Stenscholl

Staffin

Totscore

BIODA BUIDHE

Trotternish

A855

Kilt Rock Waterfall

Ellishader

Idrigill

A855

Uig

River Rha

River Conon

Marishader

BEINN EDRA
611

Garros
Culnaknock

Valtos

Rudha nam
Brathairean

Uig Bay

Earlish

Lealt

Tote

Ascrib
Islands

Loch Snizort

16

Peinlich

608
CREAG A' LAIN

Loch a' Bhràt

Trumpan

283
BEN
GEARY

Geary

Ardmore
Point

Halistra

River Hinnisdal

Hallin

451
BEINN A' SGA

RONA

DUNVEGAN HEAD

Mingay

Isay

Stein   Lusta

Loch
Bay

214
BEN DIUBAIG
Greshornish
House Hotel

Kingsburgh

A855

River Romesdal

719
Old Man
of Storr

THE
STORR

Eilean
Tigh

Boreraig

Uig

Claigan

327
BEINN BHREAC

B886

Upperglen

22

Treaslane

A850

Romesdal
Eyre

SOUND OF RAASAY

Loch
Pooltiel

Feriniquarrie

Totaig

A850

Flashader

Edinbane

Kensaleyre

River Haulton

Loch
Leathan

Eilean
Fladday

Milovaig   Glendale

Colbost

Bernisdale

B8036

16

Umac

Disgill Bay

Lephin

Black House
Folk Museum

Dunvegan

Skinidin

Kilmuir

Tote   Carbost

Skeabost   Borve

Loch
Fada

Manish Point

Loch
Arnish

Torran

Arnish

Neist
Point

Lonmore

265
BEN AKETIL

271
CRUACHAN BEINN
A' CHEARCAILL

Uigshader

Drumuie

A850

Brochel

Moonen
Bay

Rockhill

469
HEALAVAL MORE

Roag

Orbost

Vatten

Glengrasco

312

Portree

Torvaig

Hoe Rape

Ramasaig

Seafield

RAASAY

488
HEALAVAL BHEAG

Harlosh

Glen Ose

417
BEINN NA

Penifiler

412

2   3   84   4   5   6

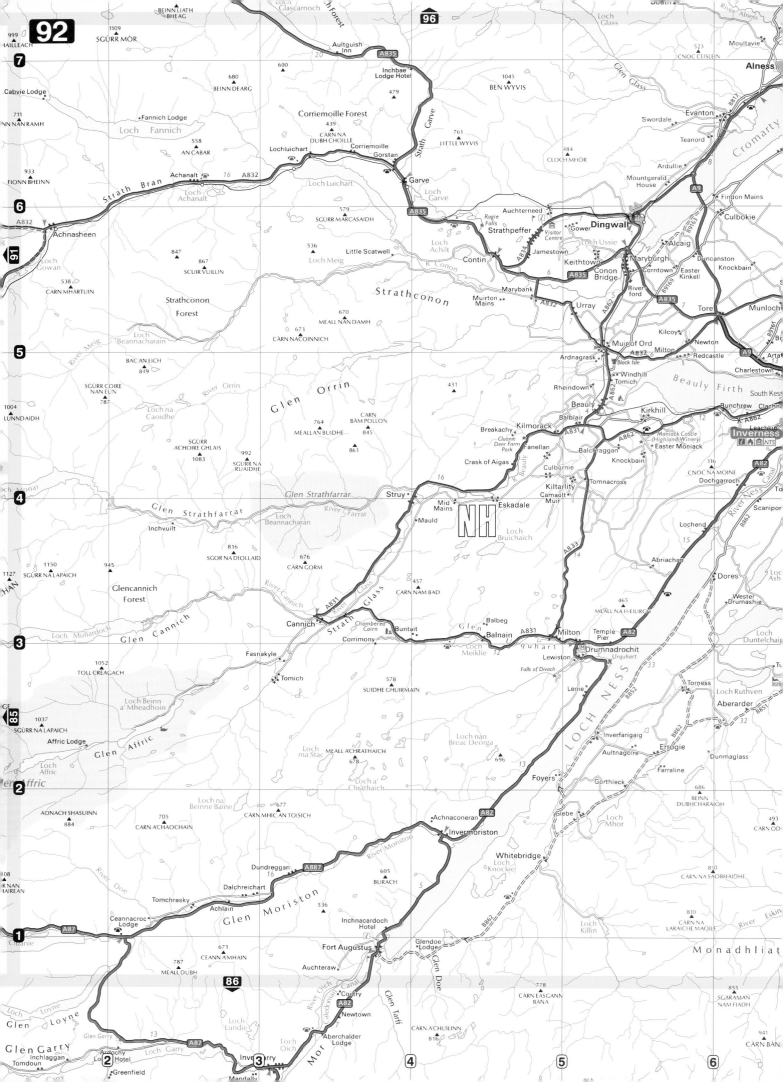

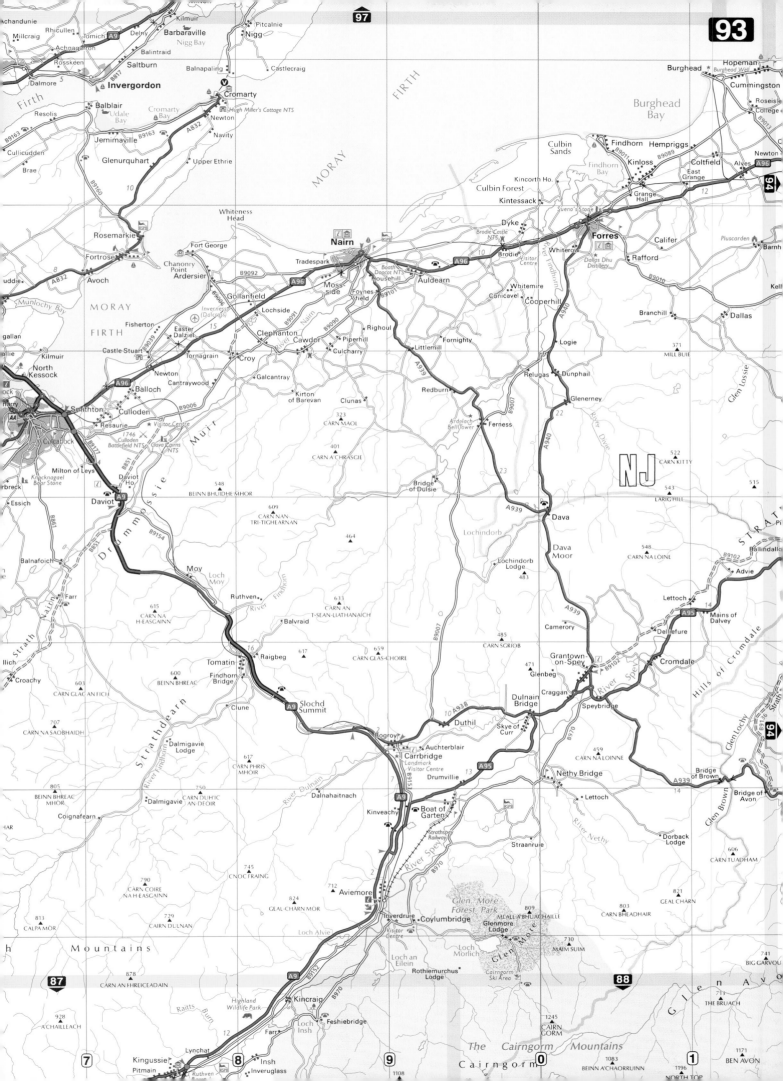

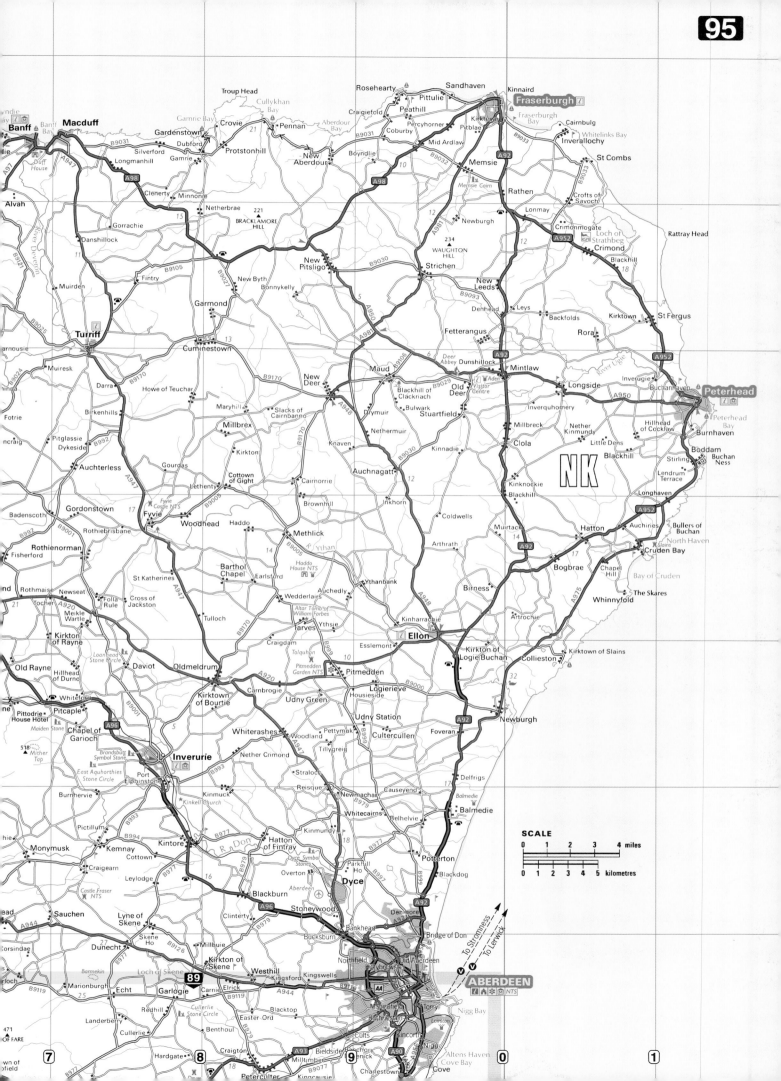

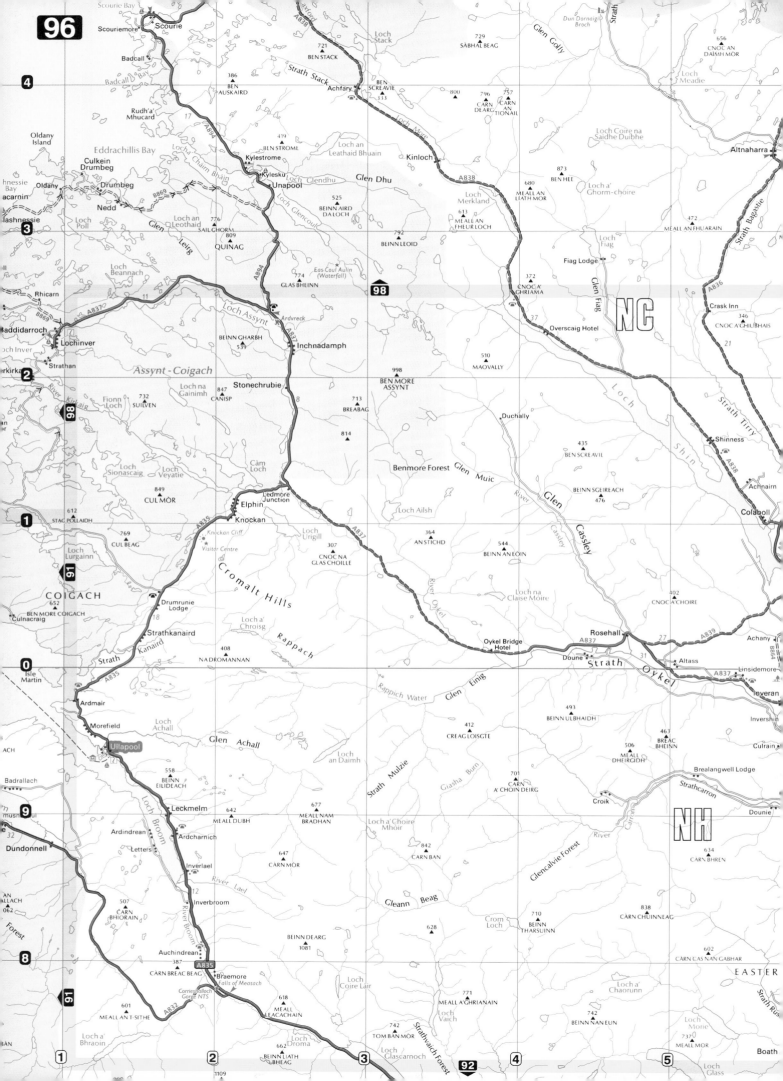

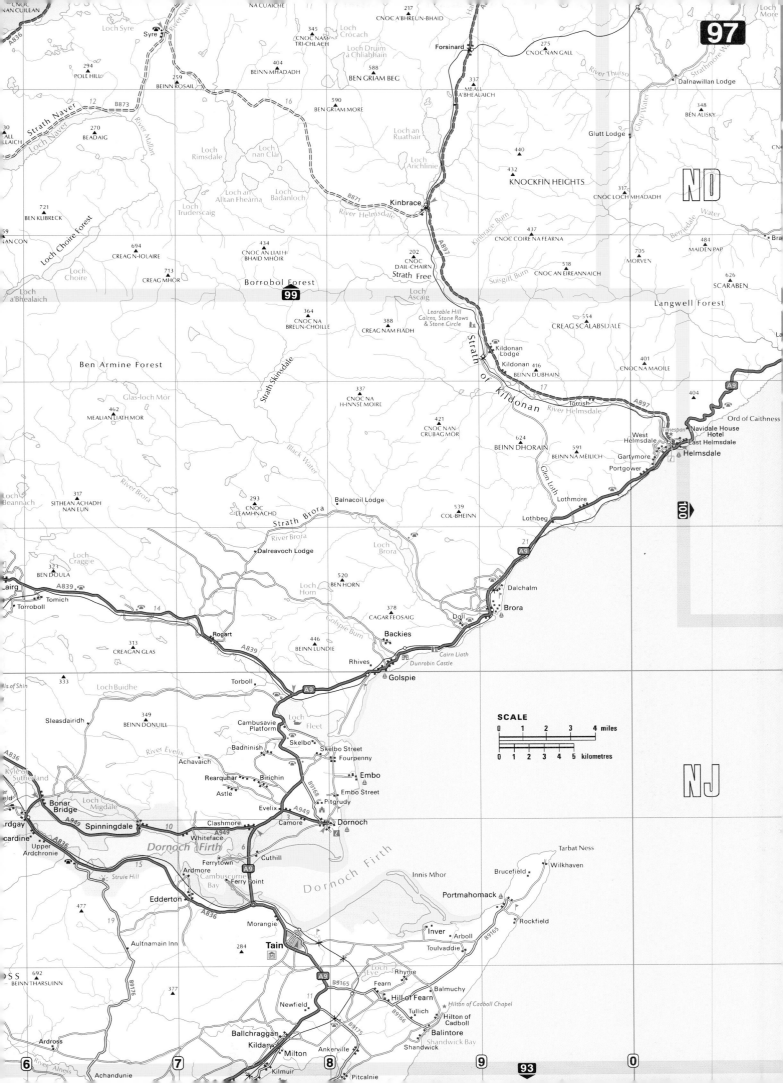

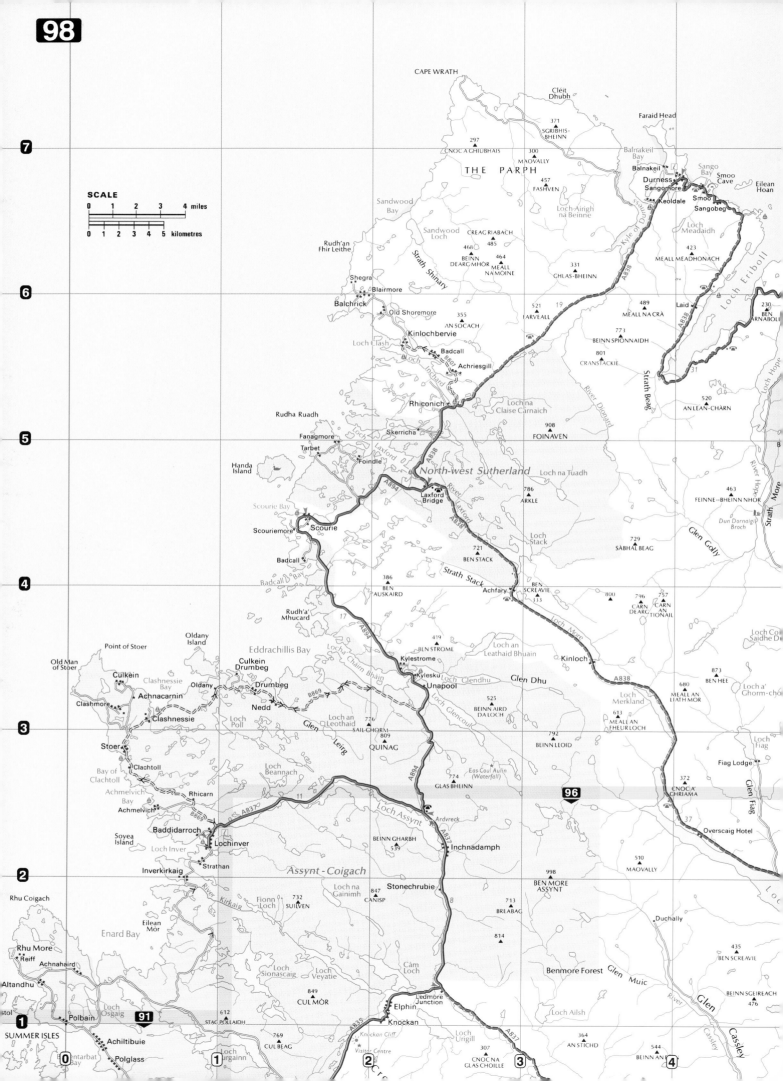

SCALE
0 1 2 3 4 miles
0 1 2 3 4 5 kilometres

7

6

5

4

3

2

1

CAPE WRATH

Cléit Dhubh

371 SGRIBHIS-BHEINN

297
CNOC A GHIUBHAIS

300 MAOVALLY

Faraid Head

Balnakeil Bay

THE PARPH

457 FASHVEN

Sandwood Bay

Sandwood Loch

Loch-Airigh na Beinne

Balnakeil
Durness
Sangomore
Keoldale
Smoo
Sango Bay
Smoo Cave
Eilean Hoan
Sangobeg

CREAG RIABACH

468 BEINN DEARG MHÒR
485
464 MEALL NA MÒINE

331 GHLAS-BHEINN

Loch Meadaidh

423 MEALL MEADHONACH

Loch Eriboll

Rudh'an Fhir Leithe

Strath Shinary

Shegra
Blairmore
Balchrick

Old Shoremore

521 FARVEALL
19

489 MEALL NA CRÀ

Laid

230 BEN ARNABOLL

355 AN SOCACH

773 BEINN SPIONNAIDH

520 AN LEAN-CHÀRN

Kinlochbervie
Badcall
Achriesgill

801 CRANSTACKIE

Loch Clash
Loch Inchard
B801

Rhiconich

Loch na Claise Carnaich

River Dionard

Strath Beag

Strath Dionard

Loch Hope

Rudha Ruadh

Fanagmore
Tarbet
Foindle

Skerricha

908 FOINAVEN

463 FEINNE-BHEINN NHOR

Handa Island

North-west Sutherland

Loch na Tuadh

31

Dun Dornaigil Broch

Scourie Bay

Laxford Bridge

786 ARKLE

River Hope

Strath More

Glen Golly

Scouriemore
Scourie

7 A894

A838

River Laxford

729 SÀBHAL BEAG

Badcall

386 BEN AUSKAIRD

721 BEN STACK

Loch Stack

Strath Stack

Glen Golly

Badcall Bay

Rudh'a' Mhucard

17

A894

Achfary
333 BEN SCREAVIE

Loch More

800 CARN DEARG
796
757 CARN AN TIONAIL

Loch Co Saidhe D

Point of Stoer
Old Man of Stoer

Oldany Island

Eddrachillis Bay

419 BEN STROME

Loch an Leathaid Bhuain

Kinloch

A838

873 BEN HEE

Loch a' Ghorm-chò

Culkein
Culkein Drumbeg
Drumbeg
Oldany
Nedd

Locha Chàrn Bhàin

Kylestrome
Kylesku
Unapool

Loch Glendhu

Glen Dhu

Loch Merkland

680 MEALL AN LIATH MOR

Achnacarnin
Clashmore
Clashnessie

B869

776 SAIL GHORM
809 QUINAG

Loch an t-Leothaid

525 BEINN AIRD DA LOCH

613 MEALL AN FHEUR LOCH

Loch Fiag

Fiag Lodge

Stoer
Clachtoll

Glen Leirg

Loch Poll

Loch Glencoul

372 CNOC A' CHRIAMA

Bay of Clachtoll

Loch Beannach

774 GLAS BHEINN

Eas Coul Aulin (Waterfall)

96

11

Achmelvich
Achmelvich Bay
Rhicarn

A837

792 BEINN LEOID

Baddidarroch
Lochinver

B869

Ardvreck

Loch Assynt

Inchnadamph

A837

27

Overscaig Hotel

Soyea Island

Loch Inver

Assynt - Coigach

BEINN GHARBH
539

Glen Fiag

Inverkirkaig
Strathan

River Kirkaig

Fionn Loch

732 SUILVEN

Loch na Gainimh

847 CANISP

Stonechrubie

8

998 BEN MORE ASSYNT

510 MAOVALLY

Rhu Coigach

Enard Bay

Eilean Mòr

814

713 BREABAG

Rhu More
Reiff
Achnahaird

Càm Loch

Benmore Forest

Glen Muic

Duchally

435 BEN SCREAVIL

Altandhu

Loch Osgaig

91

STAC POLLAIDH

849 CUL MÒR

Ledmore Junction

Elphin

A835

307 CNOC NA GLAS CHOILLE

River Cassley

BEINN SGEIREACH
476

Polbain

612

Knockan

Loch Urigill

364 AN STICHD

544 BEINN AN

SUMMER ISLES

Achiltibuie

769 CUL BEAG

Knockan Cliff

Visitor Centre

Loch Sionascaig
Loch Veyatie

Loch Ailsh

Glen Cassley

Polglass

Loch Lurgainn

A835

0 1 2 3 4

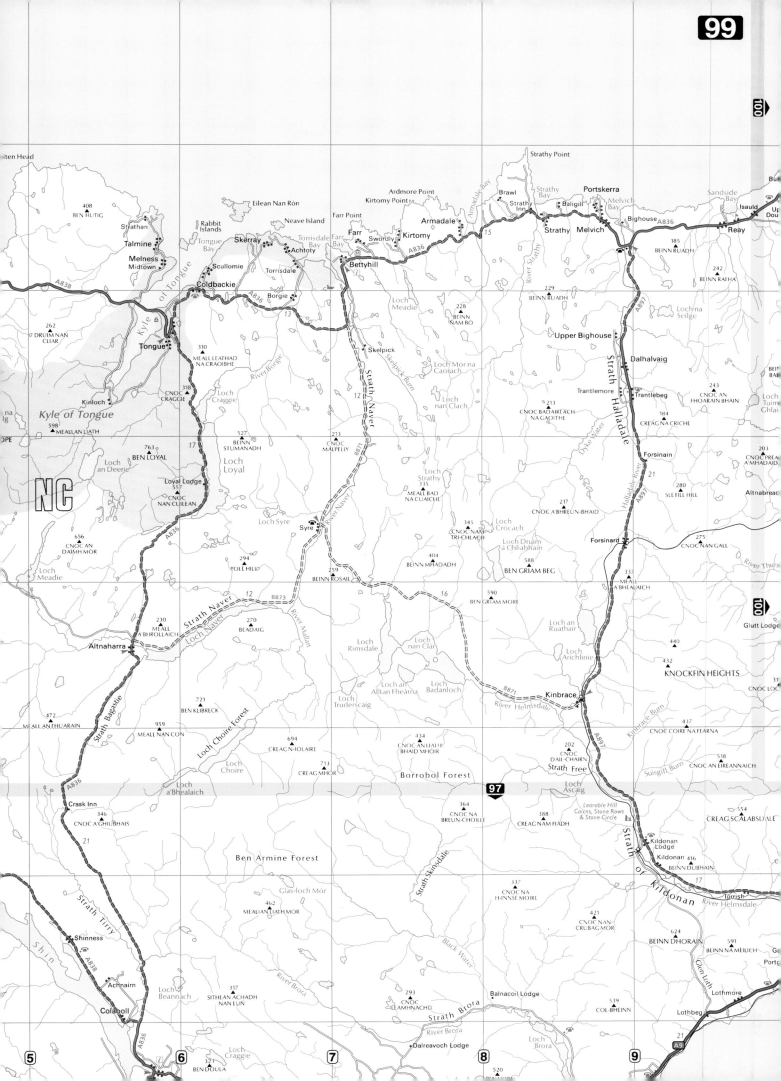

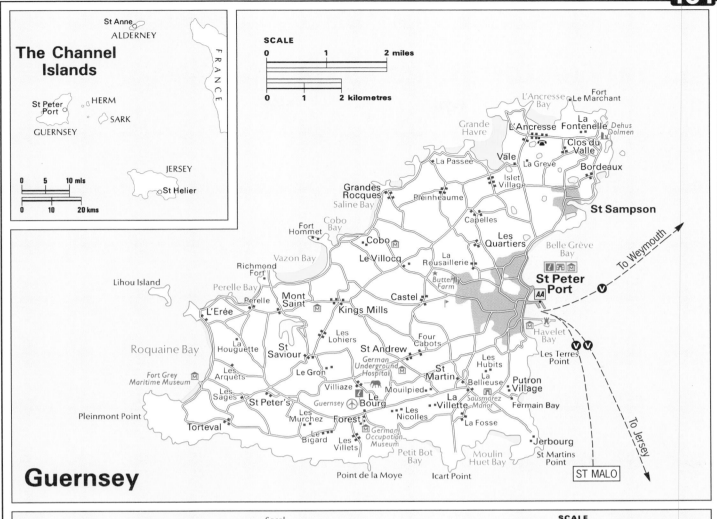

The Channel Islands

ALDERNEY — St Anne

FRANCE

St Peter Port · HERM · SARK

GUERNSEY

JERSEY · St Helier

SCALE
0 · 1 · 2 miles
0 · 1 · 2 kilometres

0 · 5 · 10 mls
0 · 10 · 20 kms

L'Ancresse Bay · Le Marchant · Fort
Grande Havre · L'Ancresse · La Fontenelle · Dehus Dolmen
La Passee · Vale · La Greve · Clos du Valle
Islet Village · Bordeaux
Grandes Rocques · Saline Bay · Pleinheaume · Capelles · **St Sampson**
Fort Hommet · Cobo Bay · Cobo · Les Quartiers · Belle Grève Bay
Vazon Bay · Le Villocq · La Rousaillerie · Butterfly Farm · **St Peter Port**
Richmond Fort · Mont Saint · Castel · AA
Lihou Island · Perelle Bay · Perelle · Kings Mills · Havelet Bay
L'Erée · Les Lohiers · St Andrew · Four Cabots · Les Hubits · Les Terres Point
Roquaine Bay · La Houguette · St Saviour · German Underground Hospital · St Martin · La Bellieuse · Putron Village
Fort Grey Maritime Museum · Les Arquets · Le Gron · Villiaze · Mouilpied · La Villette · Sausmarez Manor · Fermain Bay
Les Sages · St Peter's · Le Bourg · Guernsey · Les Nicolles · La Fosse
Pleinmont Point · Les Murchez · Forest · Les Villets
Torteval · Le Bigard · German Occupation Museum · Jerbourg · St Martins Point
Petit Bot Bay · Moulin Huet Bay
Point de la Moye · Icart Point · ST MALO

To Weymouth · To Jersey

Guernsey

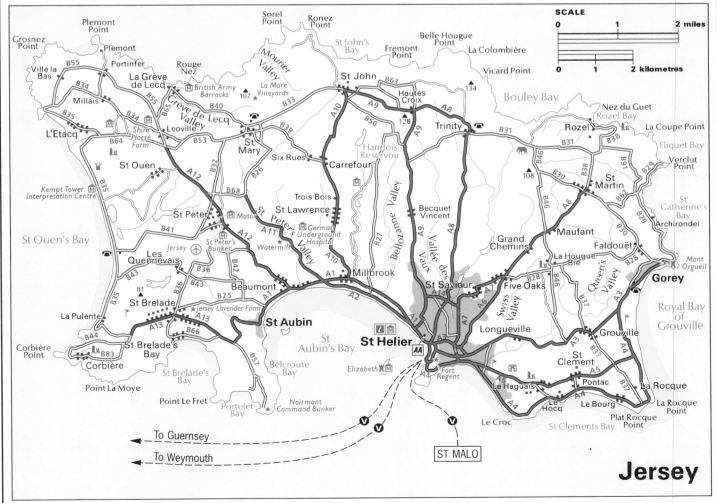

SCALE
0 · 1 · 2 miles
0 · 1 · 2 kilometres

Grosnez Point · Plemont Point · Sorel Point · Ronez Point · Belle Hougue Point · La Colombière
Plemont · St John's Bay · Fremont Point · Vicard Point
Ville la Bas · B55 · Portinfer · Rouge Nez · Mourier Valley · St John · B63 · 134 · Bouley Bay
La Grève de Lecq · British Army Barracks · La Mare Vineyards · Hautes Croix · Nez du Guet · Rozel Bay
Millais · B34 · Grève de Lecq Valley · 107 · B33 · A10 · A9 · A8 · Trinity · B31 · Rozel · La Coupe Point
L'Etacq · B35 · B64 · Shire Horse Farm · Leoville · B40 · B39 · 128 · A9 · B31 · Fliquet Bay · Verclut Point
St Ouen · B53 · St Mary · B26 · Six Rues · Carrefour · Handois Reservoir · 108 · B30 · B38 · St Martin · B29 · St Catherine's Bay
Kempt Tower Interpretation Centre · B35 · A12 · B32 · B68 · Trois Bois · B46 · A6 · B57 · Archirondel
St Peter · Motor · St Lawrence · German Underground Hospital · Becquet Vincent · Maufant · B30 · Faldouët · B28 · Mont Orgueil
St Ouen's Bay · B41 · Jersey · St Peter's Bunker · Watermill · B27 · Vallée des Vaux · Grand Chemins · La Hougue Bie · Queen's Valley · **Gorey**
Les Quennevais · St Peter's Valley · A11 · A10 · Millbrook · St Saviour · Five Oaks · B28 · A3
B43 · B36 · B42 · A1 · 81 · A14 · Swiss Valley · B37 · Royal Bay of Grouville
Beaumont · B25 · A2 · A7 · A6 · Longueville · Grouville
St Brelade · Jersey Lavender Farm · A1 · St Helier · A5
La Pulente · A13 · B66 · **St Aubin** · St Aubin's Bay · AA · St Clement · A4 · La Rocque
Corbière Point · B44 · B83 · St Brelade's Bay · Elizabeth · Fort Regent · Le Haguais · Pontac · La Rocque Point
Corbière · Belcroute Bay · Le Bourg · Plat Rocque Point
Point La Moye · St Brelade's Bay · Le Hocq
Point Le Fret · Portelet Bay · Noirmont Command Bunker · Le Croc · St Clements Bay

V · To Guernsey
V · To Weymouth · ST MALO

Jersey

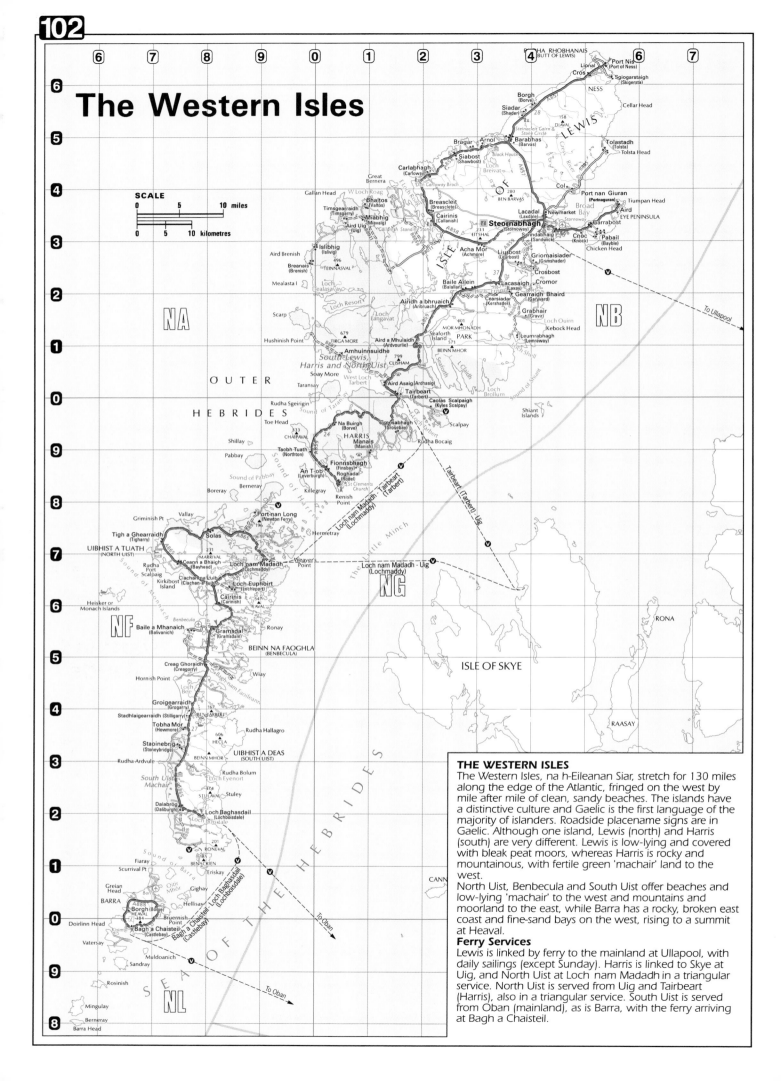

The Western Isles

THE WESTERN ISLES

The Western Isles, na h-Eileanan Siar, stretch for 130 miles along the edge of the Atlantic, fringed on the west by mile after mile of clean, sandy beaches. The islands have a distinctive culture and Gaelic is the first language of the majority of islanders. Roadside placename signs are in Gaelic. Although one island, Lewis (north) and Harris (south) are very different. Lewis is low-lying and covered with bleak peat moors, whereas Harris is rocky and mountainous, with fertile green 'machair' land to the west.

North Uist, Benbecula and South Uist offer beaches and low-lying 'machair' to the west and mountains and moorland to the east, while Barra has a rocky, broken east coast and fine-sand bays on the west, rising to a summit at Heaval.

Ferry Services

Lewis is linked by ferry to the mainland at Ullapool, with daily sailings (except Sunday). Harris is linked to Skye at Uig, and North Uist at Loch nam Madadh in a triangular service. North Uist is served from Uig and Tairbeart (Harris), also in a triangular service. South Uist is served from Oban (mainland), as is Barra, with the ferry arriving at Bagh a Chaisteil.

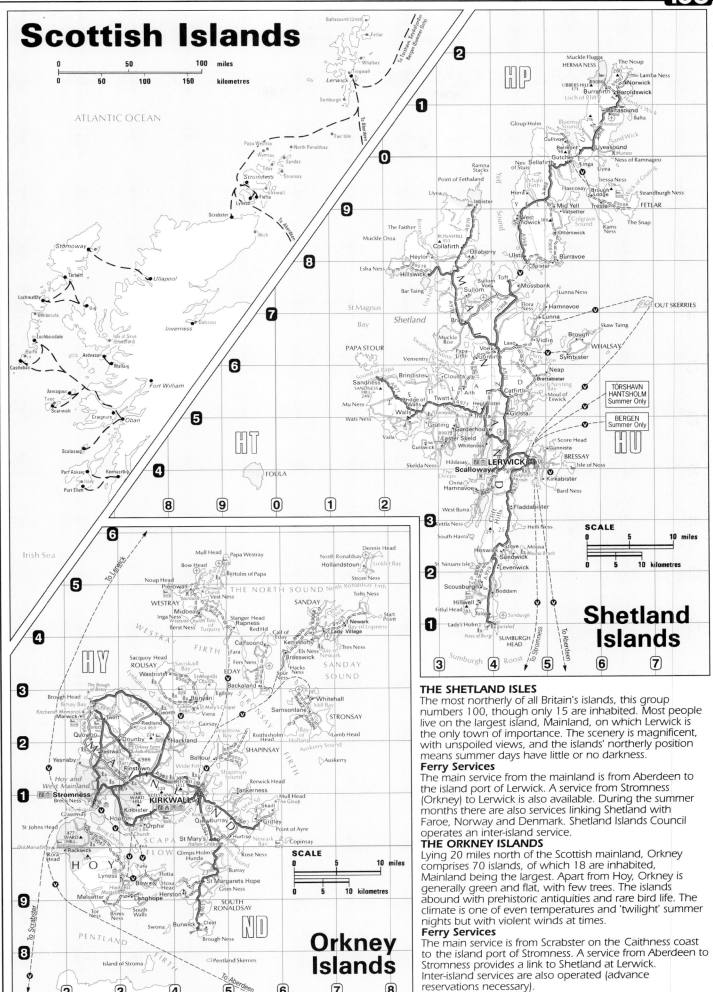

Scottish Islands

100 miles
150 kilometres

ATLANTIC OCEAN

Irish Sea

Shetland Islands

Orkney Islands

SCALE
10 miles
10 kilometres

THE SHETLAND ISLES
The most northerly of all Britain's islands, this group numbers 100, though only 15 are inhabited. Most people live on the largest island, Mainland, on which Lerwick is the only town of importance. The scenery is magnificent, with unspoiled views, and the islands' northerly position means summer days have little or no darkness.
Ferry Services
The main service from the mainland is from Aberdeen to the island port of Lerwick. A service from Stromness (Orkney) to Lerwick is also available. During the summer months there are also services linking Shetland with Faroe, Norway and Denmark. Shetland Islands Council operates an inter-island service.
THE ORKNEY ISLANDS
Lying 20 miles north of the Scottish mainland, Orkney comprises 70 islands, of which 18 are inhabited, Mainland being the largest. Apart from Hoy, Orkney is generally green and flat, with few trees. The islands abound with prehistoric antiquities and rare bird life. The climate is one of even temperatures and 'twilight' summer nights but with violent winds at times.
Ferry Services
The main service is from Scrabster on the Caithness coast to the island port of Stromness. A service from Aberdeen to Stromness provides a link to Shetland at Lerwick. Inter-island services are also operated (advance reservations necessary).

Ireland

Abbeydorney G2
Abbeyfeale G2
Abbeyleix G4
Adamstown G4
Adare G2
Adrigole H2
Ahascragh F3
Ahoghill D5
Allihies H1
Anascaul H1
Annalong E5
Annestown H4
Antrim D5
Ardagh G2
Ardara D3
Ardcath F5
Ardee E4
Ardfert G2
Ardfinnan G3
Ardglass D5
Ardgroom H1
Arklow G5
Arless G4
Armagh D4
Armoy C5
Arthurstown H4
Arvagh E4
Ashbourne F5
Ashford F5
Askeaton G2
Athboy E4
Athea G2
Athenry F3
Athleague F3
Athlone F3
Athy F4
Augher D4
Aughnacloy D4
Aughrim G5
Avoca G5

Bailieborough E4
Balbriggan F5
Balla E2
Ballacolla G4
Ballaghaderreen E3
Ballina G3
Ballina E2
Ballinafad E3
Ballinagh E4
Ballinakill G4
Ballinalee E3
Ballinamallard D4
Ballinamore E3
Ballinascarty H2
Ballinasloe F3
Ballindine E2
Ballineen H2
Ballingarry G2
Ballingarry G2
(Béal Átha an Ghaorfthaidh)
Ballinhassig H2
Ballinlough E3
Ballinrobe E2
Ballinspittle H2
Ballintober E3
Ballintra D3
Ballivor F4
Ballon G4
Ballybaun F3
Ballybay E4
Ballybofey D3
Ballybunion G2
Ballycanew G5
Ballycarry D5
Ballycastle D2
Ballycastle C5
Ballyclare D5
Ballyconneely F1
Ballycotton H3
Ballycumber F3
Ballydehob J2
Ballydesmond H2
Ballyduff H3
Ballyduff G2
Ballyfarnan E3
Ballygalley D5
Ballygar F3
Ballygawley D4
Ballygowan D5
Ballyhaise E4
Ballyhale G4
Ballyhaunis E3
Ballyhean E2
Ballyheige G2
Ballyjamesduff E4
Ballykeeran F3
Ballylanders G3
Ballylongford G2
Ballylooby G3
Ballylynan G4
Ballymahon F3
Ballymakeery H2
Ballymaloe H3
Ballymena D5
Ballymoe E3

Ballymoney C4
Ballymore F3
Ballymore Eustace F4
Ballymote E3
Ballynahinch D5
Ballynure D5
Ballyragget G4
Ballyroan D4
Ballyronan D4
Ballysadare E3
Ballyshannon D3
Ballyvaughan F2
Ballywalter D5
Balrothery F5
Baltimore J2
Baltinglass G4
Banagher F3
Banbridge D5
Bandon H2
Bangor D5
Bangor Erris E2
Bansha G3
Banteer H2
Bantry H2
Barryporeen G3
Beaufort H2
Belcoo D3
Belfast D5
Belgooly H3
Bellaghy D4
Belleek D3
Belmullet D2
(Béal an Mhuirhead)
Belturbet E4
Benburb D4
Bennettsbridge G4
Beragh D4
Birr F3
Blacklion D3
Blackwater G5
Blarney H3
Blessington F4
Boherbue H3
Borris G4
Borris-in-Ossory F3
Borrisokane F3
Borrisoleigh G3
Boyle E3
Bracknagh F4
Bray F5
Bridgetown H4
Brittas F5
Broadford G3
Broadford G2
Broughshane D5
Bruff G3
Bruree G3
Bunclody G4
Buncrana C4
Bundoran D3
Bunmahon H4
Bunnyconnellan E2
Bushmills C4
Butler's Bridge E4
Buttevant H2

Cadamstown F3
Caherconlish G3
Caherdaniel H1
Cahersiveen H1
Cahir G3
Caledon D4
Callan G4
Caltra F3
Camolin G4
Camp G1
Cappagh White G3
Cappamore G3
Cappoquin H3
Carlanstown E4
Carlingford E5
Carlow G4
Carndonagh C4
Carnew G4
Carnlough C5
Carracastle E3
Carrick D3
(An Charraig)
Carrickfergus D5
Carrickmacross E4
Carrickmore D4
Carrigahorig F3
Carrigaline H3
Carrigallen E3
Carriganimmy H2
Carrigans C4
Carrigtohill H3
Carrowkeel C4
Carryduff D5
Cashel G3
Castlebar E2
Castlebellingham E5
Castleblayney E4
Castlebridge G4
Castlecomer G4

Castle Cove H1
Castlederg D4
Castledermot G4
Castleisland G2
Castlemaine H2
Castlemartyr H3
Castleplunkett E3
Castlepollard E4
Castlerea E3
Castlerock C4
Castleshane E4
Castletown H4
Castletownbere H1
Castletownroche H3
Castletownshend J2
Castlewellan E5
Causeway G2
Cavan E4
Celbridge F4
Charlestown E3
Clady D4
Clane F4
Clara F3
Clarecastle G2
Claremorris E2
Clarinbridge F2
Clashmore H3
Claudy C4
Clifden F1
Cliffony D3
Clogh G4
Cloghan F3
Clogheen H3
Clogher D4
Clohamon G4
Clonakilty H2
Clonard F4
Clonaslee F3
Clonbulloge F4
Clonbur (An Fhairche) E2
Clondalkin F5
Clones E4
Clonmany C4
Clonmel G3
Clonmellon E4
Clonmore G3
Clonony F3
Clonoulty G3
Clonroche G4
Clontibret E4
Cloonbannin H2
Cloondara E3
Cloonkeen H2
Cloonlara G3
Clough D5
Cloughjordan F3
Cloyne H3
Coagh D4
Coalisland D4
Cobh H3
Coleraine C4
Collinstown E4
Collon E4
Collooney E3
Comber D5
Conna H3
Cookstown D4
Coole E4
Cooraclare G2
Cootehill E4
Cork H3
Cornamona F2
Corofin F2
Courtmacsherry H2
Courtown Harbour G5
Craigavon D5
Craughwell F3
Creggs E3
Cresslough C3
Croagh G3
Crolly (Croithlí) C3
Crookedwood E4
Crookhaven J1
Crookstown H2
Croom G2
Crossakeel E4
Cross Barry H2
Crosshaven H3
Crossmaglen E4
Crossmolina E2
Crumlin D5
Crusheen F2
Culdaff C4
Culleybackey D5
Curracloe G4
Curraghboy F3
Curry E3
Cushendall C5

Daingean F4
Delvin E4
Derrygonnelly D3
Derrylin E4
Dervock C5
Dingle (An Daingean) H1
Doagh D5
Donaghadee D5
Donaghmore G3

Donegal D3
Doneraile H3
Doonbeg G2
Douglas H3
Downpatrick D5
Dowra E3
Draperstown D4
Drimoleague H2
Dripsey H2
Drogheda E5
Droichead Nua F4
(Newbridge)
Dromahair D3
Dromcolliher G2
Dromore D5
Dromore E4
Dromore West D3
Drum E4
Drumconrath E4
Drumkeeran E3
Drumlish E3
Dromod E3
Drumquin D4
Drumshanbo E3
Drumsna E3
Duagh G2
Dublin F5
Duleek E5
Dunboyne F5
Duncormick H4
Dundalk E5
Dunderrow H3
Dundrum E5
Dunfanaghy C3
Dungannon D4
Dungarvan H3
Dungarvan G4
Dungiven C3
Dungloe C3
Dungourney H3
Dunkineely D3
Dun Laoghaire F5
Dunlavin F4
Dunleer E5
Dunloy C5
Dunmanway H2
Dunmore E3
Dunmore East H4
Dunmurry D5
Dunshauglin F4
Durrow G4
Durrus H2

Easky D2
Edenderry F4
Edgeworthstown E4
Eglinton D4
Elphin E3
Emyvale D4
Enfield F4
Ennis G2
Enniscorthy G4
Enniscrone D2
Enniskean H2
Enniskillen D4
Ennistymon F2
Eyrecourt F3

Farnaght E3
Farranfore H2
Feakle F3
Fenagh E3
Fermoy H3
Ferns G4
Fethard H3
Fethard G3
Finnea E4
Fintona D4
Fivemiletown D4
Fontstown F4
Foulksmills H4
Foxford E2
Foynes G2
Freemount H2
Frenchpark E3
Freshford G4
Fuerty E3

Galbally G3
Galway F2
Garrison D3
Garristown F5
Garvagh C4
Geashill F4
Gilford D5
Glandore J2
Glanworth H3
Glaslough D4

Glassan F3
Glenamaddy E3
Glenarm C5
Glenavy D5
Glenbeigh H1
Glencolumbkille D3
(Gleann Cholm Cille)
Glendalough F5
Glenealy G5
Glenfarne D3
Glengarriff H2
Glenmore G4
Glenties D3
Glenville H3
Glin G2
Glinsk F2
(Glinsce)
Golden G3
Goleen J2
Goresbridge G4
Gorey G5
Gort F2
Gortin D4
Gowran G4
Graiguenamanagh G4
Grallagh G3
Granard E4
Grange D3
Greencastle E5
Greyabbey D5
Greystones F5
Gulladuff D4

Hacketstown G4
Headford F2
Herbertstown G3
Hillsborough D5
Hilltown E5
Holycross G3
Holywood D5
Howth F5

Inch H1
Inchigeelagh H2
Inishannon H2
Irvinestown D4

Johnstown G3

Kanturk H2
Keadue E3
Keady E4
Keel E1
Keenagh E3
Kells D5
Kells E4
Kenmare H2
Kesh D3
Kilbeggan F4
Kilberry E4
Kilbrittain H2
Kilcar D3
(Cill Charthaigh)
Kilcock F5
Kilcolgan F2
Kilconnell F2
Kilconnell F2
Kilcoole F5
Kilcormac F3
Kilcullen F4
Kilcurry E5
Kildare F4
Kildavin G4
Kildorrery H3
Kildress D4
Kilfenora F2
Kilfinnane G3
Kilgarvan H2
Kilkee G2
Kilkeel E5
Kilkelly E3
Kilkenny G4
Kilkieran F2
(Cill Ciaráin)
Kilkinlea G2
Kill H4
Killadysert G2
Killala D2
Killaloe G3
Killarney H2
Killashandra E4
Killashee E3
Killeagh H3
Killeigh F4
Killenaule G3
Killimer G2
Killimor F3

Killiney F5
Killinick H4
Killorglin H2
Killough E5
Killucan F4
Killybegs D3
Killyleagh D5
Kilmacanoge F5
Kilmacrenan C3
Kilmacthomas H4
Kilmaganny G4
Kilmaine E2
Kilmallock G3
Kilmanagh G4
Kilmanahan G3
Kilmeaden H4
Kilmeage F4
Kilmeedy G2
Kilmichael H2
Kilmore Quay H4
Kilnaleck E4
Kilrea C4
Kilrush G2
Kilsheelan G3
Kiltealy G4
Kiltegan G4
Kiltimagh E2
Kiltoom F3
Kingscourt E4
Kinlough D3
Kinnegad F4
Kinnitty F3
Kinsale H3
Kinvarra F2
Kircubbin D5
Knock E3
Knockcroghery E3
Knocklofty G3
Knockmahon H4
Knocktopher G4

Lahinch F2
Lanesborough E3
Laragh F5
Larne D5
Lauragh H1
Laurencetown F3
Leap J2
Leenane E2
Leighlinbridge G4
Leitrim E3
Leixlip F4
Lemybrien H3
Letterfrack E2
Letterkenny C4
Lifford D4
Limavady C4
Limerick G3
Lisbellaw D4
Lisburn D5
Liscarroll G2
Lisdoonvarna F2
Lismore H3
Lisnaskea D4
Lisryan E4
Listowel G2
Loghill G2
Londonderry C4
Longford E3
Loughbrickland D5
Loughglinn E3
Loughrea F3
Louisburgh E2
Lucan F4
Lurgan D5
Lusk F5

Macroom H2
Maghera E5
Maghera E4
Magherafelt D4
Maguiresbridge D4
Malahide F5
Malin C4
Malin More D3
Manorhamilton D3
Markethill D4
Maynooth F4
Mazetown D5
Middletown D4
Midleton H3
Mifford D4
Millstreet H2
Milltown H3
Milltown Malbay G2
Mitchelstown H3

Moate F3
Mohill E3
Molls Gap H2
Monaghan E4
Monasterevin F4
Moneygall G3
Moneymore D4
Monivea F3
Mooncoin H4
Moorfields D5
Mount Bellew F3
Mount Charles D3
Mountmellick F4
Mountrath F4
Mountshannon F3
Mourne Abbey H2
Moville C4
Moy D4
Moylett E4
Moynalty E4
Moyvore F3
Muckross H2
Muff C4
Muine Bheag G4
Mullabohy E4
Mullagh E4
Mullinavat G4
Mullingar F4
Myshall G4

Naas F4
Nad H2
Naul F5
Navan E4
Neale E2
Nenagh G3
Newbliss E4
Newcastle D5
Newcastle West G2
Newinn G3
Newmarket H2
Newmarket-on Fergus G2
Newport E2
Newport E2
New Ross G4
Newtown G3
Newtownabbey D5
Newtownards D5
Newtownmountkennedy F5
Newtownhamilton D4
Newtownstewart D4
Newtown Butler E4
Newtown Forbes E3
Nobber E4

Oilgate G4
Oldcastle E4
Omagh D4
Omeath E5
Oola G3
Oranmore F2
Oughterard F2
Ovens H2

Pallas Grean G3
Parknasilla H1
Partry E2
Passage East H4
Passage West H3
Patrickswell G2
Paulstown G4
Pettigo D3
Plumbridge D4
Pomeroy D4
Portadown D5
Portaferry D5
Portarlington F4
Portavogie D5
Portglenone D5
Portlaoise F4
Portmarnock F5
Portrane F5
Portroe G3
Portrush C4
Portstewart C4
Portumna F3
Poyntzpass D5

Raharney F4
Randalstown D5
Rasharkin C5
Rathangen F4
Rathcoole F4
Rathcormack H3
Rathdowney G3
Rathdrum G5
Rathfriland E5

Rathkeale G2
Rath Luirc G2
(Charleville)
Rathmelton C4
Rathmolyon F4
Rathmore H2
Rathmullan C4
Rathnew F5
Rathowen E4
Rathvilly G4
Ratoath F4
Ray C4
Ring H3
(An Rinn)
Ringaskiddy H3
Riverstown F3
Rockcorry E4
Roosky E3
Rosapenna C3
Rosbercon G4
Roscommon E3
Roscrea F3
Ross Carbery J2
Roscor D3
Rosses Point D3
Rosslare Harbour H4
Roslea E4
Rostrevor E5
Roundstone F2
Roundwood F5
Rush F5

St Johnstown C4
Saintfield D5
Sallins F4
Scarriff G3
Scartaglen H2
Scarva D5
Schull J2
Scramoge E3
Scribbagh D3
Seskinore D4
Shanagolden G2
Shannonbridge F3
Shercock E4
Shillelagh G4
Shinrone F3
Shrule E2
Silvermines G3
Sion Mills D4
Sixmilebridge G2
Skerries F5
Skibbereen J2
Slane E4
Sligo D3
Smithborough E4
Sneem H1
Spiddal F2
(An Spideal)
Stewartstown D4
Stonyford G4
Strabane D4
Stradbally F4
Stradone E4
Strandhill D3
Strangford D5
Stranorlar D3
Stratford F4
Strokestown E3
Summerhill F4
Swanlinbar E4
Swatragh D4
Swinford E2
Swords F5

Taghmon G4
Tagoat H4
Tahilla H1
Tallaght F5
Tallow H3
Tallowbridge H3
Tandragee D5
Tang F3
Tarbert G2
Templemore G3
Templepatrick D5
Templetouhy G3
Termonfeckin E5
Thomas Street F3
Thomastown G4
Thurles G3
Timahoe F4
Timoleague H2
Tinahely G4
Tipperary G3
Tobercurry E3
Tobermore D4
Togher F3
Toomyvara G3
Toomore J2
Tralee G2
Tramore H4
Trim E4
Tuam F2
Tuamgraney G3
Tulla G2
Tullamore F4
Tullow G4
Tulsk E3
Turlough F2
Tyholland D4
Tyrrellspass F4

Urlingford G3

Virginia E4

Waddington H4
Warrenpoint E5
Waterford H4
Watergrasshill H3
Waterville H1
Westport E2
Wexford G4
Whitegate H3
Whitehead D5
Wicklow G5
Woodenbridge G5
Woodford F3

Youghal H3

C

D

E

1

2

Blood
Go
Isla
Dun
Aran Island
Gweebarra Bay
Ardara
Glencolumbkille (Gleann Cholm Cille)
Rossan Point
Malin More
Glencolumbkille Folk Museum
SLIEVE LEAGUE 601
Carrick (An Charraig)
Killybegs
Kilcar (Cill Charthaigh)
St John's Point
Donegal Bay
Bund
Inishmurray
Grange
Cliffony
Lissadell
BENBULBEN 525
Rosses Point
Sligo Bay
Strandhill
Sligo
Ballysadare

Erris Head
Broad Haven
Downpatrick Head
Ballycastle
Easky
Dromore West
Strandhill
Enniscrone
Killala Bay
Killala
Belmullet (Béal an Mhuirhead)
Bunnahowen
Inishkea
Bangor Erris
Carrowmore Lough
Duvillaun More
Blacksod Bay
SLIEVE MORE 672
722
Crossmolina
Ballina
Bunnyconnellan
Colloney
Achill Head
Keel
Achill Island
NEPHIN 806
Lough Feeagh
Lough Cullin
Foxford
Curry
Charlestown
Carracastle
Ballymote
Tobercurry
Swinford
Knock Regional Airport
Knock
Ballaghaderreen
Frenchp
Clare Island
Newport
Castlebar
Turlough
Kiltimagh
Kilkelly
Clew Bay
Westport
Ballyhean
Balla
Knock
Loughglinn
Inishturk
Louisburgh
CROAGH PATRICK 765
Ballyhean
Lough Carra
Castlerea
Caher Island

N314 N59 R314 R313 R315 R312 R310 R311 R294 R293 R292 R290 R284 R361 R335 R330 R322 R325 R323 R324 R320 R331 R294 N17 N59 N26 N5 N4 N83 N84 N60

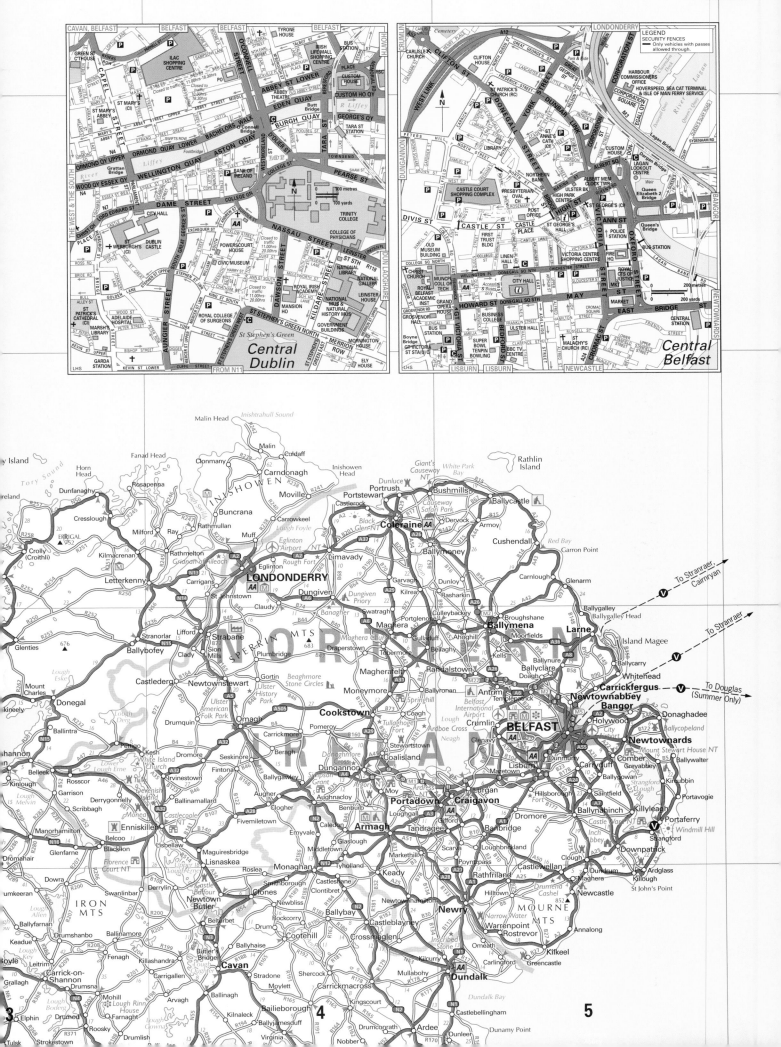

Central Dublin

Central Belfast

LEGEND
SECURITY FENCES
— Only vehicles with passes allowed through.

HOVERSPEED, SEA CAT TERMINAL & ISLE OF MAN FERRY SERVICE
HARBOUR COMMISSIONERS OFFICE

To Stranraer, Cairnryan
To Stranraer
To Douglas (Summer Only)

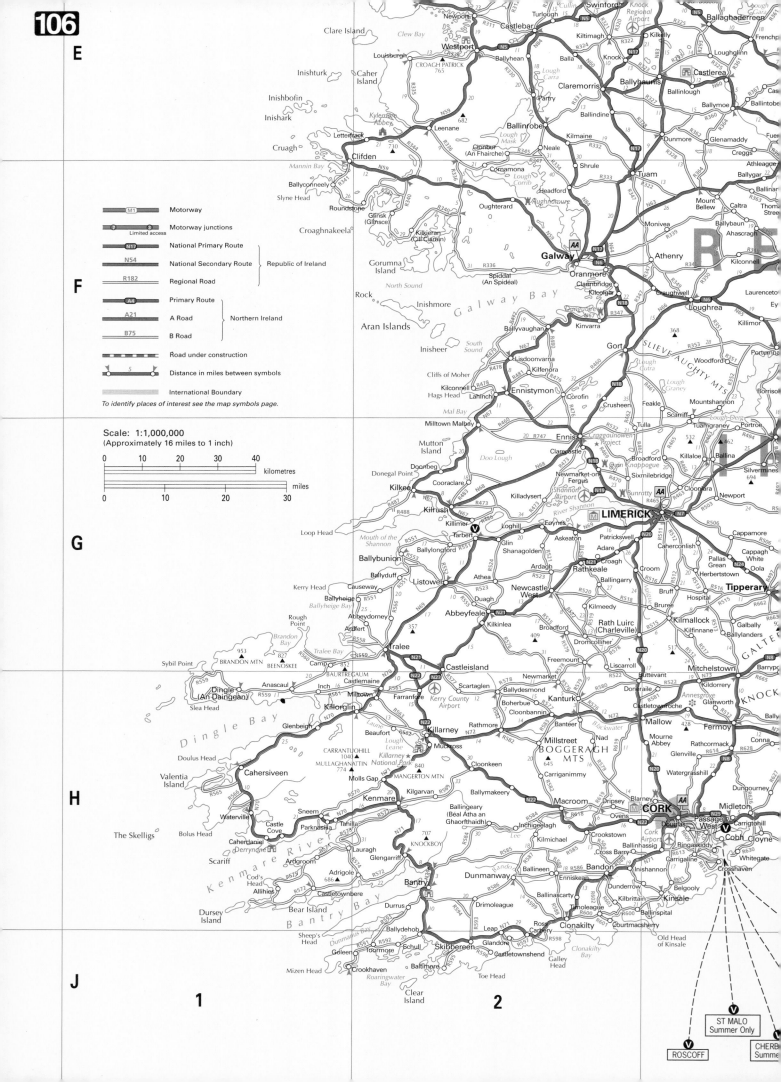

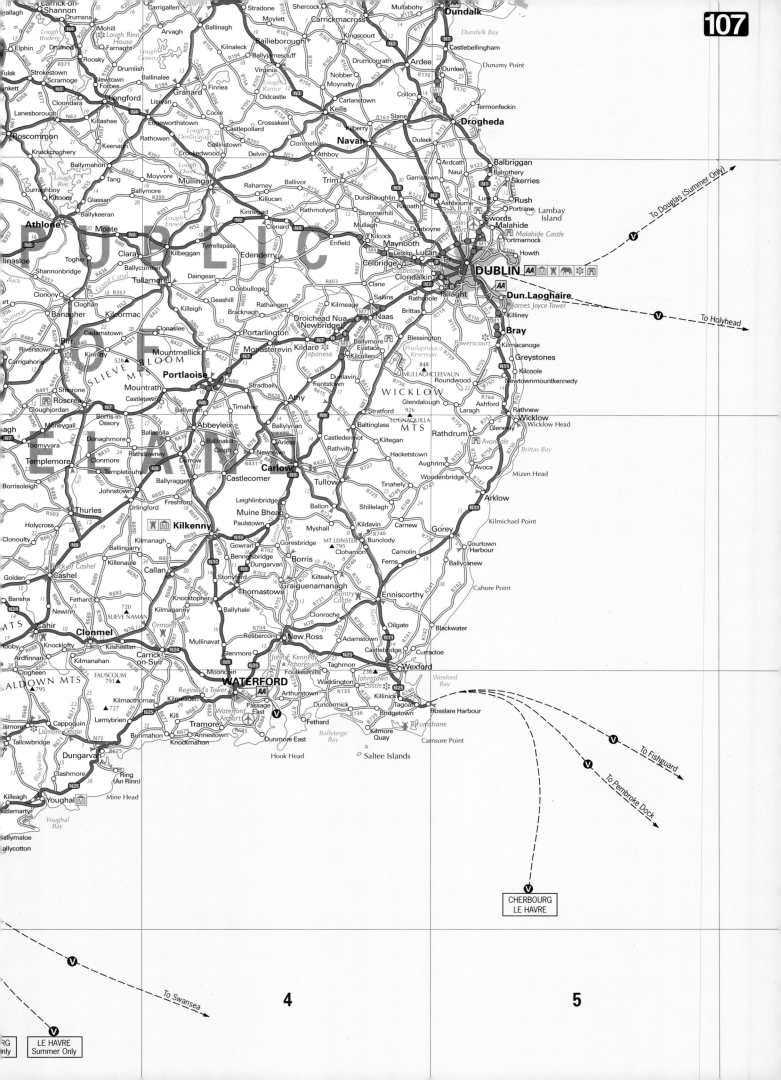

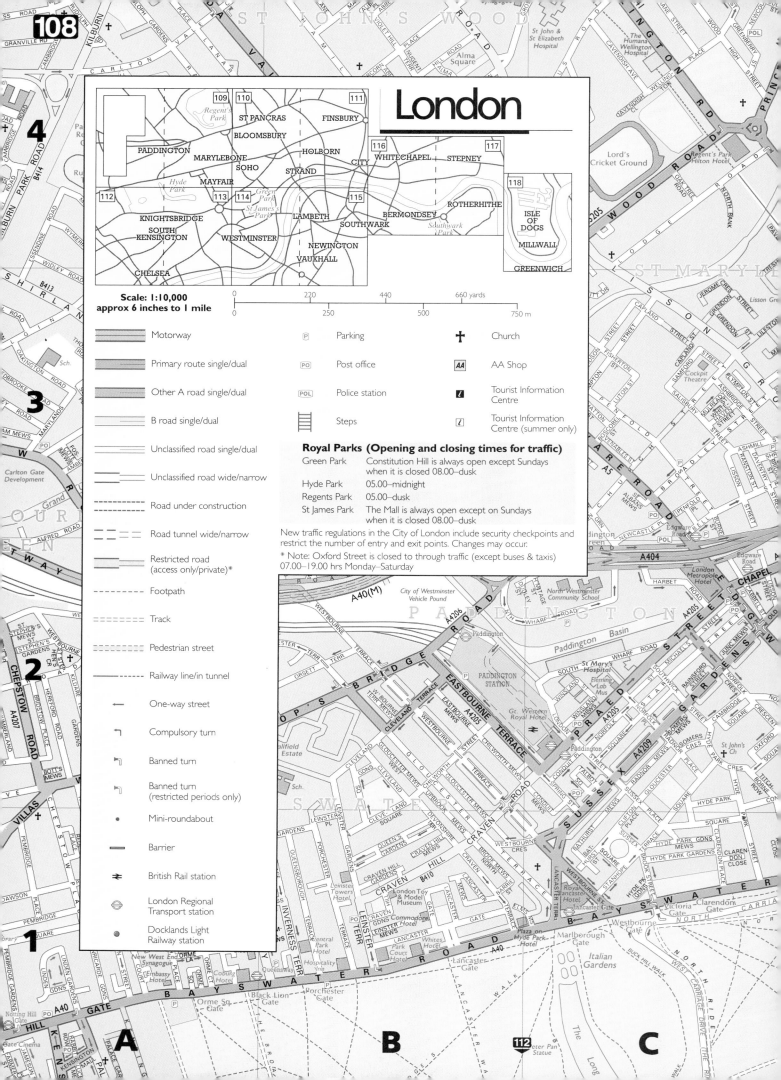

London

St John's Wood

109 110 111
Regent's Park
St Pancras
Bloomsbury
Finsbury
116 117
Paddington
Marylebone
Soho
Holborn
City
Whitechapel
Stepney
Hyde Park
Mayfair
Strand
118
112
113 114
Green Park
St James's Park
115
Isle of Dogs
Knightsbridge
South Kensington
Lambeth
Southwark
Bermondsey
Rotherhithe
Southwark Park
Millwall
Westminster
Newington
Vauxhall
Greenwich
Chelsea

Scale: 1:10,000
approx 6 inches to 1 mile

0   220   440   660 yards
0   250   500   750 m

Motorway	
Primary route single/dual	
Other A road single/dual	
B road single/dual	
Unclassified road single/dual	
Unclassified road wide/narrow	
Road under construction	
Road tunnel wide/narrow	
Restricted road (access only/private)*	
Footpath	
Track	
Pedestrian street	
Railway line/in tunnel	
One-way street	
Compulsory turn	
Banned turn	
Banned turn (restricted periods only)	
Mini-roundabout	
Barrier	
British Rail station	
London Regional Transport station	
Docklands Light Railway station	

P Parking
PO Post office
POL Police station
Steps

Church
AA AA Shop
i Tourist Information Centre
i Tourist Information Centre (summer only)

Royal Parks (Opening and closing times for traffic)

Green Park — Constitution Hill is always open except Sundays when it is closed 08.00–dusk

Hyde Park — 05.00–midnight

Regents Park — 05.00–dusk

St James Park — The Mall is always open except on Sundays when it is closed 08.00–dusk

New traffic regulations in the City of London include security checkpoints and restrict the number of entry and exit points. Changes may occur.

* Note: Oxford Street is closed to through traffic (except buses & taxis) 07.00–19.00 hrs Monday–Saturday

London street index

In the index the street names are listed in alphabetical order and written in full, but may be abbreviated on the map. Postal codes are listed where information is available. Each entry is followed by its map page number in bold type, and an arbitrary letter and grid reference number. For example for Exhibition Road SW7 **112** C3, turn to page '112. The letter 'C' refers to the grid square located at the bottom of the page. The figure '3' refers to the grid square located at the lefthand side of the page. Exhibition Road is found within the intersecting square. SW7 refers to the postcode. A proportion of street names and their references are also followed by the name of another street in italics. These entries do not appear on the map due to insufficient space but can be located adjacent to the name of the road in italics.

A

Abbey Orchard Street SW1 **114** B3
Abbey Street SE1 **116** A1
Abbots Lane SE1 **116** A2
Abchurch Lane EC4 **111** F1
Aberdour Street SE1 **115** F2
Abingdon Road W8 **112** A3
Abingdon Street SW1 **114** B3
Abingdon Villas W8 **112** A3
Achilles Way W1 **113** E4
Ackroyd Drive E3 **117** F4
Acorn Walk SE16 **117** F2
Acton Street WC1 **110** C4
Adam And Eve Court W1 **109** E1
  Oxford Street
Adam And Eve Mews W8 **112** A3
Adam Street WC2 **110** B1
Adam's Row W1 **109** E1
Adams Place E14 **118** A4
Addington Street SE1 **114** C3
Addle Hill EC4 **111** E1
Addle Street EC2 **111** E2
Adelaide Street WC2 **110** B1
  William IV Street
Adelina Grove E1 **116** D4
Adeline Place WC1 **110** B2
Adelphi Terrace WC2 **110** B1
  Adams Street
Adler Street E1 **116** B4
Admiral Place E1 **117** E2
Admirals Way E14 **118** A3
Adpar Street W2 **108** C3
Adrian Mews SW10 **112** A1
Agar Street WC2 **110** B1
Agatha Close E1 **116** C2
Agdon Street EC1 **111** D3
Agnes Street E14 **117** F4
Ainstey Street SE16 **117** D1
  Brunel Road
Air Street W1 **110** A1
Alaska Street SE1 **114** C4
Albany Mews SE5 **115** E1
Albany Road SE5 **115** E1
Albany Street NW1 **109** F4
Albatross Way SE16 **117** D1
Albemarle Street W1 **109** F1
Albemarle Way EC1 **110** C3
  Clerkenwell Road
Albert Court SW7 **112** C3
Albert Embankment SE1 **114** B1
Albert Gardens E1 **117** D3
Albert Hall Mansions SW7 **112** B3
Albert Place W8 **112** B3
Alberta Street SE17 **115** D1
Albion Close W2 **109** D1
Albion Mews W2 **109** D1
Albion Place EC1 **111** D3
Albion Street SE16 **117** D1
Albion Street W2 **109** D1
Albion Way EC1 **111** E2
Aldburgh Mews W1 **109** E2
  Marylebone Lane
Aldenham Street NW1 **110** A4
Aldermanbury EC2 **111** E2
Aldermanbury Square EC2 **111** E2
  Aldermanbury
Alderney Street SW1 **113** F2
Aldersgate Street EC1 **111** E3
Aldford Street W1 **109** E1
Aldgate EC3 **116** A3
Aldgate High Street EC3 **116** A3
Aldwych WC2 **110** C1
Alexander Place SW7 **112** C2
Alexander Square SW3 **112** C2
Alford Place N1 **111** E4
Alfred Mews W1 **110** A3
Alfred Place WC1 **110** A3

Alice Street SE1 **115** F3
Alie Street E1 **116** B3
All Hallows Lane EC4 **111** F1
All Soul's Place W1 **109** F2
  Langham Street
Allen Street W8 **112** A3
Allington Street SW1 **113** F3
Allsop Place NW1 **109** D3
Alpha Grove E14 **118** A3
Alpha Place SW3 **113** D1
Alsace Road SE17 **115** F1
Alscot Road SE1 **116** B1
Alvey Street SE17 **115** F2
Ambassador Square E14 **118** B2
Ambergate Street SE17 **115** D1
Ambrosden Avenue SW1 **114** A3
Amelia Street SE17 **115** E2
Amen Corner EC4 **111** D2
Amen Court EC4 **111** D2
America Square EC3 **116** A3
America Street SE1 **115** E4
Amoy Place E14 **117** F3
Ampton Place WC1 **110** C4
Ampton Street WC1 **110** C4
Amsterdam Road E14 **118** C2
Amwell Street EC1 **110** C4
Anderson Street SW3 **113** D2
Andrew Borde Street WC2 **110** A2
  Charing Cross Road
Angel Court EC2 **111** F2
Angel Passage EC4 **111** F1
Angel Place SE1 **115** E4
Angel Street EC1 **111** E2
Ann Moss Way SE16 **117** D1
Ansdell Street W8 **112** A3
Antill Terrace E1 **117** D4
Apothecary Street EC4 **111** D2
  New Bridge Street
Apple Tree Yard SW1 **110** A1
Appold Street EC2 **111** F3
Aquinas Street SE1 **115** D4
Arbour Square E1 **117** D4
Archangel Street SE16 **117** E1
Archer Street W1 **110** A1
Arden Crescent E14 **118** A2
Argent Street SE1 **115** E4
  Loman Street
Argyle Square WC1 **110** B4
Argyle Street WC1 **110** B4
Argyle Walk WC1 **110** B4
Argyll Road W8 **112** A3
Argyll Street W1 **109** F2
Arlington Street SW1 **113** F4
Arlington Way EC1 **111** D4
Arne Street WC2 **110** B2
Arneway Street SW1 **114** A2
Arnside Street SE17 **115** E1
Arthur Street EC4 **111** F1
Artichoke Hill E1 **116** C3
Artillery Lane E1 **116** A4
Artillery Passage E1 **116** A4
  Artillery Lane
Artillery Row SW1 **114** A3
Artizan Street E1 **116** A4
  Harrow Place
Arundel Street WC2 **110** C1
Ashbridge Street NW8 **108** C3
Ashburn Gardens SW7 **112** B2
Ashburn Mews SW7 **112** B2
Ashburn Place SW7 **112** B2
Ashby Street EC1 **111** D4
Ashdown Walk E14 **118** A2
Asher Drive E1 **116** B3
Ashfield Street E1 **116** C4
Ashland Place W1 **109** E3
Ashley Place SW1 **113** F3
Ashmill Street NW1 **108** C3
Aske Street N1 **111** F4
Aspen Way E14 **118** B4
Assam Street E1 **116** B4
Assembly Passage E1 **117** D4
Aste Street E14 **118** B3
Astell Street SW3 **113** D2
Aston Street E14 **117** E4
Astwood Mews SW7 **112** B2
Atherstone Mews SW7 **112** B2
Atterbury Street SW1 **114** B2
Attneave Street WC1 **110** C4
Auckland Street SE11 **114** C1
Augustus Street NW1 **109** F4
Aulton Place SE11 **115** D1
Austin Friars EC2 **111** F2
Austin Friars Square EC2 **111** F2
  Austin Friars
Austral Street SE11 **115** D2
Ave Maria Lane EC4 **111** E2
Aveline Street SE11 **114** C1
Avery Row W1 **109** F1
Avis Square E1 **117** E4
Avon Place SE1 **115** E3
Avonmouth Street SE1 **115** E3
Aybrook Street W1 **109** E2
Aylesbury Road SE17 **115** F1
Aylesbury Street EC1 **111** D3
Aylesford Street SW1 **114** A1
Aylward Street E1 **117** D4
Ayres Street SE1 **115** E4

B

Babmaes Street SW1 **114** A4
  Jermyn Street
Bacchus Walk N1 **111** F4
Bache's Street N1 **111** F4
Back Church Lane E1 **116** B4
Back Hill EC1 **111** D3
Bacon Grove SE1 **116** A1
Bainbridge Street WC1 **110** B2
Baker Street W1 & NW1 **109** D3
Baker's Mews W1 **109** E2
Baker's Row EC1 **111** D3
Baker's Yard EC1 **111** D3
  Baker's Row
Bakers Hall Court EC3 **116** A3
  Harp Lane
Balcombe Street NW1 **109** D3
Balderton Street W1 **109** E1
Baldwin Street EC1 **111** F4
Baldwin's Gardens EC1 **110** C3
Balfe Street N1 **110** B4
Balfour Mews W1 **109** E1
Balfour Place W1 **109** E1
Balfour Street SE17 **115** F2
Ballast Quay SE10 **118** C1

Balneil Gate SW1 **114** A1
Baltic Street EC1 **111** E3
Balvaird Place SW1 **114** B2
Bancroft Road E1 **114** C1
Bank End SE1 **115** E4
Bankside Jetty SE1 **111** E1
Banner Street EC1 **111** E3
Banyard Road SE16 **117** D1
Barbon Close WC1 **110** C3
Barge House Street SE1 **111** D1
Barkston Gardens SW5 **112** A2
Barleycorn Way E14 **117** F3
Barlow Place W1 **109** F1
Barlow Street SE17 **115** F2
Barnaby Place SW7 **112** C2
Barnardo Street E1 **117** D3
Barnby Street NW1 **110** A4
Barnes Street E14 **117** E4
Barnfield Place E14 **118** A2
Barnham Street SE1 **116** A2
Barnsdale Avenue E14 **118** A2
Baron's Place SE1 **115** D3
Barque Mews SE8 **118** A1
Barrett Street W1 **109** E2
  St Johns Wood High Street
Barrie Street W2 **108** B1
Barrow Hill Road NW8 **108** C4
Barter Street WC1 **110** B2
Barth Lane EC2 **111** E2
Bartholomew Close EC1 **111** E2
Bartholomew Lane EC2 **111** F2
Bartholomew Street SE1 **115** F3
Barton Street SW1 **114** B3
Basil Street SW3 **113** D3
Bate Street E14 **117** F3
Bateman Street W1 **110** A2
Bath Court EC1 **110** C3
  Warner Street
Bath Place N1 **111** E4
Bath Street EC1 **111** E4
Bath Terrace SE1 **115** E3
Bathurst Mews W2 **108** C1
Bathurst Street W2 **108** C1
Battle Bridge Lane SE1 **115** F4
Batty Street E1 **116** B4
Bayley Street WC1 **110** A2
Baylis Road SE1 **114** C3
Bayswater Road W2 **108** A1
Baythorne Street E3 **117** F4
Beaconsfield Road SE17 **115** F1
Beak Street W1 **110** A1
Bear Gardens SE1 **111** E1
Bear Lane SE1 **115** D4
Bear Street WC2 **110** B1
  Cranbourn Street
Beatrice Place W8 **112** A2
Beauchamp Place SW3 **113** D3
Beaumont Street EC1 **111** D3
  Brooke Street
Beaufort Gardens SW3 **113** D3
Beaufort Street SW3 **112** B1
Beaumont Mews W1 **109** E2
Beaumont Place W1 **110** A3
Beaumont Street W1 **109** E3
Beccles Street E14 **117** F3
Beckway Street SE17 **115** F2
Bedale Street SE1 **115** E3
  Borough High Street
Bedford Avenue WC1 **110** B2
Bedford Court WC2 **110** B1
Bedford Gardens W8 **112** A4
Bedford Place WC1 **110** B3
Bedford Row WC1 **110** C3
Bedford Square WC1 **110** B2
Bedford Street WC2 **110** B1
Bedford Way WC1 **110** B3
Bedfordbury WC2 **110** B1
Bedser Close SE11 **114** C1
Beech Street EC2 **111** E3
Beeston Place SW1 **113** F3
Bekesbourne Street E14 **117** E4
  Marylebone Lane
Belgrave Mews North SW1 **113** E3
Belgrave Mews South SW1 **113** E3
Belgrave Mews West SW1 **113** E3
Belgrave Place SW1 **113** E3
Belgrave Road SW1 **113** F3
Belgrave Square SW1 **113** E3
Belgrave Street E1 **117** E3
Belgrove Street WC1 **110** B4
Bell Lane E1 **116** A4
Bell Street NW1 **108** C3
Bell Yard WC2 **110** C2
Belvedere Buildings SE1 **115** E3
Belvedere Road SE1 **114** C4
Ben Jonson Road E1 **117** E4
Ben Smith Way SE16 **116** B1
Benbow Street SE8 **118** A1
Bendall Mews W1 **109** D3
Bennet's Hill EC4 **111** E1
  Castle Baynard Street
Benson Quay E1 **117** D3
Bentinck Mews W1 **109** E2
  Marylebone Lane
Bentinck Street W1 **109** E2
Bere Street E1 **117** E3
Bergen Square SE16 **117** E1
Berkeley Gardens W8 **112** A4
Berkeley Mews W1 **109** D2
Berkeley Square W1 **109** F1
Berkeley Street W1 **109** F1
Bermondsey Square SE1 **111** E2
  Long Lane
Bermondsey Street SE1 **116** A2
Bermondsey Wall East SE16 **116** B1
Bermondsey Wall West SE16 **116** B2
Bernard Street WC1 **110** B3
Berners Mews W1 **110** A2
Berners Street W1 **110** A2
Berry Street EC1 **111** E3
Berryfield Road SE17 **115** E1
Berwick Street W1 **110** A2
Bessborough Gardens SW1 **114** B2
Bessborough Place SW1 **114** A1
Bessborough Street SW1 **114** A1
Betterton Street WC2 **110** B2
Betts Street E1 **116** C3
Bevenden Street N1 **111** F4
Bevin Close SE16 **117** E2
Bevin Way WC1 **110** C4
Bevington Street SE16 **116** B1
Bevis Marks EC3 **116** A4
Bewley Street E1 **116** C3
Bickenhall Street W1 **109** D3
Bidborough Street WC1 **110** B4

Bigland Street E1 **116** C3
Billiter Square EC3 **116** A3
  Fenchurch Avenue
Billiter Street EC3 **116** A3
Billson Street E14 **118** C2
Bina Gardens SW5 **112** B2
Bingham Place W1 **109** E3
Binney Street W1 **109** E1
Birchfield Street E14 **117** E3
Birchin Lane EC3 **111** F1
Bird Street W1 **109** E2
Birdcage Walk SW1 **114** A3
Birkenhead Street WC1 **110** B4
Bishop's Court EC4 **111** D2
  Old Bailey
Bishop's Court WC2 **110** C2
  Chancery Lane
Bishop's Terrace SE11 **115** D2
Bishops Bridge Road W2 **108** B2
Bishopsgate EC2 **111** F2
Bishopsgate Arcade EC2 **116** A4
Bishopsgate Churchyard EC2 **111** F2
Bittern Street SE1 **115** E3
Black Prince Road SE1 & SE11 **114** C2
Black Swan Yard SE1 **116** A2
Blackall Street EC2 **111** F3
Blackburne's Mews W1 **109** E1
Blackfriars Bridge EC4 & SE1 **111** D1
Blackfriars Court EC4 **111** D1
Blackfriars Passage EC4 **111** D1
Blackfriars Road SE1 **115** D4
Blacklands Terrace SW3 **113** D2
Blackwall Tunnel E14 & SE1 **118** C4
Blackwall Way E14 **118** C4
Blackwood Street SE17 **115** F1
Blandford Square NW1 **109** D3
Blandford Street W1 **109** E2
Blasker Walk E14 **118** A1
Bleeding Heart Yard EC1 **111** D2
  Greville Street
Blenheim Street W1 **109** F1
  New Bond Street
Bletchley Street N1 **111** E4
Blithfield Street W8 **112** A3
Blomfield Street EC2 **111** F2
Bloomburg Street SW1 **113** F2
  Vauxhall Bridge Road
Bloomfield Place W1 **109** F1
  Bourdon Street
Bloomfield Terrace SW1 **113** E2
Bloomsbury Court WC1 **110** B2
  High Holborn
Bloomsbury Place WC1 **110** B3
  Southampton Row
Bloomsbury Square WC1 **110** B2
Bloomsbury Street WC1 **110** B2
Bloomsbury Way WC1 **110** B2
Blount Street E14 **117** E4
Blue Anchor Yard E1 **116** B3
Blyth Close E14 **118** C2
Bolsover Street W1 **109** F3
Bolt Court EC4 **111** D2
Bolton Gardens SW5 **112** A2
Bolton Gardens Mews SW10 **112** B1
Bolton Street W1 **113** F4
Bond Way SW8 **114** B1
Bonding Yard Walk SE16 **117** E1
Bonhill Street EC2 **111** F3
Bonnington Square SW8 **114** C1
Booker Close E14 **117** F4
Boot Street N1 **111** F4
Booth's Place W1 **109** F2
  Wells Street
Boreas Walk N1 **111** E4
  Nelson Place
Borough High Street SE1 **115** E3
Borough Road SE1 **115** E3
Borrett Close SE17 **115** E1
Borthwick Street SE8 **118** A1
Boscobel Place SW1 **113** E2
Boscobel Street NW8 **108** C3
Boss Street SE1 **116** A2
Boston Place NW1 **108** D3
Boswell Court WC1 **110** B3
  Boswell Street
Boswell Street WC1 **110** B3
Botolph Lane EC3 **111** F1
Bott's Mews W2 **108** A2
Boulcott Street E1 **117** E3
Boundary Lane SE17 **115** E1
Boundary Road SE1 **115** F4
Bourdon Street W1 **109** F1
Bourlet Close W1 **109** F2
Bourne Street SW1 **113** E2
Bouverie Street EC4 **111** D1
Bow Lane EC4 **111** E1
Bow Street WC2 **110** B2
Bowden Street SE11 **115** D1
Bower Street E1 **117** E3
Bowling Green Lane EC1 **111** D3
Bowling Green Place SE1 **115** F4
  Newcomen Street
Bowling Green Walk N1 **111** F4
Boyd Street E1 **116** B3
Boyfield Street SE1 **115** D3
Boyle Street W1 **109** F1
  Savile Row
Boyson Road SE17 **115** F1
Brackley Street EC1 **111** E3
Brad Street SE1 **115** D4
Bradenham Close SE17 **115** F1
Braganza Street SE17 **115** D1
Braham Street E1 **116** B3
Bramerton Street SW3 **112** C1
Bramham Gardens SW5 **112** A2
Branch Road E14 **117** E3
Brandon Street SE17 **115** E2
Brangton Road SE11 **114** C1
Brass Tally Alley SE16 **117** E1
Bray Crescent SE16 **117** D2
Bray Place SW3 **113** D2
Bread Street EC4 **111** E1
Bream's Buildings EC **110** C2
Brechin Place SW7 **112** B2
Breezer's Hill E1 **116** C3
Bremner Road SW7 **112** B3
Brendon Street W1 **109** D2
Brenton Street E14 **117** E4
Bressenden Place SW1 **113** F3
Brettell Street SE17 **115** F1
Brewer Street W1 **110** A1
Brewers' Green SW1 **114** A3
  Caxton Street
Brewhouse Lane E1 **116** C2
Brewhouse Walk SE16 **117** E2
Brick Court EC4 **110** C2
  Middle Temple Lane

Brick Street W1 .... 113 E4
Bride Lane EC4 .... 111 D2
Bridewain Street SE1 .... 116 B1
Bridewell Place EC4 .... 111 D1
Bridford Mews W1 .... 109 F3
Bridge House Quay E14 .... 118 C4
Bridge Place SW1 .... 113 F2
Bridge Street SW1 .... 114 B3
Bridge Yard SE1 .... 115 F4
Bridgeport Place E1 .... 116 B2
Kennet Street
Bridgewater Gardens EC2 .... 111 E3
Beech Street
Bridgewater Street EC2 .... 111 E3
Beech Street
Bridgeway Street NW1 .... 110 A2
Bridle Lane W1 .... 110 A1
Brightlingsea Place E14 .... 117 F3
Brill Place NW1 .... 110 A4
Briset Street EC1 .... 111 D3
Britannia Road SW6 .... 112 A2
Britannia Street WC1 .... 110 C4
Britannia Walk N1 .... 111 F4
Britten Street SW3 .... 112 C1
Britton Street EC1 .... 111 D3
Broad Court WC2 .... 110 B2
Broad Sanctuary SW1 .... 114 B3
Broad Walk W2 .... 113 E4
Broadbent Street W1 .... 109 F1
Broadley Street NW8 .... 108 C4
Broadley Terrace NW1 .... 109 D3
Broadstone Place W1 .... 109 E2
Broadwall SE1 .... 115 D4
Broadway SW1 .... 114 A3
Broadwick Street W1 .... 110 A1
Brockham Street SE1 .... 115 E3
Brodlove Lane E1 .... 117 D3
Bromley Place W1 .... 117 E4
Brompton Place SW3 .... 113 D3
Brompton Road SW3 .... 113 D3
Brompton Square SW3 .... 112 C3
Bronti Close SE17 .... 115 E1
Brook Drive SE11 .... 115 D2
Brook Gate W1 .... 109 D1
Brook Mews North W2 .... 108 B1
Brook Street W1 .... 109 E1
Brook Street W2 .... 108 C1
Brook's Mews W1 .... 109 F1
Brooke Street EC1 .... 111 D2
Brooke's Court EC1 .... 110 C2
Brooke's Market EC1 .... 111 D2
Brooke Street
Brown Hart Gardens W1 .... 109 E1
Brown Street W1 .... 109 D2
Browning Street SE17 .... 115 E2
Brownlow Mews WC1 .... 110 C3
Brownlow Street WC1 .... 110 C2
Brune Street E1 .... 116 A4
Brunel Road SE16 .... 117 D1
Brunswick Gardens W8 .... 112 A4
Brunswick Mews W1 .... 109 D2
Brunswick Place N1 .... 111 F4
Brunswick Quay SE16 .... 117 E1
Brunswick Square WC1 .... 110 B3
Brunton Place E14 .... 117 E3
Brushfield Street E1 .... 116 A4
Bruton Lane W1 .... 109 F1
Bruton Place W1 .... 109 F1
Bruton Street W1 .... 109 F1
Bryan Road SE16 .... 117 F2
Bryanston Mews East W1 .... 109 D2
Bryanston Mews West W1 .... 109 D2
Bryanston Place W1 .... 109 D2
Bryanston Square W1 .... 109 D2
Bryanston Street W1 .... 109 D2
Buck Hill Walk W2 .... 108 C1
Buck Street WC2 .... 110 B1
Buckingham Gate SW1 .... 113 F3
Buckingham Palace Road SW1 .... 113 F2
Buckingham Place SW1 .... 113 F3
Buckland Street N1 .... 111 F4
Buckle Street E1 .... 116 B4
Bucklersbury EC4 .... 111 F2
Bucknall Street WC2 .... 110 B2
Buckters Rents SE16 .... 117 E2
Budge's Walk W2 .... 108 B4
Bulleid Way SW1 .... 113 F2
Bulstrode Place W1 .... 109 E2
Marylebone Lane
Bulstrode Street W1 .... 109 E2
Bunhill Row EC1 .... 111 F3
Bunhouse Place SW1 .... 113 E2
Burbage Close SE1 .... 115 E2
Burdett Street SE1 .... 115 D3
Burge Street SE1 .... 115 F3
Burgess Street E14 .... 117 F4
Burgon Street EC4 .... 111 E2
Carter Lane
Burleigh Street WC2 .... 110 B1
Burlington Arcade W1 .... 109 F1
Burlington Gardens W1 .... 109 F1
Burne Street NW1 .... 108 C3
Burnsall Street SW3 .... 113 D1
Burnside Close SE16 .... 117 E2
Burr Close E1 .... 116 B2
Burrell Street SE1 .... 115 D4
Burrells Wharf Square E14 .... 118 A1
Burrows Mews SE1 .... 115 D4
Bursar Street SE1 .... 116 A2
Tooley Street
Burslem Street E1 .... 116 C3
Burton Grove SE17 .... 115 F1
Burton Street WC1 .... 110 B4
Burwell Close E1 .... 116 C3
Burwood Place W2 .... 109 D2
Bury Close SE16 .... 117 E2
Bury Court EC3 .... 116 A4
Bury Place WC1 .... 110 B2
Bury Street EC3 .... 116 A3
Bury Street SW1 .... 114 A4
Bury Walk SW3 .... 112 C2
Bush Lane EC4 .... 111 E1
Bushell Street E1 .... 116 B2
Wapping High Street
Butcher Row E1 .... 117 E3
Bute Street SW7 .... 112 C1
Butler Place SW1 .... 113 F3
Buckingham Gate
Butterfield Close SE16 .... 116 C1
Buttesland Street N1 .... 111 F4
Byfield Close SE16 .... 117 E2
Byng Place WC1 .... 110 A3
Byng Street E14 .... 118 A3
Byward Street EC3 .... 116 A3
Bywater Place SE16 .... 117 E2
Bywater Street SW3 .... 113 D2

C

Cabbell Street NW1 .... 108 C2
Cable Street E1 .... 116 B3
Cabot Square E14 .... 118 A4
Cadiz Street SE17 .... 115 E1
Cadogan Gardens SW3 .... 113 D2
Cadogan Gate SW1 .... 113 D2
Cadogan Lane SW1 .... 113 E3
Cadogan Place SW1 .... 113 E2
Cadogan Square SW1 .... 113 D2
Cadogan Street SW3 .... 113 D2
Cahill Street EC1 .... 111 E3
Dufferin Street
Cahir Street E14 .... 118 A2
Cale Street SW3 .... 112 C2
Caleb Street SE1 .... 115 E4
Marshalsea Road
Caledonia Street N1 .... 110 B4
Caledonian Road N1 & N7 .... 110 B4
Caledonian Wharf E14 .... 118 C2
Callingham Close E14 .... 117 F4
Callow Street SW3 .... 112 B1
Calthorpe Street WC1 .... 110 C3
Camberwell Road SE5 .... 115 E1
Cambridge Circus WC2 .... 110 B1
Cambridge Gate NW1 .... 109 F4
Cambridge Gate Mews NW1 .... 109 F4
Albany Street
Cambridge Place W8 .... 112 B3
Cambridge Square W2 .... 108 C2
Cambridge Street SW1 .... 113 F2
Cambridge Terrace Mews NW1 .... 110 F4
Chester Gate
Camdenhurst Street E14 .... 117 E4
Camera Place SW10 .... 112 B1
Cameron Place E1 .... 116 C4
Camomile Street EC3 .... 116 A4
Campden Grove W8 .... 112 A4
Campden Hill Road W8 .... 112 A3
Camperdown Street E1 .... 116 B3
Canada Square E14 .... 118 B4
Canada Street SE16 .... 117 E1
Canal Street SE5 .... 115 F1
Candover Street W1 .... 109 F2
Foley Street
Canning Passage W8 .... 112 B3
Canning Place W8 .... 112 B3
Cannon Beck Road SE16 .... 117 D2
Cannon Drive E14 .... 117 F3
Cannon Row SW1 .... 114 B3
Cannon Street EC4 .... 111 E2
Cannon Street Road E1 .... 116 C3
Canterbury Place SE17 .... 115 E2
Canvey Street SE1 .... 115 E4
Cape Yard E1 .... 116 B3
Capland Street NW8 .... 108 C4
Capper Street WC1 .... 110 A3
Capstan Square E14 .... 118 C3
Capstan Way SE16 .... 117 E2
Carbis Road E14 .... 117 F4
Carburton Street W1 .... 109 F3
Cardale Street E14 .... 118 C3
Plevina Street
Cardigan Street SE11 .... 114 C1
Cardington Street NW1 .... 110 A4
Carey Lane EC2 .... 111 E2
Carey Street WC2 .... 110 C2
Carlisle Avenue EC3 .... 116 A3
Carlisle Lane SE1 .... 114 C3
Carlisle Place SW1 .... 113 F2
Carlisle Street W1 .... 110 A2
Carlos Place W1 .... 109 E1
Carlton Gardens SW1 .... 114 A4
Carlton House Terrace SW1 .... 114 A4
Carlyle Square SW3 .... 112 C1
Carmelite Street EC4 .... 111 D1
Carnaby Street W1 .... 110 A1
Caroline Place Mews W2 .... 108 A1
Caroline Place W2 .... 117 E1
Caroline Terrace SW1 .... 113 E2
Carpenter Street W1 .... 109 E1
Carr Street E14 .... 117 E4
Carrick Mews SE8 .... 118 A1
Carrington Street W1 .... 113 E4
Shepherd Street
Carter Lane EC4 .... 111 E2
Carter Place SE17 .... 115 E1
Carter Street SE17 .... 115 E1
Carteret Street SW1 .... 114 A3
Carthusian Street EC1 .... 111 E3
Cartier Circle E14 .... 118 B4
Carting Lane WC2 .... 110 C1
Cartwright Gardens WC1 .... 110 B4
Cartwright Street E1 .... 116 B3
Casson Street E1 .... 116 B4
Castalia Square E14 .... 118 B3
Castle Baynard Street EC4 .... 111 E1
Castle Lane SW1 .... 114 A3
Castle Yard SE1 .... 115 D4
Castor Lane E14 .... 118 A4
Catesby Street SE17 .... 115 F2
Cathay Street SE16 .... 116 C1
Cathcart Road SW10 .... 112 B1
Cathedral Piazza SW1 .... 113 F3
Cathedral Street SE1 .... 115 F4
Winchester Walk
Catherine Place SW1 .... 113 F3
Catherine Street WC2 .... 110 C1
Catherine Wheel Alley E1 .... 116 A4
Catton Street WC1 .... 110 C2
Causton Street SW1 .... 114 B2
Cavaye Place SW10 .... 112 B1
Cavell Street E1 .... 116 C4
Cavendish Avenue NW8 .... 108 C4
Cavendish Close NW8 .... 108 C4
Cavendish Mews North W1 .... 109 F2
Hallam Street
Cavendish Place W1 .... 109 F2
Cavendish Square W1 .... 109 F2
Caversham Street SW3 .... 113 D1
Caxton Street SW1 .... 114 A3
Cayton Place EC1 .... 111 E4
Cayton Street
Cayton Street EC1 .... 111 E4
Cecil Court WC2 .... 110 B1
St Martin's Lane
Centaur Street SE1 .... 114 C3
Central Street EC1 .... 111 E4
Chadwell Street EC1 .... 111 D4
Chadwick Street SW1 .... 114 A3
Chagford Street NW1 .... 109 D3
Chalton Street NW1 .... 110 A4
Chamber Street E1 .... 116 B3
Chambers Street SE16 .... 116 B1
Chancel Street SE1 .... 115 D4
Chancellor Passage E14 .... 118 A4
South Colonnade
Chancery Lane WC2 .... 110 C2
Chandler Street E1 .... 116 C2
Chandos Place WC2 .... 110 B1
Chandos Street W1 .... 109 F2
Chantry Square W8 .... 112 A3
Chapel Court SE1 .... 115 F4
Chapel House Street E14 .... 118 B1
Chapel Place W1 .... 109 F2
Chapel Side W2 .... 108 A1
Chapel Street NW1 .... 108 C2
Chapel Street SW1 .... 113 E3
Chapman Street E1 .... 116 C3
Chapter Road SE17 .... 115 E1
Chapter Street SW1 .... 114 A2
Chapter Terrace SE17 .... 115 E1
Chargrove Close SE16 .... 117 D2
Charing Cross Road WC2 .... 110 B1

Charles II Street SW1 .... 114 A4
Charles Square N1 .... 111 F4
Charleston Street SE17 .... 115 E2
Charlotte Place SW1 .... 110 A1
Wilton Road
Charlotte Place W1 .... 113 F2
Goodge Street
Charlotte Road EC2 .... 111 F4
Charlotte Street W1 .... 110 A3
Charlwood Street SW1 .... 114 A1
Charnwood Gardens E14 .... 118 A2
Chart Street N1 .... 111 F4
Charterhouse Square EC1 .... 111 E3
Charterhouse Street EC1 .... 111 D2
Chaseley Street E14 .... 117 E4
Chatham Street SE17 .... 115 F2
Cheapside EC4 .... 111 E2
Chelsea Bridge SW1 & SW8 .... 113 E1
Chelsea Bridge Road SW1 .... 113 E1
Chelsea Embankment SW3 .... 113 D1
Chelsea Manor Gardens SW3 .... 113 D1
Chelsea Manor Street SW3 .... 113 D1
Chelsea Park Gardens SW3 .... 112 C1
Chelsea Square SW3 .... 112 C1
Cheltenham Terrace SW3 .... 113 D2
Chenies Mews WC1 .... 110 A3
Chenies Street WC1 .... 110 A3
Cheniston Gardens W8 .... 112 A3
Chequer Street EC1 .... 111 E3
Cherbury Street N1 .... 111 F4
Cherry Garden Street SE16 .... 116 C1
Chesham Place SW1 .... 113 E3
Chesham Street SW1 .... 113 E3
Chester Close South NW1 .... 109 F4
Chester Court NW1 .... 109 F4
Albany Street
Chester Gate NW1 .... 109 F4
Chester Mews SW1 .... 113 E3
Chester Place NW1 .... 109 F4
Chester Row SW1 .... 113 E2
Chester Square SW1 .... 113 E2
Chester Street SW1 .... 113 E3
Chester Terrace NW1 .... 109 F4
Chester Way SE11 .... 115 D2
Chesterfield Gardens W1 .... 113 E4
Chesterfield Hill W1 .... 109 E1
Chesterfield Street W1 .... 113 E4
Cheval Place SW7 .... 113 D3
Cheval Street E14 .... 118 A3
Cheyne Gardens SW3 .... 112 D1
Cheyne Walk SW3 & SW10 .... 112 C1
Chicheley Street SE1 .... 114 C4
Chichester Parade E14 .... 118 C2
Chichester Rents WC2 .... 110 C2
Chancery Lane
Chicksand Street E1 .... 116 B4
Chigwell Hill E1 .... 116 C3
The Highway
Child's Place SW5 .... 112 A2
Child's Street SW5 .... 112 A2
Chiltern Street W1 .... 109 E3
Chilworth Mews W2 .... 108 B2
Chilworth Street W2 .... 108 B2
Chipka Street E14 .... 118 B3
Chiswell Street EC1 .... 111 E3
Chitty Street W1 .... 110 A3
Christchurch Street SW3 .... 113 D1
Christian Street E1 .... 116 C3
Christopher Close SE16 .... 116 D1
Christopher Street EC2 .... 111 F3
Chudleigh Street E1 .... 117 E4
Chumleigh Street SE5 .... 115 F1
Church Place SW1 .... 113 F4
Piccadilly
Church Street NW8 .... 108 C3
Church Yard Row SE11 .... 115 D2
Churchill Gardens Road SW1 .... 113 F1
Churchill Place E14 .... 118 B4
Churchway NW1 .... 110 A4
Churton Street SW1 .... 114 A2
Cinnamon Street E1 .... 116 C2
Circus Place EC2 .... 111 F2
Finsbury Circus
Citadel Place SE11 .... 114 C2
City Garden Row N1 .... 111 E4
City Road EC1 .... 111 F3
Clabon Mews SW1 .... 113 D2
Clack Street SE16 .... 117 D1
Clanricarde Gardens W2 .... 108 A1
Clare Market WC2 .... 110 C2
Claremont Close N1 .... 111 D4
Claremont Square N1 .... 111 D4
Clarence Gardens NW1 .... 109 F4
Clarendon Close W2 .... 108 C1
Clarendon Place W2 .... 108 C1
Clarendon Road W2 .... 108 C1
Clareville Grove SW7 .... 112 B2
Clareville Street SW7 .... 112 B2
Clarges Mews W1 .... 113 F4
Clarges Street W1 .... 113 F4
Clark Street E1 .... 116 C4
Clark's Orchard SE16 .... 116 C1
Claude Street E14 .... 118 A3
Clave Street E1 .... 116 C2
Claverton Street SW1 .... 114 A1
Clay Street W1 .... 109 D2
Clayton Street SE11 .... 114 C1
Clearbrook Way E1 .... 117 D4
Cleaver Square SE11 .... 115 D1
Cleaver Street SE11 .... 115 D1
Clegg Street E1 .... 116 C2
Clemence Street E14 .... 117 F4
Clement's Inn WC2 .... 110 C2
Clement's Road SE16 .... 116 C1
Clements Lane EC4 .... 111 F1
Clenston Mews W1 .... 109 D2
Clere Street EC2 .... 111 F3
Clerkenwell Close EC1 .... 111 D3
Clerkenwell Green EC1 .... 111 D3
Clerkenwell Road EC1 .... 110 C3
Cleveland Gardens W2 .... 108 B2
Cleveland Mews W1 .... 109 F3
Cleveland Row SW1 .... 114 A4
Cleveland Square W2 .... 108 B2
Cleveland Street W1 .... 109 F3
Cleveland Terrace W2 .... 108 B2
Clifford Street W1 .... 109 F1
Clifton Place W2 .... 108 C1
Clifton Street EC2 .... 111 F3
Clink Street SE1 .... 115 F4
Clipper Close SE16 .... 117 D2
Kinburn Street
Clipstone Mews W1 .... 109 F3
Clipstone Street W1 .... 109 F3
Cliveden Place SW1 .... 113 E2
Cloak Lane EC4 .... 111 E1
Cloth Fair EC1 .... 111 E3
Cloth Street EC1 .... 111 E3
Clunbury Street N1 .... 111 F4
Cherbury Street
Cluny Place SE1 .... 115 F3
Coach & Horses Yard W1 .... 109 F1
Old Burlington Street
Cobb Street E1 .... 116 A4
Cobourg Street NW1 .... 110 A4
Cock Lane EC1 .... 111 D2

Cockpit Yard WC1 .... 110 C3
Cockspur Street SW1 .... 114 B4
Codling Close E1 .... 116 C1
Coin Street SE1 .... 115 D4
Coke Street E1 .... 116 B4
Colbeck Mews SW7 .... 112 A2
Colchester Street E1 .... 116 B4
Whitechapel High Street
Coldbath Square EC1 .... 110 C3
Coldharbour E14 .... 118 C4
Cole Street SE1 .... 115 E3
Colebrooke Row N1 .... 111 D4
Coleherne Mews SW10 .... 112 A1
Coleherne Road SW10 .... 112 A1
Coleman Street EC2 .... 111 E2
Coley Street WC1 .... 110 C3
College Hill EC4 .... 111 E1
College Street
College Street EC4 .... 111 E1
Collett Road SE16 .... 116 C1
Collier Street N1 .... 110 C4
Collingham Gardens SW5 .... 112 A2
Collingham Place SW4 .... 112 A2
Collingham Road SW5 .... 112 A2
Collinson Street SE1 .... 115 E3
Colnbrook Street SE1 .... 115 D3
Colombo Street SE1 .... 115 D4
Colonnade WC1 .... 110 B3
Colworth Grove SE17 .... 115 F2
Commercial Road E1 & E14 .... 116 B4
Commercial Street E1 .... 116 A4
Compton Passage EC1 .... 111 D3
Compton Place WC1 .... 110 B3
Compton Street EC1 .... 111 D3
Comus Street SE17 .... 115 F2
Concert Hall Approach SE1 .... 114 C4
Conduit Mews W2 .... 108 C2
Conduit Place W2 .... 108 C2
Conduit Street W1 .... 109 F1
Congreve Street SE17 .... 115 F2
Connaught Place W2 .... 109 D1
Connaught Square W2 .... 109 D2
Connaught Street W2 .... 108 C2
Cons Street SE1 .... 115 D4
Constitution Hill SW1 .... 113 E3
Content Street SE17 .... 115 F2
Conway Street W1 .... 109 F3
Cook's Road E15 .... 115 D1
Cookham Crescent SE16 .... 117 D2
Coombs Street N1 .... 111 E4
Cooper Close SE1 .... 115 D3
Cooper's Row EC3 .... 116 A3
Cope Place W8 .... 112 A3
Copeland Drive E14 .... 118 A2
Copenhagen Place E14 .... 117 F3
Copley Close SE17 .... 115 E1
Copperfield Street SE1 .... 115 E4
Copthall Avenue EC2 .... 111 F2
Coptic Street WC1 .... 110 B2
Coral Street SE1 .... 115 D3
Coram Street WC1 .... 110 B3
Cord Way E14 .... 118 A3
Cork Street W1 .... 109 F1
Corlett Street NW1 .... 108 C3
Bell Street
Corner House Street WC2 .... 114 B4
Northumberland Street
Cornhill EC3 .... 111 F2
Cornwall Gardens SW7 .... 112 A2
Cornwall Gardens Walk SW7 .... 112 A2
Cornwall Mews South SW7 .... 112 A2
Cornwall Mews West SW7 .... 112 A2
Cornwall Road SE1 .... 114 C4
Cornwall Street E1 .... 116 C3
Cornwall Terrace NW1 .... 109 D3
Cornwood Drive E1 .... 117 D4
Coronet Street N1 .... 111 F4
Corporation Row EC1 .... 111 D3
Corsham Street N1 .... 111 F4
Cosmo Place WC1 .... 110 B3
Cosser Street SE1 .... 114 C2
Cosway Street NW1 .... 109 D3
Cotham Street SE17 .... 115 E2
Cottesloe Mews SE1 .... 115 D3
Cottesmore Gardens W8 .... 112 B3
Cottingham Close SE11 .... 115 D2
Cottington Street SE11 .... 115 D2
Cottons Lane SE1 .... 115 F4
Counter Street SE1 .... 115 F4
County Street SE1 .... 115 E2
Court Street E1 .... 116 C4
Courtenay Square SE11 .... 114 C1
Courtenay Street SE11 .... 114 C1
Courtfield Gardens SW5 .... 112 A2
Courtfield Road SW7 .... 112 B2
Cousin Lane EC4 .... 111 F1
Coventry Street W1 .... 110 A1
Coverley Close E1 .... 116 B4
Cowcross Street EC1 .... 111 D3
Cowley Street SW1 .... 114 B3
Cowper Street EC2 .... 111 F3
Coxon Place SE1 .... 116 A2
Crace Street NW1 .... 110 A4
Crail Row SE17 .... 115 F2
Cramer Street W1 .... 109 E2
Crampton Street SE17 .... 115 E2
Cranbourn Street WC2 .... 110 B1
Crane Street SE10 .... 118 C1
Cranford Street E1 .... 117 E3
Cranley Gardens SW7 .... 112 B2
Cranley Mews SW7 .... 112 B2
Cranley Place SW7 .... 112 C2
Cranmer Court SW3 .... 113 D2
Cranwood Street EC1 .... 111 F4
Craven Hill W2 .... 108 B1
Craven Hill Gardens W2 .... 108 B1
Craven Hill Mews W2 .... 108 B1
Craven Road W2 .... 108 B1
Craven Street WC2 .... 110 B1
Craven Terrace W2 .... 108 B1
Crawford Passage EC1 .... 111 D3
Crawford Place W1 .... 109 D2
Crawford Street W1 .... 109 D2
Creasy Street SE1 .... 115 F3
Swan Mead
Creechurch Lane EC3 .... 116 A3
Creechurch Place EC3 .... 116 A3
Creed Lane EC4 .... 111 E2
Crescent EC3 .... 116 A3
America Square
Crescent Place SW3 .... 113 D2
Crescent Row EC1 .... 111 E3
Cresswell Place SW10 .... 112 B1
Cressy Place E1 .... 117 D4
Crestfield Street WC1 .... 110 B4
Cricketers' Court SE11 .... 115 D1
Kennington Park Road
Crimscott Street SE1 .... 116 A1
Cripplegate Street EC1 .... 109 E3
Viscount Street
Crispin Street E1 .... 116 A4
Crofts Street E1 .... 116 B3
Cromer Street WC1 .... 110 B3
Cromwell Mews SW7 .... 112 C2
Cromwell Place SW7 .... 112 C2
Cromwell Road SW7 & SW5 .... 112 A1
Crondall Street N1 .... 111 F4
Crosby Row SE1 .... 115 F3

Crosby Square EC3...... 111 F2
  Great St Helen's
Cross Keys Close W1...... 109 E2
  Marylebone Lane
Cross Lane EC3...... 116 A3
  St Dunstan's Hill
Crosslet Street SE17...... 115 F2
Crosswall EC3...... 116 A3
Crowder Street E1...... 116 C3
Crown Court WC2...... 110 B2
Crown Office Row EC4...... 111 D1
Crucifix Lane SE1...... 116 A2
Cruikshank Street WC1...... 110 C4
Crutched Friars EC3...... 116 A3
Cuba Street E14...... 118 C4
Cubitt Steps E14...... 118 A4
Cubitt Street WC1...... 110 C4
Cubitts Yard WC2...... 110 B1
  James Street
Culford Gardens SW3...... 113 D2
Culling Road SE16...... 117 D1
Cullum Street EC3...... 116 A3
Culross Street W1...... 109 E1
Culworth Street NW8...... 108 C4
Cumberland Gardens WC1...... 110 C4
  Great Percy Street
Cumberland Gate W1 & W2...... 109 D1
Cumberland Market NW1...... 109 F4
Cumberland Street SW1...... 113 F1
Cumberland Terrace NW1...... 109 E4
Cumberland Terrace Mews NW1...... 109 F4
  Albany Street
Cumming Street N1...... 110 C4
Cundy Street SW1...... 113 E2
Cureton Street SW1...... 114 B2
Curlew Street SE1...... 116 B2
Cursitor Street EC4...... 110 C2
Curzon Gate W1...... 113 E4
Curzon Place W1...... 113 E4
Curzon Street W1...... 113 E4
Cuthbert Street W2...... 108 C3
Cutler Street E1...... 116 A4
Cutlers Square E14...... 118 A2
Cyclops Mews E14...... 118 A2
Cynthia Street N1...... 110 C4
Cyrus Street EC1...... 111 D3
Czar Street SE8...... 118 A1

D

D'arblay Street W1...... 110 A2
D'oyley Street SW1...... 113 E2
Dacre Street SW1...... 114 A3
Dalgleish Street E14...... 117 E4
Dallington Street EC1...... 111 D3
Damien Street E1...... 116 C4
Dane Street WC1...... 110 C2
Dante Road SE11...... 115 D2
Daplyn Street E1...... 116 B4
Dark House Walk EC3...... 111 F1
Dartford Street SE17...... 115 E1
Dartmouth Street SW1...... 114 A3
Darwin Street SE17...... 115 F2
Date Street SE17...... 115 E1
Davenant Street E1...... 116 B4
Daventry Street NW1...... 108 C3
Davidge Street SE1...... 115 D3
Davies Mews W1...... 109 E1
Davies Street W1...... 109 E1
Dawes Street SE17...... 115 F2
De Laune Street SE17...... 115 D1
De Vere Gardens W8...... 112 B3
De Walden Street W1...... 109 E2
  Westmorland Street
Deacon Way SE17...... 115 E2
Deal Porters Way SE16...... 117 D1
Deal Street E1...... 116 B4
Dean Bradley Street SW1...... 114 B2
Dean Close SE16...... 117 E2
Dean Farrar Street SW1...... 114 A3
Dean Ryle Street SW1...... 114 B2
Dean Stanley Street SW1...... 114 B2
  Millbank
Dean Street W1...... 110 A2
Dean Trench Street SW1...... 114 B2
Dean's Buildings SE17...... 115 F2
Dean's Court EC4...... 111 D2
  Carter Lane
Dean's Mews W1...... 109 F2
Deancross Street E1...... 116 C3
Deanery Street W1...... 113 E4
Decima Street SE1...... 115 F3
Deck Close SE16...... 117 E2
Defoe Close SE16...... 117 F1
Dellow Street E1...... 116 C3
Delverton Road SE17...... 115 E1
Denbigh Street SW1...... 114 A2
Denman Street W1...... 110 A1
Denmark Place WC2...... 110 B2
  Charing Cross Road
Denmark Street WC2...... 110 B2
Denny Crescent SE11...... 115 D2
Denny Street SE11...... 115 D2
Denyer Street SW3...... 113 D2
Deptford Green SE8...... 118 A1
Derby Gate SW1...... 114 B3
Derby Street W1...... 113 E4
Dering Street W1...... 109 F2
Deverell Street SE1...... 115 F3
Devereux Court WC2...... 110 B1
  Strand
Devonport Street E1...... 117 D3
Devonshire Close W1...... 109 F3
Devonshire Mews South W1...... 109 E3
Devonshire Mews West W1...... 109 E3
Devonshire Place W1...... 109 E3
Devonshire Place W8...... 112 A3
  St Mary's Place
Devonshire Place Mews W1...... 109 E3
Devonshire Row EC2...... 116 A4
Devonshire Square EC2...... 116 A4
Devonshire Street W1...... 109 E3
Devonshire Terrace W2...... 108 B1
Diadem Court W1...... 110 A2
  Dean Street
Diana Place NW1...... 109 F3
Dickens Square SE1...... 115 E3
Dilke Street SW3...... 113 D1
Dingle Gardens E14...... 118 A4
Dingley Place EC1...... 111 E4
Dingley Road EC1...... 111 E4
Disney Place SE1...... 115 E3
Disney Street SE1...... 115 E4
  Redcross Way
Distaff Lane EC4...... 111 E1
Distin Street SE11...... 114 C2
Dixon's Alley SE16...... 116 C1
  West Lane
Dock Hill Avenue SE16...... 117 E2
Dock Street E1...... 116 B3
Dockers Tanner Road E14...... 118 A2
Dockhead SE1...... 116 B1
Dockley Road SE16...... 116 B1
Dod Street E14...... 117 F4

Doddington Grove SE17...... 115 D1
Doddington Place SE17...... 115 D1
Dodson Street SE1...... 115 D3
Dolben Street SE1...... 115 D4
Dolland Street SE11...... 114 C1
Dolphin Close SE16...... 117 D2
Dombey Street WC1...... 110 C3
Domingo Street EC1...... 111 E3
  Old Street
Dominion Street EC2...... 111 F2
Donegal Street N1...... 110 C4
Donne Place SW3...... 113 D2
Doon Street SE1...... 114 C4
Dora Street E14...... 117 F4
Doric Way NW1...... 110 A4
Dorrington Street EC1...... 111 D3
  Brooke Street
Dorset Close NW1...... 109 D3
Dorset Mews SW1...... 113 E3
Dorset Rise EC4...... 111 D1
Dorset Square NW1...... 109 D3
Dorset Street W1...... 109 D2
Doughty Mews WC1...... 110 C3
Doughty Street WC1...... 110 C3
Douglas Place SW1...... 114 A2
  Douglas Street
Douglas Street SW1...... 114 A2
Douro Place W8...... 112 B3
Dove Mews SW5...... 112 B2
Dove Walk SW1...... 113 E2
Dovehouse Street SW3...... 112 C1
Dover Street W1...... 109 F1
Dowgate Hill EC4...... 111 F1
Down Street W1...... 113 E4
Downing Street SW1...... 114 B4
Downton Road SE16...... 117 E2
Doyce Street SE1...... 115 E4
Draco Street SE17...... 115 E1
Drake Street WC1...... 110 C2
Drawdock Road SE10...... 118 C4
Draycott Avenue SW3...... 113 D2
Draycott Place SW3...... 113 D2
Draycott Terrace SW3...... 113 D2
Drayson Mews W8...... 112 A3
Drayton Gardens SW10...... 112 B1
Druid Street SE1...... 116 A2
Drummond Crescent NW1...... 110 A4
Drummond Gate SW1...... 114 A1
Drummond Road SE16...... 116 C1
Drummond Street NW1...... 109 F3
Drury Lane WC2...... 110 B2
Dryden Court SE11...... 115 D2
Duchess Mews W1...... 109 F2
Duchess Street W1...... 109 F2
Duchy Street SE1...... 115 D4
Dudley Street W2...... 108 B2
Dudmaston Mews SW3...... 112 C2
Dufferin Street EC1...... 111 E3
Dufour's Place W1...... 110 A2
Duke Of Wellington Place SW1...... 113 E3
Duke Of York Street SW1...... 110 A1
Duke Street W1...... 109 E2
Duke Street Hill SE1...... 115 F4
Duke's Lane W8...... 112 A4
Duke's Place EC3...... 116 A4
Duke's Road WC1...... 110 B4
Duke's Yard W1...... 109 E2
  Duke Street
Duncannon Street WC2...... 110 B1
Dundee Street E1...... 116 C2
Dunelm Street E1...... 117 D4
Dunlop Place SE16...... 116 B1
Dunraven Street W1...... 109 E1
Dunstable Mews W1...... 109 E3
Dunster Court EC3...... 116 A3
Dunsterville Way SE1...... 115 F3
Duplex Ride SW1...... 113 E3
Dupont Street E14...... 117 E4
Durand Gardens SW9...... — —
Durham House Street WC2...... 110 B1
Durham Row E1...... 117 E4
Durham Street SE11...... 114 C1
Durward Street E1...... 116 C4
Durweston Street W1...... 109 D2
  Crawford Street
Duthie Street E14...... 118 C4
Dyott Street WC1...... 110 B2
Dysart Street EC2...... 111 F3

E

Eagle Court EC1...... 111 D3
Eagle Street WC2...... 110 C2
Eardley Crescent SW5...... 112 A1
Earl Street EC2...... 111 F3
Earl's Court Gardens SW5...... 112 A2
Earl's Court Square SW5...... 112 A1
Earlham Street WC2...... 110 B2
Earls Court Road W8...... 112 A2
Earlstoke Street EC1...... 111 D4
  Spencer Street
Earnshaw Street WC2...... 110 B2
Easley's Mews W1...... 109 E2
  Wigmore Street
East Arbour Street E1...... 117 D4
East Ferry Road E14...... 118 B2
East India Dock Road E14...... 118 B3
East India Dock Wall Road E14...... 118 D2
East Lane SE16...... 116 B1
East Road N1...... 111 F4
East Smithfield E1...... 116 B3
East Street SE17...... 115 E1
East Tenter Street E1...... 116 B3
Eastbourne Mews W2...... 108 B2
Eastbourne Terrace W2...... 108 B2
Eastcastle Street W1...... 110 A2
Eastcheap EC3...... 111 F1
Eastney Street SE10...... 118 C1
Easton Street WC1...... 110 C3
Eaton Gate SW1...... 113 E2
Eaton Mews North SW1...... 113 E2
Eaton Mews South SW1...... 113 E2
Eaton Place SW1...... 113 E2
Eaton Row SW1...... 113 E2
Eaton Square SW1...... 113 E2
Eaton Terrace SW1...... 113 E2
Ebbisham Drive SW8...... 114 C1
Ebenezer Street N1...... 111 F4
Ebury Bridge SW1...... 113 E2
Ebury Bridge Road SW1...... 113 E1
Ebury Mews SW1...... 113 E2
Ebury Mews East SW1...... 113 E2
Ebury Square SW1...... 113 E2
Ebury Street SW1...... 113 E2
Eccleston Bridge SW1...... 113 F2
Eccleston Mews SW1...... 113 E3
Eccleston Place SW1...... 113 F2
Eccleston Square SW1...... 113 F2
Eccleston Square Mews SW1...... 113 F2
Eccleston Street SW1...... 113 E2
Edge Street W8...... 112 A4
Edgware Road W2...... 108 C3
Edward Mews NW1...... 109 E3
Edward Mews W1...... 109 E2
Edward Square SE16...... 117 E3
Egerton Crescent SW3...... 113 D2

Egerton Gardens SW3...... 112 C2
Egerton Terrace SW3...... 113 D3
Elba Place SE17...... 115 E2
Eldon Road W8...... 112 B3
Eldon Street EC2...... 111 F2
Eleanor Close SE16...... 117 D2
Elephant And Castle SE1...... 115 E2
Elephant Lane SE16...... 116 C2
Elephant Road SE17...... 115 E2
Elf Row E1...... 117 D3
Elgar Street SE16...... 117 F1
Elia Street N1...... 111 D4
Elim Street SE1...... 115 F3
Elizabeth Bridge SW1...... 113 F2
Elizabeth Square SE16...... 117 F2
Elizabeth Street SW1...... 113 E2
Ellen Street E1...... 116 B3
Elliott Road SE9...... 115 D2
Ellis Street SW1...... 113 E2
Elm Park Gardens SW10...... 112 C1
Elm Park Lane SW3...... 112 B1
Elm Park Road SW3...... 112 B1
Elm Place SW7...... 112 C1
Elm Street WC1...... 110 C3
Elm Tree Close NW8...... 108 C4
Elm Tree Road NW8...... 108 C4
Elmos Road SE16...... 117 E1
Elms Mews W2...... 108 C1
Elsa Street E1...... 117 E4
Elsted Street SE17...... 115 F2
Elvaston Mews SW7...... 112 B3
Elvaston Place SW7...... 112 B3
Elverton Street SW1...... 114 A2
Ely Place EC1...... 111 D2
Elystan Place SW3...... 113 D2
Elystan Street SW3...... 112 C2
Emba Street SE16...... 116 C1
Embankment Gardens SW3...... 113 D1
Embankment Place WC2...... 114 B4
Emerald Street WC1...... 110 C3
Emerson Street SE1...... 115 E4
Emery Hill Street SW1...... 114 A2
Emery Street SE1...... 115 D3
Emmett Street E14...... 117 F3
Emperor's Gate SW7...... 112 B2
Empire Wharf Road E14...... 118 C2
Empress Place SW6...... 112 A1
Empress Street SE17...... 115 E1
Endell Street WC2...... 110 B2
Endsleigh Gardens WC1...... 110 A3
Endsleigh Place WC1...... 110 A3
Endsleigh Street WC1...... 110 A3
Enford Street W1...... 109 D3
English Grounds SE1...... 116 A2
Enid Street SE16...... 116 B2
Ennismore Garden Mews SW7...... 112 C3
Ennismore Gardens SW7...... 112 C3
Ennismore Mews SW7...... 112 C3
Ennismore Street SW7...... 112 C3
Ensign Street E1...... 116 B3
Ensor Mews SW7...... 112 B1
Epping Close E14...... 118 A2
Epworth Street EC2...... 111 F3
Erasmus Street SW1...... 114 B2
Errol Street EC1...... 111 E3
Essex Street WC2...... 110 C1
Esterbrooke Street SW1...... 114 A2
Ethel Street SE17...... 115 E2
Europa Place EC1...... 111 E4
Euston Road NW1...... 109 F3
Euston Square NW1...... 110 A4
Euston Street NW1...... 110 A4
Evelyn Gardens SW7...... 114 B1
Evelyn Walk N1...... 111 F4
Evelyn Yard W1...... 110 A2
  Gresse Street
Eversholt Street NW1...... 110 A4
Ewer Street SE1...... 115 E4
Exchange Place EC2...... 116 A4
Exchange Square EC2...... 116 A4
Exeter Street WC2...... 110 B1
Exhibition Road SW7...... 112 C3
Exmouth Market EC1...... 111 D3
Exmouth Street E1...... 117 D4
Exon Street SE17...... 115 F2
Exton Street SE1...... 114 C4
Eyre Street Hill EC1...... 111 D3

F

Factory Place E14...... 118 B1
Fair Street SE1...... 116 A2
Fairclough Street E1...... 116 B3
Falcon Close SE1...... 115 E4
Falcon Way E14...... 118 B2
Falmouth Road SE1...... 115 E3
Fann Street EC1...... 111 E3
Fanshaw Street N1...... 111 F4
Fareham Street W1...... 110 B1
  Dean Street
Farm Street W1...... 109 E1
Farmer Street W8...... 112 A4
Farncombe Street SE16...... 116 C1
Farnell Mews SW5...... 112 A1
Farnham Place SE1...... 115 E4
Farnham Royal SE11...... 114 C1
Farrance Street E14...... 117 F3
Farringdon Lane EC1...... 111 D3
Farringdon Road EC1...... 110 C3
Farringdon Street EC4...... 111 D2
Farrins Rents SE16...... 117 E2
Farrow Place SE16...... 117 E1
Farthing Alley SE1...... 116 B1
  Wolseley Street
Farthing Fields E1...... 116 C2
  Raine Street
Fashion Street E1...... 116 B4
Faunce Street SE17...... 115 D1
Fawcett Street SW10...... 112 B1
Feather's Place SE10...... 118 C1
Featherstone Street EC1...... 111 F3
Felstead Gardens E14...... 118 B1
Fen Court EC3...... 116 A3
Fenchurch Avenue EC3...... 116 A3
Fenchurch Buildings EC3...... 111 F1
  Fenchurch Street
Fenchurch Place EC3...... 111 F1
  Fenchurch Street
Fenchurch Street EC3...... 111 F1
Fendall Street SE1...... 116 A1
Fenning Street SE1...... 115 F4
  St Thomas Street
Fernsbury Street WC1...... 110 C4
Ferry Street E14...... 118 B1
Fetter Lane EC4...... 111 D2
Field Street WC1...... 110 C4
Fieldgate Street E1...... 116 B4
Fielding Street SE17...... 115 E1
Finborough Road SW10...... 112 A1
Finch Lane EC3...... 111 F2
Finland Street SE16...... 117 E1
Finsbury Avenue EC2...... 111 F2
Finsbury Circus EC2...... 111 F2
Finsbury Pavement EC2...... 111 F2

Finsbury Square EC2...... 111 F3
Finsbury Street EC2...... 111 F3
Firtree Close SE16...... 117 E2
Fish Street Hill EC3...... 111 F1
Fish Wharf EC3...... 111 F1
Fisher Street WC1...... 110 C2
Fisherman's Walk E14...... 118 A4
Fishermans Drive SE16...... 117 E2
Fisherton Street NW8...... 108 C3
Fishmonger' Hall Wharf EC4...... 111 F1
Fitzalan Street SE11...... 114 C2
Fitzhardinge Street W1...... 109 E2
Fitzmaurice Place W1...... 109 F1
Fitzroy Square W1...... 109 F3
Fitzroy Street W1...... 109 F3
Flamborough Street E14...... 117 E4
Flank Street E1...... 116 B3
Flaxman Terrace WC1...... 110 B4
Fleet Square WC1...... 110 C4
Fleet Street EC4...... 111 D2
Fleming Road SE17...... 115 D1
Fletcher Street E1...... 116 B3
Flint Street SE17...... 115 F2
Flitcroft Street WC2...... 110 B2
Flood Street SW3...... 113 D1
Flood Walk SW3...... 113 D1
Floral Street WC2...... 110 B1
Flower And Dean Walk E1...... 116 B4
  Thrawl Street
Foley Street W1...... 109 F2
Folly Wall E14...... 118 C3
Forbes Street E1...... 116 B3
Ford Square E1...... 116 C4
Fordham Street E1...... 116 C4
Fore Street EC2...... 111 E2
Fore Street Avenue EC2...... 111 E2
Forset Street W1...... 109 D2
Forsyth Gardens SE17...... 115 D1
Fort Street E1...... 116 A4
  Artillery Lane
Fortune Street EC1...... 111 E3
Foster Lane EC2...... 111 E2
Foubert's Place W1...... 109 F1
Foulis Terrace SW7...... 112 C2
Foundry Close SE16...... 117 E2
Fountain Green Square SE16...... 116 C1
Fournier Street E1...... 116 B4
Fowey Close E1...... 116 C2
Fox And Knot Street EC1...... 111 E2
  Charterhouse Square
Frampton Street NW8...... 108 C3
Francis Close E14...... 118 C2
Francis Street SW1...... 114 A2
Franklin's Row SW3...... 113 D2
Frazier Street SE1...... 114 C3
Frean Street SE16...... 116 B1
Frederick Close W2...... 109 D1
Frederick Road SE17...... 115 E1
Frederick Square SE16...... 117 E3
Frederick Street WC1...... 110 C4
Fredericks Row EC1...... 111 D4
  Goswell Road
Fremantle Street SE17...... 115 F2
French Ordinary Court EC3...... 116 A3
  Hart Street
Friar Street EC4...... 111 E2
  Carter Lane
Friars Mead E14...... 118 B2
Friday Street EC4...... 111 E1
Friend Street EC1...... 111 D4
Frigate Mews SE8...... 118 A1
Frith Street W1...... 110 A2
Frobisher Passage E14...... 118 A4
  North Colonnade
Frostic Walk E1...... 116 B4
Frying Pan Alley E1...... 116 A4
Fulbourne Street E1...... 116 C4
Fulford Street SE16...... 116 C1
Fulham Road SW3, SW6 & SW10...... 112 C1
Furnival Street EC4...... 111 D2
Fynes Street SW1...... 114 A2

G

Gabriels Wharf SE1...... 115 D4
Gaien Place WC1...... 110 B2
Gainsford Street SE1...... 116 A2
Galbraith Street E14...... 118 B3
Galleon Close SE16...... 117 D2
  Kinburn Street
Galway Street EC1...... 111 E4
Gambia Street SE1...... 115 D4
Ganton Street W1...... 110 A1
Garbutt Place W1...... 109 E2
  Moxon Street
Gard Street EC1...... 111 E4
Garden Row SE1...... 115 D3
Garden Street E1...... 117 E4
Gardeners Lane EC4...... 111 E1
  High Timber Street
Garford Street E14...... 117 F3
Garlick Hill EC4...... 111 F1
Garnault Mews EC1...... 111 D4
Garnet Street E1...... 116 C3
Garrett Street EC1...... 111 E3
Garrick Street WC2...... 110 B1
Garter Way SE16...... 117 D2
Gaselee Street E14...... 118 C4
Gasholder Place SE11...... 114 C1
Gaspar Close SW5...... 112 B2
Gaspar Mews SW5...... 112 B2
Gate Street WC2...... 110 C2
Gateway SE17...... 115 E1
Gatliff Road SW1...... 113 E1
Gaunt Street SE1...... 115 E3
Gavel Street SE17...... 115 F2
Gayfere Street SW1...... 114 B3
Gaywood Street SE1...... 115 D3
Gaza Street SE17...... 115 D1
Gedling Place SE1...... 116 B1
Gee Street EC1...... 111 E3
Gees Court W1...... 109 E2
George Mews NW1...... 110 A4
George Row SE16...... 116 B1
George Street W1...... 109 D2
George Yard EC3...... 111 F1
George Yard W1...... 109 E1
Gerald Road SW1...... 113 E2
Geraldine Street SE11...... 115 D3
Gernon Road E3...... 110 A1
  Shaftesbury Avenue
Gerrard Street W1...... 110 A1
Gerridge Street SE1...... 115 D3
Gibson Road SE11...... 114 C2
Gilbert Place WC1...... 110 B2
Gilbert Road SE11...... 115 D2
Gilbert Street W1...... 109 E1
Gildea Street W1...... 109 F2
Gill Street E14...... 117 F3
Gillingham Street SW1...... 113 F2
Gillison Walk SE16...... 116 C1
Gilston Road SW10...... 112 B1
Giltspur Street EC1...... 111 D2

Gladstone Street
Kings Bench Street

Gladstone Street SE1 115 D3
Glamis Place E1 117 D3
Glamis Road E1 117 D3
Glangarnock Avenue E14 118 C2
Glasgow Terrace SW1 113 F1
Glasshill Street SE1 115 E3
Glasshouse Fields E1 117 D3
Glasshouse Street W1 110 A1
Glasshouse Walk SE11 114 B1
Glebe Place SW3 112 C1
Gledhow Gardens SW5 112 B2
Glenaffric Avenue E14 118 C2
Glendower Place SW7 112 C2
Glengall Grove E14 118 B3
Glentworth Street NW1 109 D3
Glenworth Avenue E14 118 C2
Globe Pond Road SE16 117 E2
Globe Street SE1 115 E3
Gloucester Arcade SW7 112 B2
Gloucester Court EC3 116 A3
Gloucester Gate Mews NW1 110 F4
Albany Street
Gloucester Mews W2 108 B2
Gloucester Mews West W2 108 B2
Gloucester Park SW7 112 B2
Gloucester Place NW1 & W1 109 D3
Gloucester Place Mews W1 109 D2
Gloucester Road SW7 112 B3
Gloucester Square W2 108 C2
Gloucester Street SW1 113 F1
Gloucester Terrace W2 108 B2
Gloucester Walk W8 112 A4
Gloucester Way EC1 111 D4
Glyn Street SE11 114 C1
Goat Street SE1 116 A2
Lafone Street
Godfrey Street SW3 113 D2
Goding Street SE11 114 B1
Godliman Street EC4 111 E1
Golden Lane EC1 111 E3
Golden Square W1 110 A1
Golding Street E1 116 C3
Gomm Road SE16 117 D1
Goodge Place W1 110 A2
Goodge Street W1 110 A2
Goodhart Place E14 117 E3
Goodman's Stile E1 116 B4
Goodman's Yard E1 116 B3
Goodwin Close SE16 116 B1
Gophir Lane EC4 111 F1
Bush Lane
Gordon Place W8 112 A4
Gordon Square WC1 110 A3
Gordon Street WC1 110 A3
Gore Street SW7 112 B3
Goring Street E1 116 A4
Bevis Marks
Gosfield Street W1 109 F2
Goslett Yard WC2 110 B2
Goswell Road EC1 111 D4
Gough Square EC4 111 D2
Gough Street WC1 110 C3
Goulston Street E1 116 B4
Gower Place WC1 110 A3
Gower Street WC1 110 A3
Gowers Walk E1 116 B3
Grace's Alley E1 116 B3
Gracechurch Street EC3 111 F1
Graces Mews NW8 108 B4
Grafton Mews W1 109 F3
Grafton Place NW1 110 A4
Grafton Street W1 109 F1
Grafton Way W1 109 A3
Graham Street N1 111 E4
Graham Terrace SW1 113 E2
Granby Terrace NW1 109 F4
Grand Avenue EC1 111 D2
Grand Junction Wharf N1 111 E4
Grange Court WC2 110 C2
Grange Road SE1 116 A1
Grange Walk SE1 116 A1
Grange Yard SE1 116 A1
Grant's Quay Wharf EC3 111 F1
Granville Place W1 109 E2
Granville Square WC1 110 C4
Granville Street WC1 110 C4
Granville Square
Grape Street WC2 110 B2
Gravel Lane E1 116 A4
Gray Street SE1 115 D3
Gray's Inn Road WC1 110 B4
Great Castle Street W1 109 F2
Great Central Street NW1 109 D3
Great Chapel Street W1 110 A2
Great College Street SW1 109 D1
Seymour Street
Great Cumberland Place W1 109 D2
Great Dover Street SE1 115 F3
Great Eastern Street EC2 111 F3
Great George Street SW1 114 B3
Great Guildford Street SE1 115 E4
Great James Street WC1 110 C3
Great Marlborough Street W1 109 F2
Great Maze Pond SE1 115 F4
Great New Street EC4 111 D2
Great Newport Street WC2 114 C2
Newport Street
Great Ormond Street WC1 110 C3
Great Percy Street WC1 110 C4
Great Peter Street SW1 114 A3
Great Portland Street W1 109 F3
Great Pulteney Street W1 110 A1
Great Queen Street WC2 110 B2
Great Russell Street WC1 110 B2
Great Scotland Yard SW1 114 B4
Great Smith Street SW1 114 B3
Great St Helen's EC3 111 F2
Great St Thomas Apostle EC4 111 E1
Queen Street
Great Suffolk Street SE1 115 E3
Great Sutton Street EC1 111 D3
Great Swan Alley EC2 111 F2
Great Tower Street EC3 116 A3
Great Trinity Lane EC4 111 E1
Garlick Hill
Great Turnstile WC1 110 B2
High Holborn
Great Winchester Street EC2 111 F2
Great Windmill Street W1 110 A1
Greatorex Street E1 116 B4
Greek Street W1 110 B2
Green Bank E1 116 C2
Green Dragon Yard E1 116 B4
Green Street W1 109 E1
Green Walk SE1 115 F3
Green Yard WC1 110 C3
Greenacre Square SE16 117 E2
Greenberry Street NW8 108 C4
Greencoat Place SW1 114 A2
Greencoat Row SW1 114 A2
Greenfield Road E1 116 B4
Greenwell Street W1 109 F3
Greenwich Park Street SE10 118 C1
Greenwich View Place E14 118 C3
Greet Street SE1 115 D4
Gregory Place W8 112 A3
Greig Terrace SE17 115 E1
Grenade Street E14 117 F3
Grendon Street NW8 108 C3
Grenville Place SW7 112 B2
Grenville Street WC1 110 B3
Gresham Street EC2 111 E2
Gresse Street W1 110 A2
Greville Street EC1 111 D2
Greycoat Place SW1 114 A3
Greycoat Street SW1 114 A2
Greystoke Place EC4 111 D2
Fetter Lane
Grigg's Place SE1 116 A1
Groom Place SW1 113 E3
Grosvenor Crescent SW1 113 E3
Grosvenor Crescent Mews SW1 113 E3
Grosvenor Gardens SW1 113 F3
Grosvenor Gate W1 109 E1
Park Lane
Grosvenor Hill W1 109 F1
Grosvenor Place SW1 113 E3
Grosvenor Road SW1 113 F1
Grosvenor Square W1 109 E1
Grosvenor Street W1 109 E1
Grosvenor Wharf Road E14 118 C2
Grove Gardens NW8 109 D4
Guildhall Buildings EC2 111 E2
Basinghall Street
Guildhall Yard EC2 111 E2
Guildhouse Street SW1 113 F2
Guilford Place WC1 110 B3
Guilford Street
Guilford Street WC1 110 B3
Guinness Square SE1 115 F2
Gulliver Street SE16 117 F1
Gulston Walk SW3 113 D2
Gun Street E1 116 A4
Gunthorpe Street E1 116 B4
Gunwhale Close SE16 117 E2
Guthrie Street SW3 112 C2
Gutter Lane EC2 111 E2
Guy Street SE1 115 F3
Gwynne Place WC1 110 C4

H

Haberdasher Street N1 111 F4
Halcrow Street E1 116 C4
Half Moon Court EC1 111 E2
Bartholomew Close
Half Moon Street W1 113 F4
Halkin Place SW1 113 E3
Halkin Street SW1 113 E3
Hall Place W2 108 C3
Hall Street EC1 111 D4
Hallam Mews W1 109 F3
Hallam Street W1 109 F3
Halley Place E14 117 E4
Halley Street E14 117 E4
Halsey Street SW3 113 D2
Hamilton Close SE16 117 E1
Hamilton Place W1 113 E4
Hamilton Square SE1 115 F3
Hammett Street EC3 116 A3
America Square
Hampstead Road NW1 109 F4
Hampton Street SE1 & SE17 115 E2
Hanbury Street E1 116 B4
Handel Street WC1 110 B3
Hankey Place SE1 115 F3
Hannibal Road E1 117 D4
Hanover Place WC2 110 B1
Long Acre
Hanover Square W1 109 F2
Hanover Street W1 109 F2
Hanover Terrace NW1 109 D4
Hanover Terrace Mews NW1 109 D4
Hans Crescent SW1 113 D3
Hans Place SW1 113 D3
Hans Road SW3 113 D3
Hans Street SW1 113 D3
Hanson Street W1 109 F2
Hanway Place W1 110 A2
Hanway Street W1 110 A2
Harbert Road W2 108 C2
Harbinger Road E14 118 A2
Harbour Exchange Square E14 118 B3
Harcourt Street W1 109 D2
Harcourt Terrace SW10 112 B1
Harding Close SE17 115 E1
Hardinge Street E1 117 D3
Hardwick Street EC1 111 D4
Hardwidge Street SE1 115 F4
Harewood Avenue NW1 109 D3
Harewood Place W1 109 F2
Harley Gardens SW10 112 B1
Harley Place W1 109 E2
Harley Street W1 109 E3
Harleyford Road SE11 114 C1
Harmsworth Street SE17 115 D1
Harp Alley EC4 111 D2
Farringdon Street
Harp Lane EC3 116 A3
Harper Road SE1 115 E3
Harpur Street WC1 110 C3
Harriet Street SW1 113 D3
Harriet Walk SW1 113 D3
Harrington Gardens SW7 112 B2
Harrington Road SW7 112 C2
Harrington Street NW1 109 F4
Harrison Street WC1 110 B4
Harrow Place E1 116 A4
Harrow Road W2, W9, W10 & NW10 108 B2
Harrowby Street W1 109 D2
Hart Street EC3 116 A3
Harwich Lane EC2 116 A4
Harwood Road NW1 109 D3
Hasker Street SW3 113 D2
Hastings Street WC1 110 B4
Hatfields SE1 115 D4
Hatherley Street SW1 114 A2
Hatteraick Street SE16 117 D2
Hatton Garden EC1 111 D3
Hatton Street NW8 108 C3
Hatton Wall EC1 111 D3
Haunch Of Venison Yard W1 108 C1
Brook Street
Havannah Street E14 118 A3
Havering Street E1 117 D3
Haverstock Street N1 111 E4
Hawkesmoor Mews E1 116 C3
Hay Hill W1 109 F1
Hay's Lane SE1 115 F4
Hay's Mews W1 109 F1
Hayes Place NW1 109 D3
Hayles Street SE11 115 D2
Haymarket SW1 110 A1
Hayne Street EC1 111 E3
Hayward's Place EC1 111 D3
Headfort Place SW1 113 E3
Heathcote Street WC1 110 C3
Heckford Street E1 117 E3
Heddon Street W1 109 F1
Heiron Street SE17 115 E1
Helena Square SE16 117 E3
Hellings Street E1 116 B2
Helmet Row EC1 111 E3
Helsinki Square SE16 117 E3
Hemp Walk SE17 115 F2
Henderson Drive NW8 108 C3
Heneage Lane EC3 116 A4
Heneage Place EC3 116 A4
Heneage Street E1 116 B4
Henniker Mews SW3 112 B1
Henrietta Place W1 109 E2
Henrietta Street WC2 110 B1
Henriques Street E1 116 B4
Henshaw Street SE17 115 F2
Herald's Place SE11 115 D2
Herbal Hill EC1 111 D3
Herbrand Street WC1 110 B3
Hercules Road SE1 114 C3
Hereford Square SW7 112 B2
Hermit Street EC1 111 D4
Hermitage Street W2 108 C2
Hermitage Wall E1 116 B2
Heron Place SE16 117 E2
Heron Quays E14 118 A4
Herrick Street SW1 114 B2
Hertford Street W1 113 E4
Hertsmere Road E14 118 A4
Hesper Mews SW5 112 A2
Hesperus Crescent E14 118 B2
Hessel Street E1 116 C3
Heygate Street SE17 115 E2
Hickin Street E14 118 B3
Hide Place SW1 114 A2
High Holborn WC1 110 B2
High Timber Street EC4 111 E1
Highbridge SE10 118 C1
Hildyard Road SW6 112 A1
Hill Street W1 109 F2
Hillery Close SE17 115 F2
Hilliard's Court E1 116 C2
Hillingdon Street SE5 & SE17 115 E1
Pelier Street
Hind Court EC4 111 D2
Hinde Street W1 109 E2
Hindmarsh Close E1 116 B3
Hobart Place SW1 113 F3
Hogarth Court EC3 111 F1
Fenchurch Street
Hogarth Place SW5 112 A2
Hogarth Road SW5 112 A2
Holbein Mews SW1 113 E2
Holbein Place SW1 113 E2
Holborn EC1 111 D2
Holborn Circus EC1 111 D2
Holborn Viaduct EC1 111 D2
Holford Place WC1 110 C4
Holford Street WC1 110 C4
Holland Street SE1 115 D4
Holland Street W8 112 A3
Hollen Street W1 110 A2
Wardour Street
Holles Street W1 109 F2
Holley Mews SW10 112 B1
Drayton Gardens
Hollywood Mews SW10 112 B1
Hollywood Road SW10 112 B1
Holyoak Road SE11 115 D2
Holyoake Court SE16 117 F2
Holyrood Street SE1 116 A2
Holywell Row EC2 111 F3
Homer Drive E14 118 A2
Homer Row W1 109 D2
Homer Street W1 109 D2
Honduras Street EC1 111 E3
Old Street
Hooper Street E1 116 B3
Hop Gardens WC2 110 B1
St Martin's Lane
Hopetown Street E1 116 B4
Hopkins Street W1 110 A1
Hopton Street SE1 115 D4
Hopwood Road SE17 115 F1
Horley Crescent SE16 117 D2
Marlow Way
Hornton Place W8 112 A3
Hornton Street W8 112 A3
Horse Guards Avenue SW1 114 B4
Horse Guards Road SW1 114 B4
Horse Ride SW1 113 F3
Horseferry Road E14 117 E3
Horseferry Road SW1 114 A3
Horselydown Lane SE1 116 A2
Horseshoe Close E14 118 B2
Hosier Lane EC1 111 D2
Hoskins Street SE10 118 C1
Hothfield Place SE16 117 D1
Hotspur Street SE11 114 C2
Houghton Street WC2 110 C1
Aldwych
Houndsditch EC3 116 A4
Howard Place SW1 110 A2
Carlisle Street
Howell Walk SE1 115 E2
Howick Place SW1 114 A3
Howland Street W1 110 A3
Howland Way SE16 117 E1
Hoxton Market N1 111 F4
Hoxton Square N1 111 F4
Huddart Street E3 117 F4
Hudson's Place SW1 113 F2
Huggin Hill EC4 111 E1
Hugh Street SW1 113 F2
Hull Close SE16 117 E2
Hull Street EC1 111 E4
Hunt's Court WC2 110 B1
Hunter Close SE1 115 F3
Prioress Street
Hunter Street WC1 110 B3
Huntley Street WC1 110 A3
Huntsman Street SE17 115 F2
Huntsworth Mews NW1 109 D3
Hutching's Street E14 118 A3
Hutton Street EC4 111 D1
Hyde Park Corner W1 113 E4
Hyde Park Crescent W2 108 C2
Hyde Park Gardens W2 108 C1
Hyde Park Gardens Mews W2 108 C1
Hyde Park Gate SW7 112 B3
Hyde Park Square W2 108 C2
Hyde Park Street W2 108 C2

I

Idol Lane EC3 116 A3
Ifield Road SW10 112 A1
Iliffe Street SE17 115 E2
Indescon Court E14 118 A3
India Street EC3 116 A3
Ingestre Place W1 110 A1
Inglebert Street EC1 111 D4
Inglewood Close E14 118 A2
Ingram Close SE11 114 C2
Inigo Place WC2 110 B1
Bedford Street
Inner Temple Lane EC4 111 D2
Insurance Street WC1 110 C4
Inverness Gardens W8 112 A4
Palace Garden Terrace
Inverness Mews W2 108 B1
Inverness Mews W8 112 A4
W8 112
Inverness Place W2 108 B1
Inverness Terrace W2 108 B1
Invicta Plaza SE1 115 D4
Inville Road SE17 115 F1
Ireland Yard EC4 111 D1
St Andrew's Hill
Ironmonger Lane EC2 111 E2
Ironmonger Place E14 118 A2
Ironmonger Row EC1 111 E4
Ironside Close SE16 117 D2
Irving Street WC2 110 B1
Isabella Street SE1 115 D4
Island Row E14 117 F3
Iverna Court W8 112 A3
Iverna Gardens W8 112 A3
Ives Street SW3 113 D2
Ivor Place NW1 109 D3
Ixworth Place SW3 112 C2

J

Jacob Street SE1 116 B2
Jamaica Road SE1 & SE16 116 B1
Jamaica Street E1 117 D4
James Street W1 109 E2
James Street WC2 110 B1
Long Acre
Jameson Street W8 112 A4
Janet Street E14 118 A3
Janeway Place SE16 116 C1
Janeway Street SE16 116 C1
Jardine Road E1 117 E3
Jay Mews SW7 112 B3
Jermyn Street SW1 114 A4
Jerome Crescent NW8 112 C3
Jewry Street EC3 116 A3
Joan Street SE1 115 D4
Jockey's Fields WC1 110 C3
John Adams Street WC2 110 B1
John Carpenter Street EC4 111 D1
John Felton Road SE16 116 B1
John Fisher Street E1 116 B3
John Islip Street 114 B2
John Maurice Close SE17 115 F2
John Princes Street W1 109 F2
John Roll Way SE16 116 C1
John Street WC1 110 C3
John's Mews WC1 110 C3
Johnson Street E1 117 D3
Johnson's Place SW1 114 A1
Joiner Street SE1 115 F4
Jonathan Street SE11 114 C2
Jubilee Crescent E14 118 C2
Jubilee Place SW3 113 D2
Jubilee Street E1 117 D4
Judd Street WC1 110 B4
Julian Place E14 118 B1
Junction Mews W2 108 C2
Juxon Street SE11 114 C2

K

Katherine Close SE16 117 D2
Kean Street WC2 110 C2
Keel Close SE16 117 E2
Keeley Street WC2 110 C2
Keeton's Road SE16 116 C1
Kelso Place W8 112 A3
Kemble Street WC2 110 C2
Kempsford Gardens SW5 112 A1
Kempsford Road SE11 115 D2
Kendal Street W2 109 C2
Kendall Place W1 109 D2
Kendrick Mews SW7 112 C2
Kendrick Place SW7 112 C2
Reece Mews
Kennet Street E1 116 B2
Kennet Wharf Lane EC4 111 E1
Kenning Street SE16 117 D2
Kennings Way SE11 115 B2
Kennington Green SE11 115 D1
Kennington Grove SE11 114 C1
Kennington Lane SE11 114 C1
Kennington Oval SE11 114 C1
Kennington Park Gardens SE11 115 D1
Kennington Park Place SE11 115 D1
Kennington Park Road SE11 115 D1
Kennington Road SE1 & SE11 114 C3
Kenrick Place W1 109 E2
Kensington Church Street W8 112 A4
Kensington Church Walk W8 112 A3
Kensington Court W8 112 A3
Kensington Court Place W8 112 A3
Kensington Gate W8 112 B3
Kensington Gore SW7 112 B3
Kensington High Street W8 & W14 112 A3
Kensington Mall W8 112 A4
Kensington Palace Gardens W8 112 A4
Kensington Road W8 & SW7 112 B3
Kensington Square W8 112 A3
Kent Passage NW1 109 D4
Kent Terrace NW1 109 D4
Kenton Street WC1 109 B3
Kenway Road SW5 112 A2
Keppel Row SE1 115 E4
Keppel Street WC1 110 B3
Keyse Road SE1 116 B1
Keystone Crescent N1 110 B4
Keyworth Street SE1 115 D3
Kinburn Street SE16 117 D2
Kinder Street E1 116 C3
King And Queen Street SE17 115 E2
King Charles Street SW1 114 B3
King David Lane E1 117 D3
King Edward Street EC1 111 E2
King Edward Walk SE1 115 D3
King James Street SE1 115 E3
King Square EC1 111 E4
King Street EC2 111 E2
King Street SW1 114 A4
King Street WC2 110 B1
King William Street EC4 111 F1
King's Bench Walk EC4 111 D1
King's Cross Road WC1 110 C4
King's Mews WC1 110 C3
King's Road SW3,SW6,SW10 113 D1
King's Scholars'Passage SW1 113 F2
King's Stairs Close SE16 116 C2
Kingfield Street E14 118 C2
Kinghorn Street EC1 111 E3
Kinglake Street SE17 115 F2
Kingly Street W1 109 F1
Kings Arms Yard EC2 111 F2
Kings Bench Street SE1 115 D3

Kingscote Street New Street

Kingscote Street EC4 111 D1
Kingsway WC2 110 C2
Kinnerton Street SW1 113 E3
Kipling Street SE1 115 F4
Kirby Grove SE1 115 F3
Kirby Street EC1 111 D3
Knaresborough Place SW5 112 A2
Knight's Walk SE11 115 D2
Knighten Street E1 116 C2
Knightrider Street EC4 111 E1
Godliman Street
Knightsbridge SW1 & SW7 113 D3
Knightsbridge Green SW1 111 F3
Lamb's Passage
Knox Street W1 109 D3
Kramer Mews SW5 112 A1
Kynance Mews SW7 112 B3

L

Lackington Street EC2 111 F3
Lafone Street SE1 116 A2
Lagado Mews SE16 117 E2
Lamb Street E1 116 A4
Lamb Walk SE1 115 F3
Lamb's Conduit Street WC1 110 C3
Lamb's Passage EC1 111 F3
Lambeth Bridge SW1 & SE11 114 B2
Lambeth High Street SE1 114 C2
Lambeth Hill EC4 111 E1
Lambeth Palace Road SE1 114 C2
Lambeth Road SE1 114 C2
Lambeth Walk SE11 114 C2
Lamlash Street SE11 115 D2
Lanark Square E14 118 B3
Lancaster Drive E14 118 B4
Lancaster Gate W2 108 B1
Lancaster Mews W2 108 B1
Lancaster Place WC2 113 D3
Lancaster Street SE1 115 D3
Lancaster Terrace W2 108 C1
Lancaster Walk W2 108 B1
Lancelot Place SW7 113 D3
Lancing Street NW1 110 A4
Landon's Close E14 118 B4
Langdale Close SE17 115 E1
Langham Place W1 109 F2
Langham Street W1 109 F2
Langley Lane SW8 114 B1
Langley Street WC2 110 B1
Langton Close WC1 110 C3
Lansdowne Row W1 109 F1
Lansdowne Terrace WC1 110 B3
Lant Street SE1 115 E3
Lanterns Court E14 118 A3
Larcom Street SE17 115 E2
Lassell Street SE10 118 C1
Launcelot Street SE1 114 C3
Lower Marsh
Launceston Place W8 112 B3
Launch Street E14 118 B3
Laurence Pountney Lane EC4 111 F1
Lavender Close SW3 112 C1
Lavender Road SE16 117 E2
Laverton Place SW5 112 A2
Lavington Street SE1 115 E4
Law Street SE1 115 F3
Lawn Lane SW8 114 B1
Lawrence Lane EC2 111 E2
Trump Street
Lawrence Street SW3 112 C1
Laxton Place NW1 109 F3
Laystall Street EC1 110 C3
Layton's Buildings SE1 115 E4
Borough High Street
Leadenhall Place EC3 111 F1
Leadenhall Street EC3 111 F2
Leake Street SE1 114 C3
Leather Lane EC1 111 D3
Leathermarket Street SE1 115 F3
Lecky Street SW7 112 C1
Leedam Drive E14 118 C2
Lees Place W1 109 E1
Leicester Court WC2 110 B1
Cranbourn Street
Leicester Place WC2 110 A1
Lisle Street
Leicester Square WC2 110 B1
Leicester Street WC2 110 B1
Leigh Hunt Street SE1 115 E3
Leigh Street WC1 110 B4
Leinster Gardens W2 108 B1
Leinster Mews W2 108 B1
Leinster Place W2 108 B1
Leinster Terrace W2 108 B1
Leman Street E1 116 B3
Lennox Gardens SW1 113 D2
Lennox Gardens Mews SW1 113 D2
Leonard Street EC2 111 F3
Leopold Street E3 117 F4
Leroy Street SE1 115 F2
Lever Street EC1 111 E4
Leverett Street SW3 113 D2
Mossop Street
Lewisham Street SW1 114 B3
Lexham Gardens W8 112 A2
Lexham Mews W8 112 A2
Lexington Street W1 110 A1
Leyden Street E1 116 A4
Leydon Close SE16 117 E2
Library Place E1 116 C3
Library Street SE1 115 D3
Lightermans Road E14 118 A3
Lilestone Street NW8 108 C3
Lillie Yard SW6 112 A1
Lime Close E1 116 B2
Lime Street EC3 111 F1
Lime Street Passage EC3 111 F1
Lime Street
Limeburner Lane EC4 111 D2
Limeharbour E14 118 B3
Limehouse Causeway E14 117 F3
Limehouse Link Tunnel E14 117 E3
Limerston Street SW10 112 B1
Lincoln Street SW3 113 D2
Lincoln's Inn Fields WC2 110 C2
Linden Gardens W2 108 A1
Lindley Street E1 116 C4
Lindsay Square SW1 114 B2
Lindsey Street EC1 111 E3
Linhope Street NW1 108 D3
Linsey Street SE16 116 B1
Lion Street E1 110 C2
Lipton Road E1 117 D3
Lisle Street W1 110 A1
Lisson Grove NW1 & NW8 108 C3
Lisson Street NW1 108 C3
Litchfield Street WC2 110 B1
Little Albany Street NW1 109 F4
Little Argyll Street W1 114 A2
Regent Street
Little Britain EC1 111 E2
Little Chester Street SW1 113 E3
Little College Street SW1 114 B3
Little Dorrit Close SE1 115 E4
Little Edward Street NW1 109 F4
Little George Street SW1 114 B3
Great George Street
Little Marlborough Street W1 109 F1
Kingly Street
Little New Street EC4 111 D2
New Street Square
Little Newport Street WC2 110 B1
Little Portland Street W1 109 F2
Little Russell Street WC1 110 B2
Little Sanctuary SW1 114 B3
Broad Sanctuary
Little Smith Street SW1 114 B3
Little Somerset Street E1 114 A3
Little St James's Street SW1 114 A4
Little Titchfield Street W1 109 F2
Little Trinity Lane EC4 111 E1
Liverpool Grove SE17 115 E1
Liverpool Street EC2 111 F2
Livingstone Place E14 118 B1
Livonia Street W2 110 A2
Lizard Street EC1 111 E4
Llewellyn Street SE16 116 B1
Lloyd Baker Street WC1 110 C4
Lloyd Square WC1 110 C4
Lloyd Street WC1 110 C4
Lloyd's Avenue EC3 116 A3
Lloyd's Row EC1 111 D4
Lockesfield Place E14 118 B1
Locksley Street E14 117 F4
Lockwood Square SE16 116 C1
Lodge Road NW8 108 C4
Loftie Street SE16 116 B1
Lolesworth Close E1 116 B4
Lollard Street SE11 114 C2
Loman Street SE1 115 E4
Lomas Street E1 116 C4
Lombard Lane EC4 111 A2
Temple Lane
London Bridge EC4 & SE1 111 F1
London Bridge Street SE1 115 F4
London Road SE1 115 D3
London Street EC3 116 A3
London Street W2 108 C2
London Wall EC2 111 E2
Long Acre WC2 110 B1
Long Lane EC1 111 E2
Long Lane SE1 115 F3
Long Walk SE1 116 A1
Long Yard WC1 110 C3
Longford Street NW1 109 F3
Longmoore Street SW1 113 F2
Longville Road SE11 115 D2
Lord North Street SW1 114 B3
Lordship Place SW3 112 C1
Lawrence Street
Lorenzo Street WC1 110 C4
Lorrimore Road SE7 115 E1
Lorrimore Square SE17 115 E1
Lothbury EC2 111 F2
Loughborough Street SE11 114 C1
Lovat Lane EC3 111 F1
Love Lane EC2 111 E2
Lovegrove Walk E14 118 B4
Lovell Place SE16 117 E1
Lovers' Walk W1 113 E4
Lowell Street E14 117 E4
Lower Belgrave Street SW1 113 E3
Lower Grosvenor Place SW1 113 F3
Lower James Street W1 110 A1
Lower John Street W1 110 A1
Lower Marsh SE1 114 C3
Lower Road SE8 & SE16 117 D1
Lower Sloane Street SW1 113 E1
Lower Thames Street EC3 111 F1
Lowndes Place SW1 113 E3
Lowndes Square SW1 113 D3
Lowndes Street SW1 113 E3
Lowood Street E1 116 C3
Bewley Street
Loxham Street WC1 110 B3
Cromer Street
Lucan Place SW3 112 C2
Lucerne Mews W8 112 A4
Lucey Road SE16 116 B1
Ludgate Broadway EC4 111 D2
Pilgrim Street
Ludgate Circus EC4 111 D2
Ludgate Square EC4 111 D2
Luke Street EC2 111 F3
Lukin Street E1 117 D3
Lumley Street W1 109 E1
Brown Hart Garden
Lupus Street SW1 113 F1
Luralda Gardens E14 118 C1
Luton Street NW8 108 C3
Luxborough Street W1 109 E3
Lyall Street SW1 113 E3
Lygon Place SW1 113 F3
Lynch Walk SE8 118 A1
Lytham Street SE17 115 F1

M

Mabledon Place WC1 110 B4
Macclesfield Road EC1 111 E4
Mackenzie Walk E14 118 A4
Macklin Street WC2 110 B2
Mackworth Street NW1 109 F4
Macleod Street SE17 115 E1
Maconochies Road E14 118 B1
Macquarie Way E14 118 B2
Maddox Street W1 109 F1
Magdalen Street SE1 116 A2
Magee Street SE11 115 D1
Maguire Street SE1 116 B2
Mahognay Close SE16 117 E2
Maiden Lane WC2 110 B1
Maiden Lane SE1 115 E4
Makins Street SW3 116 D2
Malabar Street E14 118 A3
Malet Street WC1 110 A3
Mallord Street SW3 112 C1
Mallory Street NW8 108 C3
Mallow Street EC1 111 F3
Malta Street EC1 111 D3
Maltby Street SE1 116 A1
Maltravers Street WC2 110 C1
Managers Street E14 118 C4
Manchester Grove E14 118 B2
Manchester Road E14 118 B3
Manchester Square W1 109 E2
Manchester Street W1 109 E2
Manciple Street SE1 115 F3
Mandarin Street E14 117 F3
Mandeville Place W1 109 E2
Manette Street W1 110 B2
Manilla Street E14 118 A3
Manningford Close EC1 111 D4
Manningtree Street E1 116 B4
Commercial Road
Manor Place SE17 115 E1
Manresa Road SW3 112 C1
Mansell Street E1 116 B3
Mansfield Mews W1 109 F2
Mansfield Street
Mansfield Street W1 109 F2
Mansion House Place EC4 111 A1
St Swithun's Lane
Manson Mews SW7 112 B2
Manson Place SW7 112 C2
Maple Leaf Square SE16 117 E2
Maple Street W1 109 F3
Maples Place E1 116 C4
Marble Arch W1 109 D1
Marchmont Street WC1 110 B3
Margaret Court W1 109 F2
Margaret Street
Margaret Street W1 109 F2
Margaretta Terrace SW3 112 C1
Margery Street WC1 110 C4
Marigold Street SE16 116 C1
Mariners Mews E14 118 C2
Marjorie Mews E1 117 D4
Mark Lane EC3 116 A3
Market Court W1 109 E1
Oxford Street
Market Mews W1 113 E4
Market Place W1 109 F2
Markham Square SW3 113 D2
Markham Street SW3 113 D2
Marlborough Close SE17 115 E2
Marlborough Road SW1 114 A4
Marlborough Street SW3 112 C2
Marloes Road W8 112 A3
Marlow Way SE16 117 D2
Marne Street W10 116 B1
Maroon Street E14 117 E4
Marsh Street E14 118 A2
Marsh Wall E14 118 A3
Marshall Street W1 110 A1
Marshall's Place SE16 116 B1
Marshalsea Road SE1 115 E4
Marsham Street SW1 114 B3
Marshfield Street E14 118 B3
Marsland Close SE17 115 E1
Martha Street E1 116 C3
Martin Lane EC4 111 F1
Martin's Street WC2 110 B1
Martlett Court WC2 110 B2
Marylebone High Street W1 109 E3
Marylebone Lane W1 109 E2
Marylebone Mews W1 109 E2
Marylebone Road NW1 109 D3
Marylebone Street W1 109 E2
Marylee Way SE11 114 C2
Mason Street SE17 115 F2
Mason's Arms Mews W1 109 F1
Maddox Street
Mason's Place EC1 111 E4
Mason's Yard SW1 109 E2
Duke Street St James's
Massinger Street SE17 115 F2
Mast House Terrace E14 118 A2
Master's Street E1 117 E4
Mastmaker Road E14 118 A2
Matlock Street E14 117 E4
Matthew Parker Street SW1 114 B3
Maunsel Street SW1 114 A2
May's Court WC2 110 B1
St Martin's Lane
Mayfair Place W1 113 F4
Mayflower Street SE16 117 D1
Maynards Quay E1 116 C3
McAuley Close SE1 114 C3
McCleod's Mews SW7 112 B2
Mead Row SE1 115 D3
Meadcroft Road SE11 115 D1
Meadow Row SE1 115 E2
Meard Street W1 110 A2
Mecklenburgh Place WC1 110 C3
Mecklenburgh Square WC1 110 C3
Mecklenburgh Street WC1 110 C3
Mecklenburgh Square
Medway Street SW1 114 A2
Melbury Terrace NW1 109 D3
Melcombe Place NW1 109 D3
Melcombe Street NW1 109 D3
Melior Place SE1 115 F4
Snowsfields
Mellish Street E14 118 A3
Melon Place W8 112 A4
Kensington Church Street
Melton Street NW1 110 A4
Memel Court EC1 111 E3
Baltic Street
Mepham Street SE1 114 C4
Mercer Street WC2 110 B1
Meredith Street EC1 111 D4
Merlin Street WC1 111 D4
Mermaid Court SE1 115 F4
Mermaid Row SE1 115 F3
Merrick Square SE1 115 E3
Merrington Road SW6 112 A1
Merrow Street SE17 115 E1
Methley Street SE11 115 D1
Mews Street E1 116 B2
Meymott Street SE1 115 D4
Micawber Street N1 111 E4
Middle Street EC1 111 E2
Middle Temple Lane EC4 110 C2
Middle Yard SE1 115 F4
Middlesex Street E1 116 A4
Middleton Drive SE16 117 E2
Midford Place W1 110 A3
Tottenham Court Road
Midhope Street WC1 110 B4
Midland Place E14 118 B1
Midland Road NW1 110 B4
Midship Close SE16 117 E2
Milborne Grove SW10 112 B1
Milcote Street SE1 115 D3
Mile End Road E1 116 C4
Miles Street SW8 114 B1
Milford Lane WC2 110 C1
Milk Street EC2 111 E2
Milk Yard E1 117 D3
Mill Place E14 117 F3
Mill Street SE1 116 B1
Mill Street W1 109 F1
Millbank SW1 114 B2
Millharbour E14 118 A3
Milligan Street E14 117 F3
Millman Street WC1 110 C3
Millstream Road SE1 116 A1
Millwall Dock Road E14 118 A3
Milner Street SW3 113 D2
Milton Court EC2 111 F3
Milton Street EC2 111 F3
Milverton Street SE11 115 D1
Milward Street E1 116 C4
Mincing Lane EC3 116 A3
Minera Mews SW1 113 E2
Minories EC3 116 A3
Mint Street SE1 115 E3
Miranda Close E1 116 C4
Mitchell Street EC1 111 E3
Mitre Road SE1 115 D3
Mitre Square EC3 116 A3
Mitre Street
Mitre Street EC3 116 A3
Moiety Road E14 118 A3
Molyneux Street W1 109 D2
Monck Street SW1 114 B3
Moncorvo Close SW7 112 C3
Monkton Street SE11 115 D2
Monkwell Square EC2 111 E2
Monmouth Street WC2 110 B1
Montagu Mansions W1 109 D3
Montagu Mews North W1 109 D2
Montagu Mews South W1 109 D2
Montagu Mews West W1 109 D2
Montagu Place W1 109 D2
Montagu Row W1 109 D2
Montagu Square W1 109 D2
Montagu Street W1 109 D2
Montague Close SE1 115 F4
Montague Place WC1 110 D3
Montague Street EC1 111 E2
Montague Street WC1 110 B3
Montford Place SE11 114 C1
Montpelier Mews SW7 113 D3
Montpelier Place SW7 113 D3
Montpelier Square SW7 113 D3
Montpelier Street SW7 113 D3
Montpelier Walk SW7 113 D3
Montreal Place WC2 110 C1
Montrose Court SW7 112 C3
Montrose Place SW1 113 E3
Monument Street EC3 111 F1
Monza Street E1 117 D3
Moodkee Street SE16 117 D1
Moor Lane EC2 111 F2
Moor Place EC2 111 F2
Moorfields
Moore Street SW3 110 A1
Old Compton Street
Moorfields EC2 111 F2
Moorgate EC2 111 F2
Mora Street EC1 111 E4
Morecambe Close E1 117 D4
Morecambe Street SE17 115 E2
Moreland Street EC1 111 E4
Moreton Place SW1 114 A2
Moreton Street SW1 114 A2
Moreton Terrace SW1 114 A1
Morley Street SE1 115 D3
Morocco Street SE1 115 F3
Morpeth Terrace SW1 113 F2
Morris Street E1 116 C3
Mortimer Market WC1 110 A3
Capper Street
Mortimer Street W1 109 F2
Morwell Street WC1 110 A2
Moss Close E1 116 B4
Mossop Street SW3 113 D2
Motcomb Street SW1 113 E3
Mount Pleasant WC1 110 C3
Mount Row W1 109 E1
Mount Street E1 116 C4
Mount Street W1 109 E1
Mount Terrace E1 116 C4
Moxon Street W1 109 E2
Mozart Terrace SW1 113 E2
Muirfield Crescent E14 118 B3
Mulberry Street E1 116 B4
Mulberry Walk SW3 112 C1
Mulready Street NW8 108 C3
Mulvaney Way SE1 115 F3
Mumford Court EC2 111 E2
Milk Street
Mundy Street N1 111 F4
Munster Square NW1 109 F4
Munton Road SE17 115 E2
Murphy Street SE1 114 C3
Murray Grove N1 111 E4
Musbury Street E1 117 D4
Muscovy Street EC3 116 A3
Museum Street WC1 110 B2
Myddelton Passage EC1 111 D4
Myddelton Square EC1 111 D4
Myddelton Street EC1 111 D4
Mylne Street EC1 111 D4
Myrdle Street E1 116 C4
Myrtle Walk N1 111 F4

N

Napier Avenue E14 118 A2
Narrow Street E14 117 E3
Nash Place E14 118 A4
Nash Street NW1 109 F4
Nassau Street W1 109 F2
Nathaniel Close E1 116 B4
Thrawl Street
Neal Street WC2 110 B2
Neathouse Place SW1 113 F2
Wilton Road
Nebraska Street SE1 115 E3
Neckinger SE1 116 B1
Neckinger Street SE1 116 B1
Neison Passage EC1 111 E4
Mora Street
Nelson Place N1 111 E4
Nelson Square SE1 115 D4
Nelson Street E1 116 C4
Nelson Terrace N1 111 D4
Nelson Walk SE16 117 E2
Neptune Street SE16 117 D1
Nesham Street E1 116 B3
Neston Street SE16 117 D2
Netherton Grove SW10 112 B1
Netley Street NW1 109 F4
Nevern Place SW5 112 A2
Nevern Square SW5 112 A2
Neville Street SW7 112 C2
Neville Terrace SW7 112 C1
New Bond Street W1 109 F1
New Bridge Street EC4 111 D2
New Broad Street EC2 111 F2
New Burlington Mews W1 116 A3
Hart Street
New Burlington Place W1 109 F1
New Burlington Street W1 109 F1
New Cavendish Street W1 109 E2
New Change EC4 111 E2
New Compton Street WC2 110 B2
New Crane Place E1 117 D2
New Fetter Lane EC4 111 D2
New Globe Walk SE1 115 E4
New Goulston Street E1 116 A4
New Kent Road SE1 115 E2
New King Street SE8 118 A1
New North Place EC2 111 F3
New North Road N1 111 F4
New North Street WC1 110 C3
New Oxford Street WC1 110 B2
New Quebec Street W1 109 D2
New Ride SW7 112 C3
New Road E1 116 C4
New Row WC2 110 B1
New Spring Gardens Walk SE11 114 B1
Goding Street
New Square WC2 110 C2
New Street EC2 116 A4

Street	Page	Grid
New Street Square EC4	111	D2
New Turnstile WC1	110	B2
High Holborn		
New Union Close E14	118	C3
New Union Street EC2	111	E2
Newark Street E1	116	C4
Newburgh Street W1	110	F1
Foubert's Place		
Newburn Street SE11	114	C1
Newbury Street EC1	111	E2
Newcastle Place W2	108	C3
Newcomen Street SE1	115	F4
Newell Street E14	117	F3
Newgate Street EC1	111	D2
Newington Butts SE1 & SE11	115	D2
Newington Causeway SE1	115	E3
Newlands Quay E1	117	D3
Newman Street W1	110	A2
Newman's Row WC2	110	C2
Lincoln's Inn Fields		
Newnham Terrace SE1	114	C3
Newnhams Row SE1	116	A1
Newport Place WC2	110	B1
Newport Street SE11	114	C2
Newton Street WC2	110	B2
Nicholas Lane EC4	111	F1
Nicholson Street SE1	115	D4
Nightingale Place SW10	112	B1
Nile Street N1	111	E4
Nine Elms Lane SW8	114	A1
Noble Street EC2	111	E2
Noel Street W1	110	A2
Norbiton Road E14	117	F4
Norfolk Crescent W2	108	C2
Norfolk Place W2	108	C2
Norfolk Square W2	108	C2
Norman Street EC1	111	E4
Norris Street SW1	110	A1
North Audley Street W1	109	E1
North Bank NW8	108	C4
North Colonnade E14	118	A4
North Crescent WC1	110	A3
North Flockton Street SE16	116	B1
Chambers Street		
North Gower Street NW1	110	A4
North Mews WC1	110	C3
North Ride W2	108	C1
North Row W1	109	E1
North Tenter Street E1	116	B3
North Terrace SW3	112	C2
North Wharf Road W2	108	B2
Northampton Road EC1	111	D3
Northampton Row EC1	111	D3
Exmouth Market		
Northampton Square EC1	111	D4
Northburgh Street EC1	111	D3
Northchurch SE17	115	E2
Northdown Street N1	110	C4
Northington Street WC1	110	C3
Northumberland Alley EC3	116	A3
Northumberland Avenue WC2	114	B4
Northumberland Street WC2	114	B4
Northy Street E14	117	E3
Norway Gate SE16	117	E1
Norway Place E14	117	F3
Norwich Street EC4	111	D2
Notting Hill Gate W11	108	A1
Nottingham Place W1	109	E3
Nottingham Street W1	109	E3

Street	Page	Grid
O		
O'leary Square E1	117	D4
O'meara Street SE1	115	E4
Oak Lane E14	117	F3
Oak Tree Road NW8	108	C4
Oakden Street SE11	115	D2
Oakfield Street SW10	112	B1
Oakley Crescent EC1	111	E4
Oakley Gardens SW3	113	D1
Oakley Street SW3	112	C1
Oat Lane EC2	111	E2
Observatory Gardens W8	112	A4
Occupation Road SE17	115	E1
Ocean Street E1	117	E4
Octagon Arcade EC2	111	F2
Odessa Street SE16	117	E1
Ogle Street W1	109	F2
Old Bailey EC4	111	D2
Old Bond Street W1	109	F1
Old Broad Street EC2	111	F2
Old Brompton Road SW5 & SW7	112	A1
Old Burlington Street W1	109	F1
Old Castle Street E1	116	B4
Old Cavendish Street W1	109	F2
Old Church Road E1	117	D4
Old Church Street SW3	112	C1
Old Compton Street W1	110	A1
Old Court Place W8	112	A3
Old Fleet Lane EC4	111	D2
Old Gloucester Street WC1	110	B3
Old Jamaica Road SE16	116	B1
Old Jewry EC2	111	F2
Old Marylebone Road NW1	109	D2
Old Mitre Court EC4	111	D2
Fleet Street		
Old Montagu Street E1	116	B4
Old North Street WC1	110	C3
Theobalds Road		
Old Palace Yard SW1	114	B3
Old Paradise Street SE11	114	C2
Old Park Lane W1	113	E4
Old Pye Street SW1	114	A3
Old Quebec Street W1	109	D2
Old Queen Street SW1	114	A3
Old Square WC2	110	C2
Old Street EC1	111	E3
Old Woolwich Road SE10	118	C1
Oldbury Place W1	109	E3
Olivers Yard EC1	111	F3
Olliffe Street E14	118	C2
Olney Road SE7	115	E1
Olympia Mews W2	108	B1
Onega Gate SE16	117	E1
Ongar Road SW6	112	A1
Onslow Gardens SW7	112	B2
Onslow Mews SW7	112	C2
Onslow Square SW7	112	C2
Onslow Street EC1	111	D3
Saffron Street		
Ontario Street SE1	115	E3
Ontario Way E14	118	A4
Opal Street SE11	115	D2
Orange Place SE16	117	D1
Orange Street WC2	110	B1
Orb Street SE17	115	F2
Orchard Street W1	109	E2
Orchardson Street NW8	108	C3
Orde Hall Street WC1	110	C3
Orient Street SE11	115	D2
Orme Court W2	108	A1
Orme Lane W2	108	A1
Orme Square W2	108	A1
Ormond Yard SW1	110	A1

Street	Page	Grid
Ormonde Gate SW3	113	D1
Orsett Street SE11	114	C2
Orsett Terrace W2	108	B2
Orton Street E1	116	B2
Wapping High Street		
Osbert Street SW1	114	A2
Osborne Street E1	116	B4
Oslo Square SE16	117	E1
Osnaburgh Street NW1	109	F3
Osnaburgh Terrace NW1	109	F4
Albany Street		
Ossington Buildings W1	109	E2
Moxon Street		
Ossington Street W2	108	A1
Ossulston Street NW1	110	A4
Osten Mews SW7	112	B2
Oswin Street SE11	115	D2
Othello Close SE1	115	D1
Otto Street SE17	115	D1
Oval Way SE11	114	C1
Ovex Close E14	118	C2
Ovington Gardens SW3	113	D3
Ovington Square SW3	113	D3
Ovington Street SW3	113	D2
Owen Street EC1	111	D4
Oxendon Street SW1	110	A1
Coventry Street		
Oxford Circus W1	109	F2
Regent Street		
Oxford Square W2	108	C2
Oxford Street W1	109	E1
Oystergate Walk EC4	111	F1

Street	Page	Grid
P		
Paddington Green W2	108	C3
Paddington Street W1	109	E3
Page Street SW1	114	B2
Pageantmaster Court EC4	111	D2
Ludgate Hill		
Paget Street EC1	111	D4
Pakenham Street WC1	110	C3
Palace Avenue W8	112	A4
Palace Court W2	108	A1
Palace Gardens Mews W8	112	A4
Palace Gardens Terrace W8	112	A4
Palace Gate W8	112	B3
Palace Street SW1	113	F3
Pall Mall SW1	114	A4
Pall Mall East SW1	110	B1
Palmer Street SW1	114	A3
Pancras Lane EC4	111	E2
Panton Street SW1	110	A1
Paradise Street SE16	116	C1
Paradise Walk SW3	113	D1
Paragon Mews SE1	115	F2
Searles Road		
Pardoner Street SE1	115	F3
Parfetts Street E1	116	C4
Paris Garden SE1	115	D4
Park Approach SE16	116	C1
Park Crescent W1	109	E3
Park Crescent Mews East W1	109	E3
Park Crescent Mews West W1	109	E3
Park Lane W1	109	E1
Park Place SW1	113	F4
Park Place E14	118	A4
Park Road NW1 & NW8	109	D4
Park Row SE10	118	C1
Park Square East NW1	109	F3
Park Square Mews W1	109	E3
Harley Street		
Park Square West NW1	109	E3
Park Street SE1	115	E4
Park Street W1	109	E1
Park Walk SW10	112	B1
Park West Place W2	109	D2
Parker Street WC2	110	B2
Parkers Row E1	116	B1
Parliament Square SW1	114	B3
Parliament Street SW1	114	B4
Parnham Street E14	117	E4
Parry Street SW8	114	B1
Parsonage Street E14	118	C2
Pasley Close SW1	115	E1
Passmore Street SW1	113	E2
Pastor Street SE11	115	D2
Pater Street W8	112	A3
Paternoster Row EC4	111	E2
Paternoster Square EC4	111	E2
Paul Julius Close E14	118	C4
Paul Street EC2	111	F3
Paul's Walk EC4	111	E1
Paultons Square SW3	112	C1
Paveley Street NW8	108	C4
Pavilion Road SW1	113	D2
Pavilion Street SW1	113	D2
Peabody Avenue SW1	113	F1
Peacock Street SE17	115	E2
Pear Tree Court EC1	111	D3
Pear Tree Street EC1	111	E3
Pearl Street E1	116	C2
Pearman Street SE1	115	D3
Peartree Lane E1	117	D3
Peerless Street EC1	111	E4
Pelham Crescent SW7	112	C2
Pelham Place SW7	112	C2
Pelham Street SW7	112	C2
Pelier Street SE17	115	E1
Pelling Street E14	117	F4
Pemberton Row EC4	111	D2
Pembridge Gardens W2	108	A1
Pembridge Road W11	108	A1
Pembridge Square W2	108	A1
Pembroke Mews W8	112	A2
Earls Court Road		
Penang Street E1	116	C2
Penfold Place NW1	108	C3
Penfold Street NW1 & NW8	108	C3
Pennant Mews W8	112	A2
Pennington Street E1	116	C3
Penrose Grove SE17	115	E1
Penrose Street SE17	115	E1
Penryn Street NW1	110	A4
Penton Place SE17	115	D2
Penton Rise WC1	110	C4
Pentonville Road N1	110	C4
Pepper Street SE1	115	E4
Pepper Street E14	118	B3
Pepys Street EC3	116	A3
Percival Street EC1	111	D3
Percy Circus WC1	110	C4
Percy Street W1	110	A2
Perkin's Rents SW1	114	A3
Perkins Square SE1	115	E4
Perry's Place W1	110	A2
Perryn Road SE16	116	C1
Peter Street W1	110	A1
Peter's Hill EC4	111	E2
Peter's Lane EC1	111	D3
Petersham Lane SW7	112	B3
Petersham Mews SW7	112	B3
Petersham Place SW7	112	B3
Peto Place NW1	109	F3

Street	Page	Grid
Petticoat Lane E1	116	B4
Petticoat Square E1	116	A4
Harrow Place		
Petty France SW1	114	A3
Petyward SW3	113	D2
Phelp Street SE17	115	F1
Phene Street SW3	113	D1
Philchurch Place E1	116	B3
Phillimore Walk W8	112	A3
Philpot Lane EC3	111	F1
Philpot Street E1	116	C4
Phipp Street EC2	111	F3
Phoenix Place WC1	110	C3
Phoenix Road NW1	110	A4
Phoenix Street WC2	110	B2
Charing Cross Road		
Piccadilly W1	113	F4
Piccadilly Circus W1	110	A1
Regent Street		
Pickard Street EC1	111	E4
Pickford Wharf N1	111	E4
Pickwick Street SE1	115	E3
Picton Place W1	109	E2
Pier Street E14	118	C2
Piggot Street E14	117	F3
Pilgrim Street EC4	111	D2
Pilgrimage Street SE1	115	F3
Pimlico Road SW1	113	E2
Pinchin Street E1	116	B3
Pindar Street EC2	111	F3
Pine Street EC1	111	D3
Pitfield Street N1	111	F4
Pitsea Place E1	117	E3
Pitsea Street E1	117	E3
Pitt Street W8	112	A3
Pitt's Head Mews W1	113	E4
Pixley Street E14	117	F4
Platina Street EC2	111	F3
Playhouse Yard EC4	111	D1
Plevina Street E14	118	B3
Pleydell Street EC4	111	D1
Bouverie Street		
Plough Place EC4	111	D2
Fetter Lane		
Plover Way SE16	117	E1
Plumber's Row E1	117	B4
Plumtree Court EC4	111	D2
Plymouth Wharf E14	118	C2
Plympton Street NW8	108	C3
Plympton Street		
Plymton Street NW8	108	C3
Pocock Street SE1	115	D3
Pointers Close E14	118	B1
Poland Street W1	110	A2
Pollen Street W1	109	F1
Pollitt Drive NW8	108	C3
Polygon Road NW1	110	A4
Pomwell Way E1	116	B4
Pond Place SW3	112	C2
Ponler Street E1	116	C3
Ponsonby Place SW1	114	B2
Ponsonby Terrace SW1	114	B2
Pont Street SW1	113	D3
Pont Street Mews SW1	113	D3
Poolmans Street SE16	117	D2
Poonah Street E1	117	D3
Pope Street SE1	116	A1
Poppins Court EC4	111	D2
Fleet Street		
Porchester Place W2	109	D2
Porchester Square W2	108	B2
Porchester Terrace W2	108	B1
Porchester Terrace W2	108	B2
Porlock Street SE1	115	F3
Porter Street W1	109	E3
Porter Street SE1	115	E4
Portland Place W1	109	F2
Portland Square E1	116	C2
Portland Street SE17	115	F1
Portman Close W1	109	E2
Portman Mews South W1	109	E2
Portman Road NW1	109	D2
Portman Street W1	109	E2
Portpool Lane EC1	110	C3
Portsea Place W2	109	D2
Portsmouth Street WC2	110	C2
Portsoken Street EC3	116	B3
Portugal Street WC2	110	C2
Potier Street SE1	115	F3
Pottery Street SE16	116	C1
Poultry EC2	111	E2
Praed Street W2	108	C2
Pratt Walk SE11	114	C2
Prescot Street E1	116	B3
President Street EC1	111	E4
Central Street		
Presidents Drive E1	116	C2
Prestons Road E14	118	C4
Prestwood Street N1	111	E4
Wenlock Road		
Price's Street SE1	115	D4
Prideaux Place WC1	110	C4
Primrose Hill EC4	111	D1
Hutton Street		
Primrose Street EC2	116	A4
Prince Albert Road NW1 & NW1	108	C4
Prince Consort Road SW7	112	C3
Prince Of Wales Terrace W8	112	B1
Kensington Road		
Prince's Gardens SW7	112	C3
Prince's Gate SW7	112	C3
Prince's Gate Mews SW7	112	C3
Princelet Street E1	116	B4
Princes Circus WC2	110	B2
Princes Court E1	116	C3
Princes Street EC2	111	F2
Princes Street W1	109	F2
Princess Street SE1	115	D3
Princeton Street WC1	110	C2
Printer Street EC4	111	D2
Priores Street SE1	115	F3
Priory Walk SW10	112	B1
Procter Street WC1	110	C2
Prospect Place E1	117	D2
Prospect Street SE16	116	C1
Providence Court W1	109	E1
Provost Street N1	111	F4
Prusom Street E1	116	C2
Pudding Lane EC3	111	F1
Puddle Dock EC4	111	E1
Puma Court E1	116	B4
Purbrook Street SE1	116	A1

Street	Page	Grid
Q		
Quarley Way SE15	109	D2
New Quebec Street		
Quebec Way SE16	117	E1
Queen Anne Mews W1	109	F2
Chandos Street		
Queen Anne Street W1	109	E2
Queen Anne's Gate SW1	114	A3

Street	Page	Grid
Queen Elizabeth Street SE1	116	A2
Queen Square WC1	110	B3
Queen Street EC4	111	E1
Queen Street W1	113	E4
Queen Street Place EC4	111	E1
Queen Victoria Street EC4	111	D1
Queen's Gardens SW1	113	F3
Queen's Gardens W2	108	B1
Queen's Gate SW7	112	B3
Queen's Gate Gardens SW7	112	B2
Queen's Gate Mews SW7	112	B3
Queen's Gate Place SW7	112	B2
Queen's Gate Place Mews SW7	112	B2
Queen's Gate Terrace SW7	112	B3
Queen's Row SE17	115	E1
Queen's Walk SW1	113	F4
Queenhithe EC4	111	E1
Queensberry Mews West SW7	112	B2
Queensberry Place SW7	109	F2
Harrington Street		
Queensborough Terrace W2	108	B1
Queensway W2	108	A1
Quick Street N1	111	D4

Street	Page	Grid
R		
Rabbit Row W8	112	A4
Radcot Street SE11	115	D1
Radley Mews W8	112	A2
Radnor Mews W2	108	C2
Radnor Place W2	108	C2
Radnor Street EC1	111	D3
Radnor Walk SW3	113	D1
Railway Approach SE1	115	F4
Railway Avenue SE16	117	D2
Rainbow Avenue E14	118	B1
Raine Street E1	116	C2
Rainsford Street W2	108	C2
Raleana Road E14	118	C4
Ralston Street SW3	113	D1
Ramillies Place W1	109	F2
Ramillies Street W1	116	A2
Rampart Street E1	116	C4
Rampayne Street SW1	114	A2
Randall Road SE11	114	C2
Randall Row SE11	114	C2
Ranelagh Bridge W2	108	B2
Ranelagh Grove SW1	113	E2
Ranelagh Road SW1	114	A1
Ranston Street NW1	108	C3
Raphael Street SW7	113	D3
Ratcliff Grove EC1	111	E4
Ratcliffe Cross Street E1	117	E3
Ratcliffe Lane E14	117	E3
Rathbone Place W1	110	A2
Raven Row E1	116	C4
Ravensdon Street SE11	115	D1
Ravent Road SE11	114	C2
Ravey Street EC2	111	F3
Rawlings Street SW3	113	D2
Rawstorne Place EC1	111	D4
Rawstorne Street		
Rawstorne Street EC1	111	D4
Ray Street EC1	111	D3
Reardon Path E1	116	C2
Reardon Street E1	116	C2
Rebecca Street SE16	117	D1
Rectory Square E1	117	E4
Red Lion Row SE11	115	E1
Red Lion Square WC1	110	C2
Red Lion Street WC1	110	C2
Redburn Street SW3	113	D1
Redcastle Close E1	117	D3
Redcliffe Gardens SW10 & SW5	112	A1
Redcliffe Mews SW10	112	B1
Redcliffe Place SW10	112	B1
Redcliffe Road SW10	112	B1
Redcliffe Square SW10	112	A1
Redcliffe Street SW10	112	A1
Redcross Way SE1	115	E4
Redesdale Street SW3	113	D1
Redfield Lane SW5	112	A2
Redhill Street NW1	109	F4
Redman's Road E1	117	D4
Redmead Lane E1	116	B2
Wapping High Street		
Redriff Road SE16	117	E1
Redwood Close SE16	117	E2
Reece Mews SW7	112	C2
Reedworth Street SE11	115	D2
Reeves Mews W1	109	E1
Regal Close E1	116	C4
Regan Way N1	111	F4
Regency Street SW1	114	A2
Regent Square WC1	110	B4
Regent Street W1 & SW1	109	F2
Regnart Buildings NW1	110	A4
Euston Street		
Relton Mews SW7	113	D3
Remington Street N1	111	E4
Remnant Street WC2	110	C2
Kingsway		
Renforth Street SE16	117	D1
Renfrew Road SE11	115	D2
Rennie Street SE1	111	E1
Rephidim Street SE1	115	F3
Repton Street E14	117	E4
Reston Place SW7	112	B3
Reveley Close SE16	117	E1
Rex Place W1	109	E1
Rhodeswell Road E14	117	F4
Rich Lane SW5	112	A1
Rich Street E14	117	F3
Richard's Place SW3	113	D2
Richbell Place WC1	110	C3
Emerald Street		
Richmond Buildings W1	110	A2
Dean Street		
Richmond Mews W1	110	A2
Richmond Terrace SW1	114	B4
Rickett Street SW6	112	A1
Ridgmount Gardens WC1	110	A3
Ridgmount Street WC1	110	A3
Riding House Street W1	109	F2
Riley Road SE1	116	A1
Ringwood Gardens E14	118	B2
Risborough Street SE1	115	E4
Risdon Street SE16	117	D1
River Barge Close E14	118	C3
River Street EC1	111	D4
Riverside Walk SE1	114	C4
Rivington Street EC2	111	F3
Robert Adam Street W1	109	E2
Robert Dashwood Way SE17	115	E2
Robert Street NW1	109	F4
Robert Street WC2	110	B1
Robinson Street SW3	113	D1
Flood Street		
Rochester Row SW1	114	A2
Rochester Street SW1	114	A2
Rockingham Street SE1	115	E3
Rocliffe Street N1	111	E4
Roding Mews E1	116	B2

Rodmarton Street W1 .... 109 D2
Rodney Place SE17 .... 115 E2
Rodney Road SE17 .... 115 E2
Roffey Street E14 .... 118 B3
Roger Street WC1 .... 110 C3
Roland Gardens SW7 .... 112 B1
Roland Way SE17 .... 115 F1
Roland Way SW7 .... 112 B1
Rolls Buildings EC4 .... 111 D2
Rolls Passage EC4 .... 110 C2
Romford Street E1 .... 116 C4
Romilly Street W1 .... 110 A1
Romney Street SW1 .... 114 B2
Ronald Street E1 .... 117 D3
Rood Lane EC3 .... 111 F1
Rope Street SE16 .... 117 E1
Ropemaker Road SE16 .... 117 E1
Ropemaker Street EC2 .... 111 F3
Ropemaker's Fields E14 .... 117 F3
Roper Lane SE1 .... 116 A1
Rosary Gardens SW7 .... 112 B2
Roscoe Street EC1 .... 111 E3
Rose Alley SE1 .... 115 E4
Rose Street WC2 .... 110 B1
Rosebery Avenue EC1 .... 113 D3
Rosemoor Street SW3 .... 113 D2
Roserton Street E14 .... 118 B3
Rosoman Place EC1 .... 111 D4
Rosoman Street
Rosoman Street EC1 .... 111 D4
Rossmore Road NW1 .... 109 D3
Rotary Street SE1 .... 115 D3
Rotherhithe Street SE16 .... 117 D2
Rotherhithe Tunnel Approach E3 ... 117 E3
Rotherhithe Tunnel Approach SE16 . 117 F1
Rothsay Street SE1 .... 115 F3
Rotten Row SW7 & SW1 .... 112 C4
Rotterdam Drive E14 .... 118 C2
Rouel Road SE16 .... 116 B1
Roupell Street SE1 .... 115 D4
Roxby Place SW6 .... 112 A1
Roy Square E14 .... 117 F3
Royal Avenue SW3 .... 113 D1
Royal Exchange Buildings EC3 .... 111 F2
Cornhill
Royal Hospital Road SW3 .... 113 D1
Royal Mint Place E1 .... 116 B3
Royal Mint Street E1 .... 116 B3
Royal Opera Arcade SW1 .... 114 A4
Royal Road SE17 .... 115 D1
Royal Street SE1 .... 114 C3
Rudolf Place SW8 .... 114 B1
Rufus Street N1 .... 111 F4
Rugby Street WC1 .... 110 C3
Rugg Street E14 .... 117 F3
Rum Close E1 .... 116 C3
Rupack Street SE16 .... 117 D1
Rupert Street W1 .... 110 A1
Rushworth Street SE1 .... 115 D3
Russell Place SE16 .... 117 E1
Russell Square WC1 .... 110 B3
Russell Street WC2 .... 110 C1
Russia Dock Road SE16 .... 117 E2
Russia Row EC2 .... 111 E2
Russia Walk SE16 .... 117 E1
Rutherford Street SW1 .... 114 A2
Rutland Gardens SW7 .... 113 D3
Rutland Gate SW7 .... 112 C3
Rutland Place EC1 .... 111 E3
Rutland Street SW7 .... 112 C3
Rysbrack Street SW3 .... 113 D3

S

Sackville Street W1 .... 110 A1
Saddle Yard W1 .... 113 E4
Saffron Hill EC1 .... 111 D3
Saffron Street EC1 .... 111 D3
Sage Street E1 .... 116 C3
Sage Way WC1 .... 110 C4
Sail Street SE11 .... 114 C2
St Agnes Place SE11 .... 115 D1
St Alban's Grove W8 .... 112 A3
St Alban's Street SW1 .... 110 A1
St Albans Mews W2 .... 108 C3
St Alphage Garden EC2 .... 111 E2
St Andrew Street EC4 .... 111 D2
St Andrew's Hill EC4 .... 111 D1
St Ann's Lane SW1 .... 114 A3
St Ann's Row E14 .... 117 F3
St Ann's Street SW1 .... 114 B3
St Anne Street E14 .... 117 F3
St Anne's Court W1 .... 110 A2
St Anselm's Place W1 .... 109 E1
St Anthony's Close E1 .... 116 B2
St Barnabas Street SW1 .... 113 E2
St Botolph Street EC3 .... 116 A4
St Bride Street EC4 .... 111 D2
St Chad's Place WC1 .... 110 B4
St Chad's Street WC1 .... 110 B4
St Christopher's Place W1 .... 109 E2
St Clare Street EC3 .... 116 A3
St Clement's Lane WC2 .... 110 C2
St Cross Street EC1 .... 111 D3
St Dunstan's Court EC4 .... 111 D2
Fleet Street
St Dunstan's Lane EC3 .... 111 F1
St Mary at Hill
St Dunstans Alley EC3 .... 116 A3
St Dunstans Hill
St Dunstans Hill EC3 .... 116 A3
St Ermins Hill SW1 .... 114 A3
St George Street W1 .... 109 F1
St George's Circus SE1 .... 115 D3
St George's Court EC4 .... 111 D2
St George's Drive SW1 .... 113 D3
St George's Mews SE1 .... 115 D3
St George's Road SE1 .... 115 D3
St George's Square SW1 .... 114 A1
St George's Square E14 .... 117 E3
St George's Square Mews SW1 ...... 114 A1
St Giles Circus W1 .... 110 A2
St Giles High Street WC2 .... 110 B2
St Helen's Place EC3 .... 111 F2
St Helena Street WC1 .... 110 C4
St James's Court SW1 .... 114 A3
St James's Market SW1 .... 110 A1
Haymarket
St James's Place SW1 .... 113 F4
St James's Road SE1 & SE16 .... 116 B1
St James's Row EC1 .... 111 D3
St James's Walk
St James's Square SW1 .... 114 A4
St James's Street SW1 .... 114 A4
St James's Walk EC1 .... 111 D3
St John Street EC1 .... 111 D4
St John's Lane EC1 .... 111 D3
St John's Place EC1 .... 111 D3
St John's Square EC1 .... 111 D3
St John's Villas W8 .... 112 A3
St Mary's Place
St John's Wood High Street NW8 ... 108 C4
St John's Wood Road NW8 .... 108 C4
St Katherine's Row EC3 .... 111 F1

Fenchurch Street
St Katherine's Way E1 .... 116 B1
St Lawrence Street E14 .... 118 C4
St Leonard's Terrace SW3 .... 113 D1
St Loo Avenue SW3 .... 113 D1
St Luke's Close EC1 .... 111 E3
St Luke's Street SW3 .... 112 C1
St Margaret's Street SW1 .... 114 B3
St Mark Street E1 .... 116 B3
St Martin's Court WC2 .... 110 B1
St Martin's Lane
St Martin's Lane WC2 .... 110 B1
St Martin's Place WC2 .... 110 B1
St Martin's Street WC2 .... 110 B1
St Martin's-le-grand EC1 .... 111 E2
St Mary At Hill EC3 .... 111 F1
St Mary Axe EC3 .... 116 A3
St Mary's Gardens SE11 .... 115 D2
St Mary's Gate W8 .... 112 A3
St Mary's Place W8 .... 112 A3
St Mary's Walk SE11 .... 115 D2
St Marychurch Street SE16 .... 117 D1
St Matthew Street SW1 .... 114 A3
St Michael's Street W2 .... 108 C2
St Olav's Square SE16 .... 117 D1
Albion Street
St Oswald's Place SE11 .... 114 C1
St Paul's Avenue SE16 .... 117 E2
St Paul's Churchyard EC4 .... 111 E2
St Paul's Terrace SE17 .... 115 E1
St Paul's Way E3 .... 117 F4
St Petersburgh Mews W2 .... 108 A1
St Petersburgh Place W2 .... 108 A1
St Swithin's Lane EC4 .... 111 F1
St Thomas Street SE1 .... 115 F4
St Vincent Street W1 .... 109 E2
Salamanca Place SE1 .... 114 C1
Salamanca Street SE1 & SE11 .... 114 C1
Salisbury Close SE17 .... 115 F2
Salisbury Court EC4 .... 111 D2
Salisbury Place W1 .... 109 D3
Salisbury Square EC4 .... 111 D2
Salisbury Court
Salisbury Street NW8 .... 108 C3
Salmon Lane E14 .... 117 E4
Salter Road SE16 .... 117 E1
Salter Street E14 .... 117 F3
Samford Street NW8 .... 108 C3
Sampson Street E1 .... 116 C2
Sancroft Street SE11 .... 114 C2
Sanctuary Street SE1 .... 115 E4
Marshalsea Road
Sandell Street SE1 .... 115 D4
Sandland Street WC1 .... 110 C2
Sandpiper Close SE16 .... 117 F2
Sandwich Street WC1 .... 110 B4
Sandys Row E1 .... 116 A4
Sans Walk EC1 .... 113 D3
Sardinia Street WC2 .... 110 C2
Saunders Ness Road E14 .... 118 C2
Savage Gardens EC3 .... 116 A3
Pepys Street
Savernake Close E14 .... 118 A2
Savile Row W1 .... 109 F1
Savoy Hill WC2 .... 110 C1
Savoy Way
Savoy Place WC2 .... 110 B1
Savoy Row WC2 .... 110 C1
Savoy Street
Savoy Steps WC2 .... 110 C1
Savoy Way
Savoy Street WC2 .... 110 C1
Savoy Way WC2 .... 110 C1
Sawyer Street SE1 .... 115 E4
Scala Street W1 .... 110 A2
Scandrett Street E1 .... 116 C2
Scarborough Street E1 .... 116 B3
Scarsdale Place W8 .... 112 A3
Scarsdale Villas W8 .... 112 A3
School House Lane E1 .... 117 D3
Schooner Close SE16 .... 117 D2
Scoresby Street SE1 .... 115 D4
Scotswood Street SE1 .... 113 D3
Sans Walk
Scott Lidgett Crescent SE16 .... 116 B1
Scovell Road SE1 .... 115 E3
Scrutton Street EC2 .... 111 F3
Seagrave Road SW6 .... 112 A1
Searles Road SE1 .... 115 F2
Seaton Close SE11 .... 115 D1
Sebastian Street EC1 .... 111 D4
Secker Street SE1 .... 114 C4
Sedan Way SE17 .... 115 F2
Sedding Street SW1 .... 113 E2
Sloane Square
Seddon Street WC1 .... 110 C4
Sedley Place W1 .... 109 F2
Woodstock Street
Seething Lane EC3 .... 116 A3
Sekforde Street EC1 .... 111 D3
Sellon Mews SE11 .... 114 C2
Selsdon Way E14 .... 118 B2
Selsey Street E14 .... 117 F4
Selwood Terrace SW7 .... 112 C2
Selwood Place SW7 .... 112 C1
Semley Place SW1 .... 113 E2
Senrab Street E1 .... 117 D4
Serle Street WC2 .... 110 C2
Serpentine Road W2 .... 112 C1
Seth Street SE16 .... 117 D1
Settles Street E1 .... 116 C4
Seven Dials WC2 .... 110 B2
Seville Street SW1 .... 113 D3
Knightsbridge
Seward Street EC1 .... 111 E3
Sextant Avenue E14 .... 118 C2
Seymour Mews W1 .... 109 E2
Seymour Place W1 .... 109 D2
Seymour Street W2 .... 109 D1
Seymour Walk SW10 .... 112 B1
Seyssel Street E14 .... 118 C2
Shad Thames SE1 .... 116 A2
Shadwell Pier Head E1 .... 117 D3
Shadwell Place E1 .... 116 C3
Shaftesbury Avenue W1 & WC2 .... 110 A1
Shafto Mews SW1 .... 113 D3
Shand Street SE1 .... 116 A2
Sharsted Street SE17 .... 115 D1
Shawfield Street SW3 .... 113 D1
Sheffield Street WC2 .... 110 C2
Portugal Street
Sheffield Terrace W8 .... 112 A4
Shelmerdine Close E3 .... 117 F4
Shelton Street WC2 .... 110 B2
Shepherd Market W1 .... 113 F4
Shepherd Street W1 .... 113 E4
Shepherdess Place N1 .... 111 E4
Shepherdess Walk
Shepherdess Walk N1 .... 111 E4
Sheraton Street W1 .... 110 A2
Wardour Street
Sherlock Mews W1 .... 109 E3
Sherwood Gardens E14 .... 118 A2
Sherwood Street W1 .... 110 A1
Shillibeer Place W1 .... 109 D2
Shipwright Road SE16 .... 117 E1
Shoe Lane EC4 .... 111 D2
Short Street SE1 .... 115 D4

Short's Gardens WC2 .... 110 B2
Shorter Street E1 .... 116 B3
Shoulder Of Mutton Alley E14 ...... 117 F2
Shouldham Street W1 .... 109 D2
Shroton Street NW1 .... 108 C3
Sicilian Avenue WC1 .... 110 B2
Vernon Place
Siddons Lane NW1 .... 109 D3
Sidford Place SE1 .... 114 C2
Sidmouth Street WC1 .... 110 C4
Sidney Square E1 .... 117 D4
Sidney Street E1 .... 116 C4
Silex Street SE1 .... 115 D3
Silk Street EC2 .... 111 E3
Silver Walk SE16 .... 117 F2
Silvester Street SE1 .... 115 E3
Simpson's Road E14 .... 118 B4
Singer Street EC2 .... 111 F3
Sise Lane EC4 .... 111 E2
Pancras Lane
Skinner Street EC1 .... 111 D3
Skinners Lane EC4 .... 111 E1
Queen Street
Sleaford Street SW8 .... 110 B4
Slingsby Place WC2 .... 110 B1
Slippers Place SE16 .... 116 C1
Sloane Avenue SW3 .... 113 D2
Sloane Court East SW3 .... 113 E1
Sloane Court West SW3 .... 113 E1
Sloane Gardens SW1 .... 113 E1
Sloane Square SW1 .... 113 E2
Sloane Street SW1 .... 113 D3
Sloane Terrace SW1 .... 113 E2
Sly Street E1 .... 116 C3
Cannon Street Road
Smart's Place WC2 .... 110 B2
Smeaton Street E1 .... 116 C2
Smith Close SE16 .... 117 D2
Smith Square SW1 .... 114 B3
Smith Street SW3 .... 113 D1
Smith Terrace SW3 .... 113 D1
Smithfield Street EC1 .... 111 D2
Smithy Street E1 .... 117 D4
Snow Hill EC1 .... 111 D2
Snowden Street EC2 .... 111 F3
Snowsfields SE1 .... 115 F4
Soho Square W1 .... 110 A2
Soho Street W1 .... 110 A2
Somerford Way SE16 .... 117 E1
Somers Crescent W2 .... 108 C2
Somers Mews W2 .... 108 C2
Sondes Street SE17 .... 115 F1
Sophia Square SE16 .... 117 E3
South Audley Street W1 .... 109 E1
South Bolton Gardens SW5 .... 112 B1
South Collonade E14 .... 118 A4
South Crescent WC1 .... 110 A2
Store Street
South Eaton Place SW1 .... 113 E2
South End W8 .... 112 A3
South End Row W8 .... 112 A3
South Lambeth Road SW8 .... 114 B1
South Molton Lane W1 .... 109 E1
South Molton Street W1 .... 109 E2
South Parade SW3 .... 112 C1
South Place EC2 .... 111 F2
South Street W1 .... 113 E4
South Tenter Street E1 .... 116 B3
South Terrace SW7 .... 112 C2
South Wharf Road W2 .... 108 C2
Southall Place SE1 .... 115 F3
Long Lane
Southampton Buildings WC2 .... 110 C2
Southampton Place WC1 .... 110 B2
Southampton Row WC1 .... 110 B3
Southampton Street WC2 .... 110 B1
Southsea Street SE16 .... 117 E1
Southwark Bridge EC4 & SE1 .... 111 E1
Southwark Bridge Road SE1 .... 115 E3
Southwark Park Road SE16 .... 116 C1
Southwark Street SE1 .... 115 D4
Southwell Gardens SW7 .... 112 B2
Southwick Street W2 .... 108 C2
Hyde Park Crescent
Sovereign Close E1 .... 116 C3
Spa Road SE16 .... 116 B1
Spanish Place W1 .... 109 E2
Spear Mews SW5 .... 112 A2
Spelman Street E1 .... 116 B4
Spence Close SE16 .... 117 F1
Spencer Street EC1 .... 111 D4
Spenser Street SW1 .... 114 A3
Spert Street E14 .... 117 E3
Spindrift Avenue E14 .... 118 A2
Spital Square E1 .... 116 A4
Spital Street E1 .... 116 B4
Sprimont Place SW3 .... 113 D2
Spring Gardens SW1 .... 114 B4
Spring Mews W1 .... 109 D3
Spring Street W2 .... 108 C2
Spur Road SW1 .... 113 F3
Spurgeon Street SE1 .... 115 F3
Stable Yard Road SW1 .... 114 A4
Stables Way SE11 .... 114 C1
Stacey Street WC2 .... 110 B2
Staff Street EC1 .... 111 F4
Vince Street
Stafford Place SW1 .... 113 F3
Stag Place SW1 .... 113 F3
Stainer Street SE1 .... 115 F4
Staining Lane EC2 .... 111 E2
Stalbridge Street NW1 .... 108 C3
Stalham Street SE16 .... 116 C1
Stamford Street SE1 .... 114 C4
Stanford Road W8 .... 112 A3
Stanford Street SW1 .... 114 A2
Stanhope Gardens SW7 .... 112 B2
Stanhope Gate W1 .... 113 E4
Hertford Street
Stanhope Mews East SW7 .... 112 B2
Stanhope Mews South SW7 .... 112 B2
Stanhope Mews West SW7 .... 112 B2
Stanhope Place W2 .... 109 D2
Stanhope Street NW1 .... 109 F4
Stanhope Terrace W2 .... 108 C1
Stannary Place SE11 .... 115 D1
Stannary Street SE11 .... 115 D1
Stanworth Street SE1 .... 116 B1
Staple Inn Buildings WC1 .... 110 C2
Staple Street SE1 .... 115 F3
Staples Close SE16 .... 117 E2
Star Street W2 .... 108 C2
Star Yard WC2 .... 110 C2
Starboard Way E14 .... 118 A3
Starcross Street NW1 .... 110 A4
Station Access Road EC2 .... 111 F2
Stave Yard Road SE16 .... 117 E2
Stead Street SE17 .... 115 E2
Stebondale Street E14 .... 118 C2
Steedman Street SE17 .... 115 E2
Steel's Lane E1 .... 117 D3
Steers Way SE16 .... 117 E1
Stephen Mews W1 .... 110 A2
Gresse Street
Stephen Street W1 .... 110 A2
Stephen's Row EC4 .... 111 F1
Walbrook
Stephenson Way NW1 .... 110 A3

Stepney Causeway E1 .... 117 D3
Stepney Green E1 .... 117 D4
Stepney High Street E1 .... 117 E4
Stepney Way E1 .... 116 C4
Sterling Street SW7 .... 113 D3
Montpelier Place
Sterry Street SE1 .... 115 F3
Stevedore Street E1 .... 116 C2
Stevens Street SE1 .... 116 A1
Steward Street E1 .... 116 A4
Stewart Street E14 .... 118 C3
Stewart's Grove SW3 .... 112 C2
Stillington Street SW1 .... 114 A2
Stockholm Way E1 .... 116 B2
Vaughan Way
Stocks Place E14 .... 117 F3
Stone Buildings WC2 .... 110 C2
Chancery Lane
Stone Stairs E1 .... 117 E3
Stonecutter Street EC4 .... 111 D2
Stones End Street SE1 .... 115 E3
Stoney Lane E1 .... 116 A4
Stoney Street SE1 .... 115 F4
Stopford Road SE17 .... 115 E1
Store Street WC1 .... 110 A2
Storers Quay E14 .... 118 C2
Storey's Gate SW1 .... 114 B3
Stork's Road SE16 .... 116 C1
Stourcliffe Street W1 .... 109 D2
Strafford Street E14 .... 118 A3
Strand WC2 .... 110 B1
Stratford Avenue W8 .... 112 A3
Stratford Place W1 .... 109 E2
Stratford Road W8 .... 112 A2
Strathearn Place W2 .... 108 C2
Hyde Park Square
Strathmore Gardens W8 .... 112 A4
Stratton Street W1 .... 113 F4
Strattondale Street E14 .... 118 B3
Streatham Street WC1 .... 110 B2
Dyott Street
Strutton Ground SW1 .... 114 A3
Strype Street E1 .... 116 A4
Stukeley Street WC2 .... 110 B2
Sturge Street SE1 .... 115 E3
Sturgeon Road SE17 .... 115 E1
Sturt Street N1 .... 111 E4
Stutfield Street E1 .... 116 B3
Sudeley Street N1 .... 111 D4
Sudrey Street SE1 .... 115 E3
Suffolk Lane EC4 .... 111 F1
Suffolk Place SW1 .... 110 B1
Suffolk Street
Suffolk Street SW1 .... 110 B1
Sullivan Road SE11 .... 115 D2
Summercourt Road E1 .... 117 D4
Summers Street EC1 .... 111 D3
Back Hill
Sumner Place SW7 .... 112 C2
Sumner Place Mews SW7 .... 112 C2
Sumner Street SE1 .... 115 E4
Sun Street EC2 .... 111 F3
Sun Street Passage EC2 .... 111 F2
Surrey Quays Road SE16 .... 117 D1
Surrey Row SE1 .... 115 D4
Surrey Square SE17 .... 115 F2
Surrey Street WC2 .... 110 C1
Surrey Water Road SE16 .... 117 E2
Sussex Gardens W2 .... 108 C1
Sussex Place NW1 .... 109 D4
Sussex Place W2 .... 108 C2
Sussex Square W2 .... 108 C1
Sussex Street SW1 .... 113 F1
Sutherland Row SW1 .... 113 F1
Sutherland Street
Sutherland Square SE17 .... 115 E1
Sutherland Street SW1 .... 113 F1
Sutherland Street SE17 .... 117 D3
Sutherland Walk SE17 .... 115 E1
Sutton Row W1 .... 110 B2
Swallow Street W1 .... 110 A1
Swan Lane EC4 .... 111 F1
Swan Mead SE1 .... 115 F3
Swan Road SE16 .... 117 D1
Swan Street SE1 .... 115 E3
Swan Walk SW3 .... 113 D1
Sweden Gate SE16 .... 117 E1
Swedenborg Gardens E1 .... 116 C3
Sweeney Crescent SE1 .... 116 B1
Swinton Street WC1 .... 110 C4
Swiss Court WC2 .... 110 B1
Leicester Square
Sycamore Street EC1 .... 111 E3
Old Street
Sydney Close SW3 .... 112 C2
Sydney Mews SW3 .... 112 C2
Sydney Street SW3 .... 112 C2
Symons Street SW3 .... 113 D2

T

Tabard Street SE1 .... 115 F3
Tabernacle Street EC2 .... 111 F3
Tachbrook Street SW1 .... 114 A2
Taeping Street E14 .... 118 B2
Tailworth Street E1 .... 116 B4
Chicksand Street
Talbot Square W2 .... 108 C2
Tallis Street EC4 .... 111 D1
Tamareire Street SE16 .... 117 D2
Tamworth Street SW6 .... 112 A1
Tankerton Street WC1 .... 110 B4
Cromer Street
Tanner Street SE1 .... 116 A1
Taplow Street N1 .... 111 E4
Tarbert Walk E1 .... 117 D3
Tarling Street E1 .... 116 C3
Tarrant Place W1 .... 109 D2
Tarver Road SE17 .... 115 E1
Tatum Street SE17 .... 115 F2
Taunton Mews NW1 .... 109 D3
Balcombe Street
Taunton Place NW1 .... 109 D3
Tavistock Place WC1 .... 110 B3
Tavistock Square WC1 .... 110 B3
Tavistock Street WC2 .... 110 B1
Taviton Street WC1 .... 110 A3
Tavy Close SE11 .... 115 D1
Teak Close SE16 .... 117 E2
Tedworth Square SW3 .... 113 D1
Telegraph Street EC2 .... 111 F2
Temple Avenue EC4 .... 111 D1
Temple Lane EC4 .... 111 D1
Temple Place WC2 .... 110 C1
Templeton Place SW5 .... 112 A2
Tench Street E1 .... 116 C2
Tenison Court W1 .... 109 F2
Regent Street
Tenison Way SE1 .... 114 C4
Tennis Street SE1 .... 115 F3
Tenter Ground E1 .... 116 A4
White's Row
Tenterden Street W1 .... 109 F2

Terminus Place
Zoar Street

Terminus Place SW1 113 F3
Thackeray Street W8 112 A3
Thalia Close SE10 118 C1
Thame Road SE16 117 E2
Thames Circle E14 118 A2
Thames Street SE10 118 B1
Thanet Street WC1 110 B4
Thavies Inn EC4 111 D2
Thayer Street W1 109 E2
The Boltons SW10 112 B1
The Broad Walk NW1 109 E4
The Broad Walk W8 112 B4
The Cut SE1 115 D4
The Dial Walk W8 112 B4
The Flower Walk SW7 112 B3
The Grange SE1 116 A1
The Highway E1 & E14 116 C3
The Little Boltons SW10 & SW5 111 B1
The Mall SW1 114 A4
The Mitre E14 117 F3
The Piazza WC2 110 B1
The Quarterdeck E14 118 A3
The Vale SW3 112 C1
Theed Street SE1 115 D4
Theobold's Road WC1 110 C3
Thermopylae Gate E14 118 B2
Theseus Walk N1 111 E4
Rocliffe Street
Thirleby Road SE1 114 A3
Thistle Grove SW10 112 B1
Thomas Doyle Street SE1 115 D3
Thomas More Street E1 116 B2
Thomas Place W8 112 A3
St Mary's Place
Thomas Road E14 117 F4
Thoresby Street N1 111 E4
Thorney Street SW1 114 B2
Thornton Place W1 109 D3
Thrale Street SE1 115 E4
Thrawl Street E1 116 B4
Threadneedle Street EC2 111 F2
Three Colt Street E14 117 F3
Three Cranes Walk EC4 111 E1
Three Kings Yard W1 109 E1
Three Oak Lane SE1 116 A2
Throgmorton Avenue EC2 111 F2
Throgmorton Street EC2 111 F2
Thrush Street SE17 115 E1
Thurland Road SE16 116 B1
Thurloe Close SW7 112 C2
Thurloe Place SW7 112 C2
Thurloe Place Mews SW7 112 C2
Thurloe Square SW7 112 C2
Thurloe Street SW7 112 C2
Thurlow Street SE17 115 F2
Tiller Road E14 118 A3
Tillman Street E1 116 C3
Tilney Street W1 113 E3
Timber Street EC1 111 E3
Timberland Road E1 116 C3
Timberpond Road SE16 117 E2
Tinsley Road E1 117 D4
Tinworth Street SE11 114 B2
Titchborne Row W2 108 C2
Tite Street SW3 113 D1
Tiverton Street SE1 115 E3
Tobago Street E14 118 A3
Tokenhouse Yard EC2 111 F2
Tolmers Square NW1 110 A3
Tonbridge Street WC1 110 B4
Took's Court EC4 110 C2
Tooley Street SE1 116 A2
Topham Street EC1 111 D3
Tor Gardens W8 112 A4
Torrens Street EC1 111 D4
Torrington Place E1 116 C1
Torrington Place WC1 110 A3
Tothill Street SW1 114 A3
Tottenham Court Road W1 110 A3
Tottenham Street W1 110 A3
Toulmin Street SE1 115 E3
Toussaint Walk SE16 116 B1
Tower Bridge E1 & SE1 116 A2
Tower Bridge Approach E1 116 B2
Tower Bridge Road SE1 116 A1
Tower Court WC2 110 B1
Monmouth Street
Tower Hill EC3 116 A3
Tower Hill Terrace EC3 116 A3
Gloucester Close
Tower Street WC2 110 B1
Townley Street SE17 115 E2
Townsend Street SE17 115 F2
Toynbee Street E1 116 B4
Tracey Street SE11 114 C2
Trafalgar Gardens E1 117 E4
Trafalgar Grove SE10 118 C1
Trafalgar Road SE10 118 C1
Trafalgar Square WC2 110 B1
Trafalgar Street SE17 115 F1
Trafalgar Way E14 118 B4
Transom Square E14 118 B1
Tranton Road SE16 116 C1
Trebeck Street W1 113 E4
Curzon Street
Trebovir Road SW5 112 A2
Tregunter Road SW10 112 B1
Trenchard Street SE10 118 C1
Tresham Crescent NW8 108 C4
Treveris Street SE1 115 D4
Bear Lane
Trevithick Street SE8 118 A1
Trevor Place SW7 113 D3
Trevor Square SW7 113 D3
Trevor Street SW7 113 D3
Trinidad Street E14 117 F3
Trinity Church Square SE1 115 E3
Trinity Place EC3 116 A3
Trinity Square
Trinity Square EC3 116 A3
Trinity Street SE1 115 E3
Trio Place SE1 115 E3
Triton Square NW1 109 F3
Troon Street E1 117 E4
Trumans Street SE16 116 C1
Trump Street EC2 111 E2
Tryon Street SW3 113 D2
Tudor Street EC4 111 D1
Tufton Street SW1 114 B3
Tunley Green E14 117 F4
Tunnel Avenue SE10 118 C3
Tunnel Road SE16 117 D2
Turk's Row SW3 113 E1
Turner Street E1 116 C4
Turnmill Street EC1 111 D3
Turpentine Lane SW1 113 F1
Turquand Street SE17 115 E2
Twine Court E1 116 C3
Twyford Place WC2 110 C2
Kingsway
Tyers Gate SE1 115 F3
Tyers Street SE11 114 C1
Tyers Terrace SE11 114 C1
Tysoe Street EC1 111 D4

U

Udall Street SW1 114 A2
Ufford Street SE1 115 D3
Ulster Place NW1 109 E3
Umberston Street E1 116 C4
Undershaft EC3 111 F2
Underwood Row N1 111 E4
Shepherdess Walk
Underwood Street N1 111 E4
Undine Road E14 118 B2
Union Street SE1 115 D4
University Street WC1 110 A3
Upbrook Mews W2 108 B2
Upper Belgrave Street SW1 113 E3
Upper Berkeley Street W1 109 D2
Upper Brook Street W1 109 E1
Upper Cheyne Row SW3 112 C1
Upper Grosvenor Street W1 109 E1
Upper Ground SE1 111 D1
Upper Harley Street NW1 109 E3
Upper James Street W1 110 A1
Upper John Street W1 110 A1
Upper Marsh SE1 114 C3
Upper Montagu Street W1 109 D3
Upper St Martin's Lane WC2 110 B1
Upper Tachbrook Street SW1 114 A2
Upper Thames Street EC4 111 E1
Upper Wimpole Street W1 109 E3
Upper Woburn Place WC1 110 B3

V

Valcan Square E14 118 A2
Valentine Place SE1 115 D3
Valentine Row SE1 115 D3
Vandon Passage SW1 114 A3
Vandon Street SW1 114 A3
Vandy Street EC2 111 F3
Vane Street SW1 114 A2
Varden Street E1 116 C4
Varndell Street NW1 109 F4
Vauban Street SE16 116 B1
Vaughan Street SE16 117 F1
Vaughan Way E1 116 B2
Vauxhall Bridge SW1 & SE1 114 B2
Vauxhall Bridge Road SW1 113 F2
Vauxhall Grove SW8 114 B1
Vauxhall Street SE11 114 C1
Vauxhall Street SE11 114 C2
Vauxhall Walk SE11 114 C2
Venables Street NW8 108 C3
Vere Street W1 109 E2
Vernon Place WC1 110 B2
Vernon Rise WC1 110 C4
Vernon Square WC1 110 C4
Penton Rise
Vernon Street W14 110 C4
Verulam Street WC1 110 C3
Vestry Street N1 111 F4
Vicarage Court W8 112 A4
Vicarage Gardens W8 112 A4
Vicarage Gate W8 112 A4
Victoria Avenue EC2 116 A4
Victoria Embankment SW1,
WC2 & EC4 110 C1
Victoria Grove W8 112 B3
Victoria Road W8 112 B3
Victoria Street SW1 113 F3
Victory Place SE17 115 F2
Victory Way SE16 117 E1
Vigo Street W1 110 A1
Villa Street SE17 115 F1
Villiers Street WC2 110 B1
Vince Street EC1 111 F4
Vincent Close SE16 117 E1
Vincent Square SW1 114 A2
Vincent Street SW1 114 A2
Vine Court E1 116 C4
Vine Lane SE1 116 A2
Vine Street EC3 116 A3
Vine Street W1 110 A1
Vine Street Bridge EC1 111 D3
Farringdon Lane
Vinegar Street E1 116 C2
Vineyard Walk EC1 111 D3
Pine Street
Vintner's Place EC4 111 E1
Virgil Street SE1 114 C3
Virginia Street E1 116 B3
Viscount Street EC1 111 E3

W

Wadding Street SE17 115 E2
Waithman Street EC4 111 D2
Pilgrim Street
Wakefield Mews WC1 110 B4
Wakefield Street
Wakefield Street WC1 110 B4
Wakeling Street E14 117 E3
Wakley Street EC1 111 D4
Walbrook EC4 111 F1
Walburgh Street E1 116 C3
Walcorde Avenue SE17 115 E2
Walcot Square SE11 115 D2
Walden Street E1 116 C4
Waley Street E1 117 E4
Wallgrave Road SW5 112 A2
Wallwood Street E14 117 F4
Walnut Tree Walk SE11 114 C2
Walpole Street SW3 113 D2
Walter Terrace E1 117 E4
Walton Place SW3 113 D3
Walton Street SW3 113 D2
Walworth Place SE17 115 E1
Walworth Road SE1 & SE17 115 E2
Wansey Street SE17 115 E2
Wapping Dock Street E1 116 C2
Wapping High Street E1 116 B2
Wapping Lane E1 116 C3
Wapping Walk E1 116 C3
Wapping Wall E1 117 D2
Wardour Street W1 110 A2
Warner Street EC1 110 C3
Warren Street W1 109 F3
Warwick House Street SW1 114 B4
Warwick Lane EC4 111 E2
Warwick Row SW1 113 F3
Warwick Square SW1 111 D2
Warwick Square EC4 113 F2
Warwick Street W1 110 A1
Warwick Way SW1 113 F2
Watergate EC4 111 D2
New Brodge Street
Watergate Street SE8 118 A1
Watergate Walk WC2 110 B1
Villiers Street
Waterloo Bridge WC2 & SE1 110 C1
Waterloo Place SW1 114 A4
Waterloo Road SE1 114 C4
Waterman Way E1 116 C2
Waterman's Walk EC4 111 F1
Waterside Close SE16 116 B1
Watling Street EC4 111 E2
Watney Market E1 116 C4
Watney Street E1 116 C3
Watson's Street SE8 116 C2
Waveney Close E1 116 B2
Waverton Street W1 113 E4
Weavers Lane SE1 116 A2
Webb Street SE1 115 F3
Webber Row SE1 115 D3
Webber Street SE1 115 D3
Webster Road SE16 116 C1
Weighouse Street W1 109 E1
Welbeck Street W1 109 E2
Welbeck Way W1 109 E2
Well Court EC4 111 E1
Queen Street
Welland Mews E1 116 C1
Wellclose Square E1 116 B3
Wellclose Street E1 116 C3
The Highway
Weller Street SE1 115 E3
Wellesley Street E1 117 D4
Wellesley Terrace N1 111 E4
Wellington Place NW8 108 C4
Wellington Road NW8 108 C4
Wellington Square SW3 113 D1
Wellington Street WC2 110 C1
Wells Mews W1 110 A2
Wells Square WC1 110 C4
Wells Street W1 109 F2
Wendover SE17 115 F1
Wenlock Road N1 111 E4
Wenlock Street N1 111 E4
Wentworth Market E1 116 B4
Wentworth Street
Wentworth Street E1 116 B4
Werrington Street NW1 110 A4
Wesley Close SE17 115 D2
Wesley Street W1 109 E2
Weymouth Street
West Arbour Street E1 117 D4
West Central Street WC1 110 B2
West Eaton Place SW1 113 E2
West Ferry Road E14 118 A3
West Gardens E1 116 C3
West Halkin Street SW1 113 E3
West India Avenue E14 118 A4
West India Dock Road E14 117 F3
West Lane SE16 116 C1
West Poultry Avenue EC1 111 D2
West Smithfield
West Road SW4 113 D1
West Smithfield EC1 111 D2
West Square SE11 115 D2
West Street WC2 110 B1
West Tenter Street E1 116 B3
Westbourne Crescent W2 108 B1
Westbourne Street W2 108 C1
Westbourne Terrace W2 108 B2
Westbourne Terrace Mews W2 108 B2
Westbourne Terrace Road W2 108 B2
Westcott Road SE17 115 D1
Western Place SE16 117 D2
Westferry Circus E14 118 A4
Westgate Terrace SW10 112 A1
Westland Place N1 111 F4
Westminster Bridge SW1 & SE1 114 B3
Westminster Bridge Road SE1 114 F3
Westmoreland Place SW1 113 F1
Westmoreland Road SE17 115 E1
Westmoreland Street W1 109 E2
Westmoreland Terrace SW1 113 F1
Weston Rise WC1 110 C4
Weston Street SE1 115 F3
Westport Street E1 117 E4
Westway W12 108 B2
Wetherby Gardens SW5 112 B2
Wetherby Mews SW5 112 A2
Earls Court Road
Wetherby Place SW7 112 B2
Weymouth Mews W1 109 F2
Weymouth Street W1 109 E2
Wharf Road N1 111 E4
Wharfedale Street SW10 112 A1
Wharton Street WC1 110 C4
Wheatley Street W1 109 E2
Marylebone Street
Whetstone Park WC2 110 C2
Whidborne Street WC1 110 B4
Whiskin Street EC1 111 D4
Whitcomb Street WC2 110 A1
White Church Lane E1 116 B4
White Hart Street SE11 115 D2
White Horse Lane E1 117 E4
White Horse Mews SE1 115 D3
White Horse Road E1 117 E3
White Horse Street W1 113 F4
White Kennet Street E1 116 A4
White Lion Hill EC4 111 E1
White's Grounds SE1 116 A1
White's Row E1 116 A4
Whiteadder Way E14 118 B2
Whitechapel High Street E1 116 B4
Whitechapel Road E1 116 B4
Whitecross Place EC2 111 F3
Whitecross Street EC1 111 E3
Whitefriars Street EC4 111 D2
Whitehall SW1 114 B4
Whitehall Court SW1 114 B4
Whitehall Place SW1 114 B4
Whitehaven Street NW8 108 C3
Whitehead's Grove SW3 113 D2
Whitfield Place W1 110 A3
Whitfield Street
Whitfield Street W1 110 A3
Whitgift Street SE11 114 C2
Whittaker Street SW1 113 E2
Whittington Avenue EC3 111 F2
Leadenhall Street
Whittlesey Street SE1 115 D4
Wickham Street SE11 114 C1
Wicklow Street WC1 110 C4
Widegate Street E1 116 A4
Middlesex Street
Wigmore Place W1 109 E2
Wigmore Street W1 109 E2
Wilbraham Place SW1 113 E2
Wilcox Place SW1 114 A3
Wild Court WC2 110 C2
Wild Street WC2 110 B2
Wild's Rents SE1 115 F3
Wilfred Street SW1 113 F3
Wilkes Street E1 116 B4
William IV Street WC2 110 B1
William Mews SW1 113 E3
William Road NW1 109 F4
William Square SE16 117 E3
William Street SW1 113 D3
Willoughby Passage E14 118 A4
Willoughby Street WC1 110 B2
Streatham Street
Willow Place SW1 114 A2
Willow Street EC2 111 F3
Wilmington Square WC1 111 D4
Wilmington Street WC1 111 D4
Wilson Grove SE16 116 C1
Wilson Street EC2 111 F2
Wilson's Place E14 117 F3
Wilton Crescent SW1 113 E3
Wilton Mews SW1 113 E3
Wilton Place SW1 113 E3
Wilton Road SW1 113 F2
Wilton Row SW1 113 E3
Wilton Street SW1 113 E3
Wilton Terrace SW1 113 E3
Wimpole Mews W1 109 E2
Wimpole Street W1 109 E2
Winchester Close SE17 115 D2
Winchester Square SE1 115 F4
Winchester Walk
Winchester Street SW1 113 F2
Winchester Walk SE1 115 F4
Wincott Street SE11 115 D2
Windmill Row SE11 115 D1
Windmill Street W1 110 A2
Windmill Walk SE1 115 D4
Windrose Close SE16 117 D2
Windsor Terrace N1 111 E4
Wine Close E1 116 C2
Wine Office Court EC4 111 D2
Winnett Street W1 110 A1
Rupert Street
Winsland Mews W2 108 C2
Winsland Street W2 108 C2
Winsley Street W1 110 A2
Winterton Place SW10 112 B1
Woburn Place WC1 110 B3
Woburn Square WC1 110 B3
Woburn Walk WC1 110 B3
Upper Woburn Place
Wolfe Crescent SE16 117 D1
Wolseley Street SE1 116 B1
Wood Street EC2 111 E2
Wood's Mews W1 109 E1
Wood's Place SE1 116 A1
Woodbridge Street EC1 111 D3
Woodfall Street SW3 113 D1
Woodstock Mews W1 109 E2
Westmoreland Street
Woodstock Street W1 109 F2
Woolaston Close SE1 115 E2
Wooler Street SE17 115 F1
Wootton Street SE1 115 D4
Worgan Street SE11 114 C2
Wormwood Street EC2 111 F2
Worship Street EC2 111 F3
Wren Landing E14 118 A4
Wren Street WC1 110 C3
Wright's Lane W8 112 A3
Wyatt Close SE16 117 F1
Wybert Street NW1 109 F3
Laxton Place
Wyclif Street EC1 111 D4
Wynan Road E14 118 B1
Wyndham Place W1 109 D2
Wyndham Street W1 109 D2
Wynnstay Gardens W8 112 A3
Wynyard Terrace SE11 114 C1
Wynyatt Street EC1 111 D4
Wythburn Place W1 109 D2

Y

Yabsley Street E14 118 C4
Yardley Street WC1 110 C4
Yarmouth Place W1 113 E4
Yeoman's Row SW3 113 D3
York Buildings WC2 110 B1
York Gate NW1 109 E3
York House Place W8 112 A4
York Road SE1 114 C3
York Square E14 117 E4
York Street W1 109 D3
York Terrace East NW1 109 E3
York Terrace West NW1 109 E3
Yorkshire Road E14 117 E3
Young Street W8 112 A3

Z

Zoar Street SE1 115 E4

town plans

Shetland Islands

Orkney Islands

Outer Hebrides

Coll and Tiree

Aberdeen

Glasgow

Edinburgh

Belfast

Isle of Man

Newcastle

Sunderland

Middlesbrough

York

Leeds

Liverpool

Manchester

Sheffield

DUBLIN

Nottingham

Leicester

Norwich

Birmingham

Peterborough

Coventry

Cambridge

Oxford

Swansea

Cardiff

Bristol

Reading

LONDON

Winchester

Southampton

Portsmouth

Plymouth

Isles of Scilly

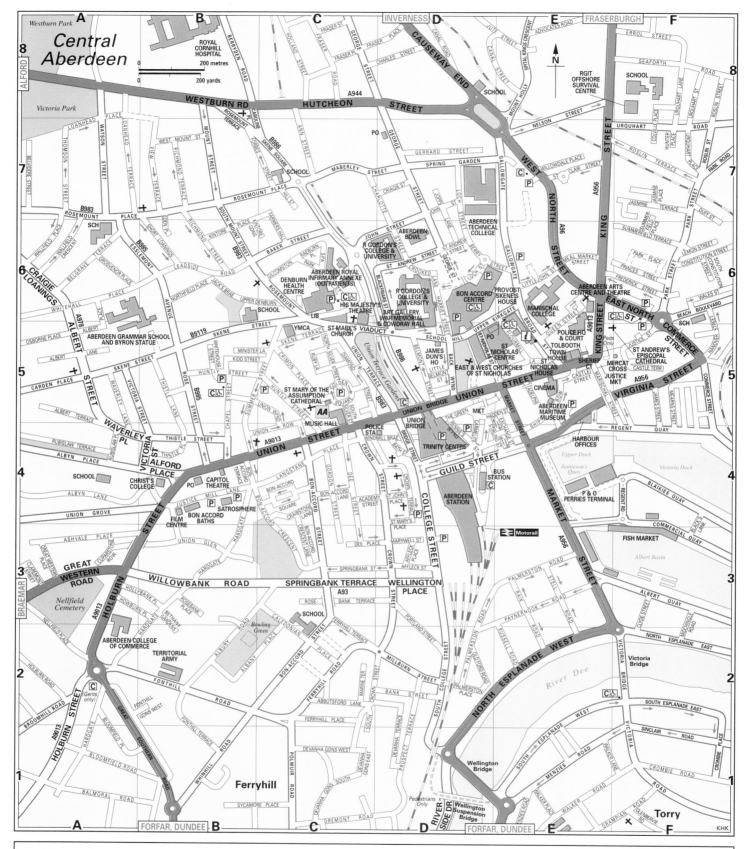

Aberdeen

Aberdeen is known as the 'Granite City', a reputation earned for the extensive use of the material and the attractiveness of its colours – white, blue, pink and grey – rather than for any suggestion of grimness. Although mostly 19th-century in character, the city is very much older. St Machar's Cathedral in Old Aberdeen was founded as far back as AD580, although rebuilt several times – principally after a devastating fire

was started on the orders of Edward III of England in 1336. Old Aberdeen, close to the River Don, is traditionally the ecclesiastical and educational hub of the city, with King's College (Aberdeen University) founded in 1494. New Aberdeen, almost as old with Marischal College (also Aberdeen University) dating from 1593, is the commercial centre and has the magnificent near-mile-long Union Street at its heart. Among its many interesting features are the impressive Art Gallery, Provost Ross's House (NTS) (Aberdeen's

third oldest building, dating from 1593, and containing the Maritime Museum), 16th-century Provost Skene's House and local history museum, the 17th-century Tolbooth Tower, and Union Bridge, one of the widest single-span arches in Britain. Aberdeen is also a major fishing port and ferry terminal for the Orkneys, Shetlands and Scandinavia, and since the North Sea oil boom it has become Britain's most important administrative and off-shore oil-rig supply and maintenance centre.

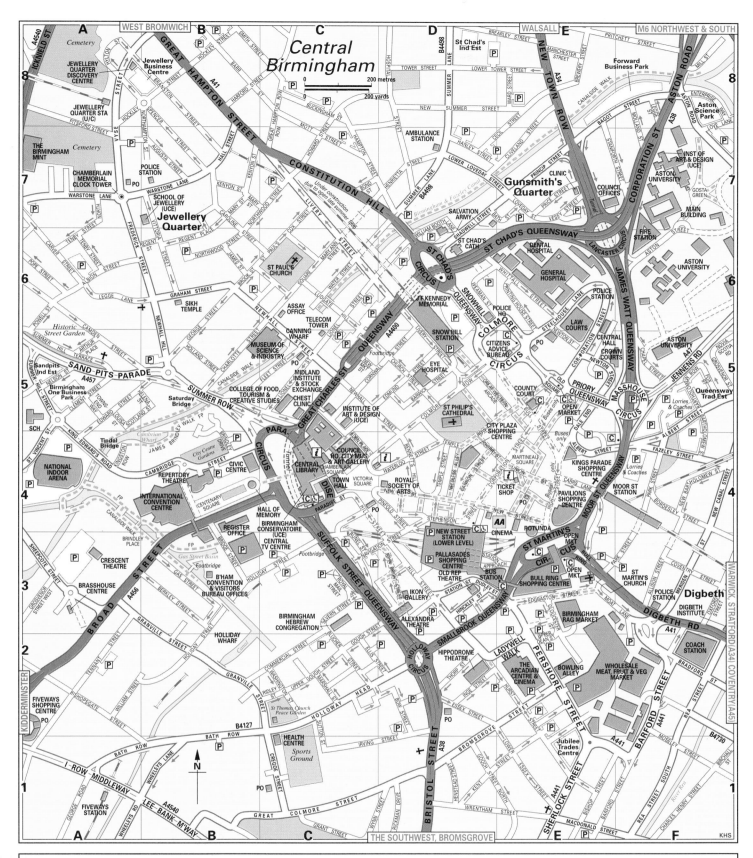

Birmingham

When the Romans were in Britain, Birmingham was little more than a staging post on Icknield Street. Throughout medieval times it was a minor agricultural centre in the middle of a heavily forested region. Timbered houses clustered together round a green that was eventually to be called the Bull Ring. But by the 16th century, although still a tiny village by today's standards, it had begun to gain a reputation as a manufacturing centre. Tens of thousands of sword blades were made here during the Civil War.

Throughout the 18th century more and more land was built on. In 1770 the Birmingham Canal was completed, expanding the possibilities of trade and dramatically increasing the town's development. All of that pales into near insignificance compared with what happened during the 19th century. Birmingham was not represented in Parliament until 1832 and had no town council until 1838. Yet by 1889 it had already

been made a city, and after only another 20 years it had become the second largest city in England. Many of Birmingham's most imposing public buildings date from the 19th century, when the city was growing rapidly. The International Convention Centre and the National Indoor Arena are two of the most recent developments. Surprisingly, the city has more miles of waterway than Venice.

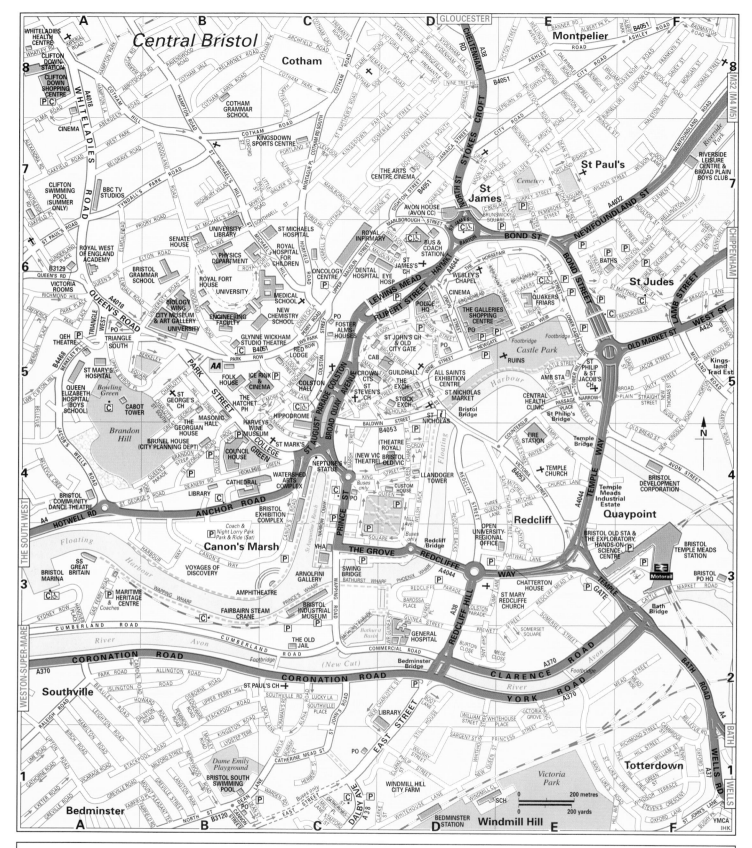

Bristol

One of Britain's most historic seaports, Bristol retains many of its visible links with the past, despite terrible damage inflicted during the bombing raids of World War II. Most imposing is the cathedral, founded as an abbey church in 1140. But perhaps even more famous than the cathedral is the Church of St Mary Redcliffe. Ranking among the finest churches in the country, it owes much of its splendour to 14th- and 15th-century merchants who bestowed huge sums of money on it. The merchant families brought wealth to the whole of Bristol, and their trading links with the world are continued through today's modern aerospace and technological industries.

Much of the best of Bristol can be seen in the area of the Floating Harbour. Several of the old warehouses have been converted into museums, galleries and exhibition centres. Scattered among them are genuinely picturesque old pubs, the best known being the Llandoger Trow, a timbered 17th-century house, the finest of its kind in Bristol. Further up the same street – King Street – is the Theatre Royal, built in 1766 and the oldest theatre in the country.

In Corn Street, the heart of the business area, is a magnificent 18th-century corn exchange. In front of it are the four pillars known as the 'nails', on which merchants used to make cash transactions - hence to 'pay on the nail'.

Forever linked with Bristol is the great engineer Isambard Kingdom Brunel. He designed the Clifton Suspension Bridge, built the Great Western Railway's line from London to Bristol's Old Station and constructed the SS *Great Britain*, the world's first screw-propelled, ocean-going iron ship – restored in the Bristol yard where she was built in 1843.

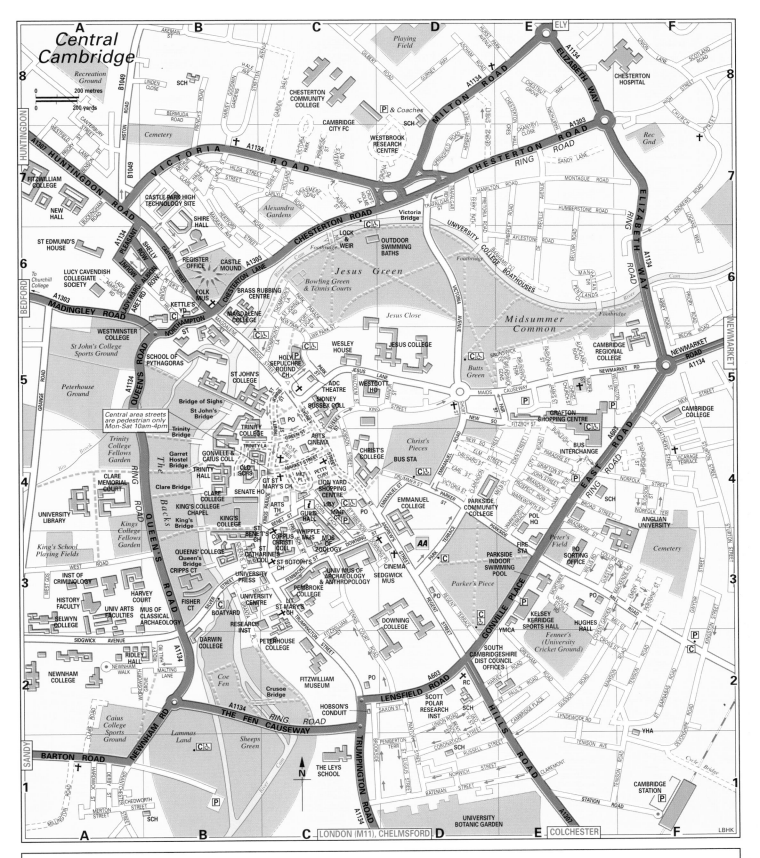

Central Cambridge

Recreation Ground

0   200 metres
0   200 yards

Cambridge

Few views in England, perhaps even in Europe, are as memorable as that from the Cambridge Backs towards the colleges. Dominating the scene in every sense is King's College Chapel. One of the finest Gothic buildings in Europe, it was built in three stages from 1446 to 1515.

No one would dispute that the chapel is Cambridge's masterpiece, but there are dozens of buildings here that would be the finest in any other town or city. Most are colleges, or are attached to colleges, and it is the university that permeates every aspect of Cambridge's landscape and life. In all, the city has 33 university colleges and nearly all have buildings and features of great architectural interest. Guided tours of the colleges are available throughout the year.

Cambridge can provide a complete history of English architecture. The oldest surviving building is the tower of St Bene't's Church, dating back to before the Norman Conquest, and its most famous church is the Church of the Holy Sepulchre, one of only four round churches of its kind.

Of the many notable museums in Cambridge, the Fitzwilliam Museum is the most prestigious. It contains some of the best collections of ceramics, paintings, coins, medals and Egyptian, Greek and Roman antiquities outside London.

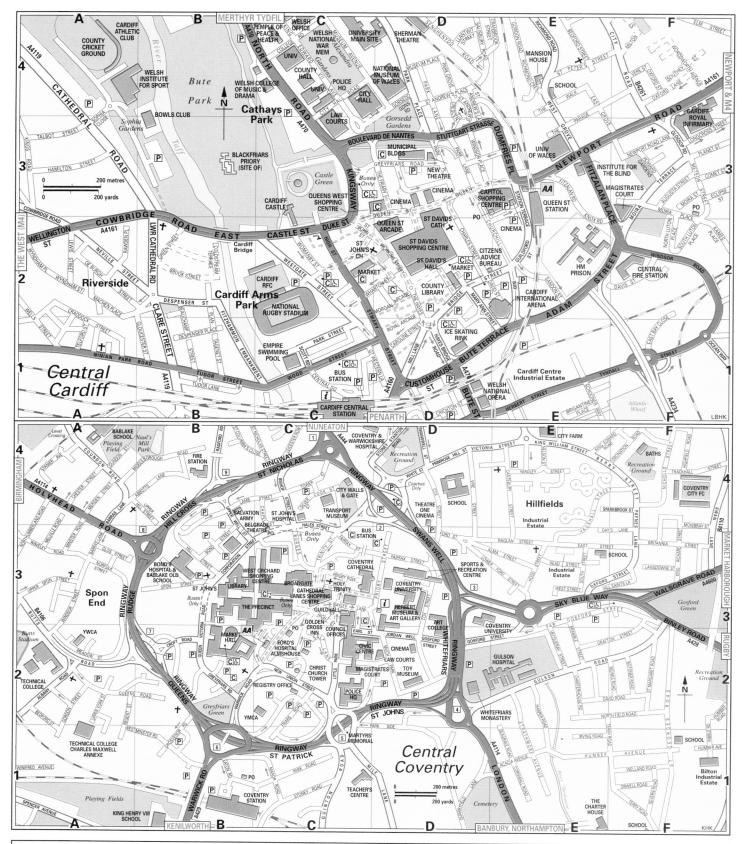

Cardiff

The coal and iron industries of the valleys made Cardiff a major export centre and by the end of the 19th century it was the world's largest coal-exporting port. Today it is a modern commercial, administrative and tourist centre, with new shopping precincts and a fine concert hall. Close to the castle, which has features from the Roman period to the last century, is the Civic Centre - a fine range of early 20th-century buildings among which is the National Museum of Wales. In the redeveloped docklands is the Welsh Industrial and Maritime Museum, and at Llandaf the 13th-century cathedral contains the work *Christ in Majesty* by Epstein. Cardiff Arms Park stadium is the home of Welsh rugby.

Coventry

Few British towns were as battered by the blitz as Coventry. The lovely old cathedral was destroyed during an air raid in November 1940, and Sir Basil Spence's impressive modern cathedral, completed in 1962, stands beside the ruins. A few medieval structures have survived intact: St Mary's Guildhall is a finely restored 14th-century building with a minstrels' gallery, and the Whitefriars Monastery now serves as a local museum. The Herbert Art Gallery and Museum has several notable collections. Today Coventry is an important car manufacturing centre with two universities; one in the city centre, the other (the University of Warwick) three miles to the south-west.

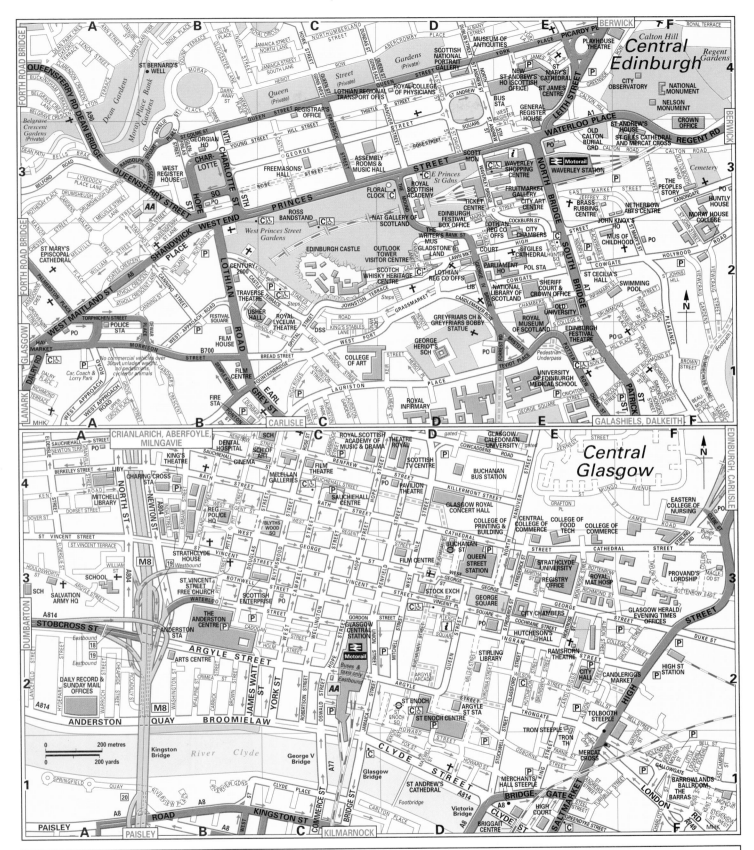

Edinburgh

Scotland's ancient capital and one of Europe's most impressive cities, Edinburgh has many historic buildings, a scenic position on the Firth of Forth below Arthur's Seat, and an international festival. Perched on a volcanic crag the historic castle stands at the western end of the Royal Mile, along which is the Old Town, with Gladstone's Land (NTS) typical of the original crowded buildings. At the other end is the royal residence, the 16th-century palace of Holyroodhouse. Below the Old Town is the Georgian New Town, built for the city's merchants and aristocrats. Here Princes Street, the main thoroughfare, is noted for its fine shops, the Gardens, and the Scott monument.

Glasgow

Scotland's largest city, Glasgow had a cathedral, university and the status of a royal burgh by 1454, and when the Industrial Revolution brought ship-building and heavy engineering it became one of the greatest industrial centres in the world. Today it is both a green and cultural city, with numerous parks. In 1988 it was the venue of Britain's third garden festival, and in recognition of its many orchestras, choirs, theatres and galleries, it was appointed European City of Culture in 1990. There are many important museums and art galleries, most notably the Burrell Collection in the Pollok Country Park, and the Art Gallery and Museum in Kelvingrove Park.

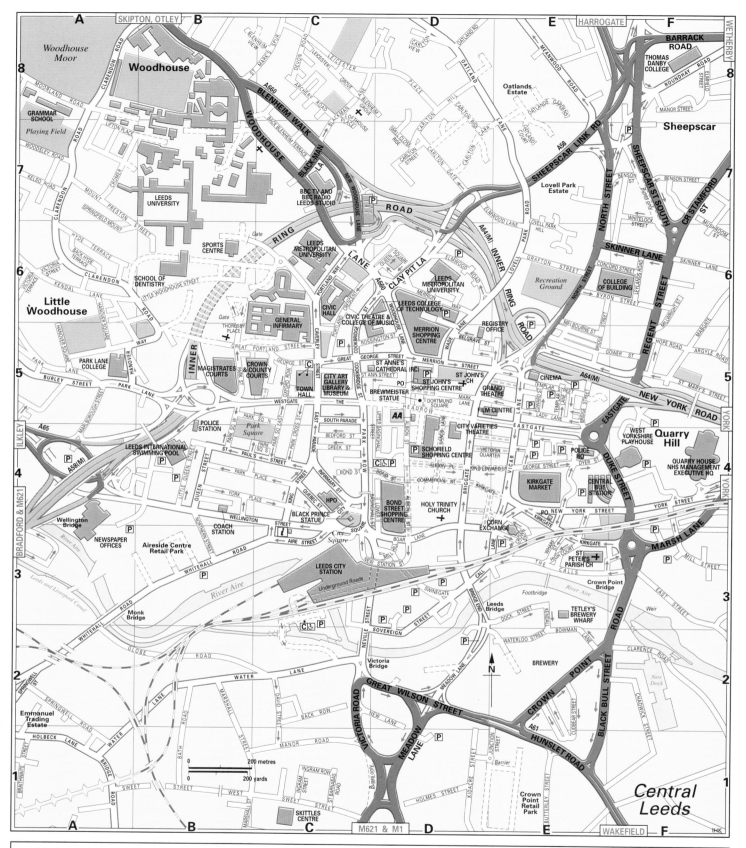

Leeds

The magnificent colonnaded Town Hall, with a 225ft-high clock-tower, is an obvious symbol of the city's pride. For centuries a major centre of the wool trade, Leeds has evolved into a city renowned for its engineering, textiles and ready-made clothes industries. Nevertheless, it also has many features to interest the tourist. The Art Gallery and Museum has sculptures by Henry Moore (a former student at the Leeds School of Art) and near by on the Headrow, the city's foremost shopping street, is the City Varieties Theatre, perhaps best known for the 'Good Old Days' TV programme. Off the Headrow are numerous attractive shopping arcades and, not far away, Kirkgate Market is the largest covered market in the North of England. The museum at Armley Mills (once the world's largest woollen mill) recalls the woollen industry, while Tetley's Brewery Wharf on the River Aire illustrates the history of the British pub. Thwaite Mills at Stourton is an industrial water-mill and the preserved Middleton Railway at Hunslet is the world's oldest non-passenger railway, authorised in 1758. At Kirkstall are the substantial remains of the 12th-century abbey and the Abbey House folk museum, while east of the city is the Tudor and Jacobean mansion of Temple Newsam House, set in a 1,200-acre park.

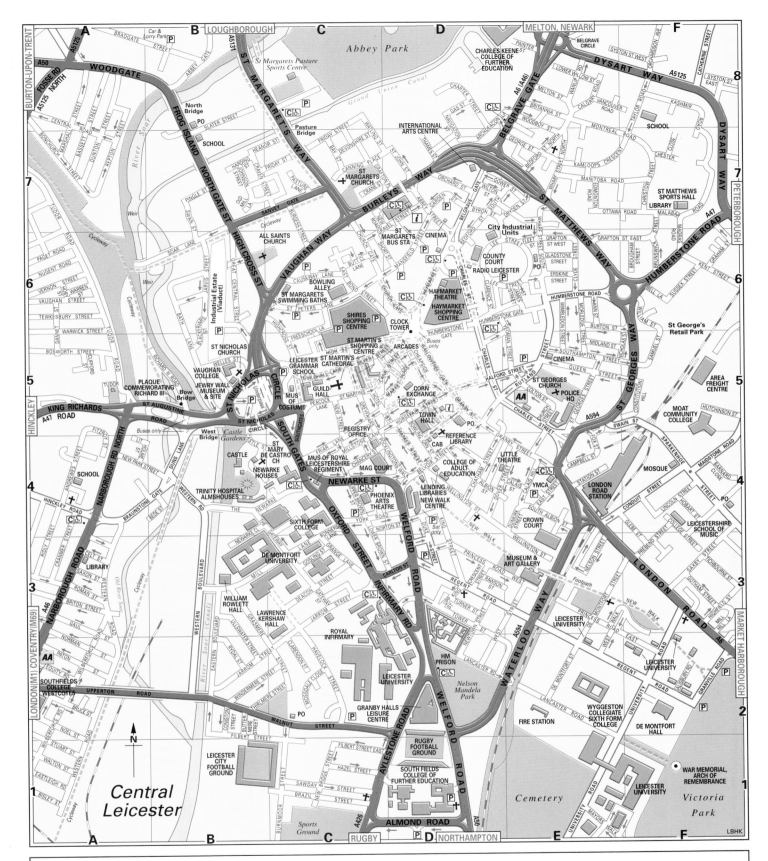

Leicester

Founded as a regional capital in Roman times and later occupied in turn by Danes, Saxons and Normans, Leicester retains many buildings from an eventful and distinguished past. Frequently visited by Richard III, it was from here that he set out, only to be killed, for the Battle of Bosworth. Today Leicester is a thriving contrast between modern shopping, leisure, academic develop-

ments and heritage. The oldest feature is the Jewry Wall, a 30ft-high section of Roman masonry, with other remains and an archaeological museum near by. Of the Norman castle little remains except the motte and great hall. The cathedral is 13th- to 15th- century, and there are several churches even older - St Nicholas being of Saxon origin. The Guildhall is a magnificent timbered building dating back in part to 1340, and Newarke Houses, two adjoining

16th-century houses, contain the museum of the city's and county's social history to the present day. Adjacent is the Museum of the Royal Leicestershire Regiment. Also of interest are the Wygston's House Museum of Costume, the 18th-century Belgrave Hall, the Leicestershire Museum of Technology and the city's Museum and Art Gallery. Situated in the northern suburbs is the Leicester north terminus of the preserved Great Central Railway to Loughborough.

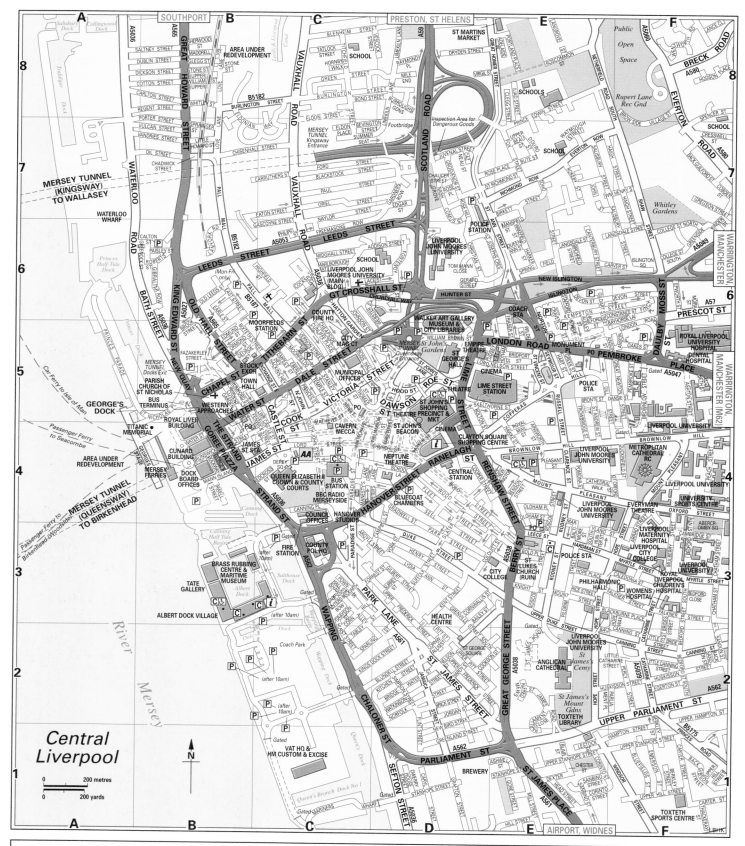

Liverpool

Although its dock area has been much reduced, Liverpool is still a thriving and successful port. Formerly the centrepiece of the docks area are three monumental buildings: the Dock Board Offices, built in 1907 with a huge copper-covered dome; the Cunard Building, dating from 1912 and decorated with an abundance of ornamental carving; and the Liver Building, with two 'liver birds' crowning its twin cupolas. The entire waterfront south of the Liver Building has been transformed into one of the north-west's biggest tourist attractions. New offices and marinas have replaced most of the old warehouses, but one outstanding group, the Albert Dock Village, has survived and contains Britains largest collection of Grade I listed buildings. Among the buildings of the 1845 dock are the Tate Gallery and the Maritime Museum and Brassrubbing Centre.

Other museums and galleries include the Walker Art Gallery, with excellent collections of European painting and sculpture, Liverpool City Libraries, one of the oldest and largest public libraries in Britain, and Bluecoat Chambers, a Queen Anne building now used as a gallery and concert hall. Liverpool has two outstanding cathedrals: the Roman Catholic, completed in 1967 in an uncompromising controversial style; and the Anglican, constructed in the great tradition of Gothic architecture, but begun in 1904 and only recently completed. Also of interest are the 450ft-high St John's Beacon, with a viewing gallery, St George's Hall, possibly Europe's finest Greco-Roman-style building, the Cavern Mecca Shopping Centre, famed for its Beatles' connections and Cavern Club reconstruction, and a new Battle of the Atlantic exhibition.

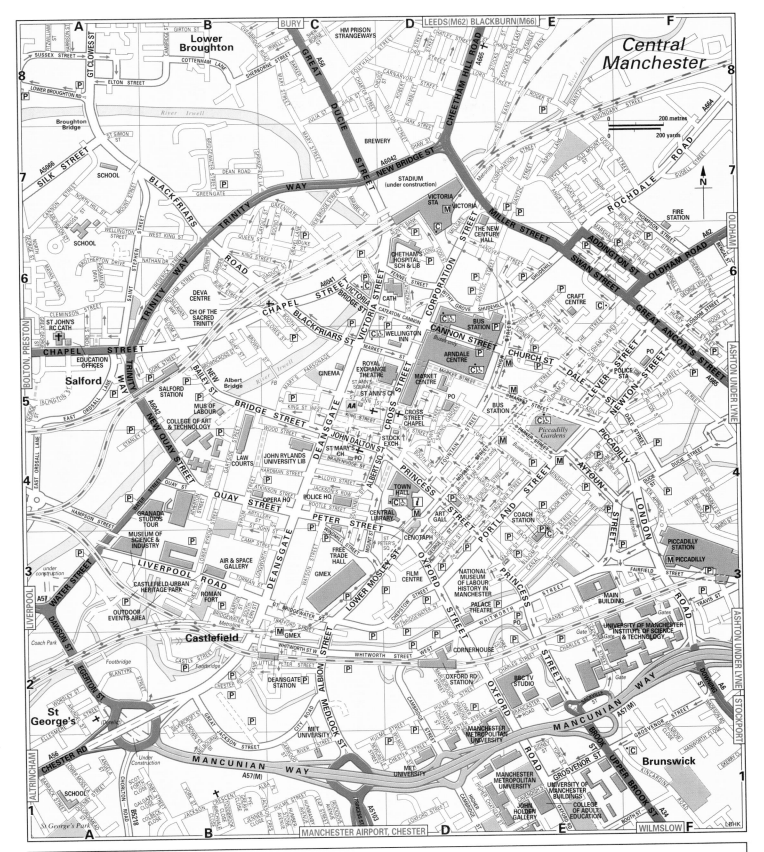

Manchester

Manchester is the regional centre for North-west England, with a population of over half a million. Commerce and industry are vital aspects of the city's character, but it is also an important cultural centre – the Hallé Orchestra has its home at the Free Trade Hall (a venue for many concerts besides classical music), there are several theatres, the John Rylands Library, which houses one of the most important collections of books in the world, and a number of museums and

galleries, including the Whitworth Gallery with its lovely watercolours.

Like many great cities it suffered badly during World War II, but some older buildings remain including the massive Gothic-style town hall of 1877. Manchester Cathedral dates mainly from the 15th century and is noted for its fine tower and outstanding carved woodwork. Near by is Chetham's Hospital, also 15th-century.

Much new development has taken place, and more is planned. The massive Arndale shopping centre caters

for the vast population, and there are huge international-standard hotels. The Museum of Science and Industry in the Castlefield Urban Heritage Park contains exhibits from the Industrial Revolution to the Space Age and includes the world's first passenger railway station. Near by are the Granada Television Studios where visitors can walk through the various film sets, including the famous 'Coronation Street', and the impressive G-Mex exhibition centre. Manchester is also the first city in Britain to reinstate an on-street tramway route as part of its new Light Rapid Transit system.

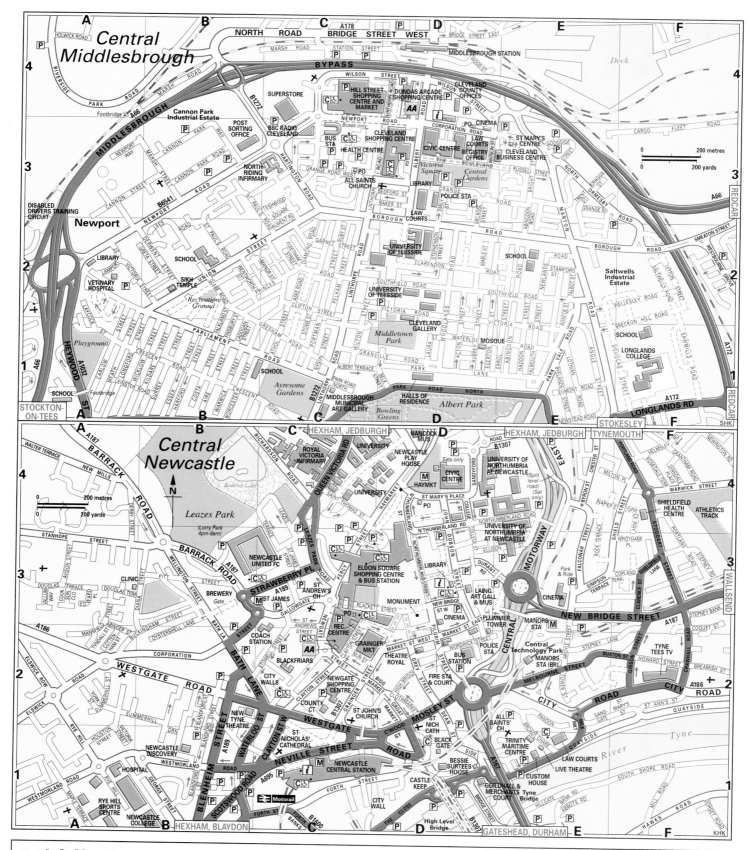

Middlesbrough

Once a major coal-exporting port and an iron- and steel-making centre, Middlesbrough is now the administrative and commercial centre for Teesside. The town's most notable structure is the Transporter Bridge across the Tees, one of only two of its type left in Britain. The Dorman Museum displays social and industrial history, and there are two major art galleries. To the south-east are 18th-century Ormesby Hall (NT) and the Captain Cook Birthplace Museum at Marton.

Newcastle

The city has six road and rail bridges across the Tyne, a massive 12th-century castle keep and a cathedral surmounted by a graceful 194ft-high crown spire. Among the many interesting buildings and streets are the elegant Central Station and Grey Street, which leads to the Grey Monument. Near by is the vast Eldon Square Shopping and Leisure Centre. Newcastle is also blessed with two universities, a host of important museums and art galleries, and a pioneering metro railway system. The Town Moor covers nearly a thousand acres.

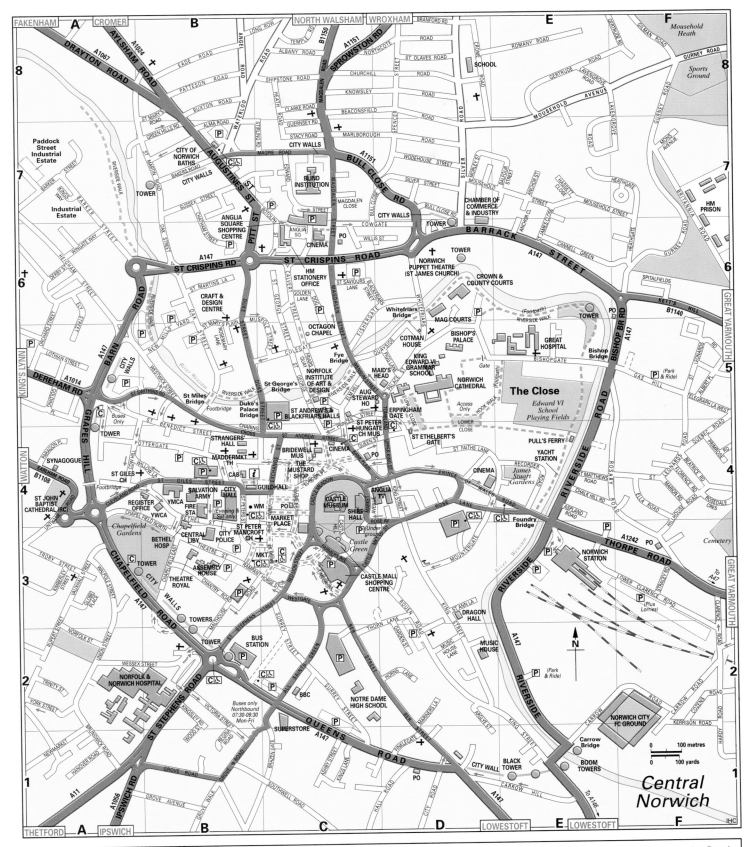

Norwich

This beautiful medieval walled city on the River Wensum has been a regional capital for centuries, and was once second only in importance to London. It is still a major commercial and administrative centre and fortunately has not been spoiled by insensitive redevelopment. Norwich still has the greatest number of surviving medieval churches (31) of any city in Europe and retains many quiet narrow streets and ways, such as Elm Hill, lined with fine old buildings.

Dominating the city centre from its substantial mound is the stone keep of the Norman castle, now in use as the Castle Museum and housing collections on local history and the Norwich school of painters. To the north-east is the magnificent Norman cathedral, a huge landmark with a graceful tower and spire soaring to 315ft and second only in height to Salisbury. Among the cathedral's many features are the largest cloisters in Britain, 800 carved roof bosses, the finely carved choir stalls and the oldest bishops' throne (possibly Saxon) in England.

Other major places of interest are the Guildhall and the late 14th-century Bridewell Museum, the Royal Norfolk Regimental Museum in the Shirehall, the St Peter Hungate Church Museum containing the Brassrubbing Centre, and Strangers' Hall, a notable 15th-century building now housing a folk museum. At the University of East Anglia, the Sainsbury Centre for Visual Arts displays 19th- and 20th-century European art and worldwide ethnographical art. Pull's Ferry (the cathedral water gate), pleasant riverside walks, extensive markets, theatres, medieval halls, Georgian buildings and two cathedral gateways are yet more reasons for visiting this fine city.

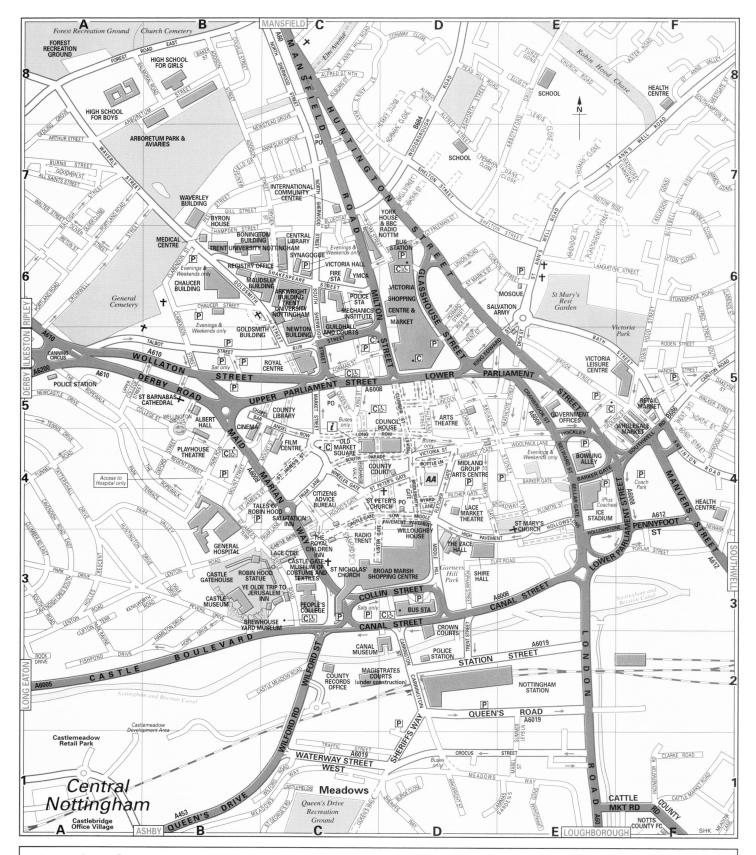

Nottingham

Hosiery and lace were the foundations upon which Nottingham's prosperity were built. The stockings came first – a knitting machine for these had been invented by a Nottinghamshire man as early as 1589 – but a machine called a 'tickler', which enabled simple patterns to be created in the stocking fabric, prompted the development of machine-made lace. The earliest fabric was produced in 1768, and an example from that period is kept in the city's Museum of Costume and Textiles in Castlegate. In fact, the entire history of lacemaking is beautifully explained in this converted row of Georgian terraces. The Industrial Museum at Wollaton Park has many other machines and exhibits tracing the development of the knitting industry, as well as displays on the other industries which have brought wealth to the city – tobacco, pharmaceuticals, engineering and printing.

Also at Wollaton Park is the Natural History Museum, while nearer the city centre are the Canal Museum and the Brewhouse Yard Museum, a marvellous collection of items from daily life in the city up to the present day. No visit to Nottingham is complete without mention of Robin Hood, the partly mythical figure whose statue stands in the castle grounds. Although the castle itself has Norman foundations, the present structure is largely Victorian and currently houses a museum.

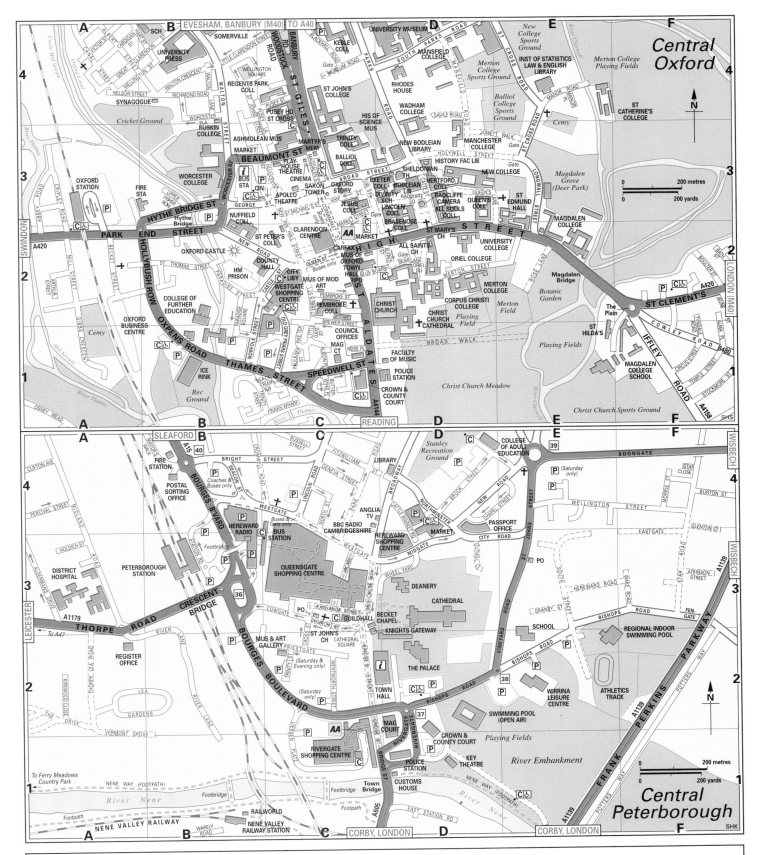

Oxford

Together with Cambridge, Oxford has probably the most famous university in the world. It was certainly the first in Britain, with Balliol, Merton and University colleges dating back to the mid-13th century. Many others followed in later centuries, creating a magnificent architectural heritage. Other buildings of note are Christ Church Cathedral, the Radcliffe Camera of 1749, the Bodleian Library (one of the world's finest) and the Ashmolean Museum, the oldest and one of the most extensive in Britain. Opened in 1621 the Botanic Gardens were also the first of their kind in the country. The city's history is displayed in the Museum of Oxford, and the Oxford Story describes the university.

Peterborough

In the heart of Peterborough the cathedral of St Peter dates back to Norman times and gave the city its name. Peterborough has expanded rapidly over the past few years from a small market town into a remarkable city, successfully blending new buildings with old. The modern Queensgate shopping centre offers an unrivalled choice of shops, while to the west the 2,000-acre Nene Park provides a focus for numerous leisure pursuits including walking, fishing, watersports and the Nene Valley Railway. To the east of the city the open landscape of the Fens is home to the Bronze Age excavations of Flag Fen.

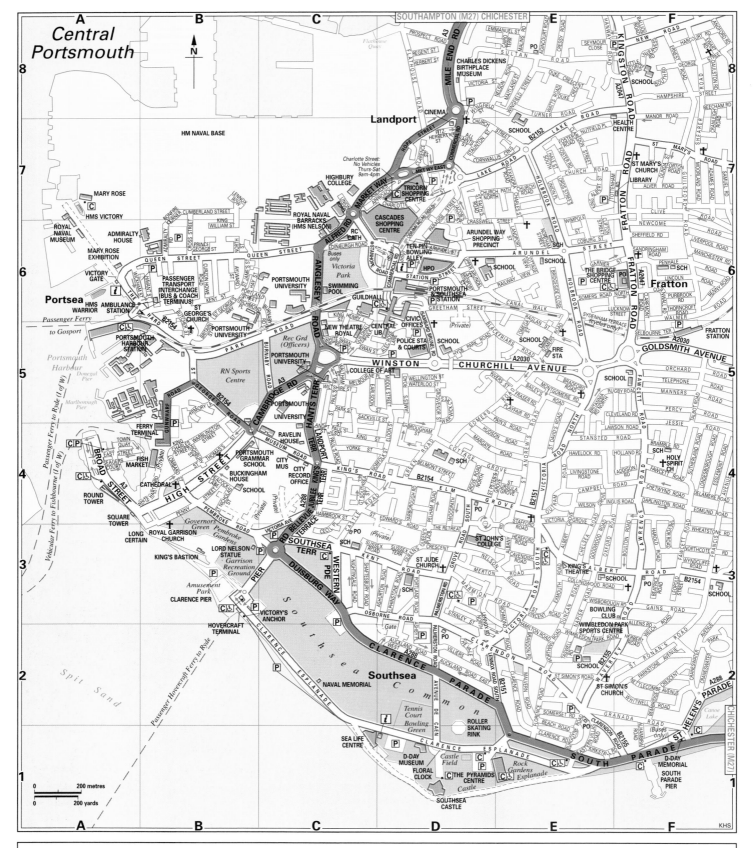

Portsmouth

A busy ferry port and one of Britain's two major naval bases, Portsmouth is world famous as the home of Nelson's flagship *Victory*, Henry VIII's *Mary Rose*, spectacularly raised from the seabed in 1982, and HMS *Warrior*, the world's first iron-hulled warship. All are located at the 300-acre dockyard, which also contains the Royal Naval and Mary Rose museums (the latter housing thousands of artefacts recovered from the ship), and many listed Georgian buildings. The city has been a naval port since the 13th century and has a cathedral dating from the 12th century. Notable fortifications are the 15th-century Round Tower, an excellent viewpoint at the harbour entrance, and Fort Nelson, one of a ring of Napoleonic defences, several of which are open to the public. The great novelist Charles Dickens was born in Portsmouth in 1805 and his birthplace is now a museum. The city was heavily bombed during World War II and the centre has been extensively rebuilt, but the old town by the harbourmouth escaped severe damage and now forms an attractive and fashionable area.

Southsea developed in the 19th century as an elegant seaside resort with fine houses and terraces, an esplanade and an extensive sea-front common where the Sea-Life Centre, Southsea Castle and Museum, the D-Day Museum (containing the 272ft-long Overlord Embroidery) and Pyramids Leisure Centre are situated. The Royal Marines Museum and the offshore Spit Bank Fort are also worth a visit.

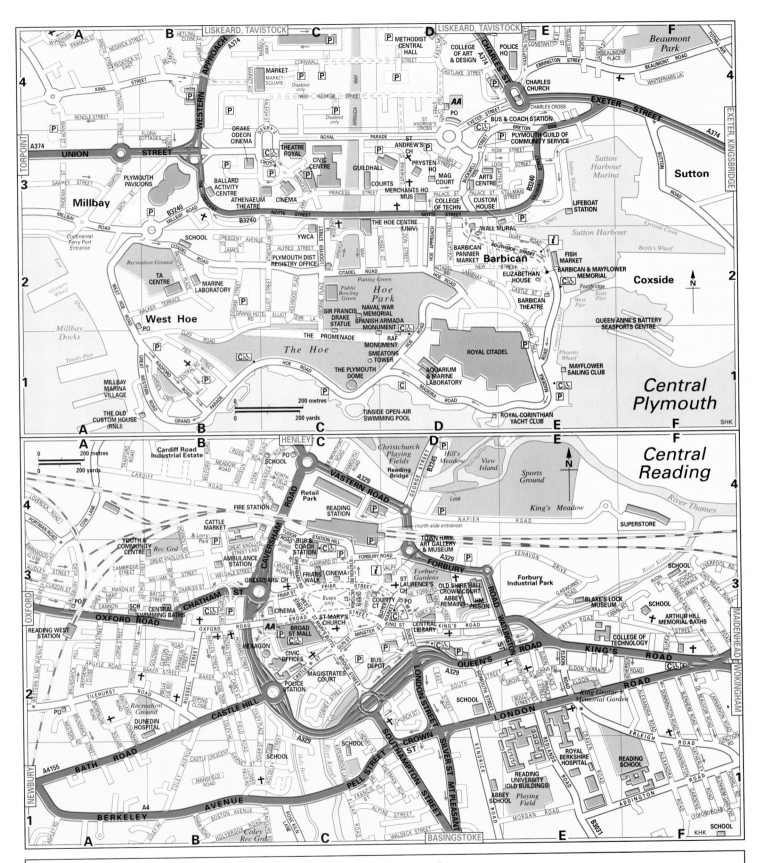

Plymouth

With a superb natural harbour, Plymouth has been a port, yachting centre and major naval base for centuries. On the Hoe are the statue of Sir Francis Drake, who sailed from here against the Spanish Armada, the Royal Naval War Memorial, Smeaton's Tower (a former Eddystone Lighthouse), the Plymouth Dome, describing the city's history, the Royal Citadel of 1666 and the Marine Laboratory Aquarium. Near by is Sutton Harbour, from where the Mayflower sailed in 1620. Plymouth was heavily bombed in World War II and its shopping centre rebuilt in a modern post-war style, but some earlier buildings survived, notably the Elizabethan and Merchant's houses, and Prysten House.

Reading

Very much a town of the present, Reading is a major commercial and administrative centre with ultra-modern office blocks contrasting with Victorian buildings, a university, county hall, large shopping centres and the well-known Hexagon Theatre. It does, however, have a long history, with the abbey founded by Henry I in 1121 becoming one of the most important in England. It suffered badly in the Dissolution and only a few ruins are left. The opening of the Kennet and Avon Canal and the coming of the Great Western Railway brought renewed prosperity to the town. Reading's history is displayed in the Blake's Lock Museum and the Museum of English Rural Life in Whiteknights Park.

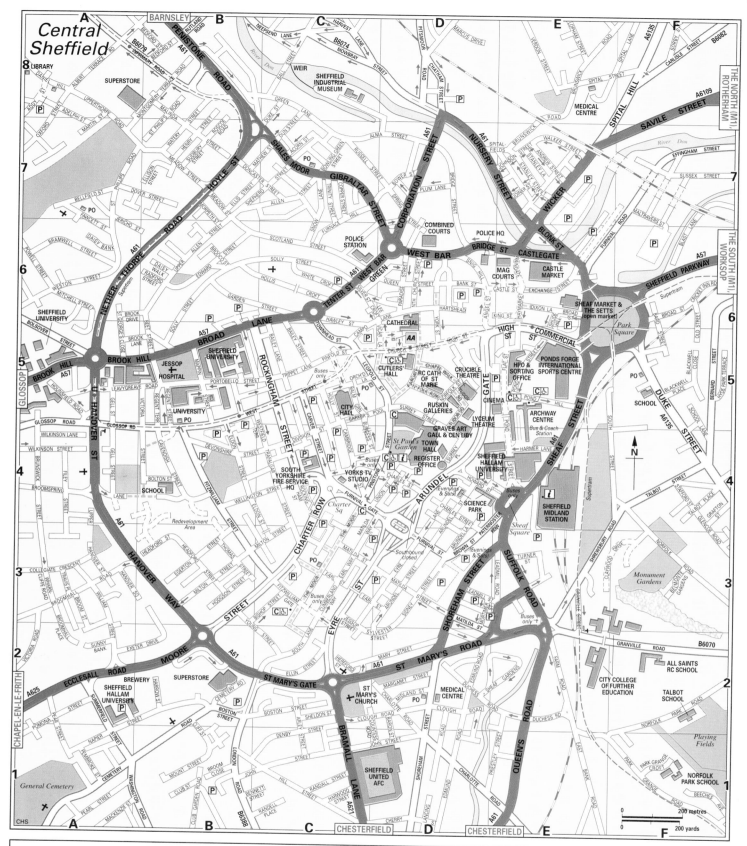

Sheffield

Cutlery – which has made Sheffield famous throughout the world – has been manufactured here since the time of Chaucer. Steel production, a vital component of the industry, was greatly improved when the crucible process was invented here in 1740 and this has created a major industry in high quality specialised steels and heavy engineering. Cutlers' Hall, the headquarters of the Honourable Company of Cutlers, has a vast display of silverware craftmanship covering every year since 1773, and the City Museum contains the world's largest collection of cutlery, dating back through time to the Paleolithic age. Abbeydale Industrial Hamlet and the Shepherd Wheel illustrate early steel and cutlery manufacture, and the city's industrial history is demonstrated in the Industrial Museum at Kelham Island.

Set on five rivers among the foothills east of the Peak District, Sheffield has many interesting and historic buildings, such as the Town Hall with a 193ft-high clock-tower, two cathedrals, two universities and a very fine and extensive shopping centre. The modern Crucible Theatre is famous as the venue of the world snooker championships. Recent developments around the city have been the Ponds Forge International Sports Centre, the Meadowhall Shopping Centre and the Don Valley Stadium used for the World Student Games in 1991. Sheffield is also the second city in Britain to construct a new supertram light railway system.

44

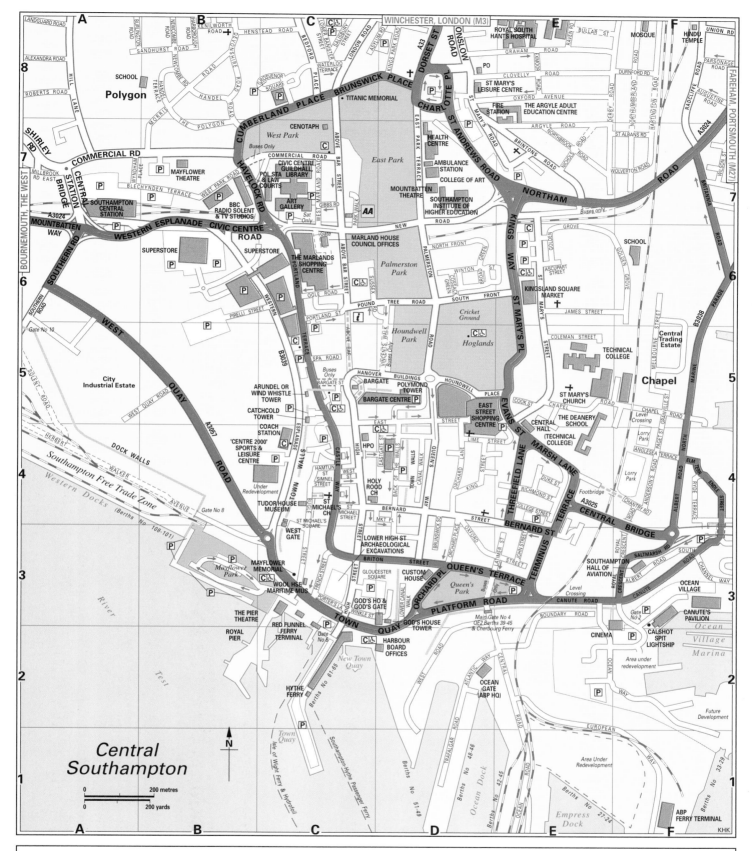

Southampton

Britain's premier passenger port in the days of the great ocean liners, Southampton is now a major container terminal and is still visited regularly by cruise ships. The unique double tide of the Solent waters, protected by the Isle of Wight, has meant that Southampton has always been a superb and important port. Although it was devastated by wartime bombing, many ancient features still survive. Outstanding are the medieval town walls, particularly impressive along the Western Esplanade. The main landward entrance to the walled town was the Bargate, a superb gateway with a guildhall (now a museum) on its upper floor. Founded in 1070, St Michael's Church is the oldest in the city and contains a rare Tournai marble font. Opposite is the Tudor House Museum, dating from the end of the 15th century, with a reconstructed Tudor garden. There are old houses along Bugle Street, with the town walls and 13th-century West Gate near by (through which Henry V passed in 1415 while embarking for Agincourt). Housed in a 14th-century warehouse is the Maritime Museum. By the Town Quay is God's House Tower, now containing the city's archaeological museum. In part of the redeveloped Eastern Docks are the popular Ocean Village Marina and Canute's Pavilion. The Hall of Aviation, built round an enormous four-engined Sandringham Flying Boat includes a Spitfire created at nearby Woolston. The impressive Civic Centre has the largest art gallery in the South of England.

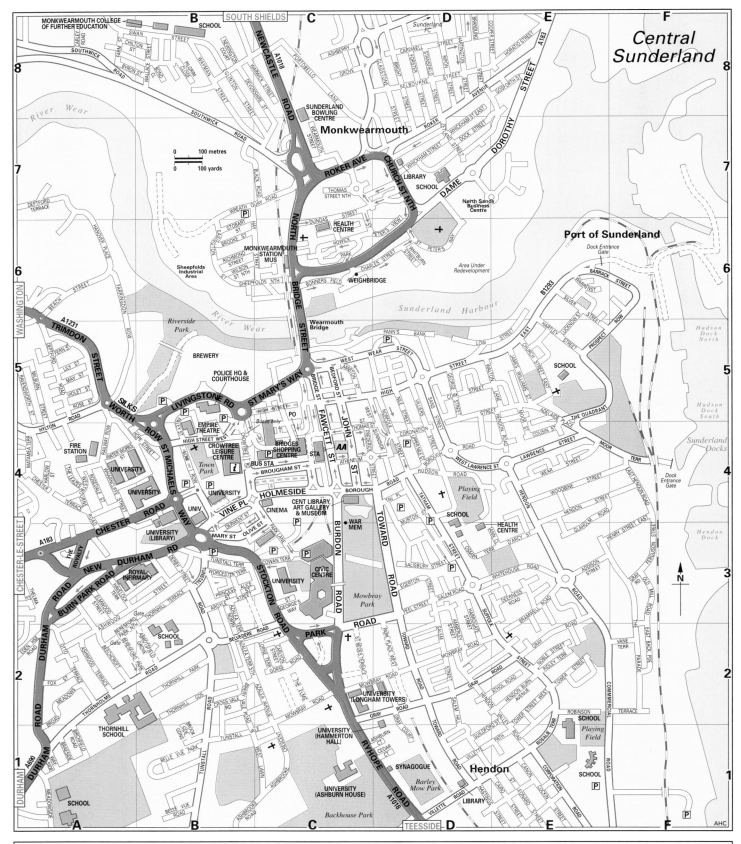

Sunderland

Sunderland was an early centre of Christianity and home of Bede, the father of English history. His church, St Peter's, was founded in 674 and the present building still retains Saxon features. Situated at the mouth of the River Wear the town developed as a port, and until recently was a major shipbuilding and coal-mining centre. In 1992 Sunderland was granted city status by HM The Queen in recognition of its recovery from the decline of its traditional industries by attracting high-tech industries, such as the Nissan car plant near Washington.

There is an excellent range of leisure facilities (such as the 160-metre ski slope at the Silksworth Sports Complex), a popular Edwardian music hall/theatre, a modern civic centre and fine beaches at Roker and Seaburn. Places of interest within the city are the art gallery and museum, Monkwearmouth Station Museum, Fulwell Mill, which dates from 1821 and is the most complete windmill in the north-east, the Grindon Museum of Edwardian period interiors, St Andrew's church at Roker, with its decorated art nouveau interior, and the Ryhope Engines Museum at a former pumping station. A little further out are the early 15th-century Hylton Castle and the impressive Grecian temple of the Penshaw Monument. At nearby Washington are the 'F' Pit Mining Museum, the 100-acre Wildfowl Trust Park on the banks of the River Wear, and Washington Old Hall (NT), rebuilt in the 17th century and notable as the ancestral home of George Washington.

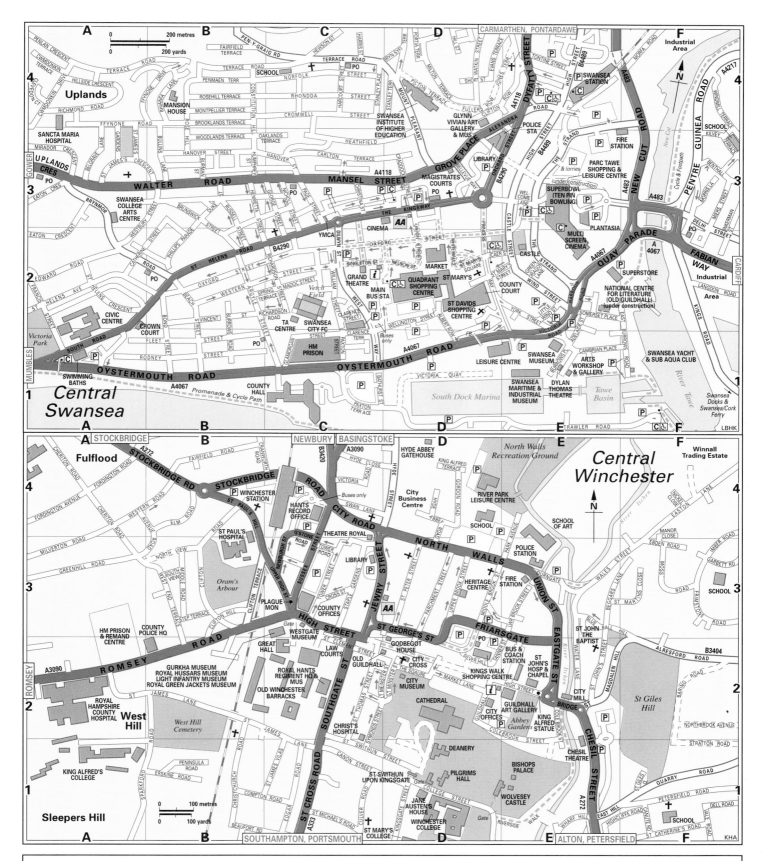

Swansea

Ironworks, smelting works, mills and factories were built here during the Industrial Revolution, with the goods exported through the city's expanding docks. Industry is still important but commerce and tourism are of increasing significance. Hundreds of acres of parkland lie in and around the city, and to the west, beyond the university, is the Gower Peninsula, one of the most beautiful areas of Wales. The history of Swansea is displayed in the Maritime and Industrial Museum and the Swansea Museum, both next to an attractive new marina in a former dock area, while the Glynn Vivian Art Gallery contains notable paintings and porcelain.

Winchester

This historic city was the capital of Saxon Wessex and of England until the late 12th century. Its impressive Norman-Gothic cathedral is one of the longest in Europe and near by are the 12th-century Wolvesey Castle and the famous public school, Winchester College, founded by Bishop William Wykeham in 1382. Adjacent is a house where the great novelist Jane Austen died in 1817. The attractive pedestrianised High Street leads up the hill towards the medieval West Gate and the site of Winchester Castle, where the surviving Great Hall contains a huge oak table once claimed to have been King Arthur's Round Table. The city also has five regimental museums.

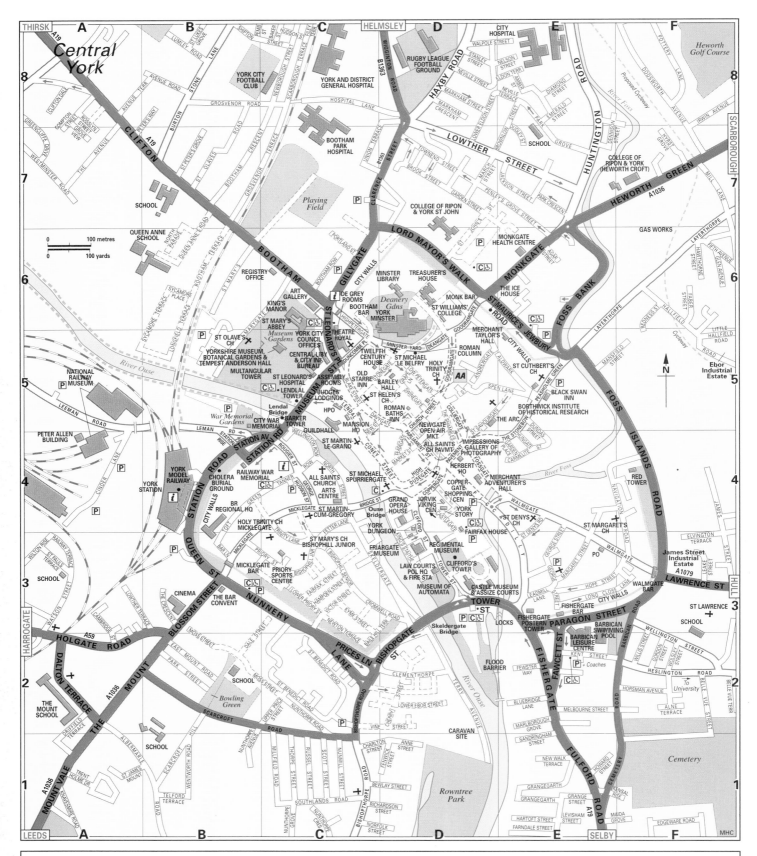

York

Unquestionably the city's outstanding glory, York Minster is considered to be one of the greatest cathedral churches in Europe. It is especially famous for its magnificent windows which contain more than half the medieval stained glass in England.

Great medieval walls enclose the historic city centre and their three-mile circuit offers impressive views of the Minster, York's numerous fine buildings, churches and the River Ouse. The ancient streets consist of a maze of alleys and lanes, some of them so narrow that the overhanging upper storeys of the houses almost touch. The most famous of these picturesque streets is The Shambles, formerly the butchers' quarter of the city, but now colonised by antique and tourist shops. York flourished throughout Tudor, Georgian and Victorian times, and handsome buildings from these periods also feature throughout the city.

The Castle Museum gives a fascinating picture of York as it used to be, and the Heritage Centre interprets the social and architectural history of the city. Other places of exceptional note in this city of riches include the Merchant Adventurer's Hall; the Treasurer's House, now owned by the National Trust and filled with fine paintings and furniture; the Jorvik Viking Centre, where there is an exciting restoration of the original Viking settlement at York; and the National Railway Museum.

index

England

1	*Avon*	**Avon**
2	*Beds*	**Bedfordshire**
3	*Berks*	**Berkshire**
5	*Bucks*	**Buckinghamshire**
6	*Cambs*	**Cambridgeshire**
8	*Ches*	**Cheshire**
9	*Cleve*	**Cleveland**
11	*Cnwll*	**Cornwall**
12	*Cumb*	**Cumbria**
13	*Derbys*	**Derbyshire**
14	*Devon*	**Devon**
15	*Dorset*	**Dorset**
17	*Dur*	**Durham**
19	*E Susx*	**East Sussex**
20	*Essex*	**Essex**
22	*Gloucs*	**Gloucestershire**
24	*Gt Lon*	**Greater London**
25	*Gt Man*	**Greater Manchester**
28	*Hants*	**Hampshire**
29	*H &W*	**Hereford & Worcester**
30	*Herts*	**Hertfordshire**
32	*Humb*	**Humberside**
33	*IOM*	**Isle of Man**
34	*IOW*	**Isle of Wight**
35	*IOS*	**Isles of Scilly**
36	*Kent*	**Kent**
37	*Lancs*	**Lancashire**
38	*Leics*	**Leicestershire**
39	*Lincs*	**Lincolnshire**
41	*Mersyd*	**Merseyside**
43	*Norfk*	**Norfolk**
44	*Nhants*	**Northamptonshire**
45	*Nthumb*	**Northumberland**
46	*N York*	**North Yorkshire**
47	*Notts*	**Nottinghamshire**
49	*Oxon*	**Oxfordshire**
52	*Shrops*	**Shropshire**
53	*Somset*	**Somerset**
55	*S York*	**South Yorkshire**
56	*Staffs*	**Staffordshire**
58	*Suffk*	**Suffolk**
59	*Surrey*	**Surrey**
61	*T & W*	**Tyne & Wear**
62	*Warwks*	**Warwickshire**
65	*W Mids*	**West Midlands**
66	*W Susx*	**West Sussex**
67	*W York*	**West Yorkshire**
68	*Wilts*	**Wiltshire**

Scotland

4	*Border*	**Borders**
7	*Cent*	**Central**
16	*D&G*	**Dumfries & Galloway**
21	*Fife*	**Fife**
23	*Gramp*	**Grampian**
31	*Highld*	**Highland**
40	*Loth*	**Lothian**
48	*Ork*	**Orkney**
51	*Shet*	**Shetland**
57	*Strath*	**Strathclyde**
60	*Tays*	**Tayside**
63	*W Isls*	**Western Isles**

Wales

10	*Clwyd*	**Clwyd**
18	*Dyfed*	**Dyfed**
26	*Gwent*	**Gwent**
27	*Gwynd*	**Gwynedd**
42	*M Glam*	**Mid Glamorgan**
50	*Powys*	**Powys**
54	*S Glam*	**South Glamorgan**
64	*W Glam*	**West Glamorgan**

Each place name entry in this index is identified by its county or region name. These are shown in italics.

A list of the abbreviated forms used is given below.

To locate a place name in the atlas turn to the map page indicated in bold type in the index and use the 4-figure grid reference.

For example, Hythe *Kent* **15** TR**1**6**3**4

is found on page 15.

The two letters 'TR' refer to the National Grid.

To pinpoint our example the first figure '1'
    is found along the bottom edge of the page.

The following figure '6' indicates how many
    imaginary tenths to move east of the line '1'.

The next bold figure '3' is found along the left-hand side of the page.

The last figure '4' shows how many imaginary tenths
    to move north of line '3'.

You will locate Hythe where these two lines intersect.

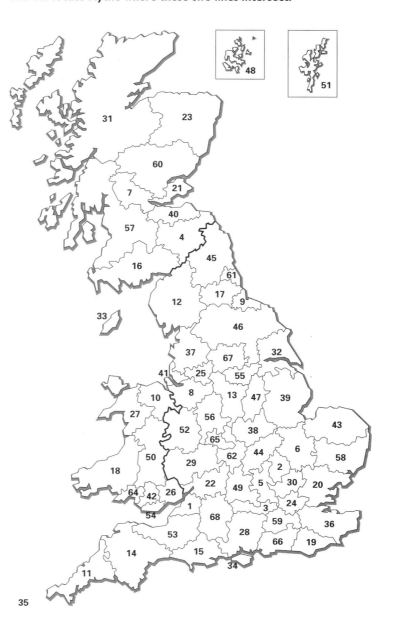

A'Chill
Apperknowle

A

A'Chill Highld 84 NG2705
Ab Kettleby Leics 40 SK7223
Abbas Combe Somset 9 ST7022
Abberley H & W 28 SO7567
Abberley Common H & W 28 SO7467
Abberton Essex 25 TM0019
Abberton H & W 28 SO9953
Abbess Roding Essex 24 TL5711
Abbey Dore H & W 27 SO3830
Abbey Green Staffs 48 SJ9757
Abbey St Bathans Border 76 NT7661
Abbey Town Cumb 67 NY1750
Abbey Village Lancs 54 SD6422
Abbey Wood Gt Lon 23 TQ4779
Abbeydale S York 49 SK3281
Abbeystead Lancs 53 SD5654
Abbot's Salford Warwks 28 SP0650
Abbotrule Border 68 NT6113
Abbots Bickington Devon 6 SS3813
Abbots Bromley Staffs 38 SK0724
Abbots Deuglie Tays 82 NO1111
Abbots Langley Herts 22 TL0901
Abbots Leigh Avon 19 ST5474
Abbots Morton H & W 28 SP0255
Abbots Ripton Cambs 31 TL2377
Abbots Worthy Hants 11 SU4932
Abbotsbury Dorset 9 SY5785
Abbotsford Border 76 NT5034
Abbotsham Devon 6 SS4226
Abbotskerswell Devon 5 SX8568
Abbotsley Cambs 31 TL2256
Abbott Street Dorset 9 ST9800
Abbotts Ann Hants 21 SU3243
Abdon Shrops 37 SO5786
Aber Gwynd 45 SH6572
Aberaeron Dyfed 34 SN4562
Aberaman M Glam 18 SO0100
Aberangell Powys 35 SH8410
Aberarder Highld 92 NH6225
Aberargie Tays 82 NO1615
Aberarth Dyfed 34 SN4763
Aberavon W Glam 18 SS7489
Abercairny Tays 82 NN9222
Abercanaid M Glam 18 SO0503
Abercarn Gwent 19 ST2194
Abercastle Dyfed 16 SM8533
Abercegir Powys 35 SH8001
Aberchalder Lodge Highld 86 NH3403
Aberchirder Gramp 94 NJ6252
Abercraf Powys 26 SN8212
Abercregan W Glam 18 SS8496
Abercwmboi M Glam 18 ST0299
Abercych Dyfed 17 SN2441
Abercynon M Glam 18 ST0794
Aberdalgie Tays 82 NO0720
Aberdare M Glam 18 SO0002
Aberdaron Gwynd 44 SH1726
Aberdeen Gramp 89 NJ9306
Aberdour Fife 82 NT1985
Aberdulais W Glam 18 SS7799
Aberdyfi Gwynd 35 SN6196
Aberedw Powys 26 SO0847
Abereiddy Dyfed 16 SM7931
Abererch Gwynd 44 SH3936
Aberfan M Glam 18 SO0700
Aberfeldy Tays 87 NN8549
Aberffraw Gwynd 44 SH3569
Aberford W York 55 SE4337
Aberfoyle Cent 81 NN5200
Abergavenny Gwent 27 SO2914
Abergele Clwyd 45 SH9477
Abergorlech Dyfed 17 SN5833
Abergwesyn Powys 26 SN8552
Abergwili Dyfed 17 SN4320
Abergwynfi W Glam 18 SS8995
Abergynolwyn Gwynd 35 SH6806
Aberkenfig M Glam 18 SS8984
Aberlady Loth 83 NT4679
Aberlemno Tays 89 NO5255
Aberllefenni Gwynd 35 SH7609
Aberllynfi Powys 27 SO1737
Aberlour Gramp 94 NJ2642
Abermule Powys 36 SO1694
Abernant Dyfed 17 SN3323
Abernethy Tays 82 NO1816
Abernyte Tays 83 NO2531
Aberporth Dyfed 17 SN2651
Abersoch Gwynd 44 SH3127
Abersychan Gwent 19 SO2603
Aberthin S Glam 18 ST0074
Abertillery Gwent 27 SO2104
Abertridwr M Glam 18 ST1289
Abertridwr Powys 36 SJ0319
Aberuthven Tays 82 NN9615
Aberystwyth Dyfed 34 SN5881
Abingdon Oxon 21 SU4997
Abinger Surrey 12 TQ1145
Abinger Hammer Surrey 12 TQ0947
Abington Nhants 30 SP7861
Abington Strath 75 NS9323
Abington Pigotts Cambs 31 TL3044
Ablington Gloucs 28 SP1007
Abney Derbys 48 SK1980
Aboyne Gramp 89 NO5298
Abram Gt Man 47 SD6001
Abriachan Highld 92 NH5535
Abridge Essex 23 TQ4696
Abson Avon 20 ST7074
Abthorpe Nhants 29 SP6446
Aby Lincs 51 TF4078
Acaster Malbis N York 56 SE5845
Acaster Selby N York 56 SE5741
Accrington Lancs 54 SD7628
Acha Strath 78 NM1854
Acha Mor W Isls 102 NB3029
Achahoish Strath 71 NR7877
Achalader Tays 88 NO1245
Achaleven Strath 80 NM9233
Achanalt Highld 92 NH2661
Achandunie Highld 92 NH6472
Achany Highld 96 NC5602
Acharacle Highld 79 NM6767
Acharn Highld 79 NM7050
Acharn Tays 87 NN7543
Achavanich Highld 100 ND1842
Achduart Highld 91 NC0403
Achfary Highld 98 NC2939
Achiltibuie Highld 91 NC0208
Achinhoan Strath 72 NR7516
Achintee Highld 85 NG9441
Achlain Highld 92 NH2812
Achmelvich Highld 98 NC0524
Achmore Highld 85 NG8533
Achmore W Isls 102 NB3029
Achnacarnin Highld 98 NC0432
Achnacarry Highld 86 NN1787
Achnacloich Highld 84 NG5908
Achnaconeran Highld 92 NH4118
Achnacroish Strath 79 NM8541
Achnadrish Lodge Strath 79 NM4652
Achnafauld Tays 82 NN8736
Achnagarron Highld 93 NH6870
Achnaha Highld 79 NM4668
Achnahaird Highld 98 NC0013
Achnairn Highld 96 NC5512
Achnalea Highld 79 NM8561
Achnamara Strath 71 NR7887
Achnasheen Highld 92 NH1658
Achnashellach Station Highld 91 NH0048
Achnastank Gramp 94 NJ2733
Achosnich Highld 79 NM4467
Achranich Highld 79 NM7047
Achreamie Highld 100 ND0166
Achriabhach Highld 86 NN1468
Achriesgill Highld 98 NC2554
Achtoty Highld 99 NC6762
Achurch Nhants 40 TL0283
Achvaich Highld 97 NH7194
Acklam Cleve 62 NZ4817
Acklam N York 56 SE7861
Ackleton Shrops 37 SO7698
Acklington Nthumb 69 NU2301
Ackton W York 55 SE4121
Ackworth Moor Top W York 55 SE4316
Acle Norfk 43 TG4010
Acock's Green W Mids 38 SP1283
Acol Kent 15 TR3067
Acomb N York 56 SE5651
Acomb Nthumb 68 NY9366
Aconbury H & W 27 SO5133
Acton Ches 47 SJ6352
Acton Gt Lon 23 TQ2080
Acton H & W 28 SO8467
Acton Staffs 38 SJ8241
Acton Suffk 32 TL8945
Acton Beauchamp H & W 28 SO6850
Acton Bridge Ches 47 SJ6075
Acton Burnell Shrops 37 SJ5302
Acton Green H & W 28 SO6950
Acton Park Clwyd 46 SJ3451
Acton Round Shrops 37 SO6395
Acton Scott Shrops 36 SO4589
Acton Trussell Staffs 38 SJ9318
Acton Turville Avon 20 ST8080
Adbaston Staffs 37 SJ7627
Adber Dorset 9 ST5920
Adbolton Notts 49 SK5938
Adderbury Oxon 29 SP4735
Adderley Shrops 37 SJ6640
Addiewell Loth 75 NS9962
Addingham W York 55 SE0749
Addington Bucks 30 SP7428
Addington Kent 14 TQ6559
Addiscombe Gt Lon 23 TQ3366
Addlestone Surrey 22 TQ0564
Addlestonemoor Surrey 22 TQ0565
Addlethorpe Lincs 51 TF5468
Adeyfield Herts 22 TL0708
Adfa Powys 36 SJ0601
Adforton H & W 36 SO4071
Adisham Kent 15 TR2253
Adlestrop Gloucs 29 SP2426
Adlingfleet Humb 56 SE8421
Adlington Lancs 54 SD6013
Admaston Shrops 37 SJ6313
Admaston Staffs 38 SK0423
Admington Warwks 29 SP2045
Adsborough Somset 8 ST2729
Adscombe Somset 19 ST1837
Adstock Bucks 30 SP7329
Adversane W Susx 12 TQ0723
Advie Highld 93 NJ1234
Adwick Le Street S York 56 SE5308
Adwick upon Dearne S York 49 SE4701
Ae D & G 66 NX9889
Ae Bridgend D & G 66 NY0186
Affleck Gramp 94 NJ5540
Affpuddle Dorset 9 SY8093
Affric Lodge Highld 92 NH1822
Afon-wen Clwyd 46 SJ1371
Afton Bridgend Strath 66 NS6213
Agglethorpe N York 61 SE0885
Aigburth Mersyd 46 SJ3886
Aike Humb 57 TA0446
Aiketgate Cumb 67 NY4846
Aikton Cumb 67 NY2753
Ailey H & W 27 SO3348
Ailsworth Cambs 40 TL1198
Ainderby Quernhow N York 62 SE3480
Ainderby Steeple N York 62 SE3392
Aingers Green Essex 25 TM1120
Ainsdale Mersyd 53 SD3112
Ainstable Cumb 67 NY5246
Ainthorpe N York 62 NZ7007
Ainville Loth 75 NT1063
Aird D & G 64 NX0960
Aird Strath 79 NM7600
Aird W Isls 102 NB5635
Aird a Mhulaidh W Isls 102 NB1810
Aird Asaig W Isls 102 NB1202
Aird of Kinloch Strath 79 NM5228
Aird of Sleat Highld 84 NG5900
Aird Uig W Isls 102 NB0533
Airdeny Strath 80 NM9929
Airdrie Strath 74 NS7565
Airdriehill Strath 74 NS7867
Airds Bay Strath 80 NM9932
Airds of Kells D & G 65 NX6770
Airidh a bhruaich W Isls 102 NB2417
Airieland D & G 65 NX7556
Airlie Tays 88 NO3150
Airmyn Humb 56 SE7224
Airntully Tays 82 NO0935
Airor Highld 85 NG7205
Airth Cent 82 NS9087
Airton N York 54 SD9059
Aisby Lincs 50 SK8692
Aisby Lincs 40 TF0138
Aish Devon 5 SX6960
Aish Devon 5 SX8458
Aisholt Somset 8 ST1935
Aiskew N York 61 SE2788
Aislaby Cleve 62 NZ4012
Aislaby N York 63 NZ8608
Aislaby N York 63 SE7785
Aisthorpe Lincs 50 SK9480
Aith Shet 103 HU3455
Akeld Nthumb 77 NT9529
Akeley Bucks 30 SP7037
Akenham Suffk 33 TM1449
Albaston Devon 4 SX4270
Alberbury Shrops 36 SJ3614
Albourne W Susx 12 TQ2516
Albrighton Shrops 37 SJ4918
Albrighton(Wolverhampton) Shrops 37 SJ8004
Alburgh Norfk 33 TM2687
Albury Herts 31 TL4324
Albury Surrey 12 TQ0447
Albury Heath Surrey 12 TQ0646
Alcaig Highld 92 NH5657
Alcaston Shrops 36 SO4587
Alcester Warwks 28 SP0857
Alciston E Susx 13 TQ5005
Alconbury Cambs 31 TL1875
Alconbury Weston Cambs 31 TL1777
Aldborough N York 55 SE4066
Aldborough Norfk 43 TG1834
Aldbourne Wilts 21 SU2676
Aldbrough Humb 57 TA2438
Aldbury Herts 30 SP9612
Aldcliffe Lancs 53 SD4660
Aldclune Tays 87 NN8964
Aldeburgh Suffk 33 TM4656
Aldeby Norfk 43 TM4493
Aldenham Herts 22 TQ1498
Alderbury Wilts 10 SU1827
Alderholt Dorset 10 SU1212
Alderley Gloucs 20 ST7690
Alderley Edge Ches 47 SJ8478
Aldermaston Berks 21 SU5965
Alderminster Warwks 29 SP2348
Aldershot Hants 22 SU8650
Alderton Gloucs 28 SP0033
Alderton Nhants 30 SP7446
Alderton Suffk 33 TM3441
Alderton Wilts 20 ST8482
Alderwasley Derbys 49 SK3053
Aldfield N York 55 SE2669
Aldford Ches 46 SJ4159
Aldgate Leics 40 SK9804
Aldham Essex 24 TL9126
Aldham Suffk 32 TM0545
Aldingbourne W Susx 12 SU9205
Aldingham Cumb 53 SD2870
Aldington H & W 28 SP0644
Aldington Kent 15 TR0736
Aldington Corner Kent 15 TR0636
Aldivalloch Gramp 94 NJ3526
Aldochlay Strath 80 NS3591
Aldreth Cambs 31 TL4473
Aldridge W Mids 38 SK0500
Aldringham Suffk 33 TM4461
Aldsworth Gloucs 28 SP1509
Aldunie Gramp 94 NJ3626
Aldwark Derbys 48 SK2257
Aldwark N York 55 SE4663
Aldwick W Susx 11 SZ9198
Aldwincle Nhants 40 TL0081
Aldworth Berks 21 SU5579
Alexandria Strath 80 NS3979
Aley Somset 19 ST1838
Alfington Devon 8 SY1197
Alfold Surrey 12 TQ0333
Alfold Crossways Surrey 12 TQ0335
Alford Gramp 94 NJ5715
Alford Lincs 51 TF4575
Alford Somset 9 ST6032
Alfreton Derbys 49 SK4155
Alfrick H & W 28 SO7453
Alfrick Pound H & W 28 SO7452
Alfriston E Susx 13 TQ5103
Algarkirk Lincs 41 TF2935
Alhampton Somset 9 ST6234
Alkborough Humb 56 SE8821
Alkham Kent 15 TR2542
Alkmonton Derbys 48 SK1838
All Cannings Wilts 20 SU0661
All Saints South Elmham Suffk 33 TM3482
All Stretton Shrops 36 SO4595
Allaleigh Devon 5 SX8053
Allanaquoich Gramp 88 NO1291
Allanbank Strath 74 NS8458
Allanton Border 77 NT8654
Allanton Strath 74 NS7454
Allanton Strath 74 NS8457
Allaston Gloucs 27 SO6304
Allbrook Hants 10 SU4521
Allen End Warwks 38 SP1696
Allen's Green Herts 31 TL4516
Allendale Nthumb 68 NY8355
Allenheads Nthumb 68 NY8645
Allensmore H & W 27 SO4635
Allenton Derbys 39 SK3732
Aller Devon 7 SS7625
Aller Somset 8 ST4029
Allerby Cumb 58 NY0839
Allercombe Devon 7 SY0494
Allerford Somset 7 SS9046
Allerston N York 63 SE8782
Allerthorpe Humb 56 SE7847
Allerton Mersyd 46 SJ3987
Allerton W York 55 SE1234
Allerton Bywater W York 55 SE4227
Allerton Mauleverer N York 55 SE4157
Allesley W Mids 39 SP3080
Allestree Derbys 49 SK3439
Allexton Leics 40 SK8100
Allgreave Ches 48 SJ9767
Allhallows Kent 24 TQ8377
Alligin Shuas Highld 91 NG8357
Allington Dorset 8 SY4693
Allington Lincs 50 SK8540
Allington Wilts 20 ST8975
Allington Wilts 20 SU0663
Allington Wilts 10 SU2039
Allithwaite Cumb 59 SD3876
Alloa Cent 82 NS8892
Allonby Cumb 58 NY0842
Alloway Strath 73 NS3318
Allowenshay Somset 8 ST3913
Alltchaorunn Highld 86 NN1951
Alltmawr Powys 26 SO0746
Alltwalis Dyfed 17 SN4431
Alltwen W Glam 18 SN7303
Alltyblaca Dyfed 17 SN5245
Allweston Dorset 9 ST6614
Almeley H & W 27 SO3351
Almeley Wooton H & W 27 SO3352
Almer Dorset 9 SY9199
Almholme S York 56 SE5808
Almington Staffs 37 SJ7034
Almondbank Tays 82 NO0625
Almondbury W York 55 SE1614
Almondsbury Avon 19 ST6084
Alne N York 55 SE4965
Alness Highld 93 NH6569
Alnham Nthumb 68 NT9810
Alnmouth Nthumb 69 NU2410
Alnwick Nthumb 69 NU1813
Alperton Gt Lon 23 TQ1883
Alphamstone Essex 24 TL8735
Alpheton Suffk 32 TL8750
Alphington Devon 5 SX9190
Alport Derbys 48 SK2264
Alpraham Ches 47 SJ5859
Alresford Essex 25 TM0621
Alrewas Staffs 38 SK1614
Alsager Ches 47 SJ7955
Alsop en le Dale Derbys 48 SK1554
Alston Cumb 68 NY7146
Alston Devon 8 ST3002
Alston Sutton Somset 19 ST4151
Alstone Gloucs 28 SO9832
Alstonefield Staffs 48 SK1355
Alswear Devon 7 SS7222
Altandhu Highld 98 NB9812
Altarnun Cnwll 4 SX2281
Altass Highld 96 NC5000
Altcreich Strath 79 NM6938
Altgaltraig Strath 80 NS0473
Althorne Essex 24 TQ9198
Althorpe Humb 56 SE8309
Altnabreac Station Highld 100 ND0045
Altnacraig Strath 79 NM8429
Altnaharra Highld 99 NC5635
Alton Derbys 49 SK3664
Alton Hants 11 SU7139
Alton Staffs 48 SK0741
Alton Barnes Wilts 20 SU1062
Alton Pancras Dorset 9 ST7002
Alton Priors Wilts 20 SU1162
Altrincham Gt Man 47 SJ7687
Altskeith Hotel Cent 81 NN4602
Alva Cent 82 NS8897
Alvah Gramp 95 NJ6760
Alvanley Ches 46 SJ4974
Alvaston Derbys 39 SK3833
Alvechurch H & W 38 SP0272
Alvecote Warwks 39 SK2404
Alvediston Wilts 9 ST9723
Alveley Shrops 37 SO7584
Alverdiscott Devon 6 SS5225
Alverstoke Hants 11 SZ6098
Alverstone IOW 11 SZ5785
Alverthorpe W York 55 SE3121
Alverton Notts 50 SK7942
Alves Gramp 93 NJ1362
Alvescot Oxon 29 SP2704
Alveston Avon 19 ST6388
Alveston Warwks 29 SP2356
Alvingham Lincs 51 TF3691
Alvington Gloucs 19 SO6000
Alwalton Cambs 40 TL1396
Alwinton Nthumb 68 NT9106
Alwoodley W York 55 SE2840
Alyth Tays 88 NO2448
Amberley Gloucs 20 SO8501
Amberley W Susx 12 TQ0213
Amble Nthumb 69 NU2604
Amblecote W Mids 38 SO8985
Ambler Thorn W York 55 SE0929
Ambleside Cumb 59 NY3704
Ambleston Dyfed 16 SN0025
Amcotts Humb 56 SE8514
Amersham Bucks 22 SU9597
Amesbury Wilts 20 SU1541
Amhuinnsuidhe W Isls 102 NB0408
Amisfield Town D & G 66 NY0082
Amlwch Gwynd 44 SH4492
Ammanford Dyfed 17 SN6212
Amotherby N York 63 SE7473
Ampfield Hants 10 SU4023
Ampleforth N York 62 SE5878
Ampney Crucis Gloucs 20 SP0601
Ampney St Mary Gloucs 20 SP0802
Ampney St Peter Gloucs 20 SP0801
Amport Hants 21 SU3044
Ampthill Beds 30 TL0337
Ampton Suffk 32 TL8671
Amroth Dyfed 17 SN1608
Amwell Herts 31 TL1613
An T-ob W Isls 102 NG0286
Anaheilt Highld 79 NM8162
Ancaster Lincs 50 SK9843
Anchor Shrops 36 SO1785
Ancroft Nthumb 77 NT9945
Ancrum Border 76 NT6224
Anderby Lincs 51 TF5275
Anderson Dorset 9 SY8897
Andover Hants 21 SU3645
Andoversford Gloucs 28 SP0219
Andreas IOM 52 SC4199
Anerley Gt Lon 23 TQ3369
Anfield Mersyd 46 SJ3692
Angarrack Cnwll 2 SW5838
Angelbank Shrops 37 SO5776
Angersleigh Somset 8 ST1918
Angle Dyfed 16 SM8603
Angmering W Susx 12 TQ0604
Angram N York 55 SE5248
Ankerville Highld 97 NH8174
Anlaby Humb 56 TA0328
Anmer Norfk 42 TF7429
Anmore Hants 11 SU6611
Anna Valley Hants 21 SU3543
Annan D & G 67 NY1966
Annat Highld 91 NG8954
Annat Strath 80 NN0322
Annathill Strath 74 NS7270
Annbank Strath 73 NS4023
Annesley Notts 49 SK5053
Annesley Woodhouse Notts 49 SK4953
Annfield Plain Dur 69 NZ1651
Anniesland Strath 74 NS5368
Ansdell Lancs 53 SD3428
Ansford Somset 9 ST6433
Ansley Warwks 39 SP3091
Anslow Staffs 39 SK2125
Anslow Gate Staffs 39 SK1924
Anstey Herts 31 TL4033
Anstey Leics 39 SK5508
Anstruther Fife 83 NO5703
Ansty W Susx 12 TQ2923
Ansty Warwks 39 SP4083
Ansty Wilts 9 ST9526
Anthorn Cumb 67 NY1958
Antingham Norfk 43 TG2533
Antony Cnwll 4 SX4054
Antrobus Ches 47 SJ6480
Anwick Lincs 50 TF1150
Anwoth D & G 65 NX5856
Aperfield Gt Lon 23 TQ4158
Apethorpe Nhants 40 TL0295
Apley Lincs 50 TF1075
Apperknowle Derbys 49 SK3878

Apperley
Backlass

Apperley Gloucs 28 SO8628
Appin Strath 86 NM9346
Appleby Humb 56 SE9514
Appleby Magna Leics 39 SK3109
Appleby Parva Leics 39 SK3008
Appleby-in-Westmorland Cumb 60 NY6820
Applecross Highld 91 NG7144
Appledore Devon 6 SS4630
Appledore Devon 7 ST0614
Appledore Kent 14 TQ9529
Appleford Oxon 21 SU5293
Applegarth Town D & G 67 NY1084
Appleshaw Hants 21 SU3048
Appleton Ches 46 SJ5186
Appleton Ches 47 SJ6184
Appleton Oxon 21 SP4401
Appleton Roebuck N York 56 SE5542
Appleton Thorn Ches 47 SJ6383
Appleton Wiske N York 62 NZ3804
Appleton-le-Moors N York 63 SE7387
Appleton-le-Street N York 63 SE7373
Appletreehall Border 76 NT5117
Appletreewick N York 55 SE0560
Appley Somset 8 ST0721
Appley Bridge Lancs 53 SD5209
Apse Heath IOW 11 SZ5683
Apsley End Beds 30 TL1232
Apuldram W Susx 11 SU8403
Arbirlot Tays 83 NO6040
Arboll Highld 97 NH8781
Arborfield Berks 22 SU7567
Arborfield Cross Berks 22 SU7666
Arbroath Tays 89 NO6441
Arbuthnott Gramp 89 NO8074
Archdeacon Newton Dur 61 NZ2517
Archencarroch Strath 81 NS4182
Archiestown Gramp 94 NJ2244
Archirondel Jersey 101 JS0000
Arclid Green Ches 47 SJ7861
Ardaily Strath 72 NR6450
Ardalanish Strath 78 NM3619
Ardanaiseig Hotel Strath 80 NN0824
Ardaneaskan Highld 85 NG8339
Ardarroch Strath 80 NS2494
Ardbeg Strath 70 NR4146
Ardbeg Strath 72 NS0766
Ardbeg Strath 80 NS1583
Ardcharnich Highld 96 NH1788
Ardchiavaig Strath 78 NM3818
Ardchonnel Strath 80 NM9812
Ardchullarie More Cent 81 NN5813
Ardechive Highld 86 NN1490
Ardeer Strath 73 NS2740
Ardeley Herts 31 TL3027
Ardelve Highld 85 NG8627
Arden Strath 80 NS3684
Ardens Grafton Warwks 28 SP1154
Ardentallen Strath 79 NM8324
Ardentinny Strath 80 NS1887
Ardentraive Strath 80 NS0374
Ardersier Highld 93 NH7855
Ardessie Highld 91 NH0689
Ardfern Strath 79 NM8004
Ardgay Highld 97 NH5990
Ardgour Highld 86 NN0163
Ardgowan Strath 80 NS2073
Ardhallow Strath 80 NS1674
Ardhasig W Isls 102 NB1202
Ardheslaig Highld 91 NG7855
Ardindrean Highld 96 NH1588
Ardingly W Susx 12 TQ3429
Ardington Oxon 21 SU4388
Ardlamont Strath 71 NR9865
Ardleigh Essex 25 TM0529
Ardleigh Heath Essex 25 TM0430
Ardler Tays 88 NO2642
Ardley Oxon 29 SP5427
Ardley End Essex 31 TL5214
Ardlui Strath 80 NN3115
Ardlussa Strath 71 NR6487
Ardmaddy Strath 80 NN0837
Ardmair Highld 96 NH1097
Ardmaleish Strath 72 NS0768
Ardminish Strath 72 NR6448
Ardmolich Highld 85 NM7172
Ardmore Highld 97 NH7086
Ardmore Strath 80 NS3178
Ardnadam Strath 80 NS1780
Ardnagrask Highld 92 NH5249
Ardnarff Highld 85 NG8935
Ardnastang Highld 79 NM8061
Ardno Strath 80 NN1508
Ardochy Lodge Hotel Highld 86 NH2002
Ardpatrick Strath 71 NR7559
Ardrishaig Strath 71 NR8585
Ardross Highld 97 NH6174
Ardrossan Strath 73 NS2342
Ardsley East W York 55 SE3025
Ardslignish Highld 79 NM5661
Ardtalla Strath 70 NR4654
Ardtoe Highld 79 NM6270
Arduaine Strath 79 NM7910
Ardvasar Highld 84 NG6303
Ardvorlich Tays 81 NN6322
Ardvourlie W Isls 102 NB1810
Ardwell D & G 64 NX1045
Ardwick Gt Man 47 SJ8597
Areley Kings H & W 28 SO7970
Arevegaig Highld 79 NM6568
Arford Hants 11 SU8236
Argoed Gwent 19 ST1799
Aribruach W Isls 102 NB2417
Aridhglas Strath 78 NM3123
Arileod Strath 78 NM1655
Arinagour Strath 78 NM2257
Ariogan Strath 79 NM8627
Arisaig Highld 85 NM6586
Arisaig House Highld 85 NM6984
Arkendale N York 55 SE3861
Arkesden Essex 31 TL4834
Arkholme Lancs 54 SD5871
Arkleton D & G 67 NY3791
Arkley Gt Lon 23 TQ2295
Arksey S York 56 SE5807
Arkwright Derbys 49 SK4270
Arle Gloucs 28 SO9223
Arlecdon Cumb 58 NY0418
Arlesey Beds 31 TL1936
Arleston Shrops 37 SJ6609
Arley Ches 47 SJ6680
Arley Warwks 39 SP2890
Arlingham Gloucs 28 SO7010
Arlington Devon 7 SS6140
Arlington E Susx 13 TQ5407
Armadale Highld 99 NC7864
Armadale Highld 85 NG6303
Armadale Loth 75 NS9368
Armaside Cumb 58 NY1527
Armathwaite Cumb 67 NY5046
Arminghall Norfk 43 TG2504
Armitage Staffs 38 SK0715
Armley W York 55 SE2833
Armston Nhants 40 TL0685
Armthorpe S York 56 SE6204
Arnabost Strath 78 NM2159
Arncliffe N York 54 SD9371
Arncroach Fife 83 NO5105
Arndilly House Gramp 94 NJ2847
Arne Dorset 9 SY9788
Arnesby Leics 39 SP6192
Arngask Tays 82 NO1410
Arnicle Strath 72 NR7138
Arnisdale Highld 85 NG8410
Arnish Highld 90 NG5948
Arniston Loth 75 NT3362
Arnol W Isls 102 NB3148
Arnold Humb 57 TA1241
Arnold Notts 49 SK5845
Arnprior Cent 81 NS6194
Arnside Cumb 59 SD4578
Aros Strath 79 NM5645
Arrad Foot Cumb 58 SD3080
Arram Humb 56 TA0344
Arrathorne N York 61 SE2093
Arreton IOW 11 SZ5386
Arrina Highld 91 NG7458
Arrington Cambs 31 TL3250
Arriundle Highld 79 NM8264
Arrochar Strath 80 NN2904
Arrow Warwks 28 SP0856
Arscott Shrops 36 SJ4307
Artafallie Highld 92 NH6349
Arthington W York 55 SE2644
Arthingworth Nhants 40 SP7581
Arthrath Gramp 95 NJ9636
Artrochie Gramp 95 NK0031
Arundel W Susx 12 TQ0106
Asby Cumb 58 NY0620
Ascog Strath 73 NS1062
Ascot Berks 22 SU9268
Ascott-under-Wychwood Oxon 29 SP3018
Asenby N York 62 SE3975
Asfordby Leics 40 SK7019
Asfordby Hill Leics 40 SK7219
Asgarby Lincs 50 TF1145
Asgarby Lincs 51 TF3366
Ash Kent 14 TQ6064
Ash Kent 15 TR2858
Ash Somset 8 ST4720
Ash Surrey 22 SU9051
Ash Green Surrey 22 SU9049
Ash Green Warwks 39 SP3384
Ash Magna Shrops 37 SJ5739
Ash Mill Devon 7 SS7823
Ash Parva Shrops 37 SJ5739
Ash Priors Somset 8 ST1529
Ash Street Suffk 32 TM0146
Ash Thomas Devon 7 ST0010
Ash Vale Surrey 22 SU8951
Ashampstead Berks 21 SU5676
Ashampstead Green Berks 21 SU5677
Ashbocking Suffk 33 TM1754
Ashbocking Green Suffk 33 TM1854
Ashbourne Derbys 48 SK1746
Ashbrittle Somset 7 ST0521
Ashburton Devon 5 SX7570
Ashbury Devon 6 SX5098
Ashbury Oxon 21 SU2685
Ashby Humb 56 SE8908
Ashby by Partney Lincs 51 TF4266
Ashby cum Fenby Humb 51 TA2500
Ashby de la Launde Lincs 50 TF0555
Ashby Folville Leics 40 SK7012
Ashby Magna Leics 39 SP5690
Ashby Parva Leics 39 SP5288
Ashby Puerorum Lincs 51 TF3271
Ashby St Ledgers Nhants 29 SP5768
Ashby St Mary Norfk 43 TG3202
Ashby-de-la-Zouch Leics 39 SK3516
Ashchurch Gloucs 28 SO9233
Ashcombe Avon 19 ST3361
Ashcombe Devon 5 SX9179
Ashcott Somset 19 ST4336
Ashdon Essex 31 TL5842
Ashe Hants 21 SU5350
Asheldham Essex 25 TL9701
Ashen Essex 32 TL7442
Ashendon Bucks 30 SP7014
Asheridge Bucks 22 SP9304
Ashfield Cent 81 NN7803
Ashfield Suffk 33 TM2062
Ashfield Green Suffk 33 TM2573
Ashford Devon 6 SS5335
Ashford Devon 5 SX6948
Ashford Kent 15 TR0142
Ashford Surrey 22 TQ0771
Ashford Bowdler Shrops 27 SO5170
Ashford Carbonel Shrops 27 SO5270
Ashford Hill Hants 21 SU5562
Ashford in the Water Derbys 48 SK1969
Ashgill Strath 74 NS7850
Ashill Devon 8 ST0811
Ashill Norfk 42 TF8804
Ashill Somset 8 ST3217
Ashingdon Essex 24 TQ8693
Ashington Nthumb 69 NZ2687
Ashington Somset 9 ST5621
Ashington W Susx 12 TQ1315
Ashkirk Border 76 NT4722
Ashleworth Gloucs 28 SO8125
Ashleworth Quay Gloucs 28 SO8125
Ashley Cambs 32 TL6961
Ashley Ches 47 SJ7784
Ashley Devon 7 SS6511
Ashley Gloucs 20 ST9394
Ashley Hants 10 SU3831
Ashley Hants 10 SZ2595
Ashley Kent 15 TR3048
Ashley Nhants 40 SP7990
Ashley Staffs 37 SJ7636
Ashley Wilts 20 ST8268
Ashley Green Bucks 22 SP9705
Ashmansworth Hants 21 SU4157
Ashmansworthy Devon 6 SS3418
Ashmore Dorset 9 ST9117
Ashmore Green Berks 21 SU5069
Ashorne Warwks 29 SP3057
Ashover Derbys 49 SK3463
Ashow Warwks 29 SP3170
Ashperton H & W 27 SO6441
Ashprington Devon 5 SX8157
Ashreigney Devon 7 SS6313
Ashtead Surrey 23 TQ1857
Ashton Ches 46 SJ5069
Ashton Cnwll 2 SW6028
Ashton Devon 5 SX8584
Ashton H & W 27 SO5164
Ashton Nhants 30 SP7649
Ashton Nhants 40 TL0588
Ashton Strath 80 NS2377
Ashton Common Wilts 20 ST8958
Ashton Keynes Wilts 20 SU0494
Ashton under Hill H & W 28 SO9937
Ashton-in-Makerfield Gt Man 47 SJ5798
Ashton-under-Lyne Gt Man 48 SJ9399
Ashurst Hants 10 SU3310
Ashurst Kent 13 TQ5138
Ashurst W Susx 12 TQ1715
Ashurstwood W Susx 13 TQ4136
Ashwater Devon 6 SX3895
Ashwell Herts 31 TL2639
Ashwell Leics 40 SK8613
Ashwell End Herts 31 TL2540
Ashwellthorpe Norfk 43 TM1497
Ashwick Somset 19 ST6348
Ashwicken Norfk 42 TF7018
Askam in Furness Cumb 58 SD2177
Askern S York 56 SE5613
Askerswell Dorset 8 SY5292
Askett Bucks 22 SP8105
Askham Cumb 59 NY5123
Askham Notts 50 SK7374
Askham Bryan N York 56 SE5548
Askham Richard N York 56 SE5347
Asknish Strath 71 NR9391
Askrigg N York 61 SD9491
Askwith N York 55 SE1648
Aslackby Lincs 40 TF0830
Aslacton Norfk 33 TM1590
Aslockton Notts 50 SK7440
Aspatria Cumb 58 NY1441
Aspenden Herts 31 TL3528
Aspley Guise Beds 30 SP9335
Aspley Heath Beds 30 SP9334
Aspull Gt Man 47 SD6108
Asselby Humb 56 SE7127
Assington Suffk 25 TL9338
Assington Green Suffk 32 TL7751
Astbury Ches 47 SJ8461
Astcote Nhants 30 SP6753
Asterby Lincs 51 TF2679
Asterley Shrops 36 SJ3707
Asterton Shrops 36 SO3991
Asthall Oxon 29 SP2811
Asthall Leigh Oxon 29 SP3013
Astle Highld 97 NH7391
Astley Gt Man 47 SD7000
Astley H & W 28 SO7867
Astley Shrops 37 SJ5218
Astley Warwks 39 SP3189
Astley Abbots Shrops 37 SO7096
Astley Bridge Gt Man 54 SD7111
Astley Cross H & W 28 SO8069
Aston Berks 22 SU7884
Aston Ches 47 SJ5578
Aston Ches 47 SJ6146
Aston Clwyd 46 SJ3067
Aston Derbys 48 SK1783
Aston H & W 36 SO4671
Aston Herts 31 TL2722
Aston Oxon 21 SP3403
Aston S York 49 SK4685
Aston Shrops 37 SJ5328
Aston Shrops 37 SJ6109
Aston Shrops 37 SO8093
Aston Staffs 37 SJ7541
Aston Staffs 38 SJ8923
Aston Staffs 38 SJ9130
Aston Abbotts Bucks 30 SP8420
Aston Botterell Shrops 37 SO6384
Aston Cantlow Warwks 28 SP1460
Aston Clinton Bucks 30 SP8812
Aston Crews H & W 28 SO6723
Aston End Herts 31 TL2724
Aston Fields H & W 28 SO9669
Aston Flamville Leics 39 SP4692
Aston Ingham H & W 28 SO6823
Aston le Walls Nhants 29 SP4950
Aston Magna Gloucs 29 SP1935
Aston Munslow Shrops 37 SO5186
Aston on Clun Shrops 36 SO3981
Aston Pigott Shrops 36 SJ3305
Aston Rogers Shrops 36 SJ3406
Aston Rowant Oxon 22 SU7299
Aston Somerville H & W 28 SP0438
Aston Subedge Gloucs 28 SP1441
Aston Tirrold Oxon 21 SU5586
Aston Upthorpe Oxon 21 SU5586
Aston-Eyre Shrops 37 SO6594
Aston-upon-Trent Derbys 39 SK4129
Astwick Beds 31 TL2138
Astwood Bucks 30 SP9547
Astwood H & W 28 SO9365
Astwood Bank H & W 28 SP0462
Aswarby Lincs 40 TF0639
Aswardby Lincs 51 TF3770
Atch Lench H & W 28 SP0350
Atcham Shrops 37 SJ5409
Athelhampton Dorset 9 SY7694
Athelington Suffk 33 TM2171
Athelney Somset 8 ST3428
Athelstaneford Loth 76 NT5377
Atherington Devon 6 SS5922
Atherstone Warwks 39 SP3097
Atherstone on Stour Warwks 29 SP2051
Atherton Gt Man 47 SD6703
Atlow Derbys 48 SK2248
Attadale Highld 85 NG9238
Atterby Lincs 50 SK9792
Attercliffe S York 49 SK3788
Atterton Leics 39 SP3598
Attleborough Norfk 42 TM0495
Attleborough Warwks 39 SP3790
Attlebridge Norfk 43 TG1216
Attleton Green Suffk 32 TL7454
Atwick Humb 57 TA1850
Atworth Wilts 20 ST8565
Aubourn Lincs 50 SK9262
Auchedly Gramp 95 NJ8933
Auchenblae Gramp 89 NO7279
Auchenbowie Cent 81 NS7987
Auchencairn D & G 66 NX7951
Auchencairn D & G 66 NX9884
Auchencairn Strath 72 NS0427
Auchencrow Border 77 NT8560
Auchendinny Loth 75 NT2561
Auchengray Strath 75 NS9954
Auchenhalrig Gramp 94 NJ3761
Auchenheath Strath 74 NS8043
Auchenhessnane D & G 66 NX8096
Auchenlochan Strath 71 NR9772
Auchenmade Strath 73 NS3548
Auchenmalg D & G 64 NX2352
Auchentibber Strath 74 NS6755
Auchentiber Strath 73 NS3647
Auchentroig Cent 81 NS5493
Auchindrean Highld 96 NH1980
Auchininna Gramp 94 NJ6546
Auchinleck Strath 74 NS5521
Auchinloch Strath 74 NS6570
Auchinstarry Strath 74 NS7176
Auchintore Highld 86 NN0972
Auchiries Gramp 95 NK0737
Auchlee Gramp 89 NO8996
Auchleven Gramp 94 NJ6224
Auchlochan Strath 74 NS7937
Auchlossan Gramp 89 NJ5601
Auchlyne Cent 81 NN5129
Auchmillan Strath 74 NS5129
Auchmithie Tays 89 NO6743
Auchmuirbridge Fife 82 NO2101
Auchnacree Tays 89 NO4663
Auchnagatt Gramp 95 NJ9241
Auchnarrow Gramp 94 NJ2023
Auchnotteroch D & G 64 NW9960
Auchroisk Gramp 94 NJ3351
Auchronie Tays 88 NO4480
Auchterarder Tays 82 NN9412
Auchteraw Highld 92 NH3507
Auchterblair Highld 93 NH9222
Auchtercairn Highld 91 NG8077
Auchterderran Fife 82 NT2195
Auchterhouse Tays 83 NO3337
Auchterless Gramp 95 NJ7141
Auchtermuchty Fife 83 NO2311
Auchterneed Highld 92 NH4959
Auchtertool Fife 82 NT2190
Auchtertyre Highld 85 NG8427
Auchtoo Cent 81 NN5520
Auckengill Highld 100 ND3663
Auckley S York 49 SE6400
Audenshaw Gt Man 48 SJ9197
Audlem Ches 47 SJ6543
Audley Staffs 47 SJ7950
Audley End Essex 31 TL5337
Audley End Suffk 32 TL8553
Aughertree Cumb 58 NY2538
Aughton Humb 56 SE7038
Aughton Lancs 46 SD3905
Aughton Lancs 53 SD5567
Aughton S York 49 SK4586
Aughton Wilts 21 SU2356
Aughton Park Lancs 46 SD4006
Auldallan Tays 88 NO3158
Auldearn Highld 93 NH9255
Aulden H & W 27 SO4654
Auldgirth D & G 66 NX9186
Auldhouse Strath 74 NS6250
Ault a' chruinn Highld 85 NG9420
Ault Hucknall Derbys 49 SK4665
Aultbea Highld 91 NG8789
Aultgrishin Highld 91 NG7485
Aultguish Inn Highld 92 NH3570
Aultmore Gramp 94 NJ4053
Aultnagoire Highld 92 NH5423
Aultnamain Inn Highld 97 NH6681
Aunsby Lincs 40 TF0438
Aust Avon 19 ST5788
Austerfield S York 49 SK6694
Austrey Warwks 39 SK2906
Austwick N York 54 SD7668
Authorpe Lincs 51 TF3980
Avebury Wilts 20 SU1069
Aveley Essex 24 TQ5680
Avening Gloucs 20 ST8898
Averham Notts 50 SK7654
Aveton Gifford Devon 5 SX6947
Aviemore Highld 93 NH8913
Avington Berks 21 SU3767
Avoch Highld 93 NH7055
Avon Dorset 10 SZ1498
Avon Dassett Warwks 29 SP4150
Avonbridge Cent 75 NS9172
Avonmouth Avon 19 ST5178
Avonwick Devon 5 SX7158
Awbridge Hants 10 SU3224
Awliscombe Devon 8 ST1301
Awre Gloucs 28 SO7008
Awsworth Notts 49 SK4844
Axbridge Somset 19 ST4354
Axford Hants 21 SU6043
Axford Wilts 21 SU2370
Axminster Devon 8 SY2998
Axmouth Devon 8 SY2591
Aycliffe Dur 61 NZ2822
Aydon Nthumb 68 NZ0065
Aylburton Gloucs 19 SO6101
Aylesbeare Devon 5 SY0392
Aylesbury Bucks 30 SP8213
Aylesby Humb 57 TA2007
Aylesford Kent 14 TQ7359
Aylesham Kent 15 TR2452
Aylestone Leics 39 SK5700
Aylmerton Norfk 43 TG1839
Aylsham Norfk 43 TG1926
Aylton H & W 27 SO6537
Aylworth Gloucs 28 SP1021
Aymestrey H & W 27 SO4265
Aynho Nhants 29 SP5133
Ayot Green Herts 31 TL2214
Ayot St Lawrence Herts 31 TL1916
Ayot St Peter Herts 31 TL2115
Ayr Strath 73 NS3321
Aysgarth N York 61 SE0088
Ayshford Devon 7 ST0415
Ayside Cumb 59 SD3983
Ayston Leics 40 SK8600
Aythorpe Roding Essex 24 TL5815
Ayton Border 77 NT9260
Azerley N York 61 SE2574

B

Babbacombe Devon 5 SX9265
Babbs Green Herts 31 TL3916
Babcary Somset 9 ST5628
Babington Somset 20 ST7051
Babraham Cambs 31 TL5150
Babworth Notts 49 SK6880
Back of Keppoch Highld 85 NM6587
Backaland Ork 103 HY5630
Backfolds Gramp 95 NK0252
Backford Ches 46 SJ3971
Backies Highld 97 NC8302
Backlass Highld 100 ND2053

Backwell Avon......................19 ST4968
Baconsthorpe Norfk..............43 TG1236
Bacton H & W......................27 SO3732
Bacton Norfk.......................43 TG3433
Bacton Suffk.......................32 TM0567
Bacup Lancs........................54 SD8622
Badachro Highld...................91 NG7873
Badbury Wilts......................21 SU1980
Badby Nhants.......................29 SP5658
Badcall Highld.....................98 NC1541
Badcall Highld.....................98 NC2455
Badcaul Highld.....................91 NH0291
Baddesley Clinton Warwks........39 SP2070
Baddesley Ensor Warwks..........39 SP2798
Baddidarroch Highld...............98 NC0822
Badenscoth Gramp..................95 NJ6938
Badenyon Gramp....................94 NJ3319
Badger Shrops......................37 SO7699
Badgeworth Gloucs..................28 SO9019
Badgworth Somset...................19 ST3952
Badicaul Highld....................85 NG7529
Badingham Suffk....................33 TM3068
Badlesmere Kent....................15 TR0153
Badlieu Border.....................75 NT0518
Badlipster Highld..................100 ND2448
Badluachrach Highld................91 NG9994
Badninish Highld...................97 NH7594
Badrallach Highld..................91 NH0691
Badsey H & W.......................28 SP0743
Badshot Lea Surrey.................22 SU8648
Badsworth W York...................55 SE4614
Badwell Ash Suffk..................32 TL9868
Bag Enderby Lincs..................51 TF3571
Bagber Dorset......................9 ST7513
Bagby N York.......................62 SE4680
Bagh a Chaisteil W Isls............102 NL6698
Bagillt Clwyd......................46 SJ2175
Baginton Warwks....................39 SP3474
Baglan W Glam......................18 SS7492
Bagley Shrops......................36 SJ4027
Bagley Somset......................19 ST4645
Bagmore Hants......................21 SU6544
Bagnall Staffs.....................48 SJ9250
Bagot Shrops.......................37 SO5873
Bagshot Surrey.....................22 SU9063
Bagstone Avon......................20 ST6987
Bagworth Leics.....................39 SK4408
Bagwy Llydiart H & W...............27 SO4426
Baildon W York.....................55 SE1539
Baildon Green W York...............55 SE1439
Baile a Mhanaich W Isls............102 NF7755
Baile Ailein W Isls................102 NB2920
Baile Mor Strath...................78 NM2824
Baillieston Strath.................74 NS6764
Bainbridge N York..................61 SD9390
Bainshole Gramp....................94 NJ6035
Bainton Cambs......................40 TF0906
Bainton Humb.......................56 SE9652
Baintown Fife......................83 NO3503
Bairnkine Border...................76 NT6515
Bakewell Derbys....................48 SK2168
Bala Gwynd.........................45 SH9235
Balallan W Isls....................102 NB2920
Balbeg Highld......................92 NH4431
Balbeggie Tays.....................82 NO1629
Balblair Highld....................92 NH5145
Balblair Highld....................93 NH7066
Balby S York.......................49 SE5600
Balcary D & G......................66 NX8149
Balchraggan Highld.................92 NH5343
Balchrick Highld...................98 NC1960
Balcombe W Susx....................12 TQ3130
Balcomie Links Fife................83 NO6209
Baldersby N York...................62 SE3578
Baldersby St James N York..........62 SE3676
Balderstone Lancs..................54 SD6332
Balderton Notts....................50 SK8151
Baldinnie Fife.....................83 NO4211
Baldinnies Tays....................82 NO0216
Baldock Herts......................31 TL2434
Baldovie Tays......................83 NO4533
Baldrine IOM.......................52 SC4281
Baldslow E Susx....................14 TQ8013
Bale Norfk.........................42 TG0136
Baledgarno Tays....................82 NO2730
Balemartine Strath.................78 NL9841
Balerno Loth.......................75 NT1666
Balfarg Fife.......................83 NO2803
Balfield Tays......................89 NO5468
Balfour Ork........................103 HY4716
Balfron Cent.......................81 NS5489
Balgaveny Gramp....................94 NJ6540
Balgavies Tays.....................89 NO5451
Balgonar Fife......................82 NT0293
Balgowan D & G.....................64 NX1142
Balgowan Highld....................87 NN6494
Balgown Highld.....................90 NG3868
Balgracie D & G....................64 NW9860
Balgray Strath.....................74 NS8824
Balgray Tays.......................83 NO4038
Balham Gt Lon......................23 TQ2873
Balhary Tays.......................88 NO2646
Balholmie Tays.....................82 NO1436
Baligill Highld....................99 NC8565
Balintore Highld...................97 NH8675
Balintore Tays.....................88 NO2859
Balintraid Highld..................93 NH7370
Balivanich W Isls..................102 NF7755
Balk N York........................62 SE4780
Balkeerie Tays.....................88 NO3244
Balkholme Humb.....................56 SE7828
Ballachulish Highld................86 NN0858
Ballanlay Strath...................72 NS0462
Ballantrae Strath..................64 NX0882
Ballasalla IOM.....................52 SC2870
Ballater Gramp.....................88 NO3695
Ballaugh IOM.......................52 SC3493
Ballchraggan Highld................97 NH7675
Ballechin Tays.....................87 NN9353
Ballencrieff Loth..................83 NT4478
Ballevullin Strath.................78 NL9546
Ballidon Derbys....................48 SK2054
Balliekine Strath..................72 NR8739
Balliemore Strath..................80 NS1099
Balligmorrie Strath................64 NX2290
Ballimore Cent.....................81 NS5317
Ballimore Strath...................71 NR9283
Ballindalloch Gramp................94 NJ1636
Ballindean Tays....................83 NO2529
Ballinger Common Bucks.............22 SP9103
Ballingham H & W...................27 SO5731
Ballingry Fife.....................82 NT1797
Ballinluig Tays....................88 NN9752
Ballinshoe Tays....................88 NO4153
Ballintuim Tays....................88 NO1055
Balloch Highld.....................93 NH7247
Balloch Strath.....................64 NX3295
Balloch Strath.....................74 NS7374

Balloch Strath.....................80 NS3982
Balloch Tays.......................82 NN8419
Ballochroy Strath..................71 NR7352
Ballogie Gramp.....................89 NO5795
Balls Cross W Susx.................12 SU9826
Balls Green E Susx.................13 TQ4936
Ballygown Strath...................79 NM4343
Ballygrant Strath..................70 NR3966
Ballyhaugh Strath..................78 NM1758
Ballymenoch Strath.................80 NS3086
Ballymichael Strath................72 NR9231
Balmacara Highld...................85 NG8028
Balmaclellan D & G.................65 NX6579
Balmae D & G.......................65 NX6844
Balmaha Cent.......................81 NS4290
Balmalcolm Fife....................83 NO3208
Balmangan D & G....................65 NX6445
Balmedie Gramp.....................95 NJ9618
Balmerino Fife.....................83 NO3524
Balmore Strath.....................74 NS5973
Balmuchy Highld....................97 NH8678
Balmuir Tays.......................89 NO5648
Balmule Fife.......................82 NT2088
Balmullo Tays......................83 NO4220
Balnacoil Lodge Highld.............97 NC8011
Balnacra Highld....................88 NO2894
Balnafoich Highld..................93 NH6835
Balnaguard Tays....................87 NN9451
Balnahard Strath...................79 NM4534
Balnahard Strath...................70 NR4199
Balnain Highld.....................92 NH4430
Balnakeil Highld...................98 NC3968
Balnapaling Highld.................93 NH7969
Balquhair Tays.....................82 NO0235
Balquhidder Cent...................81 NN5320
Balsall Common W Mids..............39 SP2376
Balsall Heath W Mids...............38 SP0784
Balscote Oxon......................29 SP3942
Balsham Cambs......................31 TL5850
Baltasound Shet....................103 HP6208
Baltersan D & G....................64 NX4261
Baltonsborough Somset..............8 ST5434
Balvarran Tays.....................88 NO0761
Balvicar Strath....................79 NM7616
Balvraid Highld....................85 NG8416
Balvraid Highld....................93 NH8231
Bamber Bridge Lancs................53 SD5625
Bamber's Green Essex...............24 TL5722
Bamburgh Nthumb....................77 NU1734
Bamff Tays.........................88 NO2251
Bamford Derbys.....................48 SK2083
Bampton Cumb.......................59 NY5118
Bampton Devon......................7 SS9522
Bampton Oxon.......................21 SP3103
Bampton Grange Cumb................59 NY5218
Banavie Highld.....................86 NN1177
Banbury Oxon.......................29 SP4540
Bancffosfelem Dyfed................17 SN4811
Banchory Gramp.....................89 NO6995
Banchory-Devenick Gramp............89 NJ9002
Bancycapel Dyfed...................17 SN4214
Bancyfelin Dyfed...................17 SN3218
Bandirran Tays.....................82 NO2030
Banff Gramp........................95 NJ6863
Bangor Gwynd.......................44 SH5772
Bangor-is-y-coed Clwyd.............46 SJ3845
Bangors Cnwll......................5 SX2099
Banham Norfk.......................32 TM0687
Bank Hants.........................10 SU2807
Bankend D & G......................66 NY0268
Bankend Strath.....................74 NS8033
Bankfoot Tays......................82 NO0635
Banglen Strath.....................65 NS5912
Bankhead Gramp.....................95 NJ9009
Bankhead Strath....................75 NS3791
Bankhead Strath....................75 NS9844
Banknock Cent......................81 NS7779
Banks Lancs........................53 SD3920
Bankshill D & G....................67 NY1982
Banningham Norfk...................43 TG2129
Bannister Green Essex..............24 TL6920
Bannockburn Cent...................82 NS8190
Banstead Surrey....................23 TQ2559
Bantham Devon......................5 SX6643
Banton Strath......................81 NS7480
Banwell Avon.......................19 ST3959
Bapchild Kent......................14 TQ9263
Bapton Wilts.......................20 ST9938
Bar Hill Cambs.....................31 TL3863
Barabhas W Isls....................102 NB3649
Barassie Strath....................73 NS3232
Barbaraville Highld................93 NH7472
Barbieston Strath..................73 NS4317
Barbon Cumb........................60 SD6282
Barbrook Devon.....................18 SS7147
Barby Nhants.......................29 SP5470
Barcaldine Strath..................86 NM9641
Barcheston Warwks..................29 SP2838
Barcombe E Susx....................13 TQ4114
Barcombe Cross E Susx..............13 TQ4115
Barden N York......................61 SE1493
Barden Park Kent...................13 TQ5746
Bardfield End Green Essex..........24 TL6231
Bardfield Saling Essex.............24 TL6826
Bardney Lincs......................50 TF1269
Bardon Leics.......................39 SK4412
Bardon Mill Nthumb.................68 NY7764
Bardowie Strath....................74 NS5873
Bardrainney Strath.................80 NS3373
Bardsea Cumb.......................58 SD3074
Bardsey W York.....................55 SE3643
Bardwell Suffk.....................32 TL9473
Bare Lancs.........................53 SD4564
Barfad D & G.......................64 NX3266
Barford Norfk......................43 TG1107
Barford Warwks.....................29 SP2606
Barford St John Oxon...............29 SP4433
Barford St Martin Wilts............10 SU0531
Barford St Michael Oxon............29 SP4332
Barfrestone Kent...................15 TR2650
Bargeddie Strath...................74 NS6964
Bargoed M Glam.....................19 ST1599
Bargrennan D & G...................64 NX3577
Barham Cambs.......................30 TL1375
Barham Kent........................15 TR2050
Barham Suffk.......................33 TM1451
Barholm Lincs......................40 TF0810
Barkby Leics.......................39 SK6309
Barkby Thorpe Leics................39 SK6309
Barkestone-le-Vale Leics...........40 SK7734
Barkham Berks......................22 SU7766
Barking Gt Lon.....................23 TQ4484
Barking Suffk......................32 TM0753
Barking Tye Suffk..................32 TM0652
Barkingside Gt Lon.................23 TQ4489
Barkisland W York..................55 SE0519
Barkla Shop Cnwll..................2 SW7350
Barkston Lincs.....................50 SK9341

Barkston Ash N York................55 SE4936
Barkway Herts......................31 TL3835
Barlanark Strath...................74 NS6664
Barlaston Staffs...................48 SJ8938
Barlavington W Susx................12 SU9716
Barlborough Derbys.................49 SK4777
Barlestone Leics...................39 SK4205
Barley Herts.......................31 TL4038
Barley Lancs.......................54 SD8240
Barleythorpe Leics.................40 SK8409
Barling Essex......................25 TQ9389
Barlings Lincs.....................50 TF0774
Barlochan D & G....................66 NX8157
Barlow Derbys......................49 SK3474
Barlow N York......................56 SE6430
Barlow T & W.......................69 NZ1561
Barmby Moor Humb...................56 SE7748
Barmby on the Marsh Humb...........56 SE6928
Barmer Norfk.......................42 TF8133
Barmollack Strath..................72 NR8043
Barmouth Gwynd.....................35 SH6116
Barmpton Dur.......................62 NZ3118
Barmston Humb......................57 TA1659
Barnacarry Strath..................80 NS0094
Barnack Cambs......................40 TF0705
Barnard Castle Dur.................61 NZ0516
Barnard Gate Oxon..................29 SP4010
Barnardiston Suffk.................32 TL7148
Barnbarroch D & G..................66 NX8456
Barnburgh S York...................56 SE4803
Barnby Suffk.......................33 TM4789
Barnby Dun S York..................56 SE6109
Barnby in the Willows Notts........50 SK8552
Barnby Moor Notts..................56 SK6684
Barncorkrie D & G..................64 NX0935
Barnes Gt Lon......................23 TQ2276
Barnes Street Kent.................13 TQ6447
Barnet Gt Lon......................23 TQ2496
Barnetby le Wold Humb..............57 TA0509
Barney Norfk.......................42 TF9932
Barnham Suffk......................32 TL8779
Barnham W Susx.....................12 SU9503
Barnham Broom Norfk................42 TG0807
Barnhead Tays......................89 NO6657
Barnhill Gramp.....................93 NJ1457
Barnhill Tays......................83 NO4731
Barnhills D & G....................64 NW9871
Barningham Dur.....................61 NZ0810
Barningham Suffk...................32 TL9676
Barnoldby le Beck Humb.............57 TA2303
Barnoldswick Lancs.................54 SD8746
Barns Green W Susx.................12 TQ1226
Barnsley Gloucs....................28 SP0704
Barnsley S York....................55 SE3406
Barnsole Kent......................15 TR2756
Barnstaple Devon...................6 SS5633
Barnston Essex.....................24 TL6419
Barnston Mersyd....................46 SJ2783
Barnstone Notts....................40 SK7335
Barnt Green H & W..................38 SP0173
Barnton Ches.......................47 SJ6375
Barnton Loth.......................75 NT1874
Barnwell All Saints Nhants.........40 TL0484
Barnwell St Andrew Nhants..........40 TL0584
Barnwood Gloucs....................28 SO8518
Barr Strath........................64 NX2794
Barrachan D & G....................64 NX3649
Barrapoll Strath...................78 NL9442
Barrasford Nthumb..................68 NY9173
Barrhead Strath....................74 NS4958
Barrhill Strath....................64 NX2382
Barrington Cambs...................31 TL3849
Barrington Somset..................8 ST3818
Barripper Cnwll....................2 SW6338
Barrock Highld.....................100 ND2570
Barrow Gloucs......................28 SO8824
Barrow Lancs.......................54 SD7338
Barrow Leics.......................40 SK8815
Barrow Somset......................9 ST7231
Barrow Suffk.......................32 TL7663
Barrow Burn Nthumb.................68 NT8610
Barrow Gurney Avon.................19 ST5268
Barrow Haven Humb..................57 TA0622
Barrow Island Cumb.................53 SD1968
Barrow upon Soar Leics.............39 SK5717
Barrow upon Trent Derbys...........39 SK3528
Barrow-in-Furness Cumb.............53 SD2068
Barrow-upon-Humber Humb............57 TA0620
Barrowby Lincs.....................40 SK8736
Barrowden Leics....................40 SK9400
Barrowford Lancs...................54 SD8539
Barry S Glam.......................18 ST1268
Barry Tays.........................83 NO5334
Barsby Leics.......................40 SK6911
Barsham Suffk......................33 TM3989
Barston W Mids.....................39 SP2078
Bartestree H & W...................27 SO5640
Barthol Chapel Gramp...............95 NJ8133
Bartholomew Green Essex............24 TL7221
Barthomley Ches....................47 SJ7652
Bartley Hants......................10 SU3012
Bartley Green W Mids...............38 SP0081
Bartlow Cambs......................31 TL5845
Barton Cambs.......................31 TL4055
Barton Ches........................46 SJ4454
Barton Devon.......................5 SX9167
Barton Gloucs......................28 SP0925
Barton Lancs.......................53 SD3509
Barton Lancs.......................53 SD5137
Barton N York......................61 NZ2208
Barton Oxon........................29 SP5507
Barton Bendish Norfk...............41 TF7105
Barton End Gloucs..................20 ST8498
Barton Hartshorn Bucks.............29 SP6430
Barton in Fabis Notts..............39 SK5132
Barton in the Beans Leics..........39 SK3906
Barton Mills Suffk.................32 TL7173
Barton on Sea Hants................10 SZ2393
Barton Seagrave Nhants.............30 SP8877
Barton St David Somset.............8 ST5432
Barton Stacey Hants................21 SU4341
Barton Town Dur....................56 SS6840
Barton Waterside Humb..............56 TA0222
Barton-le-Clay Beds................30 TL0830
Barton-le-Street N York............63 SE7274
Barton-le-Willows N York...........56 SE7163
Barton-on-the-Heath Warwks.........29 SP2532
Barton-under-
  Needwood Staffs..................38 SK1818
Barton-Upon-Humber Humb............56 TA1055
Barvas W Isls......................102 NB3649
Barway Cambs.......................31 TL5575
Barwell Leics......................39 SP4496
Barwick Devon......................6 SS5907
Barwick Somset.....................8 ST5513
Barwick in Elmet W York............55 SE4037

Baschurch Shrops...................36 SJ4221
Bascote Warwks.....................29 SP4063
Bashall Eaves Lancs................54 SD6943
Basildon Berks.....................21 SU6078
Basildon Essex.....................24 TQ7189
Basingstoke Hants..................21 SU6352
Baslow Derbys......................48 SK2572
Bason Bridge Somset................19 ST3446
Bassaleg Gwent.....................19 ST2786
Bassendean Border..................76 NT6245
Bassenthwaite Cumb.................58 NY2332
Bassett Hants......................10 SU4216
Bassingbourn Cambs.................31 TL3343
Bassingham Lincs...................50 SK9060
Bassingthorpe Leics................40 SK9628
Bassus Green Herts.................31 TL3025
Baston Lincs.......................40 TF1113
Bastwick Norfk.....................43 TG4217
Batchworth Herts...................22 TQ0694
Batcombe Dorset....................9 ST6103
Batcombe Somset....................20 ST6938
Batford Herts......................30 TL1415
Bath Avon..........................20 ST7464
Bathampton Avon....................20 ST7766
Bathealton Somset..................8 ST0823
Batheaston Avon....................20 ST7767
Bathford Avon......................20 ST7866
Bathgate Loth......................75 NS9768
Bathley Notts......................50 SK7759
Bathpool Cnwll.....................4 SX2874
Bathpool Somset....................8 ST2526
Bathville Loth.....................75 NS9367
Bathway Somset.....................19 ST5952
Batley W York......................55 SE2224
Batsford Gloucs....................29 SP1833
Battersby N York...................62 NZ5907
Battersea Gt Lon...................23 TQ2776
Battisford Tye Suffk...............32 TM0354
Battle E Susx......................14 TQ7515
Battle Powys.......................26 SO0130
Battledykes Tays...................88 NO4555
Battlesbridge Essex................24 TQ7894
Battleton Somset...................7 SS9127
Baughton H & W.....................28 SO8441
Baughurst Hants....................21 SU5860
Baulds Gramp.......................89 NO6093
Baulking Oxon......................21 SU3191
Baumber Lincs......................51 TF2274
Baunton Gloucs.....................28 SP0104
Baverstock Wilts...................10 SU0332
Bawburgh Norfk.....................43 TG1508
Bawdeswell Norfk...................42 TG0420
Bawdrip Somset.....................19 ST3439
Bawdsey Suffk......................33 TM3440
Bawtry S York......................49 SK6493
Baxenden Lancs.....................54 SD7726
Baxterley Warwks...................39 SP2896
Bayble W Isls......................102 NB5231
Baybridge Hants....................11 SU5223
Baycliff Cumb......................53 SD2872
Baydon Wilts.......................21 SU2878
Bayford Herts......................23 TL3108
Bayford Somset.....................9 ST7229
Bayhead W Isls.....................102 NF7468
Baylham Suffk......................33 TM1051
Baysham H & W......................27 SO5727
Bayston Hill Shrops................37 SJ4808
Baythorne End Essex................32 TL7242
Bayton H & W.......................37 SO6973
Bayworth Oxon......................21 SP4901
Beachampton Bucks..................30 SP7736
Beachamwell Norfk..................42 TF7505
Beacon Devon.......................8 ST1805
Beacon End Essex...................25 TL9524
Beacon's Bottom Bucks..............22 SU7895
Beaconsfield Bucks.................22 SU9490
Beacontree Gt Lon..................23 TQ4786
Beadlam N York.....................62 SE6584
Beadlow Beds.......................30 TL1038
Beadnell Nthumb....................77 NU2229
Beaford Devon......................6 SS5515
Beal N York........................56 SE5325
Beal Nthumb........................77 NU0642
Bealsmill Cnwll....................4 SX3576
Beaminster Dorset..................8 ST4701
Beamish Dur........................69 NZ2253
Beamsley N York....................55 SE0552
Beanacre Wilts.....................20 ST9066
Beanley Nthumb.....................77 NU0818
Beardon Devon......................4 SX5184
Beare Devon........................7 SS9901
Beare Green Surrey.................12 TQ1742
Bearley Warwks.....................29 SP1860
Bearpark Dur.......................69 NZ2343
Bearsden Strath....................74 NS5372
Bearstead Kent.....................14 TQ8055
Bearstone Shrops...................37 SJ7239
Bearwood W Mids....................38 SP0286
Beattock D & G.....................66 NT0802
Beauchamp Roding Essex.............24 TL5809
Beaufort Gwent.....................27 SO1611
Beaulieu Hants.....................10 SU3802
Beauly Highld......................92 NH5246
Beaumaris Gwynd....................44 SH6076
Beaumont Cumb......................67 NY3459
Beaumont Essex.....................25 TM1624
Beaumont Jersey....................101 JS0000
Beausale Warwks....................29 SP2470
Beauworth Hants....................11 SU5726
Beaver Green Kent..................15 TR0041
Beaworthy Devon....................6 SX4699
Beazley End Essex..................24 TL7429
Bebington Mersyd...................46 SJ3383
Beccles Suffk......................33 TM4289
Becconsall Lancs...................53 SD4523
Beck Row Suffk.....................32 TL6977
Beck Side Cumb.....................58 SD2382
Beckbury Shrops....................37 SJ7601
Beckenham Gt Lon...................23 TQ3769
Beckering Lincs....................50 TF1280
Beckermet Cumb.....................58 NY0106
Beckfoot Cumb......................67 NY0949
Beckford H & W.....................28 SO9736
Beckhampton Wilts..................20 SU0868
Beckingham Lincs...................50 SK8753
Beckingham Notts...................50 SK7789
Beckington Somset..................20 ST8051
Beckjay Shrops.....................36 SO3977
Beckley E Susx.....................14 TQ8523
Beckley Oxon.......................29 SP5611
Beckton Gt Lon.....................23 TQ4381
Beckwithshaw N York................55 SE2653
Becquet Vincent Jersey.............101 JS0000
Bedale N York......................61 SE2688
Bedchester Dorset..................9 ST8517
Beddau M Glam......................18 ST0585
Beddgelert Gwynd...................44 SH5948

Beddingham E Susx 13 TQ4407
Beddington Gt Lon 23 TQ3065
Beddington Corner Gt Lon 23 TQ2866
Bedfield Suffk 33 TM2166
Bedford Beds 30 TL0449
Bedham W Susx 12 TQ0122
Bedhampton Hants 11 SU7006
Bedingfield Suffk 33 TM1768
Bedingfield Street Suffk 33 TM1768
Bedlam N York 55 SE2661
Bedlam Lane Kent 14 TQ8845
Bedlington Nthumb 69 NZ2681
Bedlinog M Glam 18 SO0901
Bedminster Avon 19 ST5871
Bedminster Down Avon 19 ST5770
Bedmond Herts 22 TL0903
Bednall Staffs 38 SJ9517
Bedrule Border 76 NT6017
Bedstone Shrops 36 SO3676
Bedwas M Glam 19 ST1789
Bedwellty Gwent 19 SO1600
Bedworth Warwks 39 SP3687
Beeby Leics 39 SK6608
Beech Hants 11 SU6938
Beech Staffs 38 SJ8538
Beech Hill Berks 22 SU6964
Beechingstoke Wilts 20 SU0859
Beedon Berks 21 SU4878
Beedon Hill Berks 21 SU4877
Beeford Humb 57 TA1253
Beeley Derbys 49 SK2667
Beelsby Humb 51 TA2001
Beenham Berks 21 SU5868
Beer Devon 8 SY2289
Beer Somset 8 ST4031
Beer Hackett Dorset 9 ST6011
Beercrocombe Somset 8 ST3220
Beesands Devon 5 SX8140
Beesby Lincs 51 TF4680
Beeson Devon 5 SX8140
Beeston Beds 31 TL1648
Beeston Ches 46 SJ5358
Beeston Norfk 42 TF9015
Beeston Notts 39 SK5236
Beeston W York 55 SE2830
Beeston Regis Norfk 43 TG1642
Beeswing D & G 66 NX8969
Beetham Cumb 59 SD4979
Beetham Somset 8 ST2712
Beetley Norfk 42 TF9718
Begbroke Oxon 29 SP4614
Begelly Dyfed 16 SN1107
Beguildy Powys 36 SO1979
Beighton Norfk 43 TG3808
Beighton S York 49 SK4483
Beighton Hill Derbys 49 SK2951
Bein Inn Tays 82 NO1513
Beith Strath 73 NS3553
Bekesbourne Kent 15 TR1955
Belaugh Norfk 43 TG2818
Belbroughton H & W 38 SO9277
Belchalwell Dorset 9 ST7909
Belchalwell Street Dorset 9 ST7909
Belchamp Otten Essex 32 TL8041
Belchamp St Paul Essex 32 TL7942
Belchamp Walter Essex 32 TL8240
Belchford Lincs 51 TF2975
Belford Nthumb 77 NU1034
Belgrave Leics 39 SK5906
Belhelvie Gramp 95 NJ9417
Belhinnie Gramp 94 NJ4627
Bell Busk N York 54 SD9056
Bell End H & W 38 SO9477
Bell o' th'Hill Ches 46 SJ5245
Bellabeg Gramp 94 NJ3513
Bellanoch Strath 71 NR7992
Bellaty Tays 88 NO2359
Belle Vue Cumb 67 NY3756
Belle Vue W York 55 SE3419
Belleau Lincs 51 TF4078
Bellerby N York 61 SE1192
Bellfield Strath 74 NS8234
Bellfield Strath 75 NS9620
Bellingdon Bucks 22 SP9405
Bellingham Nthumb 68 NY8383
Belloch Strath 72 NR6737
Bellochantuy Strath 72 NR6632
Bellows Cross Dorset 10 SU0613
Bells Yew Green E Susx 13 TQ6135
Bellshill Strath 74 NS7360
Bellside Strath 74 NS8058
Bellsquarry Loth 75 NT0465
Belluton Avon 19 ST6164
Belmont Gt Lon 23 TQ2562
Belmont Lancs 54 SD6715
Belmont Shet 103 HP5600
Belmont Strath 73 NS3419
Belnacraig Gramp 94 NJ3716
Belper Derbys 49 SK3447
Belper Lane End Derbys 49 SK3349
Belsay Nthumb 68 NZ0978
Belses Border 76 NT5725
Belsford Devon 5 SX7659
Belsize Herts 22 TL0300
Belstead Suffk 33 TM1241
Belstone Devon 5 SX6293
Belthorn Lancs 54 SD7124
Beltinge Kent 15 TR1967
Beltingham Nthumb 68 NY7863
Beltoft Humb 56 SE8006
Belton Humb 56 SE7806
Belton Leics 39 SK4420
Belton Lincs 40 SK8101
Belton Lincs 40 SK9339
Belton Norfk 43 TG4802
Belvedere Gt Lon 23 TQ4978
Belvoir Leics 40 SK8133
Bembridge IOW 11 SZ6488
Bemerton Wilts 10 SU1230
Bempton Humb 57 TA1972
Ben Rhydding W York 55 SE1347
Benacre Suffk 33 TM5184
Benbuie D & G 65 NX7196
Benderloch Strath 79 NM9038
Benenden Kent 14 TQ8033
Benfield D & G 64 NX3763
Benfieldside Dur 68 NZ0952
Bengeworth H & W 28 SP0443
Benhall Green Suffk 33 TM3961
Benhall Street Suffk 33 TM3561
Benholm Gramp 89 NO8069
Beningbrough N York 55 SE5458
Benington Herts 31 TL2923
Benington Lincs 51 TF3946
Benllech Gwynd 44 SH5182
Benmore Strath 80 NS1385
Bennacott Cnwll 4 SX2992
Bennan Strath 72 NR9921

Benniworth Lincs 51 TF2081
Benover Kent 14 TQ7048
Benson Oxon 21 SU6291
Benthoul Gramp 89 NJ8003
Bentley Hants 22 SU7844
Bentley Humb 56 TA0136
Bentley S York 56 SE5605
Bentley Suffk 25 TM1138
Bentley Warwks 39 SP2895
Benton Devon 7 SS6536
Bentpath D & G 67 NY3190
Bentwichen Devon 7 SS7333
Bentworth Hants 11 SU6640
Benvie Tays 83 NO3231
Benville Dorset 8 ST5303
Benwick Cambs 41 TL3490
Beoley H & W 28 SP0669
Beoraidbeg Highld 85 NM6793
Bepton W Susx 11 SU8618
Berden Essex 31 TL4629
Bere Alston Devon 4 SX4466
Bere Ferrers Devon 4 SX4563
Bere Regis Dorset 9 SY8494
Berea Dyfed 16 SM7930
Berepper Cnwll 2 SW6523
Bergh Apton Norfk 43 TG3001
Berinsfield Oxon 21 SU5696
Berkeley Gloucs 20 ST6899
Berkhamsted Herts 22 SP9907
Berkley Somset 20 ST8049
Berkswell W Mids 39 SP2479
Bermondsey Gt Lon 23 TQ3479
Bernera Highld 85 NG8020
Bernice Strath 80 NS1391
Bernisdale Highld 90 NG4050
Berrick Prior Oxon 21 SU6294
Berrick Salome Oxon 21 SU6293
Berriedale Highld 100 ND1222
Berrier Cumb 59 NY3929
Berriew Powys 36 SJ1801
Berrington H & W 27 SO5767
Berrington Shrops 37 SJ5206
Berrington Green H & W 27 SO5766
Berrow Somset 19 ST2951
Berrow Green H & W 28 SO7458
Berry Pomeroy Devon 5 SX8261
Berryhillock Gramp 94 NJ5054
Berryhillock Gramp 94 NJ5060
Berrynarbor Devon 6 SS5646
Bersham Clwyd 46 SJ3049
Berwick E Susx 13 TQ5105
Berwick Bassett Wilts 20 SU0973
Berwick Hill Nthumb 69 NZ1775
Berwick St James Wilts 10 SU0739
Berwick St John Wilts 9 ST9422
Berwick St Leonard Wilts 9 ST9233
Berwick-upon-Tweed Nthumb 77 NT9953
Bescaby Leics 40 SK8126
Bescar Cumb 53 SD3913
Besford H & W 28 SO9144
Bessacarr S York 49 SE6100
Bessels Leigh Oxon 21 SP4501
Bessingby Humb 57 TA1566
Bessingham Norfk 43 TG1636
Besthorpe Norfk 42 TM0595
Besthorpe Notts 50 SK8264
Beswick Humb 56 TA0147
Betchworth Surrey 12 TQ2150
Bethel Gwynd 44 SH3970
Bethel Gwynd 44 SH5265
Bethersden Kent 14 TQ9240
Bethesda Dyfed 16 SN0918
Bethesda Gwynd 45 SH6266
Bethlehem Dyfed 26 SN6825
Bethnal Green Gt Lon 23 TQ3482
Betley Staffs 47 SJ7548
Betsham Kent 14 TQ6071
Betteshanger Kent 15 TR3152
Bettiscombe Dorset 8 ST3900
Bettisfield Clwyd 36 SJ4635
Bettws Gwent 19 ST2890
Bettws Bledrws Dyfed 17 SN5952
Bettws Cedewain Powys 36 SO1296
Bettws Evan Dyfed 17 SN3047
Bettws-Newydd Gwent 27 SO3606
Bettyhill Highld 99 NC7061
Betws M Glam 18 SS9086
Betws Gwerfil Goch Clwyd 45 SJ0346
Betws-y-coed Gwynd 45 SH7956
Betws-yn-Rhos Clwyd 45 SH9073
Beulah Dyfed 17 SN2846
Beulah Powys 26 SN9251
Bevercotes Notts 49 SK6972
Beverley Humb 56 TA0339
Beverston Gloucs 20 ST8694
Bewcastle Cumb 67 NY5674
Bewdley H & W 37 SO7875
Bewerley N York 55 SE1565
Bewholme Humb 57 TA1649
Bexhill E Susx 14 TQ7407
Bexley Gt Lon 23 TQ4973
Bexleyheath Gt Lon 23 TQ4875
Bexwell Norfk 41 TF6303
Beyton Suffk 32 TL9363
Beyton Green Suffk 32 TL9363
Bhaltos W Isls 102 NB0936
Bibury Gloucs 28 SP1106
Bicester Oxon 29 SP5823
Bickenhill W Mids 38 SP1882
Bicker Lincs 41 TF2237
Bickerstaffe Lancs 46 SD4404
Bickerton N York 55 SE4550
Bickford Staffs 38 SJ8814
Bickington Devon 6 SS5332
Bickington Devon 5 SX8072
Bickleigh Devon 7 SS9407
Bickleigh Devon 4 SX5262
Bickley Gt Lon 23 TQ4268
Bickley N York 63 SE9191
Bickley Moss Ches 46 SJ5448
Bicknacre Essex 24 TL7802
Bicknoller Somset 18 ST1139
Bicknor Kent 14 TQ8658
Bicton Shrops 36 SJ4415
Bicton Shrops 36 SO2983
Bidborough Kent 13 TQ5643
Biddenden Kent 14 TQ8538
Biddenham Beds 30 TL0250
Biddestone Wilts 20 ST8673
Biddisham Somset 19 ST3853
Biddlesden Bucks 29 SP6340
Biddulph Staffs 47 SJ8858
Bideford Devon 6 SS4526
Bidford-on-Avon Warwks 28 SP1052
Bielby Humb 56 SE7843
Bieldside Gramp 89 NJ8702
Bierley IOW 11 SZ5078
Bierton Bucks 30 SP8415

Big Balcraig D & G 64 NX3843
Big Carlae D & G 65 NX6597
Big Sand Highld 91 NG7578
Bigbury Devon 5 SX6646
Bigbury-on-Sea Devon 5 SX6544
Bigby Lincs 57 TA0507
Biggar Strath 75 NT0437
Biggin Derbys 48 SK1559
Biggin Derbys 48 SK2549
Biggin N York 56 SE5434
Biggin Hill Gt Lon 23 TQ4159
Biggleswade Beds 31 TL1944
Bigholms D & G 67 NY3180
Bighouse Highld 99 NC8964
Bighton Hants 11 SU6134
Biglands Cumb 67 NY2553
Bignor W Susx 12 SU9814
Bigrigg Cumb 58 NY0013
Bilborough Notts 49 SK5241
Bilbrook Somset 7 ST0341
Bilbrough N York 55 SE5346
Bilbster Highld 100 ND2853
Bildershaw Dur 61 NZ2024
Bildeston Suffk 32 TL9949
Billericay Essex 24 TQ6794
Billesdon Leics 40 SK7202
Billesley Warwks 28 SP1456
Billingborough Lincs 40 TF1133
Billinge Mersyd 46 SD5200
Billingford Norfk 42 TG0120
Billingford Norfk 33 TM1678
Billingham Cleve 62 NZ4624
Billinghay Lincs 50 TF1554
Billingley S York 55 SE4304
Billingshurst W Susx 12 TQ0825
Billingsley Shrops 37 SO7085
Billington Beds 30 SP9422
Billington Lancs 54 SD7235
Billockby Norfk 43 TG4313
Billy Row Dur 61 NZ1637
Bilsborrow Lancs 53 SD5139
Bilsby Lincs 51 TF4776
Bilsham W Susx 12 SU9702
Bilsington Kent 15 TR0434
Bilston Loth 75 NT2664
Bilston W Mids 38 SO9396
Bilstone Leics 39 SK3605
Bilton Humb 57 TA1632
Bilton N York 55 SE4749
Bilton N York 55 SE3157
Bilton Warwks 39 SP4873
Binbrook Lincs 51 TF2093
Bincombe Dorset 9 SY6884
Binegar Somset 19 ST6149
Binfield Berks 22 SU8471
Binfield Heath Oxon 22 SU7477
Bingfield Nthumb 68 NY9772
Bingham Notts 49 SK7039
Bingham's Melcombe Dorset 9 ST7702
Bingley W York 55 SE1039
Binham Norfk 42 TF9839
Binley Hants 21 SU4253
Binley W Mids 39 SP3778
Binnegar Dorset 9 SY8887
Binniehill Cent 74 NS8572
Binns Farm Gramp 94 NJ3164
Binscombe Surrey 12 SU9645
Binstead Hants 11 SU7740
Binsted W Susx 12 SU9806
Binton Warwks 28 SP1454
Bintree Norfk 42 TG0123
Birch Essex 25 TL9419
Birch Cross Staffs 38 SK1230
Birch Green Essex 25 TL9418
Birch Vale Derbys 48 SK0286
Birch Wood Somset 8 ST2414
Bircham Newton Norfk 42 TF7733
Bircham Tofts Norfk 42 TF7732
Birchanger Essex 31 TL5122
Birchburn Strath 72 NR9129
Bircher H & W 27 SO4765
Birchgrove E Susx 13 TQ4029
Birchgrove S Glam 19 ST1679
Birchgrove W Glam 18 SS7098
Birchington Kent 15 TR3069
Birchley Heath Warwks 39 SP2894
Birchover Derbys 48 SK2362
Bircotes Notts 49 SK6391
Birdbrook Essex 32 TL7041
Birdforth N York 62 SE4875
Birdham W Susx 11 SU8200
Birdingbury Warwks 29 SP4368
Birdlip Gloucs 28 SO9214
Birds Edge W York 55 SE2007
Birds Green Essex 24 TL5808
Birdsall N York 56 SE8165
Birdsgreen Shrops 37 SO7785
Birdsmoorgate Dorset 8 ST3900
Birgham Border 76 NT7939
Birichin Highld 97 NH7592
Birkby N York 62 NZ3202
Birkdale Mersyd 53 SD3214
Birkenbog Gramp 94 NJ5365
Birkenhead Mersyd 46 SJ3288
Birkenhills Gramp 95 NJ7445
Birkhall Gramp 88 NO3493
Birkhill D & G 75 NT2015
Birkhill Tays 83 NO3534
Birkin N York 56 SE5326
Birley H & W 27 SO4553
Birley Carr S York 49 SK3392
Birling Kent 14 TQ6860
Birlingham H & W 28 SO9343
Birmingham W Mids 38 SP0786
Birnam Tays 88 NO0341
Birness Gramp 95 NJ9933
Birse Gramp 89 NO5697
Birsemore Gramp 89 NO5297
Birstall Leics 39 SK5909
Birstall W York 55 SE2225
Birstwith N York 55 SE2359
Birtley H & W 27 SO3669
Birtley Nthumb 68 NY8778
Birtley T & W 69 NZ2756
Birts Street H & W 28 SO7836
Bisbrooke Leics 40 SP8899
Biscathorpe Lincs 51 TF2284
Bish Mill Devon 7 SS7425
Bisham Berks 22 SU8485
Bishampton H & W 28 SO9951
Bishop Auckland Dur 61 NZ2028
Bishop Burton Humb 56 SE9839
Bishop Middleham Dur 62 NZ3231
Bishop Monkton N York 55 SE3266
Bishop Norton Lincs 50 SK9892
Bishop Sutton Avon 19 ST5859
Bishop Thornton N York 55 SE2563

Bishop Wilton Humb 56 SE7955
Bishop's Castle Shrops 36 SO3288
Bishop's Cleeve Gloucs 28 SO9627
Bishop's Frome H & W 28 SO6648
Bishop's Green Essex 24 TL6217
Bishop's Itchington Warwks 29 SP3857
Bishop's Norton Gloucs 28 SO8424
Bishop's Nympton Devon 7 SS7523
Bishop's Offley Staffs 37 SJ7729
Bishop's Stortford Herts 31 TL4821
Bishop's Sutton Hants 11 SU6032
Bishop's Tachbrook Warwks 29 SP3161
Bishop's Tawton Devon 6 SS5729
Bishop's Waltham Hants 11 SU5517
Bishop's Wood Staffs 38 SJ8309
Bishop's Caundle Dorset 9 ST6913
Bishopbridge Lincs 50 TF0391
Bishopbriggs Strath 74 NS6070
Bishopmill Gramp 94 NJ2163
Bishops Cannings Wilts 20 SU0364
Bishops Hull Somset 8 ST2024
Bishops Lydeard Somset 8 ST1729
Bishopsbourne Kent 15 TR1852
Bishopsteignton Devon 5 SX9073
Bishopstoke Hants 10 SU4619
Bishopston W Glam 17 SS5789
Bishopstone Bucks 22 SP8010
Bishopstone E Susx 13 TQ4701
Bishopstone H & W 27 SO4143
Bishopstone Kent 23 TQ2068
Bishopstone Wilts 10 SU0625
Bishopstone Wilts 21 SU2483
Bishopstrow Wilts 20 ST8943
Bishopswood Somset 8 ST2612
Bishopsworth Avon 19 ST5768
Bishopthorpe N York 56 SE5947
Bishopton Dur 62 NZ3621
Bishopton Strath 81 NS4371
Bishton Gwent 19 ST3887
Bishton Staffs 38 SK0220
Bisley Gloucs 28 SO9005
Bisley Surrey 22 SU9559
Bissoe Cnwll 2 SW7741
Bisterne Hants 10 SU1401
Bitchfield Lincs 40 SK9828
Bittadon Devon 6 SS5441
Bittaford Devon 5 SX6656
Bitterley Shrops 37 SO5677
Bitterne Hants 10 SU4513
Bitteswell Leics 39 SP5385
Bitton Avon 20 ST6869
Bix Oxon 22 SU7284
Blaby Leics 39 SP5697
Black Bourton Oxon 29 SP2804
Black Callerton T & W 69 NZ1769
Black Corries Highld 86 NN2956
Black Crofts Strath 80 NM9234
Black Dog Devon 7 SS8009
Black Notley Essex 24 TL7620
Black Street Suffk 33 TM5186
Black Torrington Devon 6 SS4605
Blackadder Border 77 NT8452
Blackawton Devon 5 SX8051
Blackborough Devon 8 ST0909
Blackborough End Norfk 42 TF6615
Blackboys E Susx 13 TQ5220
Blackbrook Derbys 49 SK3347
Blackbrook Staffs 37 SJ7638
Blackburn Gramp 95 NJ8212
Blackburn Lancs 54 SD6827
Blackburn Loth 75 NS9865
Blackcraig Strath 66 NS6308
Blackdog Gramp 95 NJ9513
Blackdown Dorset 8 ST3903
Blackenall Heath W Mids 38 SK0002
Blacker Hill S York 49 SE3602
Blackfen Gt Lon 23 TQ4674
Blackfield Hants 10 SU4402
Blackford Somset 19 ST4147
Blackford Somset 9 ST6526
Blackford Tays 82 NN8908
Blackfordby Leics 39 SK3217
Blackhall Loth 75 NT1975
Blackhall Colliery Dur 62 NZ4539
Blackhaugh Border 76 NT4238
Blackheath Essex 23 TQ3876
Blackheath Suffk 33 TM4274
Blackheath Surrey 12 TQ0346
Blackheath W Mids 38 SO9786
Blackhill Dur 68 NZ0851
Blackhill Gramp 95 NK0039
Blackhill Gramp 95 NK0755
Blackhill Gramp 95 NK0843
Blackhill of Clackriach Gramp 95 NJ9246
Blackhorse Devon 5 SX9893
Blackland Somset 7 SS8336
Blacklaw D & G 66 NT0408
Blackley Gt Man 47 SD8502
Blacklunans Tays 88 NO1460
Blackmarstone H & W 27 SO5038
Blackmill M Glam 18 SS9386
Blackmoor Avon 19 ST4661
Blackmoor Hants 11 SU7733
Blackmoorfoot W York 55 SE0913
Blackmore Essex 24 TL6001
Blackmore End Essex 24 TL7430
Blackness Loth 82 NT0579
Blackness Berks 22 SU9568
Blackness Hants 11 SU7941
Blacko Lancs 54 SD8541
Blackpill W Glam 17 SS6190
Blackpool Devon 5 SX8547
Blackpool Lancs 53 SD3036
Blackridge Loth 74 NS8967
Blackrock Gwent 19 ST5188
Blackrod Gt Man 54 SD6110
Blacksboat Gramp 94 NJ1838
Blackshaw D & G 66 NY0465
Blackshaw Head W York 54 SD9527
Blacksnape Lancs 54 SD7121
Blackstone W Susx 12 TQ2316
Blackthorn Oxon 29 SP6219
Blackthorpe Suffk 32 TL9063
Blacktoft Humb 56 SE8324
Blacktop Gramp 89 NJ8604
Blackwall Derbys 48 SK2548
Blackwater Cnwll 2 SW7346
Blackwater Hants 22 SU8459
Blackwater IOW 11 SZ5086
Blackwater Somset 8 ST2615
Blackwaterfoot Strath 72 NR9028
Blackwell Cumb 67 NY4053
Blackwell Derbys 48 SK1272
Blackwell Derbys 49 SK4458
Blackwell H & W 38 SO9972
Blackwell Warwks 29 SP2443
Blackwood D & G 66 NX9087
Blackwood Gwent 19 ST1797

Blackwood Strath	74	NS7844
Blacon Ches	46	SJ3868
Bladnoch D & G	64	NX4254
Bladon Oxon	29	SP4514
Blaen-y-Coed Dyfed	17	SN3427
Blaen-y-cwm Gwent	26	SO1311
Blaen-y-cwm M Glam	18	SS9298
Blaenannerch Dyfed	17	SN2448
Blaenau Ffestiniog Gwynd	45	SH7045
Blaenffos Dyfed	17	SN1937
Blaenavon Gwent	27	SO2508
Blaengarw M Glam	18	SS9092
Blaengwrach W Glam	26	SN8605
Blaengwynfi W Glam	18	SS8996
Blaenpennal Dyfed	35	SN6264
Blaenplwyf Dyfed	34	SN5775
Blaenporth Dyfed	17	SN2648
Blaenrhondda M Glam	18	SS9299
Blaenwaun Dyfed	17	SN2327
Blagdon Avon	19	ST5059
Blagdon Devon	5	SX8561
Blagdon Hill Somset	8	ST2117
Blaich Highld	85	NN0376
Blain Highld	79	NM6769
Blaina Gwent	27	SO2008
Blair Atholl Tays	87	NN8665
Blair Drummond Cent	81	NS7399
Blairgowrie Tays	88	NO1745
Blairingone Fife	82	NS9896
Blairlogie Cent	82	NS8396
Blairmore Highld	98	NC1959
Blairmore Strath	80	NS1983
Blairnamarrow Gramp	94	NJ2015
Blairs Ferry Strath	71	NR9869
Blaisdon Gloucs	28	SO7017
Blake End Essex	24	TL7023
Blakebrook H & W	38	SO8276
Blakedown H & W	38	SO8878
Blakemere Ches	47	SJ5571
Blakemere H & W	27	SO3641
Blakeney Gloucs	28	SO6707
Blakeney Norfk	42	TG0243
Blakenhall Ches	47	SJ7247
Blakenhall W Mids	38	SO9197
Blakesley Nhants	29	SP6250
Blanchland Nthumb	68	NY9650
Bland Hill N York	55	SE2053
Blandford Forum Dorset	9	ST8806
Blandford St Mary Dorset	9	ST8805
Blanefield Cent	81	NS5479
Blankney Lincs	50	TF0660
Blantyre Strath	74	NS6957
Blar a' Chaorainn Highld	86	NN1066
Blargie Highld	87	NN6094
Blarmachfoldach Highld	86	NN0969
Blaston Leics	40	SP8095
Blatherwycke Nhants	40	SP9795
Blawith Cumb	58	SD2888
Blawquhairn D & G	65	NX6282
Blaxhall Suffk	33	TM3656
Blaxton S York	49	SE6700
Blaydon T & W	69	NZ1863
Bleadney Somset	19	ST4845
Bleadon Somset	19	ST3456
Blean Kent	15	TR1260
Bleasby Lincs	49	SK7149
Bleasdale Lancs	53	SD5745
Blebocraigs Fife	83	NO4214
Bleddfa Powys	27	SO2068
Bledington Gloucs	29	SP2422
Bledlow Bucks	22	SP7702
Bledlow Ridge Bucks	22	SU7997
Blegbie Loth	76	NT4861
Blencarn Cumb	60	NY6331
Blencogo Cumb	67	NY1947
Blendworth Hants	11	SU7113
Blennerhasset Cumb	58	NY1741
Bletchingdon Oxon	29	SP5018
Bletchingley Surrey	12	TQ3250
Bletchley Bucks	30	SP8633
Bletchley Shrops	37	SJ6233
Bletherston Dyfed	16	SN0721
Bletsoe Beds	30	TL0258
Blewbury Oxon	21	SU5385
Blickling Norfk	43	TG1728
Blidworth Notts	49	SK5956
Blidworth Bottoms Notts	49	SK5954
Blindcrake Cumb	58	NY1434
Blindley Heath Surrey	12	TQ3645
Blisland Cnwll	3	SX1073
Bliss Gate H & W	37	SO7472
Blissford Hants	10	SU1713
Blisworth Nhants	30	SP7253
Blithbury Staffs	38	SK0819
Blo Norton Norfk	32	TM0179
Blockley Gloucs	28	SP1634
Blofield Norfk	43	TG3309
Bloomfield Border	76	NT5824
Blore Staffs	37	SJ7234
Blore Staffs	48	SK1349
Bloxham Oxon	29	SP4336
Bloxwith W Mids	38	SJ9902
Bloxworth Dorset	9	SY8894
Blubberhouses N York	55	SE1655
Blue Anchor Somset	7	ST0243
Blue Bell Hill Kent	14	TQ7462
Blundellsands Mersyd	46	SJ3099
Blundeston Suffk	43	TM5297
Blunham Beds	30	TL1551
Blunsdon St Andrew Wilts	20	SU1389
Bluntington H & W	38	SO9074
Bluntisham Cambs	31	TL3674
Blyborough Lincs	50	SK9394
Blyford Suffk	33	TM4276
Blymhill Staffs	37	SJ8112
Blyth Notts	49	SK6287
Blyth Nthumb	69	NZ3181
Blyth Bridge Border	75	NT1345
Blythburgh Suffk	33	TM4475
Blythe Border	76	NT5849
Blyton Lincs	50	SK8594
Bo'Ness Cent	82	NT0081
Boarhills Fife	83	NO5613
Boarhunt Hants	11	SU6008
Boarstall Bucks	29	SP6214
Boat of Garten Highld	93	NH9319
Boath Highld	96	NH5774
Bobbing Kent	14	TQ8865
Bobbington Staffs	37	SO8090
Bocking Essex	24	TL7623
Bocking Churchstreet Essex	24	TL7525
Boddam Gramp	95	NK1342
Boddam Shet	103	HU3915
Boddington Gloucs	28	SO8925
Bodedern Gwynd	44	SH3380
Bodelwyddan Clwyd	45	SJ0075
Bodenham H & W	27	SO5350
Bodenham Wilts	10	SU1626

Bodenham Moor H & W	27	SO5450
Bodewryd Gwynd	44	SH4090
Bodfari Clwyd	46	SJ0970
Bodffordd Gwynd	44	SH4277
Bodfuan Gwynd	44	SH3237
Bodham Norfk	43	TG1240
Bodiam E Susx	14	TQ7825
Bodicote Oxon	29	SP4538
Bodinnick Cnwll	3	SX1352
Bodle Street Green E Susx	13	TQ6514
Bodmin Cnwll	3	SX0667
Bodsham Green Kent	15	TR1045
Bodwen Cnwll	3	SX0360
Bogallan Highld	92	NH6350
Bogbrae Gramp	95	NK0335
Boghall Loth	75	NS9867
Boghall Loth	75	NT2465
Boghead Strath	74	NS7742
Boghead Farm Gramp	94	NJ3559
Bogmoor Gramp	94	NJ3563
Bogmuir Gramp	89	NO6471
Bogniebrae Gramp	94	NJ5945
Bognor Regis W Susx	12	SZ9399
Bogroy Highld	93	NH9022
Bogue D & G	65	NX6481
Bohortha Cnwll	3	SW8532
Bohuntine Highld	86	NN2983
Bolam Dur	61	NZ1922
Bolberry Devon	5	SX6939
Boldmere W Mids	38	SP1194
Boldon T & W	69	NZ3461
Boldon Colliery T & W	69	NZ3462
Boldre Hants	10	SZ3198
Boldron Dur	61	NZ0314
Bole Notts	50	SK7987
Bolehill Derbys	49	SK2955
Bolfracks Tays	87	NN8248
Bolham Devon	7	SS9515
Bolham Water Devon	8	ST1612
Bolingey Cnwll	2	SW7653
Bollington Ches	47	SJ7286
Bollington Ches	48	SJ9377
Bolney W Susx	12	TQ2622
Bolnhurst Beds	30	TL0859
Bolshan Tays	89	NO6252
Bolsover Derbys	49	SK4770
Bolsterstone S York	49	SK2696
Boltby N York	62	SE4886
Boltenstone Gramp	94	NJ4110
Bolton Cumb	60	NY6323
Bolton Gt Man	47	SD7108
Bolton Humb	56	SE7752
Bolton Loth	76	NT5070
Bolton Nthumb	68	NU1013
Bolton Abbey N York	55	SE0754
Bolton by Bowland Lancs	54	SD7849
Bolton le Sands Lancs	53	SD4867
Bolton Low Houses Cumb	67	NY2344
Bolton Percy N York	56	SE5341
Bolton Upon Dearne S York	49	SE4502
Bolton-on-Swale N York	61	SE2599
Boltonfellend Cumb	67	NY4768
Boltongate Cumb	58	NY2340
Bolventor Cnwll	3	SX1876
Bomere Heath Shrops	37	SJ4719
Bonar Bridge Highld	97	NH6191
Bonawe Strath	80	NN0131
Bonawe Quarries Strath	80	NN0033
Bonby Humb	56	TA0015
Boncath Dyfed	17	SN2038
Bonchester Bridge Border	67	NT5812
Bondleigh Devon	7	SS6505
Bonds Lancs	53	SD4944
Bonhill Strath	80	NS3979
Boningale Shrops	38	SJ8202
Bonjedward Border	76	NT6522
Bonkle Strath	74	NS8457
Bonnington Kent	15	TR0535
Bonnington Loth	75	NT1269
Bonnington Tays	83	NO5739
Bonnybridge Cent	82	NS8279
Bonnykelly Gramp	95	NJ8653
Bonnyrigg Loth	75	NT3065
Bonnyton Tays	83	NO3338
Bonsall Derbys	49	SK2758
Bonshaw Tower D & G	67	NY2472
Bont-Dolgadfan Powys	35	SH8800
Bontnewydd Dyfed	35	SN6165
Bontnewydd Gwynd	44	SH4859
Bontuchel Clwyd	46	SJ0857
Bonvilston S Glam	18	ST0673
Boode Devon	6	SS5037
Boohay Devon	5	SX8952
Booker Bucks	22	SU8391
Booley Shrops	37	SJ5625
Boon Border	76	NT5745
Boosbeck Cleve	62	NZ6617
Boot Cumb	58	NY1700
Booth Humb	56	SE7326
Booth W York	55	SE0427
Boothby Graffoe Lincs	50	SK9859
Boothby Pagnell Lincs	40	SK9730
Boothstown Gt Man	47	SD7200
Bootle Cumb	58	SD1088
Bootle Mersyd	46	SJ3495
Boraston Shrops	27	SO6169
Bordeaux Guern	101	GN0000
Borden Kent	14	TQ8862
Bordon Hants	11	SU8035
Boreham Essex	24	TL7609
Boreham Wilts	20	ST8944
Boreham Street E Susx	13	TQ6611
Borehamwood Herts	23	TQ1996
Boreland D & G	67	NY1691
Boreraig Highld	90	NG1853
Borgh W Isls	102	NB4055
Borgh W Isls	102	NF6501
Borgie Highld	99	NC6759
Borgue D & G	65	NX6248
Borgue Highld	100	ND1326
Borley Essex	32	TL8443
Borneskitaig Highld	90	NG3770
Borness D & G	65	NX6145
Borough Green Kent	14	TQ6157
Boroughbridge N York	55	SE3966
Borrowash Derbys	39	SK4234
Borrowby N York	62	SE4289
Borrowstoun Cent	82	NS9980
Borstal Kent	14	TQ7366
Borth Dyfed	34	SN6090
Borth-y-Gest Gwynd	44	SH5637
Borthwick Loth	76	NT3659
Borthwickbrae Border	67	NT4113
Borthwickshiels Border	76	NT4315
Borve Highld	90	NG4448
Borve W Isls	102	NB4055
Borve W Isls	102	NF6501
Borve W Isls	102	NG0394

Borwick Lancs	53	SD5272
Bosbury H & W	28	SO6943
Boscastle Cnwll	4	SX0990
Boscombe Dorset	10	SZ1191
Boscombe Wilts	10	SU2038
Bosham W Susx	11	SU8003
Bosherston Dyfed	16	SR9694
Bosley Ches	48	SJ9165
Bosoughan Cnwll	3	SW8760
Bossall N York	56	SE7160
Bossiney Cnwll	4	SX0688
Bossingham Kent	15	TR1548
Bossington Somset	18	SS8947
Bostock Green Ches	47	SJ6769
Boston Lincs	51	TF3343
Boston Spa W York	55	SE4245
Boswinger Cnwll	3	SW9841
Botallack Cnwll	2	SW3732
Botany Bay Gt Lon	23	TQ2999
Botesdale Suffk	32	TM0475
Bothal Nthumb	69	NZ2386
Bothampstead Berks	21	SU5076
Bothamsall Notts	49	SK6773
Bothel Cumb	58	NY1838
Bothenhampton Dorset	8	SY4791
Bothwell Strath	74	NS7058
Botley Bucks	22	SP9802
Botley Hants	11	SU5113
Botley Oxon	29	SP4806
Botolph Claydon Bucks	30	SP7324
Botolphs W Susx	12	TQ1909
Bottesford Humb	56	SE8906
Bottesford Leics	40	SK8038
Bottisham Cambs	31	TL5460
Bottomcraig Fife	83	NO3724
Bottoms W York	54	SD0921
Botusfleming Cnwll	3	SX4061
Botwnnog Gwynd	44	SH2631
Bough Beech Kent	13	TQ4847
Boughrood Powys	26	SO1239
Boughton Nhants	30	SP7565
Boughton Norfk	42	TF7002
Boughton Notts	49	SK6768
Boughton Aluph Kent	15	TR0348
Boughton Green Kent	14	TQ7650
Boughton Lees Kent	15	TR0046
Boughton Malherbe Kent	14	TQ8849
Boughton Monchelsea Kent	14	TQ7749
Boughton Street Kent	15	TR0559
Bouldon Shrops	37	SO5485
Boulmer Nthumb	69	NU2614
Boultham Lincs	50	SK9669
Bourn Cambs	31	TL3256
Bourne Lincs	40	TF0920
Bourne End Beds	30	SP9644
Bourne End Bucks	30	TL0160
Bourne End Bucks	22	SU8987
Bourne End Herts	22	TL0206
Bournebridge Essex	23	TQ5094
Bournebrook W Mids	38	SP0483
Bournemouth Dorset	10	SZ0890
Bournes Green Essex	24	TQ9186
Bournheath H & W	38	SO9574
Bournville W Mids	38	SP0481
Bourton Dorset	9	ST7630
Bourton Oxon	21	SU2386
Bourton Shrops	37	SO5996
Bourton Wilts	20	SU0464
Bourton on Dunsmore Warwks	29	SP4370
Bourton-on-the- Hill Gloucs	29	SP1732
Bourton-on-the-Water Gloucs	28	SP1620
Bousd Strath	78	NM2563
Bouth Cumb	58	SD3285
Bouthwaite N York	55	SE1271
Bovain Cent	81	NN5430
Boveridge Dorset	10	SU0514
Bovey Tracey Devon	5	SX8178
Bovingdon Herts	22	TL0103
Bow Devon	7	SS7201
Bow Gt Lon	23	TQ3683
Bow Ork	103	ND3693
Bow Brickhill Bucks	30	SP9034
Bow of Fife Fife	83	NO3212
Bow Street Dyfed	35	SN6285
Bowbridge Gloucs	28	SO8505
Bowburn Dur	61	NZ3037
Bowcombe IOW	11	SZ4786
Bowd Devon	8	SY1090
Bowden Border	76	NT5530
Bowden Hill Wilts	20	ST9367
Bowdon Gt Man	47	SJ7686
Bower Highld	100	ND2362
Bower's Row N York	55	SE4028
Bowerchalke Wilts	10	SU0223
Bowermadden Highld	100	ND2464
Bowers Staffs	37	SJ8135
Bowers Gifford Essex	24	TQ7588
Bowershall Fife	82	NT0991
Bowes Dur	61	NY9913
Bowgreave Lancs	53	SD4943
Bowhouse D & G	66	NY0165
Bowland Border	76	NT4540
Bowley H & W	27	SO5452
Bowlhead Green Surrey	11	SU9138
Bowling Strath	81	NS4373
Bowling W York	55	SE1731
Bowmanstead Cumb	58	SD3096
Bowmore Strath	70	NR3159
Bowness-on-Solway Cumb	67	NY2262
Bowness-on-Windermere Cumb	59	SD4097
Bowriefauld Tays	89	NO5147
Bowsden Nthumb	77	NT9941
Box Gloucs	20	SO8600
Box Wilts	20	ST8268
Boxford Berks	21	SU4271
Boxford Suffk	32	TL9640
Boxgrove W Susx	11	SU9007
Boxholm Lincs	50	TF0653
Boxley Kent	14	TQ7758
Boxmoor Herts	22	TL0406
Boxted Essex	25	TL9933
Boxted Suffk	32	TL8251
Boxted Cross Essex	25	TM0032
Boxted Heath Essex	25	TM0031
Boxworth Cambs	31	TL3464
Boyden Gate Kent	15	TR2265
Boylestone Derbys	38	SK1835
Boyndie Gramp	94	NJ6463
Boyndlie Gramp	95	NJ9162
Boynton Humb	57	TA1367
Boysack Tays	89	NO6249
Boyton Cnwll	4	SX3292
Boyton Suffk	33	TM3747
Boyton Wilts	20	ST9539
Boyton Cross Essex	24	TL6409
Boyton End Suffk	32	TL7244

Bozeat Nhants	30	SP9058
Brabourne Kent	15	TR1041
Brabourne Lees Kent	15	TR0840
Brabstermire Highld	100	ND3159
Bracadale Highld	84	NG3538
Braceborough Lincs	40	TF0713
Bracebridge Heath Lincs	50	SK9867
Braceby Lincs	40	TF0135
Bracewell Lancs	54	SD8648
Brackenfield Derbys	49	SK3759
Brackenhurst Strath	74	NS7468
Brackletter Highld	86	NN1882
Brackley Nhants	29	SP5837
Bracknell Berks	22	SU8769
Braco Tays	82	NN8309
Bracobrae Gramp	94	NJ5053
Bracon Ash Norfk	43	TM1899
Bracora Highld	85	NM7192
Bracorina Highld	85	NM7292
Bradbourne Derbys	48	SK2052
Bradbury Dur	62	NZ3128
Bradden Nhants	29	SP6448
Bradenham Bucks	22	SU8297
Bradenstoke Wilts	20	SU0079
Bradfield Berks	21	SU6072
Bradfield Devon	7	ST0509
Bradfield Essex	25	TM1430
Bradfield Norfk	43	TG2733
Bradfield S York	49	SK2692
Bradfield Combust Suffk	32	TL8957
Bradfield Green Ches	47	SJ6859
Bradfield Heath Essex	25	TM1430
Bradfield St Clare Suffk	32	TL9057
Bradfield St George Suffk	32	TL9059
Bradford Devon	6	SS4207
Bradford W York	55	SE1632
Bradford Abbas Dorset	9	ST5813
Bradford Leigh Wilts	20	ST8362
Bradford Peverell Dorset	9	SY6593
Bradford-on-Avon Wilts	20	ST8261
Bradford-on-Tone Somset	8	ST1722
Bradiford Devon	6	SS5534
Brading IOW	11	SZ6087
Bradley Derbys	48	SK2246
Bradley H & W	28	SO9860
Bradley Hants	21	SU6341
Bradley Humb	57	TA2406
Bradley Staffs	38	SJ8717
Bradley W Mids	38	SO9595
Bradley Green H & W	28	SO9862
Bradley in the Moors Staffs	48	SK0541
Bradley Stoke Avon	19	ST6181
Bradmore Notts	39	SK5830
Bradninch Devon	7	SS9904
Bradnop Staffs	48	SK0155
Bradpole Dorset	8	SY4894
Bradshaw W York	55	SE0729
Bradstone Devon	4	SX3880
Bradwall Green Ches	47	SJ7563
Bradwell Bucks	30	SP8340
Bradwell Derbys	48	SK1781
Bradwell Essex	24	TL8122
Bradwell Norfk	43	TG5003
Bradwell Waterside Essex	25	TL9907
Bradwell-on-Sea Essex	25	TM0006
Bradworthy Devon	6	SS3214
Brae Highld	93	NH6662
Brae Shet	103	HU3568
Brae Roy Lodge Highld	86	NN3391
Braeface Cent	81	NS7880
Braegrum Tays	82	NO0025
Braehead D & G	64	NX4152
Braehead Strath	75	NS9550
Braehead Tays	89	NO6952
Braelangwell Lodge Highld	96	NH5192
Braemar Gramp	88	NO1591
Braemore Highld	100	ND0829
Braemore Highld	96	NH2079
Braes of Coul Tays	88	NO2857
Braes of Enzie Gramp	94	NJ3957
Braeside Strath	80	NS2374
Braeswick Ork	103	HY6137
Braevallich Strath	80	NM9507
Brafferton Dur	61	NZ2921
Brafferton N York	55	SE4370
Brafield-on-the-Green Nhants	30	SP8258
Bragar W Isls	102	NB2947
Bragbury End Herts	31	TL2621
Braidwood Strath	74	NS8448
Brailsford Derbys	48	SK2541
Braintree Essex	24	TL7523
Braiseworth Suffk	33	TM1371
Braishfield Hants	10	SU3725
Braithwaite Cumb	58	NY2323
Braithwell S York	49	SK5394
Bramber W Susx	12	TQ1810
Bramcote Warwks	39	SP4088
Bramdean Hants	11	SU6128
Bramerton Norfk	43	TG2904
Bramfield Herts	31	TL2915
Bramfield Suffk	33	TM3973
Bramford Suffk	33	TM1246
Bramhall Gt Man	48	SJ8984
Bramham W York	55	SE4242
Bramhope W York	55	SE2543
Bramley Hants	21	SU6458
Bramley S York	49	SK4892
Bramley Surrey	12	TQ0044
Bramley W York	55	SE2435
Bramley Corner Hants	21	SU6359
Bramling Kent	15	TR2256
Brampford Speke Devon	7	SX9298
Brampton Cambs	31	TL2170
Brampton Cumb	39	NY5361
Brampton Cumb	67	NY5361
Brampton Lincs	50	SK8479
Brampton Norfk	43	TG2223
Brampton S York	49	SE4101
Brampton Suffk	33	TM4381
Brampton Abbotts H & W	27	SO6026
Brampton Ash Nhants	27	SP7987
Brampton Bryan H & W	36	SO3772
Brampton-en-le-Morthen S York	49	SK4887
Bramshall Staffs	38	SK0632
Bramshaw Hants	10	SU2615
Bramshott Hants	11	SU8432
Bramwell Somset	8	ST4329
Bran End Essex	24	TL6525
Branault Highld	79	NM5269
Brancaster Norfk	42	TF7743
Brancaster Staithe Norfk	42	TF7944
Brancepeth Dur	61	NZ2237
Branchill Gramp	93	NJ0852
Branderburgh Gramp	94	NJ2371
Brandesburton Humb	57	TA1147
Brandeston Suffk	33	TM2460
Brandiston Norfk	43	TG1421

Brandon
Bucklesham

Brandon Dur 61 NZ2340
Brandon Lincs 50 SK9048
Brandon Suffk 32 TL7886
Brandon Warwks 39 SP4176
Brandon Parva Norfk 42 TG0708
Brandsby N York 56 SE5872
Brandy Wharf Lincs 50 TF0196
Branksome Dorset 10 SZ0492
Branksome Park Dorset 10 SZ0590
Bransbury Hants 21 SU4242
Bransby Lincs 50 SK8978
Branscombe Devon 8 SY1988
Bransford H & W 28 SO7952
Bransgore Hants 10 SZ1897
Bransholme Humb 57 TA1033
Bransley Shrops 37 SO6575
Branston Leics 40 SK8129
Branston Lincs 50 TF0166
Branston Staffs 39 SK2221
Branston Booths Lincs 50 TF0668
Branstone IOW 11 SZ5583
Brant Broughton Lincs 50 SK9154
Brantham Suffk 25 TM1034
Branthwaite Cumb 58 NY0525
Branthwaite Cumb 58 NY2937
Brantingham Humb 56 SE9429
Branton Nthumb 77 NU0416
Branton S York 49 SE6401
Branton Green N York 55 SE4362
Branxton Nthumb 77 NT8937
Brassington Derbys 48 SK2254
Brasted Kent 23 TQ4755
Brasted Chart Kent 13 TQ4653
Brathens Gramp 89 NO6798
Bratoft Lincs 51 TF4764
Brattleby Lincs 50 SK9481
Bratton Wilts 20 ST9152
Bratton Clovelly Devon 4 SX4691
Bratton Fleming Devon 7 SS6437
Bratton Seymour Somset 9 ST6729
Braughing Herts 31 TL3925
Braunston Leics 40 SK8306
Braunston Nhants 29 SP5466
Braunstone Leics 39 SK5502
Braunton Devon 6 SS4836
Brawby N York 63 SE7378
Brawl Highld 99 NC8166
Bray Berks 22 SU9079
Bray Shop Cnwll 4 SX3374
Braybrooke Nhants 40 SP7684
Brayford Devon 7 SS6834
Braythorn N York 55 SE2449
Brayton N York 56 SE6030
Braywick Berks 22 SU8979
Braywoodside Berks 22 SU8775
Breachwood Green Herts 30 TL1522
Breadsall Derbys 49 SK3639
Breadstone Gloucs 20 SO7000
Breage Cnwll 2 SW6128
Breakachy Highld 92 NH4644
Breamore Hants 10 SU1517
Brean Somset 19 ST2956
Breanais W Isls 102 NA9925
Brearton N York 55 SE3261
Breascleit W Isls 102 NB2135
Breasclete W Isls 102 NB2135
Breaston Derbys 39 SK4533
Brechfa Dyfed 17 SN5230
Brechin Tays 89 NO6060
Breckles Norfk 42 TL9594
Breckonside D & G 66 NX8489
Brecon Powys 26 SO0428
Bredbury Gt Man 48 SJ9291
Brede E Susx 14 TQ8218
Bredenbury H & W 27 SO6056
Bredfield Suffk 33 TM2653
Bredgar Kent 14 TQ8860
Bredhurst Kent 14 TQ7962
Bredon H & W 28 SO9236
Bredon's Hardwick H & W 28 SO9135
Bredon's Norton H & W 28 SO9339
Bredwardine H & W 27 SO3344
Breedon on the Hill Leics 39 SK4022
Breich Loth 75 NS9560
Breightmet Gt Man 54 SD7409
Breighton Humb 56 SE7033
Breinton H & W 27 SO4739
Bremhill Wilts 20 ST9773
Brenchley Kent 14 TQ6741
Brendon Devon 18 SS7748
Brenfield Strath 71 NR8482
Brenish W Isls 102 NA9925
Brent Eleigh Suffk 32 TL9448
Brent Knoll Somset 19 ST3350
Brent Mill Devon 5 SX6959
Brent Pelham Herts 31 TL4330
Brentford Gt Lon 23 TQ1777
Brentingby Leics 40 SK7818
Brentwood Essex 24 TQ5993
Brenzett Kent 15 TR0027
Brenzett Green Kent 15 TR0128
Brereton Green Ches 47 SJ7764
Bressingham Norfk 32 TM0780
Bretby Derbys 39 SK2922
Bretford Warwks 39 SP4377
Bretforton H & W 28 SP0944
Bretherdale Head Cumb 59 NY5705
Bretherton Lancs 53 SD4720
Brettabister Shet 103 HU4857
Brettenham Norfk 32 TL9383
Brettenham Suffk 32 TL9654
Bretton Clwyd 46 SJ3563
Brewood Staffs 38 SJ8808
Briantspuddle Dorset 9 SY8193
Brick Houses S York 49 SK3081
Brickendon Herts 23 TL3208
Bricket Wood Herts 22 TL1202
Bricklehampton H & W 28 SO9742
Bride IOM 52 NX4401
Bridekirk Cumb 58 NY1133
Bridestowe Devon 4 SX5189
Brideswell Gramp 94 NJ5738
Bridford Devon 5 SX8186
Bridge Cnwll 2 SW6744
Bridge Kent 15 TR1854
Bridge Hewick N York 55 SE3370
Bridge of Alford Gramp 94 NJ5617
Bridge of Allan Cent 81 NS7997
Bridge of Avon Gramp 94 NJ1835
Bridge of Avon Gramp 93 NJ1520
Bridge of Balgie Tays 87 NN5746
Bridge of Brewlands Tays 88 NO1961
Bridge of Brown Highld 93 NJ1120
Bridge of Cally Tays 88 NO1351
Bridge of Canny Gramp 89 NO6597
Bridge of Craigisla Tays 88 NO2553
Bridge of Dee D & G 65 NX7359
Bridge of Don Gramp 95 NJ9409
Bridge of Dulsie Highld 93 NH9341
Bridge of Dye Gramp 89 NO6586
Bridge of Earn Tays 82 NO1318
Bridge of Ericht Tays 87 NN5258
Bridge of Feugh Gramp 89 NO7094
Bridge of Forss Highld 100 ND0368
Bridge of Gairn Gramp 88 NO3597
Bridge of Gaur Tays 87 NN5056
Bridge of Marnoch Gramp 94 NJ5950
Bridge of Orchy Strath 80 NN2939
Bridge of Tilt Tays 87 NN8765
Bridge of Tynet Gramp 94 NJ3861
Bridge of Walls Shet 103 HU2752
Bridge of Weir Strath 73 NS3965
Bridge of Westfield Highld 100 ND0664
Bridge Sollers H & W 27 SO4142
Bridge Street Suffk 32 TL8749
Bridge Trafford Ches 46 SJ4571
Bridgehampton Somset 9 ST5624
Bridgehill Dur 68 NZ0951
Bridgemary Hants 11 SU5803
Bridgend Border 76 NT5235
Bridgend D & G 66 NT0708
Bridgend Devon 5 SX5548
Bridgend Fife 83 NO3911
Bridgend Gramp 94 NJ3731
Bridgend Gramp 94 NJ5135
Bridgend Loth 75 NT0475
Bridgend M Glam 18 SS9079
Bridgend Strath 70 NR3362
Bridgend Tays 82 NO1224
Bridgend Tays 89 NO5368
Bridgend of Lintrathen Tays 88 NO2854
Bridgerule Devon 6 SS2702
Bridgetown Somset 7 SS9233
Bridgham Norfk 32 TL9685
Bridgnorth Shrops 37 SO7193
Bridgtown Staffs 38 SJ9808
Bridgwater Somset 19 ST2937
Bridlington Humb 57 TA1866
Bridport Dorset 8 SY4692
Bridstow H & W 27 SO5824
Brierfield Lancs 54 SD8436
Brierley Gloucs 27 SO6215
Brierley W York 55 SE4010
Brierley Hill W Mids 38 SO9186
Brig o'Turk Cent 81 NN5306
Brigg Humb 56 TA0007
Briggate Norfk 43 TG3127
Briggswath N York 63 NZ8608
Brigham Cumb 58 NY0830
Brigham Humb 57 TA0753
Brighouse W York 55 SE1422
Brighstone IOW 10 SZ4282
Brighthampton Oxon 21 SP3803
Brightley Devon 6 SX6097
Brightling E Susx 14 TQ6820
Brightlingsea Essex 25 TM0817
Brighton E Susx 12 TQ3104
Brighton le Sands Mersyd 46 SJ3098
Brightons Cent 75 NS9277
Brightwalton Berks 21 SU4279
Brightwell Oxon 21 SU5790
Brightwell Suffk 33 TM2543
Brightwell Baldwin Oxon 21 SU6595
Brightwell Upperton Oxon 21 SU6594
Brignall Dur 61 NZ0712
Brigsley Humb 51 TA2501
Brigsteer Cumb 59 SD4889
Brigstock Nhants 40 SP9485
Brill Bucks 29 SP6513
Brill Cnwll 2 SW7229
Brilley H & W 27 SO2648
Brimfield H & W 27 SO5267
Brimfield Cross H & W 27 SO5368
Brimington Derbys 49 SK4073
Brimley Devon 5 SX8077
Brimpsfield Gloucs 28 SO9312
Brimpton Berks 21 SU5564
Brimscombe Gloucs 20 SO8702
Brimstage Mersyd 46 SJ3082
Brincliffe S York 49 SK3284
Brind Humb 56 SE7430
Brindister Shet 103 HU2857
Brindle Lancs 54 SD5924
Brineton Staffs 37 SJ8013
Bringhurst Leics 40 SP8492
Brington Cambs 30 TL0875
Briningham Norfk 42 TG0434
Brinkhill Lincs 51 TF3773
Brinkley Cambs 32 TL6354
Brinklow Warwks 39 SP4379
Brinkworth Wilts 20 SU0184
Brinscall Lancs 54 SD6221
Brinsley Notts 49 SK4548
Brinsworth S York 49 SK4289
Brinton Norfk 42 TG0335
Brinyan Ork 103 HY4327
Brisley Norfk 42 TF9421
Brislington Avon 19 ST6270
Brissenden Green Kent 14 TQ9439
Bristol Avon 19 ST5972
Briston Norfk 42 TG0632
Britford Wilts 10 SU1627
Brithdir Gwynd 35 SH7618
Brithdir M Glam 18 SO1401
British Legion Village Kent 14 TQ7257
Briton Ferry W Glam 18 SS7394
Britwell Salome Oxon 22 SU6792
Brixham Devon 5 SX9255
Brixton Devon 5 SX5552
Brixton Gt Lon 23 TQ3175
Brixton Deverill Wilts 20 ST8638
Brixworth Nhants 30 SP7470
Brize Norton Oxon 29 SP2907
Broad Alley H & W 28 SO8867
Broad Blunsdon Wilts 20 SU1491
Broad Campden Gloucs 28 SP1537
Broad Carr W York 55 SE0919
Broad Chalke Wilts 10 SU0325
Broad Green Essex 24 TL8823
Broad Green H & W 28 SO7756
Broad Green Suffk 32 TL7859
Broad Haven Dyfed 16 SM8613
Broad Hinton Wilts 20 SU1075
Broad Laying Hants 21 SU4362
Broad Marston H & W 28 SP1446
Broad Oak E Susx 14 TQ8219
Broad Oak H & W 27 SO4821
Broad Oak Kent 15 TR1761
Broad Oak Mersyd 46 SJ5395
Broad Street E Susx 14 TQ8616
Broad Street Kent 15 TR1139
Broad Town Wilts 20 SU0977
Broad's Green Essex 24 TL6912
Broadbridge W Susx 11 SU8105
Broadbridge Heath W Susx 12 TQ1431
Broadclyst Devon 7 SX9897
Broadfield Strath 80 NS3373
Broadford Highld 85 NG6423
Broadford Bridge W Susx 12 TQ0921
Broadgairhill Border 67 NT2010
Broadgrass Green Suffk 32 TL9663
Broadhaugh Border 77 NT8655
Broadheath Gt Man 47 SJ7689
Broadhembury Devon 8 ST1004
Broadhempston Devon 5 SX8066
Broadland Row E Susx 14 TQ8319
Broadley Gramp 94 NJ3961
Broadmayne Dorset 9 SY7286
Broadmoor Dyfed 16 SN0906
Broadoak Dorset 8 SY4396
Broadoak E Susx 13 TQ6022
Broadstairs Kent 15 TR3967
Broadstone Dorset 10 SZ0095
Broadstone Shrops 37 SO5489
Broadwas H & W 28 SO7555
Broadwater Herts 31 TL2422
Broadwater W Susx 12 TQ1404
Broadwaters H & W 38 SO8477
Broadway Dyfed 16 SM8713
Broadway H & W 28 SP0937
Broadway Somset 8 ST3215
Broadwell Gloucs 29 SP2027
Broadwell Oxon 29 SP2504
Broadwell Warwks 29 SP4565
Broadwindsor Dorset 8 ST4302
Broadwood Kelly Devon 7 SS6106
Broadwoodwidger Devon 4 SX4189
Brochel Highld 90 NG5846
Brockamin H & W 28 SO7753
Brockbridge Hants 11 SU6118
Brockdish Norfk 33 TM2179
Brockenhurst Hants 10 SU3002
Brocketsbrae Strath 74 NS8239
Brockford Street Suffk 33 TM1167
Brockhall Nhants 29 SP6362
Brockham Surrey 12 TQ1949
Brockhampton Gloucs 28 SP0322
Brockhampton H & W 27 SO5931
Brockholes W York 55 SE1510
Brocklesby Lincs 57 TA1311
Brockley Avon 19 ST4666
Brockley Suffk 32 TL8371
Brockley Green Suffk 32 TL7247
Brockley Green Suffk 32 TL8254
Brockton Shrops 36 SJ3104
Brockton Shrops 36 SO3285
Brockton Shrops 37 SO5794
Brockton Staffs 37 SJ8131
Brockweir Gwent 19 SO5401
Brockworth Gloucs 28 SO8916
Brocton Staffs 38 SJ9619
Brodick Strath 72 NS0135
Brodie Gramp 93 NH9757
Brodsworth S York 55 SE5007
Brogaig Highld 90 NG4767
Brokenborough Wilts 20 ST9189
Brokerswood Wilts 20 ST8352
Bromborough Mersyd 46 SJ3582
Brome Suffk 33 TM1376
Brome Street Suffk 33 TM1576
Bromeswell Suffk 33 TM3050
Bromfield Cumb 67 NY1746
Bromfield Shrops 37 SO4876
Bromham Beds 30 TL0051
Bromham Wilts 20 ST9665
Bromley Gt Lon 23 TQ4069
Bromley Shrops 37 SO7395
Brompton Kent 14 TQ7668
Brompton N York 62 SE3796
Brompton N York 63 SE9482
Brompton Ralph Somset 8 ST0832
Brompton Regis Somset 7 SS9531
Brompton-on-Swale N York 61 SE2199
Bromsberrow Gloucs 28 SO7433
Bromsberrow Heath Gloucs 28 SO7333
Bromsgrove H & W 28 SO9670
Bromyard H & W 27 SO6554
Bronant Dyfed 35 SN6467
Brongest Dyfed 17 SN3245
Bronington Clwyd 37 SJ4839
Bronllys Powys 26 SO1434
Bronwydd Dyfed 17 SN4123
Bronygarth Shrops 36 SJ2637
Brook Hants 10 SU2714
Brook IOW 10 SZ3983
Brook Kent 15 TR0644
Brook Surrey 12 SU9237
Brook Hill Hants 10 SU2714
Brook Street Essex 24 TQ5793
Brook Street Kent 14 TQ9333
Brook Street Suffk 32 TL8248
Brooke Leics 40 SK8405
Brooke Norfk 43 TM2899
Brookfield Strath 73 NS4164
Brookhampton Hants 11 SU7106
Brookhampton Somset 9 ST6327
Brookhouse Lancs 53 SD5464
Brookhouse S York 49 SK5188
Brookhouse Green Ches 47 SJ8161
Brookhouses Derbys 48 SK0388
Brookland Kent 15 TQ9926
Brooklands Gt Man 47 SJ7890
Brookmans Park Herts 23 TL2404
Brookthorpe Gloucs 28 SO8312
Brookwood Surrey 22 SU9557
Broom Beds 31 TL1742
Broom Dur 62 NZ2441
Broom S York 49 SK4491
Broom Warwks 28 SP0853
Broom Hill H & W 38 SO9175
Broom Hill Notts 49 SK5447
Broom Hill S York 49 SE4102
Broom Street Kent 15 TR0462
Broome H & W 38 SO9078
Broome Norfk 33 TM3591
Broome Shrops 36 SO4080
Broomedge Ches 47 SJ7085
Broomfield Essex 24 TL7010
Broomfield Kent 14 TQ8452
Broomfield Kent 15 TR1966
Broomfield Somset 8 ST2232
Broomfleet Humb 56 SE8727
Broomhaugh Nthumb 68 NZ0261
Broomhill Nthumb 69 NU2401
Brora Highld 97 NC9103
Broseley Shrops 37 SJ6701
Brotherlee Dur 60 NY9237
Brotherton N York 55 SE4825
Brotton Cleve 62 NZ6819
Broubster Highld 100 ND0359
Brough Cumb 60 NY7914
Brough Highld 100 ND2273
Brough Humb 56 SE9326
Brough Notts 50 SK8458
Brough Shet 103 HU5665
Brough Lodge Shet 103 HU5892
Brough Sowerby Cumb 60 NY7912
Broughall Shrops 37 SJ5741
Broughton Border 75 NT1136
Broughton Bucks 30 SP8939
Broughton Cambs 31 TL2878
Broughton Clwyd 46 SJ3363
Broughton Gt Man 47 SD8201
Broughton Hants 10 SU3033
Broughton Humb 56 SE9608
Broughton Lancs 53 SD5234
Broughton N York 54 SD9451
Broughton N York 63 SE7673
Broughton Nhants 30 SP8375
Broughton Oxon 29 SP4138
Broughton S Glam 18 SS9270
Broughton Staffs 37 SJ7634
Broughton Astley Leics 39 SP5292
Broughton Gifford Wilts 20 ST8763
Broughton Green H & W 28 SO9561
Broughton Hackett H & W 28 SO9254
Broughton Mains D & G 65 NX4545
Broughton Mills Cumb 58 SD2290
Broughton Moor Cumb 58 NY0533
Broughton Poggs Oxon 21 SP2303
Broughton-in-Furness Cumb 58 SD2187
Broughty Ferry Tays 83 NO4630
Brown Candover Hants 11 SU5739
Brown Edge Staffs 48 SJ9053
Brownhill Gramp 95 NJ8640
Brownhills Fife 83 NO5215
Brownhills W Mids 38 SK0405
Browninghill Green Hants 21 SU5859
Brownsham Devon 6 SS2826
Brownston Devon 5 SX6952
Broxa N York 63 SE9491
Broxbourne Herts 23 TL3606
Broxburn Loth 75 NT0872
Broxburn Loth 76 NT6977
Broxted Essex 24 TL5727
Broxwood H & W 27 SO3654
Bruan Highld 100 ND3139
Bruar Tays 87 NN8265
Brucefield Highld 97 NH9386
Bruchag Strath 73 NS1157
Bruichladdich Strath 70 NR2661
Bruisyard Suffk 33 TM3266
Bruisyard Street Suffk 33 TM3365
Brumby Humb 56 SE8909
Brund Staffs 48 SK1061
Brundall Norfk 43 TG3308
Brundish Suffk 33 TM2769
Brundish Street Suffk 33 TM2671
Brunthwaite W York 55 SE0546
Bruntingthorpe Leics 39 SP6089
Brunton Fife 83 NO3220
Brunton Nthumb 77 NU2024
Brunton Wilts 21 SU2456
Brushford Somset 7 SS9225
Brushford Barton Devon 7 SS6707
Bruton Somset 9 ST6835
Bryan's Green H & W 28 SO8868
Bryanston Dorset 9 ST8607
Bryant's Bottom Bucks 22 SU8599
Brydekirk D & G 67 NY1870
Brympton Somset 8 ST5115
Bryn W Glam 18 SS8192
Bryn Du Gwynd 44 SH3472
Bryn Gates Lancs 47 SD5901
Bryn Saith Marchog Clwyd 46 SJ0750
Bryn-coch W Glam 18 SS7499
Bryn-henllan Dyfed 16 SN0139
Bryn-mawr Gwynd 44 SH2433
Bryn-y-maen Clwyd 45 SH8376
Brynaman Dyfed 26 SN7114
Brynberian Dyfed 16 SN1035
Bryncir Gwynd 44 SH4844
Bryncroes Gwynd 44 SH2231
Bryncrug Gwynd 35 SH6103
Bryneglwys Clwyd 46 SJ1447
Brynford Clwyd 46 SJ1774
Bryngwran Gwynd 44 SH3577
Bryngwyn Gwent 27 SO3909
Bryngwyn Powys 27 SO1849
Brynhoffnant Dyfed 17 SN3351
Brynmawr Gwent 27 SO1911
Brynmenyn M Glam 18 SS9084
Brynmill W Glam 17 SS6392
Brynna M Glam 18 SS9883
Brynrefail Gwynd 44 SH5562
Brynsadler M Glam 18 ST0280
Brynsiencyn Gwynd 44 SH4867
Bualintur Highld 84 NG4020
Bubbenhall Warwks 39 SP3672
Bubwith Humb 56 SE7136
Buchanan Smithy Cent 81 NS4689
Buchanhaven Gramp 95 NK1247
Buchanty Tays 82 NN9328
Buchany Cent 81 NN7102
Buchlyvie Cent 81 NS5793
Buck's Cross Devon 6 SS3522
Buck's Mills Devon 6 SS3523
Buckabank Cumb 67 NY3749
Buckden Cambs 31 TL1967
Buckden N York 61 SD9477
Buckenham Norfk 43 TG3505
Buckerell Devon 8 ST1200
Buckfast Devon 5 SX7467
Buckfastleigh Devon 5 SX7366
Buckhaven Fife 83 NT3598
Buckholm Border 76 NT4738
Buckholt Gwent 27 SO5016
Buckhorn Weston Dorset 9 ST7524
Buckhurst Hill Essex 23 TQ4194
Buckie Gramp 94 NJ4265
Buckingham Bucks 30 SP6933
Buckland Bucks 30 SP8812
Buckland Devon 5 SX6743
Buckland Gloucs 28 SP0835
Buckland Herts 31 TL3533
Buckland Kent 15 TR3042
Buckland Oxon 21 SU3498
Buckland Surrey 12 TQ2150
Buckland Brewer Devon 6 SS4220
Buckland Common Bucks 22 SP9207
Buckland Dinham Somset 20 ST7551
Buckland Filleigh Devon 6 SS4609
Buckland in the Moor Devon 5 SX7273
Buckland Monachorum Devon 4 SX4968
Buckland Newton Dorset 9 ST6805
Buckland Ripers Dorset 9 SY6582
Buckland St Mary Somset 8 ST2613
Buckland-Tout-Saints Devon 5 SX7645
Bucklebury Berks 21 SU5570
Bucklerheads Tays 83 NO4636
Bucklers Hard Hants 10 SU4000
Bucklesham Suffk 33 TM2441

Buckley Clwyd 46 SJ2763
Bucklow Hill Ches 47 SJ7383
Buckminster Leics 40 SK8722
Bucknall Lincs 50 TF1668
Bucknall Staffs 48 SJ9047
Bucknell Oxon 29 SP5625
Bucknell Shrops 36 SO3574
Buckpool Gramp 94 NJ4165
Bucks Green W Susx 12 TQ0833
Bucks Horn Oak Hants 11 SU8041
Bucksburn Gramp 95 NJ8909
Buckton Humb 57 TA1872
Buckton Nthumb 77 NU0838
Buckworth Cambs 30 TL1476
Budbrooke Warwks 29 SP2665
Budby Notts 49 SK6169
Budd's Titson Cnwll 6 SS2401
Buddon Tays 83 NO5232
Bude Cnwll 6 SS2105
Budge's Shop Cnwll 4 SX3259
Budleigh Salterton Devon 8 SY0682
Budock Water Cnwll 2 SW7831
Buerton Ches 47 SJ6843
Bugbrooke Nhants 30 SP6757
Bugle Cnwll 3 SX0158
Bugley Dorset 9 ST7824
Bugthorpe Humb 56 SE7757
Buildwas Shrops 37 SJ6204
Builth Wells Powys 26 SO0350
Bulbridge Wilts 10 SU0830
Buldoo Highld 100 ND0067
Bulford Wilts 20 SU1643
Bulkeley Ches 46 SJ5354
Bulkington Warwks 39 SP3986
Bulkington Wilts 20 ST9458
Bulkworthy Devon 6 SS3914
Bull's Green Herts 31 TL2717
Bullbrook Berks 22 SU8869
Bullington Hants 21 SU4541
Bullington Lincs 50 TF0877
Bulmer Essex 32 TL8440
Bulmer N York 56 SE6967
Bulmer Tye Essex 24 TL8438
Bulphan Essex 24 TQ6385
Bulwark Gramp 95 NJ9345
Bulwell Notts 49 SK5343
Bulwick Nhants 40 SP9694
Bumble's Green Essex 23 TL4005
Bunacaimb Highld 85 NM6588
Bunarkaig Highld 86 NN1887
Bunbury Ches 47 SJ5657
Bunchrew Highld 92 NH6246
Bundalloch Highld 85 NG8927
Bunessan Strath 78 NM3821
Bungay Suffk 33 TM3389
Bunnahabhainn Strath 70 NR4173
Bunny Notts 39 SK5829
Buntait Highld 92 NH4030
Buntingford Herts 31 TL3629
Bunwell Norfk 33 TM1292
Bunwell Street Norfk 43 TM1193
Burbage Leics 39 SP4492
Burbage Wilts 21 SU2261
Burchett's Green Berks 22 SU8481
Burcombe Wilts 10 SU0730
Burcott Bucks 30 SP8823
Bures Suffk 24 TL9034
Burford H & W 27 SO5868
Burford Oxon 29 SP2512
Burg Strath 78 NM3845
Burgates Hants 11 SU7728
Burgess Hill W Susx 12 TQ3218
Burgh Suffk 33 TM2351
Burgh by Sands Cumb 67 NY3259
Burgh Castle Norfk 43 TG4805
Burgh Heath Surrey 23 TQ2457
Burgh Le Marsh Lincs 51 TF5065
Burgh next Aylsham Norfk 43 TG2125
Burgh St Margaret Norfk 51 TF2186
Burgh St Peter Norfk 43 TM4693
Burghclere Hants 21 SU4761
Burghead Gramp 93 NJ1168
Burghfield Berks 22 SU6668
Burghfield Common Berks 21 SU6566
Burghill H & W 27 SO4844
Burghwallis S York 56 SE5311
Burham Kent 14 TQ7262
Buriton Hants 11 SU7419
Burland Ches 47 SJ6153
Burlawn Cnwll 3 SW9970
Burleigh Berks 22 SU9169
Burleigh Gloucs 20 SO8601
Burlescombe Devon 8 ST0716
Burleston Dorset 9 SY7794
Burley Hants 10 SU2102
Burley Leics 40 SK8810
Burley Gate H & W 27 SO5947
Burley in Wharfedale W York 55 SE1646
Burley Street Hants 10 SU2004
Burley Wood Head W York 55 SE1544
Burleydam Ches 37 SJ6042
Burlingham Green Norfk 43 TG3610
Burlton Shrops 36 SJ4526
Burmarsh Kent 15 TR1032
Burmington Warwks 29 SP2637
Burn N York 56 SE5928
Burn of Cambus Cent 81 NN7102
Burnage Gt Man 47 SJ8692
Burnaston Derbys 39 SK2832
Burnbrae Strath 74 NS8759
Burnby Humb 56 SE8346
Burneside Cumb 59 SD5095
Burneston N York 61 SE3084
Burnett Avon 20 ST6665
Burnfoot Border 67 NT4113
Burnfoot Border 76 NT5116
Burnfoot D & G 66 NX9791
Burnfoot D & G 67 NY3388
Burnfoot D & G 67 NY3996
Burnfoot Tays 82 NN9904
Burnham Bucks 22 SU9282
Burnham Deepdale Norfk 42 TF8044
Burnham Green Herts 31 TL2616
Burnham Market Norfk 42 TF8342
Burnham Norton Norfk 42 TF8343
Burnham Overy Norfk 42 TF8442
Burnham Overy Staithe Norfk 42 TF8444
Burnham Thorpe Norfk 42 TF8541
Burnham-on-Crouch Essex 25 TQ9496
Burnham-on-Sea Somset 19 ST3049
Burnhaven Gramp 95 NK1244
Burnhead D & G 66 NX8695
Burnhervie Gramp 95 NJ7319
Burnhill Green Staffs 37 SJ7800
Burnhope Dur 69 NZ1948
Burnhouse Strath 73 NS3050
Burniston N York 63 TA0193

Burnley Lancs 54 SD8432
Burnmouth Border 77 NT9560
Burnopfield Dur 69 NZ1757
Burnsall N York 55 SE0361
Burnside Fife 82 NO1608
Burnside Fife 75 NT0575
Burnside Gramp 94 NJ1769
Burnside Tays 88 NO4259
Burnside Tays 89 NO5039
Burnside of Duntrune Tays 83 NO4434
Burnt Hill Berks 21 SU5774
Burnt Yates N York 55 SE2561
Burntisland Fife 83 NT2385
Burntwood Staffs 38 SK0509
Burnworthy Somset 8 ST1915
Burpham Surrey 12 TQ0152
Burpham W Susx 12 TQ0308
Burradon Nthumb 68 NT9806
Burrafirth Shet 103 HP6113
Burravoe Shet 103 HU5180
Burrells Cumb 60 NY6718
Burrelton Tays 82 NO2037
Burridge Devon 8 ST3106
Burridge Hants 11 SU5110
Burrill N York 61 SE2387
Burringham Humb 56 SE8309
Burrington Avon 7 SS6416
Burrington Devon 7 SS6416
Burrington H & W 36 SO4472
Burrough Green Cambs 32 TL6355
Burrough on the Hill Leics 40 SK7510
Burrow Lancs 59 SD6174
Burrow Somset 7 SS9342
Burrow Bridge Somset 8 ST3530
Burrowhill Surrey 22 SU9762
Burry Port Dyfed 17 SN4400
Burrygreen W Glam 17 SS4591
Burscough Lancs 53 SD4310
Burscough Bridge Lancs 53 SD4412
Bursea Humb 56 SE8033
Bursledon Hants 11 SU4809
Burslem Staffs 47 SJ8649
Burstall Suffk 33 TM0944
Burstock Dorset 8 ST4202
Burston Norfk 33 TM1383
Burstow Surrey 12 TQ3141
Burstwick Humb 57 TA2227
Burtersett N York 60 SD8989
Burtholme Cumb 67 NY5463
Burthorpe Green Suffk 32 TL7764
Burtoft Lincs 41 TF2635
Burton Ches 46 SJ3174
Burton Ches 46 SJ5063
Burton Dorset 10 SZ1694
Burton Dyfed 16 SM9805
Burton Lincs 50 SK9574
Burton Somset 19 ST1944
Burton Wilts 20 ST8179
Burton Agnes Humb 57 TA1062
Burton Bradstock Dorset 8 SY4889
Burton Coggles Lincs 40 SK9725
Burton End Essex 31 TL5323
Burton Fleming Humb 57 TA0871
Burton Hastings Warwks 39 SP4189
Burton in Lonsdale N York 54 SD6572
Burton Joyce Notts 49 SK6443
Burton Latimer Nhants 30 SP9074
Burton Lazars Leics 40 SK7716
Burton Leonard N York 55 SE3263
Burton on the Wolds Leics 39 SK5821
Burton Overy Leics 39 SP6798
Burton Pedwardine Lincs 50 TF1142
Burton Pidsea Humb 57 TA2431
Burton Salmon N York 55 SE4927
Burton upon Stather Humb 56 SE8717
Burton upon Trent Staffs 39 SK2323
Burton's Green Essex 24 TL8226
Burton-in-Kendal Cumb 59 SD5376
Burtonwood Ches 47 SJ5692
Burwardsley Ches 46 SJ5156
Burwarton Shrops 37 SO6185
Burwash E Susx 14 TQ6724
Burwash Common E Susx 13 TQ6323
Burwash Weald E Susx 13 TQ6523
Burwell Cambs 31 TL5866
Burwell Lincs 51 TF3579
Burwen Gwynd 44 SH4293
Burwick Ork 103 ND4484
Bury Cambs 41 TL2883
Bury Gt Man 54 SD8011
Bury Somset 7 SS9427
Bury W Susx 12 TQ0113
Bury Green Herts 31 TL4521
Bury St Edmunds Suffk 32 TL8564
Burythorpe N York 56 SE7964
Busby Strath 74 NS5756
Buscot Wilts 21 SU2298
Bush Gramp 89 NO7565
Bush Bank H & W 27 SO4551
Bush Hill Park Gt Lon 23 TQ3395
Bushbury W Mids 38 SJ9202
Bushey Herts 22 TQ1395
Bushey Heath Herts 22 TQ1494
Bushley H & W 28 SO8734
Bushton Wilts 20 SU0677
Bussex Somset 8 ST3535
Butcher's Pasture Essex 24 TL6024
Butcombe Avon 19 ST5161
Butleigh Somset 8 ST5233
Butleigh Wootton Somset 8 ST5035
Butlers Marston Warwks 29 SP3250
Butley Suffk 33 TM3650
Buttercrambe N York 56 SE7358
Butterdean Border 76 NT7964
Butterknowle Dur 61 NZ1025
Butterleigh Devon 7 SS9708
Buttermere Cumb 58 NY1717
Buttershaw W York 55 SE1329
Butterstone Tays 88 NO0645
Butterton Staffs 38 SJ8242
Butterton Staffs 48 SK0756
Butterwick Lincs 51 TF3845
Butterwick N York 63 SE7277
Butterwick N York 56 SE9871
Buttington Powys 36 SJ2408
Buttonoak Shrops 37 SO7578
Buxhall Suffk 32 TM0057
Buxted E Susx 13 TQ4923
Buxton Derbys 48 SK0572
Buxton Norfk 43 TG2322
Buxton Heath Norfk 43 TG1821
Bwlch Powys 27 SO1522
Bwlch-y-cibau Powys 36 SJ1717
Bwlch-y-ffridd Powys 36 SO0795
Bwlch-y-groes Dyfed 17 SN2436
Bwlch-y-sarnau Powys 36 SO0374
Bwlchgwyn Clwyd 46 SJ2653
Bwlchllan Dyfed 34 SN5758

Bwlchtocyn Gwynd 34 SH3125
Byers Green Dur 61 NZ2233
Byfield Nhants 29 SP5152
Byfleet Surrey 22 TQ0661
Byford H & W 27 SO3942
Byker T & W 69 NZ2764
Bylchau Clwyd 45 SH9762
Byley Ches 47 SJ7269
Byrewalls Border 76 NT6642
Byrness Nthumb 68 NT7602
Bystock Devon 5 SY0283
Bythorn Cambs 30 TL0575
Byton H & W 27 SO3764
Bywell Nthumb 68 NZ0461
Byworth W Susx 12 SU9821

C

Cabourne Lincs 50 TA1401
Cabrach Gramp 94 NJ3826
Cabrach Strath 70 NR4964
Cabus Lancs 53 SD4948
Cabvie Lodge Highld 92 NH1567
Cadbury Devon 7 SS9105
Cadder Strath 74 NS6072
Caddington Beds 30 TL0619
Caddonfoot Border 76 NT4535
Cade Street E Susx 13 TQ6020
Cadeby Leics 39 SK4202
Cadeby S York 49 SE5100
Cadeleigh Devon 7 SS9108
Cadgwith Cnwll 2 SW7214
Cadham Fife 83 NO2801
Cadishead Gt Man 47 SJ7091
Cadle W Glam 17 SS6296
Cadley Lancs 53 SD5231
Cadley Wilts 21 SU2066
Cadley Wilts 21 SU2453
Cadmore End Bucks 22 SU7892
Cadnam Hants 10 SU3013
Cadney Humb 56 TA0103
Cadoxton S Glam 18 ST1269
Cadoxton Juxta-
Neath W Glam 18 SS7598
Caeathro Gwynd 44 SH5061
Caenby Lincs 50 SK9989
Caeo Dyfed 26 SN6740
Caer Farchell Dyfed 16 SM7927
Caerau M Glam 18 SS8694
Caerau S Glam 18 ST1375
Caergeiliog Gwynd 44 SH3178
Caergwrle Clwyd 46 SJ3057
Caerlanrig Border 67 NT3904
Caerleon Gwent 19 ST3490
Caernarfon Gwynd 44 SH4862
Caerphilly M Glam 19 ST1587
Caersws Powys 36 SO0392
Caerwedros Dyfed 34 SN3755
Caerwent Gwent 19 ST4790
Caerwys Clwyd 46 SJ1272
Cairinis W Isls 102 NF8260
Cairinis W Isls 102 NB2133
Cairnbaan Strath 71 NR8390
Cairnbrogie Gramp 95 NJ8527
Cairnbulg Gramp 95 NK0365
Cairncross Border 77 NT8963
Cairncurran Strath 73 NS3170
Cairndow Strath 80 NN1810
Cairneyhill Fife 82 NT0486
Cairnfield House Gramp 94 NJ4162
Cairngarroch D & G 64 NX0549
Cairngrassie Gramp 89 NO9095
Cairnhall D & G 66 NX9086
Cairnie Gramp 94 NJ4844
Cairnorrie Gramp 95 NJ8641
Cairnryan D & G 64 NX0668
Cairnty Gramp 94 NJ3352
Caister-on-Sea Norfk 43 TG5112
Caistor Lincs 50 TA1101
Caistor St Edmund Norfk 43 TG2303
Calbourne IOW 10 SZ4286
Calcot Clwyd 46 SJ1674
Calcot Gloucs 28 SP0810
Calcot Row Berks 22 SU6771
Calcots Gramp 94 NJ2563
Caldbeck Cumb 58 NY3240
Caldecote Cambs 40 TL1488
Caldecote Cambs 31 TL3456
Caldecote Herts 31 TL2338
Caldecote Highfields Cambs 31 TL3559
Caldecott Leics 40 SP8693
Caldecott Nhants 30 SP9868
Caldecott Oxon 21 SU4996
Calder Bridge Cumb 58 NY0306
Calder Grove W York 55 SE3016
Calder Vale Lancs 53 SD5345
Calderbank Strath 74 NS7663
Caldercruix Strath 74 NS8167
Caldermill Strath 74 NS6641
Caldicot Gwent 19 ST4888
Caldwell N York 61 NZ1613
Calfsound Ork 103 HY5738
Calgary Strath 78 NM3751
Califer Gramp 93 NJ0857
California Cent 74 NS9076
California Derbys 39 SK3335
California Norfk 43 TG5115
Calke Derbys 39 SK3721
Callakille Highld 91 NG6955
Callander Cent 81 NN6207
Callanish W Isls 102 NB2133
Callert Cottage Highld 86 NN1060
Callestick Cnwll 2 SW7750
Calligarry Highld 84 NG6203
Callington Cnwll 4 SX3669
Callow H & W 27 SO4934
Callow End H & W 28 SO8350
Callow Hill Wilts 20 SU0384
Calmore Hants 10 SU3414
Calmsden Gloucs 28 SP0508
Calne Wilts 20 ST9971
Calshot Hants 11 SU4701
Calstock Cnwll 4 SX4368
Calstone Wellington Wilts 20 SU0268
Calthorpe Norfk 43 TG1831
Calthorpe Street Norfk 43 TG4025
Calthwaite Cumb 59 NY4640
Calton N York 54 SD9059
Calton Staffs 48 SK1049
Calveley Ches 47 SJ5958
Calver Derbys 48 SK2374
Calverhall Shrops 37 SJ6037
Calverleigh Devon 7 SS9214
Calverton Bucks 30 SP7939

Calverton Notts 49 SK6149
Calvine Tays 87 NN8065
Calvo Cumb 67 NY1453
Calzeat Border 75 NT1135
Cam Gloucs 20 ST7599
Camas Luinie Highld 85 NG9428
Camaschoirce Highld 79 NM7660
Camasine Highld 79 NM7561
Camastianavaig Highld 84 NG5039
Camasunary Highld 84 NG5118
Camault Muir Highld 92 NH5040
Camber E Susx 15 TQ9618
Camberley Surrey 22 SU8860
Camberwell Gt Lon 23 TQ3276
Camblesforth N York 56 SE6525
Cambo Nthumb 68 NZ0285
Camborne Cnwll 2 SW6440
Cambridge Cambs 31 TL4558
Cambridge Gloucs 20 SO7403
Cambrose Cnwll 2 SW6845
Cambus Cent 82 NS8594
Cambus O' May Gramp 88 NO4198
Cambusavie Platform Highld 97 NH7696
Cambusbarron Cent 81 NS7792
Cambuskenneth Cent 81 NS8094
Cambuslang Strath 74 NS6460
Cambuswallace Strath 75 NT0438
Camden Town Gt Lon 23 TQ2883
Cameley Avon 19 ST6157
Camelford Cnwll 3 SX1083
Camelon Cent 82 NS8680
Camer's Green H & W 28 SO7735
Camerory Highld 93 NJ0131
Camerton Avon 20 ST6857
Camerton Cumb 58 NY0330
Camghouran Tays 87 NN5556
Camieston Border 76 NT5730
Cammachmore Gramp 89 NO9195
Cammeringham Lincs 50 SK9482
Camore Highld 97 NH7889
Campbeltown Strath 72 NR7120
Cample D & G 66 NX8993
Campmuir Tays 82 NO2137
Camps Loth 75 NT0968
Camps End Cambs 31 TL6142
Campsall S York 56 SE5413
Campsie Strath 81 NS6079
Campsie Ash Suffk 33 TM3356
Campton Beds 30 TL1238
Camptown Border 68 NT6813
Camrose Dyfed 16 SM9220
Camserney Tays 87 NN8419
Camster Highld 100 ND2642
Camusnagaul Highld 91 NH0589
Camusnagaul Highld 86 NN0874
Camusteel Highld 91 NG7042
Camusterrach Highld 85 NG7141
Canada Hants 10 SU2818
Candacraig Gramp 88 NO3499
Candlesby Lincs 51 TF4567
Candyburn Strath 75 NT0741
Cane End Oxon 22 SU6979
Canewdon Essex 24 TQ9094
Canford Cliffs Dorset 10 SZ0589
Canford Magna Dorset 10 SZ0398
Canisbay Highld 100 ND3472
Canley W Mids 39 SP3077
Cann Dorset 9 ST8721
Cannich Highld 92 NH3331
Canning Town Gt Lon 23 TQ4081
Cannington Somset 19 ST2539
Cannock Staffs 38 SJ9810
Cannon Bridge H & W 27 SO4340
Canon Frome H & W 27 SO6443
Canon Pyon H & W 27 SO4548
Canonbie D & G 67 NY3976
Canons Ashby Nhants 29 SP5750
Canonstown Cnwll 2 SW5335
Canterbury Kent 15 TR1457
Cantley Norfk 43 TG3704
Cantley S York 49 SE6202
Canton S Glam 19 ST1676
Cantraywood Highld 93 NH7847
Cantsfield Lancs 54 SD6272
Canvey Island Essex 24 TQ7983
Canwick Lincs 50 SK9869
Canworthy Water Cnwll 4 SX2291
Caol Highld 86 NN1175
Caolas Scalpaigh W Isls 102 NG2198
Caoles Strath 78 NM0848
Caonich Highld 86 NN0692
Capel Kent 13 TQ6344
Capel Surrey 12 TQ1740
Capel Bangor Dyfed 35 SN6580
Capel Betws Lleucu Dyfed 34 SN6058
Capel Coch Gwynd 44 SH4682
Capel Curig Gwynd 45 SH7258
Capel Dewi Dyfed 17 SN4720
Capel Dewi Dyfed 17 SN4720
Capel Garmon Gwynd 45 SH8155
Capel Gwynfe Dyfed 26 SN7222
Capel Iwan Dyfed 17 SN2936
Capel le Ferne Kent 15 TR2539
Capel Mawr Gwynd 44 SH4171
Capel Seion Dyfed 35 SN6379
Capel St Andrew Suffk 33 TM3748
Capel St Mary Suffk 25 TM0838
Capel-Dewi Dyfed 35 SN6282
Capelles Guern 101 GN0000
Capelulo Gwynd 45 SH7476
Capenhurst Ches 46 SJ3673
Capheaton Nthumb 68 NZ0380
Caplaw Strath 73 NS4458
Cappercleuch Border 75 NT2423
Capton Devon 5 SX8353
Capton Somset 18 ST0839
Caputh Tays 82 NO0840
Car Colston Notts 49 SK7142
Carbeth Inn Cent 81 NS5279
Carbis Bay Cnwll 2 SW5238
Carbost Highld 84 NG3731
Carbost Highld 90 NG4248
Carbrook S York 49 SK3889
Carbrooke Norfk 42 TF9402
Cardenden Fife 82 NT2195
Cardhu Gramp 94 NJ1943
Cardiff S Glam 19 ST1876
Cardigan Dyfed 17 SN1746
Cardinal's Green Cambs 31 TL6146
Cardington Beds 30 TL0847
Cardington Shrops 37 SO5095
Cardinham Cnwll 3 SX1268
Cardrain D & G 64 NX1231
Cardrona Border 75 NT3036
Cardross Strath 80 NS3477
Cardryne D & G 64 NX1132
Cardurnock Cumb 67 NY1758

Careby

Chieveley

Careby *Lincs* **40** TF0216
Careston *Tays* **89** NO5260
Carew *Dyfed* **16** SN0403
Carew Cheriton *Dyfed* **16** SN0402
Carew Newton *Dyfed* **16** SN0404
Carey *H & W* **27** SO5730
Carfin *Strath* **74** NS7759
Carfraemill *Border* **76** NT5053
Cargate Green *Norfk* **43** TG3912
Cargen *D & G* **66** NX9672
Cargenbridge *D & G* **66** NX9575
Cargill *Tays* **82** NO1536
Cargo *Cumb* **67** NY3659
Cargreen *Cnwll* **4** SX4362
Carham *Nthumb* **76** NT7938
Carhampton *Somset* **7** ST0042
Carharrack *Cnwll* **2** SW7341
Carie *Tays* **87** NN6257
Carinish *W Isls* **102** NF8260
Carisbrooke *IOW* **11** SZ4888
Cark *Cumb* **59** SD3676
Carkeel *Cnwll* **4** SX4160
Carlabhagh *W Isls* **102** NB2043
Carlbury *Dur* **61** NZ2115
Carlby *Lincs* **40** TF0413
Carlcroft *Nthumb* **68** NT8311
Carleen *Cnwll* **2** SW6130
Carleton *N York* **54** SD9749
Carleton Forehoe *Norfk* **43** TG0905
Carleton Rode *Norfk* **43** TM1093
Carleton St Peter *Norfk* **43** TG3402
Carlincraig *Gramp* **95** NJ6743
Carlingcott *Avon* **20** ST6958
Carlisle *Cumb* **67** NY3956
Carlops *Border* **75** NT1656
Carloway *W Isls* **102** NB2043
Carlton *Beds* **30** SP9555
Carlton *Cambs* **32** TL6452
Carlton *Cleve* **62** NZ3921
Carlton *Leics* **39** SK3904
Carlton *N York* **62** NZ5004
Carlton *N York* **61** SE0684
Carlton *N York* **62** SE6086
Carlton *N York* **56** SE6423
Carlton *Notts* **49** SK6041
Carlton *S York* **55** SE3610
Carlton *Suffk* **33** TM3764
Carlton *W York* **55** SE3327
Carlton Colville *Suffk* **33** TM5189
Carlton Curlieu *Leics* **40** SP6997
Carlton Green *Cambs* **32** TL6451
Carlton Husthwaite *N York* **62** SE4976
Carlton in Lindrick *Notts* **49** SK5883
Carlton Miniott *N York* **62** SE3981
Carlton Scroop *Lincs* **50** SK9445
Carlton-le-Moorland *Lincs* **50** SK9058
Carlton-on-Trent *Notts* **50** SK7963
Carluke *Strath* **74** NS8450
Carmacoup *Strath* **74** NS7927
Carmarthen *Dyfed* **17** SN4120
Carmel *Dyfed* **17** SN5816
Carmel *Gwynd* **44** SH4954
Carmichael *Strath* **75** NS9238
Carmunnock *Strath* **74** NS5957
Carmyle *Strath* **74** NS6462
Carmyllie *Tays* **89** NO5442
Carn Brea *Cnwll* **2** SW6841
Carn-gorm *Highld* **85** NG9520
Carnaby *Humb* **57** TA1465
Carnbee *Fife* **83** NO5206
Carnbo *Tays* **82** NO0503
Carndu *Highld* **85** NG8827
Carnduff *Strath* **74** NS6646
Carnell *Strath* **73** NS4731
Carnforth *Lancs* **53** SD4970
Carnhell Green *Cnwll* **2** SW6137
Carnie *Gramp* **89** NJ8005
Carnkie *Cnwll* **2** SW7134
Carno *Powys* **35** SN9696
Carnoch *Highld* **85** NM8696
Carnock *Fife* **82** NT0489
Carnon Downs *Cnwll* **2** SW7940
Carnousie *Gramp* **94** NJ6650
Carnoustie *Tays* **83** NO5534
Carnwath *Strath* **75** NS9846
Carol Green *W Mids* **39** SP2577
Carperby *N York* **61** SE0089
Carr Gate *W York* **55** SE3123
Carr Shield *Nthumb* **68** NY8047
Carradale *Strath* **72** NR8138
Carrbridge *Highld* **93** NH9022
Carrefour *Jersey* **101** JS0000
Carreglefn *Gwynd* **44** SH3889
Carrhouse *Humb* **56** SE7706
Carrick *Strath* **71** NR9086
Carrick Castle *Strath* **80** NS1994
Carriden *Cent* **82** NT0181
Carrington *Gt Man* **47** SJ7492
Carrington *Loth* **75** NT3160
Carrog *Clwyd* **46** SJ1043
Carron *Cent* **82** NS8882
Carron *Gramp* **94** NJ2241
Carron Bridge *Cent* **81** NS7483
Carronbridge *D & G* **66** NX8698
Carronshore *Cent* **82** NS8983
Carruth House *Strath* **73** NS3566
Carrutherstown *D & G* **67** NY1071
Carrville *Dur* **69** NZ3043
Carsaig *Strath* **79** NM5421
Carscreugh *D & G* **64** NX2260
Carse Gray *Tays* **88** NO4553
Carseriggan *D & G* **64** NX3167
Carsethorn *D & G* **66** NX9959
Carshalton *Gt Lon* **23** TQ2764
Carsington *Derbys* **48** SK2553
Carskey *Strath* **72** NR6508
Carsluith *D & G* **65** NX4854
Carsphairn *D & G* **65** NX5693
Carstairs *Strath* **75** NS9345
Carstairs Junction *Strath* **75** NS9545
Carterton *Oxon* **29** SP2806
Carthew *Cnwll* **3** SX0056
Carthorpe *N York* **61** SE3083
Cartland *Strath* **74** NS8646
Cartmel *Cumb* **59** SD3878
Carway *Dyfed* **17** SN4606
Cashe's Green *Gloucs* **28** SO8205
Cassington *Oxon* **29** SP4511
Cassop Colliery *Dur* **62** NZ3438
Castel *Guern* **101** GN0000
Casterton *Lancs* **60** SD6279
Castle Acre *Norfk* **42** TF8115
Castle Ashby *Nhants* **30** SP8659
Castle Bolton *N York* **61** SE0391
Castle Bromwich *W Mids* **38** SP1489
Castle Bytham *Lincs* **40** SK9818
Castle Caereinion *Powys* **36** SJ1605
Castle Camps *Cambs* **32** TL6242
Castle Carrock *Cumb* **67** NY5455
Castle Cary *Somset* **9** ST6432
Castle Combe *Wilts* **20** ST8477
Castle Donington *Leics* **39** SK4427
Castle Douglas *D & G* **65** NX7662
Castle Eaton *Wilts* **20** SU1496
Castle Eden *Dur* **62** NZ4238
Castle Frome *H & W* **28** SO6645
Castle Gresley *Derbys* **39** SK2717
Castle Hedingham *Essex* **24** TL7835
Castle Hill *Suffk* **33** TM1446
Castle Kennedy *D & G* **64** NX1159
Castle Lachlan *Strath* **80** NS0195
Castle O'er *D & G* **67** NY2492
Castle Pulverbatch *Shrops* **36** SJ4202
Castle Rising *Norfk* **42** TF6624
Castle Stuart *Highld* **93** NH7449
Castlebay *W Isls* **102** NL6698
Castlebythe *Dyfed* **16** SN0229
Castlecary *Strath* **81** NS7878
Castlecraig *Highld* **93** NH8269
Castleford *W York* **55** SE4225
Castlehill *Border* **75** NT2135
Castlehill *Highld* **100** ND1968
Castlehill *Strath* **80** NS3875
Castlemartin *Dyfed* **16** SR9198
Castlemorton *H & W* **28** SO7937
Castleside *Dur* **68** NZ0748
Castlethorpe *Bucks* **30** SP8044
Castleton *Border* **67** NY5189
Castleton *Derbys* **48** SK1582
Castleton *Gt Man* **54** SD8810
Castleton *Gwent* **19** ST2583
Castleton *N York* **62** NZ6807
Castletown *Highld* **100** ND1967
Castletown *IOM* **52** SC2667
Castletown *T & W* **69** NZ3658
Castley *N York* **55** SE2646
Caston *Norfk* **42** TL9597
Castor *Cambs* **40** TL1298
Cat's Ash *Gwent* **19** ST3790
Catacol *Strath* **72** NR9149
Catchall *Cnwll* **2** SW4228
Catcliffe *S York* **49** SK4288
Catcomb *Wilts* **20** SU0076
Catcott *Somset* **19** ST3939
Catcott Burtle *Somset* **19** ST4043
Caterham *Surrey* **23** TQ3455
Catfield *Norfk* **43** TG3821
Catfirth *Shet* **103** HU4354
Catford *Gt Lon* **23** TQ3773
Catforth *Lancs* **53** SD4735
Cathcart *Strath* **74** NS5860
Cathedine *Powys* **26** SO1425
Catherington *Hants* **11** SU6914
Catherston Leweston *Dorset* **8** SY3694
Cathpair *Border* **76** NT4646
Catisfield *Hants* **11** SU5506
Catlodge *Highld* **87** NN6392
Catmere End *Essex* **31** TL4939
Catmore *Berks* **21** SU4580
Caton *Lancs* **53** SD5364
Caton Green *Lancs* **53** SD5565
Catrine *Strath* **74** NS5225
Catsfield *E Susx* **14** TQ7213
Catsgore *Somset* **8** ST5025
Catshill *H & W* **38** SO9573
Cattadale *Strath* **72** NR6710
Cattal *N York* **55** SE4454
Cattawade *Suffk* **25** TM1033
Catterall *Lancs* **53** SD4942
Catterick *N York* **61** SE2397
Catterick Bridge *N York* **61** SE2299
Catterlen *Cumb* **59** NY4833
Catterline *Gramp* **89** NO8678
Catterton *N York* **55** SE5145
Catteshall *Surrey* **12** SU9844
Catthorpe *Leics* **39** SP5578
Cattistock *Dorset* **9** SY5999
Catton *Cumb* **68** NY8257
Catton *N York* **62** SE3678
Catton *Norfk* **43** TG2312
Catwick *Humb* **57** TA1345
Catworth *Cambs* **30** TL0873
Caudle Green *Gloucs* **28** SO9410
Caulcott *Oxon* **29** SP5024
Cauldcots *Tays* **89** NO6547
Cauldhame *Cent* **81** NS6493
Cauldmill *Border* **76** NT5315
Cauldon *Staffs* **48** SK0749
Cauldwell *Derbys* **39** SK2517
Caulkerbush *D & G* **66** NX9257
Caulside *D & G* **67** NY4480
Caundle Marsh *Dorset* **9** ST6713
Caunton *Notts* **50** SK7460
Causeway End *D & G* **64** NX4260
Causeway End *Essex* **24** TL6819
Causewayend *Strath* **75** NT0336
Causewayhead *Cent* **81** NS8095
Causey Park *Nthumb* **69** NZ1794
Causeyend *Gramp* **95** NJ9419
Cavendish *Suffk* **32** TL8046
Cavenham *Suffk* **32** TL7670
Caversfield *Oxon* **29** SP5825
Caversham *Berks* **22** SU7274
Caverswall *Staffs* **48** SJ9542
Caverton Mill *Border* **76** NT7425
Cawdor *Highld* **93** NH8450
Cawood *N York* **56** SE5737
Cawsand *Cnwll* **4** SX4350
Cawston *Norfk* **43** TG1323
Cawthorne *S York* **55** SE2808
Caxton *Cambs* **31** TL3058
Caynham *Shrops* **37** SO5573
Caythorpe *Lincs* **50** SK9348
Caythorpe *Notts* **49** SK6845
Cayton *N York* **63** TA0583
Ceann a Bhaigh *W Isls* **102** NF7468
Ceannacroc Lodge *Highld* **92** NH2211
Cearsiadar *W Isls* **102** NB3320
Cefn *Gwent* **19** ST2788
Cefn Cribwr *M Glam* **18** SS8582
Cefn-brith *Clwyd* **45** SH9350
Cefn-mawr *Clwyd* **36** SJ2842
Cefn-y-pant *Dyfed* **17** SN1925
Cefngorwydd *Powys* **26** SN9045
Cellardyke *Fife* **83** NO5704
Cellarhead *Staffs* **48** SJ9547
Cemaes *Gwynd* **44** SH3793
Cemmaes *Powys* **35** SH8406
Cemmaes Road *Powys* **35** SH8104
Cenarth *Dyfed* **17** SN2641
Ceres *Fife* **83** NO4011
Cerne Abbas *Dorset* **9** ST6601
Cerney Wick *Gloucs* **20** SU0796
Cerrigceinwen *Gwynd* **44** SH4274
Cerrigydrudion *Clwyd* **45** SH9548
Ceunant *Gwynd* **44** SH5361
Chaceley *Gloucs* **28** SO8530
Chacewater *Cnwll* **2** SW7544
Chackmore *Bucks* **30** SP6835
Chacombe *Nhants* **29** SP4944
Chadbury *H & W* **28** SP0146
Chadderton *Gt Man* **54** SD9005
Chaddesden *Derbys* **39** SK3836
Chaddesley Corbett *H & W* **38** SO8973
Chaddlehanger *Devon* **4** SX4678
Chaddleworth *Berks* **21** SU4178
Chadlington *Oxon* **29** SP3321
Chadshunt *Warwks* **29** SP3453
Chadwell *Leics* **40** SK7824
Chadwell Heath *Gt Lon* **23** TQ4888
Chadwell St Mary *Essex* **24** TQ6478
Chadwick *H & W* **28** SO8369
Chadwick End *W Mids* **39** SP2073
Chaffcombe *Somset* **8** ST3510
Chagford *Devon* **5** SX7087
Chailey *E Susx* **13** TQ3919
Chainhurst *Kent* **14** TQ7248
Chaldon *Surrey* **23** TQ3155
Chaldon Herring or
East Chaldon *Dorset* **9** SY7983
Chale *IOW* **11** SZ4877
Chale Green *IOW* **11** SZ4879
Chalfont Common *Bucks* **22** TQ0092
Chalfont St Giles *Bucks* **22** SU9893
Chalfont St Peter *Bucks* **22** TQ0090
Chalford *Gloucs* **20** SO8903
Chalford *Wilts* **20** ST8650
Chalgrove *Oxon* **21** SU6396
Chalk *Kent* **14** TQ6773
Chalkwell *Kent* **14** TQ8963
Challacombe *Devon* **7** SS6940
Challock Lees *Kent* **15** TR0050
Chalton *Beds* **30** TL0326
Chalton *Hants* **11** SU7315
Chalvey *Berks* **22** SU9679
Chalvington *E Susx* **13** TQ5109
Chandler's Cross *Herts* **22** TQ0698
Chandler's Ford *Hants* **10** SU4319
Chantry *Somset* **20** ST7146
Chantry *Suffk* **33** TM1443
Chapel *Fife* **83** NT2593
Chapel Allerton *Somset* **19** ST4050
Chapel Allerton *W York* **55** SE3037
Chapel Amble *Cnwll* **3** SW9975
Chapel Brampton *Nhants* **30** SP7266
Chapel Chorlton *Staffs* **37** SJ8137
Chapel Green *Warwks* **29** SP4660
Chapel Haddlesey *N York* **56** SE5826
Chapel Hill *Gramp* **95** NK0635
Chapel Hill *Gwent* **37** SO5399
Chapel Hill *Lincs* **51** TF2054
Chapel Hill *N York* **55** SE3446
Chapel Lawn *Shrops* **36** SO3176
Chapel le Dale *N York* **60** SD7377
Chapel Leigh *Somset* **8** ST1229
Chapel of Garioch *Gramp* **95** NJ7124
Chapel Rossan *D & G* **64** NX1044
Chapel Row *Berks* **21** SU5769
Chapel St Leonards *Lincs* **51** TF5672
Chapel Stile *Cumb* **58** NY3205
Chapel-en-le-Frith *Derbys* **48** SK0580
Chapelend Way *Essex* **32** TL7039
Chapelhall *Strath* **74** NS7862
Chapelhope *Border* **75** NT2318
Chapelknowe *D & G* **67** NY3173
Chapelton *Devon* **6** SS5726
Chapelton *Strath* **74** NS6848
Chapelton *Tays* **89** NO6247
Chapeltown *Gramp* **94** NJ2320
Chapeltown *Lancs* **54** SD7315
Chapeltown *S York* **49** SK3596
Chapmans Well *Devon* **4** SX3593
Chapmanslade *Wilts* **20** ST8247
Chapmore End *Herts* **31** TL3216
Chappel *Essex* **24** TL8928
Chard *Somset* **8** ST3208
Chard Junction *Somset* **8** ST3404
Chardleigh Green *Somset* **8** ST3110
Chardstock *Devon* **8** ST3004
Charfield *Avon* **20** ST7292
Charing *Kent* **14** TQ9549
Charingworth *Gloucs* **29** SP1939
Charlbury *Oxon* **29** SP3519
Charlcombe *Avon* **20** ST7467
Charlcutt *Wilts* **20** ST9875
Charlecote *Warwks* **29** SP2656
Charles *Devon* **7** SS6832
Charles Tye *Suffk* **32** TM0252
Charleston *Tays* **88** NO3845
Charlestown *Cnwll* **3** SX0351
Charlestown *Fife* **82** NT0683
Charlestown *Gramp* **89** NJ9300
Charlestown *Gt Man* **47** SD8100
Charlestown *Highld* **91** NG8174
Charlestown *Highld* **92** NH6448
Charlestown *W York* **54** SD9726
Charlestown *W York* **55** SE1638
Charlesworth *Derbys* **48** SK0092
Charlinch *Somset* **19** ST2338
Charlton *Gt Lon* **23** TQ4178
Charlton *H & W* **28** SP0045
Charlton *Nhants* **29** SP5335
Charlton *Nthumb* **68** NY8184
Charlton *Oxon* **21** SU4088
Charlton *Shrops* **37** SJ5911
Charlton *Somset* **8** ST2926
Charlton *Somset* **20** ST6852
Charlton *W Susx* **11** SU8812
Charlton *Wilts* **9** ST9022
Charlton *Wilts* **20** ST9588
Charlton *Wilts* **20** SU1156
Charlton Abbots *Gloucs* **28** SP0324
Charlton Adam *Somset* **8** ST5328
Charlton Horethorne *Somset* **9** ST6623
Charlton Kings *Gloucs* **28** SO9621
Charlton Mackrell *Somset* **8** ST5328
Charlton Marshall *Dorset* **9** ST9004
Charlton Musgrove *Somset* **9** ST7229
Charlton on the Hill *Dorset* **9** ST8903
Charlton-all-Saints *Wilts* **10** SU1723
Charlton-on-Otmoor *Oxon* **29** SP5616
Charlwood *Hants* **11** SU6731
Charlwood *Surrey* **12** TQ2441
Charminster *Dorset* **9** SY6792
Charmouth *Dorset* **8** SY3693
Charndon *Bucks* **30** SP6724
Charney Bassett *Oxon* **21** SU3894
Charnock Richard *Lancs* **53** SD5515
Charsfield *Suffk* **33** TM2556
Chart Sutton *Kent* **14** TQ8049
Charter Alley *Hants* **21** SU5958
Charterhall *Border* **76** NT7647
Charterhouse *Somset* **19** ST4955
Chartershall *Cent* **81** NS7990
Chartham *Kent* **15** TR1054
Chartham Hatch *Kent* **15** TR1056
Chartridge *Bucks* **22** SP9303
Charwelton *Nhants* **29** SP5356
Chastleton *Oxon* **29** SP2429
Chasty *Devon* **6** SS3402
Chatburn *Lancs* **54** SD7644
Chatcull *Staffs* **37** SJ7934
Chatham *Kent* **14** TQ7567
Chatham Green *Essex* **24** TL7115
Chathill *Nthumb* **77** NU1827
Chattenden *Kent* **14** TQ7572
Chatteris *Cambs* **41** TL3985
Chatterton *Lancs* **54** SD7918
Chattisham *Suffk* **33** TM0942
Chatto *Border* **76** NT7717
Chatton *Nthumb* **77** NU0528
Chawleigh *Devon* **7** SS7112
Chawton *Hants* **11** SU7037
Cheadle *Gt Man* **47** SJ8688
Cheadle *Staffs* **48** SK0043
Cheadle Hulme *Gt Man* **47** SJ8786
Cheam *Gt Lon* **23** TQ2463
Chearsley *Bucks* **22** SP7110
Chebsey *Staffs* **38** SJ8528
Checkendon *Oxon* **22** SU6683
Checkley *Ches* **47** SJ7346
Checkley *Staffs* **48** SK0237
Chedburgh *Suffk* **32** TL7957
Cheddar *Somset* **19** ST4553
Cheddington *Bucks* **30** SP9217
Cheddleton *Staffs* **48** SJ9752
Cheddon Fitzpaine *Somset* **8** ST2427
Chedgrave *Norfk* **43** TM3699
Chedington *Dorset* **8** ST4805
Chediston *Suffk* **33** TM3577
Chedworth *Gloucs* **28** SP0512
Chedzoy *Somset* **19** ST3437
Cheetham Hill *Gt Man* **47** SD8401
Cheetwood *Gt Man* **47** SJ8399
Cheldon *Devon* **7** SS7313
Chelford *Ches* **47** SJ8174
Chellaston *Derbys* **39** SK3730
Chellington *Beds* **30** SP9555
Chelmarsh *Shrops* **37** SO7288
Chelmondiston *Suffk* **25** TM2037
Chelmorton *Derbys* **48** SK1169
Chelmsford *Essex* **24** TL7007
Chelmsley Wood *W Mids* **38** SP1887
Chelsea *Gt Lon* **23** TQ2778
Chelsfield *Gt Lon* **23** TQ4864
Chelsworth *Suffk* **32** TL9748
Cheltenham *Gloucs* **28** SO9422
Chelveston *Nhants* **30** SP9969
Chelvey *Avon* **19** ST4668
Chelwood *Avon* **19** ST6361
Chelwood Gate *E Susx* **13** TQ4130
Chelworth Lower
Green *Wilts* **20** SU0892
Chelworth Upper
Green *Wilts* **20** SU0893
Cheney Longville *Shrops* **36** SO4284
Chenies *Bucks* **22** TQ0198
Chepstow *Gwent* **19** ST5393
Cherhill *Wilts* **20** SU0370
Cherington *Gloucs* **20** ST9098
Cherington *Warwks* **29** SP2936
Cheriton *Hants* **11** SU5828
Cheriton *Kent* **15** TR2037
Cheriton *W Glam* **17** SS4593
Cheriton Bishop *Devon* **5** SX7793
Cheriton Fitzpaine *Devon* **7** SS8606
Cheriton or
Stackpole Elidor *Dyfed* **16** SR9897
Cherrington *Shrops* **37** SJ6619
Cherry Burton *Humb* **56** SE9841
Cherry Hinton *Cambs* **31** TL4856
Cherry Orchard *H & W* **28** SO8553
Cherry Willingham *Lincs* **50** TF0272
Chertsey *Surrey* **22** TQ0466
Cheselbourne *Dorset* **9** SY7699
Chesham *Bucks* **22** SP9601
Chesham *Gt Man* **54** SD8012
Chesham Bois *Bucks* **22** SU9699
Cheshunt *Herts* **23** TL3502
Cheslyn Hay *Staffs* **38** SJ9707
Chessetts Wood *Warwks* **38** SP1873
Chessington *Surrey* **23** TQ1863
Chester *Ches* **46** SJ4066
Chester Moor *Dur* **69** NZ2649
Chester-le-Street *Dur* **69** NZ2751
Chesterblade *Somset* **20** ST6641
Chesterfield *Derbys* **49** SK3871
Chesterfield *Staffs* **38** SK0905
Chesterhill *Loth* **76** NT3764
Chesters *Border* **76** NT6022
Chesters *Border* **68** NT6210
Chesterton *Cambs* **40** TL1295
Chesterton *Cambs* **31** TL4660
Chesterton *Gloucs* **20** SP0100
Chesterton *Oxon* **29** SP5621
Chesterton *Shrops* **37** SO7897
Chesterton Green *Warwks* **29** SP3558
Chesterwood *Nthumb* **68** NY8364
Chestfield *Kent* **15** TR1365
Cheston *Devon* **5** SX6858
Cheswardine *Shrops* **37** SJ7130
Cheswick *Nthumb* **77** NU0346
Chetnole *Dorset* **9** ST6008
Chettisham *Cambs* **41** TL5483
Chettle *Dorset* **9** ST9513
Chetton *Shrops* **37** SO6690
Chetwode *Bucks* **29** SP6429
Chetwynd *Shrops* **37** SJ7321
Chetwynd Aston *Shrops* **37** SJ7517
Cheveley *Cambs* **32** TL6861
Chevening *Kent* **23** TQ4857
Chevington *Suffk* **32** TL7859
Chevington Drift *Nthumb* **69** NZ2598
Chevithorne *Devon* **7** SS9715
Chew Magna *Avon* **19** ST5763
Chew Stoke *Avon* **19** ST5561
Chewton Keynsham *Avon* **19** ST6566
Chewton Mendip *Somset* **19** ST5953
Chicheley *Bucks* **30** SP9046
Chichester *W Susx* **11** SU8604
Chickerell *Dorset* **9** SY6480
Chicklade *Wilts* **9** ST9134
Chidden *Hants* **11** SU6517
Chiddingfold *Surrey* **12** SU9635
Chiddingly *E Susx* **13** TQ5414
Chiddingstone *Kent* **13** TQ5045
Chiddingstone
Causeway *Kent* **13** TQ5246
Chideock *Dorset* **8** SY4292
Chidham *W Susx* **11** SU7903
Chidswell *W York* **55** SE2623
Chieveley *Berks* **21** SU4774

Chignall Smealy Essex 24 TL6611
Chignall St James Essex 24 TL6610
Chigwell Essex 23 TQ4494
Chigwell Row Essex 23 TQ4693
Chilbolton Hants 21 SU3940
Chilcomb Hants 11 SU5028
Chilcombe Dorset 8 SY5291
Chilcompton Somset 19 ST6451
Chilcote Leics 39 SK2811
Child Okeford Dorset 9 ST8312
Child's Ercall Shrops 37 SJ6625
Childer Thornton Ches 46 SJ3677
Childrey Oxon 21 SU3687
Childswickham H & W 28 SP0738
Childwall Mersyd 46 SJ4189
Childwick Green Herts 22 TL1410
Chilfrome Dorset 9 SY5898
Chilgrove W Susx 11 SU8314
Chilham Kent 15 TR0653
Chillaton Devon 4 SX4381
Chillenden Kent 15 TR2753
Chillerton IOW 11 SZ4883
Chillesford Suffk 33 TM3852
Chillingham Nthumb 77 NU0525
Chillington Devon 5 SX7942
Chillington Somset 8 ST3811
Chilmark Wilts 9 ST9732
Chilmington Green Kent 15 TQ9840
Chilson Oxon 29 SP3119
Chilsworthy Cnwll 4 SX4172
Chilsworthy Devon 6 SS3206
Chilthorne Domer Somset 8 ST5219
Chilton Bucks 22 SP6811
Chilton Dur 61 NZ2829
Chilton Oxon 21 SU4885
Chilton Candover Hants 21 SU5940
Chilton Cantelo Somset 9 ST5722
Chilton Foliat Wilts 21 SU3170
Chilton Polden Somset 19 ST3740
Chilton Street Suffk 32 TL7546
Chilton Trinity Somset 19 ST2939
Chilwell Notts 39 SK5135
Chilworth Hants 10 SU4018
Chimney Oxon 21 SP3501
Chineham Hants 21 SU6555
Chingford Gt Lon 23 TQ3894
Chinley Derbys 48 SK0482
Chinnor Oxon 22 SP7501
Chipnall Shrops 37 SJ7231
Chippenham Cambs 32 TL6669
Chippenham Wilts 20 ST9173
Chipperfield Herts 22 TL0401
Chipping Herts 31 TL3531
Chipping Lancs 54 SD6243
Chipping Campden Gloucs 28 SP1539
Chipping Norton Oxon 29 SP3127
Chipping Ongar Essex 24 TL5503
Chipping Sodbury Avon 20 ST7282
Chipping Warden Nhants 29 SP4948
Chipstable Somset 7 ST0427
Chipstead Kent 23 TQ5056
Chipstead Surrey 23 TQ2756
Chirbury Shrops 36 SO2698
Chirk Clwyd 36 SJ2837
Chirnside Border 77 NT8756
Chirnsidebridge Border 77 NT8556
Chirton Wilts 20 SU0757
Chisbury Wilts 21 SU2766
Chiselborough Somset 8 ST4614
Chiseldon Wilts 21 SU1880
Chisholme Border 67 NT4112
Chislehampton Oxon 21 SU5999
Chislehurst Gt Lon 23 TQ4470
Chislet Kent 15 TR2264
Chisley W York 54 SE0028
Chiswellgreen Herts 22 TL1304
Chiswick Gt Lon 23 TQ2078
Chisworth Derbys 48 SJ9991
Chithurst W Susx 11 SU8423
Chittering Cambs 31 TL4969
Chitterne Wilts 20 ST9843
Chittlehamholt Devon 7 SS6520
Chittlehampton Devon 7 SS6325
Chittlehampton Devon 7 SS6511
Chittoe Wilts 20 ST9566
Chivelstone Devon 5 SX7838
Chlenry D & G 64 NX1260
Chobham Surrey 22 SU9762
Cholderton Wilts 21 SU2242
Cholesbury Bucks 22 SP9307
Chollerton Nthumb 68 NY9732
Cholsey Oxon 21 SU5886
Cholstrey H & W 27 SO4659
Chop Gate N York 62 SE5599
Choppington Nthumb 69 NZ2484
Chopwell T & W 69 NZ1158
Chorley Ches 47 SJ5751
Chorley Lancs 54 SD5817
Chorley Shrops 36 SO6983
Chorleywood Herts 22 TQ0396
Chorleywood West Herts 22 TQ0396
Chorlton Ches 47 SJ7250
Chorlton Lane Ches 46 SJ4547
Chorlton-cum-Hardy Gt Man 47 SJ8193
Choulton Shrops 36 SO3788
Chowley Ches 46 SJ4756
Chrishall Essex 31 TL4439
Chrisswell Strath 80 NS2274
Christchurch Cambs 41 TL4996
Christchurch Dorset 10 SZ1592
Christchurch Gwent 14 ST3489
Christian Malford Wilts 20 ST9678
Christleton Ches 46 SJ4465
Christmas Common Oxon 22 SU7193
Christon Avon 19 ST3757
Christon Bank Nthumb 77 NU2123
Christow Devon 5 SX8385
Chudleigh Devon 5 SX8679
Chudleigh Knighton Devon 5 SX8477
Chulmleigh Devon 7 SS6814
Church Lancs 54 SD7429
Church Ashton Shrops 37 SJ7317
Church Brampton Nhants 30 SP7165
Church Broughton Derbys 39 SK2033
Church Crookham Hants 22 SU8051
Church Eaton Staffs 38 SJ8417
Church End Beds 31 TL1937
Church End Essex 24 TL7228
Church End Gt Lon 23 TQ2490
Church End Hants 22 SU6756
Church Enstone Oxon 29 SP3725
Church Fenton N York 55 SE5136
Church Green Devon 8 SY1796
Church Hanborough Oxon 29 SP4213
Church Hill Ches 47 SJ6465
Church Houses N York 62 SE6697
Church Knowle Dorset 9 SY9481

Church Langton Leics 40 SP7293
Church Lawford Warwks 39 SP4576
Church Lawton Staffs 47 SJ8255
Church Leigh Staffs 38 SK0235
Church Lench H & W 28 SP0251
Church Mayfield Staffs 48 SK1544
Church Minshull Ches 47 SJ6660
Church Norton W Susx 11 SZ8795
Church Preen Shrops 37 SO5498
Church Pulverbatch Shrops 36 SJ4303
Church Stoke Powys 36 SO2794
Church Stowe Nhants 29 SP6357
Church Street Kent 14 TQ7174
Church Stretton Shrops 36 SO4593
Church Village M Glam 18 ST0885
Church Warsop Notts 49 SK5668
Churcham Gloucs 28 SO7618
Churchdown Gloucs 28 SO8819
Churchend Essex 25 TR0093
Churchfield W Mids 38 SP0197
Churchill Avon 19 ST4459
Churchill Devon 8 ST2902
Churchill H & W 38 SO8879
Churchill H & W 28 SO9253
Churchill Oxon 29 SP2824
Churchinford Devon 8 ST2112
Churchover Warwks 39 SP5180
Churchstanton Somset 8 ST1914
Churchstow Devon 5 SX7145
Churchtown Derbys 49 SK2662
Churchtown Lancs 53 SD4843
Churston Ferrers Devon 5 SX9056
Churt Surrey 11 SU8538
Churton Ches 46 SJ4156
Churwell W York 55 SE2729
Chwilog Gwynd 44 SH4338
Chyandour Cnwll 2 SW4731
Cilcain Clwyd 46 SJ1765
Cilcennin Dyfed 34 SN5260
Cilfrew W Glam 18 SN7700
Cilfynydd M Glam 18 ST0891
Cilgerran Dyfed 17 SN1942
Cilgwyn Dyfed 26 SN7429
Cilmaengwyn W Glam 26 SN7405
Cilmery Powys 26 SO0051
Cilrhedyn Dyfed 17 SN2834
Cilsan Dyfed 17 SN5922
Ciltalgarth Gwynd 45 SH8940
Cilycwm Dyfed 26 SN7539
Cimla W Glam 18 SS7696
Cinderford Gloucs 27 SO6514
Cippenham Bucks 22 SU9480
Cirencester Gloucs 20 SP0201
City Gt Lon 23 TQ3281
Clabhach Strath 78 NM1858
Clachaig Strath 80 NS1181
Clachan Highld 84 NG5436
Clachan Strath 79 NM7819
Clachan Strath 79 NM8543
Clachan Strath 71 NR7556
Clachan Mor Strath 78 NL9847
Clachan na Luib W Isls 102 NF8163
Clachan-a-Luib W Isls 102 NF8163
Clachan-Seil Strath 79 NM7718
Clachaneasy D & G 64 NX3574
Clachnaharry Highld 92 NH6446
Clachtoll Highld 98 NC0427
Clackavoid Tays 88 NO1463
Clackmannan Cent 82 NS9191
Clackmarass Gramp 94 NJ2458
Clacton-on-Sea Essex 25 TM1715
Cladich Highld 80 NN0921
Cladswell H & W 28 SP0558
Claggan Highld 79 NM7049
Claigan Highld 90 NG2354
Clanfield Hants 11 SU6916
Clanfield Oxon 21 SP2801
Clanville Hants 21 SU3148
Clanville Somset 9 ST6233
Claonaig Strath 71 NR8656
Clapgate Herts 31 TL4424
Clapham Beds 30 TL0352
Clapham Gt Lon 23 TQ2975
Clapham N York 54 SD7469
Clapham W Susx 12 TQ0906
Clapton Somset 8 ST4106
Clapton Somset 19 ST6453
Clapton-in-Gordano Avon 19 ST4773
Clapton-on-the-Hill Gloucs 28 SP1617
Claravale T & W 69 NZ1364
Clarbeston Dyfed 16 SN0521
Clarbeston Road Dyfed 16 SN0121
Clarborough Notts 50 SK7383
Clare Suffk 32 TL7745
Clarebrand D & G 65 NX7665
Clarencefield D & G 67 NY0968
Clarewood Nthumb 68 NZ0169
Clarilaw Border 76 NT5218
Clarkston Strath 74 NS5757
Clashmore Highld 98 NC0331
Clashmore Highld 97 NH7489
Clashnessie Highld 98 NC0530
Clashnoir Gramp 94 NJ2222
Clathy Tays 82 NN9920
Clathymore Tays 82 NO0121
Clatt Gramp 94 NJ5326
Clatter Powys 35 SN9994
Clatworthy Somset 7 ST0531
Claughton Lancs 53 SD5342
Claughton Lancs 53 SD5566
Claughton Mersyd 46 SJ3088
Claverdon Warwks 29 SP1965
Claverham Avon 19 ST4566
Clavering Essex 31 TL4731
Claverley Shrops 37 SO7993
Claverton Avon 20 ST7864
Clawdd-coch S Glam 18 ST0577
Clawdd-newydd Clwyd 46 SJ0852
Clawton Devon 6 SX3599
Claxby Lincs 50 TF1194
Claxton N York 56 SE6959
Claxton Norfk 43 TG3303
Clay Coton Nhants 39 SP5976
Clay Cross Derbys 49 SK3663
Clay End Herts 31 TL3024
Claybrooke Magna Leics 39 SP4988
Claydon Oxon 29 SP4549
Claydon Suffk 33 TM1349
Claygate D & G 67 NY3979
Claygate Kent 14 TQ7144
Claygate Surrey 22 TQ1563
Clayhall Surrey 23 TQ1960
Clayhanger Devon 7 ST0222
Clayhidon Devon 8 ST1615
Clayhill E Susx 14 TQ8323
Clayock Highld 100 ND1659
Claypits Gloucs 28 SO7606
Claypole Lincs 50 SK8449

Clayton S York 55 SE4507
Clayton W York 12 TQ2914
Clayton W York 55 SE1231
Clayton West W York 55 SE2510
Clayton-le-Moors Lancs 54 SD7530
Clayton-le-Woods Lancs 53 SD5622
Clayworth Notts 50 SK7387
Cleadale Highld 84 NM4789
Cleadon T & W 69 NZ3862
Clearbrook Devon 4 SX5255
Clearwell Gloucs 27 SO5608
Cleasby N York 61 NZ2512
Cleat Ork 103 ND4584
Cleatlam Dur 61 NZ1118
Cleator Cumb 58 NY0113
Cleator Moor Cumb 58 NY0115
Cleckheaton W York 55 SE1825
Clee St Margaret Shrops 37 SO5684
Cleehill Shrops 37 SO5975
Cleekhimin Strath 74 NS7658
Cleethorpes Humb 57 TA3008
Cleeton St Mary Shrops 37 SO6178
Cleeve Avon 19 ST4666
Cleeve Oxon 21 SU6081
Cleeve Hill Gloucs 28 SO9827
Cleeve Prior H & W 28 SP0849
Cleghornie Loth 83 NT5983
Clehonger H & W 27 SO4637
Cleish Tays 82 NT0998
Cleland Strath 74 NS7958
Clenamacrie Strath 80 NM9228
Clenchwarton Norfk 41 TF5920
Clent H & W 38 SO9279
Clenterty Gramp 95 NJ7760
Cleobury Mortimer Shrops 37 SO6775
Cleobury North Shrops 37 SO6286
Cleongart Strath 72 NR6734
Clephanton Highld 93 NH8150
Clerkhill D & G 67 NY2697
Cleuch-head D & G 66 NS8200
Clevancy Wilts 20 SU0575
Clevedon Avon 19 ST4171
Cleveleys Lancs 53 SD3143
Cleverton Wilts 20 ST9785
Clewer Somset 19 ST4351
Cley next the Sea Norfk 42 TG0444
Cliburn Cumb 59 NY5824
Cliddesden Hants 21 SU6349
Cliff End E Susx 14 TQ8813
Cliffe Dur 61 NZ2115
Cliffe Kent 14 TQ7376
Cliffe N York 56 SE6631
Clifford H & W 27 SO2445
Clifford W York 55 SE4344
Clifford Chambers Warwks 29 SP1952
Clifford's Mesne Gloucs 28 SO7023
Clifton Avon 19 ST5773
Clifton Beds 31 TL1639
Clifton Cent 80 NN3231
Clifton Cumb 59 NY5326
Clifton Derbys 48 SK1644
Clifton H & W 28 SO8446
Clifton Lancs 53 SD4630
Clifton N York 56 SE5953
Clifton Notts 39 SK5434
Clifton Oxon 29 SP4931
Clifton S York 49 SK4980
Clifton W York 55 SE1622
Clifton W York 55 SE1948
Clifton Campville Staffs 39 SK2510
Clifton Hampden Oxon 21 SU5495
Clifton Reynes Bucks 30 SP9051
Clifton upon
Dunsmore Warwks 39 SP5376
Clifton upon Teme H & W 28 SO7161
Cliftonville Kent 15 TR3771
Climping W Susx 12 SU9902
Clink Somset 20 ST7948
Clint N York 55 SE2659
Clint Green Norfk 42 TG0210
Clinterty Gramp 95 NJ8311
Clintmains Border 76 NT6132
Clippesby Norfk 43 TG4214
Clipsham Leics 40 SK9716
Clipston Nhants 40 SP7181
Clipston Notts 39 SK6334
Clipstone Beds 30 SP9426
Clipstone Notts 49 SK5963
Clitheroe Lancs 54 SD7441
Clive Shrops 37 SJ5124
Clixby Lincs 51 TA0904
Cloatley Wilts 20 ST9890
Clocaenog Clwyd 46 SJ0854
Clochan Gramp 94 NJ4060
Clochtow Tays 89 NO4852
Clodock H & W 27 SO3227
Clola Gramp 95 NK0043
Clophill Beds 30 TL0838
Clopton Nhants 40 TL0680
Clopton Suffk 33 TM2253
Clopton Corner Suffk 33 TM2254
Clos du Valle Guern 101 GN0000
Closeburn D & G 66 NX8992
Closeburnmill D & G 66 NX9094
Closworth Somset 9 ST5610
Clothall Herts 31 TL2731
Clotton Ches 46 SJ5264
Clough Foot W York 54 SD9123
Clough Head W York 55 SE0918
Cloughton N York 63 TA0194
Clousta Shet 103 HU3057
Clova Tays 88 NO3273
Clovelly Devon 6 SS3124
Clovenfords Border 76 NT4536
Clovulin Highld 86 NN0063
Clow Bridge Lancs 54 SD8228
Clowne Derbys 49 SK4875
Clows Top H & W 37 SO7172
Cluanie Inn Highld 85 NH0711
Cluanie Lodge Highld 85 NH0910
Clugston D & G 64 NX3557
Clun Shrops 36 SO3080
Clunas Highld 93 NH8846
Clunbury Shrops 36 SO3780
Clune Highld 93 NH7925
Clunes Highld 86 NN1988
Clungunford Shrops 36 SO3978
Clunie Gramp 94 NJ6350
Clunie Tays 88 NO1043
Clunton Shrops 36 SO3381
Clutton Avon 19 ST6259
Clutton Ches 46 SJ4654
Clutton Hill Avon 19 ST6359
Clydach Gwent 27 SO2213
Clydach W Glam 18 SN6800
Clydach Vale M Glam 18 SS9792
Clydebank Strath 74 NS4970
Clydey Dyfed 17 SN2535

Clyffe Pypard Wilts 20 SU0777
Clynder Strath 80 NS2484
Clynderwen Dyfed 16 SN1219
Clyne W Glam 18 SN8000
Clynnog-fawr Gwynd 44 SH4149
Clyro Powys 27 SO2143
Clyst Honiton Devon 5 SX9893
Clyst Hydon Devon 7 ST0301
Clyst St George Devon 5 SX9888
Clyst St Lawrence Devon 7 ST0200
Clyst St Mary Devon 5 SX9791
Cnoc W Isls 102 NB4931
Cnwch Coch Dyfed 35 SN6774
Coad's Green Cnwll 4 SX2976
Coalburn Strath 74 NS8134
Coalburns T & W 69 NZ1260
Coaley Gloucs 20 SO7701
Coalhill Essex 24 TQ7597
Coalpit Heath Avon 20 ST6780
Coalport Shrops 37 SJ6902
Coalsnaughton Cent 82 NS9195
Coaltown of Balgonie Fife 83 NT2999
Coaltown of Wemyss Fife 83 NT3295
Coalville Leics 39 SK4214
Coanwood Nthumb 68 NY6859
Coat Somset 8 ST4520
Coatbridge Strath 74 NS7365
Coatdyke Strath 74 NS7465
Coate Wilts 20 SU0462
Coate Wilts 21 SU1882
Coates Cambs 41 TL3097
Coates Gloucs 20 SO9701
Coates Lincs 50 SK9083
Coates W Susx 12 SU9917
Cobbaton Devon 7 SS6126
Coberley Gloucs 28 SO9616
Cobham Kent 14 TQ6768
Cobham Surrey 22 TQ1060
Cobnash H & W 27 SO4560
Cobo Guern 101 GN0000
Coburby Gramp 95 NJ9164
Cock Bridge Gramp 94 NJ2509
Cock Clarks Essex 24 TL8102
Cock Green Essex 24 TL6919
Cock Marling E Susx 14 TQ8718
Cockayne Hatley Beds 31 TL2649
Cockburnspath Border 76 NT7770
Cockenzie and
Port Seton Loth 76 NT4075
Cockerham Lancs 53 SD4651
Cockermouth Cumb 58 NY1230
Cockernhoe Green Herts 30 TL1223
Cockett W Glam 17 SS6394
Cockfield Dur 61 NZ1224
Cockfield Suffk 32 TL9054
Cockfosters Gt Lon 23 TQ2796
Cocking W Susx 11 SU8717
Cocking Causeway W Susx 11 SU8819
Cockington Devon 5 SX8963
Cocklake Somset 19 ST4449
Cockle Park Nthumb 69 NZ2091
Cockley Beck Cumb 58 NY2501
Cockley Cley Norfk 42 TF7904
Cockpole Green Berks 22 SU7981
Cockshutt Shrops 36 SJ4328
Cockthorpe Norfk 42 TF9842
Cockwood Devon 5 SX9780
Cockyard Derbys 48 SK0479
Coddenham Suffk 33 TM1354
Coddington H & W 28 SO7142
Coddington Notts 50 SK8354
Codford St Mary Wilts 20 ST9739
Codford St Peter Wilts 20 ST9639
Codicote Herts 31 TL2118
Codmore Hill W Susx 12 TQ0520
Codnor Derbys 49 SK4149
Codrington Avon 20 ST7278
Codsall Staffs 38 SJ8603
Codsall Wood Staffs 38 SJ8404
Coed Talon Clwyd 46 SJ2659
Coed-y-paen Gwent 19 ST3398
Coedana Gwynd 44 SH4382
Coedpoeth Clwyd 46 SJ2851
Coffinswell Devon 5 SX8968
Cofton Hackett H & W 38 SP0075
Cogan S Glam 19 ST1771
Cogenhoe Nhants 30 SP8260
Coggeshall Essex 24 TL8522
Coignafearn Highld 93 NH7018
Coilacriech Gramp 88 NO3296
Coilantogle Cent 81 NN5907
Coillore Highld 84 NG3537
Coiltry Highld 86 NH3506
Coity M Glam 18 SS9281
Col W Isls 102 NB4739
Colaboll Highld 96 NC5610
Colan Cnwll 3 SW8661
Colaton Raleigh Devon 8 SY0787
Colbost Highld 90 NG2148
Colburn N York 61 SE1999
Colby Cumb 60 NY6620
Colby IOM 52 SC2370
Colby Norfk 43 TG2231
Colchester Essex 25 TL9925
Cold Ash Berks 21 SU5169
Cold Ashby Nhants 39 SP6576
Cold Ashton Avon 20 ST7572
Cold Aston Gloucs 28 SP1219
Cold Brayfield Bucks 30 SP9252
Cold Hanworth Lincs 50 TF0383
Cold Hesledon Dur 69 NZ4146
Cold Higham Nhants 30 SP6653
Cold Kirby N York 62 SE5384
Cold Norton Essex 24 TL8500
Cold Overton Leics 40 SK8010
Coldbackie Highld 99 NC6160
Coldean E Susx 12 TQ3308
Coldeast Devon 5 SX8174
Colden W York 54 SD9628
Colden Common Hants 11 SU4822
Coldfair Green Suffk 33 TM4360
Coldharbour Surrey 12 TQ1443
Coldingham Border 77 NT9065
Coldmeece Staffs 38 SJ8532
Coldred Kent 15 TR2747
Coldridge Devon 7 SS6907
Coldstream Border 77 NT8439
Coldwaltham W Susx 12 TQ0216
Coldwell H & W 27 SO4235
Cole Somset 9 ST6733
Cole Green Herts 23 TL2811
Colebatch Shrops 36 SO3187
Colebrook Devon 7 ST0006
Colebrooke Devon 7 SX7699
Coleby Humb 56 SE8919
Coleby Lincs 50 SK9760
Coleford Devon 7 SS7701
Coleford Gloucs 27 SO5710

Coleford Somset...... 20 ST6848
Coleford Water Somset...... 8 ST1133
Colegate End Norfk...... 33 TM1987
Colehill Dorset...... 10 SU0201
Coleman's Hatch E Susx...... 13 TQ4433
Colemere Shrops...... 36 SJ4332
Colemore Hants...... 11 SU7030
Colenden Tays...... 82 NO1029
Colerne Wilts...... 20 ST8271
Colesbourne Gloucs...... 28 SP0013
Coleshill Bucks...... 22 SU9495
Coleshill Oxon...... 21 SU2393
Coleshill Warwks...... 39 SP2089
Coley Avon...... 19 ST5855
Colgate W Susx...... 12 TQ2332
Colgrain Strath...... 80 NS3280
Colinsburgh Fife...... 83 NO4703
Colinton Loth...... 75 NT2168
Colintraive Strath...... 80 NS0374
Colkirk Norfk...... 42 TF9126
Collace Tays...... 82 NO2032
Collafirth Shet...... 103 HU3482
Collaton Devon...... 5 SX7139
Collaton St Mary Devon...... 5 SX8660
College of Roseisle Gramp...... 93 NJ1466
College Town Berks...... 22 SU8560
Collessie Fife...... 83 NO2813
Collier Row Gt Lon...... 23 TQ5091
Collier Street Kent...... 14 TQ7145
Collier's End Herts...... 31 TL3720
Collieston Gramp...... 95 NK0328
Collin D & G...... 66 NY0276
Collingbourne Ducis Wilts...... 21 SU2453
Collingbourne Kingston Wilts...... 21 SU2355
Collingham W York...... 55 SE3945
Collington H & W...... 27 SO6460
Collingtree Nhants...... 30 SP7555
Collins Green Ches...... 47 SJ5594
Colliston Tays...... 89 NO6045
Colliton Devon...... 8 ST0804
Collyweston Nhants...... 40 SK9902
Colmonell Strath...... 64 NX1485
Colmworth Beds...... 30 TL1058
Coln Rogers Gloucs...... 28 SP0809
Coln St Aldwyns Gloucs...... 28 SP1405
Coln St Dennis Gloucs...... 28 SP0810
Colnbrook Berks...... 22 TQ0277
Colne Cambs...... 31 TL3775
Colne Lancs...... 54 SD8939
Colne Engaine Essex...... 24 TL8430
Colney Norfk...... 43 TG1807
Colney Heath Herts...... 23 TL2005
Colney Street Herts...... 22 TL1502
Colpy Gramp...... 95 NJ6432
Colquhar Border...... 75 NT3341
Colsterworth Lincs...... 40 SK9324
Colston Bassett Notts...... 40 SK7033
Colt's Hill Kent...... 13 TQ6443
Coltfield Gramp...... 93 NJ1163
Coltishall Norfk...... 43 TG2719
Colton Cumb...... 58 SD3185
Colton N York...... 56 SE5444
Colton Norfk...... 43 TG1009
Colton Staffs...... 38 SK0420
Colton W York...... 55 SE3732
Colva Powys...... 27 SO1952
Colvend D & G...... 66 NX8654
Colwall H & W...... 28 SO7542
Colwell Nthumb...... 68 NY9575
Colwich Staffs...... 38 SK0121
Colwinston S Glam...... 18 SS9375
Colworth W Susx...... 11 SU9103
Colwyn Bay Clwyd...... 45 SH8578
Colyford Devon...... 8 SY2592
Colyton Devon...... 8 SY2494
Combe Berks...... 21 SU3760
Combe H & W...... 27 SO3463
Combe Oxon...... 29 SP4116
Combe Fishacre Devon...... 5 SX8465
Combe Florey Somset...... 8 ST1531
Combe Hay Avon...... 20 ST7359
Combe Martin Devon...... 6 SS5846
Combe Moor H & W...... 27 SO3663
Combe Raleigh Devon...... 8 ST1502
Combe St Nicholas Somset...... 8 ST3011
Combeinteignhead Devon...... 5 SX9071
Comberbach Ches...... 47 SJ6477
Comberford Staffs...... 39 SK1907
Comberton Cambs...... 31 TL3856
Comberton H & W...... 27 SO4968
Combrook Warwks...... 29 SP3051
Combs Derbys...... 48 SK0478
Combs Suffk...... 32 TM0456
Combs Ford Suffk...... 32 TM0457
Combwich Somset...... 19 ST2542
Comers Gramp...... 95 NJ6707
Comhampton H & W...... 28 SO8367
Commercial Dyfed...... 16 SN1416
Commins Coch Powys...... 35 SH8402
Common Moor Cnwll...... 4 SX2469
Common The Wilts...... 10 SU2432
Commondale N York...... 62 NZ6610
Compstall Gt Man...... 48 SJ9690
Compstonend D & G...... 65 NX6652
Compton Berks...... 21 SU5280
Compton Devon...... 5 SX8664
Compton Hants...... 10 SU4625
Compton Staffs...... 38 SO8284
Compton Surrey...... 12 SU9546
Compton W Susx...... 11 SU7714
Compton Wilts...... 20 SU1351
Compton Abbas Dorset...... 9 ST8618
Compton Abdale Gloucs...... 28 SP0516
Compton Bassett Wilts...... 20 SU0372
Compton Beauchamp Oxon...... 21 SU2786
Compton Bishop Somset...... 19 ST3955
Compton
   Chamberlayne Wilts...... 10 SU0229
Compton Dando Avon...... 19 ST6464
Compton Dundon Somset...... 8 ST4932
Compton Durville Somset...... 8 ST4117
Compton Greenfield Avon...... 19 ST5681
Compton Martin Avon...... 9 ST5456
Compton Pauncefoot Somset...... 9 ST6426
Compton Valence Dorset...... 9 SY5993
Comrie Fife...... 82 NT0289
Comrie Tays...... 81 NN7722
Conaglen House Highld...... 86 NN0268
Conchra Highld...... 85 NG8827
Concraigie Tays...... 88 NO0944
Conderton H & W...... 28 SO9637
Condicote Gloucs...... 28 SP1528
Condorrat Strath...... 74 NS7373
Condover Shrops...... 37 SJ4905
Coney Hill Gloucs...... 28 SO8517
Coney Weston Suffk...... 32 TL9578
Coneyhurst
   Common W Susx...... 12 TQ1023

Coneysthorpe N York...... 56 SE7171
Congdon's Shop Cnwll...... 4 SX2878
Congerstone Leics...... 39 SK3605
Congham Norfk...... 42 TF7123
Congleton Ches...... 47 SJ8562
Congresbury Avon...... 19 ST4363
Conheath D & G...... 66 NX9969
Conicavel Gramp...... 93 NH9853
Coningsby Lincs...... 51 TF2257
Conington Cambs...... 40 TL1885
Conington Cambs...... 31 TL3266
Conisbrough S York...... 49 SK5098
Conisholme Lincs...... 51 TF4095
Coniston Cumb...... 58 SD3097
Coniston Humb...... 57 TA1434
Coniston Cold N York...... 54 SD9054
Conistone N York...... 54 SD9867
Connah's Quay Clwyd...... 46 SJ2969
Connel Strath...... 80 NM9134
Connel Park Strath...... 66 NS6012
Connor Downs Cnwll...... 2 SW5939
Conon Bridge Highld...... 92 NH5455
Cononley N York...... 54 SD9846
Consall Staffs...... 48 SJ9848
Consett Dur...... 68 NZ1051
Constable Burton N York...... 61 SE1690
Constantine Cnwll...... 2 SW7329
Contin Highld...... 92 NH4556
Conwy Gwynd...... 45 SH7877
Conyer's Green Suffk...... 32 TL8867
Cooden E Susx...... 14 TQ7107
Cook's Green Essex...... 25 TM1818
Cookbury Devon...... 6 SS4006
Cookham Berks...... 22 SU8985
Cookham Dean Berks...... 22 SU8685
Cookham Rise Berks...... 22 SU8885
Cookhill Warwks...... 28 SP0558
Cookley H & W...... 38 SO8480
Cookley Suffk...... 33 TM3475
Cookley Green Oxon...... 22 SU6990
Cookney Gramp...... 89 NO8693
Cooks Green Suffk...... 32 TL9753
Cooksmill Green Essex...... 24 TL6306
Coolham W Susx...... 12 TQ1122
Cooling Kent...... 14 TQ7575
Coombe Cnwll...... 5 SX9373
Coombe Devon...... 8 SY1091
Coombe Gloucs...... 20 ST7694
Coombe Hants...... 11 SU6620
Coombe Bissett Wilts...... 10 SU1026
Coombe Cellars Devon...... 5 SX9072
Coombe End Somset...... 7 ST0329
Coombe Hill Gloucs...... 28 SO8826
Coombe Keynes Dorset...... 9 SY8484
Coombe Pafford Devon...... 5 SX9166
Cooperhill Gramp...... 93 NH9953
Coopersale Common Essex...... 23 TL4702
Coopersale Street Essex...... 23 TL4701
Cop Street Kent...... 23 TQ2959
Copdock Suffk...... 33 TM1242
Copford Green Essex...... 24 TL9222
Copgrove N York...... 55 SE3463
Copister Shet...... 103 HU4879
Cople Beds...... 30 TL1048
Copley Dur...... 61 NZ0825
Copmanthorpe N York...... 56 SE5646
Compere End Staffs...... 37 SJ8029
Copp Lancs...... 53 SD4239
Coppathorne Cnwll...... 6 SS2000
Coppenhall Staffs...... 38 SJ9019
Copperhouse Cnwll...... 2 SW5637
Coppingford Cambs...... 40 TL1679
Copplestone Devon...... 7 SS7702
Coppull Lancs...... 53 SD5614
Copsale W Susx...... 12 TQ1724
Copster Green Lancs...... 54 SD6733
Copston Magna Warwks...... 39 SP4588
Copt Hewick N York...... 55 SE3471
Copthall Green Essex...... 23 TL4201
Copthorne W Susx...... 12 TQ3139
Copythorne Hants...... 10 SU3014
Corbets Tey Gt Lon...... 24 TQ5685
Corbiere Jersey...... 101 JS0000
Corbridge Nthumb...... 68 NY9964
Corby Nhants...... 40 SP8988
Corby Glen Lincs...... 40 TF0024
Cordon Strath...... 72 NS0230
Coreley Shrops...... 37 SO6173
Corfe Somset...... 8 ST2319
Corfe Castle Dorset...... 9 SY9681
Corfe Mullen Dorset...... 9 SY9896
Corfton Shrops...... 37 SO4985
Corgarff Gramp...... 94 NJ2708
Corhampton Hants...... 11 SU6120
Corley Warwks...... 39 SP2885
Corley Ash Warwks...... 39 SP2986
Cormuir Tays...... 88 NO3066
Cornard Tye Suffk...... 32 TL9041
Cornforth Dur...... 62 NZ3134
Cornhill Gramp...... 94 NJ5858
Cornhill-on-Tweed Nthumb...... 77 NT8639
Cornholme W York...... 54 SD9126
Cornoigmore Strath...... 78 NL9846
Cornsay Dur...... 69 NZ1443
Cornsay Colliery Dur...... 69 NZ1643
Corntown Highld...... 92 NH5556
Corntown M Glam...... 18 SS9177
Cornwell Oxon...... 29 SP2727
Cornwood Devon...... 5 SX6059
Cornworthy Devon...... 5 SX8255
Corpach Highld...... 86 NN0976
Corpusty Norfk...... 43 TG1129
Corrachree Gramp...... 89 NJ4604
Corran Highld...... 85 NG8409
Corran Highld...... 86 NN0263
Corrie D & G...... 67 NY2086
Corrie Strath...... 72 NS0242
Corriecravie Strath...... 72 NR9223
Corriegills Strath...... 72 NS0335
Corriegour
   Lodge Hotel Highld...... 86 NN2692
Corriemoillie Highld...... 92 NH3663
Corrimony Highld...... 91 NH3730
Corringham Essex...... 24 TQ7083
Corringham Lincs...... 50 SK8691
Corris Gwynd...... 35 SH7508
Corris Uchaf Gwynd...... 35 SH7408
Corrow Strath...... 80 NN1800
Corry Highld...... 85 SG6424
Corscombe Devon...... 7 SX6296
Corscombe Dorset...... 8 ST5105
Corse Lawn Gloucs...... 28 SO8330
Corsham Wilts...... 20 ST8770
Corsindae Gramp...... 95 NJ6808
Corsley Wilts...... 20 ST8246
Corsley Heath Wilts...... 20 ST8245
Corsock D & G...... 65 NX7675
Corston Avon...... 20 ST6965

Corston Wilts...... 20 ST9283
Corstorphine Loth...... 75 NT1972
Cortachy Tays...... 88 NO3959
Corton Suffk...... 43 TM5499
Corton Wilts...... 20 ST9340
Corton Denham Somset...... 9 ST6322
Coruanan Lodge Highld...... 86 NN0668
Corwen Clwyd...... 46 SJ0743
Coryton Devon...... 4 SX4583
Coryton Essex...... 24 TQ7382
Cosby Leics...... 39 SP5495
Coseley W Mids...... 38 SO9494
Cosgrove Nhants...... 30 SP7942
Cosham Hants...... 11 SU6505
Cosheston Dyfed...... 16 SN0003
Coshieville Tays...... 87 NN7749
Cossall Notts...... 49 SK4842
Cossington Leics...... 39 SK6013
Cossington Somset...... 19 ST3540
Costessey Norfk...... 43 TG1711
Costock Notts...... 39 SK5726
Coston Leics...... 40 SK8422
Coston Norfk...... 42 TG0506
Cote Oxon...... 21 SP3502
Cotebrook Ches...... 47 SJ5765
Cotehill Cumb...... 67 NY4650
Cotes Leics...... 39 SK5520
Cotesbach Leics...... 39 SP5382
Cotgrave Notts...... 39 SK6435
Cotham Notts...... 50 SK7946
Cotherstone Dur...... 61 NZ0119
Cothill Oxon...... 21 SU4699
Cotleigh Devon...... 8 ST2002
Cotmanhay Derbys...... 49 SK4543
Coton Cambs...... 31 TL4058
Coton Nhants...... 39 SP6771
Coton Staffs...... 37 SJ8120
Coton Clanford Staffs...... 38 SJ8723
Coton Hill Shrops...... 37 SJ4813
Coton in the Elms Derbys...... 39 SK2415
Cott Devon...... 5 SX7861
Cottage End Hants...... 21 SU4143
Cottam Lancs...... 53 SD5032
Cottam Notts...... 50 SK8179
Cottenham Cambs...... 31 TL4467
Cottered Herts...... 31 TL3129
Cotterstock Nhants...... 40 TL0490
Cottesbrooke Nhants...... 30 SP7173
Cottesmore Leics...... 40 SK9013
Cottingham Humb...... 57 TA0432
Cottingham Nhants...... 40 SP8490
Cottingley W York...... 55 SE1137
Cottisford Oxon...... 29 SP5831
Cotton Suffk...... 32 TM0666
Cottown Gramp...... 94 NJ5026
Cottown Gramp...... 95 NJ7615
Cottown of Gight Gramp...... 95 NJ8140
Cotts Devon...... 4 SX4365
Coughton Warwks...... 28 SP0860
Coulaghailtro Strath...... 71 NR7165
Coulags Highld...... 91 NG9645
Coull Gramp...... 89 NJ5102
Coulport Strath...... 80 NS2187
Coulsdon Gt Lon...... 23 TQ2959
Coulston Wilts...... 20 ST9554
Coulter Strath...... 75 NT0234
Coulton N York...... 62 SE6373
Coultra Fife...... 83 NO3523
Cound Shrops...... 37 SJ5505
Coundon Dur...... 61 NZ2329
Countersett N York...... 60 SD9187
Countess Wear Devon...... 5 SX9491
Countesthorpe Leics...... 39 SP5895
Countisbury Devon...... 18 SS7449
Coupar Angus Tays...... 82 NO2239
Coupland Nthumb...... 77 NT9330
Cour Strath...... 72 NR8248
Courance D & G...... 66 NY0590
Court Henry Dyfed...... 17 SN5522
Courteachan Highld...... 85 NM6897
Courteenhall Nhants...... 30 SP7653
Courtsend Essex...... 25 TR0293
Courtway Somset...... 8 ST2033
Cousland Loth...... 76 NT3768
Cousley Wood E Susx...... 13 TQ6533
Cove Border...... 76 NT7771
Cove Devon...... 7 SS9619
Cove Gramp...... 89 NJ9501
Cove Hants...... 22 SU8555
Cove Highld...... 91 NG8191
Cove Strath...... 80 NS2282
Covehithe Suffk...... 33 TM5282
Coven Staffs...... 38 SJ9106
Coveney Cambs...... 41 TL4882
Covenham
   St Bartholomew Lincs...... 51 TF3394
Covenham St Mary Lincs...... 51 TF3394
Coventry W Mids...... 39 SP3378
Coverack Cnwll...... 2 SW7818
Coverack Bridges Cnwll...... 2 SW6630
Coverham N York...... 61 SE1086
Covington Cambs...... 30 TL0570
Covington Strath...... 75 NS9739
Cow Honeybourne H & W...... 28 SP1143
Cowan Bridge Lancs...... 60 SD6376
Cowbeech E Susx...... 13 TQ6114
Cowbit Lincs...... 41 TF2518
Cowbridge S Glam...... 18 SS9974
Cowden Kent...... 13 TQ4640
Cowdenbeath Fife...... 82 NT1691
Cowers Lane Derbys...... 49 SK3046
Cowes IOW...... 11 SZ4996
Cowesby N York...... 62 SE4689
Cowfold W Susx...... 12 TQ2122
Cowhill Avon...... 19 ST6091
Cowie Cent...... 82 NS8389
Cowley Devon...... 7 SX9095
Cowley Gloucs...... 28 SO9614
Cowley Gt Lon...... 22 TQ0582
Cowley Oxon...... 29 SP5304
Cowling Lancs...... 54 SD5917
Cowling N York...... 54 SD9643
Cowling N York...... 61 SE2387
Cowlinge Suffk...... 32 TL7154
Cowpen Nthumb...... 69 NZ2981
Cowplain Hants...... 11 SU6810
Cowshill Dur...... 60 NY8540
Cowslip Green Avon...... 19 ST4861
Cowthorpe N York...... 55 SE4252
Coxbank Ches...... 37 SJ6541
Coxbench Derbys...... 49 SK3743
Coxford Cnwll...... 6 SX1696
Coxford Norfk...... 42 TF8529
Coxheath Kent...... 14 TQ7451
Coxhoe Dur...... 62 NZ3136
Coxley Somset...... 19 ST5343
Coxley Wick Somset...... 19 ST5243
Coxtie Green Essex...... 24 TQ5696

Coxwold N York...... 62 SE5377
Coychurch M Glam...... 18 SS9379
Coylton Strath...... 73 NS4219
Coylumbridge Highld...... 93 NH9111
Coytrahen M Glam...... 18 SS8885
Crabbs Cross H & W...... 28 SP0465
Crabtree W Susx...... 12 TQ2125
Crackenthorpe Cumb...... 60 NY6622
Crackington Haven Cnwll...... 6 SX1496
Crackleybank Shrops...... 37 SJ7611
Cracoe N York...... 54 SD9760
Craddock Devon...... 8 ST0812
Cradley H & W...... 28 SO7347
Cradley W Mids...... 38 SO9485
Cradoc Powys...... 26 SO0130
Crafthole Cnwll...... 4 SX3654
Crafton Bucks...... 30 SP8819
Cragg Vale W York...... 54 SE0023
Craggan Highld...... 93 NJ0226
Craghead Dur...... 69 NZ2150
Crai Powys...... 26 SN8924
Craibstone Gramp...... 94 NJ4959
Craichie Tays...... 89 NO5047
Craig Tays...... 89 NO6956
Craig Llangiwg W Glam...... 26 SN7204
Craigbank Strath...... 66 NS5911
Craigburn Border...... 75 NT2354
Craigcleuch D & G...... 67 NY3486
Craigdam Gramp...... 95 NJ8430
Craigdarroch D & G...... 65 NX7391
Craigdhu Strath...... 79 NM8205
Craigearn Gramp...... 95 NJ7214
Craigellachie Gramp...... 94 NJ2844
Craigend Strath...... 73 NS4670
Craigend Tays...... 82 NO1120
Craigendoran Strath...... 80 NS3181
Craighlaw D & G...... 64 NX3061
Craighouse Strath...... 70 NR5267
Craigie Strath...... 73 NS4232
Craigie Tays...... 88 NO1143
Craigiefold Gramp...... 95 NJ9165
Craigley D & G...... 65 NX7658
Craiglockhart Fife...... 75 NT2271
Craiglug Gramp...... 94 NJ3355
Craigmillar Loth...... 75 NT3071
Craigneston D & G...... 65 NX7587
Craigneuk Strath...... 74 NS7765
Craigneuk Strath...... 74 NS7756
Craignure Strath...... 79 NM7236
Craigo Tays...... 89 NO6864
Craigrothie Fife...... 83 NO3810
Craigruie Cent...... 81 NN4920
Craigo Gramp...... 89 NJ8301
Craigton Gramp...... 89 NJ8301
Craigton Strath...... 74 NS4954
Craigton Tays...... 83 NO5138
Craigton of Airlie Tays...... 88 NO3250
Crail Fife...... 83 NO6107
Crailing N York...... 76 NT6824
Crakehall N York...... 61 SE2489
Crambe N York...... 56 SE7364
Cramlington Nthumb...... 69 NZ2676
Cramond Loth...... 75 NT1976
Cramond Bridge Loth...... 75 NT1775
Cranage Ches...... 47 SJ7568
Cranberry Staffs...... 38 SJ8235
Cranborne Dorset...... 10 SU0513
Cranbrook Kent...... 14 TQ7736
Cranfield Beds...... 30 SP9542
Cranford Gt Lon...... 22 TQ1076
Cranford St Andrew Nhants...... 30 SP9277
Cranford St John Nhants...... 30 SP9276
Cranham Gloucs...... 28 SO8913
Crank Mersyd...... 46 SJ5099
Cranleigh Surrey...... 12 TQ0539
Cranmore Somset...... 20 ST6643
Cranoe Leics...... 40 SP7695
Cransford Suffk...... 33 TM3164
Cranshaws Border...... 76 NT6861
Crantock Cnwll...... 2 SW7960
Cranwell Lincs...... 50 TF0349
Cranwich Norfk...... 42 TL7794
Cranworth Norfk...... 42 TF9804
Craobh Haven Strath...... 79 NM7907
Crarae Strath...... 71 NR9897
Crask Inn Highld...... 96 NC5224
Crask of Aigas Highld...... 92 NH4642
Craster Nthumb...... 77 NU2519
Craswall H & W...... 27 SO2735
Cratfield Suffk...... 33 TM3175
Crathes Gramp...... 89 NO7596
Crathie Gramp...... 88 NO2695
Crathie Highld...... 87 NN5793
Crathorne N York...... 62 NZ4407
Craven Arms Shrops...... 36 SO4382
Crawford Strath...... 75 NS9520
Crawfordjohn Strath...... 74 NS8823
Crawick Strath...... 66 NS7811
Crawley Hants...... 10 SU4235
Crawley Oxon...... 29 SP3412
Crawley W Susx...... 12 TQ2636
Crawley Down W Susx...... 12 TQ3437
Crawshawbooth Lancs...... 54 SD8125
Crawton Gramp...... 89 NO8779
Cray N York...... 61 SD9479
Crayford Gt Lon...... 23 TQ5175
Crayke N York...... 56 SE5670
Crays Hill Essex...... 24 TQ7192
Craze Lowman Devon...... 7 SS9814
Crazies Hill Oxon...... 22 SU7980
Creacombe Devon...... 6 SS3219
Creag Ghoraidh W Isls...... 102 NF7948
Creagan Inn Strath...... 86 NM9744
Creagorry W Isls...... 102 NF7948
Creaguaineach Lodge Highld...... 86 NN3068
Creaton Nhants...... 30 SP7071
Creca D & G...... 67 NY2270
Credenhill H & W...... 27 SO4543
Crediton Devon...... 7 SS8300
Creebank D & G...... 64 NX3477
Creebridge D & G...... 64 NX4165
Creech Heathfield Somset...... 8 ST2727
Creech St Michael Somset...... 8 ST2725
Creed Cnwll...... 3 SW9347
Creekmouth Gt Lon...... 23 TQ4581
Creeting St Mary Suffk...... 33 TM0956
Creeton Lincs...... 40 TF0120
Creetown D & G...... 65 NX4759
Creggans Inn Strath...... 80 NN0902
Cregneash IOM...... 52 SC1667
Creich Fife...... 83 NO3221
Creigiau M Glam...... 18 ST0781
Cremyll Cnwll...... 4 SX4553
Cressage Shrops...... 37 SJ5904
Cressbrook Derbys...... 48 SK1673
Cresselly Dyfed...... 16 SN0606
Cressex Bucks...... 22 SU8492
Cressing Essex...... 24 TL7920
Cresswell Dyfed...... 16 SN0506

Cresswell Nthumb............69 NZ2993
Cresswell Staffs............48 SJ9739
Creswell Derbys............49 SK5274
Cretingham Suff............33 TM2260
Cretshengan Strath............71 NR7166
Crew Green Powys............36 SJ3215
Crewe Ches............46 SJ4253
Crewe Ches............47 SJ7056
Crewe Green Ches............47 SJ7255
Crewkerne Somset............8 ST4409
Crewton Derbys............39 SK3733
Crianlarich Cent............80 NN3825
Cribyn Dyfed............17 SN5250
Criccieth Gwynd............44 SH4938
Crich Derbys............49 SK3454
Crichton Loth............76 NT3862
Crick Nhants............39 SP5872
Crickadarn Powys............26 SO0942
Cricket St Thomas Somset............8 ST3708
Crickhowell Powys............27 SO2118
Cricklade Wilts............20 SU0993
Cricklewood Gt Lon............23 TQ2385
Cridling Stubbs N York............55 SE5221
Crieff Tays............82 NN8621
Criggion Powys............36 SJ2915
Crigglestone W York............55 SE3116
Crimond Gramp............95 NK0556
Crimonmogate Gramp............95 NK0358
Crimplesham Norfk............42 TF6503
Crimscote Warwks............29 SP2347
Crinan Strath............71 NR7894
Crindledyke Strath............74 NS8356
Cringleford Norfk............43 TG1905
Cringles N York............55 SE0448
Crinow Dyfed............16 SN1214
Croachy Highld............93 NH6527
Crochmare House D & G............66 NX8977
Crockenhill Kent............23 TQ5067
Crocker End Oxon............22 SU7086
Crockernwell Devon............5 SX7592
Crockerton Wilts............20 ST8642
Crocketford D & G............66 NX8372
Crockham Hill Kent............13 TQ4450
Croes-goch Dyfed............16 SM8330
Croes-lan Dyfed............17 SN3844
Croeserw W Glam............18 SS8795
Croesor Gwynd............45 SH6344
Croesyceiliog Dyfed............17 SN4016
Croesyceiliog Gwent............19 ST3096
Croft Ches............47 SJ6393
Croft Leics............39 SP5195
Croft Lincs............51 TF5061
Croft-on-Tees N York............61 NZ2809
Croftamie Cent............81 NS4785
Crofton Devon............5 SX9680
Crofton W York............55 SE3817
Crofts D & G............65 NX7365
Crofts Gramp............94 NJ2850
Crofts of Dipple Gramp............94 NJ3259
Crofts of Savoch Gramp............95 NK0460
Crofty W Glam............17 SS5294
Croggan Strath............79 NM7027
Croglin Cumb............67 NY5747
Crogo D & G............65 NX7576
Croik Highld............96 NH4591
Cromarty Highld............93 NH7867
Crombie Fife............82 NT0584
Cromdale Highld............93 NJ0728
Cromer Herts............31 TL2928
Cromer Norfk............43 TG2242
Cromford Derbys............49 SK2956
Cromhall Avon............20 ST6990
Cromor W Isls............102 NB4021
Cromwell Notts............50 SK7961
Cronberry Strath............74 NS6022
Crondall Hants............22 SU7948
Cronton Mersyd............46 SJ4988
Crook Cumb............59 SD4695
Crook Dur............61 NZ1635
Crook Inn Border............75 NT1026
Crook of Devon Tays............82 NO0400
Crooked Holme Cumb............67 NY5161
Crookedholm Strath............73 NS4537
Crookham Berks............21 SU5464
Crookham Nthumb............77 NT9138
Crookham Village Hants............22 SU7952
Crooklands Cumb............59 SD5383
Cropredy Oxon............29 SP4646
Cropston Leics............39 SK5510
Cropthorne H & W............28 SO9945
Cropton N York............63 SE7589
Cropwell Bishop Notts............39 SK6835
Cropwell Butler Notts............49 SK6837
Cros W Isls............102 NB5061
Crosbie Strath............73 NS2149
Crosbost W Isls............102 NB3924
Crosby Cumb............58 NY0738
Crosby Humb............56 SE8912
Crosby IOM............52 SC3279
Crosby Mersyd............46 SJ3198
Crosby Garret Cumb............60 NY7209
Crosby Ravensworth Cumb............60 NY6214
Croscombe Somset............19 ST5944
Cross Somset............19 ST4154
Cross Flatts W York............55 SE1040
Cross Gates W York............55 SE3534
Cross Green Suff............32 TL8353
Cross Green Suff............32 TL8955
Cross Green Suff............32 TL9852
Cross Hands Dyfed............17 SN5612
Cross Houses Shrops............37 SJ5307
Cross in Hand E Susx............13 TQ5521
Cross Inn Dyfed............34 SN3957
Cross Lane IOW............11 SZ5089
Cross Lane Head Shrops............37 SO7195
Cross o' th' hands Derbys............49 SK2846
Cross of Jackston Gramp............95 NJ7432
Cross Street Suff............33 TM1876
Cross Town Ches............47 SJ7578
Cross-at-Hand Kent............14 TQ7846
Crossaig Strath............72 NR8351
Crossapoll Strath............78 NL9943
Crosscanonby Cumb............58 NY0739
Crossdale Street Norfk............43 TG2239
Crossford Fife............82 NT0786
Crossford Strath............74 NS8246
Crossgatehall Loth............76 NT3669
Crossgates Fife............82 NT1488
Crossgates Strath............73 NS3744
Crossgill Lancs............53 SD5563
Crosshands Strath............73 NS4830
Crosshill Fife............82 NT1796
Crosshill Strath............73 NS3206
Crosshouse Strath............73 NS3938
Crosskeys Gwent............19 ST2292
Crosskeys Strath............80 NS3385
Crosskirk Highld............100 ND0369
Crosslands Cumb............59 SD3489

Crosslee Border............75 NT3018
Crosslee Strath............73 NS4066
Crossmichael D & G............65 NX7366
Crossroads Gramp............94 NJ5607
Crossroads Gramp............89 NO7594
Crosston Tays............89 NO5256
Crossway Green H & W............28 SO8468
Crosswell Dyfed............16 SN1236
Crosthwaite Cumb............59 SD4391
Croston Lancs............53 SD4818
Crostwick Norfk............43 TG2515
Crouch End Gt Lon............23 TQ3088
Crouch Hill Dorset............9 ST7010
Croucheston Wilts............10 SU0625
Croughton Nhants............29 SP5433
Crovie Gramp............95 NJ8065
Crow Edge S York............55 SE1804
Crow Green Essex............24 TQ5796
Crow Hill H & W............27 SO6326
Crowan Cnwll............2 SW6434
Crowborough E Susx............13 TQ5131
Crowcombe Somset............18 ST1436
Crowdecote Derbys............48 SK1065
Crowell Oxon............22 SU7499
Crowfield Suff............33 TM1457
Crowhill Loth............76 NT7374
Crowhurst E Susx............14 TQ7512
Crowhurst Surrey............13 TQ3847
Crowland Lincs............41 TF2410
Crowland Suff............32 TM0170
Crowlas Cnwll............2 SW5133
Crowle H & W............28 SO9256
Crowle Humb............56 SE7712
Crowle Green H & W............28 SO9516
Crowmarsh Gifford Oxon............21 SU6189
Crown Corner Suff............33 TM2570
Crownhill Devon............4 SX4858
Crownthorpe Norfk............42 TG0803
Crowntown Cnwll............2 SW6330
Crows-an-Wra Cnwll............2 SW3927
Crowthorne Berks............22 SU8464
Crowton Ches............47 SJ5774
Croxdale Dur............61 NZ2636
Croxden Staffs............48 SK0639
Croxley Green Herts............22 TQ0795
Croxton Cambs............31 TL2460
Croxton Humb............57 TA0912
Croxton Norfk............42 TF9831
Croxton Norfk............32 TL8786
Croxton Staffs............37 SJ7832
Croxton Kerrial Leics............40 SK8329
Croy Highld............93 NH7949
Croy Strath............74 NS7275
Croyde Devon............6 SS4439
Croydon Cambs............31 TL3149
Croydon Gt Lon............23 TQ3265
Crubenmore Highld............87 NN6790
Cruckmeole Shrops............36 SJ4309
Cruckton Shrops............36 SJ4310
Cruden Bay Gramp............95 NK0836
Crudgington Shrops............37 SJ6318
Crudwell Wilts............20 ST9593
Crug-y-byddar Powys............36 SO1682
Crumlin Gwent............19 ST2197
Crumplehorn Cnwll............4 SX2051
Crumpsall Gt Man............47 SD8402
Crundale Kent............15 TR0749
Crunwear Dyfed............17 SN1810
Crux Easton Hants............21 SU4256
Crwbin Dyfed............17 SN4713
Cryers Hill Bucks............22 SU8796
Crymmych Dyfed............17 SN1834
Crynant W Glam............26 SN7904
Crystal Palace Gt Lon............23 TQ3371
Cuaig Highld............91 NG7057
Cubbington Warwks............29 SP3468
Cubert Cnwll............2 SW7857
Cublington Bucks............30 SP8422
Cublington H & W............27 SO4038
Cuckfield W Susx............12 TQ3025
Cucklington Somset............9 ST7527
Cuckney Notts............49 SK5671
Cuddesdon Oxon............21 SP5903
Cuddington Bucks............22 SP7311
Cuddington Ches............47 SJ5971
Cuddington Heath Ches............46 SJ4746
Cudham Gt Lon............23 TQ4459
Cudliptown Devon............4 SX5279
Cudnell Dorset............10 SZ0696
Cudworth S York............55 SE3808
Cudworth Somset............8 ST3810
Cuffley Herts............23 TL3003
Cuil Highld............86 NM9855
Culbokie Highld............92 NH6059
Culburnie Highld............92 NH4941
Culcabock Highld............93 NH6844
Culcharry Highld............93 NH8650
Culcheth Ches............47 SJ6694
Culdrain Gramp............94 NJ5134
Culford Suff............32 TL8370
Culgaith Cumb............59 NY6029
Culham Oxon............21 SU5095
Culkein Highld............98 NC0333
Culkein Drumbeg Highld............98 NC1133
Culkerton Gloucs............20 ST9395
Cullen Gramp............94 NJ5167
Cullercoats T & W............69 NZ3570
Cullerlie Gramp............89 NJ7603
Cullicudden Highld............92 NH6463
Cullingworth W York............55 SE0636
Cullipool Strath............79 NM7413
Cullivoe Shet............103 HP5402
Culloden Highld............93 NH7246
Cullompton Devon............7 ST0207
Culm Davy Devon............8 ST1215
Culmington Shrops............37 SO4982
Culmstock Devon............8 ST1013
Culnacraig Highld............91 NC0603
Culnaightrie D & G............66 NX7750
Culnaknock Highld............90 NG5162
Culpho Suff............33 TM2149
Culrain Highld............96 NH5794
Culross Fife............82 NS9886
Culroy Strath............73 NS3114
Culsalmond Gramp............94 NJ6532
Culscadden D & G............65 NX4748
Culshabbin D & G............64 NX3051
Culswick Shet............103 HU2745
Cultercullen Gramp............95 NJ9223
Cults Gramp............89 NJ8903
Culverstone Green Kent............14 TQ6362
Culverthorpe Lincs............50 TF0240
Culworth Nhants............29 SP5446
Cumbernauld Strath............74 NS7674
Cumbernauld Village Strath............74 NS7676
Cumberworth Lincs............51 TF5073
Cuminestown Gramp............95 NJ8050
Cumledge Border............76 NT7956

Cummersdale Cumb............67 NY3953
Cummertrees D & G............67 NY1366
Cummingston Gramp............93 NJ1368
Cumnock Strath............74 NS5620
Cumnor Oxon............29 SP4504
Cumrew Cumb............67 NY5550
Cumwhinton Cumb............67 NY4552
Cumwhitton Cumb............67 NY5052
Cundall N York............55 SE4272
Cunninghamhead Strath............73 NS3741
Cupar Fife............83 NO3714
Cupar Muir Fife............83 NO3613
Curbar Derbys............48 SK2574
Curbridge Hants............11 SU5211
Curbridge Oxon............29 SP3308
Curbridge Hants............11 SU5213
Curdworth Warwks............38 SP1792
Curland Somset............8 ST2717
Curridge Berks............21 SU4972
Currie Loth............75 NT1867
Curry Mallet Somset............8 ST3221
Curry Rivel Somset............8 ST3925
Curtisden Green Kent............14 TQ7440
Curtisknowle Devon............5 SX7353
Cury Cnwll............2 SW6721
Cushnie Gramp............94 NJ5211
Cusop H & W............27 SO2441
Cutcloy D & G............65 NX4534
Cutcombe Somset............7 SS9339
Cuthill Highld............97 NH7587
Cutnall Green H & W............28 SO8868
Cutsdean Gloucs............28 SP0830
Cutthorpe Derbys............49 SK3473
Cuxham Oxon............22 SU6695
Cuxton Kent............14 TQ7066
Cuxwold Lincs............50 TA1701
Cwm Clwyd............45 SJ0677
Cwm Morgan Dyfed............17 SN2934
Cwm-cou Dyfed............17 SN2641
Cwm-Crownon Powys............26 SO1419
Cwm-Llinau Powys............35 SH8408
Cwm-y-glo Dyfed............17 SN5513
Cwm-y-glo Gwynd............44 SH5562
Cwmafan W Glam............18 SS7791
Cwmaman M Glam............18 ST0099
Cwmbach Dyfed............17 SN2526
Cwmbach M Glam............18 SO0201
Cwmbach Powys............27 SO1639
Cwmbach Llechrhyd Powys............26 SO0254
Cwmbran Gwent............19 ST2994
Cwmcarn Gwent............19 ST2293
Cwmcarvan Gwent............27 SO4707
Cwmdare M Glam............18 SN9803
Cwmdu Powys............27 SO1823
Cwmdu Powys............17 SN3731
Cwmduad Dyfed............17 SN3731
Cwmfelin M Glam............18 SO0901
Cwmfelin M Glam............18 SS8589
Cwmfelin Boeth Dyfed............17 SN1919
Cwmfelin Mynach Dyfed............19 ST6143
Cwmfelinfach Gwent............19 ST1891
Cwmffrwd Dyfed............17 SN4217
Cwmgiedd Powys............26 SN7911
Cwmgorse W Glam............26 SN7010
Cwmgwili Dyfed............17 SN5710
Cwmhiraeth Dyfed............17 SN3437
Cwmllynfell Dyfed............26 SN7412
Cwmparc M Glam............18 SS9495
Cwmpengraig Dyfed............17 SN3536
Cwmsychbant Dyfed............17 SN4746
Cwmtillery Gwent............27 SO2105
Cwmystwyth Dyfed............35 SN7874
Cwrt-newydd Dyfed............17 SN4947
Cylibebyll W Glam............26 SN7404
Cymer W Glam............18 SS8695
Cymmer M Glam............18 ST0290
Cynghordy Dyfed............26 SN8040
Cynonville W Glam............18 SS8395
Cynwyd Clwyd............36 SJ0541
Cynwyl Elfed Dyfed............17 SN3727

D

Daccombe Devon............5 SX9068
Dacre Cumb............59 NY4526
Dacre N York............55 SE1960
Dacre Banks N York............55 SE1962
Daddry Shield Dur............60 NY8937
Dadford Bucks............30 SP6638
Dadlington Leics............39 SP4097
Dagenham Gt Lon............23 TQ5084
Daglingworth Gloucs............28 SO9905
Dagnall Bucks............30 SP9916
Dailly Strath............73 NS2701
Dainton Devon............5 SX8566
Dairsie Fife............83 NO4117
Dalabrog W Isls............102 NF7521
Dalavich Strath............80 NM9612
Dalbeattie D & G............66 NX8361
Dalby IOM............52 SC2178
Dalby N York............56 SE6371
Dalcapon Tays............88 NN9754
Dalchalm Highld............97 NC9105
Dalchreichart Highld............92 NH2412
Dalchruin Tays............81 NN7116
Dalcrue Tays............82 NO0427
Dalditch Devon............8 SY0483
Dale Derbys............49 SK4338
Dale Dyfed............16 SM8005
Dalgarven Strath............73 NS2846
Dalgety Bay Fife............82 NT1683
Dalgig Strath............73 NS5512
Dalginross Tays............81 NN7721
Dalguise Tays............88 NN9847
Dalhalvaig Highld............99 NC8954
Dalham Suff............32 TL7261
Daliburgh W Isls............102 NF7521
Dalkeith Loth............75 NT3367
Dallas Gramp............93 NJ1252
Dallinghoo Suff............33 TM2655
Dallington E Susx............13 TQ6519
Dallington Nhants............30 SP7362
Dalmally Strath............80 NN1627
Dalmary Cent............81 NS5195
Dalmellington Strath............73 NS4705
Dalmeny Loth............75 NT1477
Dalmigavie Highld............93 NH7319
Dalmigavie Lodge Highld............93 NH7523
Dalmore Highld............93 NH6668
Dalmuir Strath............81 NS4871
Dalnabreck Highld............79 NM7069
Dalnacardoch Tays............87 NN7270
Dalnahaitnach Highld............93 NH8519
Dalnaspidal Tays............87 NN6473
Dalnawillan Lodge Highld............100 ND0340

Daloist Tays............87 NN7857
Dalqualurn Strath............64 NX3296
Dalreavoch Lodge Highld............97 NC7508
Dalry Strath............73 NS2909
Dalrymple Strath............73 NS3514
Dalserf Strath............74 NS7950
Dalsmeran Strath............72 NR6413
Dalston Gt Lon............23 TQ3384
Dalston Cumb............67 NY3650
Dalswinton D & G............66 NX9385
Dalton D & G............67 NY1108
Dalton N York............62 SE4376
Dalton N York............61 NZ1108
Dalton Nthumb............68 NZ1172
Dalton Piercy Cleve............62 NZ4631
Dalton-in-Furness Cumb............58 SD2274
Dalton-le-Dale Dur............69 NZ4048
Dalton-on-Tees N York............61 NZ2907
Dalveen D & G............66 NS8806
Dalveich Cent............81 NN6124
Dalwhinnie Highld............87 NN6384
Dalwood Devon............8 ST2400
Damerham Hants............10 SU1016
Damgate Norfk............43 TG4009
Danbury Essex............24 TL7805
Danby N York............62 NZ7008
Danby Wiske N York............62 SE3398
Dandaleith Gramp............94 NJ2846
Danderhall Loth............75 NT3069
Dane End Herts............31 TL3321
Dane Hills Leics............39 SK5604
Dane Street Kent............15 TR0552
Danebridge Ches............48 SJ9665
Danehill E Susx............13 TQ4027
Danshillock Gramp............95 NJ7157
Danskine Loth............76 NT5667
Darenth Kent............14 TQ5671
Daresbury Ches............47 SJ5882
Darfield S York............55 SE4104
Dargate Kent............15 TR0861
Darite Cnwll............4 SX2569
Darlaston W Mids............38 SO9796
Darlaston Green W Mids............38 SO9797
Darley N York............55 SE2059
Darley Abbey Derbys............49 SK3538
Darley Bridge Derbys............49 SK2661
Darley Green Warwks............38 SP1874
Darley Head N York............55 SE1959
Darleyhall Herts............30 TL1422
Darlingscott Warwks............29 SP2342
Darlington Dur............61 NZ2814
Darlton Notts............50 SK7773
Darowen Powys............35 SH8201
Darra Gramp............95 NJ7447
Darracott Devon............6 SS2317
Darracott Devon............6 SS4739
Darrington W York............55 SE4820
Darsham Suff............33 TM4169
Darshill Somset............19 ST6143
Dartford Kent............23 TQ5474
Dartington Devon............5 SX7862
Dartmouth Devon............5 SX8751
Darton S York............55 SE3110
Darvel Strath............74 NS5637
Darwen Lancs............54 SD6922
Datchet Berks............22 SU9877
Datchworth Herts............31 TL2619
Datchworth Green Herts............31 TL2718
Daubhill Gt Man............47 SD7007
Dauntsey Wilts............20 ST9782
Dauntsey Green Wilts............20 ST9981
Dava Highld............93 NJ0038
Davenham Ches............47 SJ6571
Daventry Nhants............29 SP5762
Davidson's Mains Loth............75 NT2175
Davidstow Cnwll............4 SX1587
Davington D & G............67 NT2302
Davington Hill Kent............15 TR0161
Daviot Gramp............95 NJ7428
Daviot Highld............93 NH7239
Daviot House Highld............93 NH7240
Davoch of Grange Gramp............94 NJ4751
Dawesgreen Surrey............12 TQ2147
Dawley Shrops............37 SJ6808
Dawlish Devon............5 SX9576
Dawlish Warren Devon............5 SX9778
Dawn Clwyd............45 SH8672
Daybrook Notts............49 SK5744
Daylesford Gloucs............29 SP2425
Deal Kent............15 TR3752
Dean Cumb............58 NY0725
Dean Devon............18 SS7048
Dean Devon............5 SX7364
Dean Hants............10 SU4431
Dean Hants............11 SU5619
Dean Oxon............29 SP3422
Dean Somset............20 ST6743
Dean Bottom Kent............14 TQ5868
Dean Court Oxon............29 SP4705
Dean Prior Devon............5 SX7363
Deanburnhaugh Border............67 NT3911
Deancombe Devon............5 SX7264
Deane Gt Man............47 SD6907
Deane Hants............21 SU5450
Deanhead W York............55 SE0415
Deanland Dorset............9 ST9918
Deanraw Nthumb............68 NY8162
Deans Loth............75 NT0369
Deanscales Cumb............58 NY0926
Deanshanger Nhants............30 SP7639
Deanshaugh Gramp............94 NJ3550
Deanston Cent............81 NN7101
Dearham Cumb............58 NY0736
Debach Suff............33 TM2454
Debden Essex............24 TL5533
Debden Essex............23 TQ4496
Debenham Suff............33 TM1763
Deblin's Green H & W............28 SO8148
Dechmont Loth............75 NT0370
Dechmont Road Loth............75 NT0269
Deddington Oxon............29 SP4631
Dedham Essex............25 TM0533
Dedworth Berks............22 SU9476
Deene Nhants............40 SP9492
Deenethorpe Nhants............40 SP9591
Deeping Gate Lincs............40 TF1509
Deeping St James Lincs............40 TF1609
Deeping St Nicholas Lincs............41 TF2115
Deerhurst Gloucs............28 SO8730
Defford H & W............28 SO9143
Defynnog Powys............26 SN9227
Deganwy Gwynd............45 SH7779
Degnish Strath............79 NM7812
Deighton N York............62 NZ3801
Deighton N York............56 SE6244
Deiniolen Gwynd............44 SH5763
Delabole Cnwll............3 SX0683
Delamere Ches............47 SJ5668

Place	Map	Grid
Delfrigs Gramp	95	NJ9620
Dell Quay W Susx	11	SU8302
Delliefure Highld	93	NJ0730
Delnashaugh Inn Gramp	94	NJ1835
Delny Highld	93	NH7372
Delves Dur	69	NZ1149
Delvine Tays	82	NO1240
Dembleby Lincs	41	TF0437
Denaby S York	49	SK4899
Denbigh Clwyd	45	SJ0566
Denbrae Fife	83	NO3818
Denbury Devon	5	SX8268
Denby Derbys	49	SK3946
Denby Dale W York	55	SE2208
Denchworth Oxon	21	SU3891
Dendron Cumb	53	SD2470
Denfield Tays	82	NN9517
Denford Nhants	30	SP9976
Dengie Essex	25	TL9802
Denham Bucks	22	TQ0487
Denham Suffk	32	TL7561
Denham Suffk	33	TM1974
Denham Green Bucks	22	TQ0488
Denhead Fife	83	NO4613
Denhead Gramp	95	NJ9952
Denhead of Gray Tays	83	NO3531
Denholm Border	76	NT5718
Denholme W York	55	SE0734
Denmead Hants	11	SU6512
Denmore Gramp	95	NJ9411
Dennington Suffk	33	TM2867
Denny Cent	81	NS8082
Dennyloanhead Cent	81	NS8080
Denside Gramp	89	NO8095
Densole Kent	15	TR2141
Denston Suffk	32	TL7652
Denstone Staffs	48	SK0940
Denstroude Kent	15	TR1061
Dent Cumb	60	SD7086
Dent-de-Lion Kent	15	TR3269
Denton Cambs	40	TL1587
Denton Dur	61	NZ2118
Denton E Susx	13	TQ4502
Denton Gt Man	48	SJ9295
Denton Kent	15	TR2147
Denton Lincs	40	SK8632
Denton N York	55	SE1448
Denton Nhants	30	SP8358
Denton Norfk	33	TM2788
Denver Norfk	41	TF6001
Denwick Nthumb	69	NU2014
Deopham Norfk	42	TG0400
Deopham Green Norfk	42	TM0499
Deptford Gt Lon	23	TQ3777
Deptford Wilts	10	SU4138
Derby Derbys	39	SK3536
Derby Devon	6	SS5633
Derbyhaven IOM	52	SC2867
Derculich Tays	87	NN8852
Deri M Glam	18	SO1201
Derringstone Kent	15	TR2049
Derrington Staffs	38	SJ8922
Derry Hill Wilts	20	ST9670
Derrythorpe Humb	56	SE8208
Dersingham Norfk	42	TF6830
Dervaig Strath	79	NM4352
Derwen Clwyd	46	SJ0750
Derwenlas Powys	35	SN7298
Desborough Nhants	40	SP8083
Desford Leics	39	SK4703
Deskford Gramp	94	NJ5061
Detling Kent	14	TQ7958
Devauden Gwent	19	ST4898
Devil's Bridge Dyfed	35	SN7376
Devizes Wilts	20	SU0061
Devonport Devon	4	SX4554
Devonside Cent	82	NS9196
Devoran Cnwll	2	SW7939
Dewarton Loth	76	NT3763
Dewlish Dorset	9	SY7798
Dewsbury W York	55	SE2421
Deytheur Powys	36	SJ2317
Dial Green W Susx	12	SU9227
Dial Post W Susx	12	TQ1519
Dibden Hants	10	SU4008
Dibden Purlieu Hants	10	SU4106
Dickleburgh Norfk	33	TM1682
Didbrook Gloucs	28	SP0531
Didcot Oxon	21	SU5290
Diddington Cambs	31	TL1965
Diddlebury Shrops	37	SO5085
Didling W Susx	11	SU8318
Didmarton Gloucs	20	ST8287
Didsbury Gt Man	47	SJ8491
Digby Lincs	50	TF0854
Digg Highld	90	NG4668
Diggle Gt Man	54	SE0007
Digmoor Lancs	46	SD4905
Dihewyd Dyfed	34	SN4855
Dilham Norfk	43	TG3325
Dilhorne Staffs	48	SJ9743
Dillington Cambs	30	TL1365
Dilston Nthumb	68	NY9763
Dilton Wilts	20	ST8548
Dilton Marsh Wilts	20	ST8449
Dilwyn H & W	27	SO4154
Dinas Dyfed	16	SN0138
Dinas Gwynd	44	SH2735
Dinas Powys S Glam	19	ST1571
Dinas-Mawddwy Gwynd	35	SH8515
Dinder Somset	19	ST5744
Dinedor H & W	27	SO5336
Dingle Mersyd	46	SJ3687
Dingley Nhants	40	SP7787
Dingwall Highld	92	NH5458
Dinnet Gramp	88	NO4598
Dinnington S York	49	SK5285
Dinnington Somset	8	ST4012
Dinnington T & W	69	NZ2073
Dinorwic Gwynd	44	SH5961
Dinton Bucks	22	SP7610
Dinton Wilts	10	SU0131
Dinwoodie D & G	67	NY1190
Dinworthy Devon	6	SS3015
Dipford Somset	8	ST2021
Dippen Strath	72	NR7937
Dippertown Devon	4	SX4284
Dippin Strath	72	NS0422
Dipple Gramp	94	NJ3258
Dipple Strath	73	NS2002
Diptford Devon	5	SX7256
Dipton Dur	69	NZ1554
Dirleton Loth	83	NT5184
Dirt Pot Nthumb	68	NY8545
Diseworth Leics	39	SK4524
Dishforth N York	62	SE3873
Disley Ches	48	SJ9784
Diss Norfk	33	TM1180
Distington Cumb	58	NY0023
Ditchampton Wilts	10	SU0831
Ditchburn Nthumb	77	NU1320
Ditcheat Somset	19	ST6236
Ditchingham Norfk	33	TM3391
Ditchling E Susx	12	TQ3215
Ditherington Shrops	37	SJ5014
Ditteridge Wilts	20	ST8169
Dittisham Devon	5	SX8655
Ditton Ches	46	SJ4986
Ditton Kent	14	TQ7158
Ditton Green Cambs	32	TL6558
Ditton Priors Shrops	37	SO6089
Dixton Gloucs	28	SO9830
Dixton Gwent	27	SO5113
Dobcross Gt Man	54	SD9906
Dobwalls Cnwll	4	SX2165
Doccombe Devon	5	SX7786
Dochgarroch Highld	92	NH6140
Docker Lancs	59	SD5774
Docking Norfk	42	TF7636
Docklow H & W	27	SO5657
Dockray Cumb	59	NY3921
Dod's Leigh Staffs	38	SK0134
Dodd's Green Ches	47	SJ6043
Doddinghurst Essex	24	TQ5999
Doddington Cambs	41	TL4090
Doddington Kent	14	TQ9357
Doddington Lincs	50	SK8970
Doddington Nthumb	77	NT9932
Doddington Shrops	37	SO6176
Doddiscombsleigh Devon	5	SX8586
Dodford H & W	38	SO9373
Dodford Nhants	29	SP6160
Dodington Avon	20	ST7580
Dodington Somset	19	ST1740
Dodleston Ches	46	SJ3661
Dodside Strath	74	NS5053
Dodworth S York	55	SE3105
Dogdyke Lincs	51	TF2055
Dogmersfield Hants	22	SU7852
Dolanog Powys	36	SJ0612
Dolbenmaen Gwynd	44	SH5043
Dolfor Powys	36	SO1087
Dolgarrog Gwynd	45	SH7767
Dolgellau Gwynd	35	SH7217
Doll Highld	97	NC8803
Dollar Cent	82	NS9698
Dollarfield Cent	82	NS9697
Dolphin Clwyd	46	SJ1973
Dolphinholme Lancs	53	SD5253
Dolphinton Strath	75	NT1046
Dolton Devon	6	SS5712
Dolwen Clwyd	45	SH8874
Dolwyddelan Gwynd	45	SH7352
Domgay Powys	36	SJ2818
Doncaster S York	56	SE5703
Donhead St Andrew Wilts	9	ST9124
Donhead St Mary Wilts	9	ST9024
Donibristle Fife	82	NT1688
Doniford Somset	18	ST0842
Donington Lincs	41	TF2035
Donington on Bain Lincs	51	TF2382
Donisthorpe Leics	39	SK3113
Donnington Berks	21	SU4668
Donnington Gloucs	29	SP1708
Donnington Shrops	37	SJ5708
Donnington Shrops	37	SJ7114
Donnington W Susx	11	SU8501
Donyatt Somset	8	ST3314
Doonfoot Strath	73	NS3219
Doonholm Strath	73	NS3317
Dorback Lodge Highld	93	NJ0716
Dorchester Dorset	9	SY6990
Dorchester Oxon	21	SU5794
Dordon Warwks	39	SK2500
Dores Highld	92	NH5934
Dorking Surrey	12	TQ1649
Dormans Land Surrey	13	TQ4041
Dormington H & W	27	SO5840
Dormston H & W	28	SO9857
Dorney Berks	22	SU9378
Dornie Highld	85	NG8826
Dornoch Highld	97	NH7989
Dornock D & G	67	NY2366
Dorrery Highld	100	ND0754
Dorridge W Mids	38	SP1775
Dorrington Lincs	50	TF0852
Dorrington Shrops	37	SJ4702
Dorrington Shrops	37	SJ7340
Dorsington Warwks	28	SP1349
Dorstone H & W	27	SO3141
Dorton Bucks	30	SP6814
Dougarie Strath	72	NR8837
Douglas IOM	52	SC3775
Douglas Strath	74	NS8330
Douglas and Angus Tays	83	NO4233
Douglas Castle Strath	74	NS8431
Douglas Pier Strath	80	NS1999
Douglas Water Strath	74	NS8736
Douglas West Strath	74	NS8231
Douglastown Tays	88	NO4147
Doulting Somset	19	ST6443
Dounby Ork	103	HY2920
Doune Cent	81	NN7201
Doune Highld	96	NC4400
Dounepark Strath	64	NX1897
Dounie Highld	96	NH5690
Dousland Devon	4	SX5369
Dove Holes Derbys	48	SK0777
Dovenby Cumb	58	NY0933
Dover Kent	15	TR3241
Dovercourt Essex	25	TM2431
Doverdale H & W	28	SO8666
Doveridge Derbys	38	SK1133
Doversgreen Surrey	12	TQ2049
Dowally Tays	88	NO0048
Dowdeswell Gloucs	28	SP0019
Dowlais M Glam	26	SO0607
Dowland Devon	6	SS5610
Dowlish Wake Somset	8	ST3712
Down Ampney Gloucs	20	SU0996
Down Hatherley Gloucs	28	SO8622
Down St Mary Devon	7	SS7604
Down Thomas Devon	4	SX5050
Downderry Cnwll	4	SX3154
Downe Gt Lon	23	TQ4361
Downend Avon	19	ST6577
Downend Gloucs	20	ST8398
Downfield Tays	83	NO3932
Downgate Cnwll	4	SX2871
Downgate Cnwll	4	SX3672
Downham Cambs	41	TL5284
Downham Essex	24	TQ7296
Downham Gt Lon	23	TQ3871
Downham Lancs	54	SD7844
Downham Market Norfk	41	TF6103
Downhead Somset	9	ST5625
Downhead Somset	19	ST6945
Downhill Tays	82	NO0930
Downholme N York	61	SE1197
Downies Gramp	89	NO9294
Downley Bucks	22	SU8495
Downside Surrey	22	TQ1057
Downton Hants	10	SZ2693
Downton Wilts	10	SU1821
Downton on the Rock H & W	36	SO4273
Dowsby Lincs	40	TF1129
Doynton Avon	20	ST7274
Draethen M Glam	19	ST2287
Draffan Strath	74	NS7945
Drakeholes Notts	49	SK7090
Drakemyre Strath	73	NS2950
Drakes Broughton H & W	28	SO9248
Draughton N York	55	SE0352
Draughton Nhants	30	SP7676
Drax N York	56	SE6726
Draycote Warwks	29	SP4433
Draycott Derbys	39	SK4433
Draycott Gloucs	29	SP1835
Draycott Somset	19	ST4751
Draycott in the Clay Staffs	38	SK1528
Draycott in the Moors Staffs	48	SJ9840
Drayton H & W	38	SO9075
Drayton Hants	11	SU6705
Drayton Leics	40	SP8392
Drayton Norfk	43	TG1813
Drayton Oxon	29	SP4241
Drayton Oxon	21	SU4894
Drayton Somset	8	ST4024
Drayton Bassett Staffs	39	SK1900
Drayton Beauchamp Bucks	22	SP9011
Drayton Parslow Bucks	30	SP8328
Drayton St Leonard Oxon	21	SU5996
Dreen Hill Dyfed	16	SM9214
Drefach Dyfed	17	SN3538
Drefach Dyfed	17	SN4945
Drefach Dyfed	17	SN5213
Dreghorn Strath	73	NS3538
Drellingore Kent	15	TR2441
Drem Loth	83	NT5079
Drewsteignton Devon	5	SX7391
Driby Lincs	51	TF3874
Driffield Gloucs	20	SU0799
Driffield Humb	56	TA0257
Drift Cnwll	2	SW4328
Drigg Cumb	58	SD0699
Drighlington W York	55	SE2228
Drimnin Highld	79	NM5554
Drimpton Dorset	8	ST4104
Drimsallie Highld	85	NM9578
Dringhouses N York	56	SE5849
Drinkstone Suffk	32	TL9561
Drinkstone Green Suffk	32	TL9660
Driver's End Herts	31	TL2220
Drointon Staffs	38	SK0226
Droitwich H & W	28	SO8963
Dron Tays	82	NO1416
Dronfield Derbys	49	SK3578
Drongan Strath	73	NS4418
Dronley Tays	83	NO3435
Droop Dorset	9	ST7508
Droxford Hants	11	SU6018
Droylsden Gt Man	48	SJ9097
Druid Clwyd	45	SJ0443
Druidston Dyfed	16	SM8616
Druimachoish Highld	86	NN1246
Druimarbin Highld	86	NN0770
Druimdrishaig Strath	71	NR7370
Druimindarroch Highld	85	NM6884
Drum Strath	71	NR9276
Drum Tays	82	NO0400
Drumalbin Strath	74	NS9038
Drumbeg Highld	98	NC1232
Drumblade Gramp	94	NJ5840
Drumblair House Gramp	94	NJ6343
Drumbreddon D & G	64	NX0843
Drumbuie Highld	85	NG7730
Drumburgh Cumb	67	NY2659
Drumburn D & G	66	NX8856
Drumchapel Strath	74	NS5270
Drumchastle Tays	87	NN6858
Drumclog Strath	74	NS6438
Drumeldrie Fife	83	NO4403
Drumelzier Border	75	NT1334
Drumfearn Highld	85	NG6716
Drumfrennie Gramp	89	NO7298
Drumguish Highld	87	NH7900
Drumhead Gramp	89	NO6092
Drumin Gramp	94	NJ1830
Drumjohn D & G	65	NX5297
Drumlamford Strath	64	NX2876
Drumlasie Gramp	89	NJ6405
Drumleaning Cumb	67	NY2751
Drumlemble Strath	72	NR6619
Drumlithie Gramp	89	NO7880
Drummoddie D & G	64	NX3845
Drummore D & G	64	NX1336
Drummore D & G	66	NX9074
Drummuir Gramp	94	NJ3843
Drumnadrochit Highld	92	NH5030
Drumnagorrach Gramp	94	NJ5252
Drumpark D & G	66	NX8779
Drumrunie Lodge Highld	96	NC1604
Drumshang Strath	73	NS2514
Drumuie Highld	90	NG4546
Drumvaich Cent	81	NN6704
Drumvillie Highld	93	NH9420
Drunzie Tays	82	NO1308
Dry Doddington Lincs	50	SK8546
Dry Drayton Cambs	31	TL3861
Drybeck Cumb	60	NY6615
Drybridge Gramp	94	NJ4362
Drybridge Strath	73	NS3536
Drybrook Gloucs	27	SO6417
Dryburgh Border	76	NT5932
Dryhope Border	75	NT2624
Drym Cnwll	2	SW6133
Drymen Cent	81	NS4788
Drymuir Gramp	95	NJ9046
Drynoch Highld	84	NG4031
Dryton Shrops	37	SJ5905
Dubford Gramp	95	NJ7963
Duchally Highld	96	NC3817
Ducklington Oxon	29	SP3507
Duddingston Loth	75	NT2872
Duddington Nhants	40	SK9800
Duddlestone Somset	8	ST2321
Duddlewick Shrops	37	SO6583
Duddo Nthumb	77	NT9342
Duddon Ches	46	SJ5164
Dudleston Shrops	36	SJ3438
Dudley T & W	69	NZ2573
Dudley W Mids	38	SO9490
Dudley Port W Mids	38	SO9691
Dudsbury Dorset	10	SZ0798
Duffield Derbys	49	SK3443
Duffryn M Glam	18	SS8495
Dufftown Gramp	94	NJ3240
Duffus Gramp	94	NJ1668
Dufton Cumb	60	NY6825
Duggleby N York	56	SE8767
Duirinish Highld	85	NG7831
Duisdalemore Highld	85	NG7013
Duisky Highld	85	NN0076
Duke Street Suffk	32	TM0742
Dukinfield Gt Man	48	SJ9397
Dulcote Somset	19	ST5644
Dulford Devon	8	ST0706
Dull Tays	87	NN8049
Dullatur Strath	74	NS7476
Dullingham Cambs	32	TL6357
Dullingham Ley Cambs	32	TL6456
Dulnain Bridge Highld	93	NH9925
Duloe Beds	30	TL1560
Duloe Cnwll	4	SX2358
Dulverton Somset	7	SS9127
Dulwich Gt Lon	23	TQ3373
Dumbarton Strath	80	NS3975
Dumbleton Gloucs	28	SP0135
Dumfries D & G	66	NX9776
Dumgoyne Cent	81	NS5283
Dummer Hants	21	SU5846
Dumpton Kent	15	TR3966
Dun Tays	89	NO6659
Dunalastair Tays	87	NN7158
Dunan Highld	84	NG5828
Dunan Strath	80	NS1571
Dunan Tays	87	NN4757
Dunaverty Strath	72	NR6807
Dunball Somset	19	ST3141
Dunbar Loth	83	NT6778
Dunbeath Highld	100	ND1629
Dunbeg Strath	79	NM8833
Dunblane Cent	81	NN7801
Dunbog Fife	83	NO2817
Duncanston Highld	92	NH5856
Duncanstone Gramp	94	NJ5726
Dunchideock Devon	5	SX8787
Dunchurch Warwks	39	SP4871
Duncow D & G	66	NX9683
Duncrievie Tays	82	NO1309
Duncton W Susx	12	SU9617
Dundee Tays	83	NO4030
Dundon Somset	8	ST4832
Dundonald Strath	73	NS3634
Dundonnell Highld	91	NH0987
Dundraw Cumb	67	NY2149
Dundreggan Highld	92	NH3214
Dundrennan D & G	65	NX7447
Dundry Avon	19	ST5666
Dunecht Gramp	95	NJ7509
Dunfermline Fife	82	NT0987
Dunfield Gloucs	20	SU1497
Dungavel Strath	74	NS6537
Dunglass Loth	76	NT7761
Dunham Notts	50	SK8074
Dunham Town Gt Man	47	SJ7387
Dunham Woodhouses Gt Man	47	SJ7282
Dunham-on-the-Hill Ches	46	SJ4772
Dunhampton H & W	28	SO8466
Dunholme Lincs	50	TF0279
Dunino Fife	83	NO5311
Dunipace Cent	81	NS8083
Dunk's Green Kent	13	TQ6152
Dunkeld Tays	88	NO0242
Dunkerton Avon	20	ST7159
Dunkeswell Devon	8	ST1407
Dunkeswick W York	55	SE3047
Dunkirk Avon	20	ST7885
Dunkirk Kent	15	TR0759
Dunlappie Tays	89	NO5867
Dunley H & W	28	SO7869
Dunlop Strath	73	NS4049
Dunmaglass Highld	92	NH5922
Dunmore Cent	82	NS8989
Dunmore Strath	71	NR7961
Dunnet Highld	100	ND2171
Dunnichen Tays	89	NO5048
Dunning Tays	82	NO0114
Dunnington Humb	57	TA1551
Dunnington N York	56	SE6652
Dunnington Warwks	28	SP0654
Dunnockshaw Lancs	54	SD8127
Dunoon Strath	80	NS1776
Dunphail Gramp	93	NJ0048
Dunragit D & G	64	NX1557
Duns Border	76	NT7853
Duns Tew Oxon	29	SP4528
Dunsby Lincs	40	TF1026
Dunscore D & G	66	NX8684
Dunsdale Cleve	62	NZ6019
Dunsden Green Oxon	22	SU7377
Dunsdon Devon	6	SS3008
Dunsfold Surrey	12	TQ0035
Dunsford Devon	5	SX8189
Dunshelt Fife	83	NO2410
Dunshillock Gramp	95	NJ9848
Dunsill Notts	49	SK4661
Dunsley N York	63	NZ8511
Dunsley Staffs	38	SO8583
Dunsmore Bucks	22	SP8605
Dunsop Bridge Lancs	54	SD6649
Dunstable Beds	30	TL0122
Dunstall Staffs	38	SK1820
Dunstan Nthumb	77	NU2419
Dunster Somset	7	SS9943
Dunston Lincs	50	TF0662
Dunston Norfk	43	TG2202
Dunston Staffs	38	SJ9217
Dunston T & W	69	NZ2362
Dunstone Devon	5	SX5951
Dunstone Devon	5	SX7175
Dunswell Humb	57	TA0735
Dunsyre Strath	75	NT0748
Dunterton Devon	4	SX3779
Duntisbourne Abbots Gloucs	28	SO9607
Duntisbourne Rouse Gloucs	28	SO9805
Duntish Dorset	9	ST6906
Duntocher Strath	74	NS4872
Dunton Beds	31	TL2344
Dunton Bucks	30	SP8224
Dunton Norfk	42	TF8830
Dunton Bassett Leics	39	SP5490
Dunton Green Kent	23	TQ5157
Duntulm Highld	90	NG4174
Dunure Strath	73	NS2515
Dunvant W Glam	17	SS5993
Dunvegan Highld	90	NG2547
Dunwich Suffk	33	TM4770

Durgan *Cnwll*	2	SW7727
Durham *Dur*	61	NZ2742
Durisdeer *D & G*	66	NS8903
Durisdeermill *D & G*	66	NS8804
Durleigh *Somset*	19	ST2736
Durley *Hants*	11	SU5116
Durley *Wilts*	21	SU2364
Durley Street *Hants*	11	SU5217
Durlock *Kent*	15	TR2757
Durlock *Kent*	15	TR3164
Durmgley *Tays*	88	NO4250
Durness *Highld*	98	NC4068
Duror *Highld*	86	NM9955
Durran *Strath*	80	NM9607
Durrington *W Susx*	12	TQ1105
Durrington *Wilts*	20	SU1544
Durris *Gramp*	89	NO7796
Dursley *Gloucs*	20	ST7598
Dursley Cross *Gloucs*	28	SO6920
Durston *Somset*	8	ST2928
Durweston *Dorset*	9	ST8508
Duston *Nhants*	30	SP7261
Duthil *Highld*	93	NH9324
Dutton *Ches*	47	SJ5779
Duxford *Cambs*	31	TL4846
Duxford *Oxon*	21	SP3600
Dwygyfylchi *Gwynd*	45	SH7376
Dwyran *Gwynd*	44	SH4465
Dyce *Gramp*	95	NJ8812
Dye House *Nthumb*	68	NY9358
Dyffryn Ardudwy *Gwynd*	34	SH5823
Dyffryn Cellwen *W Glam*	26	SN8510
Dyke *Gramp*	93	NH9858
Dyke *Lincs*	40	TF1022
Dykehead *Cent*	81	NS5997
Dykehead *Strath*	74	NS8759
Dykehead *Tays*	88	NO2453
Dykehead *Tays*	88	NO3859
Dykelands *Gramp*	89	NO7068
Dykends *Tays*	88	NO2557
Dykeside *Gramp*	95	NJ7243
Dymchurch *Kent*	15	TR1029
Dymock *Gloucs*	28	SO7031
Dyrham *Avon*	20	ST7475
Dysart *Fife*	83	NT3093
Dyserth *Clwyd*	45	SJ0578

E

Eagland Hill *Lancs*	53	SD4345
Eagle *Lincs*	50	SK8766
Eaglescliffe *Cleve*	62	NZ4215
Eaglesfield *Cumb*	58	NY0928
Eaglesfield *D & G*	67	NY2374
Eaglesham *Strath*	74	NS5751
Eagley *Gt Man*	54	SD7112
Eakring *Notts*	49	SK6762
Ealand *Humb*	56	SE7811
Ealing *Gt Lon*	23	TQ1780
Eals *Nthumb*	68	NY6756
Eamont Bridge *Cumb*	59	NY5228
Earby *Lancs*	54	SD9046
Eardington *Shrops*	37	SO7290
Eardisland *H & W*	27	SO4158
Eardisley *H & W*	27	SO3149
Eardiston *H & W*	28	SO6968
Eardiston *Shrops*	36	SJ3725
Earith *Cambs*	31	TL3875
Earl Shilton *Leics*	39	SP4697
Earl Soham *Suffk*	33	TM2363
Earl Sterndale *Derbys*	48	SK0966
Earl's Croome *H & W*	28	SO8642
Earlestown *Mersyd*	47	SJ5795
Earley *Berks*	22	SU7472
Earlish *Highld*	90	NG3861
Earls Barton *Nhants*	30	SP8563
Earls Colne *Essex*	24	TL8528
Earls Common *H & W*	28	SO9559
Earlsdon *W Mids*	39	SP3278
Earlsferry *Fife*	83	NO4800
Earlsfield *Gt Lon*	23	TQ2573
Earlsford *Gramp*	95	NJ8334
Earlsheaton *W York*	55	SE2621
Earlston *Border*	76	NT5738
Earlston *Strath*	73	NS4035
Earlswood *Surrey*	12	TQ2749
Earlswood *Warwks*	38	SP1174
Earnley *W Susx*	11	SZ8196
Earsdon *Nthumb*	69	NZ1993
Earsdon *T & W*	69	NZ3272
Earsham *Norfk*	33	TM3288
Eartham *W Susx*	12	SU9309
Easby *N York*	62	NZ5708
Easdale *Strath*	79	NM7417
Easebourne *W Susx*	11	SU9023
Easenhall *Warwks*	39	SP4679
Eashing *Surrey*	12	SU9443
Easington *Bucks*	22	SP6810
Easington *Cleve*	63	NZ7417
Easington *Dur*	69	NZ4143
Easington *Humb*	57	TA3992
Easington Colliery *Dur*	69	NZ4344
Easingwold *N York*	55	SE5269
Eassie and Nevay *Tays*	88	NO3344
East Aberthaw *S Glam*	18	ST0366
East Allington *Devon*	5	SX7748
East Anstey *Devon*	7	SS8626
East Appleton *N York*	61	SE2395
East Ashey *IOW*	11	SZ5888
East Ashling *W Susx*	11	SU8107
East Ayton *N York*	63	SE9985
East Barkwith *Lincs*	50	TF1681
East Barming *Kent*	14	TQ7254
East Barnby *N York*	63	NZ8212
East Barnet *Gt Lon*	23	TQ2795
East Barns *Loth*	76	NT7176
East Barsham *Norfk*	42	TF9133
East Beckham *Norfk*	43	TG1639
East Bedfont *Gt Lon*	22	TQ0873
East Bergholt *Suffk*	25	TM0734
East Bilney *Norfk*	42	TF9519
East Blatchington *E Susx*	13	TQ4800
East Boldon *T & W*	69	NZ3661
East Boldre *Hants*	10	SU3700
East Bradenham *Norfk*	42	TF9308
East Brent *Somset*	19	ST3451
East Bridgford *Notts*	49	SK6943
East Buckland *Devon*	7	SS6831
East Budleigh *Devon*	8	SY0684
East Butterwick *Humb*	56	SE8306
East Calder *Loth*	75	NT0867
East Carleton *Norfk*	43	TG1701
East Carlton *Nhants*	40	SP8389

East Carlton *W York*	55	SE2143
East Challow *Oxon*	21	SU3888
East Charleton *Devon*	5	SX7642
East Chelborough *Dorset*	9	ST5505
East Chiltington *E Susx*	13	TQ3715
East Chinnock *Somset*	8	ST4913
East Chisenbury *Wilts*	20	SU1452
East Clandon *Surrey*	12	TQ0651
East Claydon *Bucks*	30	SP7325
East Coker *Somset*	8	ST5412
East Combe *Somset*	8	ST1631
East Compton *Somset*	19	ST6141
East Cornworthy *Devon*	5	SX8455
East Cottingwith *Humb*	56	SE7042
East Cowes *IOW*	11	SZ5095
East Cowick *Humb*	56	SE6620
East Cowton *N York*	61	NZ3003
East Cranmore *Somset*	20	ST6743
East Creech *Dorset*	9	SY9382
East Dean *E Susx*	13	TV5598
East Dean *H & W*	27	SO6520
East Dean *Hants*	10	SU2726
East Dean *W Susx*	11	SU9012
East Dereham *Norfk*	42	TF9913
East Down *Devon*	6	SS6041
East Drayton *Notts*	50	SK7775
East Dulwich *Gt Lon*	23	TQ3375
East Dundry *Avon*	19	ST5766
East Ella *Humb*	57	TA0529
East End *Hants*	21	SU4161
East End *Hants*	10	SZ3696
East End *Kent*	14	TQ8335
East End *Oxon*	29	SP3915
East End *Somset*	20	ST6746
East Everleigh *Wilts*	21	SU2053
East Farleigh *Kent*	14	TQ7353
East Farndon *Nhants*	40	SP7184
East Ferry *Lincs*	50	SK8199
East Fortune *Loth*	83	NT5479
East Garston *Berks*	21	SU3576
East Goscote *Leics*	39	SK6413
East Grafton *Wilts*	21	SU2560
East Grange *Gramp*	93	NJ0961
East Grimstead *Wilts*	10	SU2227
East Grinstead *W Susx*	13	TQ3938
East Guldeford *E Susx*	14	TQ9321
East Haddon *Nhants*	30	SP6668
East Hagbourne *Oxon*	21	SU5288
East Halton *Humb*	57	TA1319
East Ham *Gt Lon*	23	TQ4283
East Hanney *Oxon*	21	SU4193
East Hanningfield *Essex*	24	TL7701
East Hardwick *W York*	55	SE4618
East Harling *Norfk*	32	TL9986
East Harlsey *N York*	62	SE4299
East Harnham *Wilts*	10	SU1428
East Harptree *Avon*	19	ST5655
East Hartburn *Cleve*	62	NZ4217
East Hartford *Nthumb*	69	NZ2679
East Harting *W Susx*	11	SU7919
East Hatch *Wilts*	9	ST9228
East Hatley *Cambs*	31	TL2850
East Hauxwell *N York*	61	SE1693
East Haven *Tays*	83	NO5836
East Heckington *Lincs*	50	TF1944
East Hedleyhope *Dur*	61	NZ1540
East Helmsdale *Highld*	97	ND0315
East Hendred *Oxon*	21	SU4588
East Heslerton *N York*	63	SE9276
East Hewish *Avon*	19	ST4064
East Hoathly *E Susx*	13	TQ5216
East Holme *Dorset*	9	SY8986
East Horndon *Essex*	24	TQ6389
East Horrington *Somset*	19	ST5846
East Horsley *Surrey*	12	TQ0952
East Howe *Dorset*	10	SZ0795
East Huntspill *Somset*	19	ST3445
East Hyde *Beds*	30	TL1217
East Ilsley *Berks*	21	SU4980
East Keal *Lincs*	51	TF3863
East Kennett *Wilts*	20	SU1167
East Keswick *W York*	55	SE3644
East Kilbride *Strath*	74	NS6354
East Kirkby *Lincs*	51	TF3362
East Knighton *Dorset*	9	SY8185
East Knoyle *Wilts*	9	ST8830
East Kyloe *Nthumb*	77	NU0639
East Lambrook *Somset*	8	ST4318
East Langdon *Kent*	15	TR3346
East Langton *Leics*	40	SP7292
East Laroch *Highld*	86	NN0858
East Lavant *W Susx*	11	SU8608
East Lavington *W Susx*	12	SU9416
East Layton *N York*	61	NZ1609
East Leake *Notts*	39	SK5526
East Leigh *Devon*	7	SS6905
East Leigh *Devon*	5	SX7657
East Lexham *Norfk*	42	TF8517
East Linton *Loth*	76	NT5977
East Lockinge *Oxon*	21	SU4287
East Lound *Humb*	50	SK7899
East Lulworth *Dorset*	9	SY8682
East Lutton *N York*	56	SE9469
East Lydford *Somset*	9	ST5731
East Malling *Kent*	14	TQ7056
East Marden *W Susx*	11	SU8014
East Markham *Notts*	50	SK7373
East Martin *Hants*	10	SU0719
East Marton *N York*	54	SD9050
East Meon *Hants*	11	SU6822
East Mersea *Essex*	25	TM0414
East Molesey *Surrey*	22	TQ1467
East Morden *Dorset*	9	SY9194
East Morton *D & G*	66	NS8800
East Morton *N York*	55	SE0942
East Ness *N York*	62	SE6978
East Norton *Leics*	40	SK7800
East Ogwell *Devon*	5	SX8370
East Orchard *Dorset*	9	ST8317
East Peckham *Kent*	14	TQ6648
East Pennar *Dyfed*	16	SM9602
East Pennard *Somset*	19	ST5937
East Perry *Cambs*	30	TL1566
East Portlemouth *Devon*	5	SX7538
East Prawle *Devon*	5	SX7836
East Preston *W Susx*	12	TQ0602
East Pulham *Dorset*	9	ST7209
East Putford *Devon*	6	SS3616
East Quantoxhead *Somset*	18	ST1343
East Rainton *T & W*	69	NZ3347
East Ravendale *Lincs*	51	TF2399
East Raynham *Norfk*	42	TF8825
East Rigton *W York*	55	SE3743
East Rounton *N York*	62	NZ4203
East Rudham *Norfk*	42	TF8228
East Runton *Norfk*	43	TG1942
East Ruston *Norfk*	43	TG3427
East Saltoun *Loth*	76	NT4767

East Sheen *Gt Lon*	23	TQ2075
East Shefford *Berks*	21	SU3874
East Stockwith *Lincs*	50	SK7894
East Stoke *Dorset*	9	SY8686
East Stoke *Notts*	50	SK7549
East Stour *Dorset*	9	ST8022
East Stourmouth *Kent*	15	TR2662
East Stowford *Devon*	7	SS6326
East Stratton *Hants*	21	SU5440
East Studdal *Kent*	15	TR3149
East Taphouse *Cnwll*	3	SX1863
East Thirston *Nthumb*	61	NZ1900
East Tilbury *Essex*	24	TQ6877
East Tisted *Hants*	11	SU7032
East Torrington *Lincs*	50	TF1483
East Tuddenham *Norfk*	42	TG0711
East Tytherley *Hants*	10	SU2929
East Tytherton *Wilts*	20	ST9674
East Village *Devon*	7	SS8405
East Wall *Shrops*	37	SO5293
East Walton *Norfk*	42	TF7416
East Water *Somset*	19	ST5350
East Week *Devon*	5	SX6692
East Wellow *Hants*	10	SU3020
East Wemyss *Fife*	83	NT3497
East Whitburn *Loth*	75	NS9665
East Wickham *Gt Lon*	23	TQ4677
East Williamston *Dyfed*	16	SN0904
East Winch *Norfk*	42	TF6916
East Winterslow *Wilts*	10	SU2434
East Wittering *W Susx*	11	SZ7997
East Witton *N York*	61	SE1486
East Woodburn *Nthumb*	68	NY9086
East Woodhay *Hants*	21	SU4061
East Worldham *Hants*	11	SU7538
East Wretham *Norfk*	32	TL9190
East Youlstone *Devon*	6	SS2715
Eastbourne *Dur*	61	NZ3013
Eastbourne *E Susx*	13	TV6199
Eastbridge *Suffk*	33	TM4566
Eastburn *W York*	54	SE0144
Eastbury *Berks*	21	SU3477
Eastbury *Herts*	22	TQ1092
Eastby *N York*	54	SE0154
Eastchurch *Kent*	15	TQ9871
Eastcombe *Gloucs*	28	SO8904
Eastcote *Gt Lon*	22	TQ1088
Eastcote *Nhants*	30	SP6853
Eastcote *W Mids*	39	SP1979
Eastcott *Wilts*	20	SU0255
Eastcourt *Wilts*	20	ST9792
Eastcourt *Wilts*	21	SU2361
Eastend *Essex*	25	TQ9492
Eastend *Strath*	75	NS9537
Easter Balmoral *Gramp*	88	NO2694
Easter Compton *Avon*	19	ST5782
Easter Dalziel *Highld*	93	NH7550
Easter Howgate *Loth*	75	NT2463
Easter Kinkell *Highld*	92	NH5755
Easter Moniack *Highld*	92	NH5543
Easter Ord *Gramp*	89	NJ8304
Easter Pitkierie *Fife*	83	NO5606
Easter Skeld *Shet*	103	HU3144
Eastergate *W Susx*	12	SU9405
Easterhouse *Strath*	74	NS6865
Eastern Green *W Mids*	39	SP2879
Easterton *Wilts*	20	SU0254
Eastfield *N York*	63	TA0484
Eastfield *Strath*	74	NS8964
Eastgate *Dur*	61	NY9538
Eastgate *Norfk*	43	TG1423
Easthampstead *Berks*	22	SU8667
Easthampton *H & W*	27	SO4063
Easthope *Shrops*	37	SO5695
Easthorpe *Essex*	24	TL9121
Eastington *Devon*	7	SS7408
Eastington *Gloucs*	28	SP1213
Eastington *Gloucs*	28	SO7705
Eastlands *D & G*	66	NX8172
Eastleach Martin *Gloucs*	29	SP2004
Eastleach Turville *Gloucs*	29	SP1905
Eastleigh *Devon*	6	SS4827
Eastleigh *Hants*	10	SU4519
Eastling *Kent*	15	TQ9656
Eastney *Hants*	11	SZ6698
Eastnor *H & W*	28	SO7237
Eastoft *Humb*	57	SE8016
Easton *Cambs*	30	TL1371
Easton *Cumb*	67	NY2759
Easton *Devon*	5	SX7289
Easton *Dorset*	9	SY6971
Easton *Hants*	11	SU5132
Easton *Lincs*	40	SK9326
Easton *Norfk*	43	TG1310
Easton *Somset*	19	ST5147
Easton *Suffk*	33	TM2858
Easton *Wilts*	20	ST8970
Easton Grey *Wilts*	20	ST8887
Easton Maudit *Nhants*	30	SP8858
Easton on the Hill *Nhants*	40	TF0104
Easton Royal *Wilts*	21	SU2060
Easton-in-Gordano *Avon*	19	ST5175
Eastrea *Cambs*	41	TL2997
Eastriggs *D & G*	67	NY2466
Eastrington *Humb*	56	SE7929
Eastrop *Wilts*	21	SU2092
Eastry *Kent*	15	TR3054
Eastville *Lincs*	51	TF4056
Eastwell *Leics*	40	SK7728
Eastwick *Herts*	23	TL4311
Eastwood *Essex*	24	TQ8688
Eastwood *Notts*	49	SK4646
Eastwood *W York*	54	SD9726
Eathorpe *Warwks*	29	SP3993
Eaton *Ches*	47	SJ5763
Eaton *Ches*	47	SJ8765
Eaton *Leics*	40	SK7928
Eaton *Norfk*	43	TG2006
Eaton *Notts*	50	SK7077
Eaton *Oxon*	21	SP4403
Eaton *Shrops*	37	SO5089
Eaton Bray *Beds*	30	SP9720
Eaton Constantine *Shrops*	37	SJ5906
Eaton Green *Beds*	30	SP9621
Eaton Hastings *Oxon*	21	SU2598
Eaton Mascott *Shrops*	37	SJ5305
Eaton Socon *Cambs*	31	TL1759
Eaton upon Tern *Shrops*	37	SJ6523
Ebberston *N York*	63	SE8982
Ebbesborne Wake *Wilts*	9	ST9924
Ebbw Vale *Gwent*	27	SO1609
Ebchester *Dur*	68	NZ1055
Ebford *Devon*	5	SX9887
Ebley *Gloucs*	28	SO8205
Ebnal *Ches*	46	SJ4948
Ebrington *Gloucs*	29	SP1840
Ebsworthy Town *Devon*	4	SX5090
Ecchinswell *Hants*	21	SU4959

Ecclaw *Loth*	76	NT7568
Ecclefechan *D & G*	67	NY1974
Eccles *Border*	76	NT7641
Eccles *Gt Man*	47	SJ7798
Eccles *Kent*	14	TQ7360
Eccles Road *Norfk*	32	TM0189
Ecclesall *S York*	49	SK3284
Ecclesall S *York*	49	SK3593
Ecclesalls *Staffs*	38	SJ8329
Eccleshill *W York*	55	SE1736
Ecclesmachan *Loth*	75	NT0573
Eccleston *Ches*	46	SJ4162
Eccleston *Lancs*	53	SD5217
Eccleston *Mersyd*	46	SJ4895
Echt *Gramp*	89	NJ7405
Eckford *Border*	76	NT7026
Eckington *Derbys*	49	SK4379
Eckington *H & W*	28	SO9241
Ecton *Nhants*	30	SP8263
Edale *Derbys*	48	SK1285
Edburton *W Susx*	12	TQ2311
Edderton *Highld*	97	NH7084
Eddleston *Border*	75	NT2447
Eddlewood *Strath*	74	NS7153
Eden Park *Gt Lon*	23	TQ3667
Edenbridge *Kent*	13	TQ4446
Edenfield *Lancs*	54	SD8019
Edenhall *Cumb*	59	NY5632
Edenham *Lincs*	40	TF0621
Edensor *Derbys*	48	SK2469
Edentaggart *Strath*	80	NS3293
Edenthorpe *S York*	56	SE6206
Edern *Gwynd*	44	SH2836
Edgbaston *W Mids*	38	SP0684
Edgcott *Bucks*	30	SP6722
Edgcott *Devon*	7	SS8438
Edge *Gloucs*	28	SO8409
Edge *Shrops*	36	SJ3908
Edgefield *Norfk*	43	TG0934
Edgefield Green *Norfk*	43	TG0934
Edgerton *W York*	55	SE1317
Edgeworth *Gloucs*	28	SO9406
Edgmond *Shrops*	37	SJ7119
Edgton *Shrops*	36	SO3885
Edgware *Gt Lon*	23	TQ1991
Edgworth *Lancs*	54	SD7416
Edinample *Cent*	81	NN6022
Edinbane *Highld*	90	NG3451
Edinburgh *Loth*	75	NT2573
Edingale *Staffs*	39	SK2111
Edingham *D & G*	66	NX8363
Edingley *Notts*	49	SK6655
Edingthorpe *Norfk*	43	TG3132
Edingthorpe Green *Norfk*	43	TG3031
Edington *Border*	77	NT8955
Edington *Nthumb*	69	NZ1582
Edington *Somset*	19	ST3839
Edington *Wilts*	20	ST9253
Edington Burtle *Somset*	19	ST3943
Edingworth *Somset*	19	ST3653
Edith Weston *Leics*	40	SK9205
Edithmead *Somset*	19	ST3249
Edlesborough *Bucks*	30	SP9719
Edlingham *Nthumb*	69	NU1109
Edlington *Lincs*	51	TF2371
Edmondsham *Dorset*	10	SU0611
Edmondsley *Dur*	69	NZ2349
Edmondthorpe *Leics*	40	SK8517
Edmonton *Gt Lon*	23	TQ3492
Edmundbyers *Dur*	68	NZ0150
Ednam *Border*	76	NT7337
Ednaston *Derbys*	48	SK2441
Edney *Common*		
Edradynate *Tays*	87	NN8751
Edrom *Border*	77	NT8255
Edstaston *Shrops*	37	SJ5132
Edstone *Warwks*	29	SP1861
Edwinstowe *Notts*	49	SK6266
Edworth *Beds*	31	TL2241
Edwyn Ralph *H & W*	27	SO6457
Edzell *Tays*	89	NO6068
Efail Isaf *M Glam*	18	ST0884
Efail-fach *W Glam*	18	SS7895
Efailnewydd *Gwynd*	44	SH3535
Efailwen *Dyfed*	16	SN1325
Efenechtyd *Clwyd*	46	SJ1155
Effgill *D & G*	67	NY3092
Effingham *Surrey*	12	TQ1153
Efford *Devon*	7	SS8901
Egerton *Gt Man*	54	SD7014
Egerton *Kent*	14	TQ9147
Egg Buckland *Devon*	4	SX5057
Eggesford *Devon*	7	SS6811
Eggington *Beds*	30	SP9525
Egginton *Derbys*	39	SK2628
Egglescliffe *Cleve*	62	NZ4113
Eggleston *Dur*	61	NY9923
Egham *Surrey*	22	TQ0071
Egleton *Leics*	40	SK8707
Eglingham *Nthumb*	77	NU1019
Egloshayle *Cnwll*	3	SX0072
Egloskerry *Cnwll*	4	SX2786
Eglwys Cross *Clwyd*	37	SJ4740
Eglwysbach *Gwynd*	45	SH8070
Eglwyswrw *Dyfed*	16	SN1438
Egmanton *Notts*	50	SK7368
Egremont *Cumb*	58	NY0110
Egremont *Mersyd*	46	SJ3192
Egton *N York*	63	NZ8006
Egton Bridge *N York*	63	NZ8004
Eight Ash Green *Essex*	25	TL9425
Eilanreach *Highld*	85	NG8018
Elan Village *Powys*	35	SN9364
Elberton *Avon*	19	ST6088
Elburton *Devon*	4	SX5353
Elcombe *Wilts*	20	SU1280
Eldersfield *H & W*	28	SO7931
Elderslie *Strath*	73	NS4463
Eldon *Dur*	61	NZ2328
Elfhill *Gramp*	89	NO8085
Elford *Staffs*	38	SK1810
Elgin *Gramp*	94	NJ2162
Elgol *Highld*	84	NG5213
Elham *Kent*	15	TR1744
Elie *Fife*	83	NO4900
Elim *Gwynd*	44	SH3584
Eling *Hants*	10	SU3612
Elkesley *Notts*	50	SK6975
Elkstone *Gloucs*	28	SO9612
Ella *Gramp*	94	NJ6459
Ellanbeich *Strath*	79	NM7417
Elland *W York*	55	SE1120
Ellary *Strath*	71	NR7376
Ellastone *Staffs*	48	SK1143
Ellel *Lancs*	53	SD4856
Ellemford *Border*	76	NT7260
Ellen's Green *Surrey*	12	TQ0935
Ellenhall *Staffs*	38	SJ8426
Ellerbeck *N York*	62	SE4396
Ellerby *N York*	63	NZ7914

Ellerdine Heath
Field Broughton

Ellerdine Heath Shrops 37 SJ6122
Elleric Strath 86 NN0448
Ellerker Humb 56 SE9229
Ellerton Humb 56 SE7039
Ellerton N York 61 SE2598
Ellesborough Bucks 22 SP8306
Ellesmere Shrops 36 SJ3934
Ellesmere Port Ches 46 SJ4076
Ellingham Norfk 33 TM3592
Ellingham Nthumb 77 NU1725
Ellingstring N York 61 SE1783
Ellington Cambs 31 TL1671
Ellington Nthumb 69 NZ2791
Ellington Thorpe Cambs 31 TL1670
Elliots Green Somset 20 ST7945
Ellisfield Hants 21 SU6446
Ellishader Highld 90 NG5065
Ellistown Leics 39 SK4310
Ellon Gramp 95 NJ9530
Ellonby Cumb 59 NY4235
Elloughton Humb 56 SE9428
Ellwood Gloucs 27 SO5908
Elm Cambs 41 TF4707
Elm Park Gt Lon 23 TQ5385
Elmbridge H & W 28 SO9068
Elmdon Essex 31 TL4639
Elmdon W Mids 38 SP1783
Elmers End Gt Lon 23 TQ3668
Elmesthorpe Leics 39 SP4696
Elmhurst Staffs 38 SK1112
Elmley Castle H & W 28 SO9841
Elmley Lovett H & W 28 SO8769
Elmore Gloucs 28 SO7815
Elmore Back Gloucs 28 SO7616
Elmsett Suffk 32 TM0546
Elmstead Market Essex 25 TM0624
Elmsted Court Kent 15 TR1144
Elmstone Kent 15 TR2660
Elmstone Hardwicke Gloucs 28 SO9125
Elmswell Humb 56 SE9958
Elmswell Suffk 32 TL9964
Elmton Derbys 49 SK5073
Elphin Highld 96 NC2111
Elphinstone Loth 76 NT3970
Elrick Gramp 89 NJ8106
Elrig D & G 64 NX3248
Elrington Nthumb 68 NY8563
Elsdon Nthumb 68 NY9393
Elsenham Essex 31 TL5326
Elsfield Oxon 29 SP5410
Elsham Humb 56 TA0312
Elsick House Gramp 89 NO8894
Elsing Norfk 42 TG0516
Elslack N York 54 SD9349
Elson Hants 11 SU6002
Elsrickle Strath 75 NT0643
Elstead Surrey 11 SU9043
Elsted W Susx 11 SU8119
Elsthorpe Lincs 40 TF0623
Elston Notts 50 SK7647
Elstone Devon 7 SS6716
Elstow Beds 30 TL0546
Elstree Herts 23 TQ1795
Elstronwick Humb 57 TA2232
Elswick Lancs 53 SD4238
Elswick T & W 69 NZ2263
Elsworth Cambs 31 TL3163
Elterwater Cumb 58 NY3204
Eltham Gt Lon 23 TQ4274
Eltisley Cambs 31 TL2759
Elton Cambs 40 TL0893
Elton Ches 46 SJ4575
Elton Cleve 62 NZ4017
Elton Derbys 48 SK2260
Elton H & W 27 SO4570
Elton Notts 40 SK7638
Eltringham Nthumb 68 NZ0762
Elvanfoot Strath 75 NS9517
Elvaston Derbys 39 SK4032
Elveden Suffk 32 TL8280
Elvingston Loth 76 NT4674
Elvington Kent 15 TR2750
Elvington N York 56 SE7047
Elwick Cleve 62 NZ4532
Elworth Ches 47 SJ7361
Elworthy Somset 8 ST0834
Ely Cambs 41 TL5480
Ely S Glam 18 ST1476
Emberton Bucks 30 SP8849
Embleton Nthumb 77 NU2322
Embo Highld 97 NH8192
Embo Street Highld 97 NH8091
Emborough Somset 19 ST6151
Embsay N York 54 SE0053
Emery Down Hants 10 SU2808
Emley W York 55 SE2413
Emmington Oxon 22 SP7402
Emneth Cambs 41 TF4807
Emneth Hungate Norfk 41 TF5107
Empingham Leics 40 SK9408
Empshott Hants 11 SU7531
Emsworth Hants 11 SU7406
Enborne Berks 21 SU4365
Enborne Row Hants 21 SU4463
Enderby Leics 39 SP5399
Endmoor Cumb 59 SD5384
Endon Staffs 48 SJ9253
Endon Bank Staffs 48 SJ9253
Enfield Gt Lon 23 TQ3597
Enfield Lock Gt Lon 23 TQ3698
Enfield Wash Gt Lon 23 TQ3598
Enford Wilts 20 SU1351
Engine Common Avon 20 ST6984
Englefield Berks 21 SU6272
Englefield Green Surrey 22 SU9971
Englesea-brook Ches 47 SJ7551
English Bicknor Gloucs 27 SO5815
English Frankton Shrops 36 SJ4529
Englishcombe Avon 20 ST7162
Enham-Alamein Hants 21 SU3649
Enmore Somset 8 ST2435
Enmore Green Dorset 9 ST8523
Ennerdale Bridge Cumb 58 NY0615
Enochdhu Tays 88 NO0662
Ensay Strath 78 NM3648
Ensbury Dorset 10 SZ0896
Ensdon Shrops 36 SJ4017
Ensis Devon 6 SS5626
Enstone Oxon 29 SP3724
Enterkinfoot D & G 66 NS8504
Enville Staffs 38 SO8286
Epney Gloucs 28 SO7611
Epperstone Notts 49 SK6548
Epping Essex 23 TL4502
Epping Green Essex 23 TL4305
Epping Green Herts 23 TL2906
Epping Upland Essex 23 TL4404
Eppleby N York 61 NZ1713
Epsom Surrey 23 TQ2160
Epwell Oxon 29 SP3540
Epworth Humb 56 SE7803
Erbistock Clwyd 36 SJ3541
Erdington W Mids 38 SP1191
Eridge Green E Susx 13 TQ5535
Erines Strath 71 NR8575
Eriswell Suffk 32 TL7278
Erith Gt Lon 23 TQ5177
Erlestoke Wilts 20 ST9653
Ermington Devon 5 SX6353
Erpingham Norfk 43 TG1931
Errogie Highld 92 NH5622
Errol Tays 83 NO2422
Erskine Strath 73 NS4770
Ervie D & G 64 NX0067
Erwarton Suffk 25 TM2234
Erwood Powys 26 SO0942
Eryholme N York 62 NZ3208
Eryrys Clwyd 46 SJ2057
Escomb Dur 61 NZ1830
Escrick N York 56 SE6242
Esgairgeiliog Powys 35 SH7606
Esh Dur 69 NZ1944
Esh Winning Dur 61 NZ1942
Esher Surrey 22 TQ1364
Eshott Nthumb 69 NZ2097
Eskadale Highld 92 NH4540
Eskbank Loth 75 NT3266
Eskdale Green Cumb 58 NY1400
Eskdalemuir D & G 67 NY2597
Esprick Lancs 53 SD4036
Essendine Leics 40 TF0412
Essendon Herts 23 TL2708
Essich Highld 92 NH6439
Essington Staffs 38 SJ9603
Esslemont Gramp 95 NJ9229
Eston Cleve 62 NZ5418
Etal Nthumb 77 NT9339
Etchilhampton Wilts 20 SU0460
Etchingham E Susx 14 TQ7126
Etchinghill Kent 15 TR1639
Etchinghill Staffs 38 SK0218
Etloe Gloucs 28 SO6806
Eton Wick Berks 22 SU9478
Etruria Staffs 47 SJ8647
Etteridge Highld 87 NN6892
Ettersgill Dur 60 NY8829
Ettiley Heath Ches 47 SJ7360
Ettingshall W Mids 38 SO9396
Ettington Warwks 29 SP2749
Etton Cambs 40 TF1406
Etton Humb 56 SE9743
Ettrick Border 67 NT2714
Ettrick Hill Border 67 NT2514
Ettrickbridge Border 76 NT3824
Etwall Derbys 39 SK2631
Euston Suffk 32 TL8979
Euxton Lancs 53 SD5519
Evanton Highld 92 NH6066
Evedon Lincs 50 TF0947
Evelith Shrops 37 SJ7405
Evelix Highld 97 NH7790
Evenjobb Powys 27 SO2662
Evenley Oxon 29 SP5834
Evenlode Gloucs 29 SP2129
Evenwood Dur 61 NZ1524
Evercreech Somset 19 ST6438
Everingham Humb 56 SE8042
Everleigh Wilts 21 SU2053
Evershot Beds 30 SP9833
Evershot Dorset 9 ST5704
Eversley Hants 22 SU7762
Eversley Cross Hants 22 SU7961
Everthorpe Humb 56 SE9031
Everton Beds 31 TL2051
Everton Hants 10 SZ2894
Everton Mersyd 46 SJ3491
Everton Notts 49 SK6990
Evertown D & G 67 NY3576
Evesbatch H & W 28 SO6948
Evesham H & W 28 SP0344
Evington Leics 39 SK6203
Ewden Village S York 49 SK2796
Ewell Surrey 23 TQ2262
Ewell Minnis Kent 15 TR2643
Ewelme Oxon 21 SU6491
Ewen Gloucs 20 SU0097
Ewenny M Glam 18 SS9077
Ewerby Lincs 50 TF1247
Ewesley Nthumb 68 NZ0591
Ewhurst E Susx 14 TQ7924
Ewhurst Surrey 12 TQ0940
Ewhurst Green Surrey 12 TQ0939
Ewloe Clwyd 46 SJ3066
Eworthy Devon 6 SX4495
Ewshot Hants 22 SU8149
Ewyas Harold H & W 27 SO3828
Exbourne Devon 6 SS6002
Exbury Hants 10 SU4200
Exebridge Somset 7 SS9324
Exelby N York 61 SE2987
Exeter Devon 5 SX9292
Exford Somset 7 SS8538
Exfordsgreen Shrops 36 SJ4505
Exhall Warwks 28 SP1055
Exhall Warwks 39 SP3485
Exlade Street Oxon 21 SU6581
Exminster Devon 5 SX9487
Exmouth Devon 5 SY0081
Exning Suffk 32 TL6265
Exted Kent 15 TR1744
Exton Devon 5 SX9886
Exton Hants 11 SU6120
Exton Leics 40 SK9211
Exton Somset 7 SS9233
Exwick Devon 5 SX9093
Eyam Derbys 48 SK2176
Eydon Nhants 29 SP5449
Eye Cambs 41 TF2202
Eye H & W 27 SO4964
Eye Suffk 33 TM1473
Eyemouth Border 77 NT9464
Eyeworth Beds 31 TL2545
Eyhorne Street Kent 14 TQ8354
Eyke Suffk 33 TM3151
Eynesbury Beds 31 TL1859
Eynsford Kent 23 TQ5465
Eynsham Oxon 29 SP4309
Eype Dorset 8 SY4491
Eyre Highld 90 NG4153
Eythorne Kent 15 TR2849
Eyton H & W 27 SO4761
Eyton Shrops 36 SJ3714
Eyton Shrops 36 SJ4422
Eyton Shrops 36 SO3787
Eyton on Severn Shrops 37 SJ5806
Eyton upon the
Weald Moor Shrops 37 SJ6515

F

Faccombe Hants 21 SU3857
Faceby N York 62 NZ4903
Fachwen Powys 36 SJ0316
Faddiley Ches 47 SJ5852
Fadmoor N York 62 SE6789
Faerdre W Glam 18 SN6901
Faifley Strath 74 NS4973
Failand Avon 19 ST5171
Failford Strath 73 NS4626
Failsworth Gt Man 48 SD8901
Fair Oak Hants 11 SU4918
Fair Oak Green Hants 22 SU6660
Fairbourne Gwynd 35 SH6113
Fairburn N York 55 SE4727
Fairfield Derbys 48 SK0673
Fairfield H & W 38 SO9475
Fairford Gloucs 20 SP1501
Fairgirth D & G 66 NX8756
Fairhaven Lancs 53 SD3227
Fairlie Strath 73 NS2054
Fairlight E Susx 14 TQ8511
Fairmile Devon 8 SY0897
Fairmile Surrey 22 TQ1161
Fairnilee Border 76 NT4532
Fairoak Staffs 37 SJ7632
Fairseat Kent 14 TQ6261
Fairstead Essex 24 TL7616
Fairwarp E Susx 13 TQ4626
Fairwater S Glam 18 ST1477
Fairy Cross Devon 6 SS4024
Fakenham Norfk 42 TF9229
Fakenham Magna Suffk 32 TL9176
Fala Loth 76 NT4460
Fala Dam Loth 76 NT4361
Faldingworth Lincs 50 TF0684
Faldouet Jersey 101 JS0000
Falfield Avon 20 ST6893
Falkenham Suffk 33 TM2939
Falkirk Cent 82 NS8880
Falkland Fife 83 NO2507
Fallin Cent 82 NS8391
Falloden Nthumb 77 NU1922
Fallowfield Gt Man 47 SJ8593
Fallowfield Nthumb 68 NY9268
Falls of Blarghour Strath 80 NM9913
Falmer E Susx 12 TQ3508
Falmouth Cnwll 2 SW8032
Falnash Border 67 NT3905
Falsgrave N York 63 TA0288
Falstone Nthumb 68 NY7287
Fanagmore Highld 98 NC1749
Fancott Beds 30 TL0127
Fanellan Highld 92 NH4942
Fangdale Beck N York 62 SE5694
Fangfoss Humb 56 SE7653
Fanmore Strath 78 NM4144
Fannich Lodge Highld 92 NH2266
Fans Border 76 NT6140
Far Bletchley Bucks 30 SP8533
Far Cotton Nhants 30 SP7559
Far End Cumb 58 SD3098
Far Green Gloucs 20 SO7700
Far Moor Gt Man 46 SD5204
Far Oakridge Gloucs 20 SO9203
Far Sawrey Cumb 59 SD3795
Far Thorpe Lincs 51 TF2674
Farcet Cambs 41 TL2094
Fareham Hants 11 SU5606
Farewell Staffs 38 SK0811
Faringdon Oxon 21 SU2895
Farkhill Tays 82 NO0435
Farlam Cumb 67 NY5558
Farleigh Avon 19 ST5069
Farleigh Surrey 23 TQ3760
Farleigh Hungerford Somset 20 ST8057
Farleigh Wallop Hants 21 SU6247
Farlesthorpe Lincs 51 TF4774
Farleton Cumb 59 SD5380
Farleton Lancs 53 SD5767
Farley Staffs 48 SK0644
Farley Wilts 10 SU2229
Farley Green Suffk 32 TL7353
Farley Green Surrey 12 TQ0545
Farley Hill Berks 22 SU7464
Farleys End Gloucs 28 SO7614
Farlington N York 56 SE6167
Farlow Shrops 37 SO6380
Farmborough Avon 20 ST6660
Farmcote Gloucs 28 SP0628
Farmers Dyfed 17 SN6444
Farmington Gloucs 28 SP1315
Farmoor Oxon 29 SP4506
Farmtown Gramp 94 NJ5051
Farnachty Gramp 94 NJ4261
Farnborough Berks 21 SU4381
Farnborough Gt Lon 23 TQ4464
Farnborough Hants 22 SU8753
Farnborough Warwks 29 SP4349
Farnborough Park Hants 22 SU8755
Farnborough Street Hants 22 SU8756
Farncombe Surrey 12 SU9744
Farndish Beds 30 SP9263
Farndon Ches 46 SJ4154
Farndon Notts 50 SK7651
Farnell Tays 89 NO6255
Farnham Dorset 9 ST9515
Farnham Essex 31 TL4724
Farnham N York 55 SE3460
Farnham Suffk 33 TM3660
Farnham Surrey 22 SU8346
Farnham Common Bucks 22 SU9585
Farnham Royal Bucks 22 SU9583
Farningham Kent 23 TQ5467
Farnley N York 55 SE2148
Farnley W York 55 SE2532
Farnley Tyas W York 55 SE1612
Farnsfield Notts 49 SK6456
Farnworth Ches 46 SJ5187
Farnworth Gt Man 47 SD7306
Farr Highld 99 NC7163
Farr Highld 93 NH6833
Farr Highld 87 NH8203
Farraline Highld 92 NH5621
Farringdon Devon 5 SY0191
Farrington Gurney Avon 19 ST6355
Farthinghoe Nhants 29 SP5339
Farthingstone Nhants 29 SP6154
Fartown W York 55 SE1518
Fartown W York 55 SE2233
Farway Street Devon 8 SY1895
Fasnacloich Strath 86 NN0247
Fasnakyle Highld 92 NH3128
Fassfern Highld 85 NN0278
Fatfield T & W 69 NZ2954
Fauldhouse Loth 75 NS9360
Faulkbourne Essex 24 TL7917
Faulkland Somset 20 ST7354
Fauls Shrops 37 SJ5832
Faversham Kent 15 TR0161
Fawdington N York 55 SE4372
Fawdon Nthumb 77 NU0315
Fawkham Green Kent 14 TQ5865
Fawler Oxon 29 SP3717
Fawley Berks 21 SU3981
Fawley Bucks 22 SU7586
Fawley Hants 10 SU4503
Faxfleet Humb 56 SE8624
Faygate W Susx 12 TQ2134
Fazakerley Mersyd 46 SJ3796
Fazeley Staffs 39 SK2001
Fearby N York 61 SE1981
Fearn Highld 97 NH8378
Fearnan Tays 87 NN7244
Fearnbeg Highld 91 NG7359
Fearnmore Highld 91 NG7260
Fearnoch Strath 71 NR9279
Featherstone Staffs 38 SJ9305
Featherstone W York 55 SE4221
Feckenham H & W 28 SP0162
Feering Essex 24 TL8720
Feetham N York 61 SD9898
Felbridge Surrey 13 TQ3739
Felbrigg Norfk 43 TG2039
Felcourt Surrey 13 TQ3841
Felin gwm Isaf Dyfed 17 SN5023
Felin gwm Uchaf Dyfed 17 SN5024
Felindre Dyfed 17 SN5521
Felindre Dyfed 17 SN3538
Felindre Powys 36 SO1681
Felindre W Glam 17 SN6302
Felindre Farchog Dyfed 16 SN1039
Felixkirk N York 62 SE4684
Felixstowe Suffk 25 TM3034
Felixstoweferry Suffk 25 TM3237
Felling T & W 69 NZ2762
Felmersham Beds 30 SP9957
Felmingham Norfk 43 TG2529
Felpham W Susx 12 SZ9499
Felsham Suffk 32 TL9457
Felsted Essex 24 TL6720
Feltham Gt Lon 22 TQ1073
Felthamhill Gt Lon 22 TQ0971
Felthorpe Norfk 43 TG1618
Felton Avon 19 ST5265
Felton H & W 27 SO5748
Felton Nthumb 69 NU1800
Felton Butler Shrops 36 SJ3917
Feltwell Norfk 32 TL7190
Fen Ditton Cambs 31 TL4860
Fen Drayton Cambs 31 TL3368
Fen Street Norfk 42 TL9895
Fence Lancs 54 SD8237
Fence S York 49 SK4485
Fencote N York 61 SE2893
Fencott Oxon 29 SP5716
Fendike Corner Lincs 51 TF4560
Fenham T & W 69 NZ2265
Feniscowles Lancs 54 SD6425
Feniton Devon 8 SY1099
Fenn Green Shrops 37 SO7783
Fenn Street Kent 14 TQ7975
Fenny Bentley Derbys 48 SK1749
Fenny Bridges Devon 8 SY1198
Fenny Compton Warwks 29 SP4152
Fenny Drayton Leics 39 SP3596
Fenstanton Cambs 31 TL3168
Fenstead End Suffk 32 TL8050
Fenton Cambs 41 TL3279
Fenton Cumb 67 NY5056
Fenton Lincs 50 SK8476
Fenton Lincs 50 SK8751
Fenton Notts 50 SK7982
Fenton Nthumb 77 NT9733
Fenton Staffs 48 SJ8944
Fenton Barns Loth 83 NT5181
Fenwick Nthumb 77 NU0640
Fenwick Nthumb 68 NZ0572
Fenwick S York 56 SE5916
Fenwick Strath 73 NS4643
Feock Cnwll 2 SW8238
Feolin Ferry Strath 70 NR4469
Fergushill Strath 73 NS3343
Feriniquarrie Highld 90 NG1750
Fermain Bay Guern 101 GN0000
Fern Tays 89 NO4861
Ferndale M Glam 18 SS9996
Ferndown Dorset 10 SU0700
Ferness Highld 93 NH9645
Fernham Oxon 21 SU2991
Fernhill Heath H & W 28 SO8759
Fernhurst W Susx 11 SU8928
Fernie Fife 83 NO3115
Ferniegair Strath 74 NS7354
Fernilea Highld 84 NG3732
Fernilee Derbys 48 SK0178
Ferrensby N York 55 SE3760
Ferrindonald Highld 85 NG6608
Ferring W Susx 12 TQ0902
Ferry Point Highld 97 NH7385
Ferryden Tays 89 NO7156
Ferryhill Dur 61 NZ2832
Ferryside Dyfed 17 SN3610
Ferrytown Highld 97 NH7387
Fersfield Norfk 32 TM0683
Fersit Highld 86 NN3577
Feshiebridge Highld 87 NH8504
Fetcham Surrey 22 TQ1455
Fetterangus Gramp 95 NJ9850
Fettercairn Gramp 89 NO6573
Fewston N York 55 SE1954
Ffair Rhos Dyfed 35 SN7368
Ffairfach Dyfed 17 SN6321
Ffestiniog Gwynd 45 SH7042
Fforest Dyfed 17 SN5704
Fforest Fach W Glam 17 SS6295
Ffostrasol Dyfed 17 SN3747
Ffrith Clwyd 46 SJ2855
Ffynnongroew Clwyd 46 SJ1382
Fiag Lodge Highld 98 NC4528
Fickleshole Surrey 23 TQ3860
Fiddes Gramp 89 NO8080
Fiddington Gloucs 28 SO9231
Fiddington Somset 19 ST2140
Fiddleford Dorset 9 ST8013
Fiddlers Green Cnwll 2 SW8155
Field Staffs 38 SK0233
Field Broughton Cumb 59 SD3881

Field Dalling
Garsdon

Field Dalling Norfk 42 TG0038
Field Head Leics 39 SK4909
Fife Keith Gramp 94 NJ4250
Fifehead Magdalen Dorset 9 ST7821
Fifehead Neville Dorset 9 ST7610
Fifehead St Quinton Dorset 9 ST7710
Fifield Berks 22 SU9076
Fifield Oxon 29 SP2418
Figheldean Wilts 20 SU1547
Filby Norfk 43 TG4613
Filey N York 63 TA1180
Filgrave Bucks 30 SP8648
Filkins Oxon 29 SP2304
Filleigh Devon 7 SS6627
Filleigh Devon 7 SS7410
Fillingham Lincs 50 SK9485
Fillongley Warwks 39 SP2887
Filton Avon 19 ST6079
Fimber Humb 56 SE8960
Finavon Tays 89 NO4956
Fincham Norfk 42 TF6806
Finchampstead Berks 22 SU7963
Fincharn Strath 79 NM9003
Finchdean Hants 11 SU7312
Finchingfield Essex 24 TL6832
Finchley Gt Lon 23 TQ2690
Findern Derbys 39 SK3030
Findhorn Gramp 93 NJ0364
Findhorn Bridge Highld 93 NH8027
Findo Gask Tays 82 NO0019
Findochty Gramp 94 NJ4667
Findon Gramp 89 NO9397
Findon W Susx 12 TQ1208
Findon Mains Highld 92 NH6060
Findrack House Gramp 89 NJ6004
Finedon Nhants 30 SP9172
Fingal Street Suffk 33 TM2169
Fingask Tays 82 NO1619
Fingest Bucks 22 SU7791
Finghall N York 61 SE1889
Fingland D & G 74 NS7517
Finglesham Kent 15 TR3353
Fingringhoe Essex 25 TM0220
Finlarig Cent 81 NN5733
Finmere Oxon 29 SP6332
Finnart Tays 87 NN5157
Finningham Suffk 32 TM0669
Finningley S York 49 SK6799
Finsbay W Isls 102 NG0786
Finstall H & W 28 SO9770
Finsthwaite Cumb 59 SD3687
Finstock Oxon 29 SP3616
Finstown Ork 103 HY3513
Fintry Cent 81 NS6186
Fintry Gramp 95 NJ7554
Finzean Gramp 89 NO5993
Fionnphort Strath 78 NM3023
Fionnsbhagh W Isls 102 NG0786
Fir Tree Dur 61 NZ1434
Firbank Cumb 60 SD6293
Firbeck S York 49 SK5688
Firby N York 61 SE2686
Firby N York 56 SE7466
Firsby Lincs 51 TF4562
Fishbourne IOW 11 SZ5592
Fishbourne W Susx 11 SU8304
Fishburn Dur 62 NZ3632
Fishcross Cent 82 NS8995
Fisher's Pond Hants 11 SU4820
Fisherford Gramp 95 NJ6735
Fisherrow Loth 75 NT3472
Fisherton Highld 93 NH7451
Fisherton Strath 73 NS2717
Fisherton de la Mere Wilts 10 SU0038
Fishguard Dyfed 16 SM9537
Fishlake S York 56 SE6513
Fishnish Pier Strath 79 NM6542
Fishponds Avon 19 ST6375
Fishtoft Lincs 51 TF3642
Fishtoft Drove Lincs 51 TF3148
Fishwick Border 77 NT9151
Fiskavaig Highld 84 NG3334
Fiskerton Lincs 50 TF0471
Fiskerton Notts 50 SK7351
Fittleton Wilts 20 SU1449
Fittleworth W Susx 12 TQ0019
Fitz Shrops 36 SJ4417
Fitzhead Somset 8 ST1228
Fitzwilliam W York 55 SE4115
Fiunary Highld 79 NM6246
Five Ash Down E Susx 13 TQ4723
Five Ashes E Susx 13 TQ5525
Five Bells Somset 7 ST0642
Five Oak Green Kent 13 TQ6445
Five Oaks Jersey 101 JS0000
Five Oaks W Susx 12 TQ0928
Fivehead Somset 8 ST3522
Fivelanes Cnwll 4 SX2280
Flackwell Heath Bucks 22 SU8989
Fladbury H & W 28 SO9946
Fladdabister Shet 103 HU4332
Flagg Derbys 48 SK1368
Flamborough Humb 57 TA2270
Flamstead Herts 30 TL0714
Flansham W Susx 12 SU9601
Flanshaw W York 55 SE3020
Flasby N York 54 SD9456
Flash Staffs 48 SK0266
Flashader Highld 90 NG3453
Flaunden Herts 22 TL0100
Flawborough Notts 50 SK7842
Flawith N York 55 SE4865
Flax Bourton Avon 19 ST5069
Flaxby N York 55 SE3957
Flaxley Gloucs 28 SO6815
Flaxpool Somset 8 ST1435
Flaxton N York 56 SE6762
Fleckney Leics 39 SP6493
Flecknoe Warwks 29 SP5163
Fledborough Notts 50 SK8072
Fleet Dorset 9 SY6380
Fleet Hants 22 SU8053
Fleet Lincs 41 TF3823
Fleet Hargate Lincs 41 TF3925
Fleetwood Lancs 53 SD3348
Flemingston S Glam 18 ST0169
Flemington Strath 74 NS6559
Flempton Suffk 32 TL8169
Fletchertown Cumb 58 NY2042
Fletching E Susx 13 TQ4223
Flexbury Cnwll 6 SS2107
Flexford Surrey 12 SU9350
Flimby Cumb 58 NY0233
Flimwell E Susx 14 TQ7131
Flint Clwyd 46 SJ2472
Flintham Notts 50 SK7445
Flinton Humb 57 TA2136
Flitcham Norfk 42 TF7326
Flitton Beds 30 TL0535
Flitwick Beds 30 TL0334
Flixborough Humb 56 SE8714
Flixborough Stather Humb 56 SE8614
Flixton N York 63 TA0479
Flixton Suffk 33 TM3186
Flockton W York 55 SE2314
Flockton Green W York 55 SE2515
Flodigarry Highld 90 NG4671
Flookburgh Cumb 59 SD3675
Flordon Norfk 43 TM1897
Flore Nhants 29 SP6460
Flowton Suffk 32 TM0846
Flushing Cnwll 2 SW8034
Fluxton Devon 8 SY0893
Flyford Flavell H & W 28 SO9755
Fobbing Essex 24 TQ7183
Fochabers Gramp 94 NJ3458
Fockerby Humb 56 SE8519
Foddington Somset 9 ST5729
Foel Powys 35 SH9911
Foggathorpe Humb 56 SE7537
Fogo Border 76 NT7649
Fogwatt Gramp 94 NJ2356
Foindle Highld 98 NC1948
Folda Tays 88 NO1963
Fole Staffs 48 SK0437
Foleshill W Mids 39 SP3582
Folke Dorset 9 ST6613
Folkestone Kent 15 TR2336
Folkingham Lincs 40 TF0733
Folkington E Susx 13 TQ5603
Folksworth Cambs 40 TL1489
Folkton N York 63 TA0579
Folla Rule Gramp 95 NJ7332
Follifoot N York 55 SE3452
Folly Gate Devon 6 SX5798
Fonthill Bishop Wilts 9 ST9333
Fonthill Gifford Wilts 9 ST9231
Fontmell Magna Dorset 9 ST8616
Fontmell Parva Dorset 9 ST8214
Fontwell W Susx 12 SU9407
Foolow Derbys 48 SK1976
Forbestown Gramp 94 NJ3513
Forcett N York 61 NZ1712
Ford Bucks 22 SP7709
Ford Derbys 49 SK4080
Ford Devon 6 SS4124
Ford Devon 5 SX7940
Ford Gloucs 28 SP0829
Ford Nthumb 77 NT9437
Ford Somset 8 ST0928
Ford Staffs 48 SK0653
Ford Strath 79 NM8603
Ford W Susx 12 SU9903
Ford Wilts 20 ST8475
Ford End Essex 24 TL6716
Ford Street Somset 8 ST1518
Fordcombe Kent 13 TQ5240
Fordell Fife 82 NT1588
Forden Powys 36 SJ2201
Forder Green Devon 5 SX7967
Fordham Cambs 32 TL6370
Fordham Essex 24 TL9228
Fordham Norfk 41 TL6199
Fordingbridge Hants 10 SU1414
Fordon Humb 63 TA0475
Fordoun Gramp 89 NO7475
Fordstreet Essex 24 TL9226
Fordwich Kent 15 TR1859
Fordyce Gramp 94 NJ5563
Forebridge Staffs 38 SJ9322
Foremark Derbys 39 SK3326
Forest Guern 101 GN0000
Forest Becks Lancs 54 SD7851
Forest Gate Gt Lon 23 TQ4085
Forest Green Surrey 12 TQ1241
Forest Hall T & W 69 NZ2769
Forest Hill Gt Lon 23 TQ3672
Forest Hill Oxon 29 SP5807
Forest Lane Head N York 55 SE3356
Forest Lodge Strath 86 NN2742
Forest Mill Cent 82 NS9694
Forest Row E Susx 13 TQ4234
Forestside W Susx 11 SU7612
Forfar Tays 88 NO4550
Forgandenny Tays 82 NO0818
Forge Hammer Gwent 19 ST2895
Forgie Gramp 94 NJ3854
Forgieside Gramp 94 NJ4053
Forgorig Border 76 NT7748
Formby Mersyd 46 SD3006
Forncett End Norfk 43 TM1493
Forncett St Mary Norfk 43 TM1694
Forncett St Peter Norfk 43 TM1693
Fornham All Saints Suffk 32 TL8367
Fornham St Martin Suffk 32 TL8567
Forres Gramp 93 NJ0358
Forsbrook Staffs 48 SJ9641
Forse Highld 100 ND2234
Forse House Highld 100 ND2135
Forsinain Highld 99 NC9148
Forsinard Highld 99 NC8942
Fort Augustus Highld 92 NH3709
Fort George Highld 93 NH7656
Fort Hommet Guern 101 GN0000
Fort le Marchant Guern 101 GN0000
Fort William Highld 86 NN1074
Forteviot Tays 82 NO0517
Forth Strath 75 NS9453
Forthampton Gloucs 28 SO8532
Fortingall Tays 87 NN7347
Fortnighty Highld 93 NH9350
Forton Hants 21 SU4143
Forton Lancs 53 SD4851
Forton Shrops 36 SJ4316
Forton Somset 8 ST3307
Forton Staffs 37 SJ7521
Fortrose Highld 93 NH7256
Fortuneswell Dorset 9 SY6873
Forty Hill Gt Lon 23 TQ3398
Fosbury Wilts 21 SU3157
Foscot Oxon 29 SP2421
Fosdyke Lincs 41 TF3133
Foss Tays 87 NN7858
Fossebridge Gloucs 28 SP0711
Foster Street Essex 23 TL4809
Foston Derbys 39 SK1931
Foston Leics 39 SP6094
Foston Lincs 50 SK8542
Foston N York 56 SE6965
Foston on the Wolds Humb 57 TA1055
Fotherby Lincs 51 TF3191
Fotheringhay Nhants 40 TL0593
Fotrie Gramp 94 NJ6645
Foul End Warwks 39 SP2494
Foulden Border 77 NT9355
Foulridge Lancs 54 SD8942
Foulsham Norfk 42 TG0324
Fountainhall Border 76 NT4249
Four Ashes Suffk 32 TM0070
Four Cabots Guern 101 GN0000
Four Crosses Powys 36 SJ2618
Four Elms Kent 13 TQ4648
Four Forks Somset 19 ST2336
Four Gotes Cambs 41 TF4516
Four Lanes Cnwll 2 SW6838
Four Marks Hants 11 SU6735
Four Mile Bridge Gwynd 44 SH2778
Four Oaks W Mids 39 SP2480
Four Roads Dyfed 17 SN4409
Four Throws Kent 14 TQ7729
Fourpenny Highld 97 NH8094
Fourstones Nthumb 68 NY8867
Fovant Wilts 10 SU0028
Foveran Gramp 95 NJ9723
Fowey Cnwll 3 SX1251
Fowlhall Kent 14 TQ6946
Fowlis Tays 83 NO3233
Fowlis Wester Tays 82 NN9224
Fowlmere Cambs 31 TL4245
Fownhope H & W 27 SO5834
Foxbar Strath 73 NS4561
Foxcote Somset 20 ST7155
Foxdale IOM 52 SC2778
Foxearth Essex 32 TL8344
Foxfield Cumb 58 SD2185
Foxhole Cnwll 3 SW9654
Foxholes N York 63 TA0173
Foxley Norfk 42 TG0422
Foxt Staffs 48 SK0348
Foxton Cambs 31 TL4148
Foxton Leics 40 SP7089
Foxton N York 62 SE4296
Foxwood Shrops 37 SO6276
Foy H & W 27 SO5928
Foyers Highld 92 NH4921
Foynesfield Highld 93 NH8953
Fraddon Cnwll 3 SW9158
Fradley Staffs 38 SK1513
Fradswell Staffs 38 SJ9931
Fraisthorpe Humb 57 TA1561
Framfield E Susx 13 TQ4920
Framingham Earl Norfk 43 TG2702
Framingham Pigot Norfk 43 TG2703
Framlingham Suffk 33 TM2863
Frampton Dorset 9 SY6295
Frampton Lincs 41 TF3239
Frampton Cotterell Avon 20 ST6682
Frampton Mansell Gloucs 20 SO9202
Frampton on Severn Gloucs 28 SO7407
Framsden Suffk 33 TM1959
Framwellgate Moor Dur 69 NZ2644
Frances Green Lancs 54 SD6236
Franche H & W 38 SO8278
Frankby Mersyd 46 SJ2486
Frankley H & W 38 SO9980
Frankton Warwks 29 SP4270
Frant E Susx 13 TQ5835
Fraserburgh Gramp 95 NJ9966
Frating Essex 25 TM0722
Frating Green Essex 25 TM0823
Fratton Hants 11 SU6500
Freathy Cnwll 4 SX3952
Freckenham Suffk 32 TL6672
Freckleton Lancs 53 SD4329
Freeby Leics 40 SK8020
Freefolk Hants 21 SU4848
Freeland Oxon 29 SP4112
Freethorpe Norfk 43 TG4005
Freethorpe Common Norfk 43 TG4004
Freiston Lincs 51 TF3743
Fremington Devon 6 SS5132
Fremington N York 61 SE0499
French Tays 87 NN8258
Frensham Surrey 11 SU8441
Freshfield Mersyd 46 SD2907
Freshford Avon 20 ST7860
Freshwater IOW 10 SZ3487
Fressingfield Suffk 33 TM2677
Freston Suffk 25 TM1638
Freswick Highld 100 ND3667
Fretherne Gloucs 28 SO7210
Frettenham Norfk 43 TG2417
Freuchie Fife 83 NO2806
Freystrop Dyfed 16 SM9511
Friday Bridge Cambs 41 TF4604
Friday Street Suffk 33 TM3760
Fridaythorpe Humb 56 SE8759
Friern Barnet Gt Lon 23 TQ2892
Friesland Bay Strath 78 NM1954
Friesthorpe Lincs 50 TF0683
Frieston Lincs 50 SK9347
Frieth Bucks 22 SU7990
Frilford Oxon 21 SU4497
Frilsham Berks 21 SU5473
Frimley Surrey 22 SU8757
Frindsbury Kent 14 TQ7469
Fring Norfk 42 TF7334
Fringford Oxon 29 SP6029
Frinsted Kent 14 TQ8957
Frinton-on-Sea Essex 25 TM2320
Friockheim Tays 89 NO5949
Frisby on the Wreake Leics 40 SK6917
Friskney Lincs 51 TF4655
Friston E Susx 13 TV5598
Friston Suffk 33 TM4160
Fritchley Derbys 49 SK3552
Fritham Hants 10 SU2314
Frithelstock Devon 6 SS4619
Frithelstock Stone Devon 6 SS4518
Frithville Lincs 51 TF3150
Frittenden Kent 14 TQ8140
Frittiscombe Devon 5 SX8043
Fritton Norfk 43 TG4600
Fritton Norfk 43 TM2293
Fritwell Oxon 29 SP5229
Frizinghall W York 55 SE1435
Frizington Cumb 58 NY0316
Frocester Gloucs 20 SO7803
Frodesley Shrops 37 SJ5101
Frodsham Ches 46 SJ5177
Frog End Cambs 31 TL3946
Frog Pool H & W 28 SO8065
Frogden Border 76 NT7628
Froggatt Derbys 48 SK2476
Froghall Staffs 48 SK0247
Frogmore Devon 5 SX7742
Frognall Lincs 40 TF1610
Frogwell Cnwll 4 SX3468
Frolesworth Leics 39 SP5090
Frome Somset 20 ST7747
Frome St Quintin Dorset 9 ST5902
Fromes Hill H & W 28 SO6846
Fron Isaf Clwyd 36 SJ2740
Fron-goch Gwynd 45 SH9039
Froncysyllte Clwyd 36 SJ2640
Frosterley Dur 61 NZ0237
Froxfield Wilts 21 SU2968
Froxfield Green Hants 11 SU7025
Fryern Hill Hants 10 SU4320
Fryerning Essex 24 TL6300
Fulbeck Lincs 50 SK9450
Fulbourn Cambs 31 TL5256
Fulbrook Oxon 29 SP2513
Fulflood Hants 11 SU4730
Fulford N York 56 SE6149
Fulford Somset 8 ST2029
Fulford Staffs 48 SJ9537
Fulham Gt Lon 23 TQ2576
Fulking W Susx 12 TQ2411
Full Sutton Humb 56 SE7455
Fullarton Strath 73 NS3238
Fuller Street Essex 24 TL7416
Fullerton Hants 10 SU3739
Fulletby Lincs 51 TF2973
Fullready Warwks 29 SP2846
Fullwood Strath 73 NS4450
Fulmer Bucks 22 SU9985
Fulmodeston Norfk 42 TF9930
Fulneck W York 55 SE2232
Fulnetby Lincs 50 TF0979
Fulney Lincs 41 TF2623
Fulstow Lincs 51 TF3297
Fulwell Oxon 29 SP3722
Fulwood Lancs 53 SD5431
Fulwood S York 49 SK3085
Fundenhall Norfk 43 TM1596
Funtington W Susx 11 SU8008
Funtullich Tays 81 NN7526
Furley Devon 8 ST2604
Furnace Dyfed 17 SN5001
Furnace Strath 80 NN0200
Furness Vale Derbys 48 SK0083
Furneux Pelham Herts 31 TL4327
Furzley Hants 10 SU2816
Fyfield Essex 24 TL5707
Fyfield Hants 21 SU2946
Fyfield Oxon 21 SU4298
Fyfield Wilts 20 SU1468
Fyfield Wilts 21 SU1760
Fylingthorpe N York 63 NZ9404
Fyning W Susx 11 SU8123
Fyvie Gramp 95 NJ7637

G

Gabroc Hill Strath 73 NS4550
Gaddesby Leics 39 SK6813
Gaddesden Row Herts 30 TL0512
Gadgirth Strath 73 NS4022
Gaer Powys 27 SO1721
Gaer-llwyd Gwent 19 ST4496
Gaerwen Gwynd 44 SH4871
Gailes Strath 73 NS3235
Gailey Staffs 38 SJ9110
Gainford Dur 61 NZ1716
Gainsborough Lincs 50 SK8189
Gainsford End Essex 24 TL7235
Gairloch Highld 91 NG8076
Gairlochy Highld 86 NN1784
Gairneybridge Tays 82 NT1397
Gaisby W York 55 SE1536
Gaitsgill Cumb 67 NY3846
Galashiels Border 76 NT4936
Galby Leics 40 SK6900
Galcantray Highld 93 NH8148
Galgate Lancs 53 SD4855
Galhampton Somset 9 ST6329
Gallanach Strath 78 NM2161
Gallanach Strath 79 NM8326
Gallatown Fife 83 NT2994
Galleywood Essex 24 TL7003
Gallovie Highld 87 NN5589
Gallowfauld Tays 88 NO4342
Gallowhill Tays 82 NO1635
Galltair Highld 85 NG8120
Galmisdale Highld 84 NM4784
Galmpton Devon 5 SX6940
Galmpton Devon 5 SX8856
Galphay N York 55 SE2572
Galston Strath 74 NS5036
Galton Dorset 9 SY7785
Gamblesby Cumb 59 NY6039
Gamlingay Cambs 31 TL2452
Gamlingay Great Heath Beds 31 TL2151
Gamrie Gramp 95 NJ7962
Gamston Notts 49 SK7176
Gamston Notts 49 SK5937
Ganavan Bay Strath 79 NM8632
Ganllwyd Gwynd 35 SH7324
Gannachy Tays 89 NO5970
Ganstead Humb 57 TA1434
Ganthorpe N York 56 SE6870
Ganton N York 63 SE9977
Garbity Gramp 94 NJ3152
Garboldisham Norfk 32 TM0081
Garchory Gramp 94 NJ3010
Garden Village Derbys 49 SK2698
Gardeners Green Berks 22 SU8266
Gardenstown Gramp 95 NJ8064
Garderhouse Shet 103 HU3347
Gare Hill Somset 20 ST7840
Garelochhead Strath 80 NS2491
Garford Oxon 21 SU4296
Garforth W York 55 SE4033
Gargrave N York 54 SD9354
Gargunnock Cent 81 NS7094
Garlic Street Norfk 33 TM2183
Garlieston D & G 65 NX4746
Garlinge Kent 15 TR3369
Garlinge Green Kent 15 TR1152
Garlogie Gramp 89 NJ7805
Garmond Gramp 95 NJ8052
Garmouth Gramp 94 NJ3364
Garmston Shrops 37 SJ6006
Garn-Dolbenmaen Gwynd 44 SH4943
Garnkirk Strath 74 NS6768
Garrabost W Isls 102 NB5133
Garrallan Strath 74 NS5418
Garras Cnwll 2 SW7023
Garreg Gwynd 45 SH6141
Garrigill Cumb 60 NY7441
Garroch D & G 65 NX5981
Garrochtrie D & G 64 NX1138
Garrochty Strath 73 NS0953
Garros Highld 90 NG4962
Garsdale Head Cumb 60 SD7891
Garsdon Wilts 20 ST9687

Garshall Green

Great Coxwell

Garshall Green *Staffs* 38 SJ9633
Garsington *Oxon* 21 SP5802
Garstang *Lancs* 53 SD4945
Garston *Herts* 22 TL1100
Garston *Mersyd* 46 SJ4084
Gartachossan *Strath* 70 NR3461
Gartcosh *Strath* 74 NS6967
Garth *Clwyd* 36 SJ2542
Garth *Powys* 26 SN9549
Garth Penrhyncoch *Dyfed* 35 SN6484
Garth Row *Cumb* 59 SD5297
Garthamlock *Strath* 74 NS6566
Garthmyl *Powys* 36 SO1999
Garthorpe *Humb* 56 SE8418
Garthorpe *Leics* 40 SK8320
Gartly *Gramp* 94 NJ5232
Gartmore *Cent* 81 NS5297
Gartness *Cent* 81 NS5086
Gartness *Strath* 74 NS7864
Gartocharn *Strath* 81 NS4286
Garton *Humb* 57 TA2635
Garton-on-the-Wolds *Humb* 56 SE9759
Gartsherrie *Strath* 74 NS7265
Gartymore *Highld* 97 ND0114
Garvald *Loth* 76 NT5870
Garvan *Highld* 85 NM9777
Garvard *Strath* 70 NR3791
Garve *Highld* 92 NH3961
Garvestone *Norfk* 42 TG0207
Garvock *Strath* 73 NS2570
Garway *H & W* 27 SO4522
Garway Common *H & W* 27 SO4622
Garyvard *W Isls* 102 NB3619
Gasper *Wilts* 9 ST7633
Gastard *Wilts* 20 ST8868
Gasthorpe *Norfk* 32 TL9781
Gaston Green *Essex* 31 TL4917
Gatcombe *IOW* 11 SZ4985
Gate Burton *Lincs* 50 SK8382
Gate Helmsley *N York* 56 SE6955
Gateforth *N York* 56 SE5628
Gatehead *Strath* 73 NS3936
Gatehouse *Nthumb* 68 NY7889
Gatehouse of Fleet *D & G* 65 NX5956
Gatelawbridge *D & G* 66 NX9096
Gateley *Norfk* 42 TF9624
Gatenby *N York* 62 SE3287
Gateshaw *Border* 76 NT7722
Gateshead *T & W* 69 NZ2562
Gateside *Fife* 82 NO1809
Gateside *Strath* 73 NS3653
Gateside *Strath* 73 NS4858
Gateside *Tays* 88 NO4344
Gateslack *D & G* 66 NS8902
Gatley *Gt Man* 47 SJ8488
Gatton *Surrey* 12 TQ2752
Gattonside *Border* 76 NT5435
Gauldry *Fife* 83 NO3723
Gauldswell *Tays* 88 NO2151
Gaunt's End *Essex* 24 TL5525
Gautby *Lincs* 50 TF1772
Gavinton *Border* 76 NT7652
Gawcott *Bucks* 30 SP6831
Gawsworth *Ches* 48 SJ8969
Gawthrop *Cumb* 60 SD6987
Gawthwaite *Cumb* 58 SD2784
Gaydon *Warwks* 29 SP3653
Gayhurst *Bucks* 30 SP8446
Gayle *N York* 60 SD8688
Gayles *N York* 61 NZ1207
Gayton *Nhants* 30 SP7054
Gayton *Norfk* 42 TF7219
Gayton *Staffs* 38 SJ9828
Gayton le Marsh *Lincs* 51 TF4284
Gayton Thorpe *Norfk* 42 TF7418
Gaywood *Norfk* 41 TF6320
Gazeley *Suffk* 32 TL7264
Gearraidh Bhaird *W Isls* 102 NB3619
Geary *Highld* 90 NG2661
Gedding *Suffk* 32 TL9457
Geddinge *Kent* 15 TR2346
Geddington *Nhants* 40 SP8983
Gedling *Notts* 49 SK6142
Gedney *Lincs* 41 TF4024
Gedney Broadgate *Lincs* 41 TF4022
Gedney Drove End *Lincs* 41 TF4629
Gedney Dyke *Lincs* 41 TF4126
Gedney Hill *Lincs* 41 TF3311
Geldeston *Norfk* 33 TM3991
Gell *Clwyd* 46 SH8469
Gellifor *Clwyd* 46 SJ1262
Gelligaer *M Glam* 18 ST1396
Gellilydan *Gwynd* 45 SH6839
Gellinudd *W Glam* 18 SN7303
Gellyburn *Tays* 82 NO0939
Gellywen *Dyfed* 17 SN2723
Gelston *D & G* 66 NX7758
Gelston *Lincs* 50 SK9145
Gembling *Humb* 57 TA1057
Gentleshaw *Staffs* 38 SK0511
George Green *Bucks* 22 SU9981
George Nympton *Devon* 7 SS7023
Georgefield *D & G* 67 NY2991
Georgeham *Devon* 6 SS4639
Georth *Ork* 103 HY3625
Germansweek *Devon* 6 SX4394
Gerrans *Cnwll* 3 SW8735
Gerrards Cross *Bucks* 22 TQ0088
Gerrick *Cleve* 62 NZ7012
Gestingthorpe *Essex* 24 TL8138
Geuffordd *Powys* 36 SJ2114
Gidea Park *Gt Lon* 23 TQ5290
Giffnock *Strath* 74 NS5658
Gifford *Loth* 76 NT5368
Giffordtown *Fife* 83 NO2811
Giggleswick *N York* 54 SD8063
Gilberdyke *Humb* 56 SE8329
Gilchriston *Loth* 76 NT4865
Gilcrux *Cumb* 58 NY1138
Gildersome *W York* 55 SE2429
Gildingwells *S York* 49 SK5585
Gilesgate Moor *Dur* 61 NZ2942
Gileston *S Glam* 18 ST0166
Gilfach *M Glam* 19 ST1598
Gilfach Goch *M Glam* 18 SS9790
Gilfachrheda *Dyfed* 34 SN4158
Gilgarran *Cumb* 58 NY0323
Gillamoor *N York* 62 SE6889
Gillesbie *D & G* 67 NY1691
Gilling East *N York* 62 SE6176
Gilling West *N York* 61 NZ1805
Gillingham *Dorset* 9 ST8026
Gillingham *Kent* 14 TQ7768
Gillingham *Norfk* 33 TM4191
Gillock *Highld* 100 ND2159
Gills *Highld* 100 ND3272
Gilmanscleuch *Border* 75 NT3321
Gilmerton *Loth* 75 NT2868
Gilmerton *Tays* 82 NN8823
Gilmonby *Dur* 61 NY9912
Gilmorton *Leics* 39 SP5787
Gilsland *Nthumb* 68 NY6366
Gilwern *Gwent* 27 SO2414
Gimingham *Norfk* 43 TG2836
Gipping *Suffk* 32 TM0763
Gipsey Bridge *Lincs* 51 TF2849
Girdle Toll *Strath* 73 NS3440
Girlsta *Shet* 103 HU4250
Girsby *Cleve* 62 NZ3508
Girthon *D & G* 65 NX6053
Girton *Cambs* 31 TL4262
Girton *Notts* 50 SK8265
Girvan *Strath* 64 NX1897
Gisburn *Lancs* 54 SD8248
Gisleham *Suffk* 33 TM5188
Gislingham *Suffk* 32 TM0771
Gissing *Norfk* 33 TM1485
Gittisham *Devon* 8 SY1398
Gladestry *Powys* 27 SO2355
Gladsmuir *Loth* 76 NT4573
Glais *W Glam* 18 SN7000
Glaisdale *N York* 63 NZ7705
Glamis *Tays* 88 NO3846
Glan-y-don *Clwyd* 46 SJ1679
Glanaman *Dyfed* 26 SN6713
Glandford *Norfk* 42 TG0441
Glandwr *Dyfed* 17 SN1928
Glandyfi *Dyfed* 35 SN6996
Glanton *Nthumb* 68 NU0714
Glanvilles Wootton *Dorset* 9 ST6708
Glapthorn *Nhants* 40 TL0290
Glapwell *Derbys* 49 SK4766
Glasbury *Powys* 27 SO1739
Glascwm *Powys* 27 SO1552
Glasfryn *Clwyd* 45 SH9250
Glasgow *Strath* 74 NS5865
Glasinfryn *Gwynd* 44 SH5868
Glasnacardoch Bay *Highld* 85 NM6795
Glasnakille *Highld* 84 NG5313
Glasserton *D & G* 64 NX4237
Glassford *Strath* 74 NS7247
Glasshouse *Gloucs* 28 SO7021
Glasshouses *N York* 55 SE1764
Glasson *Cumb* 67 NY2560
Glasson *Lancs* 53 SD4456
Glassonby *Cumb* 59 NY5738
Glasterlaw *Tays* 89 NO5951
Glaston *Leics* 40 SK8900
Glastonbury *Somset* 19 ST5038
Glatton *Cambs* 40 TL1586
Glazebrook *Ches* 47 SJ6992
Glazebury *Ches* 47 SJ6797
Glazeley *Shrops* 37 SO7088
Gleaston *Cumb* 53 SD2570
Glebe *Highld* 92 NH5118
Gledhow *W York* 55 SE3137
Gledpark *D & G* 65 NX6250
Gledrid *Shrops* 36 SJ3036
Glemsford *Suffk* 32 TL8348
Glen Auldyn *IOM* 52 SC4393
Glen Clunie Lodge *Gramp* 88 NO1383
Glen Maye *IOM* 52 SC2379
Glen Nevis House *Highld* 86 NN1272
Glen Parva *Leics* 39 SP5798
Glen Trool Lodge *D & G* 64 NX4080
Glenancross *Highld* 85 NM6691
Glenaros House *Strath* 79 NM5544
Glenbarr *Strath* 72 NR6736
Glenbarry *Gramp* 94 NJ5554
Glenbeg *Highld* 79 NM5862
Glenbeg *Highld* 23 NJ0028
Glenboig *Strath* 74 NS7268
Glenborrodale *Highld* 79 NM6061
Glenbranter *Strath* 80 NS1197
Glenbreck *Border* 75 NT0521
Glenbrittle House *Highld* 84 NG4121
Glenbuck *Strath* 74 NS7429
Glencally *Tays* 88 NO3562
Glencaple *D & G* 66 NX9968
Glencarron Lodge *Highld* 91 NH0650
Glencarse *Tays* 82 NO1921
Glenceitlein *Highld* 86 NN1548
Glencoe *Highld* 86 NN1058
Glencothe *Border* 75 NT0829
Glencraig *Fife* 82 NT1894
Glencrosh *D & G* 65 NX7689
Glendale *Highld* 90 NG1749
Glendaruel *Strath* 80 NR9983
Glendevon *Tays* 82 NN9904
Glendoe Lodge *Highld* 92 NH4009
Glendoick *Tays* 82 NO2022
Glenduckie *Fife* 83 NO2818
Gleneagles *Tays* 82 NN9208
Gleneagles Hotel *Tays* 82 NN9111
Glenegedale *Strath* 70 NR3351
Glenelg *Highld* 85 NG8119
Glenerney *Gramp* 93 NJ0146
Glenfarg *Tays* 82 NO1310
Glenfeshie Lodge *Highld* 87 NN8493
Glenfield *Leics* 39 SK5406
Glenfinnan *Highld* 85 NM9080
Glenfintaig Lodge *Highld* 86 NN2286
Glenfoot *Tays* 82 NO1815
Glenfyne Lodge *Strath* 80 NN2215
Glengarnock *Strath* 73 NS3252
Glengolly *Highld* 100 ND1065
Glengorm Castle *Strath* 79 NM4457
Glengrasco *Highld* 90 NG4444
Glenholm *Border* 75 NT1033
Glenhoul *D & G* 65 NX6187
Glenisla *Tays* 88 NO2160
Glenkerry *Border* 67 NT2710
Glenkin *Strath* 80 NS1280
Glenkindie *Gramp* 94 NJ4314
Glenlivet *Gramp* 94 NJ1929
Glenlochar *D & G* 65 NX7364
Glenloig *Strath* 72 NR9435
Glenlomond *Tays* 82 NO1704
Glenluce *D & G* 64 NX1957
Glenmark *Tays* 88 NO4183
Glenmassen *Strath* 80 NS1088
Glenmavis *Strath* 74 NS7467
Glenmore *Highld* 84 NG4340
Glenmore Lodge *Highld* 93 NH9709
Glenquiech *Tays* 88 NO4261
Glenralloch *Strath* 71 NR8569
Glenrothes *Fife* 83 NO2700
Glenshero Lodge *Highld* 87 NN5592
Glenstriven *Strath* 80 NS0878
Glentham *Lincs* 50 TF0090
Glentromie Lodge *Highld* 87 NN7897
Glentrool Village *D & G* 64 NX3578
Glentruim House *Highld* 87 NN6894
Glentworth *Lincs* 50 SK9488
Glenuig *Highld* 85 NM6677
Glenure *Strath* 86 NN0448
Glenurquhart *Highld* 93 NH7462
Glenvarragill *Highld* 84 NG4739
Glenwhilly *D & G* 64 NX1771
Glespin *Strath* 74 NS8127
Glewstone *H & W* 27 SO5521
Glinton *Cambs* 40 TF1505
Glooston *Leics* 40 SP7595
Glossop *Derbys* 48 SK0393
Gloster Hill *Nthumb* 69 NU2504
Gloucester *Gloucs* 28 SO8318
Glusburn *N York* 54 SE0045
Glutt Lodge *Highld* 100 ND0036
Gluvian *Cnwll* 3 SW9164
Glympton *Oxon* 29 SP4221
Glyn Ceiriog *Clwyd* 36 SJ2038
Glyn-Neath *W Glam* 26 SN8806
Glynarthen *Dyfed* 17 SN3148
Glyncorrwg *W Glam* 18 SS8798
Glynde *E Susx* 13 TQ4509
Glyndyfrdwy *Clwyd* 36 SJ1442
Glyntawe *Powys* 26 SN8416
Glynteg *Dyfed* 17 SN3637
Gnosall *Staffs* 38 SJ8220
Gnosall Heath *Staffs* 38 SJ8220
Goadby *Leics* 40 SP7598
Goadby Marwood *Leics* 40 SK7726
Goatacre *Wilts* 20 SU0276
Goatfield *Strath* 80 NN0100
Goathill *Dorset* 9 ST6717
Goathland *N York* 63 NZ8301
Goathurst *Somset* 8 ST2534
Gobowen *Shrops* 36 SJ3033
Godalming *Surrey* 12 SU9643
Goddard's Green *Kent* 14 TQ8134
Godmanchester *Cambs* 31 TL2470
Godmanstone *Dorset* 9 SY6697
Godmersham *Kent* 15 TR0550
Godney *Somset* 19 ST4842
Godolphin Cross *Cnwll* 2 SW6031
Godre'r-graig *W Glam* 26 SN7506
Godshill *IOW* 11 SZ5281
Godstone *Surrey* 12 TQ3551
Goetre *Gwent* 27 SO3206
Goff's Oak *Herts* 23 TL3202
Gofilon *Gwent* 27 SO2613
Gogar *Loth* 75 NT1672
Goginan *Dyfed* 35 SN6881
Golan *Gwynd* 44 SH5242
Golant *Cnwll* 3 SX1254
Golberdon *Cnwll* 4 SX3271
Golborne *Gt Man* 47 SJ6097
Golcar *W York* 55 SE0915
Goldcliff *Gwent* 19 ST3683
Golden Green *Kent* 13 TQ6348
Golden Pot *Hants* 11 SU7143
Golders Green *Gt Lon* 23 TQ2487
Goldhanger *Essex* 24 TL9008
Goldington *Beds* 30 TL0750
Goldsborough *N York* 63 NZ8314
Goldsborough *N York* 55 SE3856
Goldsithney *Cnwll* 2 SW5430
Goldsworth *Surrey* 22 SU9958
Goldthorpe *S York* 55 SE4604
Goldworthy *Devon* 6 SS3922
Gollanfield *Highld* 93 NH8053
Golspie *Highld* 97 NC8300
Gomeldon *Wilts* 10 SU1835
Gomshall *Surrey* 12 TQ0847
Gonalston *Notts* 49 SK6747
Gonfirth *Shet* 103 HU3661
Good Easter *Essex* 24 TL6212
Gooderstone *Norfk* 42 TF7602
Goodleigh *Devon* 6 SS6034
Goodmanham *Humb* 56 SE8843
Goodnestone *Kent* 15 TR0461
Goodnestone *Kent* 15 TR2554
Goodrich *H & W* 27 SO5719
Goodrington *Devon* 5 SX8958
Goodshaw Fold *Lancs* 54 SD8026
Goodwick *Dyfed* 16 SM9438
Goodworth Clatford *Hants* 21 SU3642
Goole *Humb* 56 SE7423
Goom's Hill *H & W* 28 SP0154
Goonbell *Cnwll* 2 SW7249
Goonhavern *Cnwll* 2 SW7853
Goonvrea *Cnwll* 2 SW7149
Goose Green *Avon* 20 ST6774
Goose Green *Essex* 25 TM1327
Goose Green *Essex* 25 TM1325
Goosecruives *Gramp* 89 NO7583
Gooseford *Devon* 5 SX6792
Goosey *Oxon* 21 SU3591
Goosnargh *Lancs* 53 SD5536
Goostrey *Ches* 47 SJ7770
Gordon *Border* 76 NT6443
Gordon Arms Hotel *Border* 75 NT3025
Gordonstown *Gramp* 94 NJ5656
Gordonstown *Gramp* 95 NJ7138
Gorebridge *Loth* 75 NT3461
Gores *Wilts* 20 SU1158
Gorey *Jersey* 101 JS0000
Goring *Oxon* 21 SU6080
Goring-by-Sea *W Susx* 12 TQ1102
Gorleston on Sea *Norfk* 43 TG5204
Gorrachie *Gramp* 95 NJ7358
Gorran *Cnwll* 3 SW9942
Gorran Haven *Cnwll* 3 SX0141
Gorse Hill *Wilts* 20 SU1586
Gorsedd *Clwyd* 46 SJ1576
Gorseinon *W Glam* 17 SS5998
Gorsgoch *Dyfed* 17 SN4850
Gorslas *Dyfed* 17 SN5713
Gorsley *Gloucs* 28 SO6925
Gorsley Common *Gloucs* 28 SO6825
Gorstan *Highld* 92 NH3862
Gorstello *Ches* 46 SJ3562
Gorsty Common *H & W* 27 SO4437
Gorsty Hill *Staffs* 38 SK1028
Gorten *Strath* 79 NM7432
Gorthleck *Highld* 92 NH5420
Gorton *Gt Man* 47 SJ8896
Gosbeck *Suffk* 33 TM1555
Gosberton *Lincs* 41 TF2331
Gosfield *Essex* 24 TL7829
Gosforth *Cumb* 58 NY0603
Gosforth *T & W* 69 NZ2368
Gospel End *Staffs* 38 SO8993
Gosport *Hants* 11 SZ6099
Gossington *Gloucs* 20 SO7302
Gotham *Notts* 39 SK5330
Gotherington *Gloucs* 28 SO9529
Gotton *Somset* 8 ST2428
Goudhurst *Kent* 14 TQ7237
Goulceby *Lincs* 51 TF2579
Gourdas *Gramp* 95 NJ7741
Gourdie *Tays* 83 NO3532
Gourdon *Gramp* 89 NO8270
Gourock *Strath* 80 NS2477
Govan *Strath* 74 NS5465
Goveton *Devon* 5 SX7546
Gowdall *Humb* 56 SE6222
Gower *Highld* 92 NH5058
Gowerton *W Glam* 17 SS5896
Gowkhall *Fife* 82 NT0589
Goxhill *Humb* 57 TA1021
Goxhill *Humb* 57 TA1844
Grabhair *W Isls* 102 NB3915
Graffham *W Susx* 12 SU9217
Grafham *Cambs* 31 TL1669
Grafham *Surrey* 12 TQ0241
Grafton *H & W* 28 SO9837
Grafton *N York* 55 SE4163
Grafton *Oxon* 21 SP2600
Grafton *Shrops* 36 SJ4319
Grafton Flyford *H & W* 28 SO9655
Grafton Regis *Nhants* 30 SP7546
Grafton Underwood *Nhants* 40 SP9280
Grafty Green *Kent* 14 TQ8748
Graig *Gwynd* 45 SH8071
Graig-fechan *Clwyd* 46 SJ1454
Grain *Kent* 14 TQ8876
Grainsby *Lincs* 51 TF2799
Grainthorpe *Lincs* 51 TF3896
Graiselound *Humb* 50 SK7698
Grampound *Cnwll* 3 SW9348
Grampound Road *Cnwll* 3 SW9150
Gramsdal *W Isls* 102 NF8155
Gramsdale *W Isls* 102 NF8155
Granborough *Bucks* 30 SP7625
Granby *Notts* 40 SK7536
Grand Chemins *Jersey* 101 JS0000
Grandborough *Warwks* 29 SP4966
Grandes Rocques *Guern* 101 GN0000
Grandtully *Tays* 87 NN9153
Grange *Cumb* 58 NY2517
Grange *Kent* 14 TQ7968
Grange *Tays* 83 NO2625
Grange Crossroads *Gramp* 94 NJ4754
Grange Hall *Gramp* 93 NJ0660
Grange Hill *Gt Lon* 23 TQ4492
Grange Lindores *Fife* 83 NO2516
Grange Moor *W York* 55 SE2215
Grange Villa *Dur* 69 NZ2352
Grange-over-Sands *Cumb* 59 SD4077
Grangehall *Strath* 75 NS9642
Grangemill *Derbys* 48 SK2457
Grangemouth *Cent* 82 NS9281
Grangepans *Cent* 82 NT0181
Grangetown *Cleve* 62 NZ5420
Gransmoor *Humb* 57 TA1259
Granston *Dyfed* 16 SM8934
Grantchester *Cambs* 31 TL4355
Grantham *Lincs* 40 SK9135
Granton *Fife* 75 NT2376
Grantown-on-Spey *Highld* 93 NJ0328
Grantshouse *Border* 76 NT8065
Grasby *Lincs* 57 TA0804
Grasmere *Cumb* 59 NY3307
Grasscroft *Gt Man* 54 SD9704
Grassendale *Mersyd* 46 SJ3985
Grassington *N York* 54 SE0063
Grassmoor *Derbys* 49 SK4067
Grassthorpe *Notts* 50 SK7967
Grateley *Hants* 21 SU2741
Graveley *Cambs* 31 TL2563
Graveley *Herts* 31 TL2327
Graveney *Kent* 15 TR0562
Gravesend *Kent* 14 TQ6574
Gravir *W Isls* 102 NB3915
Grayingham *Lincs* 50 SK9396
Grayrigg *Cumb* 59 SD5796
Grays *Essex* 24 TQ6177
Grayshott *Hants* 11 SU8735
Grayswood *Surrey* 11 SU9134
Grazeley *Berks* 22 SU6966
Greasbrough *S York* 49 SK4195
Greasby *Mersyd* 46 SJ2587
Greasley *Notts* 49 SK4846
Great Abington *Cambs* 31 TL5348
Great Addington *Nhants* 30 SP9675
Great Alne *Warwks* 28 SP1259
Great Altcar *Lancs* 46 SD3305
Great Amwell *Herts* 31 TL3712
Great Asby *Cumb* 60 NY6713
Great Ayton *N York* 62 NZ5610
Great Baddow *Essex* 24 TL7304
Great Badminton *Avon* 20 ST8082
Great Bardfield *Essex* 24 TL6730
Great Barford *Beds* 30 TL1351
Great Barrington *Gloucs* 29 SP2113
Great Barrow *Ches* 46 SJ4768
Great Barton *Suffk* 32 TL8967
Great Barugh *N York* 63 SE7479
Great Bavington *Nthumb* 68 NY9880
Great Bedwyn *Wilts* 21 SU2764
Great Bentley *Essex* 25 TM1021
Great Billing *Nhants* 30 SP8162
Great Bircham *Norfk* 42 TF7732
Great Blakenham *Suffk* 33 TM1150
Great Blencow *Cumb* 59 NY4532
Great Bolas *Shrops* 37 SJ6421
Great Bookham *Surrey* 22 TQ1354
Great Bosullow *Cnwll* 2 SW4133
Great Bourton *Oxon* 29 SP4545
Great Bowden *Leics* 40 SP7488
Great Bradley *Suffk* 32 TL6753
Great Braxted *Essex* 24 TL8614
Great Bricett *Suffk* 32 TM0350
Great Brickhill *Bucks* 30 SP9030
Great Bridgeford *Staffs* 38 SJ8827
Great Brington *Nhants* 30 SP6665
Great Bromley *Essex* 25 TM0826
Great Broughton *Cumb* 58 NY0731
Great Broughton *N York* 62 NZ5405
Great Budworth *Ches* 47 SJ6677
Great Burdon *Dur* 62 NZ3116
Great Burstead *Essex* 24 TQ6892
Great Busby *N York* 62 NZ5205
Great Canfield *Essex* 24 TL5918
Great Carlton *Lincs* 51 TF4085
Great Casterton *Leics* 40 TF0008
Great Chart *Kent* 15 TQ9841
Great Chatfield *Wilts* 20 ST8563
Great Chatwell *Staffs* 37 SJ7914
Great Chesterford *Essex* 31 TL5042
Great Cheverell *Wilts* 20 ST9854
Great Chishill *Cambs* 31 TL4238
Great Clacton *Essex* 25 TM1716
Great Cliffe *W York* 55 SE3015
Great Clifton *Cumb* 58 NY0429
Great Coates *Humb* 57 TA2309
Great Comberton *H & W* 28 SO9542
Great Corby *Cumb* 67 NY4754
Great Cornard *Suffk* 32 TL8840
Great Cowden *Humb* 57 TA2342
Great Coxwell *Oxon* 21 SU2693

Great Cransley
Handcross

Great Cransley Nhants 30 SP8376
Great Cressingham Norfk 42 TF8501
Great Crosthwaite Cumb 58 NY2524
Great Cubley Derbys 48 SK1638
Great Dalby Leics 40 SK7414
Great Doddington Nhants 30 SP8864
Great Dunham Norfk 42 TF8714
Great Dunmow Essex 24 TL6222
Great Durnford Wilts 10 SU1338
Great Easton Essex 24 TL6025
Great Easton Leics 40 SP8492
Great Eccleston Lancs 53 SD4240
Great Ellingham Norfk 42 TM0196
Great Elm Somset 20 ST7449
Great Englebourne Devon 5 SX7756
Great Everdon Nhants 29 SP5957
Great Eversden Cambs 31 TL3653
Great Finborough Suffk 32 TM0158
Great Fransham Norfk 42 TF8913
Great Gaddesden Herts 22 TL0211
Great Gidding Cambs 40 TL1183
Great Givendale Humb 56 SE8153
Great Glemham Suffk 33 TM3361
Great Glen Leics 39 SP6597
Great Gonerby Lincs 40 SK8938
Great Gransden Cambs 31 TL2655
Great Green Cambs 31 TL2844
Great Green Suffk 32 TL9155
Great Green Suffk 32 TL9365
Great Habton N York 63 SE7576
Great Hale Lincs 50 TF1442
Great Hallingbury Essex 31 TL5119
Great Hanwood Shrops 36 SJ4409
Great Harrowden Nhants 30 SP8770
Great Harwood Lancs 54 SD7332
Great Haseley Oxon 21 SP6401
Great Hatfield Humb 57 TA1842
Great Haywood Staffs 38 SJ9922
Great Heck N York 56 SE5920
Great Henny Essex 24 TL8637
Great Hinton Wilts 20 ST9059
Great Hockham Norfk 32 TL9592
Great Holland Essex 25 TM2019
Great Horkesley Essex 25 TL9731
Great Hormead Herts 31 TL4029
Great Horton W York 55 SE1431
Great Horwood Bucks 30 SP7731
Great Houghton Nhants 30 SP7958
Great Houghton S York 55 SE4206
Great Hucklow Derbys 48 SK1777
Great Kelk Humb 57 TA1058
Great Kimble Bucks 22 SP8205
Great Kingshill Bucks 22 SU8797
Great Langdale Cumb 58 NY2906
Great Langton N York 61 SE2996
Great Leighs Essex 24 TL7217
Great Limber Lincs 57 TA1308
Great Linford Bucks 30 SP8542
Great Livermere Suffk 32 TL8871
Great Longstone Derbys 48 SK2071
Great Lumley T & W 69 NZ2949
Great Malvern H & W 28 SO7746
Great Maplestead Essex 24 TL8034
Great Marton Lancs 53 SD3235
Great Massingham Norfk 42 TF7922
Great Milton Oxon 21 SP6202
Great Missenden Bucks 22 SP8901
Great Mitton Lancs 54 SD7138
Great Mongeham Kent 15 TR3551
Great Moulton Norfk 33 TM1690
Great Musgrave Cumb 60 NY7613
Great Ness Shrops 36 SJ3919
Great Oak Gwent 27 SO3810
Great Oakley Essex 25 TM1927
Great Oakley Nhants 40 SP8785
Great Offley Herts 30 TL1427
Great Ormside Cumb 60 NY7017
Great Orton Cumb 67 NY3254
Great Ouseburn N York 55 SE4461
Great Oxendon Nhants 40 SP7383
Great Oxney Green Essex 24 TL6606
Great Paxton Cambs 31 TL2063
Great Plumpton Lancs 53 SD3833
Great Plumstead Norfk 43 TG3010
Great Ponton Lincs 40 SK9230
Great Preston W York 55 SE4029
Great Raveley Cambs 41 TL2581
Great Rissington Gloucs 29 SP1917
Great Rollright Oxon 29 SP3231
Great Ryburgh Norfk 42 TF9527
Great Ryle Nthumb 68 NU0212
Great Ryton Shrops 37 SJ4803
Great Saling Essex 24 TL6925
Great Salkeld Cumb 59 NY5536
Great Sampford Essex 24 TL6435
Great Saughall Ches 46 SJ3669
Great Shefford Berks 21 SU3875
Great Shelford Cambs 31 TL4651
Great Smeaton N York 62 NZ3404
Great Snoring Norfk 42 TF9434
Great Somerford Wilts 20 ST9682
Great Soudley Shrops 37 SJ7229
Great Stainton Dur 62 NZ3322
Great Stambridge Essex 24 TQ8991
Great Staughton Cambs 30 TL1264
Great Steeping Lincs 51 TF4364
Great Strickland Cumb 59 NY5522
Great Stukeley Cambs 31 TL2274
Great Sturton Lincs 51 TF2176
Great Swinburne Nthumb 68 NY9375
Great Tew Oxon 29 SP4028
Great Tey Essex 24 TL8925
Great Torrington Devon 6 SS4919
Great Tosson Nthumb 68 NU0200
Great Totham Essex 24 TL8611
Great Totham Essex 24 TL8713
Great Urswick Cumb 58 SD2674
Great Wakering Essex 25 TQ9487
Great Waldingfield Suffk 32 TL9144
Great Walsingham Norfk 42 TF9437
Great Waltham Essex 24 TL6913
Great Warley Essex 24 TQ5890
Great Washbourne Gloucs 28 SO9834
Great Weeke Devon 5 SX7187
Great Weldon Nhants 40 SP9289
Great Wenham Suffk 25 TM0738
Great Whittington Nthumb 68 NZ0070
Great Wigborough Essex 25 TL9615
Great Wilbraham Cambs 31 TL5557
Great Wishford Wilts 10 SU0735
Great Witcombe Gloucs 28 SO9114
Great Witley H & W 28 SO7566
Great Wolford Warwks 29 SP2534
Great Wratting Essex 32 TL6848
Great Wymondley Herts 31 TL2128
Great Wyrley Staffs 38 SJ9907
Great Yarmouth Norfk 43 TG5207
Great Yeldham Essex 24 TL7638
Greatford Lincs 40 TF0811
Greatgate Staffs 48 SK0539
Greatham Cleve 62 NZ4927
Greatham Hants 11 SU7730
Greatham W Susx 12 TQ0415
Greatstone-on-Sea Kent 15 TR0822
Greatworth Nhants 29 SP5542
Green End Herts 31 TL3222
Green End Herts 31 TL3333
Green End Warwks 39 SP2686
Green Hammerton N York 55 SE4556
Green Heath Staffs 38 SJ9913
Green Moor S York 49 SK2899
Green Ore Somset 19 ST5750
Green Quarter Cumb 59 NY4603
Green Street H & W 28 SO8749
Green Street Herts 31 TL4521
Green Street Herts 23 TQ1998
Green Street Green Kent 14 TQ5870
Green Tye Herts 31 TL4418
Greenburn Loth 75 NS9360
Greenfield Beds 30 TL0534
Greenfield Clwyd 46 SJ1977
Greenfield Highld 86 NH2000
Greenfield Strath 80 NS2490
Greenford Gt Lon 22 TQ1482
Greengairs Strath 74 NS7870
Greengates W York 55 SE1937
Greenhalgh Lancs 53 SD4035
Greenham Somset 8 ST0820
Greenhaugh Nthumb 68 NY7987
Greenhill Cent 82 NS8279
Greenhill D & G 67 NY1079
Greenhill Kent 15 TR1666
Greenhill Strath 75 NS9332
Greenhithe Kent 14 TQ5875
Greenholm Strath 74 NS5437
Greenhouse Border 76 NT5523
Greenhow Hill N York 55 SE1164
Greenland Highld 100 ND2367
Greenland S York 49 SK3988
Greenlaw Border 76 NT7146
Greenlea D & G 66 NY0375
Greenloaning Tays 82 NN8307
Greenmount Gt Man 54 SD7714
Greenock Strath 80 NS2876
Greenodd Cumb 58 SD3182
Greens Norton Nhants 30 SP6649
Greenshields Strath 75 NT0243
Greenside T & W 69 NZ1362
Greenside W York 55 SE1716
Greenstead Essex 25 TM0125
Greenstead Green Essex 24 TL8227
Greensted Essex 24 TL5403
Greenway Somset 8 ST3124
Greenwich Gt Lon 23 TQ3877
Greet Gloucs 28 SP0230
Greete Shrops 27 SO5770
Greetham Leics 40 SK9214
Greetham Lincs 51 TF3070
Greetland W York 55 SE0821
Greinton Somset 19 ST4136
Grenaby IOM 52 SC2672
Grendon Nhants 30 SP8760
Grendon Warwks 39 SP2799
Grendon Underwood Bucks 30 SP6820
Grenoside S York 49 SK3393
Greosabhagh W Isls 102 NG1593
Gresford Clwyd 46 SJ3454
Gresham Norfk 43 TG1638
Greshornish
House Hotel Highld 90 NG3454
Gressenhall Norfk 42 TF9615
Gressenhall Green Norfk 42 TF9616
Gressingham Lancs 53 SD5769
Greta Bridge Dur 61 NZ0813
Gretna D & G 67 NY3167
Gretna Green D & G 67 NY3168
Gretton Gloucs 28 SP0030
Gretton Nhants 40 SP8994
Gretton Shrops 37 SO5195
Grewelthorpe N York 61 SE2376
Grey's Green Oxon 22 SU7182
Greyrigg D & G 66 NY0888
Greysouthen Cumb 58 NY0729
Greystoke Cumb 59 NY4430
Greystone Tays 89 NO5343
Greywell Hants 22 SU7151
Griff Warwks 39 SP3689
Griffithstown Gwent 19 ST2998
Grimeford Village Lancs 54 SD6112
Grimesthorpe S York 49 SK3689
Grimethorpe S York 55 SE4109
Grimley H & W 28 SO8360
Grimmet Strath 73 NS3210
Grimoldby Lincs 51 TF3988
Grimpo Shrops 36 SJ3526
Grimsargh Lancs 54 SD5834
Grimsby Humb 57 TA2710
Grimscote Nhants 29 SP6553
Grimscott Cnwll 6 SS2606
Grimshader W Isls 102 NB4025
Grimsthorpe Lincs 40 TF0422
Grimston Leics 39 SK6821
Grimston Norfk 42 TF7222
Grimstone Dorset 9 SY6394
Grimstone End Suffk 32 TL9368
Grindale Humb 57 TA1271
Grindleford Derbys 48 SK2477
Grindleton Lancs 54 SD7545
Grindley Brook Shrops 37 SJ5242
Grindlow Derbys 48 SK1877
Grindon Staffs 48 SK0854
Gringley on the Hill Notts 50 SK7390
Grinsdale Cumb 67 NY3758
Grinshill Shrops 37 SJ5223
Grinton N York 61 SE0498
Griomaisiader W Isls 102 NB4025
Grishipoll Strath 78 NM1859
Gristhorpe N York 63 TA0981
Griston Norfk 42 TL9499
Gritley Ork 103 HY5504
Grittenham Wilts 20 SU0382
Grittleton Wilts 20 ST8580
Grizebeck Cumb 58 SD2384
Grizedale Cumb 59 SD3394
Groby Leics 39 SK5207
Groes Clwyd 45 SJ0064
Groes-faen M Glam 18 ST0680
Groes-Wen M Glam 18 ST1286
Groesffordd Marli Clwyd 45 SJ0073
Grogarry W Isls 102 NF7739
Grogport Strath 72 NR8144
Groigearraidh W Isls 102 NF7739
Gronant Clwyd 46 SJ0983
Groombridge E Susx 13 TQ5337
Grosebay W Isls 102 NG1593
Grosmont Gwent 27 SO4024
Grosmont N York 63 NZ8305
Groton Suffk 32 TL9641
Grouville Jersey 101 JS0000
Grove Notts 50 SK7479
Grove Oxon 21 SU4090
Grove Park Gt Lon 23 TQ4072
Grovesend W Glam 17 SN5900
Gruinard Highld 91 NG9489
Gruinart Strath 70 NR2966
Grula Highld 84 NG3826
Gruline Strath 79 NM5440
Grundisburgh Suffk 33 TM2251
Gruting Shet 103 HU2749
Gualachulain Highld 86 NN1145
Guardbridge Fife 83 NO4518
Guarlford H & W 28 SO8145
Guay Tays 88 NN9948
Guestling Green E Susx 14 TQ8513
Guestling Thorn E Susx 14 TQ8516
Guestwick Norfk 42 TG0626
Guide Lancs 54 SD7025
Guide Post Nthumb 69 NZ2585
Guilden Morden Cambs 31 TL2744
Guilden Sutton Ches 46 SJ4468
Guildford Surrey 12 SU9949
Guildtown Tays 82 NO1331
Guilsborough Nhants 30 SP6772
Guilsfield Powys 36 SJ2211
Guiltreehill Strath 73 NS3610
Guineaford Devon 6 SS5537
Guisborough Cleve 62 NZ6015
Guiseley W York 55 SE1942
Guist Norfk 42 TG0025
Guiting Power Gloucs 28 SP0924
Gullane Loth 83 NT4882
Gulval Cnwll 2 SW4831
Gulworthy Devon 4 SX4572
Gumfreston Dyfed 16 SN1001
Gumley Leics 39 SP6889
Gun Hill E Susx 13 TQ5614
Gunby Lincs 40 SK9121
Gunby Lincs 51 TF4666
Gundleton Hants 11 SU6133
Gunn Devon 7 SS6333
Gunnerside N York 61 SD9598
Gunnerton Nthumb 68 NY9074
Gunness Humb 56 SE8411
Gunnislake Cnwll 4 SX4371
Gunnista Shet 103 HU5043
Gunthorpe Norfk 42 TG0134
Gunthorpe Notts 49 SK6844
Gunwalloe Cnwll 2 SW6522
Gurnard IOW 11 SZ4795
Gurney Slade Somset 19 ST6249
Gurnos W Glam 26 SN7709
Gussage All Saints Dorset 10 SU0010
Gussage St Andrew Dorset 9 ST9714
Gussage St Michael Dorset 9 ST9811
Guston Kent 15 TR3244
Gutcher Shet 103 HU5499
Guthrie Tays 89 NO5650
Guyhirn Cambs 41 TF4003
Guyzance Nthumb 69 NU2103
Gwaenysgor Clwyd 46 SJ0781
Gwalchmai Gwynd 44 SH3876
Gwaun-Cae-Gurwen W Glam 26 SN6911
Gweek Cnwll 2 SW7026
Gwenddwr Powys 26 SO0643
Gwennap Cnwll 2 SW7340
Gwernaffield Clwyd 46 SJ2065
Gwernesney Gwent 19 SO4101
Gwernogle Dyfed 17 SN5333
Gwernymynydd Clwyd 46 SJ2162
Gwespyr Clwyd 46 SJ1183
Gwinear Cnwll 2 SW5937
Gwithian Cnwll 2 SW5841
Gwyddelwern Clwyd 46 SJ0746
Gwyddgrug Dyfed 17 SN4635
Gwytherin Clwyd 45 SH8761

H

Habberley H & W 37 SO8177
Habberley Shrops 36 SJ3903
Habergham Lancs 54 SD8033
Habertoft Lincs 51 TF5069
Habrough Humb 57 TA1413
Hacconby Lincs 40 TF1025
Haceby Lincs 40 TF0236
Hacheston Suffk 33 TM3059
Hackbridge Gt Lon 23 TQ2865
Hackenthorpe S York 49 SK4183
Hackford Norfk 42 TG0502
Hackforth N York 61 SE2492
Hackland Ork 103 HY3920
Hackleton Nhants 30 SP8055
Hacklinge Kent 15 TR3454
Hackness N York 63 SE9790
Hackney Gt Lon 23 TQ3484
Hackthorn Lincs 50 SK9982
Hackthorpe Cumb 59 NY5423
Hadden Border 76 NT7836
Haddenham Bucks 22 SP7308
Haddenham Cambs 31 TL4675
Haddington Lincs 50 SK9162
Haddington Loth 76 NT5173
Haddiscoe Norfk 43 TM4497
Haddo Gramp 95 NJ8337
Haddon Cambs 40 TL1392
Hadham Ford Herts 31 TL4321
Hadleigh Essex 24 TQ8187
Hadleigh Suffk 32 TM0242
Hadley H & W 28 SO8564
Hadley End Staffs 38 SK1320
Hadley Wood Gt Lon 23 TQ2698
Hadlow Kent 13 TQ6350
Hadlow Down E Susx 13 TQ5324
Hadnall Shrops 37 SJ5220
Hadstock Essex 31 TL5644
Hadzor H & W 28 SO9162
Hafodunos Clwyd 45 SH8666
Haggerston Nthumb 77 NU0443
Haggs Cent 81 NS7879
Hagley H & W 27 SO5641
Hagley H & W 38 SO9180
Hagworthingham Lincs 51 TF3469
Hail Weston Cambs 31 TL1662
Haile Cumb 58 NY0308
Hailey Oxon 29 SP3512
Hailsham E Susx 13 TQ5909
Hainault Gt Lon 23 TQ4591
Hainford Norfk 43 TG2218
Hainton Lincs 50 TF1884
Haisthorpe Humb 57 TA1264
Hakin Dyfed 16 SM8905
Halam Notts 49 SK6754
Halbeath Fife 82 NT1288
Halberton Devon 7 ST0112
Halcro Highld 100 ND2360
Hale Ches 46 SJ4782
Hale Cumb 59 SD5078
Hale Gt Man 47 SJ7786
Hale Hants 10 SU1818
Hale Surrey 22 SU8448
Hale Green E Susx 13 TQ5514
Hale Street Kent 14 TQ6749
Hales Norfk 43 TM3797
Hales Staffs 37 SJ7134
Hales Place Kent 15 TR1459
Halesowen W Mids 38 SO9683
Halesworth Suffk 33 TM3877
Halewood Mersyd 46 SJ4585
Halford Devon 5 SX8174
Halford Shrops 36 SO4383
Halford Warwks 29 SP2645
Halfpenny Green Staffs 38 SO8291
Halfway House Shrops 36 SJ3411
Halfway Houses Kent 14 TQ9372
Halifax W York 55 SE0925
Halistra Highld 90 NG2459
Halkirk Highld 100 ND1359
Halkyn Clwyd 46 SJ2171
Hall Strath 73 NS4154
Hall Dunnerdale Cumb 58 SD2195
Hall Green W Mids 38 SP1181
Hall's Green Herts 31 TL2728
Halland E Susx 13 TQ4916
Hallaton Leics 40 SP7896
Hallatrow Avon 19 ST6357
Hallbankgate Cumb 67 NY5859
Hallen Avon 19 ST5580
Hallgarth Dur 69 NZ3243
Hallin Highld 90 NG2558
Halling Kent 14 TQ7063
Hallington Lincs 51 TF3085
Hallington Nthumb 68 NY9875
Halliwell Gt Man 54 SD6910
Halloughton Notts 49 SK6951
Hallow H & W 28 SO8258
Hallrule Border 67 NT5914
Hallsands Devon 5 SX8138
Hallyne Border 75 NT1940
Halnaker W Susx 11 SU9007
Halsall Lancs 53 SD3710
Halse Nhants 29 SP5640
Halse Somset 8 ST1428
Halsetown Cnwll 2 SW5038
Halsham Humb 57 TA2727
Halstead Essex 24 TL8130
Halstead Kent 23 TQ4861
Halstead Leics 40 SK7505
Halstock Dorset 8 ST5308
Halsway Somset 18 ST1337
Haltham Lincs 51 TF2463
Halton Bucks 22 SP8710
Halton Clwyd 36 SJ3039
Halton Lancs 53 SD5064
Halton Nthumb 68 NY9967
Halton W York 55 SE3533
Halton East N York 55 SE0454
Halton Gill N York 60 SD8776
Halton Holegate Lincs 51 TF4165
Halton Lea Gate Nthumb 68 NY6458
Halton Shields Nthumb 68 NZ0168
Halton West N York 54 SD8454
Haltwhistle Nthumb 68 NY7064
Halvergate Norfk 43 TG4106
Halwell Devon 5 SX7753
Halwill Devon 6 SX4299
Halwill Junction Devon 6 SS4400
Ham Devon 8 ST2301
Ham Gloucs 20 ST6898
Ham Gt Lon 23 TQ1772
Ham Kent 15 TR3254
Ham Somset 8 ST2825
Ham Wilts 21 SU3262
Ham Green H & W 28 SP0163
Ham Street Somset 9 ST5534
Hamble Hants 11 SU4806
Hambleden Bucks 22 SU7886
Hambledon Hants 11 SU6414
Hambledon Surrey 12 SU9638
Hambleton Lancs 53 SD3742
Hambleton N York 56 SE5530
Hambridge Somset 8 ST3921
Hambrook W Susx 11 SU7806
Hamels Herts 31 TL3724
Hameringham Lincs 51 TF3167
Hamerton Cambs 40 TL1379
Hamilton Strath 74 NS7255
Hamlet Dorset 9 ST5908
Hammersmith Gt Lon 23 TQ2378
Hammerwich Staffs 38 SK0707
Hammoon Dorset 9 ST8114
Hamnavoe Shet 103 HU3735
Hamnavoe Shet 103 HU4971
Hampden Park E Susx 13 TQ6002
Hampden Row Bucks 22 SP8501
Hamperden End Essex 24 TL5730
Hampnett Gloucs 28 SP0915
Hampole S York 55 SE5010
Hampreston Dorset 10 SZ0598
Hampstead Gt Lon 23 TQ2685
Hampstead Norrey's Berks 21 SU5276
Hampsthwaite N York 55 SE2559
Hampton Gt Lon 22 TQ1369
Hampton H & W 28 SP0243
Hampton Kent 15 TR1568
Hampton Shrops 37 SO7486
Hampton Wilts 21 SU1892
Hampton Bishop H & W 27 SO5637
Hampton Heath Ches 46 SJ5049
Hampton in Arden W Mids 39 SP2080
Hampton Lovett H & W 28 SO8865
Hampton Lucy Warwks 29 SP2557
Hampton on the Hill Warwks 29 SP2564
Hampton Poyle Oxon 29 SP5015
Hampton Wick Gt Lon 23 TQ1769
Hamptworth Wilts 10 SU2419
Hamsey E Susx 13 TQ4012
Hamstall Ridware Staffs 38 SK1019
Hamstead Marshall Berks 21 SU4165
Hamsterley Dur 69 NZ1156
Hamsterley Dur 61 NZ1231
Hamstreet Kent 15 TR0033
Hamworthy Dorset 9 SY9991
Hanbury H & W 28 SO9664
Hanbury Staffs 38 SK1727
Hanchurch Staffs 38 SJ8441
Hand and Pen Devon 7 SY0495
Handbridge Ches 46 SJ4065
Handcross W Susx 12 TQ2629

Place	Page	Grid Ref
Handforth Ches	47	SJ8583
Handley Ches	46	SJ4657
Handley Derbys	49	SK3761
Handsworth S York	49	SK4186
Handsworth W Mids	38	SP0489
Hanging Langford Wilts	10	SU0337
Hangleton E Susx	12	TQ2607
Hanham Avon	19	ST6472
Hankelow Ches	47	SJ6645
Hankerton Wilts	20	ST9790
Hanley Staffs	47	SJ8847
Hanley Castle H & W	28	SO8442
Hanley Child H & W	27	SO6565
Hanley Swan H & W	28	SO8142
Hanley William H & W	28	SO6766
Hanlith N York	54	SD8961
Hanmer Clwyd	36	SJ4539
Hannaford Devon	6	SS6029
Hannington Hants	21	SU5355
Hannington Nhants	30	SP8170
Hannington Wilts	21	SU1793
Hannington Wick Wilts	21	SU1795
Hanslope Bucks	30	SP8046
Hanthorpe Lincs	40	TF0823
Hanwell Gt Lon	22	TQ1579
Hanwell Oxon	29	SP4343
Hanworth Gt Lon	22	TQ1271
Hanworth Norfk	43	TG1935
Happendon Strath	74	NS8533
Happisburgh Norfk	43	TG3831
Happisburgh Common Norfk	43	TG3728
Hapsford Ches	46	SJ4774
Hapton Lancs	54	SD7931
Hapton Norfk	43	TM1796
Harberton Devon	5	SX7758
Harbertonford Devon	5	SX7856
Harbledown Kent	15	TR1357
Harborne W Mids	38	SP0284
Harborough Magna Warwks	39	SP4778
Harbottle Nthumb	68	NT9304
Harbourneford Devon	5	SX7162
Harbury Warwks	29	SP3759
Harby Leics	40	SK7431
Harby Notts	50	SK8770
Harcombe Devon	5	SX8881
Harcombe Devon	8	SY1590
Harcombe Bottom Devon	8	SY3395
Harden W York	55	SE0838
Hardgate D & G	66	NX8167
Hardgate Gramp	89	NJ7901
Hardgate Strath	74	NS5072
Hardham W Susx	12	TQ0317
Hardingham Norfk	42	TG0403
Hardingstone Nhants	30	SP7657
Hardington Somset	20	ST7452
Hardington Mandeville Somset	8	ST5111
Hardington Marsh Somset	8	ST5009
Hardington Moor Somset	8	ST5112
Hardisworthy Devon	6	SS2320
Hardley Hants	10	SU4205
Hardley Street Norfk	43	TG3701
Hardraw N York	60	SD8691
Hardstoft Derbys	49	SK4363
Hardway Hants	11	SU6001
Hardway Somset	9	ST7234
Hardwick Bucks	30	SP8019
Hardwick Cambs	31	TL3758
Hardwick Nhants	30	SP8469
Hardwick Norfk	33	TM2289
Hardwick Oxon	29	SP3806
Hardwick Oxon	29	SP5729
Hardwicke Gloucs	28	SO7912
Hardwicke Gloucs	28	SO9027
Hardy's Green Essex	25	TL9320
Hare Croft W York	55	SE0835
Hare Green Essex	25	TM1025
Hare Hatch Berks	22	SU8077
Hare Street Essex	23	TL4209
Hare Street Essex	15	TL5300
Hare Street Herts	31	TL3929
Hareby Lincs	51	TF3365
Harefield Gt Lon	22	TQ0590
Harehill Derbys	38	SK1735
Harehills W York	55	SE3135
Harelaw Border	76	NT5323
Harescombe Gloucs	28	SO8310
Haresfield Gloucs	28	SO8010
Harestock Hants	10	SU4631
Harewood W York	55	SE3245
Harewood End H & W	27	SO5227
Harford Devon	5	SX6359
Hargrave Ches	46	SJ4862
Hargrave Nhants	30	TL0370
Hargrave Suffk	32	TL7759
Hargrave Green Suffk	25	TM1834
Harkstead Suffk	25	TM1834
Harlaston Staffs	39	SK2110
Harlaxton Lincs	40	SK8832
Harlech Gwynd	44	SH5831
Harlescott Shrops	37	SJ4916
Harlesden Gt Lon	23	TQ2183
Harlesthorpe Derbys	49	SK4976
Harleston Devon	5	SX7945
Harleston Norfk	33	TM2483
Harleston Suffk	32	TM0160
Harlestone Nhants	30	SP7064
Harley S York	49	SK3698
Harlington Beds	30	TL0330
Harlington Gt Lon	22	TQ0877
Harlington S York	49	SE4802
Harlosh Highld	84	NG2841
Harlow Essex	23	TL4410
Harlow Hill Nthumb	68	NZ0768
Harlthorpe Humb	56	SE7337
Harlton Cambs	31	TL3852
Harlyn Bay Cnwll	3	SW8775
Harman's Cross Dorset	9	SY9880
Harmby N York	61	SE1289
Harmer Green Herts	31	TL2515
Harmer Hill Shrops	37	SJ4822
Harmston Lincs	50	SK9662
Harnage Shrops	37	SJ5604
Harnhill Gloucs	20	SP0600
Harold Hill Gt Lon	23	TQ5392
Harold Wood Gt Lon	23	TQ5890
Haroldston West Dyfed	16	SM8615
Haroldswick Shet	103	HP6312
Harome N York	62	SE6481
Harpenden Herts	30	TL1314
Harpford Devon	8	SY0990
Harpham Humb	57	TA0861
Harpley H & W	28	SO6861
Harpley Norfk	42	TF7825
Harpole Nhants	30	SP6961
Harpsdale Highld	100	ND1355
Harpsden Oxon	22	SU7680
Harpswell Lincs	50	SK9389
Harpurhey Gt Man	47	SD8501
Harraby Cumb	67	NY4154
Harracott Devon	6	SS5527
Harrapool Highld	85	NG6523
Harrietfield Tays	82	NN9829
Harrietsham Kent	14	TQ8652
Harringay Gt Lon	23	TQ3188
Harrington Lincs	51	TF3671
Harrington Nhants	40	SP7780
Harringworth Nhants	40	SP9197
Harrogate N York	55	SE3054
Harrold Beds	30	SP9457
Harrow Gt Lon	22	TQ1588
Harrow Green Suffk	32	TL8654
Harrow on the Hill Gt Lon	22	TQ1587
Harrow Weald Gt Lon	22	TQ1591
Harrowbarrow Cnwll	4	SX4070
Harston Cambs	31	TL4250
Harston Leics	40	SK8331
Harswell Humb	56	SE8240
Hart Cleve	62	NZ4734
Hartburn Nthumb	68	NZ0885
Hartest Suffk	32	TL8352
Hartfield E Susx	13	TQ4735
Hartford Cambs	31	TL2572
Hartford Ches	47	SJ6372
Hartford End Essex	24	TL6817
Hartfordbridge Hants	22	SU7757
Hartforth N York	61	NZ1606
Harthill Ches	46	SJ4955
Harthill N York	74	NS9064
Harthill S York	49	SK4980
Hartington Derbys	48	SK1260
Hartland Devon	6	SS2524
Hartland Quay Devon	6	SS2224
Hartlebury H & W	38	SO8471
Hartlepool Cleve	62	NZ5032
Hartley Cumb	60	NY7808
Hartley Kent	14	TQ6066
Hartley Kent	14	TQ7634
Hartley Wespall Hants	22	SU6958
Hartley Wintney Hants	22	SU7656
Hartlip Kent	14	TQ8464
Harton N York	56	SE7061
Harton T & W	69	NZ3765
Hartpury Gloucs	28	SO7924
Hartshead W York	55	SE1822
Hartshill Staffs	47	SJ8546
Hartshill Warwks	39	SP3194
Hartshorne Derbys	39	SK3221
Hartside Nthumb	77	NT9716
Hartwell Nhants	30	SP7850
Hartwith N York	55	SE2161
Hartwood Strath	74	NS8459
Hartwoodmyres Border	76	NT4324
Harvel Kent	14	TQ6563
Harvington H & W	38	SO8775
Harvington H & W	28	SP0549
Harwell Notts	49	SK6891
Harwell Oxon	21	SU4989
Harwich Essex	25	TM2531
Harwood Dale N York	63	SE9695
Harworth Notts	49	SK6191
Hasbury W Mids	38	SO9582
Hascombe Surrey	12	TQ0039
Haselbeach Nhants	30	SP7177
Haselbury Plucknett Somset	8	ST4710
Haseley Warwks	29	SP2367
Haselor Warwks	28	SP1257
Hasfield Gloucs	28	SO8227
Haskayne Lancs	46	SD3508
Hasketon Suffk	33	TM2450
Haslemere Surrey	11	SU9032
Haslingden Lancs	54	SD7823
Haslingfield Cambs	31	TL4052
Haslington Ches	47	SJ7355
Hassingham Norfk	43	TG3605
Hassocks W Susx	12	TQ3015
Hassop Derbys	48	SK2272
Haster Highld	100	ND3251
Hastingleigh Kent	15	TR0945
Hastings E Susx	14	TQ8209
Hastingwood Essex	23	TL4807
Hastoe Herts	22	SP9209
Haswell Dur	69	NZ3743
Haswell Plough Dur	62	NZ3742
Hatch Beauchamp Somset	8	ST3020
Hatch End Gt Lon	22	TQ1390
Hatchmere Ches	47	SJ5571
Hatcliffe Humb	51	TA2100
Hatfield H & W	27	SO5959
Hatfield Herts	23	TL2308
Hatfield S York	56	SE6609
Hatfield Broad Oak Essex	24	TL5416
Hatfield Heath Essex	31	TL5215
Hatfield Peverel Essex	24	TL7911
Hatfield Woodhouse S York	56	SE6708
Hatford Oxon	21	SU3395
Hatherden Hants	21	SU3450
Hatherleigh Devon	6	SS5404
Hathern Leics	39	SK5022
Hatherop Gloucs	28	SP1505
Hathersage Derbys	48	SK2381
Hathersage Booths Derbys	48	SK2480
Hatherton Ches	47	SJ6847
Hatherton Staffs	38	SJ9510
Hatley St George Cambs	31	TL2751
Hatt Cnwll	4	SX4062
Hatton Ches	47	SJ5982
Hatton Derbys	39	SK2130
Hatton Gramp	95	NK0537
Hatton Gt Lon	22	TQ0975
Hatton Lincs	50	TF1776
Hatton Shrops	37	SO4790
Hatton Tays	89	NO4642
Hatton Warwks	29	SP2367
Hatton of Fintray Gramp	95	NJ8316
Haugh Strath	74	NS4925
Haugh of Glass Gramp	94	NJ4238
Haugh of Urr D & G	66	NX8066
Haugham Lincs	51	TF3381
Haughhead Inn Strath	81	NS6079
Haughley Suffk	32	TM0262
Haughley Green Suffk	32	TM0264
Haughton Shrops	36	SJ3726
Haughton Shrops	37	SJ7408
Haughton Staffs	38	SJ8620
Haughton le Skerne Dur	62	NZ3116
Haughton Moss Ches	47	SJ5756
Haultwick Herts	31	TL3323
Haunton Staffs	39	SK2310
Hautes Croix Jersey	101	JS0000
Hauxley Nthumb	69	NU2303
Hauxton Cambs	31	TL4452
Havant Hants	11	SU7106
Havenstreet IOW	11	SZ5690
Havercroft W York	55	SE3813
Haverfordwest Dyfed	16	SM9515
Haverhill Suffk	32	TL6745
Haverigg Cumb	58	SD1578
Havering-atte-Bower Essex	23	TQ5193
Haversham Bucks	30	SP8242
Haverthwaite Cumb	59	SD3483
Havyat Avon	19	ST4761
Hawarden Clwyd	46	SJ3165
Hawbush Green Essex	24	TL7820
Hawe's Green Norfk	43	TM2399
Hawen Dyfed	17	SN3446
Hawes N York	60	SD8789
Hawford H & W	28	SO8460
Hawick Border	67	NT5014
Hawkchurch Devon	8	ST3400
Hawkedon Suffk	32	TL7953
Hawkeridge Wilts	20	ST8653
Hawkesbury Avon	20	ST7686
Hawkesbury Upton Avon	20	ST7789
Hawkhurst Kent	14	TQ7530
Hawkinge Kent	15	TR2139
Hawkley Hants	11	SU7429
Hawkridge Devon	7	SS8630
Hawkshead Cumb	59	SD3598
Hawkshead Hill Cumb	59	SD3398
Hawksland Strath	74	NS8439
Hawkspur Green Essex	24	TL6532
Hawkstone Shrops	37	SJ5830
Hawksworth Notts	50	SK7543
Hawksworth W York	55	SE1641
Hawkwell Essex	24	TQ8591
Hawley Hants	22	SU8657
Hawling Gloucs	28	SP0622
Hawnby N York	62	SE5489
Haworth W York	55	SE0337
Hawstead Suffk	32	TL8559
Hawthorn Dur	69	NZ4145
Hawthorn Hill Lincs	51	TF2155
Hawton Notts	50	SK7851
Haxby N York	56	SE6058
Haxey Humb	50	SK7799
Hay Green Norfk	41	TF5418
Hay Street Herts	31	TL3926
Hay-on-Wye Powys	27	SO2342
Haydock Mersyd	47	SJ5697
Haydon Dorset	9	ST6715
Haydon Bridge Nthumb	68	NY8464
Haydon Wick Wilts	20	SU1387
Hayes Gt Lon	22	TQ0980
Hayes Gt Lon	23	TQ4066
Hayes End Gt Lon	22	TQ0882
Hayfield Derbys	48	SK0386
Hayfield Strath	80	NN0723
Hayhillock Tays	89	NO5242
Hayle Cnwll	2	SW5537
Hayley Green W Mids	38	SO9582
Hayne Devon	7	SS9515
Hayne Devon	5	SX7685
Haynes Beds	30	TL0740
Haynes West End Beds	30	TL0640
Hayscastle Dyfed	16	SM8925
Hayscastle Cross Dyfed	16	SM9125
Hayton Cumb	58	NY1041
Hayton Cumb	67	NY5157
Hayton Humb	56	SE8245
Hayton Notts	49	SK7284
Haytor Vale Devon	5	SX7777
Haytown Devon	6	SS3814
Haywards Heath W Susx	12	TQ3324
Haywood S York	56	SE5812
Hazel Grove Gt Man	48	SJ9287
Hazelbank Strath	74	NS8345
Hazelbury Bryan Dorset	9	ST7408
Hazeleigh Essex	24	TL8203
Hazelton Walls Fife	83	NO3322
Hazelwood Derbys	49	SK3245
Hazlemere Bucks	22	SU8895
Hazleton Gloucs	28	SP0718
Heacham Norfk	42	TF6737
Headbourne Worthy Hants	11	SU4832
Headcorn Kent	14	TQ8344
Headingley W York	55	SE2836
Headington Oxon	29	SP5207
Headlam Dur	61	NZ1818
Headlesscross Strath	75	NS9158
Headley Hants	21	SU5162
Headley Hants	11	SU8236
Headley Surrey	23	TQ2054
Headon Notts	50	SK7476
Heads Strath	74	NS7247
Heads Nook Cumb	67	NY5054
Heage Derbys	49	SK3750
Healaugh N York	55	SE0199
Healaugh N York	55	SE5047
Heald Green Gt Man	47	SJ8485
Heale Somset	8	ST2420
Heale Somset	7	ST3825
Healey N York	61	SE1780
Healeyfield Dur	68	NZ0648
Healing Humb	57	TA2110
Heamoor Cnwll	2	SW4631
Heanor Derbys	49	SK4346
Heanton Punchardon Devon	6	SS5035
Heapham Lincs	50	SK8788
Heasley Mill Devon	7	SS7332
Heast Highld	85	NG6417
Heath Derbys	49	SK4567
Heath W York	55	SE3520
Heath and Reach Beds	30	SP9228
Heath End Surrey	22	SU8549
Heath Green H & W	38	SP0771
Heath Hill Shrops	37	SJ7613
Heath Town W Mids	38	SO9399
Heathcote Derbys	48	SK1460
Heather Leics	39	SK3910
Heathfield E Susx	13	TQ5821
Heathfield Somset	8	ST1626
Heathton Shrops	37	SO8192
Heatley Staffs	38	SK0626
Heaton Staffs	48	SJ9562
Heaton T & W	69	NZ2666
Heaton W York	55	SE1335
Heaton's Bridge Lancs	53	SD4011
Heaverham Kent	14	TQ5758
Heavitree Devon	5	SX9492
Hebburn T & W	69	NZ3164
Hebden N York	55	SE0263
Hebden Bridge W York	54	SD9927
Hebing End Herts	31	TL3122
Hebron Dyfed	17	SN1827
Hebron Nthumb	69	NZ1989
Heckfield Hants	22	SU7260
Heckfield Green Suffk	33	TM1875
Heckfordbridge Essex	25	TL9421
Heckington Lincs	50	TF1444
Heckmondwike W York	55	SE1824
Heddington Wilts	20	ST9966
Heddon-on-the-Wall Nthumb	69	NZ1366
Hedenham Norfk	43	TM3193
Hedge End Hants	11	SU4912
Hedgerley Bucks	22	SU9687
Hedging Somset	8	ST3029
Hedley on the Hill Nthumb	68	NZ0759
Hednesford Staffs	38	SJ9912
Hedon Humb	57	TA1928
Hedsor Bucks	22	SU9086
Heglibister Shet	103	HU3851
Heighington Dur	61	NZ2422
Heighington Lincs	50	TF0269
Heightington H & W	37	SO7671
Heiton Border	76	NT7130
Hele Devon	6	SS5347
Hele Devon	7	SS9902
Hele Devon	8	ST1824
Helensburgh Strath	80	NS2982
Helenton Strath	73	NS3830
Helford Cnwll	2	SW7526
Helford Passage Cnwll	2	SW7626
Helhoughton Norfk	42	TF8626
Helions Bumpstead Essex	32	TL6541
Helland Cnwll	3	SX0771
Hellescott Cnwll	4	SX2888
Hellesdon Norfk	43	TG2010
Hellidon Nhants	29	SP5158
Hellifield N York	54	SD8556
Hellingly E Susx	13	TQ5812
Helm Nthumb	69	NZ1896
Helmdon Nhants	29	SP5943
Helme W York	55	SE0912
Helmingham Suffk	33	TM1857
Helmsdale Highld	97	ND0315
Helmshore Lancs	54	SD7821
Helmsley N York	62	SE6183
Helmswell Cliff Lincs	50	SK9489
Helperby N York	55	SE4469
Helperthorpe N York	56	SE9570
Helpringham Lincs	40	TF1440
Helpston Cambs	40	TF1205
Helsby Ches	46	SJ4975
Helsey Lincs	51	TF5170
Helston Cnwll	2	SW6527
Helstone Cnwll	3	SX0881
Helton Cumb	59	NY5021
Hemblington Norfk	43	TG3411
Hemel Hempstead Herts	22	TL0507
Hemerdon Devon	5	SX5657
Hemingbrough N York	56	SE6730
Hemingby Lincs	51	TF2374
Hemingford Abbots Cambs	31	TL2871
Hemingford Grey Cambs	31	TL2970
Hemingstone Suffk	33	TM1454
Hemington Nhants	40	TL0985
Hemington Somset	20	ST7253
Hemley Suffk	33	TM2842
Hemlington Cleve	62	NZ5014
Hempnall Norfk	43	TM2494
Hempnall Green Norfk	43	TM2493
Hemprigs Gramp	93	NJ1063
Hempstead Essex	24	TL6338
Hempstead Kent	14	TQ7964
Hempstead Norfk	43	TG1037
Hempstead Norfk	43	TG4028
Hempton Norfk	42	TF9129
Hempton Oxon	29	SP4431
Hemsby Norfk	43	TG4917
Hemswell Lincs	50	SK9290
Hemsworth W York	55	SE4213
Hemyock Devon	8	ST1313
Henderside Park Border	76	NT7435
Hendon Gt Lon	23	TQ2389
Hendy Dyfed	17	SN5803
Henfield W Susx	12	TQ2115
Hengoed M Glam	18	ST1594
Hengoed Powys	27	SO2253
Hengrave Suffk	32	TL8268
Henham Essex	24	TL5428
Henhurst Kent	14	TQ6669
Heniarth Powys	36	SJ1208
Henlade Somset	8	ST2623
Henley Dorset	9	ST6904
Henley Somset	8	ST4232
Henley Suffk	33	TM1551
Henley W Susx	11	SU8925
Henley's Down E Susx	14	TQ7312
Henley-in-Arden Warwks	28	SP1566
Henley-on-Thames Oxon	22	SU7682
Henllan Clwyd	45	SJ0268
Henllan Dyfed	17	SN3540
Henllys Gwent	19	ST2691
Henlow Beds	31	TL1738
Hennock Devon	5	SX8381
Henny Street Essex	24	TL8738
Henry's Moat (Castell Hendre) Dyfed	16	SN0427
Henryd Gwynd	45	SH7774
Hensall N York	56	SE5923
Henshaw Nthumb	68	NY7664
Hensingham Cumb	58	NX9816
Henstead Suffk	33	TM4685
Hensting Hants	11	SU4922
Henstridge Somset	9	ST7219
Henstridge Ash Somset	9	ST7220
Henton Oxon	22	SP7602
Henton Somset	19	ST4945
Henwick H & W	28	SO8355
Henwood Cnwll	4	SX2673
Heol-y-Cyw M Glam	18	SS9484
Hepple Nthumb	68	NT9901
Hepscott Nthumb	69	NZ2284
Heptonstall W York	54	SD9828
Hepworth Suffk	32	TL9874
Hepworth W York	55	SE1606
Herbrandston Dyfed	16	SM8707
Hereford H & W	27	SO5139
Hereson Kent	15	TR3865
Heribusta Highld	90	NG3970
Heriot Loth	76	NT3953
Hermiston Loth	75	NT1870
Hermitage Berks	21	SU5072
Hermitage Border	67	NY5095
Hermitage Dorset	9	ST6506
Hermon Dyfed	17	SN2031
Hermon Gwynd	44	SH3968
Herne Kent	15	TR1865
Herne Bay Kent	15	TR1768
Herne Hill Gt Lon	23	TQ3274
Herne Pound Kent	14	TQ6654
Herner Devon	6	SS5826
Hernhill Kent	15	TR0660
Herodsfoot Cnwll	4	SX2160
Heronden Kent	15	TR2954
Heronsford Strath	64	NX1283
Herriard Hants	22	SU6646
Herringfleet Suffk	43	TM4797
Herringswell Suffk	32	TL7270
Herringthorpe S York	49	SK4492
Herrington T & W	69	NZ3453
Hersden Kent	15	TR2062
Hersham Surrey	22	TQ1164

Herstmonceux *E Susx*...... 13 TQ6312
Herston *Ork*...... 103 ND4191
Hertford *Herts*...... 31 TL3212
Hertford Heath *Herts*...... 23 TL3510
Hesketh Lane *Lancs*...... 54 SD6141
Hesleden *Dur*...... 62 NZ4438
Heslington *N York*...... 56 SE6250
Hessay *N York*...... 55 SE5253
Hessett *Suffk*...... 32 TL9361
Hessle *Humb*...... 56 TA0326
Hessle *W York*...... 55 SE4317
Heston *Gt Lon*...... 22 TQ1277
Hestwall *Ork*...... 103 HY2618
Heswall *Mersyd*...... 46 SJ2681
Hethe *Oxon*...... 29 SP5929
Hethersett *Norfk*...... 43 TG1404
Hethersgill *Cumb*...... 67 NY4767
Hethpool *Nthumb*...... 77 NT8928
Hett *Dur*...... 61 NZ2836
Hetton *N York*...... 54 SD9658
Hetton-le-Hole *T & W*...... 62 NZ3547
Heugh *Nthumb*...... 68 NZ0873
Heugh Head *Border*...... 77 NT8762
Heughhead *Gramp*...... 94 NJ3811
Heveningham *Suffk*...... 33 TM3372
Hever *Kent*...... 13 TQ4745
Heversham *Cumb*...... 59 SD4983
Hevingham *Norfk*...... 43 TG1921
Hewas Water *Cnwll*...... 3 SW9649
Hewelsfield *Gloucs*...... 19 SO5602
Hewish *Avon*...... 19 ST4064
Hewish *Somset*...... 8 ST4208
Hewood *Dorset*...... 8 ST3502
Hexham *Nthumb*...... 68 NY9364
Hextable *Kent*...... 13 TQ5170
Hexthorpe *S York*...... 49 SE5602
Hexton *Herts*...... 30 TL1030
Hexworthy *Cnwll*...... 4 SX3581
Hexworthy *Devon*...... 5 SX6572
Heybridge *Essex*...... 24 TL8508
Heybridge *Essex*...... 24 TQ6398
Heybrook Bay *Devon*...... 4 SX4949
Heydon *Cambs*...... 31 TL4339
Heydon *Norfk*...... 43 TG1127
Heydour *Lincs*...... 40 TF0039
Heylipoll *Strath*...... 78 NL9743
Heylor *Shet*...... 103 HU2980
Heysham *Lancs*...... 53 SD4160
Heyshott *W Susx*...... 11 SU8917
Heytesbury *Wilts*...... 20 ST9242
Heythrop *Oxon*...... 29 SP3527
Heywood *Gt Man*...... 54 SD8510
Heywood *Wilts*...... 20 ST8753
Hibaldstow *Humb*...... 50 SE9702
Hickleton *S York*...... 55 SE4805
Hickling *Norfk*...... 43 TG4124
Hickling *Notts*...... 40 SK6928
Hickling Green *Norfk*...... 43 TG4123
Hickstead *W Susx*...... 12 TQ2620
Hidcote Bartrim *Gloucs*...... 29 SP1742
Hidcote Boyce *Gloucs*...... 29 SP1742
High Ackworth *W York*...... 55 SE4417
High Ardwell *D & G*...... 64 NX0745
High Auldgirth *D & G*...... 66 NX9187
High Bankhill *Cumb*...... 59 NY5542
High Beach *Essex*...... 23 TQ4198
High Bentham *N York*...... 54 SD6669
High Bickington *Devon*...... 6 SS6020
High Biggins *Cumb*...... 59 SD6078
High Blantyre *Strath*...... 74 NS6756
High Bonnybridge *Cent*...... 82 NS8379
High Bray *Devon*...... 7 SS6934
High Brooms *Kent*...... 13 TQ5941
High Casterton *Cumb*...... 60 SD6278
High Catton *Humb*...... 56 SE7153
High Coniscliffe *Dur*...... 61 NZ2215
High Crosby *Cumb*...... 67 NY4559
High Cross *Hants*...... 11 SU7126
High Cross *Herts*...... 31 TL3618
High Cross *Strath*...... 73 NS4046
High Cross *Warwks*...... 29 SP2067
High Drummore *D & G*...... 64 NX1235
High Easter *Essex*...... 24 TL6214
High Ellington *N York*...... 61 SE2083
High Ercall *Shrops*...... 37 SJ5917
High Etherley *Dur*...... 61 NZ1728
High Garrett *Essex*...... 24 TL7727
High Grantley *N York*...... 55 SE2369
High Green *H & W*...... 28 SO8745
High Green *Norfk*...... 43 TG1305
High Green *Norfk*...... 33 TM1689
High Halden *Kent*...... 14 TQ8937
High Halstow *Kent*...... 14 TQ7875
High Ham *Somset*...... 8 ST4231
High Harrogate *N York*...... 55 SE3155
High Hatton *Shrops*...... 37 SJ6124
High Hawsker *N York*...... 63 NZ9207
High Hesket *Cumb*...... 67 NY4744
High Hoyland *S York*...... 55 SE2710
High Hurstwood *E Susx*...... 13 TQ4926
High Hutton *N York*...... 56 SE7568
High Ireby *Cumb*...... 58 NY2237
High Kilburn *N York*...... 55 SE5179
High Lands *Dur*...... 61 NZ1226
High Lane *Gt Man*...... 48 SJ9585
High Lane *H & W*...... 28 SO6760
High Lanes *Cnwll*...... 2 SW5637
High Laver *Essex*...... 23 TL5208
High Legh *Ches*...... 47 SJ7084
High Leven *Cleve*...... 62 NZ4512
High Littleton *Avon*...... 19 ST6458
High Lorton *Cumb*...... 58 NY1625
High Marnham *Notts*...... 50 SK8070
High Melton *S York*...... 49 SE5001
High Mickley *Nthumb*...... 68 NZ0761
High Newport *T & W*...... 69 NZ3754
High Newton *Cumb*...... 59 SD4082
High Nibthwaite *Cumb*...... 58 SD2989
High Offley *Staffs*...... 37 SJ7826
High Ongar *Essex*...... 24 TL5603
High Onn *Staffs*...... 38 SJ8216
High Park Corner *Essex*...... 25 TM0320
High Pennyvenie *Strath*...... 73 NS4907
High Roding *Essex*...... 24 TL6017
High Salvington *W Susx*...... 12 TQ1206
High Spen *T & W*...... 69 NZ1359
High Street *Cnwll*...... 3 SW9653
High Street *Kent*...... 15 TR0862
High Street *Suffk*...... 33 TM4355
High Toynton *Lincs*...... 51 TF2869
High Trewhitt *Nthumb*...... 68 NU0105
High Urpeth *Dur*...... 69 NZ2354
High Valleyfield *Fife*...... 82 NT0086
High Wray *Cumb*...... 59 SD3799
High Wych *Herts*...... 31 TL4614
High Wycombe *Bucks*...... 22 SU8693
Higham *Derbys*...... 49 SK3859

Higham *Kent*...... 13 TQ6048
Higham *Kent*...... 14 TQ7171
Higham *Lancs*...... 54 SD8136
Higham *S York*...... 55 SE3107
Higham *Suffk*...... 32 TL7465
Higham *Suffk*...... 25 TM0335
Higham Dykes *Nthumb*...... 69 NZ1375
Higham Ferrers *Nhants*...... 30 SP9668
Higham Gobion *Beds*...... 30 TL1032
Higham Hill *Gt Lon*...... 23 TQ3590
Higham on the Hill *Leics*...... 39 SP3895
Highampton *Devon*...... 6 SS4804
Highams Park *Gt Lon*...... 23 TQ3891
Highbridge *Somset*...... 19 ST3247
Highbrook *W Susx*...... 12 TQ3630
Highburton *W York*...... 55 SE1813
Highbury *Gt Lon*...... 23 TQ3185
Highbury *Somset*...... 20 ST6949
Highclere *Hants*...... 21 SU4359
Highcliffe *Dorset*...... 10 SZ2193
Highcliffiane *Derbys*...... 49 SK2947
Higher Ansty *Dorset*...... 9 ST7604
Higher Bartle *Lancs*...... 53 SD5033
Higher Bockhampton *Dorset*...... 9 SY7292
Higher Brixham *Devon*...... 5 SX9155
Higher Chillington *Somset*...... 8 ST3810
Higher Combe *Somset*...... 7 SS9030
Higher Gabwell *Devon*...... 5 SX9169
Higher Irlam *Gt Man*...... 47 SJ7295
Higher Kinnerton *Clwyd*...... 46 SJ3261
Higher Muddiford *Devon*...... 6 SS5638
Higher Penwortham *Lancs*...... 53 SD5128
Higher Town *Cnwll*...... 2 SW8044
Higher Town *Cnwll*...... 3 SX0061
Higher Town *IOS*...... 2 SV9215
Higher Walton *Ches*...... 47 SJ5985
Higher Walton *Lancs*...... 53 SD5727
Higher Wambrook *Somset*...... 8 ST2908
Higher Waterston *Dorset*...... 9 SY7295
Higher Wheelton *Lancs*...... 54 SD6022
Higher Whitley *Ches*...... 47 SJ6180
Higher Wraxhall *Dorset*...... 9 ST5601
Higher Wych *Ches*...... 46 SJ4943
Highfield *Strath*...... 73 NS3150
Highfield *T & W*...... 69 NZ1458
Highgate *Gt Lon*...... 23 TQ2887
Highlane *S York*...... 49 SK4081
Highleadon *Gloucs*...... 28 SO7623
Highleigh *W Susx*...... 11 SZ8498
Highley *Shrops*...... 37 SO7483
Highmoor *Oxon*...... 22 SU7084
Highmoor Cross *Oxon*...... 22 SU7084
Highnam *Gloucs*...... 28 SO7817
Highnam Green *Gloucs*...... 28 SO7920
Highsted *Kent*...... 14 TQ9061
Highstreet Green *Essex*...... 24 TL7634
Highstreet Green *Surrey*...... 12 SU9835
Hightae *D & G*...... 67 NY0978
Hightown *Mersyd*...... 46 SD3003
Hightown Green *Suffk*...... 32 TL9756
Highweek *Devon*...... 5 SX8472
Highwood Hill *Gt Lon*...... 23 TQ2193
Highworth *Wilts*...... 21 SU2092
Hilden Park *Kent*...... 13 TQ5747
Hildenborough *Kent*...... 13 TQ5648
Hildersham *Cambs*...... 31 TL5448
Hilderstone *Staffs*...... 38 SJ9534
Hilderthorpe *Humb*...... 57 TA1766
Hilfield *Dorset*...... 9 ST6305
Hilgay *Norfk*...... 41 TL6298
Hill *Avon*...... 19 ST6495
Hill *Warwks*...... 29 SP4566
Hill Brow *Hants*...... 11 SU7926
Hill Chorlton *Staffs*...... 37 SJ7939
Hill Common *Somset*...... 8 ST1426
Hill Dyke *Lincs*...... 51 TF3447
Hill End *Fife*...... 82 NT0395
Hill End *Gloucs*...... 28 SO9037
Hill Green *Kent*...... 14 TQ8362
Hill Head *Hants*...... 11 SU5402
Hill of Beath *Fife*...... 82 NT1590
Hill of Fearn *Highld*...... 97 NH8377
Hill Ridware *Staffs*...... 38 SK0817
Hill Side *W York*...... 55 SE1717
Hill Top *W York*...... 55 SE3315
Hillam *N York*...... 55 SE5028
Hillbutts *Dorset*...... 9 ST9901
Hillcott *Wilts*...... 20 SU1158
Hillend *Fife*...... 82 NT1483
Hillend *Loth*...... 75 NT2566
Hillend *Strath*...... 74 NS8267
Hillesden *Bucks*...... 30 SP6828
Hillesley *Gloucs*...... 20 ST7689
Hillfarrance *Somset*...... 8 ST1624
Hillfoot *Strath*...... 74 NS5472
Hillhead *Strath*...... 75 NS9840
Hillhead of Cocklaw *Gramp*...... 95 NK0844
Hillhead of Durno *Gramp*...... 95 NJ7128
Hilliclay *Highld*...... 100 ND1764
Hillingdon *Gt Lon*...... 22 TQ0782
Hillington *Norfk*...... 42 TF7225
Hillington *Strath*...... 74 NS5164
Hillmorton *Warwks*...... 39 SP5373
Hillowton *D & G*...... 66 NX7763
Hills Town *Derbys*...... 49 SK4869
Hillside *Gramp*...... 89 NO9197
Hillside *T & W*...... 89 NO6960
Hillstreet *Hants*...... 10 SU3416
Hillswick *Shet*...... 103 HU2877
Hilltown *Devon*...... 4 SX5380
Hillwell *Shet*...... 103 HU3714
Hilmarton *Wilts*...... 20 SU0175
Hilperton *Wilts*...... 20 ST8759
Hilsea *Hants*...... 11 SU6503
Hilston *Humb*...... 57 TA2833
Hilton *Border*...... 77 NT8750
Hilton *Cambs*...... 31 TL2966
Hilton *Cleve*...... 62 NZ4611
Hilton *Cumb*...... 60 NY7320
Hilton *Derbys*...... 39 SK2430
Hilton *Dorset*...... 9 ST7802
Hilton *Dur*...... 61 NZ1622
Hilton *Shrops*...... 37 SO7795
Hilton of Cadboll *Highld*...... 97 NH8776
Himbleton *H & W*...... 28 SO9458
Himley *Staffs*...... 38 SO8891
Hincaster *Cumb*...... 59 SD5084
Hinchley Wood *Surrey*...... 23 TQ1565
Hinckley *Leics*...... 39 SP4294
Hinderclay *Suffk*...... 32 TM0276
Hinderwell *N York*...... 63 NZ7916
Hindhead *Surrey*...... 11 SU8835
Hindley *Gt Man*...... 47 SD6104
Hindlip *H & W*...... 28 SO8858
Hindolveston *Norfk*...... 42 TG0329
Hindon *Wilts*...... 9 ST9132
Hindringham *Norfk*...... 42 TF9836
Hingham *Norfk*...... 42 TG0202

Hinnington *Shrops*...... 37 SJ7404
Hinstock *Shrops*...... 37 SJ6925
Hintlesham *Suffk*...... 32 TM0843
Hinton *Avon*...... 20 ST7376
Hinton *H & W*...... 27 SO3338
Hinton *Shrops*...... 37 SJ4008
Hinton Ampner *Hants*...... 11 SU6027
Hinton Blewett *Somset*...... 19 ST5956
Hinton Charterhouse *Avon*...... 20 ST7758
Hinton Martell *Dorset*...... 10 SU0106
Hinton on the Green *H & W*...... 28 SP0240
Hinton Parva *Wilts*...... 21 SU2383
Hinton St George *Somset*...... 8 ST4212
Hinton St Mary *Dorset*...... 9 ST7816
Hinton Waldrist *Oxon*...... 21 SU3799
Hints *Shrops*...... 28 SO6374
Hints *Staffs*...... 38 SK1502
Hinwick *Beds*...... 30 SP9361
Hinxhill *Kent*...... 15 TR0442
Hinxton *Cambs*...... 31 TL4945
Hinxworth *Herts*...... 31 TL2340
Hipperholme *W York*...... 55 SE1225
Hipswell *N York*...... 61 SE1898
Hirn *Gramp*...... 89 NJ7200
Hirnant *Powys*...... 36 SJ0422
Hirst *Nthumb*...... 69 NZ2787
Hirst Courtney *N York*...... 56 SE6124
Hirwaun *M Glam*...... 26 SN9505
Hiscott *Devon*...... 6 SS5426
Histon *Cambs*...... 31 TL4463
Hitcham *Suffk*...... 32 TL9851
Hitcham Causeway *Suffk*...... 32 TL9852
Hitcham Street *Suffk*...... 32 TL9851
Hitchin *Herts*...... 31 TL1829
Hither Green *Gt Lon*...... 23 TQ3874
Hittisleigh *Devon*...... 7 SX7395
Hive *Humb*...... 56 SE8230
Hixon *Staffs*...... 38 SK0025
Hoaden *Kent*...... 15 TR2759
Hoar Cross *Staffs*...... 38 SK1323
Hoarwithy *H & W*...... 27 SO5429
Hoath *Kent*...... 15 TR2064
Hobarris *Shrops*...... 36 SO3178
Hobkirk *Border*...... 67 NT5811
Hobson *Dur*...... 69 NZ1756
Hoby *Leics*...... 39 SK6617
Hockering *Norfk*...... 42 TG0713
Hockerton *Notts*...... 49 SK7156
Hockley *Essex*...... 24 TQ8392
Hockley Heath *W Mids*...... 38 SP1572
Hockliffe *Beds*...... 30 SP9726
Hockwold cum Wilton *Norfk*...... 32 TL7388
Hockworthy *Devon*...... 7 ST0319
Hoddesdon *Herts*...... 23 TL3708
Hoddleston *Lancs*...... 54 SD7122
Hoddom Cross *D & G*...... 67 NY1873
Hoddom Mains *D & G*...... 67 NY1572
Hodgeston *Dyfed*...... 16 SS0399
Hodnet *Shrops*...... 37 SJ6128
Hodsall Street *Kent*...... 14 TQ6263
Hodsock *Notts*...... 49 SK6185
Hodson *Wilts*...... 21 SU1780
Hodthorpe *Derbys*...... 49 SK5376
Hoe *Norfk*...... 42 TF9916
Hogben's Hill *Kent*...... 15 TR0356
Hoggeston *Bucks*...... 30 SP8024
Hoghton *Lancs*...... 54 SD6125
Hognaston *Derbys*...... 48 SK2350
Hogrill's End *Warwks*...... 39 SP2292
Hogsthorpe *Lincs*...... 51 TF5372
Holbeach *Lincs*...... 41 TF3624
Holbeach Drove *Lincs*...... 41 TF3212
Holbeach Hurn *Lincs*...... 41 TF3926
Holbeach St Johns *Lincs*...... 41 TF3518
Holbeach St Mark's *Lincs*...... 41 TF3731
Holbeach St Matthew *Lincs*...... 41 TF4132
Holbeck *Notts*...... 49 SK5473
Holberrow Green *H & W*...... 28 SP0259
Holbeton *Devon*...... 5 SX6150
Holborn *Gt Lon*...... 23 TQ3181
Holbrook *Derbys*...... 49 SK3644
Holbrook *Suffk*...... 25 TM1636
Holbrook Moor *Derbys*...... 49 SK3645
Holbury *Hants*...... 10 SU4303
Holcombe *Devon*...... 5 SX9574
Holcombe *Somset*...... 20 ST6749
Holcombe Rogus *Devon*...... 7 ST0518
Holcot *Nhants*...... 30 SP7969
Holden *Lancs*...... 54 SD7749
Holdenby *Nhants*...... 30 SP6967
Holder's Green *Essex*...... 24 TL6328
Holdgate *Shrops*...... 37 SO5689
Holdingham *Lincs*...... 50 TF0547
Holditch *Dorset*...... 8 ST3402
Hole *Devon*...... 6 SS3402
Holford *Somset*...... 19 ST1541
Holgate *N York*...... 56 SE5851
Holker *Cumb*...... 59 SD3676
Holkham *Norfk*...... 42 TF8943
Hollacombe *Devon*...... 6 SS3702
Holland Fen *Lincs*...... 51 TF2349
Holland-on-Sea *Essex*...... 25 TM1916
Hollandstoun *Ork*...... 103 HY7553
Hollesley *Suffk*...... 33 TM3544
Hollicombe *Devon*...... 5 SX8962
Hollingbourne *Kent*...... 14 TQ8455
Hollingbury *E Susx*...... 12 TQ3107
Hollingdon *Bucks*...... 30 SP8727
Hollington *Derbys*...... 48 SK2239
Hollington *Staffs*...... 48 SK0538
Hollingworth *Gt Man*...... 47 SK0096
Hollins Green *Ches*...... 47 SJ6990
Hollinsclough *Staffs*...... 48 SK0666
Hollocombe *Devon*...... 7 SS6311
Holloway *Derbys*...... 49 SK3256
Holloway *Gt Lon*...... 23 TQ3086
Hollowell *Nhants*...... 30 SP6971
Hollowmoor Heath *Ches*...... 46 SJ4868
Holly Green *H & W*...... 28 TF1135
Hollybush *Gwent*...... 19 SO1603
Hollybush *H & W*...... 28 SO7536
Hollybush *Strath*...... 73 NS3915
Hollym *Humb*...... 57 TA3425
Holmbridge *W York*...... 55 SE1206
Holmbury St Mary *Surrey*...... 12 TQ1143
Holmbush *Cnwll*...... 3 SX0352
Holmcroft *Staffs*...... 38 SJ9024
Holme *Cambs*...... 40 TL1987
Holme *Cumb*...... 59 SD5278
Holme *N York*...... 62 SE3582
Holme *Notts*...... 50 SK8059
Holme *W York*...... 55 SE1105
Holme Chapel *Lancs*...... 54 SD8728
Holme Green *N York*...... 56 SE5541
Holme Hale *Norfk*...... 42 TF8807
Holme Lacy *H & W*...... 27 SO5535
Holme Marsh *H & W*...... 27 SO3454
Holme next the Sea *Norfk*...... 42 TF7043

Holme on the Wolds *Humb*...... 56 SE9646
Holme Pierrepont *Notts*...... 49 SK6238
Holme St Cuthbert *Cumb*...... 67 NY1047
Holme upon Spalding
  Moor *Humb*...... 56 SE8038
Holmer *H & W*...... 27 SO5042
Holmer Green *Bucks*...... 22 SU9097
Holmes Chapel *Ches*...... 47 SJ7667
Holmesfield *Derbys*...... 49 SK3277
Holmeswood *Lancs*...... 53 SD4316
Holmethorpe *Surrey*...... 12 TQ2851
Holmewood *Derbys*...... 49 SK4365
Holmfirth *W York*...... 55 SE1408
Holmhead *Strath*...... 74 NS5620
Holmpton *Humb*...... 57 TA3623
Holmrook *Cumb*...... 58 SD0799
Holmwood *Surrey*...... 12 TQ1647
Holne *Devon*...... 5 SX7069
Holnest *Dorset*...... 9 ST6510
Holnicote *Somset*...... 7 SS9146
Holsworthy *Devon*...... 6 SS3403
Holsworthy Beacon *Devon*...... 6 SS3608
Holt *Clwyd*...... 46 SJ4053
Holt *Dorset*...... 10 SU0303
Holt *H & W*...... 28 SO8362
Holt *Norfk*...... 42 TG0838
Holt *Wilts*...... 20 ST8661
Holt End *H & W*...... 28 SO0769
Holt Heath *H & W*...... 28 SO8163
Holtby *N York*...... 56 SE6754
Holton *Oxon*...... 29 SP6006
Holton *Somset*...... 9 ST6826
Holton *Suffk*...... 33 TM4077
Holton cum Beckering *Lincs*...... 50 TF1181
Holton le Clay *Lincs*...... 51 TA2802
Holton le Moor *Lincs*...... 50 TF0697
Holton St Mary *Suffk*...... 25 TM0536
Holwell *Dorset*...... 9 ST6911
Holwell *Herts*...... 31 TL1633
Holwell *Leics*...... 40 SK7323
Holwell *Oxon*...... 29 SP2309
Holwick *Dur*...... 60 NY9126
Holy Island *Nthumb*...... 77 NU1241
Holybourne *Hants*...... 11 SU7340
Holyhead *Gwynd*...... 44 SH2482
Holymoorside *Derbys*...... 49 SK3369
Holyport *Berks*...... 22 SU8977
Holystone *Nthumb*...... 68 NT9502
Holytown *Strath*...... 74 NS7660
Holywell *Cambs*...... 31 TL3370
Holywell *Clwyd*...... 46 SJ1875
Holywell *Cnwll*...... 2 SW7659
Holywell *Dorset*...... 9 ST5904
Holywell Green *W York*...... 55 SE0819
Holywell Lake *Somset*...... 8 ST1020
Holywell Row *Suffk*...... 32 TL7177
Holywood *D & G*...... 66 NX9480
Homer *Shrops*...... 37 SJ6101
Homer Green *Mersyd*...... 46 SD3402
Homersfield *Suffk*...... 33 TM2885
Homington *Wilts*...... 10 SU1226
Honey Tye *Suffk*...... 25 TL9535
Honeybourne *H & W*...... 28 SP1144
Honeychurch *Devon*...... 7 SS6303
Honeystreet *Wilts*...... 20 SU1061
Honiley *Warwks*...... 39 SP2372
Honing *Norfk*...... 43 TG3227
Honingham *Norfk*...... 43 TG1011
Honington *Lincs*...... 50 SK9443
Honington *Suffk*...... 32 TL9174
Honington *Warwks*...... 29 SP2642
Honiton *Devon*...... 8 ST1600
Honley *W York*...... 55 SE1311
Hoo *Kent*...... 14 TQ7872
Hoo End *Herts*...... 31 TL1820
Hoo Green *Ches*...... 47 SJ7182
Hooe *Devon*...... 4 SX5052
Hooe *E Susx*...... 14 TQ6809
Hooe Common *E Susx*...... 14 TQ6910
Hoohill *Lancs*...... 53 SD3237
Hook *Dyfed*...... 16 SM9711
Hook *Hants*...... 22 SU7254
Hook *Humb*...... 56 SE7625
Hook *Kent*...... 14 TQ6170
Hook *Surrey*...... 23 TQ1864
Hook *Wilts*...... 20 SU0784
Hook Green *Kent*...... 13 TQ6535
Hook Norton *Oxon*...... 29 SP3533
Hooke *Dorset*...... 8 ST5300
Hookway *Devon*...... 7 SX8598
Hooton Levitt *S York*...... 49 SK5591
Hooton Pagnell *S York*...... 55 SE4807
Hooton Roberts *S York*...... 49 SK4897
Hope *Clwyd*...... 46 SJ3058
Hope *Derbys*...... 48 SK1783
Hope *Devon*...... 5 SX6740
Hope *Shrops*...... 37 SO5974
Hope *Staffs*...... 48 SK1254
Hope Bowdler *Shrops*...... 37 SO4792
Hope End Green *Essex*...... 24 TL5720
Hope Mansell *H & W*...... 27 SO6219
Hope under Dinmore *H & W*...... 27 SO5052
Hopehouse *Border*...... 75 NT2916
Hopeman *Gramp*...... 93 NJ1469
Hopesay *Shrops*...... 36 SO3983
Hopperton *N York*...... 55 SE4256
Hopstone *Shrops*...... 37 SO7894
Hopton *Derbys*...... 49 SK2653
Hopton *Staffs*...... 38 SJ9426
Hopton *Suffk*...... 32 TL9979
Hopton Cangeford *Shrops*...... 37 SO5480
Hopton Castle *Shrops*...... 36 SO3678
Hopton on Sea *Norfk*...... 43 TM5299
Hopton Wafers *Shrops*...... 37 SO6376
Hoptonheath *Shrops*...... 36 SO3377
Hopwas *Staffs*...... 38 SK1804
Hopwood *H & W*...... 38 SP0375
Horam *E Susx*...... 13 TQ5717
Horbling *Lincs*...... 40 TF1135
Horbury *W York*...... 55 SE2918
Horden *Dur*...... 62 NZ4440
Hordle *Hants*...... 10 SZ2795
Hordley *Shrops*...... 36 SJ3831
Horfield *Avon*...... 19 ST5976
Horham *Suffk*...... 33 TM2072
Horkesley Heath *Essex*...... 25 TL9829
Horkstow *Humb*...... 56 SE9817
Horley *Oxon*...... 29 SP4144
Horley *Surrey*...... 12 TQ2842
Hornblotton Green *Somset*...... 9 ST5833
Hornby *Lancs*...... 54 SD5868
Hornby *N York*...... 62 NZ3605
Hornby *N York*...... 61 SE2233
Horncastle *Lincs*...... 51 TF2669
Hornchurch *Gt Lon*...... 23 TQ5387
Horndean *Border*...... 77 NT9049
Horndean *Hants*...... 11 SU7013
Horndon *Devon*...... 4 SX5280

Horndon on the Hill *Essex* 24 TQ6683
Horne *Surrey* 12 TQ3344
Horner *Somset* 7 SS9045
Horning *Norfk* 43 TG3417
Horninghold *Leics* 40 SP8097
Horninglow *Staffs* 39 SK2425
Horningsea *Cambs* 31 TL4962
Horningsham *Wilts* 20 ST8141
Horningtoft *Norfk* 42 TF9323
Horns Cross *Devon* 6 SS3823
Hornsea *Humb* 57 TA1947
Hornsey *Gt Lon* 23 TQ3089
Hornton *Oxon* 29 SP3945
Horra *Shet* 103 HU4693
Horrabridge *Devon* 4 SX5169
Horridge *Devon* 5 SX7674
Horringer *Suffk* 32 TL8261
Horrocksford *Lancs* 54 SD7543
Horsebridge *Devon* 4 SX4075
Horsebridge *E Susx* 13 TQ5811
Horsebridge *Hants* 10 SU3430
Horsebridge *Shrops* 36 SJ3606
Horseheath *Cambs* 31 TL6147
Horsehouse *N York* 61 SE0480
Horsell *Surrey* 22 SU9959
Horseman's Green *Clwyd* 36 SJ4441
Horsenden *Bucks* 22 SP7902
Horsey *Norfk* 43 TG4622
Horsey *Somset* 19 ST3239
Horsford *Norfk* 43 TG1916
Horsforth *W York* 55 SE2338
Horsham *H & W* 28 SO7358
Horsham *W Susx* 12 TQ1731
Horsham St Faith *Norfk* 43 TG2115
Horsington *Lincs* 50 TF1968
Horsington *Somset* 9 ST7023
Horsley *Derbys* 49 SK3744
Horsley *Gloucs* 20 ST8497
Horsley *Nthumb* 68 NY8496
Horsley *Nthumb* 68 NZ0965
Horsley Woodhouse *Derbys* 49 SK3944
Horsleycross Street *Essex* 25 TM1228
Horsleyhill *Border* 76 NT5319
Horsmonden *Kent* 14 TQ7040
Horspath *Oxon* 29 SP5705
Horstead *Norfk* 43 TG2619
Horsted Keynes *W Susx* 13 TQ3828
Horton *Avon* 20 ST7584
Horton *Berks* 22 TQ0175
Horton *Bucks* 30 SP9219
Horton *Dorset* 10 SU0307
Horton *Lancs* 54 SD8550
Horton *Nhants* 30 SP8154
Horton *Shrops* 37 SJ6814
Horton *Somset* 8 ST3214
Horton *Staffs* 48 SJ9457
Horton *W Glam* 17 SS4785
Horton *Wilts* 20 SU0463
Horton Green *Ches* 46 SJ4549
Horton in Ribblesdale *N York* 54 SD8071
Horton Kirby *Kent* 14 TQ5668
Horton-cum-Studley *Oxon* 29 SP5912
Horwich *Gt Man* 54 SD6311
Horwood *Devon* 6 SS5027
Hoscote *Border* 67 NT3911
Hose *Leics* 40 SK7329
Hosh *Tays* 82 NN8523
Hoswick *Shet* 103 HU4123
Hotham *Humb* 56 SE8934
Hothfield *Kent* 15 TQ9644
Hoton *Leics* 39 SK5722
Hott *Nthumb* 68 NY7785
Hough *Ches* 47 SJ7151
Hough *Ches* 46 SJ4886
Hough-on-the-Hill *Lincs* 50 SK9246
Hougham *Lincs* 50 SK8844
Houghton *Cambs* 31 TL2872
Houghton *Dyfed* 16 SM9807
Houghton *Hants* 10 SU3432
Houghton *W Susx* 12 TQ0111
Houghton Conquest *Beds* 30 TL0441
Houghton Green *E Susx* 14 TQ9222
Houghton le Spring *T & W* 69 NZ3449
Houghton on the Hill *Leics* 39 SK6703
Houghton Regis *Beds* 30 TL0123
Houghton St Giles *Norfk* 42 TF9235
Hound Green *Hants* 22 SU7359
Houndslow *Border* 76 NT6347
Houndwood *Border* 77 NT8463
Hounslow *Gt Lon* 22 TQ1375
Hounslow Green *Essex* 24 TL6518
Househill *Highld* 93 NH8855
Houses Hill *W York* 55 SE1916
Housieside *Gramp* 95 NJ8926
Houston *Strath* 73 NS4066
Houstry *Highld* 100 ND1534
Houton *Ork* 103 HY3104
Hove *E Susx* 12 TQ2804
Hoveringham *Notts* 49 SK6946
Hoveton *Norfk* 43 TG3018
Hovingham *N York* 62 SE6675
How *Cumb* 67 NY5056
How Caple *H & W* 27 SO6030
Howden *Humb* 56 SE7428
Howden-le-Wear *Dur* 61 NZ1633
Howe *Highld* 100 ND3061
Howe *N York* 62 SE3580
Howe *Norfk* 43 TM2799
Howe Green *Essex* 24 TL7403
Howe of Teuchar *Gramp* 95 NJ7946
Howe Street *Essex* 16 TL6914
Howe Street *Essex* 24 TL6934
Howegreen *Essex* 24 TL8301
Howell *Lincs* 50 TF1346
Howes *D & G* 67 NY1866
Howey *Powys* 26 SO0558
Howgate *Loth* 75 NT2457
Howick *Nthumb* 77 NU2517
Howle *Dur* 61 NZ0926
Howle *Shrops* 37 SJ6923
Howle Hill *H & W* 27 SO6020
Howlett End *Essex* 24 TL5834
Howley *Somset* 8 ST2609
Howmore *W Isls* 102 NF7536
Hownam *Border* 76 NT7719
Howsham *Humb* 57 TA0404
Howsham *N York* 62 SE7362
Howtel *Nthumb* 77 NT8934
Howwood *Strath* 73 NS3960
Hoxne *Suffk* 33 TM1777
Hoylake *Mersyd* 46 SJ2189
Hoyland Nether *S York* 49 SE3700
Hoyland Swaine *S York* 55 SE2604
Huby *N York* 55 SE2747
Huby *N York* 56 SE5665
Hucclecote *Gloucs* 28 SO8717
Hucking *Kent* 14 TQ8458
Hucknall *Notts* 49 SK5349

Huddersfield *W York* 55 SE1416
Huddington *H & W* 28 SO9457
Hudswell *N York* 61 NZ1400
Huggate *Humb* 56 SE8855
Hugh Town *IOS* 2 SV9010
Hughenden Valley *Bucks* 22 SU8697
Hughley *Shrops* 37 SO5698
Huish *Devon* 6 SS5311
Huish *Wilts* 20 SU1463
Huish Champflower *Somset* 7 ST0529
Huish Episcopi *Somset* 8 ST4326
Hulcott *Bucks* 30 SP8516
Hulham *Devon* 5 SY0183
Hull *Humb* 57 TA0829
Hulland *Derbys* 48 SK2446
Hulland Ward *Derbys* 48 SK2546
Hullavington *Wilts* 20 ST8981
Hullbridge *Essex* 24 TQ8095
Hulme *Staffs* 48 SJ9345
Hulme *Gt Man* 47 SJ8396
Hulme End *Staffs* 48 SK1059
Hulme Walfield *Ches* 47 SJ8465
Hulverstone *IOW* 10 SZ3984
Hulver Street *Suffk* 33 TM4686
Humberston *Humb* 57 TA3105
Humberstone *Leics* 39 SK6305
Humbie *Loth* 76 NT4662
Humbleton *Humb* 57 TA2234
Humby *Lincs* 40 TF0032
Hume *Border* 76 NT7041
Humshaugh *Nthumb* 68 NY9171
Huna *Highld* 100 ND3573
Huncote *Leics* 39 SP5197
Hundalee *Border* 76 NT6418
Hunderthwaite *Dur* 61 NY9821
Hundleby *Lincs* 51 TF3966
Hundleton *Dyfed* 16 SM9600
Hundon *Suffk* 32 TL7348
Hundred End *Lancs* 53 SD4122
Hundred House *Powys* 26 SO1154
Hungarton *Leics* 40 SK6907
Hungerford *Berks* 21 SU3368
Hungerford *Somset* 7 ST0440
Hungerford Newtown *Berks* 21 SU3571
Hungerstone *H & W* 27 SO4435
Hunmanby *N York* 63 TA0977
Hunningham *Warwks* 29 SP3767
Hunsdon *Herts* 31 TL4114
Hunsingore *N York* 55 SE4253
Hunslet *W York* 55 SE3130
Hunsonby *Cumb* 59 NY5835
Hunstanton *Norfk* 42 TF6740
Hunstanworth *Dur* 68 NY9448
Hunston *Suffk* 32 TL9768
Hunston *W Susx* 11 SU8601
Hunstrete *Avon* 19 ST6462
Hunsworth *W York* 55 SE1827
Hunters Quay *Strath* 80 NS1879
Hunterston *Ches* 47 SJ6946
Huntham *Somset* 8 ST3134
Hunthill Lodge *Tays* 89 NO4771
Huntingdon *Cambs* 31 TL2471
Huntingdon *H & W* 27 SO2553
Huntingfield *Suffk* 33 TM3374
Huntington *Loth* 76 NT4874
Huntington *N York* 56 SE6156
Huntington *Staffs* 38 SJ9712
Huntley *Gloucs* 28 SO7219
Huntly *Gramp* 94 NJ5339
Hunton *Hants* 21 SU4840
Hunton *Kent* 14 TQ7149
Hunton *N York* 61 SE1892
Huntscott *Somset* 7 SS9144
Huntscott *Somset* 7 ST0020
Huntsham *Devon* 6 SS5023
Huntshaw *Devon* 19 ST3145
Huntspill *Somset* 8 ST2633
Huntstile *Somset* 8 ST2633
Huntworth *Somset* 8 ST3134
Hunwick *Dur* 61 NZ1832
Hunworth *Norfk* 42 TG0635
Hurdcott *Wilts* 10 SU1733
Hurdsfield *Ches* 48 SJ9274
Hurley *Berks* 22 SU8283
Hurley *Warwks* 39 SP2495
Hurley Common *Warwks* 39 SP2496
Hurlford *Strath* 73 NS4536
Hurn *Dorset* 10 SZ1296
Hursley *Hants* 10 SU4225
Hurst *Berks* 22 SU7973
Hurst Green *E Susx* 14 TQ7327
Hurst Green *Essex* 25 TM0916
Hurst Green *Lancs* 54 SD6838
Hurst Green *Surrey* 13 TQ3951
Hurstbourne Priors *Hants* 21 SU4346
Hurstbourne Tarrant *Hants* 21 SU3853
Hurstley *H & W* 27 SO3548
Hurstpierpoint *W Susx* 12 TQ2716
Hurstwood *Lancs* 54 SD8831
Hurtiso *Ork* 103 HY5001
Hurworth-on-Tees *Dur* 61 NZ3009
Husbands Bosworth *Leics* 39 SP6484
Husborne Crawley *Beds* 30 SP9635
Husthwaite *N York* 62 SE5175
Huthwaite *Notts* 49 SK4659
Huttoft *Lincs* 51 TF5176
Hutton *Avon* 19 ST3558
Hutton *Border* 77 NT9053
Hutton *Essex* 24 TQ6395
Hutton *Humb* 56 TA0253
Hutton *Lancs* 53 SD4926
Hutton Bonville *N York* 62 NZ3300
Hutton Buscel *N York* 63 SE9784
Hutton Conyers *N York* 62 SE3273
Hutton Cranswick *Humb* 56 TA0252
Hutton End *Cumb* 59 NY4538
Hutton Henry *Dur* 62 NZ4236
Hutton Lowcross *Cleve* 62 NZ5914
Hutton Magna *Dur* 61 NZ1212
Hutton Roof *Cumb* 59 NY3734
Hutton Roof *Cumb* 59 SD5677
Hutton Rudby *N York* 62 NZ4606
Hutton Sessay *N York* 62 SE4776
Hutton Wandesley *N York* 55 SE5050
Hutton-le-Hole *N York* 62 SE7090
Huxham *Devon* 7 SX9497
Huxley *Ches* 46 SJ5061
Huyton *Mersyd* 46 SJ4490
Hycemoor *Cumb* 58 SD0989
Hyde *Gt Man* 48 SJ9494
Hyde Heath *Bucks* 22 SP9300
Hyde Lea *Staffs* 38 SJ9120
Hyndford Bridge *Strath* 75 NS9141
Hynish *Strath* 78 NL9839
Hyssington *Powys* 36 SO3194
Hythe *Hants* 10 SU4207
Hythe *Kent* 15 TR1634
Hythe End *Berks* 22 TQ0172

Ibberton *Dorset* 9 ST7807
Ible *Derbys* 48 SK2457
Ibsley *Hants* 10 SU1509
Ibstock *Leics* 39 SK4009
Ibstone *Bucks* 22 SU7593
Ibthorpe *Hants* 21 SU3753
Iburndale *N York* 63 NZ8707
Ibworth *Hants* 21 SU5654
Ickburgh *Norfk* 42 TL8195
Ickenham *Gt Lon* 22 TQ0786
Ickford *Bucks* 29 SP6407
Ickham *Kent* 15 TR2258
Ickleford *Herts* 31 TL1831
Icklesham *E Susx* 14 TQ8716
Ickleton *Cambs* 31 TL4943
Icklingham *Suffk* 32 TL7772
Ickornshaw *N York* 54 SD9642
Ickwell Green *Beds* 30 TL1545
Icomb *Gloucs* 29 SP2122
Idbury *Oxon* 29 SP2319
Iddesleigh *Devon* 6 SS5708
Ide *Devon* 5 SX8990
Ide Hill *Kent* 13 TQ4851
Ideford *Devon* 5 SX8977
Iden *E Susx* 14 TQ9123
Iden Green *Kent* 14 TQ7437
Iden Green *Kent* 14 TQ8031
Idle *W York* 55 SE1737
Idless *Cnwll* 2 SW8147
Idlicote *Warwks* 29 SP2844
Idmiston *Wilts* 10 SU1937
Idridgehay *Derbys* 49 SK2849
Idrigill *Highld* 90 NG3863
Idstone *Oxon* 21 SU2584
Iffley *Oxon* 21 SP5203
Ifield *W Susx* 12 TQ2537
Iford *Dorset* 10 SZ1393
Iford *E Susx* 13 TQ4007
Ifton *Gwent* 19 ST4688
Ightham *Kent* 14 TQ5956
Ightfield *Shrops* 37 SJ5938
Iken *Suffk* 33 TM4155
Ilam *Staffs* 48 SK1350
Ilchester *Somset* 8 ST5222
Ilderton *Nthumb* 77 NU0121
Ilford *Gt Lon* 23 TQ4486
Ilford *Somset* 8 ST3617
Ilfracombe *Devon* 6 SS5247
Ilkeston *Derbys* 49 SK4641
Ilketshall St Andrew *Suffk* 33 TM3887
Ilketshall St Margaret *Suffk* 33 TM3485
Ilkley *W York* 55 SE1147
Illand *Cnwll* 4 SX2878
Illey *W Mids* 38 SO9881
Illogan *Cnwll* 2 SW6743
Illston on the Hill *Leics* 40 SP7099
Ilmer *Bucks* 22 SP7605
Ilmington *Warwks* 29 SP2143
Ilminster *Somset* 8 ST3614
Ilsington *Devon* 5 SX7875
Ilston *W Glam* 17 SS5590
Ilton *N York* 61 SE1978
Ilton *Somset* 8 ST3517
Imachar *Strath* 72 NR8640
Immingham *Humb* 57 TA1814
Immingham Dock *Humb* 57 TA1916
Ince *Ches* 46 SJ4576
Ince Blundell *Mersyd* 46 SD3203
Ince-in-Makerfield *Gt Man* 47 SD5904
Inchbae Lodge Hotel *Highld* 92 NH4069
Inchbare *Tays* 89 NO6065
Inchberry *Gramp* 94 NJ3055
Inchinnan *Strath* 73 NS4769
Inchlaggan *Highld* 86 NH1701
Inchmichael *Tays* 83 NO2425
Inchnacardoch Hotel *Highld* 86 NH3810
Inchnadamph *Highld* 96 NC2521
Inchture *Tays* 83 NO2228
Inchvuilt *Highld* 92 NH2438
Inchyra *Tays* 82 NO1820
Indian Queens *Cnwll* 3 SW9159
Ingatestone *Essex* 24 TQ6499
Ingbirchworth *S York* 55 SE2205
Ingestre *Staffs* 38 SJ9724
Ingham *Lincs* 50 SK9483
Ingham *Norfk* 43 TG3926
Ingham *Suffk* 32 TL8570
Ingham Corner *Norfk* 43 TG3927
Ingleby *Derbys* 39 SK3426
Ingleby Arncliffe *N York* 62 NZ4400
Ingleby Barwick *Cleve* 62 NZ4414
Ingleby Greenhow *N York* 62 NZ5806
Ingleigh Green *Devon* 6 SS6007
Inglesbatch *Avon* 20 ST7061
Inglesham *Wilts* 21 SU2098
Ingleston *D & G* 66 NX6048
Ingleston *D & G* 66 NX9865
Ingleton *Dur* 61 NZ1720
Ingleton *N York* 54 SD6972
Inglewhite *Lancs* 53 SD5439
Ingoe *Nthumb* 68 NZ0374
Ingoldisthorpe *Norfk* 42 TF6832
Ingoldmells *Lincs* 51 TF5668
Ingoldsby *Lincs* 40 TF0129
Ingram *Nthumb* 77 NU0115
Ingrow *W York* 55 SE0539
Ingst *Avon* 19 ST5887
Ingthorpe *Leics* 40 SK9908
Ingworth *Norfk* 43 TG1929
Inkberrow *H & W* 28 SP0157
Inkhorn *Gramp* 95 NJ9239
Inkpen *Berks* 21 SU3664
Inkstack *Highld* 100 ND2570
Innellan *Strath* 73 NS1570
Innerleithen *Border* 75 NT3336
Innerleven *Fife* 83 NO3700
Innermessan *D & G* 64 NX0862
Innerwick *Loth* 76 NT7273
Innsworth *Gloucs* 28 SO8419
Insch *Gramp* 94 NJ2863
Innesmill *Gramp* 94 NJ6228
Insh *Highld* 87 NH8101
Inskip *Lancs* 53 SD4637
Instow *Devon* 6 SS4730
Intake *S York* 49 SK3884
Inver *Gramp* 88 NO2293
Inver *Highld* 97 NH8682
Inver *Tays* 88 NO0142
Inver-boyndie *Gramp* 94 NJ6664
Inveralort *Highld* 85 NM7681
Inveralligin *Highld* 91 NG8457

Inverallochy *Gramp* 95 NK0365
Inveran *Highld* 96 NH5797
Inveraray *Strath* 80 NN0908
Inverarish *Highld* 84 NG5535
Inverarity *Tays* 88 NO4544
Inverarnan *Cent* 80 NN3118
Inveravon *Cent* 82 NS9579
Inverawe *Strath* 80 NN0231
Inverbervie *Gramp* 89 NO8272
Inverbroom *Highld* 96 NH1883
Invercreran
House Hotel *Strath* 86 NN0146
Inverdruie *Highld* 93 NH8911
Inveresk *Loth* 75 NT3471
Inveresragan *Strath* 80 NM9835
Inverey *Gramp* 88 NO0089
Inverfarigaig *Highld* 92 NH5123
Inverfolla *Strath* 86 NM9544
Invergarry *Highld* 86 NH3001
Invergelder *Tays* 81 NN7327
Invergloy *Highld* 86 NN2288
Invergordon *Highld* 93 NH7068
Invergowrie *Tays* 83 NO3430
Inverguseran *Highld* 85 NG7407
Inverhadden *Tays* 87 NN6757
Inverherive Hotel *Cent* 80 NN3626
Inverie *Highld* 85 NG7600
Inverinan *Strath* 80 NM9917
Inverinate *Highld* 85 NG9221
Inverkeilor *Tays* 89 NO6649
Inverkeithing *Fife* 82 NT1383
Inverkeithny *Gramp* 94 NJ6247
Inverkip *Strath* 80 NS2072
Inverkirkaig *Highld* 98 NC0719
Inverlael *Highld* 96 NH1885
Inverlair *Highld* 86 NN3479
Inverliever Lodge *Strath* 79 NM8905
Inverlochy *Strath* 80 NN1927
Invermarkie *Gramp* 94 NJ4239
Invermoriston *Highld* 92 NH4216
Inverneg *Strath* 80 NS3497
Inverness *Highld* 93 NH6645
Invernoaden *Strath* 80 NS1297
Inveroran Hotel *Strath* 86 NN2741
Inverquharity *Tays* 88 NO4057
Inverquhomery *Gramp* 95 NK0146
Inverroy *Highld* 86 NN2581
Inversanda *Highld* 86 NM9459
Invershiel *Highld* 85 NG9319
Invershin *Highld* 96 NH5796
Invershore *Highld* 100 ND2435
Inversnaid Hotel *Cent* 80 NN3308
Inverugie *Highld* 95 NK0048
Inveruglas *Strath* 80 NN3109
Inveruglass *Highld* 87 NH8000
Inverurie *Gramp* 95 NJ7721
Inwardleigh *Devon* 6 SX5699
Inworth *Essex* 24 TL8717
Iping *W Susx* 11 SU8522
Ipplepen *Devon* 5 SX8366
Ipsden *Oxon* 21 SU6285
Ipstones *Staffs* 48 SK0149
Ipswich *Suffk* 33 TM1644
Irby *Mersyd* 46 SJ2584
Irby in the Marsh *Lincs* 51 TF4663
Irby upon Humber *Humb* 57 TA1904
Irchester *Nhants* 30 SP9265
Ireby *Cumb* 58 NY2338
Ireby *Lancs* 60 SD6575
Ireland *Beds* 30 TL1341
Ireleth *Cumb* 58 SD2277
Ireshopeburn *Dur* 60 NY8638
Ireton Wood *Derbys* 49 SK2847
Irlam *Gt Man* 47 SJ7294
Irnham *Lincs* 40 TF0226
Iron Acton *Avon* 20 ST6783
Ironbridge *Shrops* 37 SJ6703
Ironmacannie *D & G* 65 NX6675
Ironville *Derbys* 48 SK4351
Irstead *Norfk* 43 TG3620
Irthington *Cumb* 67 NY4961
Irthlingborough *Nhants* 30 SP9470
Irton *N York* 63 TA0184
Irvine *Strath* 73 NS3238
Isbister *Shet* 103 HU3790
Isfield *E Susx* 13 TQ4417
Isham *Nhants* 30 SP8873
Isle Abbotts *Somset* 8 ST3520
Isle Brewers *Somset* 8 ST3621
Isle of Dogs *Gt Lon* 23 TQ3779
Isle of Whithorn *D & G* 65 NX4736
Isleham *Cambs* 32 TL6474
Isleornsay *Highld* 85 NG7012
Islesteps *D & G* 66 NX9672
Islet Village *Guern* 101 GN0000
Isley Walton *Leics* 39 SK4224
Islibhig *W Isls* 102 NB0029
Islington *Gt Lon* 23 TQ3184
Islip *Nhants* 40 SP9879
Islip *Oxon* 29 SP5214
Islivig *W Isls* 102 NB0029
Isombridge *Shrops* 37 SJ6113
Itchen Abbas *Hants* 11 SU5333
Itchen Stoke *Hants* 11 SU5532
Itchingfield *W Susx* 12 TQ1328
Itteringham *Norfk* 43 TG1430
Itton *Devon* 7 SX6899
Itton *Gwent* 19 ST4995
Ivegill *Cumb* 67 NY4143
Iver *Bucks* 22 TQ0381
Iver Heath *Bucks* 22 TQ0283
Iveston *Dur* 69 NZ1350
Ivinghoe *Bucks* 30 SP9416
Ivinghoe Aston *Bucks* 30 SP9517
Ivington *H & W* 27 SO4756
Ivington Green *H & W* 27 SO4656
Ivy Hatch *Kent* 14 TQ5854
Ivybridge *Devon* 5 SX6356
Ivychurch *Kent* 15 TR0327
Iwade *Kent* 14 TQ9067
Iwerne Courtney or
Shroton *Dorset* 9 ST8512
Iwerne Minster *Dorset* 9 ST8614
Ixworth *Suffk* 32 TL9370
Ixworth Thorpe *Suffk* 32 TL9173

Jack-in-the-Green *Devon* 7 SY0195
Jackton *Strath* 74 NS5952
Jacobstow *Cnwll* 6 SX1995
Jacobstowe *Devon* 6 SS5801

Jameston Dyfed	16	SS0598
Jamestown Highld	92	NH4756
Jamestown Strath	80	NS3981
Janets-town Highld	100	ND3551
Janetstown Highld	100	ND1932
Jardine Hall D & G	67	NY1088
Jarrow T & W	69	NZ3364
Jasper's Green Essex	24	TL7226
Jawcraig Cent	74	NS8475
Jaywick Essex	25	TM1413
Jedburgh Border	76	NT6420
Jeffreston Dyfed	16	SN0906
Jemimaville Highld	93	NH7165
Jerbourg Guern	101	GN0000
Jesmond T & W	69	NZ2566
Jevington E Susx	13	TQ5601
Jockey End Herts	30	TL0413
John O'Groats Highld	100	ND3872
Johnby Cumb	59	NY4332
Johnshaven Gramp	89	NO7967
Johnston Dyfed	16	SM9310
Johnstone D & G	67	NT2400
Johnstone Strath	73	NS4263
Johnstonebridge D & G	67	NY1092
Johnstown Clwyd	46	SJ3046
Joppa Dyfed	34	SN5666
Joppa Strath	73	NS4119
Jordanston Dyfed	16	SM9132
Joyden's Wood Kent	23	TQ5072
Juniper Green Loth	75	NT1968
Jurby IOM	52	SC3598

K

Kaber Cumb	60	NY7911
Kames Strath	71	NR9771
Kames Strath	74	NS6926
Kea Cnwll	2	SW8142
Keal Cotes Lincs	51	TF3660
Kearsley Gt Man	47	SD7504
Kearsley Nthumb	68	NZ0275
Kearsney Kent	15	TR2844
Kearstwick Cumb	59	SD6079
Kedington Suffk	32	TL7046
Kedleston Derbys	49	SK3040
Keelby Lincs	57	TA1610
Keele Staffs	47	SJ8045
Keelham W York	55	SE0732
Keeston Dyfed	16	SM9019
Keevil Wilts	20	ST9258
Kegworth Leics	39	SK4826
Kehelland Cnwll	2	SW6241
Keig Gramp	94	NJ6119
Keighley W York	55	SE0541
Keillour Tays	82	NN9725
Keiloch Gramp	88	NO1891
Keils Strath	70	NR5268
Keinton Mandeville Somset	8	ST5430
Keir Mill D & G	66	NX8593
Keisley Cumb	60	NY7124
Keiss Highld	100	ND3461
Keith Gramp	94	NJ4250
Keithick Tays	82	NO2038
Keithock Tays	89	NO6063
Keithtown Gramp	92	NH5256
Kelbrook Lancs	54	SD9044
Kelburn Strath	73	NS2156
Kelby Lincs	50	TF0041
Keld N York	60	NY8900
Kelfield N York	56	SE5938
Kelham Notts	50	SK7755
Kelhead D & G	67	NY1469
Kellamergh Lancs	53	SD4029
Kellas Gramp	94	NJ1654
Kellas Tays	83	NO4535
Kellaton Devon	5	SX8039
Kelling Norfk	43	TG0942
Kellington N York	56	SE5524
Kelloe Dur	62	NZ3436
Kelly Devon	4	SX3981
Kelmarsh Nhants	40	SP7379
Kelmscot Oxon	21	SU2499
Kelsale Suffk	33	TM3865
Kelsall Ches	46	SJ5268
Kelshall Herts	31	TL3336
Kelsick Cumb	67	NY1950
Kelso Border	76	NT7234
Kelstedge Derbys	49	SK3363
Kelstern Lincs	51	TF2489
Kelston Avon	20	ST7067
Keltneyburn Tays	87	NN7749
Kelty Fife	82	NT1494
Kelvedon Essex	24	TL8619
Kelvedon Hatch Essex	24	TQ5698
Kelynack Cnwll	2	SW3729
Kemback Fife	83	NO4115
Kemberton Shrops	37	SJ7204
Kemble Gloucs	20	ST9897
Kemerton H & W	28	SO9536
Kemeys Commander Gwent	27	SO3404
Kemnay Gramp	95	NJ7316
Kemp Town E Susx	12	TQ3303
Kempley Gloucs	28	SO6629
Kempley Green Gloucs	28	SO6728
Kempsey H & W	28	SO8549
Kempsford Gloucs	20	SU1696
Kempshott Hants	21	SU6050
Kempston Beds	30	TL0347
Kempton Shrops	36	SO3682
Kemsing Kent	23	TQ5558
Kenardington Kent	15	TQ9732
Kenchester H & W	27	SO4342
Kencot Oxon	29	SP2504
Kendal Cumb	59	SD5192
Kenfig M Glam	33	SS8283
Kenilworth Warwks	39	SP2871
Kenley Gt Lon	23	TQ3260
Kenley Shrops	37	SJ5500
Kenmore Highld	91	NG7557
Kenmore Tays	87	NN7745
Kenn Avon	19	ST4268
Kenn Devon	5	SX9285
Kennacraig Strath	71	NR8262
Kennerleigh Devon	7	SS8107
Kennerleigh Green Mersyd	46	SD3801
Kennet Cent	82	NS9291
Kennethmont Gramp	94	NJ5428
Kennett Cambs	32	TL7068
Kennford Devon	5	SX9186
Kenninghall Norfk	32	TM0386
Kennington Kent	15	TR0245
Kennington Oxon	21	SP5201
Kennoway Fife	83	NO3502
Kenny Somset	8	ST3117
Kennyhill Suffk	32	TL6679

Kennythorpe N York	56	SE7865
Kenovay Strath	78	NL9946
Kensaleyre Highld	90	NG4151
Kensington Gt Lon	23	TQ2579
Kensworth Beds	30	TL0319
Kensworth Common Beds	30	TL0317
Kent's Green Gloucs	28	SO7423
Kent's Oak Hants	10	SU3224
Kentallen Highld	86	NN0057
Kentchurch H & W	27	SO4125
Kentford Suffk	32	TL7066
Kentisbeare Devon	7	ST0608
Kentisbury Devon	7	SS6243
Kentish Town Gt Lon	23	TQ2884
Kentmere Cumb	59	NY4504
Kenton Devon	5	SX9583
Kenton Gt Lon	23	TQ1788
Kenton Suffk	33	TM1965
Kenton T & W	69	NZ2267
Kentra Highld	79	NM6569
Kenwyn Cnwll	2	SW8145
Keoldale Highld	98	NC3866
Keppoch Highld	85	NG8924
Kepwick N York	62	SE4690
Keresley W Mids	39	SP3282
Kerris Cnwll	2	SW4427
Kerry Powys	36	SO1490
Kerrycroy Strath	73	NS1061
Kersall Notts	49	SK7162
Kersbrook Devon	5	SY0683
Kersey Suffk	32	TM0044
Kershader W Isls	102	NB3320
Kershopefoot D & G	67	NY4782
Kerswell Devon	8	ST0806
Kerswell Green H & W	28	SO8646
Kesgrave Suffk	33	TM2245
Kessingland Suffk	33	TM5286
Kestle Cnwll	3	SW9845
Kestle Mill Cnwll	3	SW8459
Keston Gt Lon	23	TQ4164
Keswick Cumb	58	NY2623
Keswick Norfk	43	TG2004
Ketsby Lincs	51	TF3676
Kettering Nhants	30	SP8678
Ketteringham Norfk	43	TG1603
Kettins Tays	83	NO2338
Kettlebaston Suffk	32	TL9650
Kettlebridge Fife	83	NO3007
Kettleburgh Suffk	33	TM2660
Kettleholm D & G	67	NY1577
Kettleshulme Ches	48	SJ9879
Kettlesing N York	55	SE2356
Kettlesing Bottom N York	55	SE2357
Kettlestoft Ork	103	HY6538
Kettlestone Norfk	42	TF9631
Kettlethorpe Lincs	50	SK8475
Kettlewell N York	54	SD9672
Ketton Leics	40	SK9704
Kew Gt Lon	23	TQ1876
Kewstoke Avon	19	ST3363
Kexby Lincs	50	SK8785
Kexby N York	56	SE7050
Key Green Ches	48	SJ8963
Key Street Kent	14	TQ8764
Keyham Leics	39	SK6706
Keyhaven Hants	10	SZ3091
Keyingham Humb	57	TA2425
Keymer W Susx	12	TQ3115
Keynsham Avon	19	ST6568
Keysoe Row Beds	30	TL0861
Keyston Cambs	30	TL0475
Keyworth Notts	39	SK6130
Kibblesworth T & W	69	NZ2456
Kibworth Beauchamp Leics	39	SP6893
Kibworth Harcourt Leics	39	SP6894
Kidbrooke Gt Lon	23	TQ4176
Kidderminster H & W	38	SO8376
Kidlington Oxon	29	SP4913
Kidmore End Oxon	22	SU6979
Kidsdale D & G	64	NX4336
Kidsgrove Staffs	47	SJ8454
Kidwelly Dyfed	17	SN4006
Kiel Crofts Strath	79	NM9039
Kielder Nthumb	68	NY6293
Kiells Strath	70	NR4168
Kilbarchan Strath	73	NS4063
Kilbeg Highld	85	NG6506
Kilberry Strath	71	NR7164
Kilbirnie Strath	73	NS3154
Kilbride Strath	79	NM8525
Kilbride Strath	71	NR7279
Kilbride Strath	72	NS0367
Kilburn Derbys	49	SK3845
Kilburn Gt Lon	23	TQ2483
Kilburn N York	62	SE5179
Kilby Leics	39	SP6295
Kilchamaig Strath	71	NR8060
Kilchattan Strath	70	NR3795
Kilchattan Strath	73	NS1054
Kilcheran Strath	79	NM8239
Kilchoan Highld	79	NM4863
Kilchrenan Strath	80	NN0322
Kilconquhar Fife	83	NO4802
Kilcot Gloucs	28	SO6925
Kilcoy Highld	92	NH5751
Kilcreggan Strath	80	NS2480
Kildale N York	62	NZ6009
Kildalloig Strath	72	NR7518
Kildary Highld	97	NH7674
Kildavaig Strath	72	NR9866
Kildavanan Strath	72	NS0266
Kildonan Highld	97	NC9120
Kildonan Strath	72	NS0321
Kildonan Lodge Highld	97	NC9022
Kildonnan Highld	84	NM4885
Kildrochet House D & G	64	NX0856
Kildrummy Gramp	94	NJ4617
Kildwick N York	55	SE0046
Kilfinan Strath	71	NR9378
Kilfinnan Highld	86	NN2795
Kilgetty Dyfed	16	SN1207
Kilgrammie Strath	73	NS2502
Kilgwrrwg Common Gwent	19	ST4797
Kilham Humb	57	TA0664
Kilkenneth Strath	78	NL9444
Kilkenzie Strath	72	NR6724
Kilkhampton Cnwll	6	SS2511
Killamarsh Derbys	49	SK4581
Killay W Glam	17	SS6092
Killerby Dur	61	NZ1919
Killerton Devon	7	SS9700
Killichonan Tays	87	NN5458
Killiechronan Strath	79	NM5441
Killiecrankie Tays	87	NN9162
Killilan Highld	85	NG9430
Killin Cent	81	NN5733
Killinghall N York	55	SE2858

Killington Cumb	59	SD6188
Killingworth T & W	69	NZ2770
Killochyett Border	76	NT4545
Kilmacolm Strath	73	NS3567
Kilmahog Cent	81	NN6108
Kilmahumaig Strath	71	NR7893
Kilmaluag Highld	90	NG4374
Kilmany Fife	83	NO3821
Kilmarie Highld	84	NG5517
Kilmarnock Strath	73	NS4237
Kilmartin Strath	71	NR8398
Kilmaurs Strath	73	NS4141
Kilmelford Strath	79	NM8512
Kilmeny Strath	70	NR3965
Kilmersdon Somset	20	ST6952
Kilmeston Hants	11	SU5825
Kilmichael Strath	71	NR8593
Kilmichael Strath	71	NR6922
Kilmichael of Inverlussa Strath	71	NR7786
Kilmington Devon	8	SY2797
Kilmington Wilts	20	ST7736
Kilmington Common Wilts	9	ST7735
Kilmington Street Wilts	9	ST7835
Kilmorack Highld	92	NH4944
Kilmore Highld	85	NG6507
Kilmore Strath	79	NM5270
Kilmore Strath	79	NM8825
Kilmory Highld	71	NR7074
Kilmory Strath	72	NR9621
Kilmuir Highld	90	NG2547
Kilmuir Highld	90	NG3770
Kilmuir Highld	93	NH6749
Kilmuir Highld	97	NH7573
Kilmun Strath	80	NS1781
Kiln Green Berks	22	SU8178
Kiln Pit Hill Nthumb	68	NZ0355
Kilnave Strath	70	NR2871
Kilncadzow Strath	74	NS8848
Kilndown Kent	14	TQ7035
Kilninver Strath	79	NM8221
Kilnsea Humb	57	TA4115
Kilnsey N York	54	SD9767
Kilnwick Humb	56	SE9949
Kiloran Strath	70	NR3996
Kilpatrick Strath	72	NR9026
Kilpeck H & W	27	SO4430
Kilpin Humb	56	SE7726
Kilrenny Fife	83	NO5704
Kilsby Nhants	39	SP5671
Kilspindie Tays	82	NO2125
Kilstay D & G	64	NX1238
Kilsyth Strath	81	NS7178
Kiltarlity Highld	92	NH5041
Kilton Cleve	62	NZ7018
Kilton Thorpe Cleve	62	NZ6917
Kilvaxter Highld	90	NG3869
Kilve Somset	18	ST1442
Kilvington Notts	50	SK8042
Kilwinning Strath	73	NS3043
Kimberley Norfk	42	TG0603
Kimberley Notts	49	SK4944
Kimberworth S York	49	SK4093
Kimblesworth Dur	69	NZ2547
Kimbolton Cambs	30	TL1067
Kimbolton H & W	27	SO5261
Kimcote Leics	39	SP5886
Kimmeridge Dorset	9	SY9179
Kimpton Hants	21	SU2746
Kimpton Herts	31	TL1718
Kinbrace Highld	99	NC8631
Kinbuck Cent	81	NN7905
Kincaple Fife	83	NO4618
Kincardine Fife	82	NS9387
Kincardine Highld	97	NH6089
Kincardine O'Neil Tays	89	NO5999
Kinclaven Tays	82	NO1538
Kincorth Gramp	89	NJ9403
Kincorth House Gramp	93	NJ0161
Kincraig Highld	87	NH8305
Kincraigie Tays	88	NN9849
Kindallachan Tays	88	NN9949
Kinerarach Strath	71	NR6553
Kineton Gloucs	28	SP0926
Kineton Warwks	29	SP3350
Kinfauns Tays	82	NO1622
Kinfig M Glam	18	SS8081
Kinfold Strath	73	NS3634
King's Bromley Staffs	38	SK1216
King's Cliffe Nhants	40	TL0097
King's Coughton Warwks	28	SP0859
King's Heath W Mids	38	SP0781
King's Lynn Norfk	41	TF6120
King's Mills Guern	101	GN0000
King's Norton Leics	39	SK6800
King's Norton W Mids	38	SP0579
King's Nympton Devon	7	SS6819
King's Pyon H & W	27	SO4450
King's Somborne Hants	10	SU3531
King's Stag Dorset	9	ST7210
King's Stanley Gloucs	20	SO8103
King's Sutton Oxon	29	SP4936
King's Walden Herts	31	TL1623
Kingarth Strath	73	NS0956
Kingcausie Gramp	89	NO8699
Kingcoed Gwent	27	SO4305
Kingerby Lincs	50	TF0592
Kingford Devon	6	SS2806
Kingham Oxon	29	SP2624
Kingholm Quay D & G	66	NX9773
Kinghorn Fife	83	NT2686
Kinglassie Fife	82	NT2298
Kingoldrum Tays	88	NO3355
Kingoodie Tays	83	NO3329
Kings Caple H & W	27	SO5528
Kings House Hotel Highld	86	NO2654
Kings Langley Herts	22	TL0702
Kings Meaburn Cumb	60	NY6221
Kings Muir Border	75	NT2539
Kings Newnham Warwks	39	SP4577
Kings Ripton Cambs	31	TL2676
Kings Weston Avon	19	ST5477
Kings Worthy Hants	11	SU4932
Kingsand Cnwll	4	SX4350
Kingsbarns Fife	83	NO5912
Kingsbridge Devon	5	SX7344
Kingsbridge Somset	7	SS9837
Kingsburgh Highld	90	NG3955
Kingsbury Gt Lon	23	TQ1988
Kingsbury Warwks	39	SP2196
Kingsbury Episcopi Somset	8	ST4321
Kingsclere Hants	21	SU5258
Kingscote Gloucs	20	ST8196
Kingscott Devon	6	SS5318
Kingscross Strath	72	NS0428
Kingsdon Somset	8	ST5126
Kingsdowh Kent	15	TR3748
Kingsdown Wilts	20	ST8167
Kingsdown Wilts	20	SU1688

Kingseat Fife	82	NT1290
Kingsey Bucks	22	SP7406
Kingsfold W Susx	12	TQ1636
Kingsford Gramp	89	NJ8506
Kingsford Strath	73	NS4447
Kingsgate Kent	15	TR3970
Kingshall Street Suffk	32	TL9161
Kingsheanton Devon	6	SS5537
Kingshouse Hotel Cent	81	NN5620
Kingskerswell Devon	5	SX8767
Kingskettle Fife	83	NO3008
Kingsland Gwynd	44	SH2581
Kingsland H & W	27	SO4461
Kingsley Ches	47	SJ5574
Kingsley Hants	11	SU7838
Kingsley Staffs	48	SK0146
Kingsley Green W Susx	11	SU8930
Kingsley Park Nhants	30	SP7762
Kingsmuir Tays	83	NO5308
Kingsnorth Kent	89	NO4849
Kingsteignton Devon	15	TR0039
Kingsthorne H & W	5	SX8773
Kingsthorpe Nhants	27	SO4931
Kingston Cambs	30	SP7563
Kingston Cnwll	31	TL3455
Kingston Devon	4	SX3675
Kingston Dorset	5	SX6347
Kingston Dorset	7	ST7509
Kingston IOW	9	SY9579
Kingston Kent	11	SZ4781
Kingston Loth	15	TR1950
Kingston Bagpuize Oxon	83	NT5482
Kingston Blount Oxon	21	SU4098
Kingston by Sea W Susx	22	SU7399
Kingston Deverill Wilts	12	TQ2305
Kingston Lisle Oxon	20	ST8437
Kingston near Lewes E Susx	21	SU3287
Kingston on Soar Notts	13	TQ3908
Kingston on Spey Gramp	39	SK5027
Kingston Russell Dorset	94	NJ3365
Kingston Seymour Avon	9	SY5791
Kingston St Mary Somset	19	ST4066
Kingston upon Thames Gt Lon	8	ST2229
Kingstone H & W	23	TQ1869
Kingstone Somset	27	SO4235
Kingstone Staffs	8	ST3713
Kingswear Devon	38	SK0629
Kingswells Gramp	5	SX8851
Kingswinford W Mids	89	NJ8606
Kingswood Avon	38	SO8888
Kingswood Bucks	19	ST6473
Kingswood Gloucs	30	SP6919
Kingswood Surrey	20	ST7491
Kingswood Warwks	18	ST1037
Kingswood Common Staffs	23	TQ2455
Kingthorpe Lincs	38	SP1871
Kington Avon	38	SJ8302
Kington H & W	50	TF1275
Kington H & W	19	ST6290
Kington Langley Wilts	27	SO2956
Kington Magna Dorset	28	SO2956
Kington St Michael Wilts	20	ST9276
Kingussie Highld	9	ST7622
Kingweston Somset	20	ST9077
Kinharrachie Gramp	87	NH7500
Kinharvie D & G	8	ST5230
Kinkell Bridge Tays	95	NJ9231
Kinknockie Gramp	66	NX9266
Kinleith Loth	82	NN9316
Kinlet Shrops	95	NK0041
Kinloch Highld	75	NT1866
Kinloch Highld	37	SO7180
Kinloch Highld	98	NC3434
Kinloch Highld	99	NC5552
Kinloch Tays	84	NM4099
Kinloch Tays	88	NO1444
Kinloch Hourn Highld	88	NO2644
Kinloch Rannoch Tays	85	NG9506
Kinlochard Cent	87	NH6658
Kinlochbervie Highld	81	NN4502
Kinlochcoil Highld	98	NC2256
Kinlochewe Highld	85	NM9779
Kinlochiaggan Highld	91	NH0261
Kinlochleven Highld	87	NN5289
Kinlochmoidart Highld	86	NN1861
Kinlochnanuagh Highld	85	NM7072
Kinloss Gramp	85	NM7384
Kinmel Bay Clwyd	93	NJ0661
Kinmount House D & G	45	SH9880
Kinmuck Gramp	67	NY1368
Kinmundy Gramp	95	NJ8119
Kinnabus Strath	95	NJ8817
Kinnadie Gramp	70	NR2942
Kinnaird Tays	95	NJ9743
Kinnaird Castle Tays	88	NN9559
Kinneddar Gramp	83	NO2428
Kinnelhead D & G	94	NO6357
Kinnell Tays	94	NJ2269
Kinnerley Shrops	66	NT0201
Kinnersley H & W	89	NO6150
Kinnersley H & W	36	SJ3320
Kinnerton Powys	27	SO3449
Kinnesswood Tays	27	SO8743
Kinninvie Dur	26	SO2463
Kinnordy Tays	82	NO1702
Kinoulton Notts	61	NZ0521
Kinross Tays	88	NO3655
Kinrossie Tays	50	SK6730
Kinsbourne Green Herts	82	NO1102
Kinsham H & W	82	NO1832
Kinsham H & W	27	SO3665
Kinsley W York	50	SO9335
Kinson Dorset	55	SE4114
Kintbury Berks	10	SZ0796
Kintessack Gramp	21	SU3866
Kintillo Tays	93	NJ0060
Kinton H & W	82	NO1317
Kinton Shrops	38	SO4174
Kintore Gramp	36	SJ3719
Kintour Strath	91	NJ7916
Kintra Strath	70	NR4551
Kintraw Strath	78	NM3125
Kinveachy Highld	79	NM8204
Kinver Staffs	93	NH9018
Kippax W York	38	SO8483
Kippen Cent	55	SE4130
Kippford or Scaur D & G	81	NS6494
Kipping's Cross Kent	66	NX8354
Kirbister Ork	13	TQ6440
Kirby Bedon Norfk	103	HY3607
Kirby Bellars Leics	43	TG2705
Kirby Cane Norfk	40	SK7117
Kirby Cross Essex	43	TM3794
Kirby Fields Leics	25	TM2120
Kirby Grindalythe N York	39	SK5203
Kirby Hill N York	56	SE9067
	61	NZ1406

Kirby Hill *N York*	55	SE3968
Kirby Knowle *N York*	62	SE4687
Kirby le Soken *Essex*	25	TM2121
Kirby Misperton *N York*	63	SE7779
Kirby Muxloe *Leics*	39	SK5104
Kirby Row *Norfk*	33	TM3792
Kirby Sigston *N York*	62	SE4194
Kirby Underdale *Humb*	56	SE8462
Kirby Wiske *N York*	62	SE3784
Kirconnel *D & G*	66	NX9868
Kirdford *W Susx*	12	TQ0126
Kirk *Highld*	100	ND2859
Kirk Bramwith *S York*	56	SE6211
Kirk Deighton *N York*	55	SE3950
Kirk Ella *Humb*	56	TA0129
Kirk Hallam *Derbys*	49	SK4540
Kirk Hammerton *N York*	55	SE4655
Kirk Ireton *Derbys*	49	SK2650
Kirk Langley *Derbys*	49	SK2838
Kirk Merrington *Dur*	61	NZ2631
Kirk Michael *IOM*	52	SC3190
Kirk of Shotts *Strath*	74	NS8462
Kirk Sandall *S York*	56	SE6108
Kirk Smeaton *N York*	55	SE5216
Kirk Yetholm *Border*	77	NT8228
Kirkabister *Shet*	103	HU4938
Kirkandrews *D & G*	65	NX6048
Kirkandrews upon Eden *Cumb*	67	NY3558
Kirkbampton *Cumb*	67	NY3056
Kirkbean *D & G*	66	NX9759
Kirkbride *Cumb*	67	NY2256
Kirkbuddo *Tays*	89	NO5043
Kirkburn *Border*	75	NT2938
Kirkburn *Humb*	56	SE9855
Kirkburton *W York*	55	SE1912
Kirkby *Lincs*	50	TF0592
Kirkby *Mersyd*	46	SJ4099
Kirkby *N York*	62	NZ5305
Kirkby Fleetham *N York*	61	SE2894
Kirkby Green *Lincs*	50	TF0857
Kirkby in Ashfield *Notts*	49	SK4856
Kirkby in Ashfield *Notts*	50	TF0946
Kirkby la Thorpe *Lincs*	50	TF0946
Kirkby Lonsdale *Cumb*	59	SD6178
Kirkby Malham *N York*	54	SD8960
Kirkby Mallory *Leics*	39	SK4500
Kirkby Malzeard *N York*	61	SE2374
Kirkby on Bain *Lincs*	51	TF2462
Kirkby Overblow *N York*	55	SE3249
Kirkby Stephen *Cumb*	60	NY7708
Kirkby Thore *Cumb*	60	NY6325
Kirkby Underwood *Lincs*	40	TF0727
Kirkby Wharf *N York*	55	SE5041
Kirkby-in-Furness *Cumb*	58	SD2282
Kirkbymoorside *N York*	62	SE6986
Kirkcaldy *Fife*	83	NT2892
Kirkcambeck *Cumb*	67	NY5368
Kirkchrist *D & G*	65	NX6751
Kirkcolm *D & G*	64	NX0268
Kirkconnel *D & G*	66	NS7311
Kirkconnell *D & G*	65	NX6760
Kirkcowan *D & G*	64	NX3260
Kirkcudbright *D & G*	65	NX6850
Kirkdale *Mersyd*	46	SJ3493
Kirkfieldbank *Strath*	74	NS8643
Kirkgunzeon *D & G*	66	NX8666
Kirkham *Lancs*	53	SD4232
Kirkham *N York*	56	SE7365
Kirkhamgate *W York*	55	SE2922
Kirkharle *Nthumb*	68	NZ0182
Kirkhaugh *Nthumb*	68	NY6949
Kirkheaton *Nthumb*	68	NZ0177
Kirkheaton *W York*	55	SE1818
Kirkhill *Highld*	92	NH5545
Kirkhope *Strath*	66	NS9606
Kirkibost *Highld*	84	NG5518
Kirkinch *Tays*	88	NO3044
Kirkinner *D & G*	64	NX4251
Kirkintilloch *Strath*	74	NS6573
Kirkland *Cumb*	58	NY0718
Kirkland *D & G*	66	NS7213
Kirkland *D & G*	64	NX4356
Kirkland *D & G*	66	NX8190
Kirkland *D & G*	66	NY0389
Kirkleatham *Cleve*	62	NZ5921
Kirklevington *Cleve*	62	NZ4309
Kirkley *Suffk*	33	TM5391
Kirklington *N York*	62	SE3181
Kirklington *Notts*	49	SK6757
Kirklinton *Cumb*	67	NY4367
Kirkliston *Loth*	75	NT1274
Kirkmabreck *D & G*	65	NX4856
Kirkmaiden *D & G*	64	NX1236
Kirkmichael *Strath*	73	NS3408
Kirkmichael *Tays*	88	NO0759
Kirkmuirhill *Strath*	74	NS7842
Kirknewton *Loth*	75	NT1166
Kirknewton *Nthumb*	77	NT9130
Kirkney *Gramp*	94	NJ5132
Kirkoswald *Cumb*	59	NY5541
Kirkoswald *Strath*	73	NS2407
Kirkpatrick *D & G*	66	NX9090
Kirkpatrick Durham *D & G*	66	NX7870
Kirkpatrick-Fleming *D & G*	67	NY2770
Kirksanton *Cumb*	58	SD1380
Kirkstall *W York*	55	SE2635
Kirkstead *Lincs*	50	TF1762
Kirkstile *D & G*	67	NY3690
Kirkstile *Gramp*	94	NJ5235
Kirkstyle *Highld*	100	ND3472
Kirkthorpe *W York*	55	SE3621
Kirkton *D & G*	66	NX9781
Kirkton *Fife*	83	NO3625
Kirkton *Gramp*	94	NJ6425
Kirkton *Gramp*	95	NJ8243
Kirkton *Highld*	85	NG8227
Kirkton *Highld*	85	NG9141
Kirkton *Tays*	82	NN9618
Kirkton Manor *Border*	75	NT2238
Kirkton of Airlie *Tays*	88	NO3151
Kirkton of Auchterhouse *Tays*	83	NO3438
Kirkton of Barevan *Highld*	93	NH8347
Kirkton of Collace *Tays*	82	NO1931
Kirkton of Glenbuchat *Gramp*	94	NJ3715
Kirkton of Logie Buchan *Gramp*	95	NJ9829
Kirkton of Menmuir *Tays*	89	NO5364
Kirkton of Monikie *Tays*	83	NO5138
Kirkton of Rayne *Gramp*	95	NJ6930
Kirkton of Skene *Gramp*	95	NJ8007
Kirkton of Strathmartine *Tays*	83	NO3735
Kirkton of Tealing *Tays*	83	NO4038
Kirktown *Gramp*	95	NJ9965
Kirktown *Gramp*	95	NK0852
Kirktown of Bourtie *Gramp*	95	NJ8025
Kirktown of Fetteresso *Gramp*	89	NO8486
Kirktown of Mortlach *Gramp*	94	NJ3138
Kirktown of Slains *Gramp*	95	NK0329
Kirkwall *Ork*	103	HY4411
Kirkwhelpington *Nthumb*	68	NY9984
Kirmington *Humb*	57	TA1011
Kirmond le Mire *Lincs*	50	TF1892
Kirn *Strath*	80	NS1878
Kirriemuir *Tays*	88	NO3853
Kirstead Green *Norfk*	43	TM2997
Kirtlebridge *D & G*	67	NY2372
Kirtling *Cambs*	32	TL6857
Kirtling Green *Suffk*	32	TL6855
Kirtlington *Oxon*	29	SP4919
Kirtomy *Highld*	99	NC7463
Kirton *Gramp*	94	NJ6113
Kirton *Lincs*	41	TF3038
Kirton *Notts*	49	SK6969
Kirton *Suffk*	33	TM2740
Kirton in Lindsey *Lincs*	50	SK9398
Kirtonhill *Strath*	80	NS3875
Kirwaugh *D & G*	64	NX4054
Kishorn *Highld*	85	NG8440
Kislingbury *Nhants*	30	SP6959
Kittisford *Somset*	8	ST0822
Kittybrewster *Gramp*	95	NJ9207
Kivernoll *H & W*	27	SO4632
Knaith *Lincs*	50	SK8284
Knap Corner *Dorset*	9	ST8023
Knaphill *Surrey*	22	SU9658
Knaplock *Somset*	7	SS8633
Knapp *Somset*	8	ST3025
Knapton *N York*	56	SE5652
Knapton *N York*	63	SE8876
Knapton *Norfk*	43	TG3034
Knapwell *Cambs*	31	TL3362
Knaresborough *N York*	55	SE3557
Knarsdale *Nthumb*	68	NC4159
Knaven *Gramp*	95	NJ8943
Knayton *N York*	62	SE4387
Knebworth *Herts*	31	TL2520
Knedlington *Humb*	56	SE7327
Kneesall *Notts*	49	SK7064
Kneesworth *Cambs*	31	TL3444
Kneeton *Notts*	49	SK7146
Knelston *W Glam*	17	SS4988
Knenhall *Staffs*	48	SJ9237
Knightcote *Warwks*	29	SP4054
Knightley *Staffs*	37	SJ8125
Knighton *Dorset*	9	ST6111
Knighton *Dorset*	39	SK6001
Knighton *Powys*	36	SO2872
Knighton *Somset*	19	ST1944
Knighton *Staffs*	37	SJ7240
Knighton *Staffs*	37	SJ7527
Knighton on Teme *H & W*	27	SO6369
Knightwick *H & W*	28	SO7356
Knill *H & W*	27	SO2960
Knipton *Leics*	40	SK8231
Kniveton *Derbys*	48	SK2050
Knock *Cumb*	60	NY6727
Knock *Gramp*	94	NJ5452
Knock *Highld*	85	NG6709
Knock *W Isls*	102	NB4331
Knock Castle *Strath*	73	NS1963
Knockally *Highld*	100	ND1429
Knockan *Highld*	96	NC2110
Knockan *Highld*	94	NJ1941
Knockando *Gramp*	92	NH5543
Knockbain *Highld*	92	NH6256
Knockdee *Highld*	100	ND1760
Knockdown *Wilts*	20	ST8388
Knockeen *Strath*	64	NX3195
Knockenkelly *Strath*	72	NS0427
Knockentiber *Strath*	73	NS4039
Knockespock House *Gramp*	94	NJ5423
Knockholt *Kent*	23	TQ4658
Knockholt Pound *Kent*	23	TQ4859
Knockin *Shrops*	36	SJ3322
Knockinlaw *Strath*	73	NS4439
Knocknain *D & G*	64	NW9764
Knocksheen *D & G*	65	NX5882
Knockvennie Smithy *D & G*	65	NX7571
Knodishall *Suffk*	33	TM4262
Knole *Somset*	8	ST4825
Knolls Green *Ches*	47	SJ8079
Knolton *Clwyd*	36	SJ3739
Knook *Wilts*	20	ST9341
Knossington *Leics*	40	SK8008
Knott End-on-Sea *Lancs*	53	SD3548
Knotting *Beds*	30	TL0063
Knotting Green *Beds*	30	TL0062
Knottingley *W York*	55	SE5023
Knowbury *Shrops*	37	SO5775
Knowe *D & G*	64	NX3171
Knowehead *D & G*	65	NX6090
Knoweside *Strath*	73	NS2512
Knowl Hill *Berks*	22	SU8279
Knowle *Avon*	19	ST6070
Knowle *Devon*	6	SS4938
Knowle *Devon*	7	SS7801
Knowle *Devon*	7	ST0007
Knowle *Devon*	8	SY0582
Knowle *Shrops*	37	SO5973
Knowle *Somset*	7	SS9643
Knowle *W Mids*	38	SP1876
Knowle Green *Lancs*	54	SD6388
Knowle St Giles *Somset*	8	ST3411
Knowlefield *Cumb*	67	NY4057
Knowlton *Kent*	15	TR2853
Knowsley *Mersyd*	46	SJ4395
Knowstone *Devon*	7	SS8323
Knox Bridge *Kent*	14	TQ7840
Knucklas *Powys*	36	SO2574
Knuston *Nhants*	30	SP9266
Knutsford *Ches*	47	SJ7578
Krumlin *W York*	55	SE0518
Kuggar *Cnwll*	2	SW7216
Kyle of Lochalsh *Highld*	85	NG7627
Kyleakin *Highld*	85	NG7526
Kylerhea *Highld*	85	NG7820
Kyles Scalpay *W Isls*	102	NG2198
Kylesku *Highld*	98	NC2233
Kylesmorar *Highld*	85	NM8093
Kylestrome *Highld*	98	NC2234
Kynnersley *Shrops*	37	SJ6716
Kyrewood *H & W*	27	SO5967

L

L'Ancresse *Guern*	101	GN0000
L'Eree *Guern*	101	GN0000
L'Etacq *Jersey*	101	JS0000
La Beilleuse *Guern*	101	SY5206
La Fontenelle *Guern*	101	GN0000
La Fosse *Guern*	101	GN0000
La Greve *Guern*	101	GN0000
La Greve de Lecq *Jersey*	101	JS0000
La Hougue Bie *Jersey*	101	JS0000
La Passee *Guern*	101	GN0000
La Pulente *Jersey*	101	JS0000
La Rocque *Jersey*	101	JS0000
La Rousaillerie *Guern*	101	GN0000
La Villette *Guern*	101	GN0000
Lacadal *W Isls*	102	NB4234
Lacasaigh *W Isls*	102	NB3321
Lacey Green *Bucks*	22	SP8200
Lach Dennis *Ches*	47	SJ7071
Lackford *Suffk*	32	TL7970
Lackford Green *Suffk*	32	TL7970
Lacock *Wilts*	20	ST9168
Ladbroke *Warwks*	29	SP4158
Laddingford *Kent*	14	TQ6948
Ladock *Cnwll*	3	SW9050
Lady Hall *Cumb*	58	SD1986
Lady Village *Ork*	103	HY4841
Ladybank *Fife*	83	NO3009
Ladygill *Strath*	75	NS9428
Ladykirk *Border*	77	NT8847
Ladykirk Ho *Border*	77	NT8845
Ladywood *H & W*	28	SO8661
Ladywood *W Mids*	38	SP0586
Lag *D & G*	66	NX8786
Laga *Highld*	79	NM6361
Lagavulin *Strath*	70	NR4045
Lagg *Strath*	72	NR9521
Laggan *Highld*	86	NN2997
Laggan *Highld*	87	NN6194
Laggan *Strath*	64	NX0982
Laid *Highld*	98	NC4159
Laide *Highld*	91	NG9091
Laig *Highld*	84	NM4687
Laigh Church *Strath*	73	NS4647
Laigh Fenwick *Strath*	73	NS4542
Laigh Glenmuir *Strath*	74	NS6120
Laighstonehall *Strath*	74	NS7054
Laindon *Essex*	24	TQ6889
Lairg *Highld*	96	NC5806
Laisterdyke *W York*	55	SE1932
Lake *Dorset*	9	SY9990
Lake *Wilts*	10	SU1339
Lakenheath *Suffk*	32	TL7182
Lakesend *Norfk*	41	TL5196
Laleston *M Glam*	18	SS8779
Lamancha *Border*	75	NT2052
Lamarsh *Essex*	24	TL8835
Lamas *Norfk*	43	TG2423
Lambden *Border*	76	NT7443
Lamberhurst *Kent*	14	TQ6736
Lamberhurst Down *Kent*	14	TQ6735
Lamberton *Border*	77	NT9658
Lambeth *Gt Lon*	23	TQ3178
Lambfair Green *Suffk*	32	TL7153
Lambley *Notts*	49	SK6345
Lambley *Nthumb*	68	NY6658
Lambourn *Berks*	21	SU3278
Lambourne End *Essex*	23	TQ4794
Lambs Green *W Susx*	12	TQ2136
Lamerton *Devon*	4	SX4577
Lamesley *T & W*	69	NZ2557
Lamington *Strath*	75	NS9731
Lamlash *Strath*	72	NS0231
Lamonby *Cumb*	59	NY4036
Lamorna *Cnwll*	2	SW4424
Lamorran *Cnwll*	3	SW8741
Lampeter *Dyfed*	17	SN5747
Lampeter Velfrey *Dyfed*	17	SN1514
Lamphey *Dyfed*	16	SN0100
Lamplugh *Cumb*	58	NY0820
Lamport *Nhants*	30	SP7574
Lamyatt *Somset*	19	ST6536
Lanark *Strath*	74	NS8843
Lancaster *Lancs*	53	SD4761
Lanchester *Dur*	69	NZ1647
Lancing *W Susx*	12	TQ1804
Land-hallow *Highld*	100	ND1833
Landbeach *Cambs*	31	TL4765
Landcross *Devon*	6	SS4523
Landerberry *Gramp*	89	NJ7404
Landewednack *Cnwll*	2	SW7012
Landford *Wilts*	10	SU2519
Landimore *W Glam*	17	SS4692
Landkey *Devon*	6	SS6031
Landkey Town *Devon*	6	SS5931
Landore *W Glam*	18	SS6695
Landrake *Cnwll*	4	SX3760
Landscove *Devon*	5	SX7766
Landulph *Cnwll*	4	SX4261
Lane *Cnwll*	2	SW8260
Lane End *Bucks*	22	SU8091
Lane End *Wilts*	20	STB145
Lane End Waberthwaite *Cumb*	58	SD1093
Lane Ends *Derbys*	39	SK2334
Lane Head *Dur*	61	NZ1211
Laneast *Cnwll*	4	SX2283
Laneham *Notts*	50	SK8076
Lanehead *Dur*	60	NY8441
Langaller *Somset*	8	ST2626
Langar *Notts*	40	SK7234
Langbank *Strath*	80	NS3873
Langbar *N York*	55	SE0951
Langcliffe *N York*	54	SD8264
Langdale End *N York*	63	SE9391
Langdon *Hants*	10	SU4206
Langdown *Hants*	83	NO3304
Langdyke *Fife*	25	TM0018
Langenhoe *Essex*	31	TL1841
Langford *Beds*	7	SO203
Langford *Devon*	24	TL8309
Langford *Notts*	50	SK8258
Langford *Oxon*	21	SP2402
Langford Budville *Somset*	8	ST1122
Langford End *Beds*	31	TL1753
Langham *Essex*	25	TM0333
Langham *Leics*	40	SK8411
Langham *Norfk*	42	TG0141
Langham *Suffk*	32	TL9769
Langho *Lancs*	54	SD7034
Langholm *D & G*	67	NY3684
Langley *Berks*	22	TQ0178
Langley *Essex*	31	TL4334
Langley *Hants*	10	SU4401
Langley *Herts*	31	TL2122
Langley *Kent*	14	TQ8052
Langley *Nthumb*	68	NY8261
Langley *Somset*	8	ST0828
Langley *W Susx*	11	SU8029
Langley *Warwks*	29	SP1962
Langley Burrell *Wilts*	20	ST9375
Langley Green *Essex*	24	TL8722
Langley Marsh *Somset*	8	ST0729
Langley Park *Dur*	69	NZ2145
Langley Street *Norfk*	43	TG3601
Langleybury *Herts*	22	TL0700
Langney *E Susx*	13	TQ6302
Langold *Notts*	49	SK5886
Langore *Cnwll*	4	SX2986
Langport *Somset*	8	ST4226
Langrick *Lincs*	51	TF2648
Langridge *Avon*	20	ST7469
Langrigg *Cumb*	67	NY1645
Langrish *Hants*	11	SU7023
Langsett *S York*	48	SE2100
Langshaw *Border*	76	NT5139
Langside *Tays*	81	NN7913
Langstone *Gwent*	19	ST3789
Langstone *Hants*	11	SU7204
Langthorne *N York*	61	SE2491
Langthorpe *N York*	55	SE3867
Langthwaite *N York*	61	NZ0001
Langtoft *Humb*	56	TA0066
Langtoft *Lincs*	40	TF1212
Langton *Dur*	61	NZ1619
Langton *Lincs*	51	TF2368
Langton *Lincs*	51	TF3970
Langton *N York*	56	SE7966
Langton by Wragby *Lincs*	50	TF1476
Langton Green *Kent*	13	TQ5439
Langton Herring *Dorset*	9	SY6182
Langton Matravers *Dorset*	10	SZ0078
Langtree *Devon*	6	SS4515
Langwathby *Cumb*	59	NY5733
Langwell House *Highld*	100	ND1122
Langworth *Lincs*	50	TF0676
Lanivet *Cnwll*	3	SX0464
Lank *Cnwll*	3	SX0875
Lanlivery *Cnwll*	3	SX0759
Lanner *Cnwll*	2	SW7139
Lanreath *Cnwll*	3	SX1857
Lansallos *Cnwll*	3	SX1751
Lanteglos *Cnwll*	3	SX0882
Lanteglos Highway *Cnwll*	3	SX1453
Lanton *Border*	76	NT6221
Lanton *Nthumb*	77	NT9231
Lapford *Devon*	7	SS7308
Laphroaig *Strath*	70	NR3845
Lapley *Staffs*	38	SJ8712
Lapworth *Warwks*	38	SP1671
Larachbeg *Highld*	79	NM6948
Larbert *Cent*	82	NS8582
Largie *Gramp*	94	NJ6131
Largiemore *Strath*	71	NR9486
Largoward *Fife*	83	NO4607
Largs *Strath*	73	NS2059
Largybeg *Strath*	72	NS0423
Largymore *Strath*	72	NS0424
Larkfield *Kent*	14	TQ7058
Larkfield *Strath*	80	NS2475
Larkhall *Strath*	74	NS7651
Larkhill *Wilts*	20	SU1244
Larling *Norfk*	32	TL9889
Lartington *Dur*	61	NZ0117
Lasham *Hants*	11	SU6742
Lask Edge *Staffs*	48	SJ9156
Lassodie *Fife*	82	NT1292
Lasswade *Loth*	75	NT3065
Lastingham *N York*	63	SE7290
Latchingdon *Essex*	24	TL8800
Latchley *Cnwll*	4	SX4173
Latebrook *Staffs*	47	SJ8453
Lathbury *Bucks*	30	SP8744
Latheron *Highld*	100	ND2033
Latheronwheel *Highld*	100	ND1832
Lathones *Fife*	83	NO4708
Latimer *Bucks*	22	TQ0099
Latteridge *Avon*	20	ST6684
Lattiford *Somset*	9	ST6926
Latton *Wilts*	20	SU0995
Lauder *Border*	76	NT5347
Laugharne *Dyfed*	17	SN3010
Laughterton *Lincs*	50	SK8375
Laughton *E Susx*	13	TQ4913
Laughton *Leics*	39	SP6688
Laughton *Lincs*	50	SK8497
Laughton *Lincs*	40	TF0731
Laughton-en-le-Morthen *S York*	49	SK5187
Launcells *Cnwll*	6	SS2405
Launceston *Cnwll*	4	SX3384
Launton *Oxon*	29	SP6022
Laurencekirk *Gramp*	89	NO7171
Laurieston *Cent*	82	NS9179
Laurieston *D & G*	65	NX6864
Lavendon *Bucks*	30	SP9153
Lavenham *Suffk*	32	TL9149
Lavernock *S Glam*	19	ST1868
Laversdale *Cumb*	67	NY4762
Laverstock *Wilts*	10	SU1630
Laverstoke *Hants*	21	SU4948
Laverton *Gloucs*	28	SP0735
Laverton *N York*	61	SE2273
Laverton *Somset*	20	ST7753
Lavister *Clwyd*	46	SJ3758
Law *Strath*	74	NS8252
Law Hill *Strath*	74	NS8251
Lawers *Tays*	81	NN6739
Lawford *Essex*	25	TM0831
Lawford *Somset*	8	ST1336
Lawgrove *Tays*	82	NO0926
Lawhitton *Cnwll*	4	SX3582
Lawkland *N York*	54	SD7766
Lawrenny *Dyfed*	16	SN0106
Lawshall *Suffk*	32	TL8654
Laxay *W Isls*	102	NB3321
Laxdale *W Isls*	102	NB4234
Laxey *IOM*	52	SC4384
Laxfield *Suffk*	33	TM2972
Laxford Bridge *Highld*	98	NC2346
Laxo *Shet*	103	HU4463
Laxton *Humb*	56	SE7925
Laxton *Nhants*	40	SP9596
Laxton *Notts*	49	SK7267
Laycock *W York*	55	SE0341
Layer Breton *Essex*	25	TL9417
Layer Marney *Essex*	24	TL9217
Layer-de-la-Haye *Essex*	25	TL9620
Layham *Suffk*	32	TM0240
Laymore *Dorset*	8	ST3804
Laytham *Humb*	56	SE7439
Laythes *Cumb*	67	NY2455
Lazonby *Cumb*	59	NY5439
Le Bigard *Guern*	101	GN0000
Le Bourg *Guern*	101	GN0000
Le Bourg *Jersey*	101	JS0000
Le Gron *Guern*	101	GN0000
Le Haquais *Jersey*	101	JS0000
Le Hocq *Jersey*	101	JS0000
Le Villocq *Guern*	101	GN0000
Lea *Derbys*	49	SK3257
Lea *H & W*	27	SO6521
Lea *Lincs*	50	SK8286
Lea *Shrops*	36	SO3589

Lea
Littlestone-on-Sea

Lea Wilts 20 ST9586
Lea Marston Warwks 39 SP2093
Leachkin Highld 92 NH6344
Leadburn Loth 75 NT2355
Leaden Roding Essex 24 TL5913
Leadenham Lincs 50 SK9452
Leadgate Dur 69 NZ1251
Leadhills Strath 74 NS8815
Leafield Oxon 29 SP3115
Leagrave Beds 30 TL0523
Leake Common Side Lincs 51 TF3952
Lealholm N York 63 NZ7607
Lealt Highld 90 NG5060
Leamington Hastings Warwks 29 SP4467
Leamington Spa Warwks 29 SP3265
Leasgill Cumb 59 SD4983
Leasingham Lincs 50 TF0548
Leasingthorne Dur 61 NZ2530
Leatherhead Surrey 23 TQ1656
Leathley N York 55 SE2347
Leaton Shrops 36 SJ4618
Leaveland Kent 15 TR0053
Leavenheath Suffk 25 TL9537
Leavening N York 56 SE7863
Leaves Green Gt Lon 23 TQ4161
Lebberston N York 63 TA0782
Lechlade Gloucs 21 SU2199
Leck Lancs 60 SD6476
Leck Gruinart Strath 70 NR2768
Leckbuie Tays 81 NN7040
Leckford Hants 10 SU3737
Leckhampstead Berks 21 SU4375
Leckhampstead Bucks 30 SP7237
Leckhampstead Thicket Berks 21 SU4276
Leckhampton Gloucs 28 SO9419
Leckmelm Highld 96 NH1689
Leconfield Humb 56 TA0143
Ledaig Strath 79 NM9037
Ledburn Bucks 30 SP9021
Ledbury H & W 28 SO7137
Ledgemoor H & W 27 SO4150
Ledmore Junction Highld 96 NC2412
Ledsham W York 55 SE4529
Ledston W York 55 SE4328
Ledwell Oxon 29 SP4128
Lee Devon 6 SS4846
Lee Gt Lon 23 TQ3875
Lee Brockhurst Shrops 37 SJ5427
Lee Chapel Essex 24 TQ6987
Lee Clump Bucks 22 SP9004
Lee Mill Devon 5 SX5955
Lee-on-the-Solent Hants 11 SU5600
Leebotwood Shrops 37 SO4798
Leece Cumb 53 SD2469
Leeds Kent 14 TQ8253
Leeds W York 55 SE2932
Leedstown Cnwll 2 SW6034
Leek Staffs 48 SJ9856
Leek Wootton Warwks 29 SP2868
Leeming N York 61 SE2989
Leeming Bar N York 61 SE2889
Lees Derbys 49 SK2637
Lees Gt Man 54 SD9504
Lees Green Derbys 49 SK2637
Leesthorpe Leics 40 SK7813
Leeswood Clwyd 46 SJ2660
Leetown Tays 82 NO2121
Leftwich Ches 47 SJ6672
Legbourne Lincs 51 TF3784
Legerwood Border 76 NT5843
Legsby Lincs 50 TF1385
Leicester Leics 39 SK5804
Leicester Forest East Leics 39 SK5202
Leigh Dorset 9 ST6108
Leigh Gloucs 28 SO8626
Leigh Gt Man 47 SJ6599
Leigh H & W 28 SO7853
Leigh Kent 13 TQ5446
Leigh Surrey 12 TQ2246
Leigh Wilts 20 SU0692
Leigh Beck Essex 24 TQ8183
Leigh Delamere Wilts 20 ST8879
Leigh Green Kent 14 TQ9033
Leigh Knoweglass Strath 74 NS6350
Leigh Park Dorset 10 SZ0299
Leigh Sinton H & W 28 SO7750
Leigh upon Mendip Somset 20 ST6947
Leigh Woods Avon 19 ST5672
Leigh-on-Sea Essex 24 TQ8286
Leighterton Gloucs 20 ST8290
Leighton Powys 36 SJ2306
Leighton Shrops 37 SJ6105
Leighton Bromswold Cambs 30 TL1175
Leighton Buzzard Beds 30 SP9225
Leinthall Earls H & W 27 SO4467
Leinthall Starkes H & W 27 SO4369
Leintwardine H & W 36 SO4074
Leire Leics 39 SP5290
Leiston Suffk 33 TM4462
Leitfie Tays 88 NO2545
Leith Loth 75 NT2776
Leitholm Border 76 NT7944
Lelant Cnwll 2 SW5437
Lelley Humb 57 TA2032
Lem Hill H & W 37 SO7275
Lempitlaw Border 76 NT7832
Lemreway W Isls 102 NB3711
Lemsford Herts 31 TL2212
Lenchwick H & W 28 SP0347
Lendalfoot Strath 64 NX1390
Lendrick Cent 81 NN5506
Lendrum Terrace Gramp 95 NK1141
Lenham Kent 14 TQ8952
Lenham Heath Kent 14 TQ9149
Lenie Highld 92 NH5126
Lennel Border 77 NT8540
Lennox Plunton D & G 65 NX6051
Lennoxlove Loth 76 NT5172
Lennoxtown Strath 74 NS6277
Lenton Lincs 40 TF0230
Lenzie Strath 74 NS6572
Leochel-Cushnie Gramp 94 NJ5210
Leominster H & W 27 SO4959
Leonard Stanley Gloucs 20 SO8003
Leoville Jersey 101 JS0000
Lephin Highld 90 NG1749
Leppington N York 56 SE7661
Lepton W York 55 SE2015
Lerryn Cnwll 3 SX1457
Lerwick Shet 103 HU4741
Les Arquets Guern 101 GN0000
Les Hubits Guern 101 GN0000
Les Lohiers Guern 101 GN0000
Les Murchez Guern 101 GN0000
Les Nicolles Guern 101 GN0000
Les Quartiers Guern 101 GN0000
Les Quennevais Jersey 101 JS0000
Les Sages Guern 101 GN0000
Les Villets Guern 101 GN0000
Lesbury Nthumb 69 NU2311
Leslie Fife 83 NO2501
Leslie Gramp 94 NJ5924
Lesmahagow Strath 74 NS8139
Lesnewth Cnwll 4 SX1390
Lessingham Norfk 43 TG3928
Lessonhall Cumb 67 NY2250
Leswalt D & G 64 NX0163
Letchmore Heath Herts 22 TQ1597
Letchworth Herts 31 TL2232
Letcombe Bassett Oxon 21 SU3784
Letcombe Regis Oxon 21 SU3886
Letham Border 68 NT6709
Letham Fife 83 NO3014
Letham Tays 89 NO5348
Letham Grange Tays 89 NO6345
Lethenty Gramp 94 NJ5820
Lethenty Gramp 95 NJ8140
Letheringham Suffk 33 TM2757
Letheringsett Norfk 42 TG0638
Letterfearn Highld 85 NG8823
Letterfinlay Lodge
Hotel Highld 86 NN2491
Lettermorar Highld 85 NM7389
Letters Highld 96 NH1687
Lettershaw Strath 74 NS8920
Letterston Dyfed 16 SM9429
Lettoch Highld 93 NJ0219
Lettoch Highld 93 NJ1032
Letton H & W 27 SO3346
Letty Green Herts 23 TL2810
Letwell S York 49 SK5686
Leuchars Fife 83 NO4521
Leurbost W Isls 102 NB3725
Levedale Staffs 38 SJ8916
Level's Green Essex 31 TL4724
Leven Fife 83 NO3800
Leven Humb 57 TA1045
Levencorroch Strath 72 NS0021
Levens Cumb 59 SD4886
Levens Green Herts 31 TL3522
Levenshulme Gt Man 47 SJ8794
Levenwick Shet 103 HU4021
Leverburgh W Isls 102 NG0286
Leverington Cambs 41 TF4411
Leverstock Green Herts 22 TL0806
Leverton Lincs 51 TF4047
Levington Suffk 33 TM2339
Levisham N York 63 SE8390
Lew Oxon 29 SP3206
Lewannick Cnwll 4 SX2780
Lewdown Devon 4 SX4586
Lewes E Susx 13 TQ4110
Leweston Dyfed 16 SM9322
Lewisham Gt Lon 23 TQ3774
Lewiston Highld 92 NH5129
Lewknor Oxon 22 SU7197
Lewson Street Kent 15 TQ9661
Lewtrenchard Devon 4 SX4586
Lexworthy Somset 8 ST2535
Ley Hill Bucks 22 SP9902
Leybourne Kent 14 TQ6858
Leyburn N York 61 SE1190
Leygreen Herts 31 TL1624
Leyland Lancs 53 SD5422
Leylodge Gramp 95 NJ7613
Leys Gramp 95 NK0052
Leys Tays 83 NO2537
Leys of Cossans Tays 88 NO3849
Leysdown-on-Sea Kent 15 TR0370
Leysmill Tays 89 NO6047
Leysters H & W 27 SO5664
Leyton Gt Lon 23 TQ3786
Leytonstone Gt Lon 23 TQ3987
Lezant Cnwll 4 SX3479
Lezayre IOM 52 SC4294
Lhanbryde Gramp 94 NJ2761
Libanus Powys 26 SN9925
Libberton Strath 75 NS9943
Liberton Loth 75 NT2769
Lichfield Staffs 38 SK1109
Lickey H & W 38 SO9975
Lickey End H & W 38 SO9772
Lickfold W Susx 12 SU9226
Liddesdale Highld 79 NM7759
Liddington Wilts 21 SU2081
Lidgate Suffk 32 TL7258
Lidlington Beds 30 SP9939
Liff Tays 83 NO3332
Lifford W Mids 38 SP0580
Lifton Devon 4 SX3885
Liftondown Devon 4 SX3685
Lighthorne Warwks 29 SP3355
Lightwater Surrey 22 SU9362
Lilbourne Nhants 39 SP5676
Lilleshall Shrops 37 SJ7315
Lilley Herts 30 TL1126
Lilliesleaf Border 76 NT5325
Lillingstone Dayrell Bucks 30 SP7039
Lillingstone Lovell Bucks 30 SP7140
Lillington Dorset 9 ST6212
Lilliput Dorset 10 SZ0489
Lilstock Somset 19 ST1645
Limbury Beds 30 TL0724
Lime Street H & W 28 SO8130
Limekilnburn Strath 74 NS7050
Limekilns Fife 82 NT0883
Limerigg Cent 74 NS8571
Limerstone IOW 10 SZ4482
Limington Somset 8 ST5422
Limmerhaugh Strath 74 NS6127
Limpenhoe Norfk 43 TG3903
Limpley Stoke Wilts 20 ST7860
Limpsfield Surrey 13 TQ4053
Limpsfield Chart Surrey 13 TQ4251
Linby Notts 49 SK5351
Linchmere W Susx 11 SU8630
Lincluden D & G 66 NX9677
Lincoln Lincs 50 SK9771
Lincomb H & W 28 SO8268
Lindal in Furness Cumb 58 SD2475
Lindale Cumb 59 SD4180
Lindfield W Susx 12 TQ3425
Lindford Hants 11 SU8036
Lindley W York 55 SE1217
Lindley Green N York 55 SE2248
Lindores Fife 83 NO2616
Lindridge H & W 28 SO6769
Lindsell Essex 24 TL6427
Lindsey Suffk 32 TL9745
Lindsey Tye Suffk 32 TL9845
Lingdale Cleve 62 NZ6716
Lingen H & W 27 SO3667
Lingfield Surrey 13 TQ3843
Lingwood Norfk 43 TG3508
Linicro Highld 90 NG3966
Linkend H & W 28 SO8231
Linkenholt Hants 21 SU3657
Linkinhorne Cnwll 4 SX3173
Linktown Fife 83 NT2790
Linkwood Gramp 94 NJ2361
Linley Shrops 36 SO3592
Linley Green H & W 28 SO6953
Linleygreen Shrops 37 SO6898
Linlithgow Loth 75 NS9977
Linsidemore Highld 96 NH5499
Linslade Beds 30 SP9125
Linstead Parva Suffk 33 TM3377
Linstock Cumb 67 NY4258
Linthurst H & W 38 SO9972
Linthwaite W York 55 SE1014
Lintlaw Border 77 NT8258
Lintmill Gramp 94 NJ5165
Linton Border 76 NT7726
Linton Cambs 31 TL5646
Linton Derbys 39 SK2716
Linton H & W 28 SO6625
Linton Kent 14 TQ7550
Linton N York 54 SD9962
Linton W York 55 SE3946
Linton Hill Gloucs 28 SO6624
Linton-on-Ouse N York 55 SE4860
Linwood Lincs 50 TF1186
Linwood Strath 73 NS4464
Lional W Isls 102 NB5263
Liphook Hants 11 SU8431
Liscard Mersyd 46 SJ2991
Liscombe Somset 7 SS8732
Liskeard Cnwll 4 SX2564
Liss Hants 11 SU7727
Lissett Humb 57 TA1458
Lissington Lincs 50 TF1083
Lisvane S Glam 19 ST1883
Liswerry Gwent 14 ST3487
Litcham Norfk 42 TF8817
Litchborough Nhants 29 SP6354
Litchfield Hants 21 SU4653
Litherland Mersyd 46 SJ3397
Litlington Cambs 31 TL3142
Litlington E Susx 13 TQ5201
Little Abington Cambs 31 TL5349
Little Addington Nhants 30 SP9673
Little Airies D & G 64 NX4248
Little Alne Warwks 28 SP1461
Little Altcar Mersyd 46 SD3006
Little Amwell Herts 23 TL3511
Little Asby Cumb 60 NY6909
Little Aston Staffs 38 SK0900
Little Ayton N York 62 NZ5610
Little Baddow Essex 24 TL7707
Little Badminton Avon 20 ST8084
Little Bampton Cumb 67 NY2755
Little Bardfield Essex 24 TL6531
Little Barford Beds 31 TL1756
Little Barningham Norfk 43 TG1333
Little Barrington Gloucs 29 SP2012
Little Barrow Ches 46 SJ4769
Little Bavington Nthumb 68 NY9878
Little Bedwyn Wilts 21 SU2866
Little Bentley Essex 25 TM1125
Little Berkhamsted Herts 23 TL2907
Little Billing Nhants 30 SP8061
Little Billington Beds 30 SP9322
Little Birch H & W 27 SO5130
Little Blakenham Suffk 33 TM1048
Little Blencow Cumb 59 NY4532
Little Bognor W Susx 12 TQ0020
Little Bolehill Derbys 49 SK2954
Little Bookham Surrey 22 TQ1254
Little Bourton Oxon 29 SP4544
Little Bradley Suffk 32 TL6852
Little Brampton Shrops 36 SO3681
Little Braxted Essex 24 TL8314
Little Brechin Tays 89 NO5862
Little Brickhill Bucks 30 SP9132
Little Brington Nhants 30 SP6663
Little Bromley Essex 25 TM0928
Little Broughton Cumb 58 NY0731
Little Budworth Ches 47 SJ5965
Little Burstead Essex 24 TQ6692
Little Bytham Lincs 40 TF0118
Little Canfield Essex 24 TL5821
Little Carlton Lincs 51 TF3985
Little Casterton Leics 40 TF0109
Little Cawthorpe Lincs 51 TF3583
Little Chalfont Bucks 22 SU9997
Little Chart Kent 14 TQ9446
Little Chesterford Essex 31 TL5141
Little Cheverell Wilts 20 ST9953
Little Chishill Cambs 31 TL4137
Little Clacton Essex 25 TM1618
Little Clifton Cumb 58 NY0528
Little Comberton H & W 28 SO9643
Little Common E Susx 14 TQ7107
Little Compton Warwks 29 SP2630
Little Cornard Suffk 32 TL9039
Little Cowarne H & W 27 SO6051
Little Coxwell Oxon 21 SU2893
Little Crakehall N York 61 SE2390
Little Cressingham Norfk 42 TF8700
Little Crosby Mersyd 46 SD3201
Little Cubley Derbys 48 SK1537
Little Dalby Leics 40 SK7714
Little Dens Gramp 95 NK0643
Little Dewchurch H & W 27 SO5231
Little Ditton Cambs 32 TL6658
Little Driffield Humb 56 TA0058
Little Dunham Norfk 42 TF8612
Little Dunkeld Tays 88 NO0342
Little Dunmow Essex 24 TL6521
Little Durnford Wilts 10 SU1234
Little Eaton Derbys 49 SK3641
Little Ellingham Norfk 42 TM0099
Little Everdon Nhants 29 SP5957
Little Eversden Cambs 31 TL3753
Little Faringdon S York 21 SP2201
Little Fencote N York 61 SE2893
Little Fenton N York 55 SE5235
Little Fransham Norfk 42 TF9011
Little Gaddesden Herts 30 SP9913
Little Glemham Suffk 33 TM3458
Little Gorsley H & W 28 SO6924
Little Gransden Cambs 31 TL2755
Little Green Somset 20 ST7248
Little Grimsby Lincs 51 TF3291
Little Hadham Herts 31 TL4322
Little Hale Lincs 50 TF1441
Little Hallam Derbys 49 SK4640
Little Hallingbury Essex 31 TL5017
Little Harrowden Nhants 30 SP8771
Little Haseley Oxon 21 SP6400
Little Hatfield Humb 57 TA1743
Little Haven Dyfed 16 SM8512
Little Hay Staffs 38 SK1102
Little Haywood Staffs 38 SK0021
Little Heath W Mids 39 SP3482
Little Hereford H & W 27 SO5568
Little Horkesley Essex 25 TL9532
Little Hormead Herts 31 TL4028
Little Horsted E Susx 13 TQ4718
Little Horton W York 55 SE1531
Little Horwood Bucks 30 SP7930
Little Houghton Nhants 30 SP8059
Little Houghton S York 55 SE4205
Little Hucklow Derbys 48 SK1678
Little Hutton N York 62 SE4576
Little Irchester Nhants 30 SP9066
Little Keyford Somset 20 ST7746
Little Kimble Bucks 22 SP8207
Little Kineton Warwks 29 SP3350
Little Kingshill Bucks 22 SU8999
Little Knox D & G 66 NX8060
Little Langdale Cumb 58 NY3103
Little Langford Wilts 10 SU0436
Little Lashbrook Devon 6 SS4007
Little Laver Essex 24 TL5409
Little Leigh Ches 47 SJ6175
Little Leighs Essex 24 TL7117
Little Lever Gt Man 47 SD7507
Little Linford Bucks 30 SP8444
Little Load Somset 8 ST4724
Little London E Susx 13 TQ5620
Little London Essex 31 TL4729
Little London Hants 21 SU3749
Little London Hants 21 SU6259
Little Longstone Derbys 48 SK1871
Little Malvern H & W 28 SO7640
Little Maplestead Essex 24 TL8234
Little Marcle H & W 28 SO6736
Little Marlow Bucks 22 SU8787
Little Massingham Norfk 42 TF7824
Little Melton Norfk 43 TG1607
Little Mill Gwent 19 SO3203
Little Milton Oxon 21 SP6100
Little Missenden Bucks 22 SU9299
Little Musgrave Cumb 60 NY7612
Little Ness Shrops 36 SJ4019
Little Newcastle Dyfed 16 SM9829
Little Newsham Dur 61 NZ1217
Little Norton Somset 8 ST4715
Little Oakley Essex 25 TM2129
Little Oakley Nhants 40 SP8985
Little Onn Staffs 38 SJ8315
Little Orton Cumb 67 NY3555
Little Packington Warwks 39 SP2184
Little Pannell Wilts 20 SU0053
Little Paxton Cambs 31 TL1862
Little Petherick Cnwll 3 SW9172
Little Plumstead Norfk 43 TG3112
Little Ponton Lincs 40 SK9232
Little Preston Nhants 29 SP5854
Little Raveley Cambs 41 TL2579
Little Reedness Humb 56 SE8022
Little Ribston N York 55 SE3853
Little Rissington Gloucs 29 SP1819
Little Rollright Oxon 29 SP2930
Little Ryburgh Norfk 42 TF9628
Little Salkeld Cumb 59 NY5636
Little Sampford Essex 24 TL6533
Little Saughall Ches 46 SJ3768
Little Saxham Suffk 32 TL8063
Little Scatwell Highld 92 NH3856
Little Sessay N York 62 SE4674
Little Shelford Cambs 31 TL4551
Little Silver Devon 7 SS8601
Little Singleton Lancs 53 SD3739
Little Skipwith N York 56 SE6538
Little Smeaton N York 55 SE5216
Little Snoring Norfk 42 TF9532
Little Sodbury Avon 20 ST7582
Little Somborne Hants 10 SU3832
Little Somerford Wilts 20 ST9684
Little Soudley Shrops 37 SJ7128
Little Stainton Dur 62 NZ3420
Little Staughton Beds 30 TL1062
Little Steeping Lincs 51 TF4362
Little Stonham Suffk 33 TM1160
Little Stretton Leics 39 SK6600
Little Stretton Shrops 36 SO4491
Little Strickland Cumb 59 NY5619
Little Stukeley Cambs 31 TL2175
Little Sugnall Staffs 37 SJ8031
Little Swinburne Nthumb 68 NY9477
Little Sypland D & G 65 NX7253
Little Tew Oxon 29 SP3828
Little Tey Essex 24 TL8923
Little Thetford Cambs 31 TL5376
Little Thorpe Dur 62 NZ4242
Little Thurlow Green Suffk 32 TL6851
Little Thurrock Essex 24 TQ6277
Little Torrington Devon 6 SS4916
Little Town Lancs 54 SD6635
Little Urswick Cumb 58 SD2673
Little Wakering Essex 25 TQ9388
Little Walden Essex 31 TL5441
Little Waldingfield Suffk 32 TL9245
Little Walsingham Norfk 42 TF9337
Little Waltham Essex 24 TL7012
Little Washbourne Gloucs 28 SO9833
Little Weighton Humb 56 SE9833
Little Weldon Nhants 40 SP9289
Little Wenham Suffk 32 TM0839
Little Wenlock Shrops 37 SJ6406
Little Weston Somset 9 ST6225
Little Whitefield IOW 11 SZ5889
Little Wilbraham Cambs 31 TL5458
Little Witcombe Gloucs 28 SO9115
Little Witley H & W 28 SO7863
Little Wittenham Oxon 21 SU5693
Little Wolford Warwks 29 SP2635
Little Woodcote Surrey 23 TQ2861
Little Wratting Suffk 32 TL6847
Little Wymington Beds 30 SP9565
Little Wymondley Herts 31 TL2127
Little Wyrley Staffs 38 SK0105
Little Yeldham Essex 32 TL7839
Littleborough Gt Man 54 SD9316
Littleborough Notts 50 SK8282
Littlebourne Kent 15 TR2057
Littlebredy Dorset 9 SY5889
Littlebury Essex 31 TL5139
Littlebury Green Essex 31 TL4838
Littledean Gloucs 28 SO6713
Littleham Devon 6 SS4323
Littleham Devon 5 SY0381
Littlehampton W Susx 12 TQ0201
Littlehempston Devon 5 SX8162
Littlemill Gramp 88 NO3295
Littlemill Highld 93 NH9150
Littlemore Oxon 21 SP5302
Littleover Derbys 39 SK3334
Littleport Cambs 41 TL5686
Littlestone-on-Sea Kent 15 TR0824

Littlethrope

Longwood

Littlethorpe *Leics* 39 SP5496
Littlethorpe *N York* 55 SE3269
Littleton *Ches* 46 SJ4466
Littleton *D & G* 65 NX6355
Littleton *Hants* 10 SU4532
Littleton *Somset* 8 ST4930
Littleton *Surrey* 22 TQ0668
Littleton *Tays* 88 NO3350
Littleton Drew *Wilts* 20 ST8380
Littleton-on-Severn *Avon* 19 ST5989
Littletown *Dur* 69 NZ3343
Littlewick Green *Berks* 22 SU8379
Littleworth *H & W* 28 SO8850
Littleworth *Oxon* 21 SU3197
Littleworth *Staffs* 38 SJ9323
Littley Green *Essex* 24 TL6917
Litton *Derbys* 48 SK1675
Litton *N York* 60 SD9074
Litton *Somset* 19 ST5954
Litton Cheney *Dorset* 8 SY5490
Liurbost *W Isls* 102 NB3725
Liverpool *Mersyd* 46 SJ3490
Liversedge *W York* 55 SE1923
Liverton *Cleve* 63 NZ7115
Liverton *Devon* 5 SX8075
Livingston *Loth* 75 NT0668
Livingston Village *Loth* 75 NT0366
Lixton *Devon* 5 SX6950
Lixwm *Clwyd* 46 SJ1671
Lizard *Cnwll* 2 SW7012
Llanaelhaearn *Gwynd* 44 SH3844
Llanafan *Dyfed* 35 SN6872
Llanallgo *Gwynd* 44 SH5085
Llanarmon
Dyffryn Ceiriog *Clwyd* 36 SJ1532
Llanarmon-yn-Ial *Clwyd* 46 SJ1956
Llanarth *Dyfed* 34 SN4257
Llanarth *Gwent* 27 SO3710
Llanarthne *Dyfed* 17 SN5320
Llanasa *Clwyd* 46 SJ1081
Llanbadarn Fawr *Dyfed* 34 SN6081
Llanbadarn Fynydd *Powys* 36 SO0977
Llanbadoc *Gwent* 19 ST3799
Llanbeder *Gwent* 19 ST3890
Llanbedr *Gwynd* 44 SH5826
Llanbedr *Powys* 27 SO2320
Llanbedr-Dyffryn-Clwyd *Clwyd* 46 SJ1459
Llanbedr-y-cennin *Gwynd* 45 SH7669
Llanbedrgoch *Gwynd* 44 SH5180
Llanbedrog *Gwynd* 44 SH3231
Llanberis *Gwynd* 44 SH5760
Llanbethery *S Glam* 18 ST0369
Llanbister *Powys* 36 SO1173
Llanblethian *S Glam* 18 SS9873
Llanboidy *Dyfed* 17 SN2123
Llanbradach *M Glam* 18 ST1490
Llanbrynmair *Powys* 35 SH8902
Llancadle *S Glam* 18 ST0368
Llancarfan *S Glam* 18 ST0470
Llancloudy *H & W* 27 SO4921
Llandaff *S Glam* 19 ST1577
Llandanwg *Gwynd* 44 SH5728
Llanddanielfab *Gwynd* 44 SH4970
Llanddarog *Dyfed* 17 SN5016
Llanddeiniol *Dyfed* 34 SN5571
Llanddeiniolen *Gwynd* 44 SH5465
Llandderfel *Gwynd* 45 SH9837
Llanddeusant *Gwynd* 44 SH3485
Llanddew *Powys* 26 SO0530
Llanddewi *W Glam* 17 SS4588
Llanddewi Brefi *Dyfed* 26 SN6655
Llanddewi Rhydderch *Gwent* 27 SO3512
Llanddewi Velfrey *Dyfed* 16 SN1415
Llanddewi Ystradenni *Powys* 26 SO1068
Llanddoget *Gwynd* 45 SH8063
Llanddona *Gwynd* 44 SH5779
Llanddowror *Dyfed* 17 SN2514
Llanddulas *Clwyd* 45 SH9178
Llanddwywe *Gwynd* 34 SH5822
Llanddyfnan *Gwynd* 44 SH5078
Llandefaelogtrer-graig *Powys* 26 SO1229
Llandefalle *Powys* 26 SO1035
Llandegai *Gwynd* 44 SH5971
Llandegfan *Gwynd* 44 SH5674
Llandegla *Clwyd* 46 SJ2051
Llandegley *Powys* 26 SO1463
Llandegveth *Gwent* 19 ST3395
Llandeilo *Dyfed* 17 SN6222
Llandeilo Graban *Powys* 26 SO0944
Llandeloy *Dyfed* 16 SM8626
Llandenny *Gwent* 27 SO4104
Llandevaud *Gwent* 19 ST4090
Llandevenny *Gwent* 19 ST4186
Llandinam *Powys* 35 SO0288
Llandissilio *Dyfed* 16 SN1221
Llandogo *Gwent* 19 SO5203
Llandough *S Glam* 18 SS9972
Llandough *S Glam* 19 ST1673
Llandovery *Dyfed* 26 SN7634
Llandow *S Glam* 18 SS9473
Llandre *Dyfed* 35 SN6286
Llandre *Dyfed* 26 SN6741
Llandre Isaf *Dyfed* 16 SN1328
Llandrillo *Clwyd* 36 SJ0337
Llandrillo-yn-Rhos *Clwyd* 45 SH8380
Llandrindod Wells *Powys* 26 SO0561
Llandrinio *Powys* 36 SJ2817
Llandudno *Gwynd* 45 SH7882
Llandudno Junction *Gwynd* 45 SH7977
Llandudwen *Gwynd* 44 SH2736
Llandulas *Powys* 26 SN8841
Llandwrog *Gwynd* 44 SH4555
Llandybie *Dyfed* 17 SN6115
Llandyfaelog *Dyfed* 17 SN4111
Llandyfriog *Dyfed* 17 SN3341
Llandygwydd *Dyfed* 17 SN2443
Llandyrnog *Clwyd* 46 SJ1065
Llandyssil *Powys* 36 SO1995
Llandysul *Dyfed* 17 SN4140
Llanedeyrn *S Glam* 19 ST2181
Llanegryn *Gwynd* 34 SH6005
Llanegwad *Dyfed* 17 SN5221
Llaneilian *Gwynd* 44 SH4692
Llanelian-yn-Rhos *Clwyd* 45 SH8676
Llanelidan *Clwyd* 46 SJ1150
Llanelieu *Powys* 27 SO1834
Llanelli *Dyfed* 17 SN5000
Llanelltyd *Gwynd* 35 SH7119
Llanelwedd *Powys* 26 SO0451
Llanenddwyn *Gwynd* 34 SH5823
Llanengan *Gwynd* 44 SH2926
Llanerchymedd *Gwynd* 44 SH4184
Llanerfyl *Powys* 36 SJ0309
Llanfachraeth *Gwynd* 44 SH3182
Llanfachreth *Gwynd* 35 SH7522
Llanfaelog *Gwynd* 44 SH3373
Llanfaelrhys *Gwynd* 44 SH2026
Llanfaethlu *Gwynd* 44 SH3186
Llanfair *Gwynd* 44 SH5728
Llanfair Caereinion *Powys* 36 SJ1006
Llanfair Clydogau *Dyfed* 26 SN6251
Llanfair Dyffryn Clwyd *Clwyd* 46 SJ1355
Llanfair P G *Gwynd* 44 SH5271
Llanfair Talhaiarn *Clwyd* 45 SH9270
Llanfair Waterdine *Shrops* 36 SO2376
Llanfair-is-gaer *Gwynd* 44 SH5065
Llanfair-y-Cwmmwd *Gwynd* 44 SH4466
Llanfair-yn-Neubwll *Gwynd* 44 SH3076
Llanfairfechan *Gwynd* 45 SH6874
Llanfairynghornwy *Gwynd* 44 SH3290
Llanfallteg *Dyfed* 17 SN1520
Llanfallteg West *Dyfed* 16 SN1419
Llanfarian *Dyfed* 34 SN5877
Llanfechain *Powys* 36 SJ1920
Llanfechell *Gwynd* 44 SH3791
Llanferres *Clwyd* 46 SJ1860
Llanfihangel Glyn Myfyr *Clwyd* 45 SH9849
Llanfihangel Nant Bran *Powys* 26 SN9434
Llanfihangel Rhydithon *Powys* 27 SO1566
Llanfihangel Rogiet *Gwent* 19 ST4587
Llanfihangel yn
Nhowyn *Gwynd* 44 SH3277
Llanfihangel-ar-Arth *Dyfed* 17 SN4540
Llanfihangel-y-Creuddyn *Dyfed* 35 SN6675
Llanfihangel-y-traethau *Gwynd* 44 SH5934
Llanfihangel-yng-
Ngwynfa *Powys* 36 SJ0816
Llanfilo *Powys* 26 SO1132
Llanfoist *Gwent* 27 SO2813
Llanfor *Gwynd* 45 SH9336
Llanfrechfa *Gwent* 19 ST3293
Llanfrynach *Powys* 26 SO0725
Llanfwrog *Clwyd* 46 SJ1157
Llanfwrog *Gwynd* 44 SH3084
Llanfyllin *Powys* 36 SJ1419
Llanfynydd *Clwyd* 46 SJ2856
Llanfynydd *Dyfed* 17 SN5527
Llanfyrnach *Dyfed* 17 SN2231
Llangadfan *Powys* 35 SJ0110
Llangadog *Dyfed* 26 SN7028
Llangadwaladr *Gwynd* 44 SH3869
Llangaffo *Gwynd* 44 SH4468
Llangammarch Wells *Powys* 26 SN9346
Llangan *S Glam* 18 SS9577
Llangarron *H & W* 27 SO5220
Llangathen *Dyfed* 17 SN5822
Llangattock *Powys* 27 SO2117
Llangattock Lingoed *Gwent* 27 SO3620
Llangedwyn *Clwyd* 36 SJ1824
Llangefni *Gwynd* 44 SH4675
Llangeinor *M Glam* 18 SS9187
Llangeinwen *Gwynd* 44 SH4465
Llangeitho *Dyfed* 35 SN6259
Llangeler *Dyfed* 17 SN3739
Llangelynin *Gwynd* 34 SH5707
Llangendeirne *Dyfed* 17 SN4513
Llangennech *Dyfed* 17 SN5601
Llangernyw *Clwyd* 45 SH8767
Llangian *Gwynd* 44 SH2928
Llangloffan *Dyfed* 16 SM9032
Llanglydwen *Dyfed* 17 SN1826
Llangoed *Gwynd* 44 SH6079
Llangollen *Clwyd* 36 SJ2141
Llangolman *Dyfed* 16 SN1127
Llangors *Powys* 26 SO1327
Llangower *Gwynd* 45 SH9032
Llangranog *Dyfed* 34 SN3154
Llangristiolus *Gwynd* 44 SH4373
Llangrove *H & W* 27 SO5219
Llangunllo *Powys* 36 SO2171
Llangunnor *Dyfed* 17 SN4320
Llangurig *Powys* 35 SN9079
Llangwm *Clwyd* 45 SH9644
Llangwm *Dyfed* 16 SM9909
Llangwm *Gwent* 19 ST4299
Llangwm-isaf *Gwent* 19 SO4300
Llangwnnadl *Gwynd* 44 SH2033
Llangwyryfon *Dyfed* 34 SN5970
Llangybi *Dyfed* 17 SN6053
Llangybi *Gwent* 19 ST3796
Llangybi *Gwynd* 44 SH4341
Llangynhafal *Clwyd* 46 SJ1263
Llangynidr *Powys* 27 SO1519
Llangynin *Dyfed* 17 SN2517
Llangynog *Dyfed* 17 SN3314
Llangynog *Powys* 36 SJ0526
Llangynwyd *M Glam* 18 SS8588
Llanhamlach *Powys* 26 SO0926
Llanharan *M Glam* 18 ST0083
Llanharry *M Glam* 18 ST0080
Llanhennock *Gwent* 19 ST3592
Llanhilleth *Gwent* 19 SO2100
Llanidloes *Powys* 35 SN9584
Llaniestyn *Gwynd* 44 SH2733
Llanigon *Powys* 27 SO2139
Llanilar *Dyfed* 35 SN6275
Llanilid *M Glam* 18 SS9781
Llanina *Dyfed* 34 SN4059
Llanishen *Gwent* 19 SO4703
Llanishen *S Glam* 19 ST1781
Llanllechid *Gwynd* 45 SH6268
Llanllowell *Gwent* 19 ST3998
Llanllugan *Powys* 36 SJ0502
Llanllwch *Dyfed* 17 SN3818
Llanllwchaiarn *Powys* 36 SO1292
Llanllwni *Dyfed* 17 SN4741
Llanllyfni *Gwynd* 44 SH4751
Llanmadoc *W Glam* 17 SS4493
Llanmaes *S Glam* 18 SS9769
Llanmartin *Gwent* 19 ST3989
Llanmiloe *Dyfed* 17 SN2408
Llanmorlais *W Glam* 17 SS5294
Llannefydd *Clwyd* 45 SH9870
Llannon *Dyfed* 17 SN5308
Llannor *Gwynd* 44 SH3537
Llanon *Dyfed* 34 SN5166
Llanover *Gwent* 27 SO3109
Llanpumsaint *Dyfed* 17 SN4229
Llanrhaeadr-ym-
Mochnant *Clwyd* 36 SJ1226
Llanrhidian *W Glam* 17 SS4992
Llanrhychwyn *Gwynd* 45 SH7761
Llanrhyddlad *Gwynd* 44 SH3389
Llanrhystud *Dyfed* 34 SN5369
Llanrian *Dyfed* 16 SM8231
Llanrothal *H & W* 27 SO4718
Llanrug *Gwynd* 44 SH5363
Llanrumney *S Glam* 19 ST2280
Llanrwst *Gwynd* 45 SH8061
Llansadurnen *Dyfed* 17 SN2810
Llansadwrn *Dyfed* 26 SN6931
Llansadwrn *Gwynd* 44 SH5575
Llansaint *Dyfed* 17 SN3808
Llansamlet *W Glam* 18 SS6897
Llansanffraid
Glan Conwy *Gwynd* 45 SH8076
Llansannan *Clwyd* 45 SH9365
Llansantffraed *Powys* 26 SO1223
Llansantffraed-
Cwmdeuddwr *Powys* 35 SN9667
Llansantffraed-in-Elvel *Powys* 26 SO0954
Llansantffraid *Dyfed* 34 SN5167
Llansantffraid-ym-
Mechain *Powys* 36 SJ2220
Llansawel *Dyfed* 17 SN6136
Llansilin *Clwyd* 36 SJ2128
Llansoy *Gwent* 19 SO4402
Llanspyddid *Powys* 26 SO0128
Llanstadwell *Dyfed* 16 SM9404
Llansteffan *Dyfed* 17 SN3510
Llantarnam *Gwent* 19 ST3093
Llanteg *Dyfed* 17 SN1810
Llanthewy Skirrid *Gwent* 27 SO3416
Llanthony *Gwent* 27 SO2827
Llantilio Pertholey *Gwent* 27 SO3116
Llantilio-Crossenny *Gwent* 27 SO3914
Llantrisant *Gwent* 19 ST3996
Llantrisant *M Glam* 18 ST0483
Llantrithyd *S Glam* 18 ST0472
Llantwit Fardre *M Glam* 18 ST0886
Llantwit Major *S Glam* 18 SS9668
Llanuwchllyn *Gwynd* 45 SH8730
Llanvaches *Gwent* 19 ST4391
Llanvair Discoed *Gwent* 19 ST4492
Llanvapley *Gwent* 27 SO3614
Llanvetherine *Gwent* 27 SO3617
Llanvihangel Crucorney *Gwent* 27 SO3220
Llanwddyn *Powys* 35 SJ0219
Llanwenog *Dyfed* 17 SN4945
Llanwern *Gwent* 19 ST3688
Llanwinio *Dyfed* 17 SN2626
Llanwnda *Dyfed* 16 SM9339
Llanwnda *Gwynd* 44 SH4758
Llanwnnen *Dyfed* 17 SN5347
Llanwnog *Powys* 35 SO0293
Llanwrda *Dyfed* 26 SN7131
Llanwrin *Powys* 35 SH7803
Llanwrthwl *Powys* 35 SN9763
Llanwrtyd Wells *Powys* 26 SN8846
Llanwyddelan *Powys* 36 SJ0801
Llanyblodwel *Shrops* 36 SJ2323
Llanybri *Dyfed* 17 SN3312
Llanybydder *Dyfed* 17 SN5244
Llanycefn *Dyfed* 16 SN0923
Llanychaer Bridge *Dyfed* 16 SM9835
Llanymawddwy *Gwynd* 35 SH9019
Llanymynech *Shrops* 36 SJ2621
Llanynghenedl *Gwynd* 44 SH3181
Llanynis *Powys* 26 SN9950
Llanynys *Clwyd* 46 SJ1062
Llanyre *Powys* 26 SO0462
Llanystumdwy *Gwynd* 44 SH4738
Llanywern *Powys* 26 SO1028
Llawhaden *Dyfed* 16 SN0717
Llawnt *Shrops* 36 SJ2430
Llawryglyn *Powys* 35 SN9291
Llay *Clwyd* 46 SJ3355
Llechryd *Dyfed* 17 SN2143
Llechylched *Gwynd* 44 SH3476
Lledrod *Dyfed* 35 SN6470
Llithfaen *Gwynd* 44 SH3542
Lloc *Clwyd* 46 SJ1376
Llowes *Powys* 27 SO1941
Llwydcoed *M Glam* 26 SN9904
Llwydiarth *Powys* 36 SJ0315
Llwyncelyn *Dyfed* 34 SN4459
Llwyndafydd *Dyfed* 34 SN3755
Llwyngwril *Gwynd* 34 SH5909
Llwynmawr *Clwyd* 36 SJ2237
Llwynypia *M Glam* 18 SS9993
Llynclys *Shrops* 36 SJ2824
Llynfaes *Gwynd* 44 SH4178
Llys-y-fran *Dyfed* 16 SN0424
Llysfaen *Clwyd* 45 SH8977
Llyswen *Powys* 26 SO1337
Llysworney *S Glam* 18 SS9673
Llywel *Powys* 26 SN8630
Loan *Cent* 75 NS9675
Loanhead *Loth* 75 NT2865
Loaningfoot *D & G* 66 NX9655
Loans *Strath* 73 NS3431
Lobhillcross *Devon* 4 SX4686
Loch Baghasdail *W Isls* 102 NF7919
Loch Euphoirt *W Isls* 102 NF8563
Loch Katrine Pier *Cent* 81 NN4907
Loch Loyal Lodge *Highld* 99 NC6146
Loch Maree Hotel *Highld* 91 NG9170
Loch nam Madadh *W Isls* 102 NF9169
Lochailort *Highld* 85 NM7682
Lochaline *Highld* 79 NM6744
Lochans *D & G* 64 NX0656
Locharbriggs *D & G* 66 NX9980
Lochavich *Strath* 80 NM9415
Lochawe *Strath* 80 NN1227
Lochboisdale *W Isls* 102 NF7919
Lochbuie *Strath* 79 NM6025
Lochcarron *Highld* 85 NG8939
Lochdon *Strath* 79 NM7233
Lochdonhead *Strath* 79 NM7233
Lochead *Strath* 71 NR7778
Lochearnhead *Cent* 81 NN5823
Lochee *Tays* 83 NO3731
Locheilside Station *Highld* 85 NM9978
Lochend *Highld* 92 NH5937
Locheport *W Isls* 102 NF8563
Lochfoot *D & G* 66 NX8973
Lochgair *Strath* 71 NR9290
Lochgelly *Fife* 82 NT1893
Lochgilphead *Strath* 71 NR8688
Lochgoilhead *Strath* 80 NN2001
Lochieheads *Fife* 83 NO2513
Lochill *Gramp* 94 NJ2964
Lochindorb Lodge *Highld* 93 NH9635
Lochinver *Highld* 98 NC0922
Lochluichart *Highld* 92 NH3363
Lochmaben *D & G* 66 NY0882
Lochmaddy *W Isls* 102 NF9169
Lochore *Fife* 82 NT1796
Lochranza *Strath* 72 NR9350
Lochside *Gramp* 89 NO7364
Lochside *Highld* 93 NH8152
Lochton *Strath* 64 NX2579
Lochty *Fife* 83 NO5208
Lochty *Tays* 89 NO5362
Lochuisge *Highld* 79 NM7955
Lochwinnoch *Strath* 73 NS3559
Lochwood *D & G* 66 NY0896
Lockengate *Cnwll* 3 SX0361
Lockerbie *D & G* 67 NY1381
Lockeridge *Wilts* 20 SU1467
Lockerley *Hants* 10 SU3025
Locking *Avon* 19 ST3659
Lockington *Humb* 56 SE9947
Lockleywood *Shrops* 37 SJ6928
Locksbottom *Gt Lon* 23 TQ4265
Lockton *N York* 63 SE8489
Loddington *Leics* 40 SK7902
Loddington *Nhants* 30 SP8178
Loddiswell *Devon* 5 SX7248
Loddon *Norfk* 43 TM3698
Lode *Cambs* 31 TL5362
Lode Heath *W Mids* 38 SP1580
Loders *Dorset* 8 SY4994
Lodsworth *W Susx* 12 SU9223
Lofthouse Gate *W York* 55 SE3324
Lofthouse *N York* 61 SE1073
Lofthouse *W York* 55 SE3325
Loftus *Cleve* 63 NZ7218
Logan *Strath* 74 NS5820
Loganlea *Loth* 75 NS9762
Loggerheads *Staffs* 37 SJ7336
Logie *Fife* 83 NO4020
Logie *Gramp* 93 NJ0150
Logie *Tays* 89 NO6963
Logie Coldstone *Gramp* 88 NJ4304
Logie Pert *Tays* 89 NO6664
Logierait *Tays* 88 NN9752
Logierieve *Gramp* 95 NJ9127
Login *Dyfed* 17 SN1623
Lolworth *Cambs* 31 TL3664
Lonbain *Highld* 91 NG6852
Londesborough *Humb* 56 SE8645
London *Gt Lon* 23 TQ2879
London Apprentice *Cnwll* 3 SX0049
London Colney *Herts* 23 TL1803
Londonderry *N York* 61 SE3087
Londonthorpe *Lincs* 40 SK9537
Londubh *Highld* 91 NG8680
Long Ashton *Avon* 19 ST5570
Long Bank *H & W* 37 SO7674
Long Bennington *Lincs* 50 SK8344
Long Bredy *Dorset* 9 SY5690
Long Buckby *Nhants* 29 SP6367
Long Clawson *Leics* 40 SK7227
Long Compton *Staffs* 38 SJ8522
Long Compton *Warwks* 29 SP2832
Long Crendon *Bucks* 22 SP6908
Long Crichel *Dorset* 9 ST9710
Long Ditton *Surrey* 23 TQ1766
Long Duckmanton *Derbys* 49 SK4471
Long Eaton *Derbys* 39 SK4833
Long Green *Ches* 46 SJ4770
Long Green *H & W* 28 SO8433
Long Hanborough *Oxon* 29 SP4114
Long Itchington *Warwks* 29 SP4165
Long Lawford *Warwks* 39 SP4776
Long Load *Somset* 8 ST4623
Long Marston *Herts* 30 SP8915
Long Marston *N York* 55 SE5051
Long Marston *Warwks* 28 SP1548
Long Marton *Cumb* 60 NY6624
Long Melford *Suffk* 32 TL8645
Long Newnton *Gloucs* 20 ST9192
Long Newton *Loth* 76 NT5164
Long Preston *N York* 54 SD8358
Long Riston *Humb* 57 TA1242
Long Stratton *Norfk* 33 TM1992
Long Street *Bucks* 30 SP7947
Long Sutton *Hants* 22 SU7347
Long Sutton *Lincs* 41 TF4322
Long Sutton *Somset* 8 ST4725
Long Thurlow *Suffk* 32 TM0068
Long Waste *Shrops* 37 SJ6115
Long Whatton *Leics* 39 SK4723
Long Wittenham *Oxon* 21 SU5493
Longbenton *T & W* 69 NZ2668
Longborough *Gloucs* 29 SP1729
Longbridge *W Mids* 38 SP0177
Longbridge Deverill *Wilts* 20 ST8640
Longburton *Dorset* 9 ST6412
Longcliffe *Derbys* 48 SK2255
Longcombe *Devon* 5 SX8359
Longcot *Oxon* 21 SU2790
Longden *Shrops* 36 SJ4406
Longdon *H & W* 28 SO8336
Longdon *Staffs* 38 SK0714
Longdon Green *Staffs* 38 SK0813
Longdon upon Tern *Shrops* 37 SJ6115
Longdown *Devon* 5 SX8691
Longdowns *Cnwll* 2 SW7434
Longfield *Kent* 14 TQ6069
Longford *Derbys* 48 SK2137
Longford *Gloucs* 28 SO8320
Longford *Shrops* 37 SJ6434
Longford *Shrops* 37 SJ7218
Longforgan *Tays* 83 NO2929
Longformacus *Border* 76 NT6957
Longframlington *Nthumb* 69 NU1300
Longham *Dorset* 10 SZ0698
Longham *Norfk* 42 TF9416
Longhaven *Gramp* 95 NJ9538
Longhaven *Gramp* 95 NK1039
Longhirst *Nthumb* 69 NZ2289
Longhope *Gloucs* 28 SO6918
Longhope *Ork* 103 ND3190
Longhorsley *Nthumb* 69 NZ1494
Longhoughton *Nthumb* 77 NU2415
Longlane *Derbys* 48 SK2437
Longlevens *Gloucs* 28 SO8519
Longley *W York* 55 SE0522
Longleys *Tays* 88 NO2643
Longmanhill *Gramp* 95 NJ7362
Longmoor Camp *Hants* 11 SU7931
Longmorn *Gramp* 94 NJ2358
Longnewton *Border* 76 NT5827
Longnewton *Cleve* 62 NZ3816
Longney *Gloucs* 28 SO7612
Longniddry *Loth* 76 NT4476
Longnor *Shrops* 37 SJ4800
Longnor *Staffs* 48 SK0864
Longparish *Hants* 21 SU4345
Longridge *Lancs* 54 SD6037
Longridge *Loth* 75 NS9462
Longriggend *Strath* 74 NS8270
Longrock *Cnwll* 2 SW5031
Longsdon *Staffs* 48 SJ9654
Longside *Gramp* 95 NK0347
Longstanton *Cambs* 31 TL3966
Longstock *Hants* 10 SU3537
Longstowe *Cambs* 31 TL3054
Longstreet *Wilts* 20 SU1451
Longthorpe *Cambs* 40 TL1698
Longthwaite *Cumb* 59 NY4323
Longton *Lancs* 53 SD4825
Longton *Staffs* 48 SJ9143
Longtown *Cumb* 67 NY3768
Longtown *H & W* 27 SO3229
Longueville *Jersey* 101 JS0000
Longville in the Dale *Shrops* 37 SO5393
Longwick *Bucks* 22 SP7905
Longwitton *Nthumb* 68 NZ0788
Longwood *D & G* 65 NX7060

Longworth *Oxon* 21 SU3899
Longyester *Loth* 76 NT5465
Lonmay *Gramp* 95 NK0159
Lonmore *Highld* 90 NG2646
Looe *Cnwll* 4 SX2553
Loose *Kent* 14 TQ7552
Loosley Row *Bucks* 22 SP8100
Lootcherbrae *Gramp* 94 NJ6053
Lopen *Somset* 8 ST4214
Loppington *Shrops* 36 SJ4629
Lords Wood *Kent* 14 TQ7762
Lornty *Tays* 88 NO1746
Loscoe *Derbys* 49 SK4247
Lossiemouth *Gramp* 94 NJ2370
Lostock Gralam *Ches* 47 SJ6974
Lostock Green *Ches* 47 SJ6973
Lostwithiel *Cnwll* 3 SX1059
Lothbeg *Highld* 97 NC9410
Lothersdale *N York* 54 SD9545
Lothmore *Highld* 97 NC9611
Loughborough *Leics* 39 SK5319
Loughor *W Glam* 17 SS5698
Loughton *Bucks* 30 SP8337
Loughton *Essex* 23 TQ4296
Loughton *Shrops* 37 SO6182
Lound *Lincs* 40 TF0618
Lound *Notts* 49 SK6986
Lound *Suffk* 43 TM5099
Lount *Leics* 39 SK3819
Louth *Lincs* 51 TF3287
Love Clough *Lancs* 54 SD8127
Lovedean *Hants* 11 SU6812
Lover *Wilts* 10 SU2120
Loversall *S York* 49 SK5798
Loves Green *Essex* 24 TL6404
Loveston *Dyfed* 16 SN0808
Lovington *Somset* 7 ST5930
Low Ackworth *W York* 55 SE4517
Low Barbeth *D & G* 64 NX0166
Low Bentham *N York* 54 SD6469
Low Biggins *Cumb* 54 SD6477
Low Borrowbridge *Cumb* 59 NY6101
Low Bradfield *S York* 49 SK2691
Low Bradley *N York* 54 SE0048
Low Burnham *Humb* 50 SE7802
Low Catton *Humb* 56 SE7053
Low Crosby *Cumb* 67 NY4459
Low Dinsdale *Dur* 62 NZ3411
Low Eggborough *N York* 56 SE5623
Low Ellington *N York* 61 SE1983
Low Gartachorrans *Cent* 81 NS4685
Low Grantley *N York* 55 SE2370
Low Ham *Somset* 8 ST4329
Low Harrogate *N York* 55 SE2955
Low Hesket *Cumb* 67 NY4646
Low Hill *H & W* 38 SO8473
Low Hutton *N York* 56 SE7667
Low Lorton *Cumb* 58 NY1525
Low Marnham *Notts* 50 SK8069
Low Mill *N York* 62 SE6795
Low Moorsley *T & W* 69 NZ3446
Low Mowthorpe *N York* 56 SE8966
Low Newton *Cumb* 59 SD4082
Low Row *Cumb* 67 NY5863
Low Row *N York* 61 SD9797
Low Salchrie *D & G* 64 NX0365
Low Santon *Humb* 56 SE9412
Low Tharston *Norfk* 43 TM1895
Low Torry *Fife* 83 NT0186
Low Worsall *N York* 62 NZ3909
Low Wray *Cumb* 59 NY3701
Lowdham *Notts* 49 SK6646
Lower Aisholt *Somset* 8 ST2035
Lower Ansty *Dorset* 9 ST7603
Lower Apperley *Gloucs* 28 SO8527
Lower Ashton *Devon* 5 SX8484
Lower Assendon *Oxon* 22 SU7484
Lower Bartle *Lancs* 53 SD4933
Lower Beeding *W Susx* 12 TQ2127
Lower Benefield *Nhants* 40 SP9988
Lower Bentley *H & W* 28 SO9865
Lower Boddington *Nhants* 29 SP4852
Lower Bourne *Surrey* 22 SU8444
Lower Brailes *Warwks* 29 SP3139
Lower Breakish *Highld* 85 NG6723
Lower Broadheath *H & W* 28 SO8157
Lower Bullingham *H & W* 27 SO5138
Lower Burgate *Hants* 10 SU1515
Lower Caldecote *Beds* 31 TL1746
Lower Cam *Gloucs* 20 SO7400
Lower Catesby *Nhants* 29 SP5159
Lower Chapel *Powys* 26 SO0235
Lower Chicksgrove *Wilts* 9 ST7729
Lower Chute *Wilts* 21 SU3153
Lower Clapton *Gt Lon* 23 TQ3485
Lower Clent *H & W* 38 SO9279
Lower Cumberworth *W York* ... 55 SE2209
Lower Dean *Beds* 30 TL0569
Lower Diabaig *Highld* 91 NG7960
Lower Dicker *E Susx* 13 TQ5511
Lower Down *Shrops* 36 SO3484
Lower Dunsforth *N York* 55 SE4464
Lower Egleton *H & W* 27 SO6245
Lower End *Bucks* 30 SP9238
Lower Eythorne *Kent* 15 TR2849
Lower Failand *Avon* 19 ST5173
Lower Farringdon *Hants* 11 SU7035
Lower Feltham *Gt Lon* 22 TQ0971
Lower Froyle *Hants* 22 SU7544
Lower Gabwell *Devon* 5 SX9169
Lower Gledfield *Highld* 96 NH5890
Lower Godney *Somset* 19 ST4742
Lower Gravenhurst *Beds* 30 TL1035
Lower Green *Kent* 13 TQ5640
Lower Green *Kent* 13 TQ6341
Lower Halliford *Surrey* 22 TQ0866
Lower Halstow *Kent* 14 TQ8567
Lower Hamworthy *Dorset* 9 SY9990
Lower Hardres *Kent* 15 TR1553
Lower Hartwell *Bucks* 30 SP7912
Lower Hergest *H & W* 27 SO2755
Lower Heyford *Oxon* 29 SP4824
Lower Irlam *Gt Man* 47 SJ7193
Lower Killeyan *Strath* 70 NR2742
Lower Kinnerton *Ches* 46 SJ3462
Lower Langford *Avon* 19 ST4560
Lower Largo *Fife* 83 NO4102
Lower Leigh *Staffs* 38 SK0135
Lower Loxhore *Devon* 7 SS6137
Lower Lydbrook *Gloucs* 27 SO5916
Lower Lye *H & W* 27 SO4066
Lower Machen *Gwent* 19 ST2288
Lower Middleton
  Cheney *Nhants* 29 SP5041
Lower Moor *W Mids* 28 SO9747
Lower Morton *Avon* 19 ST6491
Lower Nazeing *Essex* 23 TL3906
Lower Penarth *S Glam* 19 ST1869

Lower Penn *Staffs* 38 SO8796
Lower Peover *Ches* 47 SJ7474
Lower Pond Street *Essex* 31 TL4537
Lower Quinton *Warwks* 29 SP1847
Lower Raydon *Suffk* 25 TM0338
Lower Roadwater *Somset* 7 ST0339
Lower Seagry *Wilts* 20 ST9580
Lower Shelton *Beds* 30 SP9942
Lower Shiplake *Oxon* 22 SU7679
Lower Shuckburgh *Warwks* 29 SP4862
Lower Slaughter *Gloucs* 29 SP1622
Lower Standen *Kent* 15 TR2340
Lower Stanton
  St Quintin *Wilts* 20 ST9180
Lower Stoke *Kent* 14 TQ8375
Lower Stone *Gloucs* 20 ST6794
Lower Stow Bedon *Norfk* 42 TL9694
Lower Street *Dorset* 9 SY8399
Lower Street *Norfk* 43 TG2635
Lower Street *Suffk* 33 TM1052
Lower Sundon *Beds* 30 TL0526
Lower Swanwick *Hants* 11 SU4909
Lower Swell *Gloucs* 29 SP1725
Lower Tean *Staffs* 48 SK0138
Lower Town *Devon* 5 SX7172
Lower Town *Dyfed* 16 SM9637
Lower Tysoe *Warwks* 29 SP3445
Lower Upcott *Devon* 5 SX8880
Lower Upham *Hants* 11 SU5219
Lower Vexford *Somset* 8 ST1135
Lower Weare *Somset* 19 ST4053
Lower Westmancote *H & W* 28 SO9337
Lower Whatley *Somset* 20 ST7447
Lower Whitley *Ches* 47 SJ6179
Lower Wield *Hants* 21 SU6340
Lower Willingdon *E Susx* 13 TQ5803
Lower Winchendon *Bucks* 30 SP7312
Lower Woodford *Wilts* 10 SU1235
Lower Wraxhall *Dorset* 9 ST5700
Lowesby *Leics* 40 SK7207
Lowestoft *Suffk* 43 TM5493
Loweswater *Cumb* 58 NY1421
Lowfield Heath *W Susx* 12 TQ2739
Lowick *Nhants* 40 SP9881
Lowick *Nthumb* 77 NU0139
Lowick Green *Cumb* 58 SD2985
Lowsonford *Warwks* 29 SP1868
Lowther *Cumb* 59 NY5323
Lowthorpe *Humb* 57 TA0860
Lowton *Somset* 8 ST1918
Loxbeare *Devon* 7 SS9116
Loxhill *Surrey* 12 TQ0038
Loxhore *Devon* 7 SS6138
Loxhore Cott *Devon* 7 SS6138
Loxley *Warwks* 29 SP2553
Loxton *Avon* 19 ST3755
Loxwood *W Susx* 12 TQ0331
Lubenham *Leics* 40 SP7087
Lucas Green *Surrey* 22 SU9460
Luccombe *Somset* 7 SS9243
Luccombe Village *IOW* 11 SZ5879
Lucker *Nthumb* 77 NU1530
Luckett *Cnwll* 4 SX3873
Lucking Street *Essex* 24 TL8134
Luckington *Wilts* 20 ST8383
Luckwell Bridge *Somset* 7 SS9038
Lucton *H & W* 27 SO4364
Ludborough *Lincs* 51 TF2995
Ludbrook *Devon* 5 SX6654
Ludchurch *Dyfed* 16 SN1411
Luddenden *W York* 55 SE0426
Luddenden Foot *W York* 55 SE0325
Luddesdown *Kent* 14 TQ6666
Luddington *Humb* 56 SE8316
Luddington *Warwks* 28 SP1652
Luddington in the
  Brook *Nhants* 40 TL1083
Ludford *Lincs* 51 TF1989
Ludford *Shrops* 37 SO5174
Ludgershall *Bucks* 29 SP6517
Ludgershall *Wilts* 21 SU2650
Ludgvan *Cnwll* 2 SW5033
Ludham *Norfk* 43 TG3818
Ludlow *Shrops* 37 SO5175
Ludney *Somset* 8 ST3812
Ludwell *Wilts* 9 ST9122
Ludworth *Dur* 62 NZ3641
Luffincott *Devon* 6 SX3394
Luffness *Loth* 83 NT4780
Lugar *Strath* 74 NS5921
Luggate Burn *Loth* 76 NT5974
Luggiebank *Strath* 74 NS7672
Lugton *Strath* 73 NS4152
Lugwardine *H & W* 27 SO5540
Luib *Highld* 84 NG5627
Lulham *H & W* 27 SO4141
Lullington *Derbys* 39 SK2412
Lullington *Somset* 20 ST7851
Lulsgate Bottom *Avon* 19 ST5165
Lulsley *H & W* 28 SO7455
Lumb *Lancs* 54 SD8324
Lumb *W York* 55 SE0221
Lumby *N York* 55 SE4830
Lumloch *Strath* 74 NS6370
Lumphanan *Gramp* 89 NJ5804
Lumphinnans *Fife* 82 NT1792
Lumsden *Gramp* 94 NJ4722
Lunan *Tays* 89 NO6851
Lunanhead *Tays* 89 NO4752
Luncarty *Tays* 82 NO0929
Lund *Humb* 56 SE9647
Lund *N York* 56 SE6532
Lundford Magna *Lincs* 50 TF1989
Lundie *Cent* 81 NN7304
Lundie *Tays* 83 NO2836
Lundin Links *Fife* 83 NO4002
Lunna *Shet* 103 HU4869
Lunsford *Kent* 14 TQ6959
Lunsford's Cross *E Susx* 14 TQ7210
Lunt *Mersyd* 46 SD3402
Luppitt *Devon* 8 ST1606
Lupridge *Devon* 5 SX7153
Lupset *W York* 55 SE3119
Lupton *Cumb* 59 SD5581
Lurgashall *W Susx* 12 SU9326
Lurley *Devon* 7 SS9215
Luscombe *Devon* 5 SX7957
Luss *Strath* 80 NS3692
Lusta *Highld* 90 NG2656
Lustleigh *Devon* 5 SX7881
Luston *H & W* 27 SO4863
Luthermuir *Gramp* 89 NO6568
Luthrie *Fife* 83 NO3319
Luton *Beds* 30 TL0921
Luton *Devon* 5 ST0802
Luton *Devon* 5 SX9076
Luton *Kent* 14 TQ7766
Lutterworth *Leics* 39 SP5484

Lutton *Devon* 5 SX5959
Lutton *Devon* 5 SX6961
Lutton *Lincs* 41 TF4325
Lutton *Nhants* 40 TL1187
Luxborough *Somset* 7 SS9738
Luxulyan *Cnwll* 3 SX0558
Lybster *Highld* 100 ND2435
Lydbury North *Shrops* 36 SO3486
Lydd *Kent* 15 TR0420
Lydden *Kent* 15 TR2645
Lydden *Kent* 15 TR3567
Lyddington *Leics* 40 SP8797
Lyde Green *Hants* 22 SU7057
Lydford *Devon* 4 SX5185
Lydford on Fosse *Somset* 9 ST5630
Lydgate *W York* 54 SD9225
Lydham *Shrops* 36 SO3391
Lydiard Millicent *Wilts* 20 SU0986
Lydiard Tregoze *Wilts* 20 SU1085
Lydiate *Mersyd* 46 SD3604
Lydiate Ash *H & W* 38 SO9775
Lydlinch *Dorset* 9 ST7413
Lydney *Gloucs* 19 SO6303
Lydstep *Dyfed* 16 SS0898
Lye *W Mids* 38 SO9284
Lye Green *E Susx* 13 TQ5134
Lye Green *Warwks* 29 SP1965
Lye's Green *Wilts* 20 ST8146
Lyford *Oxon* 21 SU3994
Lymbridge Green *Kent* 15 TR1244
Lyme *Border* 75 NT2041
Lyme Regis *Dorset* 8 SY3492
Lyminge *Kent* 15 TR1641
Lymington *Hants* 10 SZ3295
Lyminster *W Susx* 12 TQ0204
Lymm *Ches* 47 SJ6887
Lympne *Kent* 15 TR1135
Lympsham *Somset* 19 ST3354
Lympstone *Devon* 5 SX9984
Lynch Green *Norfk* 43 TG1505
Lynchat *Highld* 87 NH7801
Lyndhurst *Hants* 10 SU3008
Lyndon *Leics* 40 SK9004
Lyne *Surrey* 22 TQ0166
Lyne of Skene *Gramp* 95 NJ7610
Lyneal *Shrops* 36 SJ4433
Lyneham *Oxon* 29 SP2720
Lyneham *Wilts* 20 SU0278
Lyness *Ork* 103 ND3094
Lyng *Norfk* 42 TG0617
Lyng *Somset* 8 ST3329
Lynmouth *Devon* 18 SS7249
Lynn of Shenval *Gramp* 94 NJ2129
Lynsted *Kent* 14 TQ9460
Lynton *Devon* 18 SS7249
Lyon's Gate *Dorset* 9 ST6505
Lyonshall *H & W* 27 SO3355
Lytchett Matravers *Dorset* 9 SY9495
Lytchett Minster *Dorset* 9 SY9693
Lyth *Highld* 100 ND2762
Lytham *Lancs* 53 SD3627
Lytham St Anne's *Lancs* 53 SD3427
Lythe *N York* 63 NZ8413
Lythmore *Highld* 100 ND0566

M

Mabe Burnthouse *Cnwll* 2 SW7634
Mabie *D & G* 66 NX9570
Mablethorpe *Lincs* 51 TF5085
Macclesfield *Ches* 48 SJ9173
Macclesfield Forest *Ches* 48 SJ9772
Macduff *Gramp* 95 NJ7064
Macharioch *Strath* 72 NR7309
Machen *M Glam* 19 ST2189
Machire *Strath* 70 NR2164
Machrie *Strath* 72 NR8934
Machrihanish *Strath* 72 NR6320
Machrins *Strath* 70 NR3693
Machynlleth *Powys* 35 SH7400
Machynys *Dyfed* 17 SS5198
Mackworth *Derbys* 49 SK3137
Macmerry *Loth* 76 NT4372
Maddaford *Devon* 6 SX5494
Madderty *Tays* 82 NN9522
Maddiston *Cent* 75 NS9476
Madeley *Staffs* 47 SJ7744
Madingley *Cambs* 31 TL3960
Madley *H & W* 27 SO4238
Madresfield *H & W* 28 SO8047
Madron *Cnwll* 2 SW4531
Maen-y-groes *Dyfed* 34 SN3858
Maenclochog *Dyfed* 16 SN0827
Maendy *S Glam* 18 ST0076
Maentwrog *Gwynd* 45 SH6640
Maer *Staffs* 37 SJ7938
Maerdy *M Glam* 18 SS9798
Maesbrook *Shrops* 36 SJ3021
Maesbury Marsh *Shrops* 36 SJ3125
Maesllyn *Dyfed* 17 SN3644
Maesteg *M Glam* 18 SS8590
Maesybont *Dyfed* 17 SN5616
Maesycwmmer *M Glam* 19 ST1594
Magdalen Laver *Essex* 23 TL5108
Maggieknockater *Gramp* 94 NJ3145
Maggots End *Essex* 31 TL4827
Magham Down *E Susx* 13 TQ6011
Maghull *Mersyd* 46 SD3703
Magor *Gwent* 19 ST4286
Maiden Bradley *Wilts* 20 ST8038
Maiden Head *Avon* 19 ST5666
Maiden Newton *Dorset* 9 SY5997
Maiden Wells *Dyfed* 16 SR9799
Maidencombe *Devon* 5 SX9268
Maidenhayne *Devon* 8 SY2795
Maidenhead *Berks* 22 SU8980
Maidens *Strath* 73 NS2107
Maidenwell *Lincs* 51 TF3179
Maidford *Nhants* 29 SP6052
Maids Moreton *Bucks* 30 SP7035
Maidstone *Kent* 14 TQ7555
Maidwell *Nhants* 30 SP7476
Mainclee *Gwent* 14 ST3288
Mains of Bainakettle *Gramp* ... 89 NO6274
Mains of Balhall *Tays* 89 NO5163
Mains of Dalvey *Highld* 93 NJ1132
Mains of Haulkerton *Gramp* 89 NO7172
Mainsforth *Dur* 62 NZ3131
Mainsriddle *D & G* 66 NX9456
Mainstone *Shrops* 36 SO2787
Maisemore *Gloucs* 28 SO8121
Makeney *Derbys* 49 SK3544
Malborough *Devon* 5 SX7139

Malden *Surrey* 23 TQ2166
Maldon *Essex* 24 TL8506
Malham *N York* 54 SD9063
Mallaig *Highld* 85 NM6796
Mallaigvaig *Highld* 85 NM6897
Malltraeth *Gwynd* 44 SH4068
Mallwyd *Gwynd* 35 SH8612
Malmesbury *Wilts* 20 ST9387
Malmsmead *Somset* 18 SS7947
Malpas *Ches* 46 SJ4847
Malpas *Cnwll* 3 SW8442
Malpas *Gwent* 19 ST3090
Maltby *Cleve* 62 NZ4613
Maltby *S York* 49 SK5592
Maltby le Marsh *Lincs* 51 TF4681
Malting Green *Essex* 25 TL9701
Maltman's Hill *Kent* 14 TQ9043
Malton *N York* 56 SE7872
Malvern Link *H & W* 28 SO7947
Malvern Wells *H & W* 28 SO7742
Malzie *D & G* 64 NX3754
Mamble *H & W* 37 SO6871
Mamhilad *Gwent* 19 SO3003
Manaccan *Cnwll* 2 SW7624
Manafon *Powys* 36 SJ1102
Manais *W Isls* 102 NG1089
Manaton *Devon* 5 SX7581
Manby *Lincs* 51 TF3986
Mancetter *Warwks* 39 SP3296
Manchester *Gt Man* 47 SJ8497
Mancot *Clwyd* 46 SJ3167
Mandally *Highld* 86 NH2900
Manea *Cambs* 41 TL4789
Maney *W Mids* 38 SP1195
Manfield *N York* 61 NZ2113
Mangotsfield *Avon* 20 ST6676
Mangrove Green *Herts* 30 TL1224
Manish *W Isls* 102 NG1089
Manley *Ches* 46 SJ5071
Manmoel *Gwent* 19 SO1803
Mannel *Strath* 78 NL9840
Manning's Heath *W Susx* 12 TQ2028
Manningford Bohune *Wilts* 20 SU1357
Manningford Bruce *Wilts* 20 SU1358
Manningham *W York* 55 SE1435
Mannington *Dorset* 10 SU0605
Manningtree *Essex* 25 TM1031
Mannofield *Gramp* 89 NJ9104
Manor Park *Gt Lon* 23 TQ4285
Manorbier *Dyfed* 16 SS0697
Manorbier Newton *Dyfed* 16 SN0400
Manorhill *Border* 76 NT6632
Manorowen *Dyfed* 16 SM9336
Mansell Gamage *H & W* 27 SO3944
Mansell Lacy *H & W* 27 SO4245
Mansfield *Notts* 49 SK5361
Mansfield *Strath* 66 NS6214
Mansfield Woodhouse *Notts* 49 SK5363
Manston *Dorset* 9 ST8115
Manston *W York* 55 SE3634
Manswood *Dorset* 9 ST9708
Manthorpe *Lincs* 40 TF0715
Manton *Humb* 50 SE9302
Manton *Leics* 40 SK8704
Manton *Wilts* 21 SU1768
Manuden *Essex* 31 TL4926
Maperton *Somset* 9 ST6726
Maplebeck *Notts* 49 SK7060
Mapledurham *Oxon* 22 SU6976
Mapledurwell *Hants* 22 SU6851
Maplehurst *W Susx* 12 TQ1824
Maplescombe *Kent* 14 TQ5664
Mapleton *Derbys* 48 SK1647
Mapperley *Derbys* 49 SK4342
Mapperley Park *Notts* 49 SK5842
Mapperton *Dorset* 8 SY5099
Mappleborough
  Green *Warwks* 28 SP0866
Mappleton *Humb* 57 TA2243
Mapplewell *S York* 55 SE3210
Mappowder *Dorset* 9 ST7306
Marazanvose *Cnwll* 2 SW7950
Marazion *Cnwll* 2 SW5130
Marbury *Ches* 47 SJ5645
March *Cambs* 41 TL4196
March *Strath* 66 NS9914
Marcham *Oxon* 21 SU4596
Marchamley *Shrops* 37 SJ5929
Marchington *Staffs* 38 SK1330
Marchwiel *Clwyd* 46 SJ3547
Marchwood *Hants* 10 SU3810
Marcross *S Glam* 18 SS9269
Marden *H & W* 27 SO5146
Marden *Kent* 14 TQ7444
Marden *Wilts* 20 SU0857
Marden Thorn *Kent* 14 TQ7642
Mardy *Gwent* 27 SO3015
Mareham le Fen *Lincs* 51 TF2761
Mareham on the Hill *Lincs* 51 TF2867
Marehill *W Susx* 12 TQ0618
Maresfield *E Susx* 13 TQ4624
Marfleet *Humb* 57 TA1429
Marford *Clwyd* 46 SJ3556
Margam *W Glam* 18 SS7887
Margaret Marsh *Dorset* 9 ST8218
Margaretting *Essex* 24 TL6701
Margaretting Tye *Essex* 24 TL6800
Margate *Kent* 15 TR3571
Margnaheglish *Strath* 72 NS0332
Margrie *D & G* 65 NX5950
Margrove Park *Cleve* 62 NZ6515
Marham *Norfk* 42 TF7009
Marhamchurch *Cnwll* 6 SS2203
Marholm *Cambs* 40 TF1401
Mariansleigh *Devon* 7 SS7422
Marine Town *Kent* 14 TQ9274
Marionburgh *Gramp* 89 NJ7006
Marishader *Highld* 90 NG4963
Maristow *Devon* 4 SX4764
Marjoriebanks *D & G* 66 NY0883
Mark *D & G* 64 NX1157
Mark *Somset* 19 ST3847
Mark Cross *E Susx* 13 TQ5010
Mark Cross *E Susx* 13 TQ5831
Markbeech *Kent* 13 TQ4742
Markby *Lincs* 51 TF4878
Market Bosworth *Leics* 39 SK4003
Market Deeping *Lincs* 40 TF1310
Market Drayton *Shrops* 37 SJ6734
Market Harborough *Leics* 40 SP7387
Market Lavington *Wilts* 20 SU0154
Market Overton *Leics* 40 SK8816
Market Rasen *Lincs* 51 TF1089
Market Stainton *Lincs* 51 TF2279
Market Street *Norfk* 43 TG2921
Market Weighton *Humb* 56 SE8741
Market Weston *Suffk* 32 TL9877

Markfield
Minffordd

Markfield Leics 39 SK4809
Markham Gwent 19 SO1601
Markham Moor Notts 49 SK7173
Markinch Fife 83 NO2901
Markington N York 55 SE2865
Marks Tey Essex 24 TL9023
Marksbury Avon 20 ST6662
Markshall Essex 24 TL8425
Markyate Herts 30 TL0616
Marlborough Wilts 21 SU1868
Marlcliff Warwks 28 SP0950
Marldon Devon 5 SX8663
Marlesford Suffk 33 TM3258
Marlingford Norfk 43 TG1309
Marloes Dyfed 16 SM7908
Marlow Bucks 22 SU8486
Marlpit Hill Kent 13 TQ4347
Marnhull Dorset 9 ST7818
Marple Gt Man 48 SJ9588
Marr S York 55 SE5105
Marrick N York 61 SE0798
Marsden T & W 69 NZ3964
Marsden W York 55 SE0411
Marsh Baldon Oxon 21 SU5699
Marsh Gibbon Bucks 29 SP6422
Marsh Green Devon 8 SY0493
Marsh Green Kent 13 TQ4344
Marsh Lane Derbys 49 SK4079
Marsh Street Somset 7 SS9944
Marshalswick Herts 23 TL1608
Marsham Norfk 43 TG1923
Marshborough Kent 15 TR3057
Marshbrook Shrops 36 SO4489
Marshchapel Lincs 51 TF3599
Marshfield Avon 20 ST7873
Marshfield Gwent 19 ST2582
Marshgate Cnwll 4 SX1592
Marshland St James Norfk 41 TF5209
Marshwood Dorset 8 SY3899
Marske N York 61 NZ1000
Marske-by-the-Sea Cleve 62 NZ6322
Marston H & W 27 SO3557
Marston Lincs 50 SK8943
Marston Oxon 29 SP5208
Marston Staffs 38 SJ9227
Marston Wilts 20 ST9656
Marston Green W Mids 38 SP1785
Marston Magna Somset 9 ST5922
Marston Meysey Wilts 20 SU1297
Marston Montgomery Derbys 48 SK1337
Marston Moretaine Beds 30 SP9941
Marston on Dove Derbys 39 SK2329
Marston St Lawrence Nhants 29 SP5341
Marston Stannet H & W 27 SO5655
Marston Trussell Nhants 40 SP6985
Marstow H & W 27 SO5518
Marsworth Bucks 30 SP9114
Marten Wilts 21 SU2860
Marthall Ches 47 SJ7975
Martham Norfk 43 TG4518
Martin Hants 10 SU0619
Martin Kent 15 TR3447
Martin Lincs 50 TF1259
Martin Lincs 51 TF2466
Martin Hussingtree H & W 28 SO8860
Martinhoe Devon 18 SS6648
Martinstown Dorset 9 SY6489
Martlesham Suffk 33 TM2547
Martletwy Dyfed 16 SN0310
Martley H & W 28 SO7560
Martock Somset 8 ST4619
Marton Ches 47 SJ8568
Marton Cleve 62 NZ5115
Marton Humb 57 TA1739
Marton Lincs 50 SK8381
Marton N York 55 SE4162
Marton N York 63 SE7383
Marton Shrops 36 SJ2802
Marton Warwks 29 SP4068
Marton-le-Moor N York 55 SE3770
Martyr Worthy Hants 11 SU5132
Martyr's Green Surrey 22 TQ0857
Marwick Ork 103 HY2324
Marwood Devon 6 SS5437
Mary Tavy Devon 4 SX5079
Marybank Highld 92 NH4853
Maryburgh Highld 92 NH5456
Maryculter Gramp 89 NO8599
Marygold Border 77 NT8159
Maryhill Gramp 95 NJ8245
Maryhill Strath 74 NS5669
Marykirk Gramp 89 NO6865
Marylebone Gt Lon 23 TQ2782
Marylebone Gt Man 47 SD5807
Marypark Gramp 94 NJ1938
Maryport Cumb 58 NY0336
Maryport D & G 64 NX1434
Marystow Devon 4 SX4382
Maryton Tays 89 NO6856
Marywell Gramp 89 NO9399
Marywell Tays 89 NO5895
Marywell Tays 89 NO6544
Masham N York 61 SE2280
Masongill N York 60 SD6675
Mastin Moor Derbys 49 SK4575
Matching Essex 31 TL5212
Matching Green Essex 23 TL5311
Matching Tye Essex 23 TL5111
Matfen Nthumb 68 NZ0371
Matfield Kent 13 TQ6541
Mathern Gwent 19 ST5290
Mathon H & W 28 SO7346
Mathry Dyfed 16 SM8832
Matlaske Norfk 43 TG1534
Matlock Derbys 49 SK3059
Matson Gloucs 28 SO8515
Mattersey Notts 49 SK6889
Mattingley Hants 22 SU7357
Mattishall Norfk 42 TG0511
Mattishall Burgh Norfk 42 TG0512
Mauchline Strath 74 NS4927
Maud Gramp 95 NJ9148
Maufant Jersey 101 JS0000
Maugersbury Gloucs 29 SP2025
Maughold IOM 52 SC4991
Mauld Highld 92 NH4038
Maulden Beds 30 TL0538
Maulds Meaburn Cumb 60 NY6216
Maunby N York 62 SE3586
Maund Bryan H & W 27 SO5650
Maundown Somset 7 ST0628
Mautby Norfk 43 TG4812
Mavesyn Ridware Staffs 38 SK0816
Mavis Enderby Lincs 51 TF3666
Mawbray Cumb 66 NY0846
Mawdesley Lancs 53 SD4914
Mawdlam M Glam 18 SS8081
Mawgan Cnwll 2 SW7025
Mawgan Porth Cnwll 3 SW8567
Mawla Cnwll 2 SW7045
Mawnan Cnwll 2 SW7827
Mawnan Smith Cnwll 2 SW7728
Maxey Cambs 40 TF1208
Maxstoke Warwks 39 SP2386
Maxted Street Kent 15 TR1244
Maxton Border 76 NT6130
Maxton Kent 15 TR3041
Maxwell Town D & G 66 NX9676
Maxworthy Cnwll 4 SX2593
May Bank Staffs 47 SJ8547
Maybole Strath 73 NS2909
Maybury Surrey 22 TQ0159
Mayfield E Susx 13 TQ5826
Mayfield Loth 75 NT3565
Mayfield Staffs 48 SK1545
Mayford Surrey 22 SU9956
Maynard's Green E Susx 13 TQ5818
Maypole Green Norfk 43 TM4195
Maypole Green Suffk 32 TL9159
Meadgate Avon 20 ST6758
Meadle Bucks 22 SP8005
Meadowfield Dur 61 NZ2439
Meadwell Devon 4 SX4081
Mealrigg Cumb 67 NY1345
Meamskirk Strath 74 NS5455
Meanwood W York 55 SE2837
Meare Somset 19 ST4541
Meare Green Somset 8 ST3326
Meare Green Somset 8 ST2922
Mears Ashby Nhants 30 SP8366
Measham Leics 39 SK3311
Meathop Cumb 59 SD4380
Meavy Devon 4 SX5467
Medbourne Leics 40 SP8093
Meden Vale Notts 49 SK5870
Medmenham Berks 22 SU8084
Medomsley Dur 69 NZ1154
Medstead Hants 11 SU6537
Meerbrook Staffs 48 SJ9860
Meesden Herts 31 TL4332
Meeth Devon 6 SS5408
Meeting House Hill Norfk 43 TG3028
Meidrim Dyfed 17 SN2920
Meifod Powys 36 SJ1513
Meigle Tays 88 NO2844
Meikle Carco D & G 66 NS7813
Meikle Earnock Strath 74 NS7053
Meikle Kilmory Strath 72 NS0560
Meikle Obney Tays 82 NO0337
Meikle Wartle Gramp 95 NJ7230
Meikleour Tays 82 NO1539
Meinciau Dyfed 17 SN4610
Meir Staffs 48 SJ9342
Melbourn Cambs 31 TL3844
Melbourne Derbys 39 SK3825
Melbourne Humb 56 SE7543
Melbury Abbas Dorset 9 ST8820
Melbury Bubb Dorset 9 ST5906
Melbury Osmond Dorset 9 ST5707
Melchbourne Beds 30 TL0265
Melcombe Bingham Dorset 9 ST7602
Meldon Devon 5 SX5692
Meldon Nthumb 69 NZ1183
Meldreth Cambs 31 TL3746
Meldrum Cent 81 NS7299
Melfort Strath 79 NM8313
Melgund Castle Tays 89 NO5455
Meliden Clwyd 45 SJ0680
Melin-y-wig Clwyd 45 SJ0448
Melkinthorpe Cumb 59 NY5525
Melkridge Nthumb 68 NY7364
Melksham Wilts 20 ST9063
Melling Lancs 54 SD5970
Melling Mersyd 46 SD3800
Mellis Suffk 33 TM0974
Mellon Charles Highld 91 NG8491
Mellon Udrigle Highld 91 NG8996
Mellor Gt Man 48 SJ9888
Mellor Lancs 54 SD6530
Mellor Brook Lancs 54 SD6431
Mells Somset 20 ST7248
Melmerby Cumb 59 NY6137
Melmerby N York 61 SE0785
Melmerby N York 62 SE3376
Melness Highld 99 NC5861
Melplash Dorset 8 SY4898
Melrose Border 76 NT5434
Melsetter Ork 103 ND2689
Melsonby N York 61 NZ1908
Meltham S York 55 SE1010
Melton Humb 56 SE9726
Melton Suffk 33 TM2850
Melton Constable Norfk 42 TG0432
Melton Mowbray Leics 40 SK7518
Melton Ross Humb 57 TA0610
Melvaig Highld 91 NG7486
Melverley Shrops 36 SJ3316
Melvich Highld 99 NC8764
Membury Devon 8 ST2803
Memsie Gramp 95 NJ9762
Memus Tays 88 NO4259
Menai Bridge Gwynd 44 SH5571
Mendham Suffk 33 TM2782
Mendlesham Suffk 33 TM1065
Mendlesham Green Suffk 33 TM0963
Menheniot Cnwll 4 SX2863
Mennock D & G 66 NS8107
Menston W York 55 SE1643
Menstrie Cent 82 NS8597
Mentmore Bucks 30 SP9019
Meoble Highld 85 NM7987
Meole Brace Shrops 37 SJ4810
Meonstoke Hants 11 SU6119
Meopham Kent 14 TQ6466
Mepal Cambs 41 TL4481
Meppershall Beds 30 TL1336
Mere Ches 47 SJ7281
Mere Wilts 9 ST8132
Mere Brow Lancs 53 SD4218
Mereclough Lancs 54 SD8730
Mereworth Kent 13 TQ6553
Meriden W Mids 39 SP2482
Merkadale Highld 84 NG3931
Merrion Dyfed 16 SR9397
Merriott Somset 8 ST4412
Merrow Surrey 12 TQ0250
Merry Hill Herts 22 TQ1394
Merryhill W Mids 38 SO8897
Merrymeet Cnwll 4 SX2766
Mersham Kent 15 TR0540
Merston W Susx 11 SU8902
Merstone IOW 11 SZ5285
Merther Cnwll 3 SW8644
Merthyr Cynog Powys 26 SN9837
Merthyr Mawr M Glam 18 SS8877
Merthyr Tydfil M Glam 26 SO0406
Merthyr Vale M Glam 18 ST0799
Merton Devon 6 SS5212
Merton Gt Lon 23 TQ2570
Merton Norfk 42 TL9098
Merton Oxon 29 SP5717
Meshaw Devon 7 SS7619
Messing Essex 24 TL8918
Messingham Humb 56 SE8904
Metfield Suffk 33 TM2980
Metherell Cnwll 4 SX4069
Metheringham Lincs 50 TF0661
Methil Fife 83 NT3799
Methilhill Fife 83 NO3500
Methley W York 55 SE3926
Methlick Gramp 95 NJ8537
Methven Tays 82 NO0225
Methwold Norfk 42 TL7394
Methwold Hythe Norfk 42 TL7194
Mettingham Suffk 33 TM3689
Metton Norfk 43 TG2037
Mevagissey Cnwll 3 SX0144
Mexborough S York 49 SE4700
Mey Highld 100 ND2872
Meylltyrn Gwynd 44 SH2332
Meysey Hampton Gloucs 20 SP1100
Miabhig W Isls 102 NB0834
Miavaig W Isls 102 NB0834
Michaelchurch H & W 27 SO5225
Michaelchurch Escley H & W 27 SO3134
Michaelston-le-Pit S Glam 19 ST1572
Michaelstone-y-Fedw Gwent 19 ST2484
Michaelstow Cnwll 3 SX0778
Micheldever Hants 11 SU5139
Micheldever Station Hants 21 SU5143
Michelmersh Hants 10 SU3426
Mickfield Suffk 33 TM1361
Mickle Trafford Ches 46 SJ4469
Micklebring S York 49 SK5194
Mickleby N York 63 NZ8012
Micklefield W York 55 SE4432
Mickleham Surrey 12 TQ1653
Mickleover Derbys 39 SK3033
Mickleton Dur 61 NY9623
Mickleton Gloucs 28 SP1643
Mickletown W York 55 SE4027
Mickley N York 61 SE2576
Mickley Green Suffk 32 TL8457
Mickley Square Nthumb 68 NZ0762
Mid Ardlaw Gramp 95 NJ9463
Mid Beltie Gramp 89 NJ6200
Mid Calder Loth 75 NT0767
Mid Clyth Highld 100 ND2937
Mid Lavant W Susx 11 SU8508
Mid Mains Highld 92 NH4239
Mid Yell Shet 103 HU5190
Midbea Ork 103 HY4444
Middle Aston Oxon 29 SP4726
Middle Barton Oxon 29 SP4325
Middle Chinnock Somset 8 ST4713
Middle Claydon Bucks 30 SP7225
Middle Duntisbourne Gloucs 28 SO9806
Middle Handley Derbys 49 SK4077
Middle Kames Strath 71 NR9189
Middle Mayfield Staffs 48 SK1444
Middle Rasen Lincs 50 TF0889
Middle Rocombe Devon 5 SX9069
Middle Stoke Kent 14 TQ8275
Middle Street Essex 23 TL4005
Middle Town IOS 2 SV8808
Middle Tysoe Warwks 29 SP3444
Middle Wallop Hants 10 SU2937
Middle Winterslow Wilts 10 SU2333
Middle Woodford Wilts 10 SU1136
Middlebie D & G 67 NY2176
Middlebridge Tays 87 NN8866
Middleham N York 61 SE1287
Middlehill Wilts 20 ST8168
Middlehope Shrops 37 SO4988
Middlemarsh Dorset 9 ST6707
Middlesbrough Cleve 62 NZ4919
Middleshaw Cumb 59 SD5588
Middlesmoor N York 61 SE0973
Middlestone Dur 61 NZ2531
Middlestown W York 55 SE2617
Middlethird Border 76 NT6843
Middleton Cleve 62 NZ5233
Middleton Derbys 48 SK1963
Middleton Derbys 49 SK2755
Middleton Essex 32 TL8639
Middleton Gt Man 47 SD8705
Middleton H & W 27 SO5469
Middleton Hants 21 SU4244
Middleton Loth 76 NT3758
Middleton N York 63 SE7885
Middleton Nhants 40 SP8489
Middleton Norfk 42 TF6616
Middleton Nthumb 68 NZ0584
Middleton Shrops 37 SO5477
Middleton Strath 78 NL9443
Middleton Strath 73 NS3952
Middleton Suffk 33 TM4267
Middleton Tays 82 NO1206
Middleton W Glam 17 SS4287
Middleton W York 55 SE1249
Middleton W York 55 SE3028
Middleton Warwks 38 SP1798
Middleton Cheney Nhants 29 SP4941
Middleton Moor Suffk 33 TM4167
Middleton on the Hill H & W 27 SO5364
Middleton One Row Dur 62 NZ3512
Middleton Quernhow N York 62 SE3378
Middleton Scriven Shrops 37 SO6887
Middleton St George Dur 62 NZ3412
Middleton Stoney Oxon 29 SP5323
Middleton Tyas N York 61 NZ2205
Middleton-in-Teesdale Dur 61 NY9425
Middleton-on-Sea W Susx 12 SU9600
Middleton-on-the-Wolds Humb 56 SE9449
Middletown Powys 36 SJ3012
Middlewich Ches 47 SJ7066
Middlewood Cnwll 4 SX2775
Middlewood H & W 27 SO2844
Middlewood Green Suffk 33 TM0961
Middleyard Strath 74 NS5132
Middlezoy Somset 8 ST3733
Midford Avon 20 ST7660
Midgham Berks 21 SU5567
Midgley W York 55 SE0226
Midgley W York 55 SE2714
Midhopestones S York 48 SK2399
Midhurst W Susx 11 SU8821
Midlem Border 76 NT5227
Midpark Strath 72 NS0259
Midsomer Norton Avon 20 ST6654
Midtown Highld 99 NC5861
Midtown Brae Highld 91 NG8284
Migvie Gramp 88 NJ4306
Milborne Port Somset 9 ST6718
Milborne St Andrew Dorset 9 SY8097
Milborne Wick Somset 9 ST6620
Milbourne Nthumb 69 NZ1175
Milbourne Wilts 20 ST9587
Milburn Cumb 60 NY6529
Milbury Heath Avon 20 ST6790
Milby N York 55 SE4067
Milcombe Oxon 29 SP4134
Milden Suffk 32 TL9546
Mildenhall Suffk 32 TL7174
Mildenhall Wilts 21 SU2069
Mile Oak E Susx 12 TQ2407
Mile Town Kent 14 TQ9274
Mileham Norfk 42 TF9119
Miles Hope H & W 27 SO5764
Miles Platting Gt Man 47 SJ8599
Milesmark Fife 82 NT0688
Milfield Nthumb 77 NT9333
Milford Derbys 49 SK3545
Milford Staffs 38 SJ9720
Milford Surrey 12 SU9442
Milford Haven Dyfed 16 SM9005
Milford on Sea Hants 10 SZ2891
Milkwall Gloucs 27 SO5809
Mill Bank W York 55 SE0321
Mill Brow Gt Man 48 SJ9789
Mill End Bucks 22 SU7885
Mill End Herts 31 TL3332
Mill Green Cambs 32 TL6245
Mill Green Essex 24 TL6301
Mill Green Lincs 41 TF2223
Mill Green Suffk 32 TL9542
Mill Green Suffk 32 TL9957
Mill Green Suffk 33 TM1360
Mill Hill Gt Lon 23 TQ2292
Mill Meece Staffs 38 SJ8333
Mill of Drummond Tays 82 NN8315
Mill of Haldane Strath 80 NS3982
Mill Street Suffk 32 TM0672
Millais Jersey 101 JS0000
Milland W Susx 11 SU8328
Millbreck Gramp 95 NK0044
Millbrex Gramp 95 NJ8144
Millbridge Surrey 11 SU8442
Millbrook Beds 30 TL0138
Millbrook Cnwll 4 SX4252
Millbrook Hants 10 SU3813
Millbrook Jersey 101 JS0000
Millbuie Gramp 95 NJ7909
Millburn Strath 73 NS4429
Millcorner E Susx 14 TQ8223
Millcraig Highld 93 NH6571
Milldale Staffs 48 SK1354
Miller's Dale Derbys 48 SK1473
Millerhill Loth 75 NT3269
Millerston Strath 74 NS6467
Millhalf H & W 27 SO2747
Millheugh Strath 74 NS7450
Millhouse Strath 71 NR9570
Millhouse Green S York 55 SE2203
Millhousebridge D & G 67 NY1085
Millhouses S York 49 SK3484
Milliken Park Strath 73 NS4162
Millington Humb 56 SE8351
Millom Cumb 58 SD1780
Millport Strath 73 NS1654
Millthrop Cumb 60 SD6591
Milltimber Gramp 89 NJ8501
Milltown D & G 67 NY3375
Milltown Devon 6 SS5538
Milltown Gramp 94 NJ2609
Milltown Gramp 94 NJ4716
Milltown of Campfield Gramp 89 NJ6500
Milltown of Edinvillie Gramp 94 NJ2640
Milltown of Learney Gramp 89 NJ6303
Milnathort Tays 82 NO1204
Milngavie Strath 74 NS5574
Milnrow Gt Man 54 SD9212
Milnthorpe Cumb 59 SD4981
Milovaig Highld 90 NG1549
Milson Shrops 37 SO6472
Milsted Kent 14 TQ9058
Milston Wilts 20 SU1645
Milton Avon 19 ST3462
Milton Cambs 31 TL4762
Milton Cent 81 NN5001
Milton Cumb 67 NY5560
Milton D & G 64 NX2154
Milton D & G 66 NX8470
Milton Derbys 39 SK3126
Milton Dyfed 16 SN0403
Milton Gramp 94 NJ5163
Milton Highld 100 ND3451
Milton Highld 91 NG7043
Milton Highld 92 NH4930
Milton Highld 92 NH5749
Milton Highld 97 NH7674
Milton Kent 14 TQ6674
Milton Notts 49 SK7173
Milton Oxon 21 SU4892
Milton Somset 8 ST4621
Milton Strath 73 NS3569
Milton Strath 73 NS4274
Milton Tays 88 NO1357
Milton Abbas Dorset 9 ST8002
Milton Abbot Devon 4 SX4079
Milton Bridge Loth 75 NT2562
Milton Bryan Beds 30 SP9730
Milton Clevedon Somset 20 ST6637
Milton Combe Devon 4 SX4866
Milton Damerel Devon 6 SS3810
Milton Ernest Beds 30 TL0156
Milton Green Ches 46 SJ4658
Milton Hill Oxon 21 SU4790
Milton Keynes Bucks 30 SP8537
Milton Lilbourne Wilts 21 SU1960
Milton Malsor Nhants 30 SP7355
Milton Morenish Tays 81 NN6135
Milton of Auchinhove Gramp 89 NJ5503
Milton of Balgonie Fife 83 NO3200
Milton of Buchanan Cent 81 NS4490
Milton of Campsie Strath 74 NS6576
Milton of Leys Highld 93 NH6942
Milton of Tullich Gramp 88 NO3897
Milton on Stour Dorset 9 ST7928
Milton Regis Kent 14 TQ9064
Milton-under-Wychwood Oxon 29 SP2618
Milverton Somset 8 ST1225
Milverton Warwks 29 SP3166
Milwich Staffs 38 SJ9632
Minard Strath 71 NR9796
Minchinhampton Gloucs 20 SO8700
Minehead Somset 7 SS9646
Minera Clwyd 46 SJ2751
Minety Wilts 20 SU0290
Minffordd Gwynd 44 SH5938

Place	Page	Grid
Mingarry Park Highld	79	NM6869
Miningsby Lincs	51	TF3264
Minions Cnwll	4	SX2671
Minishant Strath	73	NS3314
Minllyn Gwynd	35	SH8514
Minnigaff D & G	64	NX4166
Minnonie Gramp	95	NJ7760
Minskip N York	55	SE3864
Minstead Hants	10	SU2811
Minsted W Susx	11	SU8520
Minster Kent	14	TQ9573
Minster Kent	15	TR3064
Minster Lovell Oxon	36	SP3111
Minsterley Shrops	36	SJ3705
Minsterworth Gloucs	28	SO7817
Minterne Magna Dorset	9	ST6504
Minting Lincs	50	TF1873
Mintlaw Gramp	95	NJ9948
Minto Border	76	NT5620
Minton Shrops	36	SO4390
Mirehouse Cumb	58	NX9715
Mirfield W York	55	SE2019
Miserden Gloucs	28	SO9308
Miskin M Glam	18	ST0480
Misson Notts	49	SK6895
Misterton Leics	39	SP5583
Misterton Notts	50	SK7694
Misterton Somset	8	ST4508
Mistley Essex	25	TM1231
Mitcham Gt Lon	23	TQ2768
Mitchel Troy Gwent	27	SO4910
Mitcheldean Gloucs	28	SO6618
Mitchell Cnwll	3	SW8554
Mitchellslacks D & G	66	NX9696
Mitford Nthumb	69	NZ1786
Mithian Cnwll	2	SW7450
Mixbury Oxon	29	SP6033
Mobberley Ches	47	SJ7879
Mobberley Staffs	48	SK0041
Moccas H & W	27	SO3543
Mochdre Powys	36	SO0788
Mochrum D & G	64	NX3446
Mockbeggar Kent	14	TQ7146
Mockerkin Cumb	58	NY0923
Modbury Devon	5	SX6651
Moddershall Staffs	38	SJ9236
Moelfre Clwyd	36	SJ1828
Moelfre Gwynd	44	SH5186
Moffat D & G	66	NT0805
Mogerhanger Beds	30	TL1449
Mol-chlach Highld	84	NG4513
Molash Kent	15	TR0251
Mold Clwyd	46	SJ2363
Moldgreen W York	55	SE1516
Molehill Green Essex	24	TL5624
Molescroft Humb	56	TA0140
Molesworth Cambs	30	TL0775
Molland Devon	7	SS8028
Mollington Ches	46	SJ3870
Mollington Oxon	29	SP4447
Mollinsburn Strath	74	NS7171
Mondynes Gramp	89	NO7779
Monewden Suffk	33	TM2358
Moneydie Tays	82	NO0629
Moniaive D & G	66	NX7890
Monifieth Tays	83	NO4932
Monikie Tays	83	NO4938
Monimail Fife	83	NO2914
Monk Fryston N York	55	SE5029
Monk Sherborne Hants	21	SU6056
Monk Soham Suffk	33	TM2165
Monk Street Essex	24	TL6128
Monk's Gate W Susx	12	TQ2027
Monken Hadley Gt Lon	23	TQ2497
Monkhide H & W	27	SO6144
Monkhill Cumb	67	NY3458
Monkhopton Shrops	37	SO6293
Monkland H & W	27	SO4557
Monkleigh Devon	6	SS4520
Monknash S Glam	18	SS9170
Monkokehampton Devon	6	SS5805
Monks Eleigh Suffk	32	TL9647
Monks Heath Ches	47	SJ8474
Monks Horton Kent	14	TQ8356
Monks Kirby Warwks	39	SP4683
Monkseaton T & W	69	NZ3472
Monksilver Somset	10	ST0737
Monksthorpe Lincs	51	TF4465
Monkswood Gwent	19	SO3402
Monkton E Susx	8	ST1803
Monkton Kent	15	TR2964
Monkton Strath	73	NS3527
Monkton T & W	69	NZ3363
Monkton Combe Avon	20	ST7762
Monkton Deverill Wilts	20	ST8537
Monkton Farleigh Wilts	20	ST8065
Monkton Heathfield Somset	8	ST2526
Monkton Wyld Dorset	8	SY3396
Monkwearmouth T & W	69	NZ3958
Monkwood Hants	11	SU6630
Monmore Green W Mids	38	SO9297
Monmouth Gwent	27	SO5012
Monnington on Wye H & W	27	SO3743
Monreith D & G	64	NX3541
Mont Saint Guern	101	GN0000
Montacute Somset	8	ST4916
Montford Shrops	36	SJ4114
Montford Bridge Shrops	36	SJ4215
Montgarrie Gramp	94	NJ5717
Montgarswood Strath	74	NS5227
Montgomery Powys	36	SO2296
Montgreenan Strath	73	NS3343
Montrose Tays	89	NO7157
Monxton Hants	21	SU3144
Monyash Derbys	48	SK1566
Monymusk Gramp	95	NJ6815
Monzie Tays	82	NN8725
Moodiesburn Strath	74	NS6970
Moonzie Fife	83	NO3317
Moor Allerton W York	55	SE3038
Moor Crichel Dorset	9	ST9908
Moor End W York	55	SE0528
Moor Green Herts	31	TL3226
Moor Head W York	55	SE1337
Moor Monkton N York	55	SE5156
Moorby Lincs	51	TF2964
Moordown Dorset	10	SZ0994
Moore Ches	47	SJ5784
Moorends S York	56	SE6915
Moorgreen Notts	49	SK4847
Moorhouse Cumb	67	NY3356
Moorhouse Notts	50	SK7566
Moorhouse Bank Surrey	13	TQ4353
Moorlinch Somset	19	ST3936
Moorsholm Cleve	62	NZ6814
Moorside Dorset	9	ST7919
Moorswater Cnwll	4	SX2364
Moorthorpe W York	55	SE4611

Place	Page	Grid
Moortown Lincs	50	TF0798
Moortown W York	55	SE2939
Morangie Highld	97	NH7683
Morar Highld	85	NM6793
Morborne Cambs	40	TL1391
Morchard Bishop Devon	7	SS7707
Morcombelake Dorset	8	SY4094
Morcott Leics	40	SK9200
Morda Shrops	36	SJ2827
Morden Dorset	9	SY9195
Morden Gt Lon	23	TQ2666
Mordiford H & W	27	SO5737
Mordon Dur	62	NZ3226
More Shrops	36	SO3491
Morebath Devon	7	SS9525
Morebattle Border	76	NT7724
Morecambe Lancs	53	SD4364
Moredon Wilts	20	SU1487
Morefield Highld	96	NH1195
Morehall Kent	15	TR2136
Moreleigh Devon	5	SX7652
Morenish Tays	81	NN6035
Moresby Cumb	58	NX9921
Morestead Hants	11	SU5025
Moreton Dorset	9	SY8089
Moreton Essex	23	TL5307
Moreton H & W	27	SO5064
Moreton Mersyd	46	SJ2689
Moreton Oxon	22	SP6904
Moreton Corbet Shrops	37	SJ5623
Moreton Jeffries H & W	27	SO6048
Moreton Morrell Warwks	29	SP3155
Moreton on Lugg H & W	27	SO5045
Moreton Pinkney Nhants	29	SP5749
Moreton Say Shrops	37	SJ6334
Moreton Valence Gloucs	28	SO7809
Moreton-in-Marsh Gloucs	29	SP2032
Moretonhampstead Devon	5	SX7586
Morfa Nefyn Gwynd	44	SH2840
Morham Loth	76	NT5571
Morland Cumb	59	NY6022
Morley Ches	47	SJ8282
Morley Derbys	49	SK3940
Morley W York	55	SE2627
Morley Green Ches	47	SJ8281
Morley St Botolph Norfk	42	TM0799
Morningside Loth	75	NT2470
Morningside Strath	74	NS8355
Morningthorpe Norfk	33	TM2192
Morpeth Nthumb	69	NZ1986
Morphie Gramp	89	NO7164
Morrey Staffs	38	SK1218
Morriston W Glam	18	SS6697
Morston Norfk	42	TG0043
Mortehoe Devon	6	SS4545
Morthen S York	49	SK4788
Mortimer Berks	21	SU6564
Mortimer West End Hants	21	SU6363
Mortimer's Cross H & W	27	SO4263
Mortlake Gt Lon	23	TQ2075
Morton Cumb	67	NY3854
Morton Derbys	49	SK4060
Morton Lincs	50	SK8091
Morton Lincs	40	TF0923
Morton Norfk	43	TG1216
Morton Notts	49	SK7251
Morton Shrops	36	SJ2924
Morton-on-Swale N York	62	SE3291
Morvah Cnwll	2	SW4035
Morval Cnwll	4	SX2556
Morvich Highld	85	NG9621
Morville Shrops	37	SO6794
Morwenstow Cnwll	6	SS2015
Mosborough S York	49	SK4281
Moscow Strath	73	NS4840
Moseley H & W	28	SO8159
Moseley W Mids	38	SO9498
Moseley W Mids	38	SP0783
Moss S York	56	SE5914
Moss Strath	78	NL9544
Moss Bank Mersyd	46	SJ5197
Moss Edge Lancs	53	SD4243
Moss-side Highld	93	NH8555
Mossat Gramp	94	NJ4719
Mossbank Shet	103	HU4575
Mossbay Cumb	58	NX9927
Mossblown Strath	73	NS4024
Mossburnford Border	76	NT6616
Mossdale D & G	65	NX6670
Mossdale Strath	73	NS4904
Mossend Strath	74	NS7460
Mossgiel Strath	73	NS4828
Mossknowe D & G	67	NY2769
Mossley Gt Man	48	SD9701
Mosspaul Hotel Border	67	NY3999
Mosstodloch Gramp	94	NJ3259
Mossy Lea Lancs	53	SD5312
Mossyard D & G	65	NX5451
Mosterton Dorset	8	ST4505
Moston Gt Man	47	SD8701
Mostyn Clwyd	46	SJ1580
Motcombe Dorset	9	ST8525
Mothecombe Devon	5	SX6047
Motherby Cumb	59	NY4228
Motherwell Strath	74	NS7457
Motspur Park Gt Lon	23	TQ2267
Mottingham Gt Lon	23	TQ4272
Mottisfont Hants	10	SU3226
Mottistone IOW	10	SZ4083
Mottram in Longdendale Gt Man	48	SJ9995
Mottram St Andrew Ches	47	SJ8778
Mouilpied Guern	101	GN0000
Mouldsworth Ches	46	SJ5071
Moulin Tays	87	NN9459
Moulscoomb E Susx	12	TQ3307
Moulsford Oxon	21	SU5883
Moulsoe Bucks	30	SP9141
Moultavie Highld	92	NH6371
Moulton Ches	47	SJ6569
Moulton Lincs	41	TF3023
Moulton N York	61	NZ2303
Moulton Nhants	30	SP7866
Moulton S Glam	18	ST0770
Moulton Suffk	32	TL6964
Moulton Chapel Lincs	41	TF2918
Moulton Seas End Lincs	41	TF3227
Moulton St Mary Norfk	43	TG3907
Mount Cnwll	3	SX1468
Mount Ambrose Cnwll	2	SW7043
Mount Bures Essex	24	TL9032
Mount Hawke Cnwll	2	SW7147
Mount Lothian Loth	75	NT2757
Mount Pleasant Derbys	49	SK3448
Mount Pleasant Suffk	32	TL7347
Mount Tabor W York	55	SE0527
Mountain W York	55	SE0930
Mountain Ash M Glam	18	ST0499
Mountain Cross Border	75	NT1547

Place	Page	Grid
Mountfield E Susx	14	TQ7320
Mountgerald House Highld	92	NH5661
Mountjoy Cnwll	3	SW8760
Mountnessing Essex	24	TQ6297
Mounton Gwent	19	ST5193
Mountsorrel Leics	39	SK5814
Mountstuart Strath	73	NS1159
Mousehill Surrey	12	SU9441
Mousehole Cnwll	2	SW4626
Mouswald D & G	66	NY0672
Mowhaugh Border	76	NT8120
Mowsley Leics	39	SP6489
Mowtie Gramp	89	NO8388
Moy Highld	93	NH7634
Moy Highld	86	NN4282
Moye Highld	85	NG8818
Moylgrove Dyfed	16	SN1144
Muasdale Strath	72	NR6840
Much Birch H & W	27	SO5030
Much Cowarne H & W	27	SO6147
Much Dewchurch H & W	27	SO4831
Much Hadham Herts	31	TL4219
Much Hoole Lancs	53	SD4723
Much Marcle H & W	27	SO6532
Much Wenlock Shrops	37	SO6299
Muchalls Gramp	89	NO9092
Muchelney Somset	8	ST4224
Muchelney Ham Somset	8	ST4423
Muchlarnick Cnwll	4	SX2156
Mucklestone Staffs	37	SJ7237
Muckton Lincs	51	TF3781
Mucomir Highld	86	NN1884
Muddiford Devon	6	SS5638
Muddles Green E Susx	13	TQ5413
Mudeford Dorset	10	SZ1892
Mudford Somset	9	ST5719
Mudford Sock Somset	9	ST5519
Mugdock Cent	74	NS5577
Mugeary Highld	84	NG4439
Mugginton Derbys	49	SK2842
Muggleswick Dur	68	NZ0449
Muir of Fowlis Gramp	94	NJ5612
Muir of Miltonduff Gramp	94	NJ1859
Muir of Ord Highld	92	NH5250
Muir of Thorn Tays	82	NO0637
Muirden Gramp	95	NJ7054
Muirdrum Tays	83	NO5637
Muiresk Gramp	95	NJ6948
Muirhead Fife	83	NO2605
Muirhead Strath	74	NS6869
Muirhead Tays	83	NO3434
Muirhouses Cent	82	NT0180
Muirkirk Strath	74	NS6927
Muirmill Cent	81	NS7283
Muirshearlich Highld	86	NN1380
Muirtack Gramp	95	NJ9937
Muirton Tays	82	NN9211
Muirton Mains Highld	92	NH4553
Muirton of Ardblair Tays	88	NO1643
Muker N York	60	SD9097
Mulbarton Norfk	43	TG1901
Mulben Gramp	94	NJ3550
Mulindry Strath	70	NR3659
Mullion Cnwll	2	SW6719
Mullion Cove Cnwll	2	SW6617
Mumby Lincs	51	TF5174
Muncher's Green Herts	31	TL3126
Munderfield Row H & W	27	SO6651
Munderfield Stocks H & W	27	SO6550
Mundesley Norfk	43	TG3136
Mundford Norfk	42	TL8093
Mundham Norfk	43	TM3397
Mundon Hill Essex	24	TL8602
Mungrisdale Cumb	59	NY3630
Munlochy Highld	92	NH6453
Munnoch Strath	73	NS2548
Munsley H & W	28	SO6640
Munslow Shrops	37	SO5287
Murchington Devon	5	SX6888
Murcott Oxon	29	SP5815
Murkle Highld	100	ND1668
Murlaggan Highld	85	NN0192
Murroes Tays	83	NO4635
Murrow Cambs	41	TF3707
Mursley Bucks	30	SP8128
Murthill Tays	89	NO4657
Murthly Tays	82	NO1038
Murton Cumb	60	NY7221
Murton Dur	69	NZ3847
Murton N York	56	SE6452
Murton Nthumb	77	NT9748
Musbury Devon	8	SY2794
Musselburgh Loth	75	NT3472
Muston Leics	40	SK8237
Muston N York	63	TA0979
Mustow Green H & W	38	SO8774
Muswell Hill Gt Lon	23	TQ2889
Mutehill D & G	65	NX6848
Mutford Suffk	33	TM4888
Muthill Tays	82	NN8717
Mybster Highld	100	ND1652
Myddfai Dyfed	26	SN7730
Myddle Shrops	36	SJ4623
Mydroilyn Dyfed	34	SN4555
Mylor Cnwll	2	SW8135
Mylor Bridge Cnwll	2	SW8036
Mynachlog ddu Dyfed	16	SN1430
Myndtown Shrops	36	SO3989
Mynydd Llandygai Gwynd	44	SH6065
Mynydd-bach Gwent	19	ST4894
Mynydd-bach W Glam	18	SS6597
Myrebird Gramp	89	NO7398
Myredykes Border	67	NY5998
Mytchett Surrey	22	SU8855
Mytholm W York	54	SD9827
Mytholmroyd W York	54	SE0126
Myton-on-Swale N York	55	SE4366

N

Place	Page	Grid
Na Buirgh W Isls	102	NG0394
Naast Highld	91	NG8283
Naburn N York	56	SE5945
Nackington Kent	15	TR1554
Nacton Suffk	33	TM2240
Nafferton Humb	57	TA0559
Nag's Head Gloucs	20	ST8898
Nailbourne Somset	8	ST2128
Nailsea Avon	19	ST4770
Nailstone Leics	39	SK4106
Nailsworth Gloucs	20	ST8499
Nairn Highld	93	NH8856
Nannerch Clwyd	46	SJ1669
Nanpantan Leics	39	SK5017

Place	Page	Grid
Nanpean Cnwll	3	SW9556
Nanstallon Cnwll	3	SX0367
Nant Peris Gwynd	44	SH6058
Nant-y-moel M Glam	18	SS9392
Nanternis Dyfed	34	SN3756
Nantgaredig Dyfed	17	SN4921
Nantglyn Clwyd	45	SJ0061
Nantmel Powys	26	SO0366
Nantmor Gwynd	44	SH6046
Nantwich Ches	47	SJ6552
Naphill Bucks	22	SU8496
Napleton H & W	28	SO8648
Napton on the Hill Warwks	29	SP4661
Narberth Dyfed	16	SN1015
Narborough Leics	39	SP5499
Narborough Norfk	42	TF7412
Nasareth Gwynd	44	SH4749
Naseby Nhants	30	SP6978
Nash Bucks	30	SP7833
Nash Gwent	19	ST3483
Nash Shrops	37	SO6071
Nash's Green Hants	22	SU6745
Nassington Nhants	40	TL0696
Nasty Herts	31	TL3524
Nateby Cumb	60	NY7706
Nateby Lancs	53	SD4644
Natland Cumb	59	SD5289
Naughton Suffk	32	TM0249
Naunton Gloucs	28	SP1123
Naunton H & W	28	SO8645
Naunton H & W	28	SO8739
Naunton Beauchamp H & W	28	SO9652
Navenby Lincs	50	SK9858
Navestock Essex	23	TQ5397
Navestock Side Essex	24	TQ5697
Navidale House Hotel Highld	97	ND0316
Navity Highld	93	NH7864
Nawton N York	62	SE6584
Nayland Suffk	25	TL9734
Nazeing Essex	23	TL4106
Neap Shet	103	HU5058
Near Cotton Staffs	48	SK0646
Near Sawry Cumb	59	SD3795
Neasden Gt Lon	23	TQ2185
Neasham Dur	62	NZ3210
Neath W Glam	18	SS7597
Neatham Hants	11	SU7440
Neatishead Norfk	43	TG3420
Nebo Dyfed	34	SN5465
Nebo Gwynd	44	SH4850
Nebo Gwynd	45	SH8355
Nebo Gwynd	44	SH4690
Necton Norfk	42	TF8709
Nedd Highld	98	NC1331
Nedging Suffk	32	TL9948
Nedging Tye Suffk	32	TM0149
Needham Norfk	33	TM2281
Needham Market Suffk	32	TM0855
Needingworth Cambs	31	TL3472
Neen Savage Shrops	37	SO6677
Neen Sollars Shrops	37	SO6672
Neenton Shrops	37	SO6388
Nefyn Gwynd	44	SH3040
Neilston Strath	73	NS4857
Nelson Lancs	54	SD8638
Nelson M Glam	18	ST1195
Nemphlar Strath	74	NS8544
Nempnett Thrubwell Avon	19	ST5260
Nenthead Cumb	68	NY7743
Nenthorn Border	76	NT6837
Nercwys Clwyd	46	SJ2360
Nereabolls Strath	70	NR2255
Nerston Strath	74	NS6456
Nesbit Nthumb	77	NT9833
Nesfield N York	55	SE0949
Nesscliffe Shrops	36	SJ3819
Neston Ches	46	SJ2977
Neston Wilts	20	ST8668
Netchwood Shrops	37	SO6291
Nether Alderley Ches	47	SJ8476
Nether Blainslie Border	76	NT5443
Nether Broughton Notts	40	SK6925
Nether Cerne Dorset	9	SY6798
Nether Compton Dorset	9	ST5917
Nether Crimond Gramp	95	NJ8222
Nether Dallachy Gramp	94	NJ3563
Nether Exe Devon	7	SS9300
Nether Fingland Strath	66	NS9310
Nether Handwick Tays	88	NO3641
Nether Haugh S York	49	SK4196
Nether Headon Notts	50	SK7477
Nether Heage Derbys	49	SK3650
Nether Heyford Nhants	30	SP6658
Nether Howcleugh Strath	66	NT0312
Nether Kellet Lancs	53	SD5068
Nether Kinmundy Gramp	95	NK0543
Nether Langwith Notts	49	SK5370
Nether Moor Derbys	49	SK3866
Nether Padley Derbys	48	SK2478
Nether Poppleton N York	56	SE5654
Nether Silton N York	62	SE4592
Nether Stowey Somset	19	ST1939
Nether Wallop Hants	10	SU3036
Nether Wasdale Cumb	58	NY1204
Nether Wellwood Strath	74	NS6526
Nether Westcote Oxon	29	SP2220
Nether Whitacre Warwks	39	SP2392
Nether Whitecleuch Strath	74	NS8319
Netheravon Wilts	20	SU1448
Netherbrae Gramp	95	NJ7959
Netherburn Strath	74	NS7947
Netherbury Dorset	8	SY4799
Netherby N York	55	SE3346
Nethercleuch D & G	67	NY1186
Netherend Gloucs	19	SO5900
Netherfield E Susx	14	TQ7019
Netherfield Road E Susx	14	TQ7417
Netherhampton Wilts	10	SU1029
Netherhay Dorset	8	ST4105
Netherlaw D & G	65	NX7444
Netherley Gramp	89	NO8593
Nethermill D & G	66	NY0487
Nethermuir Gramp	95	NJ9044
Netherplace Strath	74	NS5255
Netherseal Derbys	39	SK2812
Netherthong W York	55	SE1309
Netherton Cent	81	NS5579
Netherton Devon	5	SX8971
Netherton Nthumb	68	NT9807
Netherton Tays	89	SO7382
Netherton Tays	88	NO1452
Netherton Tays	89	NO5457
Netherton W Mids	38	SO9488
Netherton W York	55	SE2816
Netherton Cumb	58	NX9907
Nethertown Highld	100	ND3578
Nethertown Staffs	38	SK1017

Netherwitton North Walsham

Netherwitton *Nthumb* 68 NZ0990
Nethy Bridge *Highld* 93 NJ0020
Netley *Hants* 10 SU4508
Netley Marsh *Hants* 10 SU3313
Nettlebed *Oxon* 22 SU6986
Nettlebridge *Somset* 19 ST6448
Nettlecombe *Dorset* 8 SY5195
Nettleden *Herts* 22 TL0110
Nettleham *Lincs* 50 TF0075
Nettlestead *Kent* 14 TQ6852
Nettlestead Green *Kent* 14 TQ6850
Nettlestone *IOW* 11 SZ6290
Nettlesworth *Dur* 69 NZ2547
Nettleton *Lincs* 50 TA1100
Nettleton *Wilts* 20 ST8278
Netton *Wilts* 10 SU1336
Nevern *Dyfed* 16 SN0840
Nevill Holt *Leics* 40 SP8193
New Abbey *D & G* 66 NX9666
New Aberdour *Gramp* 95 NJ8863
New Addington *Gt Lon* 23 TQ3763
New Alresford *Hants* 11 SU5832
New Alyth *Tays* 88 NO2447
New Ash Green *Kent* 14 TQ6065
New Balderton *Notts* 50 SK8152
New Barn *Kent* 14 TQ6169
New Barnet *Gt Lon* 23 TQ2695
New Bewick *Nthumb* 77 NU0620
New Bilton *Warwks* 39 SP4875
New Bolingbroke *Lincs* 51 TF3057
New Boultham *Lincs* 50 SK9670
New Bradwell *Bucks* 30 SP8341
New Brampton *Derbys* 49 SK3771
New Brancepeth *Dur* 61 NZ2241
New Brighton *Mersyd* 46 SJ3093
New Buckenham *Norfk* 32 TM0890
New Byth *Gramp* 95 NJ8254
New Costessey *Norfk* 43 TG1810
New Crofton *W York* 55 SE3817
New Cross *Gt Lon* 23 TQ3676
New Cross *Somset* 8 ST4119
New Cumnock *Strath* 66 NS6213
New Deer *Gramp* 95 NJ8847
New Denham *Bucks* 22 TQ0484
New Duston *Nhants* 30 SP7162
New Earswick *N York* 56 SE6155
New Edlington *S York* 49 SK5398
New Elgin *Gramp* 94 NJ2261
New Ellerby *Humb* 57 TA1639
New Eltham *Gt Lon* 23 TQ4472
New End *H & W* 28 SP0560
New Fletton *Cambs* 40 TL1997
New Galloway *D & G* 65 NX6377
New Gilston *Fife* 83 NO4208
New Grimsby *IOS* 2 SV8815
New Haw *Surrey* 22 TQ0563
New Holkham *Norfk* 42 TF8839
New Holland *Humb* 57 TA0823
New Houghton *Derbys* 49 SK4965
New Houghton *Norfk* 42 TF7927
New Hutton *Cumb* 59 SD5691
New Inn *Dyfed* 17 SN4736
New Inn *Gwent* 19 ST3099
New Invention *Shrops* 36 SO2976
New Kelso *Highld* 91 NG9442
New Lanark *Strath* 74 NS8842
New Langholm *D & G* 67 NY3684
New Leake *Lincs* 51 TF4057
New Leeds *Gramp* 95 NJ9954
New Luce *D & G* 64 NX1764
New Malden *Gt Lon* 23 TQ2168
New Marske *Cleve* 62 NZ6121
New Marston *Oxon* 29 SP5407
New Mill *Cnwll* 2 SW4534
New Mill *Gramp* 89 NO7883
New Mill *W York* 55 SE1609
New Mills *Cnwll* 3 SW8952
New Mills *Derbys* 48 SK0085
New Mills *Powys* 36 SJ0901
New Milton *Hants* 10 SZ2495
New Mistley *Essex* 25 TM1131
New Moat *Dyfed* 16 SN0625
New Ollerton *Notts* 49 SK6667
New Pitsligo *Gramp* 95 NJ8855
New Prestwick *Strath* 73 NS3424
New Quay *Dyfed* 34 SN3959
New Rackheath *Norfk* 43 TG2812
New Radnor *Powys* 27 SO2161
New Ridley *Nthumb* 68 NZ0559
New Romney *Kent* 15 TR0624
New Rossington *S York* 49 SK6198
New Scone *Tays* 82 NO1326
New Sharlston *W York* 55 SE3819
New Silksworth *T & W* 69 NZ3853
New Somerby *Lincs* 40 SK9235
New Stevenston *Strath* 74 NS7659
New Town *Beds* 31 TL1945
New Town *Dorset* 9 ST8318
New Town *Dorset* 9 ST9515
New Town *Dorset* 9 ST9918
New Town *E Susx* 13 TQ4720
New Town *Loth* 76 NT4470
New Town *Somset* 8 ST2712
New Tredegar *M Glam* 18 SO1403
New Trows *Strath* 74 NS8038
New Walsoken *Cambs* 41 TF4609
New Waltham *Humb* 57 TA2804
New Wimpole *Cambs* 31 TL3549
New Winton *Loth* 76 NT4271
New York *Lincs* 51 TF2455
New Zealand *Derbys* 39 SK3336
Newall *W York* 55 SE1946
Newark *D & G* 66 NS7808
Newark *Ork* 103 HY7142
Newark-on-Trent *Notts* 50 SK7953
Newarthill *Strath* 74 NS7859
Newbattle *Loth* 75 NT3365
Newbie *D & G* 67 NY1764
Newbiggin *Cumb* 59 NY4729
Newbiggin *Cumb* 67 NY5549
Newbiggin *Cumb* 60 NY6228
Newbiggin *Dur* 60 NY9127
Newbiggin *N York* 61 SE0086
Newbiggin-by-the-Sea *Nthumb* 69 NZ3087
Newbiggin-on-Lune *Cumb* 60 NY7005
Newbigging *Strath* 75 NT0145
Newbigging *Tays* 88 NO2841
Newbigging *Tays* 83 NO4237
Newbold *Derbys* 49 SK3672
Newbold on Stour *Warwks* 29 SP2446
Newbold Pacey *Warwks* 29 SP2957
Newbold Verdon *Leics* 39 SK4403
Newborough *Cambs* 41 TF2005
Newborough *Gwynd* 44 SH4265
Newborough *Staffs* 38 SK1325
Newbourne *Suffk* 33 TM2743
Newbridge *Cnwll* 2 SW4231
Newbridge *D & G* 66 NX9479
Newbridge *Gwent* 19 ST2097
Newbridge *Hants* 10 SU2915
Newbridge *IOW* 10 SZ4187
Newbridge *Loth* 75 NT1272
Newbridge Green *H & W* 28 SO8439
Newbridge on Wye *Powys* 26 SO0158
Newbrough *Nthumb* 68 NY8767
Newbuildings *Devon* 7 SS7903
Newburgh *Fife* 83 NO2318
Newburgh *Gramp* 95 NJ9659
Newburgh *Gramp* 95 NJ9925
Newburgh *Lancs* 53 SD4810
Newburgh Priory *N York* 62 SE5476
Newburn *T & W* 69 NZ1665
Newbury *Berks* 21 SU4766
Newbury *Somset* 20 ST6949
Newby *Cumb* 59 NY5921
Newby *Lancs* 54 SD8146
Newby *N York* 62 NZ5012
Newby *N York* 54 SD7269
Newby Bridge *Cumb* 59 SD3686
Newby East *Cumb* 67 NY4758
Newby West *Cumb* 67 NY3753
Newby Wiske *N York* 62 SE3687
Newcastle *Gwent* 27 SO4417
Newcastle *Shrops* 36 SO2582
Newcastle Emlyn *Dyfed* 17 SN3040
Newcastle upon Tyne *T & W* 69 NZ2464
Newcastle-under-Lyme *Staffs* 47 SJ8445
Newcastleton *D & G* 67 NY4887
Newchapel *Dyfed* 17 SN2239
Newchapel *Surrey* 12 TQ3641
Newchurch *Gwent* 19 ST4597
Newchurch *IOW* 11 SZ5685
Newchurch *Kent* 15 TR0531
Newchurch *Powys* 27 SO2150
Newchurch *Staffs* 38 SK1423
Newcraighall *Loth* 75 NT3272
Newdigate *Surrey* 12 TQ1942
Newell Green *Berks* 22 SU8770
Newenden *Kent* 14 TQ8327
Newent *Gloucs* 28 SO7225
Newfield *Dur* 61 NZ2033
Newfield *Highld* 97 NH7877
Newgale *Dyfed* 16 SM8522
Newgate Street *Herts* 23 TL3005
Newhall *Ches* 47 SJ6145
Newhaven *E Susx* 13 TQ4401
Newholm *N York* 63 NZ8610
Newhouse *Strath* 74 NS7961
Newick *E Susx* 13 TQ4121
Newington *Kent* 14 TQ8564
Newington *Kent* 15 TR1837
Newington *Oxon* 21 SU6096
Newland *Gloucs* 27 SO5509
Newland *H & W* 28 SO7948
Newland *Humb* 57 TA0631
Newland *N York* 56 SE6824
Newland *Somset* 7 SS8238
Newlandrig *Loth* 76 NT3762
Newlands *Border* 67 NY5094
Newlands *Nthumb* 68 NZ0855
Newlands of Dundurcas *Gramp* 94 NJ2951
Newlyn *Cnwll* 2 SW4628
Newmachar *Gramp* 95 NJ8919
Newmains *Strath* 74 NS8256
Newman's Green *Suffk* 32 TL8843
Newmarket *Cumb* 59 NY3438
Newmarket *Suffk* 32 TL6463
Newmarket *W Isls* 102 NB4235
Newmill *Border* 67 NT4510
Newmill *Gramp* 94 NJ4352
Newmill of Inshewan *Tays* 88 NO4260
Newmillerdam *W York* 55 SE3215
Newmills *Fife* 82 NT0186
Newmills *Gwent* 27 SO5107
Newmills *Loth* 75 NT1667
Newmiln *Tays* 82 NO1230
Newmilns *Strath* 74 NS5337
Newney Green *Essex* 24 TL6507
Newnham *Gloucs* 28 SO6911
Newnham *H & W* 27 SO6469
Newnham *Hants* 22 SU7053
Newnham *Herts* 31 TL2437
Newnham *Kent* 14 TQ9557
Newnham *Nhants* 29 SP5859
Newport *Cnwll* 4 SX3285
Newport *Devon* 6 SS5632
Newport *Dyfed* 16 SN0539
Newport *Essex* 31 TL5234
Newport *Gloucs* 20 ST7097
Newport *Gwent* 19 ST3188
Newport *Highld* 100 ND1324
Newport *Humb* 56 SE8530
Newport *IOW* 11 SZ5089
Newport *Shrops* 37 SJ7419
Newport Pagnell *Bucks* 30 SP8743
Newport-on-Tay *Fife* 83 NO4228
Newquay *Cnwll* 2 SW8161
Newseat *Gramp* 95 NJ7032
Newsham *Lancs* 53 SD5136
Newsham *N York* 61 NZ1010
Newsham *N York* 62 SE3784
Newsham *Nthumb* 69 NZ3080
Newsholme *Humb* 56 SE7129
Newstead *Border* 76 NT5634
Newstead *Notts* 49 SK5152
Newstead *Nthumb* 77 NU1527
Newtack *Gramp* 94 NJ4446
Newthorpe *N York* 55 SE4632
Newton *Beds* 31 TL2344
Newton *Border* 76 NT6020
Newton *Cambs* 41 TF4314
Newton *Cambs* 31 TL4349
Newton *Ches* 46 SJ4167
Newton *Ches* 46 SJ5059
Newton *Cumb* 53 SD2271
Newton *Derbys* 49 SK4459
Newton *Gramp* 94 NJ1663
Newton *Gramp* 94 NJ3362
Newton *H & W* 27 SO3432
Newton *H & W* 27 SO5153
Newton *Highld* 92 NH5850
Newton *Highld* 93 NH7448
Newton *Highld* 93 NH7866
Newton *Lancs* 53 SD4430
Newton *Lancs* 59 SD5974
Newton *Lancs* 54 SD6950
Newton *Lincs* 40 TF0436
Newton *Loth* 75 NT0977
Newton *M Glam* 18 SS8377
Newton *Nhants* 40 SP8883
Newton *Norfk* 42 TF8315
Newton *Notts* 49 SK6841
Newton *Nthumb* 68 NZ0364
Newton *Somset* 18 ST1038
Newton *Staffs* 38 SK0325
Newton *Strath* 80 NS0498
Newton *Strath* 74 NS6760
Newton *Strath* 75 NS9331
Newton *Suffk* 32 TL9240
Newton *Warwks* 39 SP5378
Newton Abbot *Devon* 5 SX8571
Newton Arlosh *Cumb* 67 NY2055
Newton Aycliffe *Dur* 61 NZ2724
Newton Bewley *Cleve* 62 NZ4626
Newton Blossomville *Bucks* 30 SP9251
Newton Bromswold *Beds* 30 SP9966
Newton Burgoland *Leics* 39 SK3708
Newton by Toft *Lincs* 50 TF0487
Newton Ferrers *Cnwll* 4 SX3466
Newton Ferrers *Devon* 5 SX5548
Newton Ferry *W Isls* 102 NF8978
Newton Flotman *Norfk* 43 TM2198
Newton Harcourt *Leics* 39 SP6497
Newton Heath *Gt Man* 47 SD8700
Newton Kyme *N York* 55 SE4644
Newton Longville *Bucks* 30 SP8431
Newton Mearns *Strath* 74 NS5355
Newton Morrell *N York* 61 NZ2309
Newton Mountain *Dyfed* 16 SM9808
Newton of Balcanquhal *Tays* 82 NO1610
Newton on Ouse *N York* 55 SE5159
Newton on Trent *Lincs* 50 SK8373
Newton Poppleford *Devon* 8 SY0889
Newton Purcell *Oxon* 29 SP6230
Newton Regis *Warwks* 39 SK2707
Newton Reigny *Cumb* 59 NY4731
Newton Row *Highld* 100 ND3449
Newton Solney *Derbys* 39 SK2825
Newton St Cyres *Devon* 7 SX8898
Newton St Faith *Norfk* 43 TG2217
Newton St Loe *Avon* 20 ST7064
Newton St Petrock *Devon* 6 SS4112
Newton Stacey *Hants* 21 SU4140
Newton Stewart *D & G* 64 NX4065
Newton Toney *Wilts* 21 SU2140
Newton Tracey *Devon* 6 SS5226
Newton under Roseberry *Cleve* 62 NZ5713
Newton upon Derwent *Humb* 56 SE7149
Newton Valence *Hants* 11 SU7232
Newton Wamphray *D & G* 67 NY1195
Newton-by-the-Sea *Nthumb* 77 NU2325
Newton-le-Willows *Mersyd* 47 SJ5995
Newton-le-Willows *N York* 61 SE2189
Newton-on-the-Moor *Nthumb* 69 NU1705
Newtongarry Croft *Gramp* 94 NJ5735
Newtongrange *Loth* 75 NT3364
Newtonhill *Gramp* 89 NO9193
Newtonloan *Loth* 75 NT3362
Newtonmill *Tays* 89 NO6064
Newtonmore *Highld* 87 NN7098
Newtown *Ches* 47 SJ6247
Newtown *Ches* 48 SJ9060
Newtown *Cumb* 67 NY1048
Newtown *Cumb* 67 NY5062
Newtown *D & G* 66 NS7710
Newtown *Devon* 7 SY0699
Newtown *Devon* 7 SS7625
Newtown *Dorset* 10 SZ0393
Newtown *Gloucs* 20 SO6702
Newtown *Gt Man* 47 SD5604
Newtown *H & W* 27 SO5333
Newtown *H & W* 27 SO6145
Newtown *H & W* 28 SO7037
Newtown *H & W* 28 SO8755
Newtown *Hants* 11 SU6013
Newtown *Highld* 86 NH3504
Newtown *IOW* 10 SZ4290
Newtown *Nthumb* 68 NU0300
Newtown *Nthumb* 77 NU0425
Newtown *Powys* 36 SO1091
Newtown *Shrops* 36 SJ4222
Newtown *Shrops* 37 SJ4731
Newtown *Wilts* 9 ST9129
Newtown Linford *Leics* 39 SK5209
Newtown of Beltrees *Strath* 73 NS3758
Newtown St Boswells *Border* 76 NT5732
Newtyle *Tays* 88 NO2941
Newyork *Strath* 80 NM9611
Neyland *Dyfed* 16 SM9605
Nicholashayne *Devon* 8 ST1016
Nicholaston *W Glam* 17 SS5288
Nidd *N York* 55 SE3060
Nigg *Gramp* 89 NJ9402
Nigg *Highld* 93 NH8071
Nightcott *Devon* 7 SS8925
Nine Elms *Wilts* 20 SU1085
Ninebanks *Nthumb* 68 NY7853
Nineveh *H & W* 27 SO6265
Ninfield *E Susx* 14 TQ7012
Ningwood *IOW* 10 SZ3989
Nisbet *Border* 76 NT6725
Nisbet Hill *Border* 76 NT7950
Niton *IOW* 11 SZ5076
Nitshill *Strath* 74 NS5260
No Man's Heath *Ches* 46 SJ5148
No Man's Heath *Warwks* 39 SK2808
Nocton *Lincs* 50 TF0564
Noke *Oxon* 29 SP5413
Nolton *Dyfed* 16 SM8618
Nolton Haven *Dyfed* 16 SM8618
Nomansland *Devon* 7 SS8313
Nomansland *Wilts* 10 SU2517
Noneley *Shrops* 37 SJ4828
Nonington *Kent* 15 TR2552
Nook *Cumb* 59 SD5481
Norbiton *Gt Lon* 23 TQ1969
Norbury *Ches* 47 SJ5547
Norbury *Derbys* 48 SK1241
Norbury *Gt Lon* 23 TQ3069
Norbury *Shrops* 36 SO3692
Norbury *Staffs* 37 SJ7823
Norchard *H & W* 28 SO8568
Nordelph *Norfk* 41 TF5501
Nordley *Shrops* 37 SO6996
Norham *Nthumb* 77 NT9047
Norland Town *W York* 55 SE0622
Norley *Ches* 47 SJ5772
Norleywood *Hants* 10 SZ3597
Norman's Green *Devon* 7 ST0503
Normanby *Cleve* 62 NZ5418
Normanby *Humb* 56 SE8816
Normanby *Lincs* 50 SK9988
Normanby *N York* 63 SE7381
Normanby le Wold *Lincs* 50 TF1295
Normandy *Surrey* 12 SU9351
Normanton *Derbys* 39 SK3433
Normanton *Leics* 50 SK8140
Normanton *Lincs* 50 SK9446
Normanton *Notts* 49 SK7054
Normanton *W York* 55 SE3822
Normanton le Heath *Leics* 39 SK3712
Normanton on Soar *Notts* 39 SK5122
Normanton on the Wolds *Notts* 39 SK6232
Normanton on Trent *Notts* 50 SK7868
Norney *Surrey* 12 SU9444
North Anston *S York* 49 SK5184
North Aston *Oxon* 29 SP4828
North Baddesley *Hants* 10 SU3920
North Ballachulish *Highld* 86 NN0560
North Barrow *Somset* 9 ST6129
North Barsham *Norfk* 42 TF9135
North Benfleet *Essex* 24 TQ7588
North Bersted *W Susx* 12 SU9201
North Berwick *Loth* 83 NT5485
North Boarhunt *Hants* 11 SU6010
North Bovey *Devon* 5 SX7484
North Bradley *Wilts* 20 ST8555
North Brentor *Devon* 4 SX4881
North Brewham *Somset* 20 ST7236
North Buckland *Devon* 6 SS4840
North Burlingham *Norfk* 43 TG3609
North Cadbury *Somset* 9 ST6327
North Carlton *Lincs* 50 SK9477
North Carlton *Notts* 49 SK5984
North Cave *Humb* 56 SE8932
North Cerney *Gloucs* 28 SP0107
North Charford *Hants* 10 SU1919
North Charlton *Nthumb* 77 NU1622
North Cheam *Gt Lon* 23 TQ2365
North Cheriton *Somset* 9 ST6925
North Chideock *Dorset* 8 SY4294
North Cliffe *Humb* 56 SE8736
North Clifton *Notts* 50 SK8272
North Cockerington *Lincs* 51 TF3790
North Collingham *Notts* 50 SK8362
North Common *E Susx* 13 TQ3921
North Connel *Strath* 79 NM9034
North Cornelly *M Glam* 18 SS8181
North Corry *Highld* 79 NM8353
North Cotes *Lincs* 51 TA3400
North Cove *Suffk* 33 TM4689
North Cowton *N York* 61 NZ2803
North Crawley *Bucks* 30 SP9244
North Creake *Norfk* 42 TF8538
North Curry *Somset* 8 ST3125
North Dalton *Humb* 56 SE9351
North Deighton *N York* 55 SE3951
North Duffield *N York* 56 SE6837
North Duntulm *Highld* 90 NG4274
North Elham *Kent* 15 TR1844
North Elmham *Norfk* 42 TF9820
North Elmsall *W York* 55 SE4712
North End *Essex* 24 TL6618
North End *Hants* 10 SU1016
North End *Hants* 11 SU6502
North End *Nhants* 30 SP9668
North End *W Susx* 12 SU9703
North Erradale *Highld* 91 NG7480
North Evington *Leics* 39 SK6204
North Fambridge *Essex* 24 TQ8597
North Ferriby *Humb* 56 SE9826
North Frodingham *Humb* 57 TA1053
North Gorley *Hants* 10 SU1611
North Green *Suffk* 33 TM3162
North Grimston *N York* 56 SE8467
North Hayling *Hants* 11 SU7303
North Hill *Cnwll* 4 SX2776
North Hillingdon *Gt Lon* 22 TQ0784
North Hinksey *Oxon* 29 SP4905
North Huish *Devon* 5 SX7156
North Hykeham *Lincs* 50 SK9465
North Kelsey *Humb* 50 TA0401
North Kessock *Highld* 93 NH6548
North Killingholme *Humb* 57 TA1417
North Kilvington *N York* 62 SE4285
North Kilworth *Leics* 39 SP6183
North Kyme *Lincs* 50 TF1552
North Landing *Humb* 57 TA2471
North Lee *Bucks* 22 SP8308
North Leigh *Oxon* 29 SP3813
North Leverton with Habblesthorpe *Notts* 50 SK7882
North Lopham *Norfk* 32 TM0382
North Luffenham *Leics* 40 SK9303
North Marden *W Susx* 11 SU8016
North Marston *Bucks* 30 SP7722
North Middleton *Loth* 75 NT3559
North Milmain *D & G* 64 NX0852
North Molton *Devon* 7 SS7329
North Moreton *Oxon* 21 SU5689
North Mundham *W Susx* 11 SU8702
North Muskham *Notts* 50 SK7958
North Newbald *Humb* 56 SE9136
North Newington *Oxon* 29 SP4240
North Newnton *Wilts* 20 SU1257
North Newton *Somset* 8 ST3031
North Nibley *Gloucs* 20 ST7495
North Ormesby *Cleve* 62 NZ5119
North Ormsby *Lincs* 51 TF2893
North Otterington *N York* 62 SE3689
North Owersby *Lincs* 50 TF0594
North Perrott *Somset* 8 ST4709
North Petherton *Somset* 8 ST2833
North Petherwin *Cnwll* 4 SX2789
North Pickenham *Norfk* 42 TF8606
North Piddle *H & W* 28 SO9654
North Pool *Devon* 5 SX7741
North Poorton *Dorset* 8 SY5298
North Quarme *Somset* 7 SS9236
North Queensferry *Fife* 82 NT1380
North Radworthy *Devon* 7 SS7534
North Rauceby *Lincs* 50 TF0246
North Reston *Lincs* 51 TF3883
North Rigton *N York* 55 SE2749
North Rode *Ches* 47 SJ8866
North Runcton *Norfk* 42 TF6416
North Scarle *Lincs* 50 SK8466
North Shian *Strath* 79 NM9143
North Shields *T & W* 69 NZ3568
North Shoebury *Essex* 24 TQ9286
North Shore *Lancs* 53 SD3037
North Side *Cambs* 41 TL2799
North Somercotes *Lincs* 51 TF4296
North Stainley *N York* 61 SE2876
North Stifford *Essex* 24 TQ6080
North Stoke *Avon* 20 ST7069
North Stoke *Oxon* 21 SU6186
North Stoke *W Susx* 12 TQ0110
North Street *Berks* 21 SU6371
North Street *Kent* 15 TR0157
North Sunderland *Nthumb* 77 NU2131
North Tamerton *Cnwll* 6 SX3197
North Tawton *Devon* 7 SS6601
North Third *Cent* 81 NS7589
North Thoresby *Lincs* 51 TF2998
North Tidworth *Wilts* 21 SU2349
North Town *Berks* 22 SU8882
North Town *Devon* 6 SS5109
North Town *Somset* 19 ST5642
North Tuddenham *Norfk* 42 TG0314
North Walsham *Norfk* 43 TG2830

North Waltham *Hants* 21 SU5646
North Warnborough *Hants* 22 SU7351
North Weald Basset *Essex* 23 TL4904
North Wheatley *Notts* 50 SK7585
North Widcombe *Somset* 19 ST5758
North Willingham *Lincs* 50 TF1688
North Wingfield *Derbys* 49 SK4065
North Witham *Lincs* 40 SK9221
North Wootton *Dorset* 9 ST6514
North Wootton *Norfk* 42 TF6424
North Wootton *Somset* 19 ST5641
North Wraxall *Wilts* 20 ST8175
Northall *Bucks* 30 SP9520
Northallerton *N York* 62 SE3694
Northam *Devon* 6 SS4529
Northam *Hants* 10 SU4312
Northampton *H & W* 28 SO8365
Northampton *Nhants* 30 SP7560
Northaw *Herts* 23 TL2702
Northay *Somset* 8 ST2811
Northborough *Cambs* 40 TF1507
Northbourne *Kent* 15 TR3352
Northbrook *Hants* 11 SU5139
Northchapel *W Susx* 12 SU9529
Northchurch *Herts* 22 SP9708
Northcott *Devon* 4 SX3392
Northcourt *Oxon* 21 SU4998
Northdown *Kent* 15 TR3770
Northend *Warwks* 29 SP3952
Northenden *Gt Man* 47 SJ8289
Northfield *Gramp* 95 NJ9008
Northfield *Humb* 56 TA0326
Northfield *W Mids* 38 SP0279
Northfields *Lincs* 40 TF0208
Northfleet *Kent* 14 TQ6374
Northiam *E Susx* 14 TQ8324
Northill *Beds* 30 TL1446
Northington *Hants* 11 SU5637
Northlands *Lincs* 51 TF3453
Northleach *Gloucs* 28 SP1118
Northleigh *Devon* 8 SY1995
Northlew *Devon* 6 SX5099
Northmoor *Oxon* 21 SP4202
Northmuir *Tays* 88 NO3854
Northney *Hants* 11 SU7303
Northolt *Gt Lon* 22 TQ1384
Northop *Clwyd* 46 SJ2468
Northop Hall *Clwyd* 46 SJ2667
Northorpe *Lincs* 50 SK8997
Northorpe *Lincs* 41 TF2036
Northowram *W York* 55 SE1126
Northport *Dorset* 9 SY9288
Northrepps *Norfk* 43 TG2439
Northton *W Isls* 102 NF9989
Northway *Somset* 8 ST1329
Northwich *Ches* 47 SJ6673
Northwick *H & W* 28 SO8458
Northwold *Norfk* 42 TL7597
Northwood *Gt Lon* 22 TQ0990
Northwood *IOW* 11 SZ4992
Northwood *Shrops* 36 SJ4633
Northwood End *Beds* 30 TL0941
Northwood Green *Gloucs* 28 SO7216
Norton *Cleve* 62 NZ4421
Norton *E Susx* 13 TQ4701
Norton *Gloucs* 28 SO8524
Norton *H & W* 28 SO8751
Norton *H & W* 28 SP0447
Norton *N York* 56 SE7971
Norton *Nhants* 29 SP5963
Norton *Notts* 49 SK5771
Norton *Powys* 27 SO3067
Norton *S York* 56 SE5415
Norton *Shrops* 37 SJ7200
Norton *Suffk* 32 TL9565
Norton *W Susx* 12 SU9206
Norton *Wilts* 20 ST8884
Norton Bavant *Wilts* 20 ST9043
Norton Bridge *Staffs* 38 SJ8630
Norton Canes *Staffs* 38 SK0107
Norton Canon *H & W* 27 SO3847
Norton Disney *Lincs* 50 SK8859
Norton Fitzwarren *Somset* 8 ST1925
Norton Green *IOW* 10 SZ3488
Norton Hawkfield *Avon* 19 ST5964
Norton Heath *Essex* 24 TL6004
Norton in Hales *Shrops* 37 SJ7038
Norton Lindsey *Warwks* 29 SP2263
Norton Little Green *Suffk* 32 TL9766
Norton Malreward *Avon* 19 ST6064
Norton St Philip *Somset* 20 ST7755
Norton sub Hamdon *Somset* 8 ST4615
Norton Subcourse *Norfk* 43 TM4198
Norton Wood *H & W* 27 SO3648
Norton-Juxta-Twycross *Leics* 39 SK3207
Norton-le-Clay *N York* 55 SE4071
Norwell *Notts* 50 SK7761
Norwell Woodhouse *Notts* 50 SK7362
Norwich *Norfk* 43 TG2308
Norwick *Shet* 103 HP6414
Norwood *Cent* 82 NS8793
Norwood Green *Gt Lon* 22 TQ1378
Norwood Hill *Surrey* 12 TQ2343
Noseley *Leics* 40 SP7398
Noss Mayo *Devon* 5 SX5547
Nosterfield *N York* 61 SE2780
Nostie *Highld* 85 NG8527
Notgrove *Gloucs* 28 SP1020
Nottage *M Glam* 18 SS8177
Notter *Cnwll* 4 SX3960
Nottingham *Notts* 49 SK5739
Notton *W York* 55 SE3413
Notton *Wilts* 20 ST9169
Noutard's Green *H & W* 28 SO8066
Nox *Shrops* 36 SJ4110
Nuffield *Oxon* 22 SU6687
Nun Monkton *N York* 55 SE5057
Nunburnholme *Humb* 56 SE8447
Nuneaton *Warwks* 39 SP3691
Nuneham Courtenay *Oxon* 21 SU5599
Nunhead *Gt Lon* 23 TQ3475
Nunkeeling *Humb* 57 TA1449
Nunney *Somset* 20 ST7345
Nunnington *N York* 62 SE6679
Nunsthorpe *Humb* 57 TA2607
Nunthorpe *Cleve* 62 NZ5314
Nunthorpe *Cleve* 56 SE6050
Nunthorpe Village *Cleve* 62 NZ5413
Nunton *Wilts* 10 SU1526
Nunwick *N York* 62 SE3274
Nursling *Hants* 10 SU3716
Nutbourne *W Susx* 11 SU7705
Nutbourne *W Susx* 12 TQ0753
Nutfield *Surrey* 12 TQ3050
Nuthall *Notts* 49 SK5243
Nuthampstead *Herts* 31 TL4034
Nuthurst *W Susx* 12 TQ1925
Nutley *E Susx* 13 TQ4427

Nybster *Highld* 100 ND3663
Nyetimber *W Susx* 11 SZ8998
Nyewood *W Susx* 11 SU8021
Nymet Rowland *Devon* 7 SS7108
Nymet Tracey *Devon* 7 SS7200
Nympsfield *Gloucs* 20 SO8000
Nyton *W Susx* 12 SU9305

O

Oad Street *Kent* 14 TQ8762
Oadby *Leics* 39 SK6200
Oak Cross *Devon* 6 SX5399
Oakamoor *Staffs* 48 SK0444
Oakbank *Loth* 75 NT0766
Oakdale *Gwent* 19 ST1898
Oake *Somset* 8 ST1525
Oaken *Staffs* 38 SJ8602
Oakenclough *Lancs* 53 SD5447
Oakengates *Shrops* 37 SJ7010
Oakenshaw *Dur* 61 NZ1937
Oakenshaw *W York* 55 SE1727
Oaker Side *Derbys* 49 SK2760
Oakford *Devon* 7 SS9121
Oakford *Dyfed* 34 SN4558
Oakham *Leics* 40 SK8608
Oakhanger *Hants* 11 SU7635
Oakhill *Somset* 19 ST6347
Oakington *Cambs* 31 TL4164
Oakle Street *Gloucs* 28 SO7517
Oakley *Beds* 30 TL0153
Oakley *Bucks* 29 SP6412
Oakley *Fife* 82 NT0289
Oakley *Hants* 21 SU5650
Oakley *Suffk* 33 TM1677
Oakridge *Gloucs* 20 SO9103
Oaksey *Wilts* 20 ST9993
Oakthorpe *Leics* 39 SK3212
Oakwoodhill *Surrey* 12 TQ1337
Oakworth *W York* 55 SE0338
Oare *Kent* 15 TR0063
Oare *Somset* 18 SS7947
Oare *Wilts* 20 SU1563
Oasby *Lincs* 40 TF0039
Oath *Somset* 8 ST3827
Oathlaw *Tays* 89 NO4756
Oatlands Park *Surrey* 22 TQ0865
Oban *Strath* 79 NM8629
Obley *Shrops* 36 SO3377
Obney *Tays* 82 NO0237
Oborne *Dorset* 9 ST6518
Occlestone Green *Ches* 47 SJ6962
Occold *Suffk* 33 TM1570
Occumster *Highld* 100 ND2635
Ochiltree *Strath* 74 NS5021
Ockbrook *Derbys* 39 SK4235
Ockham *Surrey* 22 TQ0756
Ockle *Highld* 79 NM5570
Ockley *Surrey* 12 TQ1440
Ocle Pychard *H & W* 27 SO5945
Odcombe *Somset* 8 ST5015
Odd Down *Avon* 20 ST7462
Oddingley *H & W* 28 SO9159
Oddington *Gloucs* 29 SP2225
Oddington *Oxon* 29 SP5515
Odell *Beds* 30 SP9657
Odiham *Hants* 22 SU7451
Odsal *W York* 55 SE1529
Odsey *Herts* 31 TL2938
Odstock *Wilts* 10 SU1426
Odstone *Leics* 39 SK3907
Offchurch *Warwks* 29 SP3565
Offenham *H & W* 28 SP0546
Offham *E Susx* 13 TQ4012
Offham *Kent* 14 TQ6557
Offham *W Susx* 12 TQ0208
Offord Cluny *Cambs* 31 TL2267
Offord Darcy *Cambs* 31 TL2266
Offton *Suffk* 32 TM0649
Offwell *Devon* 8 SY1999
Ogbourne Maizey *Wilts* 21 SU1871
Ogbourne St Andrew *Wilts* 21 SU1872
Ogbourne St George *Wilts* 21 SU2074
Ogle *Nthumb* 69 NZ1378
Oglet *Mersyd* 46 SJ4181
Ogmore *M Glam* 18 SS8876
Ogmore Vale *M Glam* 18 SS9390
Ogmore-by-Sea *M Glam* 18 SS8675
Okeford Fitzpaine *Dorset* 9 ST8010
Okehampton *Devon* 6 SX5995
Old *Nhants* 30 SP7872
Old Aberdeen *Gramp* 95 NJ9407
Old Alresford *Hants* 11 SU5834
Old Auchenbrack *D & G* 65 NX7597
Old Basford *Notts* 49 SK5543
Old Basing *Hants* 22 SU6652
Old Bewick *Nthumb* 77 NU0621
Old Bolingbroke *Lincs* 51 TF3565
Old Bramhope *W York* 55 SE2343
Old Brampton *Derbys* 49 SK3371
Old Bridge of Urr *D & G* 66 NX7767
Old Buckenham *Norfk* 32 TM0691
Old Burghclere *Hants* 21 SU4657
Old Byland *N York* 62 SE5585
Old Church Stoke *Powys* 36 SO2894
Old Clee *Humb* 57 TA2808
Old Cleeve *Somset* 7 ST0441
Old Clipstone *Notts* 49 SK6064
Old Dailly *Strath* 64 NX2299
Old Dalby *Leics* 39 SK6723
Old Deer *Gramp* 95 NJ9747
Old Edington *S York* 49 SK5397
Old Ellerby *Humb* 57 TA1637
Old Felixstowe *Suffk* 25 TM3135
Old Fletton *Cambs* 40 TL1997
Old Forge *H & W* 27 SO5518
Old Grimsby *IOS* 2 SV8915
Old Hall Green *Herts* 31 TL3722
Old Harlow *Essex* 23 TL4711
Old Hill *W Mids* 38 SO9586
Old Hunstanton *Norfk* 42 TF6842
Old Hutton *Cumb* 59 SD5688
Old Kea *Cnwll* 3 SW8441
Old Kilpatrick *Strath* 81 NS4672
Old Knebworth *Herts* 31 TL2320
Old Langho *Lancs* 54 SD7035
Old Leake *Lincs* 51 TF4050
Old Malton *N York* 56 SE7972
Old Micklefield *W York* 55 SE4433
Old Milverton *Warwks* 29 SP2967
Old Newton *Suffk* 32 TM0562
Old Radnor *Powys* 27 SO2558
Old Rayne *Gramp* 95 NJ6728
Old Romney *Kent* 15 TR0325

Old Shoreham *W Susx* 12 TQ2006
Old Shoremore *Highld* 98 NC2058
Old Sodbury *Avon* 20 ST7581
Old Somerby *Lincs* 40 SK9633
Old Stratford *Nhants* 30 SP7741
Old Swinford *W Mids* 38 SO9083
Old Thirsk *N York* 62 SE4382
Old Town *Cumb* 59 SD5982
Old Town *E Susx* 13 TV5999
Old Town *IOS* 2 SV9110
Old Trafford *Gt Man* 47 SJ8196
Old Warden *Beds* 30 TL1343
Old Weston *Cambs* 30 TL0977
Old Wick *Highld* 100 ND3649
Old Windsor *Berks* 22 SU9874
Old Wives Lees *Kent* 15 TR0754
Old Woking *Surrey* 22 TQ0157
Oldany *Highld* 98 NC0932
Oldberrow *Warwks* 28 SP1265
Oldbury *Shrops* 37 SO7791
Oldbury *W Mids* 38 SO9888
Oldbury *Warwks* 39 SP3194
Oldbury on the Hill *Gloucs* 20 ST8188
Oldbury-on-Severn *Avon* 19 ST6092
Oldcastle *Gwent* 27 SO3224
Oldcotes *Notts* 49 SK5888
Oldfield *H & W* 28 SO8464
Oldford *Somset* 20 ST7850
Oldhall Green *Suffk* 32 TL8956
Oldham *Gt Man* 54 SD9204
Oldhamstocks *Loth* 76 NT7470
Oldhurst *Cambs* 31 TL3077
Oldland *Avon* 20 ST6771
Oldmeldrum *Gramp* 95 NJ8127
Oldmill *Cnwll* 4 SX3673
Oldmixon *Avon* 19 ST3358
Oldstead *N York* 62 SE5379
Oldwall *Cumb* 67 NY4761
Oldwalls *W Glam* 17 SS4891
Olive Green *Staffs* 38 SK1118
Oliver *Border* 75 NT0924
Oliver's Battery *Hants* 10 SU4527
Ollaberry *Shet* 103 HU3680
Ollach *Highld* 84 NG5137
Ollerton *Ches* 47 SJ7776
Ollerton *Notts* 49 SK6567
Ollerton *Shrops* 37 SJ6425
Olney *Bucks* 30 SP8951
Olrig House *Highld* 100 ND1866
Olton *W Mids* 38 SP1382
Olveston *Avon* 19 ST6086
Ombersley *H & W* 28 SO8463
Ompton *Notts* 49 SK6865
Onchan *IOM* 52 SC3978
Onecote *Staffs* 48 SK0455
Onibury *Shrops* 36 SO4579
Onich *Highld* 86 NN0261
Onllwyn *W Glam* 18 SN8410
Onneley *Staffs* 37 SJ7542
Onslow Village *Surrey* 12 SU9849
Onston *Ches* 47 SJ5873
Opinan *Highld* 91 NG7472
Orbliston *Gramp* 94 NJ3057
Orbost *Highld* 90 NG2543
Orby *Lincs* 51 TF4967
Orchard Portman *Somset* 8 ST2421
Orcheston *Wilts* 20 SU0545
Orcop *H & W* 27 SO4726
Orcop Hill *H & W* 27 SO4727
Ord *Gramp* 94 NJ6258
Ordhead *Gramp* 94 NJ6610
Ordie *Gramp* 88 NJ4501
Ordiequish *Gramp* 94 NJ3357
Ordley *Nthumb* 68 NY9459
Ordsall *Notts* 49 SK7079
Ore *E Susx* 14 TQ8311
Orford *Ches* 47 SJ6190
Orford *Suffk* 33 TM4250
Organford *Dorset* 9 SY9392
Orlestone *Kent* 15 TR0034
Orleton *H & W* 27 SO4967
Orleton *H & W* 28 SO7067
Orlingbury *Nhants* 30 SP8572
Ormesby *Cleve* 62 NZ5317
Ormesby St Margaret *Norfk* 43 TG4914
Ormesby St Michael *Norfk* 43 TG4714
Ormiscaig *Highld* 91 NG8590
Ormiston *Loth* 76 NT4169
Ormsaigmore *Highld* 79 NM4763
Ormsary *Strath* 71 NR7472
Ormskirk *Lancs* 46 SD4108
Oronsay *Strath* 70 NR3588
Orphir *Ork* 103 HY3404
Orpington *Gt Lon* 23 TQ4666
Orrell *Gt Man* 46 SD5303
Orrell *Mersyd* 46 SJ3496
Orroland *D & G* 65 NX7746
Orsett *Essex* 24 TQ6482
Orslow *Staffs* 37 SJ8015
Orston *Notts* 50 SK7740
Orton *Cumb* 60 NY6208
Orton *Nhants* 40 SP8079
Orton *Staffs* 38 SO8795
Orton Longueville *Cambs* 40 TL1796
Orton Waterville *Cambs* 40 TL1595
Orton-on-the-Hill *Leics* 39 SK3003
Orwell *Cambs* 31 TL3650
Osbaldeston *Lancs* 54 SD6431
Osbaldwick *N York* 56 SE6251
Osbaston *Leics* 39 SK4204
Osbaston *Shrops* 36 SJ3222
Osbournby *Lincs* 40 TF0638
Oscroft *Ches* 46 SJ5060
Osgathorpe *Leics* 39 SK4319
Osgodby *Lincs* 50 TF0792
Osgodby *N York* 56 SE6433
Osgodby *N York* 63 TA0584
Oskaig *Highld* 84 NG5438
Oskamull *Strath* 79 NM4540
Osmaston *Derbys* 48 SK1943
Osmington *Dorset* 9 SY7283
Osmington Mills *Dorset* 9 SY7381
Osmondthorpe *W York* 55 SE3333
Osmotherley *N York* 62 SE4596
Osney *Oxon* 29 SP4906
Ospringe *Kent* 15 TR0060
Ossett *W York* 55 SE2720
Ossington *Notts* 50 SK7564
Oswaldkirk *N York* 62 SE6278
Oswaldtwistle *Lancs* 54 SD7327
Oswestry *Shrops* 36 SJ2929
Otford *Kent* 23 TQ5359
Otham *Kent* 14 TQ7953
Othery *Somset* 8 ST3831
Otley *Suffk* 33 TM2055
Otley *W York* 55 SE2045
Otter Ferry *Strath* 71 NR9384
Otterbourne *Hants* 10 SU4522

Otterburn *N York* 54 SD8857
Otterburn *Nthumb* 68 NY8893
Otterham *Cnwll* 4 SX1690
Otterhampton *Somset* 19 ST2443
Ottershaw *Surrey* 22 TQ0263
Otterswick *Shet* 103 HU5285
Otterton *Devon* 8 SY0684
Ottery *Devon* 4 SX4475
Ottery St Mary *Devon* 8 SY1095
Ottinge *Kent* 15 TR1642
Ottringham *Humb* 57 TA2624
Oughterside *Cumb* 58 NY1140
Oughtibridge *S York* 49 SK3093
Oughtrington *Ches* 47 SJ6987
Oulston *N York* 62 SE5474
Oulton *Cumb* 67 NY2502
Oulton *Norfk* 43 TG1328
Oulton *Staffs* 38 SJ9035
Oulton *Suffk* 33 TM5294
Oulton Broad *Suffk* 33 TM5192
Oulton Street *Norfk* 43 TG1527
Oundle *Nhants* 40 TL0388
Ousdale *Highld* 38 SO8693
Ousby *Cumb* 59 NY6134
Ousden *Suffk* 32 TL7459
Ousefleet *Humb* 56 SE8323
Ouston *Dur* 69 NZ2554
Out Rawcliffe *Lancs* 53 SD4041
Outgate *Cumb* 59 SD3599
Outhgill *Cumb* 60 NY7801
Outhill *Warwks* 28 SP1066
Outlane *W York* 55 SE0817
Outwell *Norfk* 41 TF5103
Outwood *Surrey* 12 TQ3145
Outwoods *Staffs* 37 SJ7817
Ouzlewell Green *W York* 55 SE3326
Over *Cambs* 31 TL3770
Over Compton *Dorset* 9 ST5816
Over Green *Warwks* 38 SP1694
Over Haddon *Derbys* 48 SK2066
Over Kellet *Lancs* 53 SD5169
Over Kiddington *Oxon* 29 SP4021
Over Norton *Oxon* 29 SP3128
Over Silton *N York* 62 SE4493
Over Stenton *Fife* 83 NT2799
Over Stowey *Somset* 19 ST1838
Over Stratton *Somset* 8 ST4315
Over Wallop *Hants* 10 SU2838
Over Whitacre *Warwks* 39 SP2590
Over Worton *Oxon* 29 SP4329
Overbury *H & W* 28 SO9537
Overleigh *Somset* 8 ST4835
Overpool *Ches* 46 SJ3877
Overscaig Hotel *Highld* 96 NC4123
Overseal *Derbys* 38 SK2915
Oversland *Kent* 15 TR0557
Overstone *Nhants* 30 SP7966
Overstrand *Norfk* 43 TG2440
Overthorpe *Nhants* 29 SP4840
Overton *Clwyd* 36 SJ3741
Overton *Gramp* 95 NJ8714
Overton *Hants* 21 SU5149
Overton *Lancs* 53 SD4358
Overton *N York* 56 SE5555
Overton *Shrops* 36 SO5072
Overton *W Glam* 17 SS4685
Overton *W York* 55 SE2516
Overtown *Lancs* 60 SD6275
Overtown *Strath* 74 NS8053
Oving *Bucks* 30 SP7821
Oving *W Susx* 11 SU9004
Ovingdean *E Susx* 12 TQ3503
Ovingham *Nthumb* 68 NZ0863
Ovington *Dur* 61 NZ1314
Ovington *Essex* 32 TL7642
Ovington *Hants* 11 SU5631
Ovington *Norfk* 42 TF9202
Ovington *Nthumb* 68 NZ0663
Ower *Hants* 10 SU3215
Owermoigne *Dorset* 9 SY7685
Owlerton *S York* 49 SK3389
Owlsmoor *Berks* 22 SU8462
Owlswick *Bucks* 22 SP7806
Owmby *Lincs* 57 TA0704
Owmby *Lincs* 50 TF0087
Owslebury *Hants* 11 SU5123
Owston *Leics* 40 SK7707
Owston *S York* 56 SE5511
Owston Ferry *Humb* 56 SE8000
Owstwick *Humb* 57 TA2732
Owthorne *Humb* 57 TA3328
Owthorpe *Notts* 39 SK6733
Oxborough *Norfk* 42 TF7401
Oxbridge *Dorset* 8 SY4797
Oxcombe *Lincs* 51 TF3177
Oxen End *Essex* 24 TL6629
Oxen Park *Cumb* 58 SD3187
Oxenhope *W York* 55 SE0334
Oxenpill *Somset* 8 ST4441
Oxenton *Gloucs* 28 SO9531
Oxenwood *Wilts* 21 SU3058
Oxford *Oxon* 29 SP5106
Oxhey *Herts* 22 TQ1295
Oxhill *Warwks* 29 SP3146
Oxley *W Mids* 38 SJ9001
Oxley Green *Essex* 24 TL9014
Oxley's Green *E Susx* 14 TQ6921
Oxlode *Cambs* 41 TL4886
Oxnam *Border* 76 NT6918
Oxnead *Norfk* 43 TG2224
Oxshott *Surrey* 22 TQ1460
Oxspring *S York* 49 SE2601
Oxted *Surrey* 13 TQ3852
Oxton *Border* 76 NT4953
Oxton *N York* 55 SE5042
Oxton *Notts* 49 SK6351
Oxwich *W Glam* 17 SS4986
Oxwich Green *W Glam* 17 SS4985
Oykel Bridge Hotel *Highld* 96 NC3801
Oyne *Gramp* 95 NJ6725
Oystermouth *W Glam* 17 SS6187

P

Pabail *W Isls* 102 NB5231
Packington *Leics* 39 SK3614
Padanaram *Tays* 88 NO4251
Padbury *Bucks* 30 SP7230
Paddington *Gt Lon* 23 TQ2681
Paddlesworth *Kent* 14 TQ6862
Paddlesworth *Kent* 15 TR1939
Paddock Wood *Kent* 14 TQ6744
Padiham *Lancs* 54 SD7933
Padside *N York* 55 SE1659

Place	Map	Grid
Padstow Cnwll	3	SW9175
Padworth Berks	21	SU6166
Pagham W Susx	11	SZ8897
Paglesham Essex	24	TQ9293
Paignton Devon	5	SX8860
Pailton Warwks	39	SP4781
Painscastle Powys	27	SO1646
Painshawfield Nthumb	68	NZ0560
Painsthorpe Humb	56	SE8158
Painswick Gloucs	28	SO8609
Painter's Forstal Kent	15	TQ9958
Paisley Strath	73	NS4864
Pakefield Suffk	33	TM5390
Pakenham Suffk	32	TL9267
Paley Street Berks	22	SU8776
Palgrave Suffk	33	TM1178
Pallington Dorset	9	SY7891
Palmerston Strath	74	NS5019
Palnackie D & G	66	NX8157
Palnure D & G	65	NX4563
Palterton Derbys	49	SK4768
Pamber End Hants	21	SU6158
Pamber Green Hants	21	SU6159
Pamber Heath Hants	21	SU6162
Pamington Gloucs	28	SO9433
Pamphill Dorset	9	ST9900
Pampisford Cambs	31	TL4948
Panbride Tays	83	NO5635
Pancrasweek Devon	6	SS2905
Pandy Gwent	27	SO3322
Pandy Tudur Clwyd	45	SH8564
Panfield Essex	24	TL7325
Pangbourne Berks	21	SU6376
Pangdean W Susx	12	TQ2911
Pannal N York	55	SE3051
Pannal Ash N York	55	SE2953
Pannanich Wells Hotel Gramp	88	NO4097
Pant Shrops	36	SJ2722
Pant-glas Gwynd	44	SH4747
Pant-glas Shrops	35	SN9874
Pant-y-dwr Powys	46	SJ1964
Pant-y-mwyn Clwyd	46	SJ1675
Pantasaph Clwyd	35	SN7797
Pantglas Powys	50	TF1778
Panton Lincs	43	TG3513
Panxworth Norfk	58	NY1031
Papcastle Cumb	100	ND3851
Papigoe Highld	76	NT5972
Papple Loth	49	SK5451
Papplewick Notts	31	TL2862
Papworth Everard Cambs	31	TL2664
Papworth St Agnes Cambs	3	SX0753
Par Cnwll	53	SD4911
Parbold Lancs	7	ST5736
Parbrook Somset	45	SH8834
Parc Gwynd	19	ST4091
Parc Seymour Gwent	58	NY0924
Pardshaw Cumb	33	TM3060
Parham Suffk	66	NX9091
Park D & G	89	NO7898
Park Gramp	68	NY6861
Park Nthumb	22	SU6988
Park Corner Oxon	11	SU5108
Park Gate Hants	55	SE1841
Park Gate W York	23	TQ1982
Park Royal Gt Lon	27	SO6108
Parkend Gloucs	13	TQ6148
Parkers Green Kent	46	SJ2878
Parkgate Ches	66	NY0288
Parkgate D & G	12	TQ2043
Parkgate Surrey	81	NS4871
Parkhall Strath	6	SS3921
Parkham Devon	95	NJ8914
Parkhill House Gramp	17	SS5489
Parkmill W Glam	69	NZ4248
Parkside Dur	74	NS8058
Parkside Strath	10	SZ0391
Parkstone Dorset	23	TL4308
Parndon Essex	47	SD7001
Parr Bridge Gt Man	7	SS6745
Parracombe Devon	41	TF3708
Parson Drove Cambs	25	TM0226
Parson's Heath Essex	74	NS5467
Partick Strath	47	SJ7191
Partington Gt Man	51	TF4068
Partney Lincs	67	NY2750
Parton Cumb	58	NX9820
Parton Cumb	65	NX6970
Parton D & G	12	TQ1919
Partridge Green W Susx	48	SK1854
Parwich Derbys	30	SP7839
Passenham Nhants	11	SU8234
Passfield Hants	43	TG3234
Paston Norfk	12	TQ3008
Patcham E Susx	12	TQ0806
Patching W Susx	19	ST6082
Patchway Avon	55	SE1565
Pateley Bridge N York	82	NO0711
Path of Condie Tays	83	NT2992
Pathhead Fife	76	NT3964
Pathhead Loth	66	NS6114
Pathhead Strath	73	NS4110
Patna Strath	20	SU0758
Patney Wilts	52	SC2482
Patrick IOM	61	SE2190
Patrick Brompton N York	47	SJ7597
Patricroft Gt Man	57	TA3122
Patrington Humb	15	TR1855
Patrixbourne Kent	59	NY3915
Patterdale Cumb	38	SO8299
Pattingham Staffs	30	SP6754
Pattishall Nhants	24	TL8124
Pattiswick Green Essex	2	SW4627
Paul Cnwll	10	SU1432
Paul's Dene Wilts	30	SP7145
Paulerspury Bucks	57	TA1626
Paull Humb	19	ST6556
Paulton Avon	68	NZ1099
Pauperhaugh Nthumb	30	SP9955
Pavenham Beds	19	ST2942
Pawlett Somset	29	SP1837
Paxford Gloucs	77	NT9353
Paxton Border	8	ST0901
Payhembury Devon	54	SD8251
Paythorne Lancs	13	TQ4101
Peacehaven E Susx	48	SK1179
Peak Forest Derbys	40	TF1606
Peakirk Cambs	85	NM7180
Peanmeanach Highld	12	TQ2633
Pease Pottage W Susx	20	ST7057
Peasedown St John Avon	42	TG0516
Peaseland Green Norfk	21	SU4577
Peasemore Berks	33	TM3569
Peasenhall Suffk	12	TQ0844
Peaslake Surrey	46	SJ5294
Peasley Cross Mersyd	14	TQ8822
Peasmarsh E Susx	83	NO4509
Peat Inn Fife	95	NJ9366
Peathill Gramp		
Peatling Magna Leics	39	SP5992
Peatling Parva Leics	39	SP5889
Pebmarsh Essex	24	TL8533
Pebworth H & W	28	SP1347
Pecket Well W York	54	SD9929
Peckforton Ches	46	SJ5356
Peckham Gt Lon	23	TQ3476
Peckleton Leics	39	SK4701
Pedlinge Kent	15	TR1335
Pedmore W Mids	38	SO9182
Pedwell Somset	19	ST4236
Peebles Border	75	NT2540
Peel IOM	52	SC2483
Peene Kent	15	TR1837
Pegsdon Beds	30	TL1130
Pegswood Nthumb	69	NZ2287
Pegwell Kent	15	TR3664
Peinchorran Highld	84	NG5233
Peinlich Highld	90	NG4158
Pelaw T & W	69	NZ3061
Peldon Essex	25	TL9816
Pelsall W Mids	38	SK0203
Pelton Dur	69	NZ2553
Pelynt Cnwll	4	SX2055
Pemberton Dyfed	17	SN5300
Pemberton Gt Man	47	SD5503
Pembrey Dyfed	17	SN4301
Pembridge H & W	27	SO3958
Pembroke Dyfed	16	SM9801
Pembroke Dock Dyfed	16	SM9603
Pembury Kent	13	TQ6240
Pen Rhiwfawr W Glam	26	SN7410
Pen-bont Rhydybeddau Dyfed	35	SN6783
Pen-ffordd Dyfed	16	SN0722
Pen-rhiw Dyfed	17	SN2440
Pen-twyn Gwent	27	SO5209
Pen-y-bont Clwyd	36	SJ2123
Pen-y-Bont-Fawr Powys	36	SJ0824
Pen-y-bryn Gwynd	17	SN1742
Pen-y-clawdd Gwent	27	SO4507
Pen-y-coedcae M Glam	18	ST0587
Pen-y-cwn Dyfed	16	SM8523
Pen-y-felin Clwyd	46	SJ1569
Pen-y-graig Gwynd	44	SH2033
Pen-y-stryt Clwyd	46	SJ1952
Penallt Gwent	27	SO5210
Penally Dyfed	16	SS1199
Penalt H & W	27	SO5629
Penarth S Glam	19	ST1871
Penbryn Dyfed	17	SN2951
Pencader Dyfed	17	SN4436
Pencaitland Loth	76	NT4468
Pencarnisiog Gwynd	44	SH3573
Pencarreg Dyfed	17	SN5445
Pencelli Powys	26	SO0925
Pencelli Powys	17	SS5495
Penclawdd W Glam	18	SS5595
Pencoed M Glam	17	SS9581
Pencombe H & W	27	SO5952
Pencraig H & W	27	SO5620
Pencraig Powys	36	SJ0426
Pendeen Cnwll	2	SW3834
Penderyn M Glam	18	SN9408
Pendine Dyfed	17	SN2208
Pendlebury Gt Man	47	SD7802
Pendleton Lancs	54	SD7539
Pendock H & W	28	SO7832
Pendoggett Cnwll	3	SX0279
Pendomer Somset	8	ST5210
Pendoylan S Glam	18	ST0576
Penegoes Powys	35	SH7600
Pengam Gwent	19	ST1597
Pengam S Glam	19	ST2177
Penge Gt Lon	23	TQ3570
Pengelly Cnwll	3	SX0783
Pengrugla Cnwll	3	SW9947
Penhallow Cnwll	2	SW7651
Penhalvean Cnwll	2	SW7038
Penhill Wilts	20	SU1588
Penhow Gwent	19	ST4290
Penicuik Loth	75	NT2359
Penifiler Highld	84	NG4841
Peninver Strath	72	NR7524
Penistone S York	55	SE2403
Penkill Strath	64	NX2398
Penkridge Staffs	38	SJ9213
Penlean Cnwll	6	SX2098
Penley Clwyd	36	SJ4040
Penllyn S Glam	18	SS9775
Penmachno Gwynd	45	SH7950
Penmaen Gwent	19	ST1897
Penmaen W Glam	17	SS5288
Penmaenmawr Gwynd	45	SH7276
Penmaenpool Gwynd	35	SH6918
Penmark S Glam	18	ST0568
Penmorfa Gwynd	44	SH5540
Penmynydd Gwynd	44	SH5074
Penn Bucks	22	SU9193
Penn Street Bucks	22	SU9295
Pennal Gwynd	35	SH6900
Pennan Gramp	95	NJ8465
Pennant Powys	35	SN8897
Pennard W Glam	17	SS5688
Pennerley Shrops	36	SO3599
Pennington Cumb	58	SD2677
Pennorth Powys	26	SO1125
Penny Bridge Cumb	58	SD3083
Penny Hill Lincs	41	TF3526
Pennycross Strath	79	NM5025
Pennyghael Strath	79	NM5125
Pennyglen Strath	73	NS2710
Pennymoor Devon	7	SS8611
Penparc Dyfed	17	SN2047
Penperlleni Gwent	27	SO3204
Penpoll Cnwll	3	SX1454
Penponds Cnwll	2	SW6339
Penpont D & G	66	NX8494
Penrhiw-pal Dyfed	17	SN3445
Penrhiwceiber M Glam	18	ST0597
Penrhiwllan Dyfed	17	SN3641
Penrhos Gwent	27	SO4111
Penrhos Gwynd	44	SH3433
Penrhyn Bay Gwynd	45	SH8281
Penrhyncoch Dyfed	35	SN6484
Penrhyndeudraeth Gwynd	45	SH6139
Penrice W Glam	17	SS4987
Penrioch Strath	72	NR8744
Penrith Cumb	59	NY5130
Penrose Cnwll	3	SW8770
Penruddock Cumb	59	NY4227
Penryn Cnwll	2	SW7834
Pensarn Clwyd	45	SH9578
Pensax H & W	28	SO7269
Penselwood Somset	9	ST7531
Pensford Avon	19	ST6263
Pensham H & W	28	SO9444
Penshurst Kent	13	TQ5243
Pensilva Cnwll	4	SX2970
Pentewan Cnwll	3	SX0147
Pentir Gwynd	44	SH5766
Pentire Cnwll	2	SW7861
Pentlow Essex	32	TL8146
Pentney Norfk	42	TF7214
Penton Mewsey Hants	21	SU3247
Pentraeth Gwynd	44	SH5278
Pentre M Glam	18	SS9696
Pentre Shrops	36	SJ3617
Pentre Berw Gwynd	44	SH4772
Pentre Hodrey Shrops	36	SO3277
Pentre Llanrhaeadr Clwyd	46	SJ0863
Pentre Meyrick S Glam	18	SS9675
Pentre-ba^ch Powys	26	SN9132
Pentre-celyn Clwyd	46	SJ1453
Pentre-celyn Powys	35	SH8905
Pentre-chwyth W Glam	18	SS6794
Pentre-cwrt Dyfed	17	SN3838
Pentre-Gwenlais Dyfed	17	SN6016
Pentre-tafarn-y-fedw Gwynd	45	SH8162
Pentrebach M Glam	26	SO0604
Pentredwr Clwyd	46	SJ1946
Pentrefelin Gwynd	44	SH5239
Pentrefoelas Clwyd	45	SH8751
Pentregat Dyfed	17	SN3551
Pentrich Derbys	49	SK3852
Pentridge Hill Dorset	10	SU0317
Pentyrch M Glam	18	ST1081
Penwithick Cnwll	3	SX0256
Penybanc Dyfed	17	SN6123
Penybont Powys	26	SO1164
Penycae Clwyd	46	SJ2745
Penyffordd Clwyd	46	SJ3061
Penygarnedd Powys	36	SJ1023
Penygraig M Glam	18	SS9990
Penygroes Dyfed	17	SN5813
Penygroes Gwynd	44	SH4752
Penysarn Gwynd	44	SH4590
Penywaun M Glam	26	SN9804
Penzance Cnwll	2	SW4730
Peopleton H & W	28	SO9350
Peover Heath Ches	47	SJ7973
Peper Harow Surrey	12	SU9344
Peplow Shrops	37	SJ6224
Pepperstock Beds	30	TL0817
Perceton Strath	73	NS3540
Percie Gramp	89	NO5992
Percyhorner Gramp	95	NJ9665
Perelle Guern	101	GN0000
Periton Somset	7	SS9545
Perivale Gt Lon	23	TQ1682
Perkins Village Devon	5	SY0291
Perlethorpe Notts	49	SK6470
Perranarworthal Cnwll	2	SW7738
Perranporth Cnwll	2	SW7554
Perranuthnoe Cnwll	2	SW5329
Perranwell Cnwll	2	SW7739
Perranzabuloe Cnwll	2	SW7752
Perry Barr W Mids	38	SP0791
Perry Green Wilts	20	ST9689
Pershall Staffs	37	SJ8129
Pershore H & W	28	SO9446
Perth Tays	82	NO1123
Perthy Shrops	36	SJ3633
Perton H & W	27	SO5940
Perton Staffs	38	SO8699
Pertwood Wilts	20	ST8936
Peter Tavy Devon	4	SX5177
Peter's Green Herts	30	TL1419
Peterborough Cambs	40	TL1998
Peterchurch H & W	27	SO3438
Peterculter Gramp	89	NJ8300
Peterhead Gramp	95	NK1246
Peterlee Dur	62	NZ4241
Peters Marland Devon	6	SS4713
Petersfield Hants	11	SU7423
Petersham Gt Lon	23	TQ1873
Peterston-Super-Ely S Glam	18	ST0876
Peterston Wentlooge Gwent	19	ST2679
Peterstow H & W	27	SO5624
Petham Kent	15	TR1251
Petherwin Gate Cnwll	4	SX2889
Petrockstow Devon	6	SS5109
Pett E Susx	14	TQ8714
Pettaugh Suffk	33	TM1659
Petterden Tays	83	NO4240
Pettinain Strath	75	NS9543
Pettistree Suffk	33	TM3055
Petton Devon	7	ST0124
Petts Wood Gt Lon	23	TQ4567
Pettycur Fife	83	NT2686
Pettymuk Gramp	95	NJ9023
Petworth W Susx	12	SU9721
Pevensey E Susx	13	TQ6405
Pewsey Wilts	20	SU1660
Pheasant's Hill Bucks	22	SU7887
Phepson H & W	28	SO9459
Philham Devon	6	SS2522
Philiphaugh Border	76	NT4327
Phillack Cnwll	2	SW5638
Philleigh Cnwll	3	SW8639
Philpot End Essex	24	TL6118
Philpstoun Loth	75	NT0577
Phoenix Green Hants	22	SU7555
Phoines Highld	87	NN7093
Pibsbury Somset	8	ST4426
Pica Cumb	58	NY0222
Pickering N York	63	SE7984
Pickford W Mids	39	SP2881
Pickhill N York	62	SE3483
Picklescott Shrops	36	SO4399
Pickmere Ches	47	SJ6977
Pickney Somset	8	ST1929
Pickup Bank Lancs	54	SD7122
Pickwell Leics	40	SK7811
Pickworth Lincs	40	SK9913
Pickworth Lincs	40	TF0433
Pictillum Gramp	95	NJ7317
Picton Ches	46	SJ4371
Picton N York	62	NZ4107
Piddinghoe E Susx	13	TQ4303
Piddington Nhants	30	SP8054
Piddington Oxon	29	SP6317
Piddlehinton Dorset	9	SY7197
Piddletrenthide Dorset	9	SY7099
Pidley Cambs	31	TL3377
Piercebridge Dur	62	NZ2115
Pierowall Ork	103	HY4348
Pilgrims Hatch Essex	24	TQ5895
Pilham Lincs	50	SK8693
Pillaton Cnwll	4	SX3664
Pillerton Hersey Warwks	29	SP2948
Pillerton Priors Warwks	29	SP2947
Pilley Hants	10	SZ3298
Pilley S York	49	SE3300
Pillgwenlly Gwent	19	ST3186
Pilling Lancs	53	SD4048
Pilning Avon	19	ST5684
Pilsbury Derbys	48	SK1163
Pilsdon Dorset	8	SY4199
Pilsley Derbys	48	SK2371
Pilsley Derbys	49	SK4262
Pilson Green Norfk	43	TG3713
Piltdown E Susx	13	TQ4422
Pilton Devon	6	SS5534
Pilton Leics	40	SK9102
Pilton Nhants	40	TL0284
Pilton Somset	19	ST5941
Pimperne Dorset	9	ST9009
Pin Green Herts	31	TL2525
Pinchbeck Lincs	41	TF2425
Pinhoe Devon	7	SX9694
Pinley Green Warwks	29	SP2066
Pinminnoch Strath	64	NX1993
Pinmore Strath	64	NX2091
Pinn Devon	8	SY1086
Pinner Gt Lon	22	TQ1289
Pinner Green Gt Lon	22	TQ1289
Pinvin H & W	28	SO9549
Pinwherry Strath	64	NX2086
Pinxton Derbys	49	SK4554
Pipe and Lyde H & W	27	SO5043
Pipe Gate Shrops	37	SJ7340
Piperhill Highld	93	NH8650
Pipewell Nhants	40	SP8485
Pirbright Surrey	22	SU9455
Pirnie Border	76	NT6528
Pirnmill Strath	72	NR8744
Pirton H & W	28	SO8847
Pirton Herts	30	TL1431
Pishill Oxon	22	SU7389
Pistyll Gwynd	44	SH3241
Pitagowan Tays	87	NN8165
Pitblae Gramp	95	NJ9864
Pitcairngreen Tays	82	NO0627
Pitcalnie Highld	93	NH8072
Pitcaple Gramp	95	NJ7225
Pitcarity Tays	88	NO3365
Pitch Green Bucks	22	SP7703
Pitch Place Surrey	11	SU8839
Pitchcombe Gloucs	28	SO8508
Pitchcott Bucks	30	SP7720
Pitchford Shrops	37	SJ5303
Pitchroy Gramp	94	NJ1738
Pitcombe Somset	9	ST6732
Pitcox Loth	76	NT6475
Pitfichie Gramp	95	NJ6716
Pitglassie Gramp	95	NJ6943
Pitgrudy Highld	97	NH7991
Pitkennedy Tays	89	NO5454
Pitlessie Fife	83	NO3309
Pitlochry Tays	87	NN9458
Pitmachie Gramp	95	NJ6728
Pitmain Highld	87	NH7400
Pitmedden Gramp	95	NJ8827
Pitmuies Tays	89	NO5649
Pitmunie Gramp	94	NJ6614
Pitney Somset	8	ST4528
Pitroddie Tays	82	NO2125
Pitscottie Fife	83	NO4112
Pitsea Essex	24	TQ7488
Pitsford Nhants	30	SP7567
Pitt Devon	7	ST0316
Pittarrow Gramp	89	NO7274
Pittenweem Fife	83	NO5502
Pitteuchar Fife	83	NT2899
Pittington Dur	69	NZ3244
Pittodrie House Hotel Gramp	95	NJ6924
Pitton Wilts	10	SU2131
Pittulie Gramp	95	NJ9567
Pity Me Dur	69	NZ2645
Pixham Surrey	12	TQ1750
Plains Strath	74	NS7966
Plaish Shrops	37	SO5296
Plaistow Derbys	49	SK3456
Plaistow Gt Lon	23	TQ4082
Plaistow W Susx	12	TQ0030
Platford Hants	10	SU2719
Plas Cymyran Gwynd	44	SH2975
Plastow Green Hants	21	SU5361
Platt Kent	14	TQ6257
Plawsworth Dur	69	NZ2647
Plaxtol Kent	13	TQ6053
Play Hatch Oxon	22	SU7376
Playden E Susx	14	TQ9221
Playford Suffk	33	TM2147
Playing Place Cnwll	2	SW8141
Playley Green Gloucs	28	SO7631
Plealey Shrops	36	SJ4206
Plean Cent	82	NS8386
Pleasance Fife	83	NO2312
Pleasington Lancs	54	SD6426
Pleasley Derbys	49	SK5064
Pleinheaume Guern	101	GN0000
Plemont Jersey	101	JS0000
Plemstall Ches	46	SJ4570
Pleshey Essex	24	TL6614
Plockton Highld	85	NG8033
Ploughfield H & W	27	SO3841
Plowden Shrops	36	SO3887
Ploxgreen Shrops	36	SJ3604
Pluckley Kent	14	TQ9245
Pluckley Thorne Kent	14	TQ9244
Plumbland Cumb	58	NY1539
Plumley Ches	47	SJ7274
Plumpton Cumb	59	NY4937
Plumpton E Susx	12	TQ3613
Plumpton Nhants	29	SP5948
Plumpton End Nhants	30	SP7245
Plumpton Green E Susx	12	TQ3616
Plumstead Gt Lon	23	TQ4478
Plumstead Norfk	43	TG1334
Plumtree Notts	39	SK6132
Plungar Leics	40	SK7634
Plurenden Kent	14	TQ9337
Plush Dorset	9	ST7102
Plwmp Dyfed	17	SN3652
Plymouth Devon	4	SX4754
Plympton Devon	4	SX5456
Plymstock Devon	4	SX5152
Plymtree Devon	7	ST0502
Pockley N York	62	SE6385
Pocklington Humb	56	SE8048
Podimore Somset	8	ST5424
Podington Beds	30	SP9462
Podmore Staffs	37	SJ7835
Pointon Lincs	40	TF1131
Pokesdown Dorset	10	SZ1292
Polbain Highld	91	NB9910
Polbathic Cnwll	4	SX3456
Polbeth Loth	75	NT0264
Pole Elm H & W	28	SO8450
Polebrook Nhants	40	TL0686
Polegate E Susx	13	TQ5804
Polesworth Warwks	39	SK2602
Polglass Highld	91	NC0307
Polgooth Cnwll	3	SW9950

Polgown D & G 66 NS7103
Poling W Susx 12 TQ0404
Poling Corner W Susx 12 TQ0405
Polkerris Cnwll 3 SX0952
Pollington Humb 56 SE6119
Polloch Highld 79 NM7668
Pollokshaws Strath 74 NS5661
Pollokshields Strath 74 NS5763
Polmassick Cnwll 3 SW9745
Polmont Cent 82 NS9378
Polnish Highld 85 NM7582
Polperro Cnwll SX2051
Polruan Cnwll 3 SX1250
Polstead Suffk 25 TL9938
Poltalloch Strath 71 NR8196
Poltimore Devon 7 SX9696
Polton Loth 75 NT2864
Polwarth Border 76 NT7450
Polyphant Cnwll 4 SX2682
Polzeath Cnwll 3 SW9378
Pomathorn Loth 75 NT2459
Ponders End Gt Lon 23 TQ3596
Pondersbridge Cambs 41 TL2692
Ponsanooth Cnwll 2 SW7537
Ponsworthy Devon 5 SX7073
Pont Robert Powys 36 SJ1012
Pont-ar-gothi Dyfed 17 SN5021
Pont-faen Powys 26 SN9934
Pont-Nedd-Fechan Powys 26 SN9007
Pont-rhyd-y-fen W Glam 18 SS7994
Pont-y-pant Gwynd 45 SH7554
Pontac Jersey 101 JS0000
Pontantwn Dyfed 17 SN4412
Pontardawe W Glam 26 SN7204
Pontarddulais W Glam 17 SN5903
Pontarsais Dyfed 17 SN4428
Pontblyddyn Clwyd 46 SJ2760
Pontefract W York 55 SE4521
Ponteland Nthumb 69 NZ1672
Ponterwyd Dyfed 35 SN7481
Pontesbury Shrops 36 SJ3906
Pontesford Shrops 36 SJ4106
Pontfadog Clwyd 36 SJ2338
Pontfaen Dyfed 16 SN0234
Pontgarreg Dyfed 17 SN3353
Ponthenry Dyfed 17 SN4709
Ponthir Gwent 19 ST3292
Ponthirwaun Dyfed 17 SN2645
Pontlliw W Glam 17 SS6199
Pontllanfraith Gwent 19 ST1895
Pontlyfni Gwynd 44 SH4352
Pontnewydd Gwent 19 ST2896
Pontop Dur 69 NZ1453
Pontrhydfendigaid Dyfed 35 SN7366
Pontrhydygroes Dyfed 35 SN7472
Pontrilas H & W 27 SO3927
Ponts Green E Susx 14 TQ6715
Pontshaen Dyfed 17 SN4446
Pontshill H & W 27 SO6421
Pontsticill M Glam 26 SO0511
Pontwelly Dyfed 17 SN4140
Pontyates Dyfed 17 SN4708
Pontyberem Dyfed 17 SN5010
Pontybodkin Clwyd 46 SJ2759
Pontyclun M Glam 18 ST0381
Pontycymer M Glam 18 SS9091
Pontypool Gwent 19 SO2800
Pontypridd M Glam 18 ST0789
Pontywaun Gwent 19 ST2292
Pool Cnwll 2 SW6641
Pool W York 55 SE2445
Pool of Muckhart Cent 82 NO0000
Pool Street Essex 24 TL7636
Poole Dorset 10 SZ0090
Poole Keynes Wilts 20 ST9995
Poolewe Highld 91 NG8580
Pooley Bridge Cumb 59 NY4724
Poolfold Staffs 48 SJ8959
Poolhill Gloucs 28 SO7229
Popham Hants 21 SU5543
Poplar Gt Lon 23 TQ3780
Porchfield IOW 10 SZ4491
Poringland Norfk 43 TG2701
Porkellis Cnwll 2 SW6933
Porlock Somset 7 SS8846
Porlock Weir Somset 18 SS8647
Port Appin Strath 79 NM9045
Port Askaig Strath 70 NR4369
Port Bannatyne Strath 72 NS0767
Port Carlisle Cumb 67 NY2461
Port Charlotte Strath 70 NR2558
Port Driseach Strath 80 NR9973
Port Einon W Glam 17 SS4685
Port Ellen Strath 70 NR3645
Port Elphinstone Gramp 95 NJ7720
Port Erin IOM 52 SC1969
Port Gaverne Cnwll 3 SX0080
Port Glasgow Strath 80 NS3274
Port Henderson Highld 91 NG7573
Port Isaac Cnwll 3 SW9980
Port Logan D & G 64 NX0940
Port Mor Highld 84 NM4279
Port Na Craig Tays 87 NN9357
Port nan Giuran W Isls 102 NB5537
Port nan Long W Isls 102 NF8978
Port Nis W Isls 102 NB5363
Port of Menteith Cent 81 NN5801
Port of Ness W Isls 102 NB5363
Port Quin Cnwll 3 SW9780
Port Ramsay Strath 79 NM8845
Port Soderick IOM 52 SC3472
Port St Mary IOM 52 SC2067
Port Talbot W Glam 18 SS7689
Port Wemyss Strath 70 NR1651
Port William D & G 64 NX3343
Port-an-Eorna Highld 85 NG7732
Portachoillan Strath 71 NR7557
Portavadie Strath 71 NR9369
Portbury Avon 19 ST5075
Portchester Hants 11 SU6105
Portencalzie D & G 64 NX0171
Portencross Strath 73 NS1748
Portesham Dorset 9 SY6085
Portessie Gramp 94 NJ4366
Portfield Gate Dyfed 16 SM9215
Portgate Devon 4 SX4285
Portgordon Gramp 94 NJ3964
Portgower Highld 97 ND0013
Porth Cnwll 3 SW8362
Porth M Glam 18 ST0291
Porth Navas Cnwll 2 SW7527
Porthallow Cnwll 2 SW7923
Porthcawl M Glam 18 SS8177
Porthcothan Cnwll 3 SW8672
Porthcurno Cnwll 2 SW3822
Porthgain Dyfed 16 SM8132
Porthgwarra Cnwll 2 SW3721

Porthkerry S Glam 18 ST0866
Porthleven Cnwll 2 SW6225
Porthmadog Gwynd 44 SH5638
Porthoustock Cnwll 2 SW8021
Porthpean Cnwll 3 SX0250
Porthtowan Cnwll 2 SW6947
Porthyrhyd Dyfed 17 SN5215
Portincaple Strath 80 NS2393
Portinfer Jersey 101 JS0000
Portington Humb 56 SE7831
Portinnisherrich Strath 80 NM9711
Portinscale Cumb 58 NY2523
Portishead Avon 19 ST4675
Portknockie Gramp 94 NJ4868
Portlethen Gramp 89 NO9196
Portling D & G 66 NX8753
Portloe Cnwll 3 SW9339
Portmahomack Highld 97 NH9184
Portmellon Cnwll 3 SX0144
Portnacroish Strath 79 NM9247
Portnaguran W Isls 102 NB5537
Portnahaven Strath 70 NR1652
Portnalong Highld 84 NG3434
Portobello Loth 75 NT3073
Portobello W Mids 38 SO9598
Porton Wilts 10 SU1836
Portpatrick D & G 64 NW9954
Portreath Cnwll 2 SW6545
Portree Highld 90 NG4843
Portscatho Cnwll 3 SW8635
Portsea Hants 11 SU6300
Portskerra Highld 99 NC8765
Portskewett Gwent 19 ST4988
Portslade E Susx 12 TQ2506
Portslade-by-Sea E Susx 12 TQ2605
Portslogan D & G 64 NW9858
Portsmouth Hants 11 SU6400
Portsmouth W York 54 SD9026
Portsonachan Hotel Strath 80 NN0420
Portsoy Gramp 94 NJ5866
Portswood Hants 10 SU4214
Portuairk Highld 79 NM4368
Portway H & W 38 SP0872
Portwrinkle Cnwll 4 SX3553
Portyerrock D & G 65 NX4738
Poslingford Suffk 32 TL7648
Posso Border 75 NT2033
Postbridge Devon 5 SX6579
Postcombe Oxon 22 SP7000
Postling Kent 15 TR1439
Postwick Norfk 43 TG2907
Potarch Gramp 89 NO6097
Potsgrove Beds 30 SP9530
Pott Shrigley Ches 48 SJ9479
Potter Brompton N York 63 SE9777
Potter Heigham Norfk 43 TG4119
Potter's Green Herts 31 TL3520
Potterhanworth Lincs 50 TF0566
Potterhanworth Booths Lincs 50 TF0767
Potterne Wilts 20 ST9958
Potterne Wick Wilts 20 ST9957
Potters Bar Herts 23 TL2401
Potters Crouch Herts 22 TL1105
Potters Marston Leics 39 SP4996
Pottersheath Herts 31 TL2318
Potterspury Nhants 30 SP7543
Potterton Gramp 95 NJ9415
Potto N York 62 NZ4703
Potton Beds 31 TL2249
Poughill Cnwll 6 SS2207
Poughill Devon 7 SS8508
Poulshot Wilts 20 ST9659
Poulton Gloucs 20 SP0901
Poulton-le-Fylde Lancs 53 SD3439
Pound Green E Susx 13 TQ5123
Pound Green Suffk 32 TL7153
Pound Hill W Susx 12 TQ2937
Poundffald W Glam 17 SS5694
Poundon Bucks 29 SP6425
Poundstock Cnwll 5 SX7072
Pouton D & G 65 NX4645
Povey Cross Surrey 12 TQ2642
Powburn Nthumb 77 NU0616
Powderham Devon 5 SX9684
Powerstock Dorset 8 SY5196
Powfoot D & G 67 NY1465
Powhill Cumb 67 NY2355
Powick H & W 28 SO8351
Powmill Tays 82 NT0297
Poxwell Dorset 9 SY7384
Poyle Surrey 22 TQ0376
Poynings W Susx 12 TQ2611
Poyntington Dorset 9 ST6520
Poynton Ches 48 SJ9283
Poynton Green Shrops 37 SJ5618
Poys Street Suffk 33 TM3570
Praa Sands Cnwll 2 SW5828
Pratt's Bottom Gt Lon 23 TQ4762
Praze-an-Beeble Cnwll 2 SW6335
Prees Shrops 37 SJ5533
Prees Green Shrops 37 SJ5531
Preesall Lancs 53 SD3647
Pren-gwyn Dyfed 17 SN4244
Prendwick Nthumb 68 NU0012
Prenteg Gwynd 44 SH5841
Prescot Mersyd 46 SJ4692
Prescott Devon 8 ST0814
Presnerby Tays 88 NO1866
Prestatyn Clwyd 45 SJ0682
Prestbury Ches 48 SJ8976
Prestbury Gloucs 28 SO9723
Presteigne Powys 27 SO3164
Prestleigh Somset 19 ST6340
Preston Border 76 NT7957
Preston Devon 5 SX8574
Preston Devon 5 SX8962
Preston Dorset 9 SY7083
Preston E Susx 12 TQ3106
Preston Gloucs 20 SP0400
Preston Herts 31 TL1824
Preston Humb 57 TA1830
Preston Kent 15 TR0260
Preston Kent 15 TR2460
Preston Lancs 53 SD5329
Preston Leics 40 SK8602
Preston Loth 76 NT5977
Preston Nthumb 77 NU1825
Preston Somset 8 ST0935
Preston Suffk 32 TL9450
Preston Wilts 21 SU2774
Preston Bagot Warwks 29 SP1765
Preston Bissett Bucks 29 SP6529
Preston Bowyer Somset 8 ST1326
Preston Brook Ches 47 SJ5680
Preston Candover Hants 21 SU6041
Preston Capes Nhants 29 SP5754
Preston Green Warwks 28 SP1665

Preston Gubbals Shrops 37 SJ4919
Preston on Stour Warwks 29 SP2049
Preston on the Hill Ches 47 SJ5780
Preston on Wye H & W 27 SO3842
Preston Patrick Cumb 59 SD5483
Preston Plucknett Somset 8 ST5316
Preston upon
the Weald Moors Shrops 37 SJ6815
Preston Wynne H & W 27 SO5546
Preston-under-Scar N York 61 SE0691
Prestonpans Loth 76 NT3874
Prestwich Gt Man 47 SD8104
Prestwick Strath 73 NS3525
Prestwood Bucks 22 SP8700
Prickwillow Cambs 41 TL5982
Priddy Somset 19 ST5250
Priest Hutton Lancs 59 SD5273
Priestland Strath 74 NS5737
Priestweston Shrops 36 SO2997
Primrosehill Border 76 NT7857
Primsidemill Border 76 NT8126
Princes Risborough Bucks 22 SP8003
Princethorpe Warwks 29 SP4070
Princetown Devon 5 SX5873
Priors Hardwick Warwks 29 SP4756
Priors Marston Warwks 29 SP4957
Priors Norton Gloucs 28 SO8624
Priston Avon 20 ST6960
Prittlewell Essex 24 TQ8687
Privett Hants 11 SU6727
Probus Cnwll 3 SW8947
Prospect Cumb 58 NY1140
Prospidnick Cnwll 2 SW6431
Protstonhill Gramp 95 NJ8163
Prudhoe Nthumb 68 NZ0962
Publow Avon 19 ST6264
Puckeridge Herts 31 TL3823
Pucklechurch Avon 20 ST6976
Puddington Ches 46 SJ3273
Puddington Devon 7 SS8310
Puddletown Dorset 9 SY7594
Pudsey W York 55 SE2232
Pulborough W Susx 12 TQ0418
Pulford Ches 46 SJ3758
Pulham Dorset 9 ST7008
Pulham Market Norfk 33 TM1986
Pulham St Mary Norfk 33 TM2085
Pulloxhill Beds 30 TL0634
Pumpherston Loth 75 NT0669
Pumsaint Dyfed 26 SN6540
Puncheston Dyfed 16 SN0129
Puncknowle Dorset 8 SY5388
Punnett's Town E Susx 13 TQ6220
Purbrook Hants 11 SU6707
Purfleet Essex 24 TQ5578
Puriton Somset 19 ST3041
Purleigh Essex 24 TL8402
Purley Berks 22 SU6675
Purley Gt Lon 23 TQ3161
Purse Caundle Dorset 9 ST6917
Purtington Somset 8 ST3908
Purton Gloucs 28 SO6904
Purton Gloucs 28 SO6705
Purton Wilts 20 SU0987
Purton Stoke Wilts 20 SU0990
Pury End Nhants 30 SP7145
Pusey Oxon 21 SU3596
Putley H & W 27 SO6337
Putley Green H & W 27 SO6437
Putloe Gloucs 28 SO7709
Putney Gt Lon 23 TQ2374
Putron Village Guern 101 GN0000
Puttenham Surrey 12 SU9247
Puxley Nhants 30 SP7542
Puxton Avon 19 ST4063
Pwll Dyfed 17 SN4801
Pwll Trap Dyfed 17 SN2616
Pwll-du Gwent 27 SO2411
Pwll-glas Clwyd 46 SJ1154
Pwll-y-glaw W Glam 18 SS7993
Pwllgloyw Powys 26 SO0333
Pwllheli Gwynd 44 SH3735
Pwllmeyric Gwent 19 ST5292
Pye Bridge Derbys 49 SK4452
Pye Corner Herts 31 TL4412
Pyecombe W Susx 12 TQ2813
Pyle M Glam 18 SS8282
Pyleigh Somset 8 ST1330
Pylle Somset 19 ST6038
Pymore Cambs 41 TL4986
Pymore Dorset 8 SY4694
Pyrford Surrey 22 TQ0358
Pyrton Oxon 22 SU6896
Pytchley Nhants 30 SP8574
Pyworthy Devon 6 SS3102

Q

Quabbs Shrops 36 SO2180
Quadring Lincs 41 TF2233
Quainton Bucks 30 SP7420
Quarley Hants 21 SU2743
Quarndon Derbys 49 SK3340
Quarrier's Homes Strath 73 NS3366
Quarrington Lincs 50 TF0544
Quarrington Hill Dur 62 NZ3337
Quarry Bank W Mids 38 SO9386
Quarrywood Gramp 94 NJ1763
Quarter Strath 74 NS7251
Quarter Strath 73 NS1961
Quatford Shrops 38 SO7391
Quatt Shrops 38 SO7588
Quebec Dur 69 NZ1743
Quedgeley Gloucs 28 SO8014
Queen Adelaide Cambs 41 TL5681
Queen Camel Somset 19 ST5924
Queen Charlton Avon 19 ST6367
Queen Oak Dorset 9 ST7831
Queen Street Kent 14 TQ6845
Queen's Bower IOW 11 SZ5684
Queenborough Kent 14 TQ9172
Queenhill H & W 28 SO8537
Queensbury W York 55 SE1030
Queensferry Clwyd 46 SJ3168
Queenslie Strath 74 NS6565
Queenzieburn Strath 74 NS6977
Quendon Essex 31 TL5130
Queniborough Leics 39 SK6412
Quenington Gloucs 28 SP1404
Quethiock Cnwll 4 SX3164
Quidenham Norfk 32 TM0287
Quidhampton Wilts 10 SU1030
Quina Brook Shrops 37 SJ5232
Quinton Nhants 30 SP7754

R

Quintrell Downs Cnwll 3 SW8460
Quither Devon 4 SX4481
Quixwood Border 76 NT7863
Quoditch Devon 6 SX4097
Quorndon Leics 39 SK5616
Quothquan Strath 75 NS9939
Quoybrray Ork 103 HY5005
Quoyloo Ork 103 HY2420

Rableyheath Herts 31 TL2319
Rachan Mill Border 75 NT1134
Rachub Gwynd 45 SH6267
Rackenford Devon 7 SS8518
Rackham W Susx 12 TQ0413
Rackheath Norfk 43 TG2814
Rackwick Ork 103 ND2099
Radbourne Derbys 39 SK2836
Radcliffe Gt Man 47 SD7806
Radcliffe on Trent Notts 49 SK6439
Radclive Bucks 30 SP6734
Radernie Fife 83 NO4609
Radford Semele Warwks 29 SP3464
Radlett Herts 23 TL1600
Radley Oxon 21 SU5398
Radley Green Essex 24 TL6205
Radnage Bucks 22 SU7897
Radstock Avon 20 ST6854
Radstone Nhants 29 SP5840
Radway Warwks 29 SP3648
Radwell Beds 30 TL0057
Radwell Herts 31 TL2335
Radwinter Essex 24 TL6037
Radyr S Glam 18 ST1280
Rafford Gramp 93 NJ0556
Ragdale Leics 39 SK6619
Raglan Gwent 27 SO4107
Ragnall Notts 50 SK8073
Raigbeg Highld 93 NH8128
Rainbow Hill H & W 28 SO8555
Rainford Mersyd 46 SD4700
Rainham Gt Lon 23 TQ5282
Rainham Kent 14 TQ8165
Rainhill Mersyd 46 SJ4991
Rainhill Stoops Mersyd 46 SJ5090
Rainow Ches 48 SJ9475
Rainton N York 62 SE3675
Rainworth Notts 49 SK5858
Raisthorpe N York 56 SE8561
Rait Tays 82 NO2226
Raithby Lincs 51 TF3084
Raithby Lincs 51 TF3766
Rake W Susx 11 SU8027
Ralia Highld 87 NN7097
Ramasaig Highld 90 NG1644
Rame Cnwll 2 SW7233
Rame Cnwll 4 SX4249
Rampisham Dorset 9 ST5602
Rampside Cumb 53 SD2366
Rampton Cambs 31 TL4267
Rampton Notts 50 SK8078
Ramridge End Beds 30 TL1023
Ramsbottom Gt Man 54 SD7916
Ramsbury Wilts 21 SU2771
Ramscraigs Highld 100 ND1427
Ramsdean Hants 11 SU7022
Ramsdell Hants 21 SU5857
Ramsden Oxon 29 SP3515
Ramsden Bellhouse Essex 24 TQ7194
Ramsey Cambs 41 TL2885
Ramsey Essex 25 TM2130
Ramsey IOM 52 SC4594
Ramsey Forty Foot Cambs 41 TL3087
Ramsey Heights Cambs 41 TL2484
Ramsey Island Essex 25 TL9405
Ramsey Mereside Cambs 41 TL2889
Ramsey St Mary's Cambs 41 TL2587
Ramsgate Kent 15 TR3865
Ramsgill N York 55 SE1170
Ramshope Nthumb 68 NT7304
Ramshorn Staffs 48 SK0845
Ramsnest Common Surrey 12 SU9432
Ranby Lincs 51 TF2278
Ranby Notts 49 SK6580
Rand Lincs 50 TF1078
Randwick Gloucs 28 SO8306
Ranfurly Strath 73 NS3865
Rangemore Staffs 38 SK1822
Rangeworthy Avon 20 ST6986
Rankinston Strath 73 NS4513
Rann Lancs 54 SD7124
Rannoch Station Tays 86 NN4257
Ranochan Highld 85 NM8282
Ranscombe Somset 7 SS9443
Ranskill Notts 49 SK6587
Ranton Staffs 38 SJ8524
Ranton Green Staffs 38 SJ8423
Ranworth Norfk 43 TG3514
Raploch Cent 81 NS7894
Rapness Ork 103 HY5141
Rapps Somset 8 ST3316
Rascarrel D & G 66 NX7948
Rashfield Strath 80 NS1483
Rashwood H & W 28 SO9165
Raskelf N York 55 SE4971
Ratagan Highld 85 NG9119
Ratby Leics 39 SK5105
Ratcliffe Culey Leics 39 SP3299
Ratcliffe on Soar Notts 39 SK4928
Ratcliffe on the Wreake Leics 39 SK6314
Rathen Gramp 95 NJ9960
Rathillet Fife 83 NO3620
Rathmell N York 54 SD8059
Ratho Loth 75 NT1370
Rathven Gramp 94 NJ4465
Ratley Warwks 29 SP3847
Ratling Kent 15 TR2453
Ratlinghope Shrops 36 SO4096
Rattar Highld 100 ND2673
Rattery Devon 5 SX7461
Rattlesden Suffk 32 TL9758
Ratton Village E Susx 13 TQ5901
Rattray Tays 88 NO1845
Raunds Nhants 30 SP9972
Raven Meols Mersyd 46 SD2905
Ravenfield S York 49 SK4895
Ravenglass Cumb 58 SD0896
Raveningham Norfk 43 TM3996
Ravenscar N York 63 NZ9801
Ravenscliffe Staffs 47 SJ8452
Ravensden Beds 30 TL0754
Ravenshead Notts 49 SK5654

Ravensthorpe Nhants	30	SP6670
Ravensthorpe W York	55	SE2220
Ravenstone Bucks	30	SP8451
Ravenstone Leics	39	SK4013
Ravenstonedale Cumb	60	NY7203
Ravenstruther Strath	75	NS9245
Ravensworth N York	61	NZ1308
Rawcliffe Humb	56	SE6822
Rawcliffe N York	56	SE5854
Rawdon W York	55	SE2139
Rawling Street Kent	14	TQ9059
Rawmarsh S York	49	SK4396
Rawreth Essex	24	TQ7893
Rawridge Devon	8	ST2006
Rawtenstall Lancs	54	SD8123
Raydon Suffk	25	TM0438
Rayleigh Essex	24	TQ8090
Rayne Essex	24	TL7222
Raynes Park Gt Lon	23	TQ2368
Reach Cambs	31	TL5666
Read Lancs	54	SD7634
Reading Berks	22	SU7173
Reading Street Kent	14	TQ9230
Reading Street Kent	15	TR3869
Reagill Cumb	59	NY6017
Rearquhar Highld	97	NH7492
Rearsby Leics	39	SK6514
Reay Highld	99	NC9664
Reculver Kent	15	TR2269
Red Ball Devon	8	ST0917
Red Hill Dorset	10	SZ0995
Red Hill Warwks	28	SP1356
Red Lodge Suffk	32	TL6970
Red Roses Dyfed	17	SN2011
Red Row T & W	69	NZ2599
Red Wharf Bay Gwynd	44	SH5281
Redberth Dyfed	16	SN0804
Redbourn Herts	30	TL1012
Redbourne Lincs	50	SK9799
Redbrook Clwyd	37	SJ5041
Redbrook Gloucs	27	SO5309
Redbrook Street Kent	14	TQ9336
Redburn Highld	93	NH9447
Redcar Cleve	62	NZ6024
Redcastle D & G	66	NX8165
Redcastle Highld	92	NH5849
Redding Cent	82	NS9278
Reddingmuirhead Cent	75	NS9177
Redditch H & W	28	SP0467
Rede Suffk	32	TL8055
Redenhall Norfk	33	TM2684
Redesmouth Nthumb	68	NY8682
Redford Gramp	89	NO7570
Redford Tays	89	NO5644
Redford W Susx	11	SU8626
Redfordgreen Border	76	NT3616
Redgorton Tays	82	NO0828
Redgrave Suffk	32	TM0477
Redhill Avon	19	ST4962
Redhill Gramp	89	NJ7704
Redhill Herts	31	TL3033
Redhill Surrey	12	TQ2750
Redisham Suffk	33	TM4084
Redland Avon	19	ST5775
Redland Ork	103	HY3724
Redlingfield Suffk	33	TM1870
Redlingfield Green Suffk	33	TM1871
Redlynch Somset	9	ST7033
Redlynch Wilts	10	SU2021
Redmarley H & W	28	SO7666
Redmarley D'Abitot Gloucs	28	SO7531
Redmarshall Cleve	62	NZ3821
Redmile Leics	40	SK7935
Redmire N York	61	SE0491
Redmyre Gramp	89	NO7575
Rednal Shrops	36	SJ3628
Redpath Border	76	NT5835
Redruth Cnwll	2	SW6942
Redstone Tays	82	NO1834
Redwick Avon	19	ST5486
Redwick Gwent	19	ST4184
Redworth Dur	61	NZ2423
Reed Herts	31	TL3636
Reedham Norfk	43	TG4201
Reedness Humb	56	SE7923
Reepham Lincs	50	TF0473
Reepham Norfk	43	TG1022
Reeth N York	61	SE0399
Reeves Green W Mids	39	SP2677
Reiff Highld	98	NB9614
Reigate Surrey	12	TQ2550
Reighton N York	63	TA1375
Reisque Gramp	95	NJ8819
Reiss Highld	100	ND3354
Relubbus Cnwll	2	SW5631
Relugas Gramp	93	NH9948
Remenham Berks	22	SU7684
Remenham Hill Berks	22	SU7882
Rempstone Notts	39	SK5724
Rendcomb Gloucs	28	SP0209
Rendham Suffk	33	TM3464
Renfrew Strath	74	NS5067
Renhold Beds	30	TL0952
Renishaw Derbys	49	SK4577
Rennington Nthumb	77	NU2118
Renton Strath	80	NS3877
Renwick Cumb	67	NY5943
Repps Norfk	43	TG4217
Repton Derbys	39	SK3026
Resaurie Highld	93	NH7045
Rescassa Cnwll	3	SW9842
Resipole Highld	79	NM7264
Reskadinnick Cnwll	2	SW6341
Resolis Highld	93	NH6765
Resolven W Glam	18	SN8302
Rest and be Thankful Strath	80	NN2307
Reston Border	77	NT8862
Reswallie Tays	89	NO5051
Retford Notts	49	SK7081
Rettendon Essex	24	TQ7698
Revesby Lincs	51	TF2961
Rew Street IOW	11	SZ4794
Rewe Devon	7	SX9499
Reydon Suffk	33	TM4977
Reymerston Norfk	42	TG0206
Reynalton Dyfed	16	SN0908
Reynoldston W Glam	17	SS4889
Rezare Cnwll	4	SX3677
Rhandirmwyn Dyfed	26	SN7843
Rhayader Powys	35	SN9768
Rheindown Highld	92	NH5147
Rhes-y-cae Clwyd	46	SJ1871
Rhewl Clwyd	46	SJ1060
Rhewl Clwyd	46	SJ1744
Rhicarn Highld	98	NC0825
Rhiconich Highld	98	NC2552
Rhicullen Highld	93	NH6971
Rhigos M Glam	26	SN9205
Rhireavach Highld	91	NH0295
Rhives Highld	97	NC8200
Rhiwbina S Glam	19	ST1682
Rhiwderyn Gwent	19	ST2687
Rhiwlas Gwynd	44	SH5765
Rhoden Green Kent	14	TQ6845
Rhodes Minnis Kent	15	TR1542
Rhodiad-y-brenin Dyfed	16	SM7627
Rhonehouse D & G	65	NX7459
Rhoose S Glam	18	ST0666
Rhos Dyfed	17	SN3835
Rhos W Glam	18	SN7302
Rhos-on-Sea Clwyd	45	SH8480
Rhos-y-gwaliau Gwynd	45	SH9434
Rhosbeirio Gwynd	44	SH3991
Rhoscolyn Gwynd	44	SH2267
Rhoscrowther Dyfed	16	SM9002
Rhosesmor Clwyd	46	SJ2168
Rhosgoch Powys	27	SO1847
Rhoshill Dyfed	17	SN1940
Rhoshirwaun Gwynd	44	SH2029
Rhoslefain Gwynd	34	SH5705
Rhosllanerchrugog Clwyd	46	SJ2946
Rhosmeirch Gwynd	44	SH4677
Rhosneigr Gwynd	44	SH3173
Rhossili W Glam	17	SS4187
Rhostryfan Gwynd	44	SH4957
Rhostyllen Clwyd	46	SJ3148
Rhosybol Gwynd	44	SH4288
Rhosymedre Clwyd	36	SJ2842
Rhu Strath	80	NS0864
Rhuallt Clwyd	46	SJ0775
Rhubodach Strath	80	NS0273
Rhuddlan Clwyd	45	SJ0278
Rhunahaorine Strath	72	NR7048
Rhyd Gwynd	45	SH6341
Rhyd-Ddu Gwynd	44	SH5652
Rhyd-uchaf Gwynd	45	SH9037
Rhyd-y pennau Dyfed	35	SN6385
Rhyd-y-clafdy Gwynd	44	SH3234
Rhyd-y-foel Clwyd	45	SH9176
Rhyd-y-groes Gwynd	44	SH5867
Rhydargaeau Dyfed	17	SN4326
Rhydcymerau Dyfed	17	SN5738
Rhydlewis Dyfed	17	SN3561
Rhydowen Dyfed	17	SN4445
Rhydyfro W Glam	18	SN7105
Rhyl Clwyd	45	SJ0081
Rhymney M Glam	26	SO1107
Rhynd Tays	82	NO1520
Rhynie Gramp	94	NJ4927
Rhynie Highld	97	NH8479
Ribbesford H & W	37	SO7874
Ribbleton Lancs	53	SD5631
Ribchester Lancs	54	SD6535
Riby Lincs	57	TA1807
Riccall N York	56	SE6237
Riccarton Border	67	NY5494
Riccarton Strath	73	NS4236
Richards Castle H & W	27	SO4969
Richmond N York	61	NZ1701
Richmond S York	49	SK4085
Richmond Fort Guern	101	GN0000
Richmond upon Thames Gt Lon	23	TQ1774
Rickerscote Staffs	38	SJ9220
Rickford Avon	19	ST4859
Rickham Devon	5	SX7537
Rickinghall Suffk	32	TM0475
Rickling Essex	31	TL4931
Rickling Green Essex	31	TL5129
Rickmansworth Herts	22	TQ0694
Riddell Border	76	NT5124
Riddlecombe Devon	7	SS6113
Riddlesden W York	55	SE0742
Ridge Dorset	9	SY9386
Ridge Herts	23	TL2100
Ridge Wilts	9	ST9531
Ridge Lane Warwks	39	SP2994
Ridgehill Avon	19	ST5462
Ridgeway Derbys	49	SK4081
Ridgeway Derbys	32	TL7340
Ridgewell Essex	13	TQ4719
Ridgewood E Susx	30	SP9736
Ridgmont Beds	68	NZ0161
Riding Mill Nthumb	40	SK8402
Ridlington Leics	43	TG3430
Ridlington Norfk	68	NY9084
Ridsdale Nthumb	62	SE5785
Rievaulx N York	81	NY2966
Rigg D & G	74	NS7670
Riggend Strath	93	NH8851
Righoul Highld	51	TF4375
Rigsby Lincs	54	SD6225
Rigside Strath	4	SX2973
Riley Green Lancs	63	SE8574
Rilla Mill Cnwll	54	SD8045
Rillington N York	9	ST6121
Rimington Lancs	54	TA3128
Rimpton Somset	16	SM9825
Rimswell Humb	37	SO7395
Rinaston Dyfed	65	NX6957
Rindleford Shrops	43	TG1313
Ringford D & G	13	TQ4412
Ringland Norfk	5	SX6546
Ringmer E Susx	5	SX9272
Ringmore Devon	94	NJ2644
Ringmore Devon	33	TM4088
Ringorm Gramp	33	TM4087
Ringsfield Suffk	30	SP9814
Ringsfield Corner Suffk	32	TM0452
Ringshall Bucks	32	TM0551
Ringshall Suffk	30	SP9875
Ringshall Stocks Suffk	42	TF7040
Ringstead Nhants	10	SU1505
Ringstead Norfk	15	TR3548
Ringwood Hants	13	TQ5110
Ringwould Kent	49	SK3950
Ripe E Susx	10	SZ1698
Ripley Derbys	55	SE2860
Ripley Hants	22	TQ0556
Ripley N York	11	SU6623
Ripley Surrey	55	SE3171
Riplington Hants	40	TF0927
Ripon N York	28	SO8737
Rippingale Lincs	15	TR3550
Ripple H & W	55	SE0319
Ripple Kent	70	NR3143
Ripponden W York	27	SO5455
Risabus Strath	32	TL8066
Risbury H & W	19	SJ9267
Risby Suffk	57	TA1542
Risca Gwent	41	TF2129
Rise Humb	30	TL0462
Risegate Lincs	22	SU7263
Riseley Beds	33	TM1668
Riseley Berks	54	SD7230
Rishangles Suffk		
Rishton Lancs		
Rishworth W York	55	SE0318
Risley Ches	47	SJ6592
Risley Derbys	39	SK4535
Risplith N York	55	SE2468
River Kent	15	TR3043
River W Susx	12	SU9323
Riverford Highld	92	NH5454
Riverhead Kent	23	TQ5156
Rivington Lancs	54	SD6214
Road Weedon Nhants	29	SP6359
Roade Nhants	30	SP7651
Roadside Highld	100	ND1560
Roadside Strath	74	NS5717
Roadwater Somset	7	ST0338
Roag Highld	90	NG2644
Roan of Craigoch Strath	73	NS2904
Roast Green Essex	31	TL4632
Roath S Glam	19	ST1977
Roberton Border	67	NT4214
Roberton Strath	75	NS9428
Robertsbridge E Susx	14	TQ7423
Roberttown W York	55	SE1922
Robeston Wathen Dyfed	16	SN0815
Robgill Tower D & G	67	NY2471
Robin Hood's Bay N York	63	NZ9505
Roborough Devon	6	SS5717
Roborough Devon	4	SX5062
Roby Mersyd	46	SJ4390
Rocester Staffs	48	SK1039
Roch Dyfed	16	SM8821
Rochdale Gt Man	54	SD8913
Roche Cnwll	3	SW9860
Rochester Kent	14	TQ7468
Rochester Nthumb	68	NY8298
Rochford Essex	24	TQ8790
Rochford H & W	27	SO6268
Rochville Strath	80	NS2390
Rock Cnwll	3	SW9375
Rock H & W	37	SO7371
Rock Nthumb	77	NU2020
Rock Ferry Mersyd	46	SJ3386
Rockbeare Devon	7	SY0194
Rockbourne Hants	10	SU1118
Rockcliffe Cumb	67	NY3561
Rockcliffe D & G	66	NX8454
Rockfield Gwent	27	SO4814
Rockfield Highld	97	NH9282
Rockford Devon	18	SS7547
Rockhampton Gloucs	19	ST6593
Rockhill Shrops	36	SO2078
Rockingham Nhants	40	SP8691
Rockland All Saints Norfk	42	TL9996
Rockland St Mary Norfk	43	TG3104
Rockland St Peter Norfk	42	TL9897
Rockley Notts	49	SK7174
Rockley Wilts	20	SU1571
Rockwell End Bucks	22	SU7988
Rodborough Gloucs	28	SO8404
Rodbourne Wilts	20	SU1485
Rodbourne Wilts	20	ST9383
Rodden Dorset	9	SY6184
Rode Somset	20	ST8053
Rode Heath Ches	47	SJ8056
Rodel W Isls	102	NG0483
Roden Shrops	37	SJ5716
Rodhuish Somset	7	ST0139
Rodington Shrops	37	SJ5814
Rodington Heath Shrops	37	SJ5814
Rodley Gloucs	28	SO7411
Rodmarton Gloucs	20	ST9498
Rodmell E Susx	13	TQ4106
Rodmersham Kent	14	TQ9261
Rodmersham Green Kent	14	TQ9161
Rodney Stoke Somset	19	ST4849
Rodsley Derbys	48	SK2040
Roe Green Herts	23	TL2107
Roe Green Herts	31	TL3133
Roecliffe N York	55	SE3665
Roehampton Gt Lon	23	TQ2273
Roffey W Susx	12	TQ1932
Rogart Highld	97	NC7202
Rogate W Susx	11	SU8023
Rogerstone Gwent	19	ST2787
Roghadal W Isls	102	NG0483
Rogiet Gwent	19	ST4587
Roke Oxon	21	SU6293
Roker T & W	69	NZ4058
Rollesby Norfk	43	TG4416
Rolleston Leics	40	SK7300
Rolleston Staffs	39	SK2327
Rolston Humb	57	TA2144
Rolvenden Kent	14	TQ8431
Rolvenden Layne Kent	14	TQ8530
Romaldkirk Dur	61	NY9922
Romanby N York	62	SE3693
Romanno Bridge Border	75	NT1647
Romansleigh Devon	7	SS7220
Romesdal Highld	90	NG4053
Romford Dorset	10	SU0709
Romford Gt Lon	23	TQ5188
Romiley Gt Man	48	SJ9490
Romsey Hants	10	SU3521
Romsley H & W	38	SO9680
Romsley Shrops	37	SO7883
Ronachan Strath	71	NR7454
Rookhope Dur	61	NY9342
Rookley IOW	11	SZ5084
Rooks Bridge Somset	19	ST3652
Rooks Nest Somset	8	ST0933
Rookwith N York	61	SE2086
Roos Humb	57	TA2830
Roothams Green Beds	30	TL0957
Ropley Hants	11	SU6431
Ropley Dean Hants	11	SU6232
Ropsley Lincs	40	SK9933
Rora Gramp	95	NK0650
Rorrington Shrops	36	SJ3000
Rosarie Gramp	94	NJ3850
Rose Cnwll	2	SW7754
Rose Ash Devon	7	SS7921
Rose Green Essex	25	TL9028
Rose Green Suffk	25	TL9337
Rose Green Suffk	32	TL9741
Rose Green W Susx	11	SZ9099
Rose Hill Lancs	54	SD8231
Rose Lands E Susx	13	TQ6200
Rosebank Strath	74	NS8049
Rosebush Dyfed	16	SN0729
Rosedale Abbey N York	63	SE7296
Rosehall Highld	96	NC4702
Rosehearty Gramp	95	NJ9267
Roseisle Gramp	93	NJ1466
Rosemarket Dyfed	16	SM9508
Rosemarkie Highld	93	NH7357
Rosemary Lane Devon	8	ST1514
Rosemount Tays	88	NO1843
Rosenannon Cnwll	3	SW9566
Rosewell Loth	75	NT2862
Roseworth Cleve	62	NZ4221
Rosgill Cumb	59	NY5316
Roshven Highld	85	NM7078
Roskhill Highld	90	NG2744
Rosley Cumb	67	NY3245
Roslin Loth	75	NT2763
Rosliston Derbys	39	SK2416
Rosneath Strath	80	NS2583
Ross D & G	65	NX6444
Ross-on-Wye H & W	27	SO5923
Rossett Clwyd	46	SJ3657
Rossett Green N York	55	SE2952
Rossington N York	49	SK6298
Rosskeen Highld	93	NH6869
Rossland Strath	73	NS4370
Roster Highld	100	ND2639
Rostherne Ches	47	SJ7483
Rosthwaite Cumb	58	NY2514
Roston Derbys	48	SK1340
Rosyth Loth	82	NT1082
Rothbury Nthumb	68	NU0501
Rotherby Leics	39	SK6716
Rotherfield E Susx	13	TQ5529
Rotherfield Greys Oxon	22	SU7282
Rotherfield Peppard Oxon	22	SU7182
Rotherham S York	49	SK4392
Rothersthorpe Nhants	30	SP7156
Rotherwick Hants	22	SU7156
Rothes Gramp	94	NJ2749
Rothesay Strath	73	NS0864
Rothiebrisbane Gramp	95	NJ7437
Rothiemay Gramp	94	NJ5548
Rothiemurchus Lodge Highld	93	NH9407
Rothienorman Gramp	95	NJ7235
Rothley Leics	39	SK5812
Rothmaise Gramp	95	NJ6832
Rothwell Lincs	50	TF1499
Rothwell Nhants	40	SP8181
Rothwell W York	55	SE3428
Rottal Lodge Tays	88	NO3769
Rottingdean E Susx	12	TQ3602
Rottington Cumb	58	NX9613
Roucan D & G	66	NY0277
Rough Common Kent	15	TR1259
Rougham Norfk	42	TF8320
Rougham Green Suffk	32	TL9061
Roughpark Gramp	94	NJ3412
Roughton Lincs	51	TF2464
Roughton Norfk	43	TG2136
Roughton Shrops	37	SO7594
Roundbush Green Essex	24	TL5814
Roundham Somset	8	ST4209
Roundhay W York	55	SE3337
Roundway Wilts	20	SU0163
Roundhill Tays	88	NO3750
Rous Lench H & W	28	SP0153
Rousdon Devon	8	SY2991
Rousham Oxon	29	SP4724
Routenburn Strath	73	NS1961
Routh Humb	57	TA0942
Row Cnwll	3	SX0976
Row Cumb	59	SD4589
Row Green Essex	24	TL7420
Rowanburn D & G	67	NY4177
Rowardennan Hotel Cent	80	NS3698
Rowardennan Lodge Cent	80	NS3598
Rowarth Derbys	48	SK0189
Rowberrow Somset	19	ST4558
Rowde Wilts	20	ST9762
Rowen Gwynd	45	SH7671
Rowfoot Nthumb	68	NY6860
Rowington Warwks	29	SP2069
Rowland Derbys	48	SK2172
Rowland's Castle Hants	11	SU7310
Rowland's Gill T & W	69	NZ1658
Rowledge Surrey	11	SU8243
Rowley Dur	68	NZ0848
Rowley Humb	56	SE9732
Rowley Green W Mids	39	SP3483
Rowley Regis W Mids	38	SO9787
Rowlstone H & W	27	SO3727
Rowner Hants	11	SU5801
Rowney Green H & W	38	SP0471
Rownhams Hants	10	SU3817
Rowrah Cumb	58	NY0518
Rowsham Bucks	30	SP8417
Rowsley Derbys	48	SK2565
Rowston Lincs	50	TF0856
Rowton Ches	46	SJ4464
Rowton Shrops	37	SJ6119
Roxburgh Border	76	NT6930
Roxby Humb	56	SE9116
Roxton Beds	31	TL1554
Roxwell Essex	24	TL6408
Roy Bridge Highld	86	NN2681
Roydon Essex	23	TL4010
Roydon Norfk	42	TF7023
Roydon Norfk	33	TM1080
Roydon Hamlet Essex	23	TL4107
Royston Herts	31	TL3540
Royston S York	55	SE3611
Royton Gt Man	54	SD9107
Rozel Jersey	101	JS0000
Ruabon Clwyd	46	SJ3043
Ruaig Strath	78	NM0747
Ruan Lanihorne Cnwll	3	SW8942
Ruan Major Cnwll	2	SW7016
Ruan Minor Cnwll	2	SW7115
Ruardean Gloucs	27	SO6217
Ruardean Hill Gloucs	27	SO6317
Ruardean Woodside Gloucs	27	SO6216
Rubery H & W	38	SO9977
Ruckinge Kent	15	TR0233
Ruckley Shrops	37	SJ5300
Rudby N York	62	NZ4706
Rudchester Nthumb	69	NZ1167
Ruddington Notts	39	SK5732
Rudge Somset	20	ST8251
Rudgeway Avon	19	ST6386
Rudgwick W Susx	12	TQ0834
Rudley Green Essex	24	TL8303
Rudloe Wilts	20	ST8470
Rudry M Glam	19	ST2086
Rudston Humb	57	TA0967
Rudyard Staffs	48	SJ9557
Ruecastle Border	76	NT6120
Rufford Lancs	53	SD4615
Rufforth N York	55	SE5251
Rugby Warwks	39	SP5075
Rugeley Staffs	38	SK0418
Ruishton Somset	8	ST2625
Ruislip Gt Lon	22	TQ0987
Ruletown Head Border	68	NT6113
Rumbach Gramp	94	NJ3852
Rumbling Bridge Tays	82	NT0199
Rumburgh Suffk	33	TM3481
Rumford Cent	75	NS9377

Rumford Cnwll	3	SW8970
Rumney S Glam	19	ST2178
Runcorn Ches	46	SJ5182
Runcton W Susx	11	SU8802
Runcton Holme Norfk	41	TF6109
Runfold Surrey	22	SU8647
Runhall Norfk	42	TG0507
Runham Norfk	43	TG4610
Runnington Somset	8	ST1221
Runswick N York	63	NZ8016
Runtaleave Tays	88	NO2867
Runwell Essex	24	TQ7594
Ruscombe Berks	22	SU7976
Rush Green Essex	25	TM1515
Rush Green Gt Lon	23	TQ5187
Rushall H & W	27	SO6435
Rushall Norfk	33	TM1982
Rushall Wilts	20	SU1255
Rushbrooke Suffk	32	TL8961
Rushbury Shrops	37	SO5191
Rushden Herts	31	TL3031
Rushden Nhants	30	SP9566
Rushford Norfk	32	TL9281
Rushlake Green E Susx	13	TQ6218
Rushmere Suffk	33	TM4986
Rushmoor Surrey	11	SU8740
Rushock H & W	27	SO3058
Rushock H & W	38	SO8871
Rusholme Gt Man	47	SJ8594
Rushton Ches	47	SJ5863
Rushton Nhants	40	SP8482
Rushton Spencer Staffs	48	SJ9362
Rushwick H & W	28	SO8254
Rushyford Dur	61	NZ2728
Ruskie Cent	81	NN6600
Ruskington Lincs	50	TF0851
Rusland Cumb	59	SD3488
Rusper W Susx	12	TQ2037
Ruspidge Gloucs	28	SO6611
Russ Hill Surrey	12	TQ2240
Russell's Water Oxon	22	SU7089
Rusthall Kent	13	TQ5639
Rustington W Susx	12	TQ0402
Ruston N York	63	SE9583
Ruston Parva Humb	57	TA0661
Ruswarp N York	63	NZ8809
Rutherford Border	76	NT6430
Rutherglen Strath	74	NS6161
Ruthernbridge Cnwll	3	SX0166
Ruthin Clwyd	46	SJ1258
Ruthrieston Gramp	89	NJ9204
Ruthven Gramp	94	NJ5046
Ruthven Highld	93	NH8132
Ruthven Highld	87	NN7699
Ruthven Tays	88	NO2848
Ruthven House Tays	88	NO3047
Ruthvoes Cnwll	3	SW9260
Ruthwell D & G	67	NY0967
Ruyton-XI-Towns Shrops	36	SJ3922
Ryal Nthumb	68	NZ0174
Ryall Dorset	8	SY4095
Ryall H & W	28	SO8640
Ryarsh Kent	14	TQ6660
Rydal Cumb	59	NY3606
Ryde IOW	11	SZ5992
Rye E Susx	14	TQ9220
Rye Foreign E Susx	14	TQ8922
Rye Street H & W	28	SO7835
Ryhall Leics	40	TF0310
Ryhill W York	55	SE3814
Ryhope T & W	69	NZ4152
Ryland Lincs	50	TF0179
Rylands Notts	39	SK5335
Rylstone N York	54	SD9658
Ryme Intrinseca Dorset	9	ST5810
Ryther N York	56	SE5539
Ryton Shrops	37	SJ7602
Ryton T & W	69	NZ1564
Ryton-on-Dunsmore Warwks	39	SP3874

S

Sabden Lancs	54	SD7837
Sacombe Herts	31	TL3319
Sacombe Green Herts	31	TL3419
Sacriston T & W	69	NZ2447
Sadberge Dur	62	NZ3416
Saddell Strath	72	NR7832
Saddington Leics	39	SP6691
Saddle Bow Norfk	41	TF6015
Saddlescombe W Susx	12	TQ2711
Saffron Walden Essex	24	TL5438
Sageston Dyfed	16	SN0503
Saham Hills Norfk	42	TF9003
Saham Toney Norfk	42	TF8901
Saighton Ches	46	SJ4462
St Abbs Border	77	NT9167
St Agnes Cnwll	2	SW7150
St Agnes Loth	76	NT6763
St Albans Herts	22	TL1407
St Allen Cnwll	2	SW8250
St Andrew Guern	101	GN0000
St Andrew's Major S Glam	18	ST1371
St Andrews Fife	83	NO5116
St Andrews Well Dorset	8	SY4793
St Ann's D & G	66	NY0793
St Ann's Chapel Devon	5	SX6647
St Anne's Lancs	53	SD3228
St Anthony Cnwll	2	SW7825
St Anthony's Hill E Susx	13	TQ6201
St Arvans Gwent	19	ST5296
St Asaph Clwyd	45	SJ0374
St Athan S Glam	18	ST0167
St Aubin Jersey	101	JS0000
St Austell Cnwll	3	SX0152
St Bees Cumb	58	NX9711
St Blazey Cnwll	3	SX0654
St Boswells Border	76	NT5930
St Brelade Jersey	101	JS0000
St Brelades Bay Jersey	101	JS0000
St Breock Cnwll	3	SW9771
St Breward Cnwll	3	SX0977
St Briavels Gloucs	27	SO5604
St Bride's Major M Glam	18	SS8974
St Brides super-Ely S Glam	18	ST0977
St Brides Wentlooge Gwent	19	ST2982
St Budeaux Devon	5	SX4558
St Buryan Cnwll	2	SW4025
St Catherines Strath	80	NN1207
St Chloe Gloucs	20	SO8401
St Clears Dyfed	17	SN2816
St Cleer Cnwll	4	SX2468
St Clement Cnwll	3	SW8543
St Clement Jersey	101	JS0000

St Clether Cnwll	4	SX2084
St Colmac Strath	72	NS0467
St Columb Major Cnwll	3	SW9163
St Columb Minor Cnwll	3	SW8362
St Columb Road Cnwll	3	SW9157
St Combs Gramp	95	NK0563
St Cross South Elmham Suffk	33	TM2984
St Cyrus Gramp	89	NO7464
St David's Tays	82	NN9420
St Davids Dyfed	16	SM7525
St Day Cnwll	2	SW7242
St Decumans Somset	7	ST0642
St Dennis Cnwll	3	SW9557
St Dogmaels Dyfed	17	SN1645
St Dominick Cnwll	4	SX4067
St Donats S Glam	18	SS9368
St Endellion Cnwll	3	SW9978
St Enoder Cnwll	3	SW8956
St Erme Cnwll	3	SW8449
St Erney Cnwll	4	SX3759
St Erth Cnwll	2	SW5535
St Erth Praze Cnwll	2	SW5735
St Ervan Cnwll	3	SW8970
St Ewe Cnwll	3	SW9746
St Fagans S Glam	18	ST1277
St Fergus Gramp	95	NK0952
St Fillans Tays	81	NN6924
St Florence Dyfed	16	SN0801
St Gennys Cnwll	6	SX1497
St George Clwyd	45	SH9775
St George's S Glam	18	ST1076
St Georges Avon	19	ST3762
St Germans Cnwll	4	SX3657
St Giles in the Wood Devon	6	SS5319
St Giles-on-the-Heath Cnwll	4	SX3690
St Harmon Powys	35	SN9872
St Helen Auckland Dur	61	NZ1826
St Helena Norfk	43	TG1816
St Helens IOW	11	SZ6289
St Helens Mersyd	46	SJ5195
St Helier Gt Lon	23	TQ2567
St Helier Jersey	101	JS0000
St Hilary Cnwll	2	SW5431
St Hilary S Glam	18	ST0173
St Illtyd Gwent	19	SO2202
St Ippolitts Herts	31	TL1927
St Ishmaels Dyfed	16	SM8307
St Issey Cnwll	3	SW9271
St Ive Cnwll	4	SX3167
St Ives Cambs	31	TL3171
St Ives Cnwll	2	SW5140
St Jame's End Nhants	30	SP7460
St James South Elmham Suffk	33	TM3281
St John Cnwll	4	SX4053
St John Jersey	101	JS0000
St John's IOM	52	SC2781
St John's Chapel Devon	6	SS5329
St John's Chapel Dur	60	NY8837
St John's Fen End Norfk	41	TF5312
St John's Kirk Strath	75	NS9836
St John's Town of Dalry D & G	65	NX6281
St John's Wood Gt Lon	23	TQ2683
St Johns H & W	28	SO8454
St Johns Kent	23	TQ5356
St Johns Surrey	22	SU9857
St Jude's IOM	52	SC3996
St Just Cnwll	2	SW3731
St Just-in-Roseland Cnwll	3	SW8435
St Katherines Gramp	95	NJ7834
St Keverne Cnwll	2	SW7921
St Kew Cnwll	3	SX0276
St Kew Highway Cnwll	3	SX0375
St Keyne Cnwll	4	SX2461
St Laurence Kent	15	TR3665
St Lawrence Essex	25	TL9604
St Lawrence IOW	11	SZ5376
St Lawrence Jersey	101	JS0000
St Leonards Bucks	22	SP9007
St Leonards Dorset	10	SU1103
St Leonards E Susx	14	TQ8009
St Levan Cnwll	2	SW3822
St Lythans S Glam	18	ST1072
St Mabyn Cnwll	3	SX0473
St Madoes Tays	82	NO1921
St Margaret South Elmham Suffk	33	TM3183
St Margaret's at Cliffe Kent	15	TR3544
St Margarets H & W	27	SO3533
St Margarets Herts	23	TL3811
St Margarets Hope Ork	103	ND4493
St Marks IOM	52	SC2974
St Martin Cnwll	4	SX2555
St Martin Guern	101	GN0000
St Martin Jersey	101	JS0000
St Martin's Tays	82	NO1530
St Martins Shrops	36	SJ3236
St Mary Jersey	101	JS0000
St Mary Bourne Hants	21	SU4250
St Mary Church S Glam	18	ST0071
St Mary Cray Gt Lon	23	TQ4768
St Mary in the Marsh Kent	15	TR0627
St Mary's Ork	103	HY4701
St Mary's Bay Kent	15	TR0827
St Mary's Hoo Kent	14	TQ8076
St Marychurch Devon	5	SX9166
St Maughans Green Gwent	27	SO4717
St Mawes Cnwll	3	SW8433
St Mawgan Cnwll	3	SW8765
St Mellion Cnwll	4	SX3965
St Mellons S Glam	19	ST2281
St Merryn Cnwll	3	SW8874
St Mewan Cnwll	3	SW9951
St Michael Caerhays Cnwll	3	SW9642
St Michael Church Somset	8	ST3030
St Michael Penkevil Cnwll	3	SW8541
St Michael South Elmham Suffk	33	TM3483
St Michael's on Wyre Lancs	53	SD4641
St Michaels H & W	27	SO5865
St Michaels Kent	14	TQ8835
St Minver Cnwll	3	SW9677
St Monans Fife	83	NO5201
St Neot Cnwll	3	SX1868
St Neots Cambs	31	TL1860
St Newlyn East Cnwll	2	SW8256
St Nicholas Dyfed	16	SM9035
St Nicholas S Glam	18	ST0974
St Nicholas at Wade Kent	15	TR2666
St Ninians Cent	81	NS7991
St Olaves Norfk	43	TM4599
St Osyth Essex	25	TM1215
St Ouen Jersey	101	JS0000
St Owens Cross H & W	27	SO5324
St Paul's Walden Herts	31	TL1922
St Pauls Cray Gt Lon	23	TQ4768
St Peter Jersey	101	JS0000
St Peter Port Guern	101	GN0000
St Peter's Guern	101	GN0000
St Peter's Kent	15	TR3868

St Pinnock Cnwll	4	SX2063
St Quivox Strath	73	NS3723
St Sampson Guern	101	GN0000
St Saviour Guern	101	GN0000
St Saviour Jersey	101	JS0000
St Stephen Cnwll	3	SW9453
St Stephen's Coombe Cnwll	3	SW9451
St Stephens Cnwll	4	SX3285
St Stephens Cnwll	4	SX4158
St Teath Cnwll	3	SX0680
St Tudy Cnwll	3	SX0676
St Twynnells Dyfed	16	SR9597
St Veep Cnwll	3	SX1455
St Vigeans Tays	89	NO6443
St Wenn Cnwll	3	SW9664
St Weonards H & W	27	SO4924
Saintbury Gloucs	28	SP1139
Salachail Strath	86	NN0551
Salcombe Devon	5	SX7439
Salcombe Regis Devon	8	SY1588
Salcott Essex	25	TL9413
Sale Gt Man	47	SJ7991
Sale Green H & W	28	SO9358
Saleby Lincs	51	TF4578
Salehurst E Susx	14	TQ7524
Salem Dyfed	35	SN6684
Salem Gwynd	44	SH5456
Salen Highld	79	NM6864
Salen Strath	79	NM5743
Salford Beds	30	SP9339
Salford Gt Man	47	SJ8197
Salford Oxon	29	SP2828
Salford Priors Warwks	28	SP0751
Salfords Surrey	12	TQ2846
Salhouse Norfk	43	TG3114
Saline Fife	82	NT0292
Salisbury Wilts	10	SU1429
Salkeld Dykes Cumb	59	NY5437
Salle Norfk	43	TG1024
Salmonby Lincs	51	TF3273
Salperton Gloucs	28	SP0720
Salsburgh Strath	74	NS8262
Salt Staffs	38	SJ9527
Saltaire W York	55	SE1438
Saltash Cnwll	4	SX4258
Saltburn Highld	93	NH7270
Saltburn-by-the-Sea Cleve	62	NZ6621
Saltby Leics	40	SK8526
Saltcoats Strath	73	NS2441
Saltdean E Susx	13	TQ3802
Salterbeck Cumb	58	NX9926
Salterforth Lancs	54	SD8845
Salterton Wilts	10	SU1336
Saltfleet Lincs	51	TF4593
Saltfleetby All Saints Lincs	51	TF4590
Saltfleetby St Clements Lincs	51	TF4691
Saltfleetby St Peter Lincs	51	TF4489
Saltford Avon	20	ST6867
Salthouse Norfk	42	TG0743
Saltmarshe Humb	56	SE7824
Saltney Ches	46	SJ3865
Salton N York	63	SE7179
Saltrens Devon	6	SS4522
Saltwood Kent	15	TR1535
Salvington W Susx	12	TQ1205
Salwarpe H & W	28	SO8762
Salwayash Dorset	8	SY4596
Sambourne Warwks	28	SP0662
Sambrook Shrops	37	SJ7124
Samlesbury Lancs	54	SD5930
Sampford Arundel Somset	8	ST1118
Sampford Brett Somset	18	ST0741
Sampford Courtenay Devon	7	SS6301
Sampford Moor Somset	8	ST1118
Sampford Peverell Devon	7	ST0314
Sampford Spiney Devon	4	SX5372
Samsonlane Ork	103	HY6526
Samuelston Loth	76	NT4870
Sanaigmore Strath	70	NR2370
Sancreed Cnwll	2	SW4129
Sancton Humb	56	SE8939
Sand Hills W York	55	SE3739
Sand Hole Humb	56	SE8137
Sand Hutton N York	56	SE6958
Sandaig Highld	85	NG7102
Sandal Magna W York	55	SE3417
Sandavore Highld	84	NM4785
Sandbach Ches	47	SJ7560
Sandbank Strath	80	NS1680
Sandbanks Dorset	10	SZ0487
Sandend Gramp	94	NJ5566
Sanderstead Gt Lon	23	TQ3461
Sandford Avon	19	ST4259
Sandford Cumb	60	NY7316
Sandford Devon	7	SS8202
Sandford Hants	10	SU1601
Sandford IOW	11	SZ5381
Sandford Strath	74	NS7143
Sandford Orcas Dorset	9	ST6220
Sandford St Martin Oxon	29	SP4226
Sandford-on-Thames Oxon	21	SP5301
Sandgate Kent	15	TR2035
Sandhaven Gramp	95	NJ9667
Sandhead D & G	64	NX0949
Sandhills Surrey	12	SU9337
Sandhoe Nthumb	68	NY9666
Sandhole Strath	80	NS0098
Sandholme Humb	56	SE8230
Sandhurst Berks	22	SU8361
Sandhurst Gloucs	28	SO8223
Sandhurst Kent	14	TQ8028
Sandhutton N York	62	SE3881
Sandilands Lincs	51	TF5280
Sandleheath Hants	10	SU1215
Sandleigh Oxon	21	SP4701
Sandley Dorset	9	ST7724
Sandness Shet	103	HU1957
Sandon Essex	24	TL7404
Sandon Herts	31	TL3234
Sandon Staffs	38	SJ9429
Sandon Bank Staffs	38	SJ9428
Sandown IOW	11	SZ5984
Sandplace Cnwll	4	SX2557
Sandridge Herts	23	TL1710
Sandringham Norfk	42	TF6928
Sandsend N York	63	NZ8612
Sandtoft Humb	56	SE7408
Sandway Kent	14	TQ8950
Sandwich Kent	15	TR3358
Sandwick Cumb	58	NY0846
Sandwick W Isls	102	NB4432
Sandwith Cumb	58	NX9614
Sandy Beds	31	TL1649
Sandy Lane Wilts	20	ST9668
Sandy Park Devon	5	SX7189
Sandyford D & G	67	NY2093
Sandygate Devon	5	SX8674
Sandygate IOM	52	SC3797

Sandyhills D & G	66	NX8855
Sandylands Lancs	53	SD4263
Sangobeg Highld	98	NC4266
Sangomore Highld	98	NC4067
Sankyn's Green H & W	28	SO7965
Sanna Bay Highld	79	NM4469
Sannox Strath	72	NS0145
Sanquhar D & G	66	NS7809
Santon Bridge Cumb	58	NY1101
Santon Downham Suffk	32	TL8187
Sapcote Leics	39	SP4893
Sapey Common H & W	28	SO7064
Sapiston Suffk	32	TL9175
Sapperton Gloucs	20	SO9403
Sapperton Lincs	40	TF0133
Saracen's Head Lincs	41	TF3427
Sarclet Highld	100	ND3443
Sarisbury Hants	11	SU5008
Sarn Gwynd	44	SH2432
Sarn Powys	35	SN9597
Sarn Powys	36	SO2090
Sarnau Dyfed	17	SN3150
Sarnau Powys	36	SJ2315
Sarnesfield H & W	27	SO3750
Saron Dyfed	17	SN6012
Saron Gwynd	44	SH5365
Sarratt Herts	22	TQ0499
Sarre Kent	15	TR2565
Sarsden Oxon	29	SP2822
Satley Dur	69	NZ1143
Satterleigh Devon	7	SS6622
Satterthwaite Cumb	59	SD3392
Sauchen Gramp	95	NJ7011
Saucher Tays	82	NO1933
Sauchieburn Gramp	89	NO6669
Saul Gloucs	28	SO7409
Saundby Notts	50	SK7888
Saundersfoot Dyfed	16	SN1304
Saunderton Bucks	22	SP7901
Saunton Devon	6	SS4637
Sausthorpe Lincs	51	TF3868
Savile Town W York	55	SE2420
Sawbridge Warwks	29	SP5065
Sawbridgeworth Herts	31	TL4814
Sawdon N York	63	SE9485
Sawley Lancs	54	SD7746
Sawley N York	55	SE2467
Sawston Cambs	31	TL4849
Sawtry Cambs	40	TL1683
Saxby Leics	40	SK8219
Saxby Lincs	50	TF0086
Saxby All Saints Humb	56	SE9816
Saxelbye Leics	40	SK6921
Saxham Street Suffk	32	TM0861
Saxilby Lincs	50	SK8975
Saxlingham Norfk	42	TG0239
Saxlingham Green Norfk	43	TM2396
Saxlingham Nethergate Norfk	43	TM2297
Saxlingham Thorpe Norfk	43	TM2197
Saxmundham Suffk	33	TM3863
Saxon Street Cambs	32	TL6759
Saxondale Notts	49	SK6839
Saxtead Suffk	33	TM2665
Saxtead Green Suffk	33	TM2564
Saxtead Little Green Suffk	33	TM2466
Saxthorpe Norfk	43	TG1130
Saxton N York	55	SE4736
Sayers Common W Susx	12	TQ2618
Scackleton N York	56	SE6472
Scaftworth Notts	49	SK6691
Scagglethorpe N York	56	SE8372
Scalasaig Strath	70	NR3993
Scalby Humb	56	SE8429
Scalby N York	63	TA0090
Scaldwell Nhants	30	SP7672
Scaleby Cumb	67	NY4463
Scalebyhill Cumb	67	NY4463
Scales Cumb	59	NY3426
Scales Cumb	53	SD2772
Scalford Leics	40	SK7624
Scaling N York	63	NZ7413
Scalloway Shet	103	HU4039
Scamblesby Lincs	51	TF2778
Scamodale Highld	85	NM8373
Scampston N York	63	SE8575
Scampton Lincs	50	SK9579
Scaniport Highld	92	NH6239
Scapegoat Hill W York	55	SE0916
Scarborough N York	63	TA0488
Scarcewater Cnwll	3	SW9154
Scarcliffe Derbys	49	SK4968
Scarcroft Hill W York	55	SE3741
Scarfskerry Highld	100	ND2674
Scargill Dur	61	NZ0510
Scarinish Strath	78	NM0444
Scarisbrick Lancs	53	SD3713
Scarning Norfk	42	TF9512
Scarrington Notts	50	SK7341
Scartho Humb	57	TA2606
Scawby Humb	56	SE9605
Scawsby S York	56	SE5404
Scawthorpe S York	56	SE5506
Scawton N York	62	SE5483
Scayne's Hill W Susx	12	TQ3623
Scethrog Powys	26	SO1025
Scholes Gt Man	47	SD5905
Scholes S York	49	SK3895
Scholes W York	55	SE1507
Scissett W York	55	SE2410
Scleddau Dyfed	16	SM9434
Scofton Notts	49	SK6280
Scole Norfk	33	TM1579
Sconser Highld	84	NG5132
Scoonie Fife	83	NO3801
Scopwick Lincs	50	TF0757
Scoraig Highld	91	NH0096
Scorborough Humb	56	TA0145
Scorrier Cnwll	2	SW7244
Scorton Lancs	53	SD5048
Scorton N York	61	NZ2500
Scot's Gap Nthumb	68	NZ0386
Scotby Cumb	67	NY4455
Scotch Corner N York	61	NZ2105
Scotforth Lancs	53	SD4859
Scothern Lincs	50	TF0377
Scotland Well Tays	82	NO1801
Scotlandwell Tays	82	NO1801
Scotscalder Station Highld	100	ND0956
Scotsmill Gramp	94	NJ5618
Scotstoun Strath	74	NS5267
Scotswood T & W	69	NZ2063
Scotter Lincs	50	SE8800
Scotterthorpe Lincs	50	SE8701
Scotton Lincs	50	SK8899
Scotton N York	61	SE1895
Scotton N York	55	SE3259
Scoulton Norfk	42	TF9800
Scourie Highld	98	NC1544
Scouriemore Highld	98	NC1443

Scousburgh Shet 103 HU3717
Scrabster Highld 100 ND1070
Scraesburgh Border 76 NT6718
Scrane End Lincs 51 TF3841
Scraptoft Leics 39 SK6405
Scratby Norfk 43 TG5015
Scrayingham N York 56 SE7359
Scredington Lincs 50 TF0940
Screel D & G 66 NX8053
Scremby Lincs 51 TF4467
Scremerston Nthumb 77 NU0049
Screveton Notts 50 SK7343
Scriven N York 55 SE3458
Scrooby Notts 49 SK6590
Scropton Derbys 39 SK1930
Scrub Hill Lincs 51 TF2355
Scruschloch Tays 88 NO2357
Scruton N York 61 SE2992
Sculthorpe Norfk 42 TF8930
Scunthorpe Humb 56 SE8910
Sea Palling Norfk 43 TG4226
Seaborough Dorset 8 ST4206
Seabrook Kent 15 TR1835
Seaburn T & W 69 NZ4059
Seacroft W York 55 SE3635
Seafield Highld 90 NG4743
Seafield Loth 75 NT0066
Seaford E Susx 13 TV4899
Seaforth Mersyd 46 SJ3297
Seagrave Leics 39 SK6117
Seaham Dur 69 NZ4149
Seahouses Nthumb 77 NU2231
Seal Kent 23 TQ5556
Seale Surrey 22 SU8947
Seamer N York 62 NZ4910
Seamer N York 63 TA0183
Seamill Strath 73 NS2047
Searby Lincs 57 TA0705
Seasalter Kent 15 TR0864
Seascale Cumb 58 NY0301
Seathwaite Cumb 58 SD2295
Seatoller Cumb 58 NY2413
Seaton Cnwll 4 SX3054
Seaton Cumb 58 NY0130
Seaton Devon 8 SY2490
Seaton Humb 57 TA1646
Seaton Kent 15 TR2258
Seaton Leics 40 SP9098
Seaton Nthumb 69 NZ3276
Seaton Delaval Nthumb 69 NZ3075
Seaton Ross Humb 56 SE7840
Seaton Sluice Nthumb 69 NZ3376
Seatown Dorset 8 SY4291
Seave Green N York 62 NZ5500
Seaview IOW 11 SZ6291
Seaville Cumb 67 NY1553
Seavington St Mary Somset 8 ST4014
Seavington St Michael Somset 8 ST4015
Sebergham Cumb 59 NY3641
Seckington Warwks 39 SK2507
Sedbergh Cumb 60 SD6591
Sedbury Gloucs 19 ST5493
Sedbusk N York 60 SD8891
Sedgeberrow H & W 28 SP0238
Sedgebrook Lincs 40 SK8537
Sedgefield Dur 62 NZ3528
Sedgeford Norfk 42 TF7036
Sedgehill Wilts 9 ST8627
Sedgley W Mids 38 SO9193
Sedgwick Cumb 59 SD5186
Sedlescombe E Susx 14 TQ7818
Sedrup Bucks 22 SP8011
Seend Wilts 20 ST9460
Seend Cleeve Wilts 20 ST9360
Seer Green Bucks 22 SU9692
Seething Norfk 43 TM3197
Sefton Mersyd 46 SD3501
Seighford Staffs 38 SJ8825
Seion Gwynd 44 SH5466
Seisdon Staffs 38 SO8495
Selattyn Shrops 36 SJ2633
Selborne Hants 11 SU7433
Selby N York 56 SE6132
Selham W Susx 12 SU9320
Selhurst Gt Lon 23 TQ3267
Selkirk Border 76 NT4728
Sellack H & W 27 SO5627
Sellafirth Shet 103 HU5198
Sellick's Green Somset 8 ST2119
Sellindge Kent 15 TR0938
Selling Kent 15 TR0456
Sells Green Wilts 20 ST9462
Selly Oak W Mids 38 SP0482
Selmeston E Susx 13 TQ5007
Selsdon Gt Lon 23 TQ3562
Selsey W Susx 11 SZ8593
Selside N York 60 SD7875
Selsted Kent 15 TR2144
Selston Notts 49 SK4553
Selworthy Somset 7 SS9246
Semer Suffk 32 TL9946
Semington Wilts 20 ST8960
Semley Wilts 9 ST8926
Send Surrey 22 TQ0155
Senghenydd M Glam 18 ST1190
Sennen Cnwll 2 SW3525
Sennen Cove Cnwll 2 SW3526
Sennybridge Powys 26 SN9228
Sessay N York 62 SE4575
Setchey Norfk 41 TF6313
Seton Mains Loth 76 NT4275
Settle N York 54 SD8163
Settrington N York 56 SE8370
Seven Ash Somset 8 ST1533
Seven Kings Gt Lon 23 TQ4587
Seven Sisters W Glam 26 SN8208
Seven Wells Gloucs 28 SP1134
Sevenhampton Gloucs 28 SP0321
Sevenhampton Wilts 21 SU2090
Sevenoaks Kent 23 TQ5255
Sevenoaks Weald Kent 13 TQ5250
Severn Beach Avon 19 ST5484
Severn Stoke H & W 28 SO8644
Sevington Kent 15 TR0340
Sewards End Essex 24 TL5738
Sewell Beds 30 SP9922
Sewerby Humb 57 TA1968
Seworgan Cnwll 2 SW7030
Sewstern Leics 40 SK8821
Sgiogarstaigh W Isls 102 NB5461
Shabbington Bucks 22 SP6606
Shackerstone Leics 39 SK3706
Shackleford Surrey 12 SU9345
Shader W Isls 102 NB3854
Shadforth Dur 62 NZ3440
Shadingfield Suffk 33 TM4384
Shadoxhurst Kent 15 TQ9737
Shadwell Norfk 32 TL9383

Shaftenhoe End Herts 31 TL4037
Shaftesbury Dorset 9 ST8623
Shafton S York 55 SE3911
Shalbourne Wilts 21 SU3163
Shalden Hants 11 SU6941
Shaldon Devon 5 SX9372
Shalfleet IOW 10 SZ4189
Shalford Essex 24 TL7229
Shalford Surrey 12 TQ0047
Shalford Green Essex 24 TL7127
Shalmsford Street Kent 15 TR0954
Shalstone Bucks 29 SP6436
Shamley Green Surrey 12 TQ0343
Shandford Tays 89 NO4962
Shandon Strath 80 NS1930
Shandwick Highld 97 NH8575
Shangton Leics 40 SP7196
Shanklin IOW 11 SZ5881
Shap Cumb 59 NY5615
Shapwick Dorset 9 ST9301
Shapwick Somset 19 ST4138
Shardlow Derbys 39 SK4330
Shareshill Staffs 38 SJ9406
Sharlston W York 55 SE3918
Sharnbrook Beds 30 SP9959
Sharnford Leics 39 SP4891
Sharoe Green Lancs 53 SD5333
Sharow N York 55 SE3371
Sharpenhoe Beds 30 TL0630
Sharperton Nthumb 68 NT9503
Sharpness Gloucs 20 SO6702
Sharrington Norfk 42 TG0337
Shatterford H & W 37 SO7981
Shaugh Prior Devon 4 SX5463
Shavington Ches 47 SJ6951
Shaw Berks 21 SU4768
Shaw Gt Man 54 SD9308
Shaw Wilts 20 ST8965
Shaw Mills N York 55 SE2562
Shawbost W Isls 102 NB2646
Shawbury Shrops 37 SJ5521
Shawell Leics 39 SP5480
Shawford Hants 10 SU4625
Shawhead D & G 66 NX8675
Shawsburn Strath 74 NS7750
Shearington D & G 66 NY0266
Shearsby Leics 39 SP6290
Shearston Somset 8 ST2830
Shebbear Devon 6 SS4409
Shebdon Staffs 37 SJ7625
Shebster Highld 100 ND0164
Sheddens Strath 74 NS5757
Shedfield Hants 11 SU5613
Sheen Derbys 48 SK1161
Sheepscar W York 55 SE3134
Sheepscombe Gloucs 28 SO8910
Sheepstor Devon 5 SX5667
Sheepwash Devon 6 SS4806
Sheepy Magna Leics 39 SK3201
Sheepy Parva Leics 39 SK3301
Sheering Essex 31 TL5014
Sheerness Kent 14 TQ9174
Sheerwater Surrey 22 TQ0461
Sheet Hants 11 SU7524
Sheffield S York 49 SK3587
Shefford Beds 30 TL1439
Shefford English Hants 10 SU2922
Shegra Highld 98 NC1860
Sheinton Shrops 37 SJ6003
Shelderton Shrops 36 SO4077
Sheldon Derbys 48 SK1768
Sheldon Devon 8 ST1208
Sheldon W Mids 38 SP1584
Sheldwich Kent 15 TR0156
Shelfanger Norfk 33 TM1083
Shelford Notts 49 SK6642
Shellacres Border 77 NT8943
Shelley Suffk 25 TM0038
Shelley W York 55 SE2011
Shellingford Oxon 21 SU3193
Shellow Bowells Essex 24 TL6007
Shelsley Beauchamp H & W 28 SO7363
Shelsley Walsh H & W 28 SO7263
Shelton Beds 30 TL0368
Shelton Norfk 33 TM2291
Shelton Notts 50 SK7844
Shelton Under Harley Staffs 37 SJ8139
Shelve Shrops 36 SO3399
Shelwick H & W 27 SO5242
Shenfield Essex 24 TQ6095
Shenington Oxon 29 SP3742
Shenley Herts 23 TL1800
Shenley Brook End Bucks 30 SP8335
Shenley Church End Bucks 30 SP8336
Shenmore H & W 27 SO3937
Shennanton D & G 64 NX3363
Shenstone H & W 38 SO8673
Shenstone Staffs 38 SK1004
Shenton Leics 39 SK3800
Shephall Herts 31 TL2623
Shepherd's Bush Gt Lon 23 TQ2380
Shepherd's Green Oxon 22 SU7183
Shepherdswell Kent 15 TR2647
Shepley W York 55 SE1909
Shepperton Surrey 22 TQ0766
Shepreth Cambs 31 TL3947
Shepshed Leics 39 SK4819
Shepton Beauchamp Somset 8 ST4017
Shepton Mallet Somset 19 ST6143
Shepton Montague Somset 9 ST6831
Shepway Kent 14 TQ7753
Sheraton Dur 62 NZ4435
Sherborne Dorset 9 ST6316
Sherborne Gloucs 28 SP1614
Sherborne H & W 19 ST5855
Sherborne St John Hants 21 SU6255
Sherbourne Warwks 29 SP2661
Sherburn Dur 62 NZ3142
Sherburn N York 63 SE9576
Sherburn Hill Dur 62 NZ3342
Sherburn in Elmet N York 55 SE4933
Shere Surrey 12 TQ0747
Shereford Norfk 42 TF8829
Sherfield English Hants 10 SU2922
Sherfield on Loddon Hants 22 SU6858
Sherford Devon 5 SX7844
Sherford Dorset 9 SY9193
Sheriff Hutton N York 56 SE6566
Sheriffhales Shrops 37 SJ7512
Sheringham Norfk 43 TG1543
Sherington Bucks 30 SP8846
Shermanbury Norfk 42 TF7132
Sherrington Wilts 20 ST9639
Sherston Wilts 20 ST8586
Sherwood Notts 49 SK5643
Shettleston Strath 74 NS6464
Shevington Gt Man 47 SD5408
Sheviock Cnwll 4 SX3755
Shibden Head W York 55 SE0928

Shide IOW 11 SZ5088
Shidlaw Nthumb 76 NT8037
Shiel Bridge Highld 85 NG9318
Shieldaig Highld 91 NG8154
Shieldhill Cent 74 NS8976
Shieldhill D & G 66 NY0385
Shieldhill House Hotel Strath 75 NS7755
Shields Strath 74 NS7555
Shielhill Strath 80 NS2472
Shielhill Tays 88 NO4257
Shifnal Shrops 37 SJ7407
Shilbottle Nthumb 69 NU1908
Shildon Dur 61 NZ2226
Shillford Strath 73 NS4556
Shillingford Devon 7 SS9824
Shillingford Oxon 21 SU5992
Shillingford Abbot Devon 5 SX9088
Shillingford St George Devon 5 SX9087
Shillingstone Dorset 9 ST8211
Shillington Beds 30 TL1234
Shilton Oxon 29 SP2608
Shilton Warwks 39 SP4084
Shimpling Norfk 33 TM1583
Shimpling Suffk 32 TL8651
Shimpling Street Suffk 32 TL8753
Shincliffe Dur 61 NZ2940
Shinfield Berks 22 SU7368
Shinness Highld 96 NC5215
Shipbourne Kent 13 TQ5952
Shipdham Norfk 42 TF9507
Shipham Somset 19 ST4457
Shiphay Devon 5 SX8965
Shiplake Oxon 22 SU7678
Shiplake Row Oxon 22 SU7478
Shipley W Susx 12 TQ1421
Shipley W York 55 SE1537
Shipley Bridge Surrey 12 TQ3040
Shipmeadow Suffk 33 TM3790
Shippon Oxon 21 SU4898
Shipston on Stour Warwks 29 SP2540
Shipton Gloucs 28 SP0318
Shipton N York 56 SE5558
Shipton Shrops 37 SO5692
Shipton Bellinger Hants 21 SU2345
Shipton Gorge Dorset 8 SY4991
Shipton Green W Susx 11 SZ8099
Shipton Moyne Gloucs 20 ST8989
Shipton-on-Cherwell Oxon 29 SP4716
Shipton-under-Wychwood Oxon 29 SP2817
Shiptonthorpe Humb 56 SE8543
Shirburn Oxon 22 SU6995
Shirdley Hill Lancs 53 SD3612
Shirebrook Derbys 49 SK5267
Shiregreen S York 49 SK3691
Shirehampton Avon 19 ST5376
Shiremoor T & W 69 NZ3171
Shirenewton Gwent 19 ST4793
Shireoaks Notts 49 SK5580
Shirland Derbys 49 SK4058
Shirley Derbys 48 SK2141
Shirley Gt Lon 23 TQ3565
Shirley Hants 10 SU4014
Shirley W Mids 38 SP1278
Shirrell Heath Hants 11 SU5714
Shirven Strath 71 NR8784
Shirwell Devon 6 SS6037
Shiskine Strath 72 NR9129
Shobdon H & W 27 SO4062
Shobrooke Devon 7 SS8601
Shoby Leics 39 SK6820
Shocklach Ches 46 SJ4349
Shoeburyness Essex 25 TQ9385
Sholden Kent 15 TR3552
Sholing Hants 10 SU4511
Shop Cnwll 6 SS2214
Shop Cnwll 3 SW8773
Shop Street Suffk 33 TM2268
Shoreditch Gt Lon 23 TQ3382
Shoreditch Somset 8 ST2422
Shoreham Kent 23 TQ5161
Shoreham-by-Sea W Susx 12 TQ2105
Shorley Hants 11 SU5726
Shorne Kent 14 TQ6971
Shortgate E Susx 13 TQ4915
Shortlanesend Cnwll 2 SW8047
Shorwell IOW 10 SZ4583
Shoscombe Avon 20 ST7156
Shotesham Norfk 33 TM2499
Shotgate Essex 24 TQ7592
Shotley Suffk 25 TM2335
Shotley Bridge Nthumb 68 NZ0953
Shotley Gate Suffk 25 TM2433
Shotley Street Suffk 25 TM2335
Shottenden Kent 15 TR0454
Shottery Warwks 29 SP1854
Shotteswell Warwks 29 SP4245
Shottisham Suffk 33 TM3244
Shottle Derbys 49 SK3149
Shottlegate Derbys 49 SK3147
Shotton Clwyd 46 SJ3168
Shotton Dur 62 NZ4139
Shotts Strath 74 NS8759
Shotwick Ches 46 SJ3371
Shougle Gramp 94 NJ2155
Shouldham Norfk 42 TF6709
Shouldham Thorpe Norfk 42 TF6607
Shoulton H & W 28 SO8159
Shrawardine Shrops 36 SJ3915
Shrawley H & W 28 SO8065
Shrewley Warwks 29 SP2167
Shrewton Wilts 37 SJ4912
Shrewton Wilts 20 SU0743
Shripney W Susx 12 SU9302
Shrivenham Oxon 21 SU2389
Shropham Norfk 32 TL9893
Shucknall H & W 27 SO5842
Shudy Camps Cambs 32 TL6244
Shurdington Gloucs 28 SO9218
Shurlock Row Berks 22 SU8374
Shurrery Highld 100 ND0458
Shurrery Lodge Highld 100 ND0456
Shurton Somset 19 ST2044
Shustoke Warwks 39 SP2290
Shut Heath Staffs 38 SJ8621
Shute Devon 8 SY2597
Shutford Oxon 29 SP3840
Shuthonger Gloucs 28 SO8935
Shutlanger Nhants 29 SP7249
Shuttington Warwks 39 SK2505
Shuttleworth Lancs 54 SK4673
Siabost W Isls 102 NB2646
Siadar W Isls 102 NB3854
Sibbertoft Nhants 39 SP6882
Sibdon Carwood Shrops 36 SO4183
Sibford Ferris Oxon 29 SP3537
Sibford Gower Oxon 29 SP3537

Sible Hedingham Essex 24 TL7734
Sibley's Green Essex 24 TL6128
Sibsey Lincs 51 TF3550
Sibson Cambs 40 TL0997
Sibson Leics 39 SK3500
Sibster Highld 100 ND3253
Sibthorpe Notts 50 SK7273
Sibthorpe Notts 50 SK7645
Sicklesmere Suffk 32 TL8760
Sicklinghall N York 55 SE3448
Sidbury Devon 8 SY1391
Sidbury Shrops 37 SO6885
Sidcot Somset 19 ST4257
Sidcup Gt Lon 23 TQ4672
Siddington Ches 47 SJ8470
Siddington Gloucs 20 SU0399
Sidestrand Norfk 43 TG2539
Sidford Devon 8 SY1390
Sidlesham W Susx 11 SZ8599
Sidley E Susx 14 TQ7408
Sidmouth Devon 8 SY1287
Sigglesthorne Humb 57 TA1545
Sigingstone S Glam 18 SS9771
Silchester Hants 21 SU6261
Sileby Leics 39 SK6015
Silecroft Cumb 58 SD1381
Silfield Norfk 43 TM1299
Silk Willoughby Lincs 50 TF0542
Silkstone S York 55 SE2805
Silkstone Common S York 55 SE2904
Silksworth T & W 69 NZ3752
Silloth Cumb 67 NY1153
Silpho N York 63 SE9692
Silsden W York 55 SE0446
Silsoe Beds 30 TL0835
Silton Dorset 9 ST7829
Silver End Beds 30 TL1042
Silver End Essex 24 TL8119
Silver Street H & W 28 SP0776
Silverburn Loth 75 NT2060
Silverdale Lancs 53 SD4674
Silverdale Staffs 47 SJ8146
Silverford Gramp 95 NJ7763
Silverstone Nhants 30 SP6743
Silverton Devon 7 SS9502
Silvington Shrops 37 SO6279
Simonburn Nthumb 68 NY8773
Simons Burrow Devon 8 ST1416
Simonsbath Somset 7 SS7739
Simonstone Lancs 54 SD7734
Simprim Border 77 NT8445
Simpson Bucks 30 SP8836
Simpson Cross Dyfed 16 SM8919
Sinclair's Hill Border 76 NT8150
Sinclairston Strath 73 NS4716
Sinderby N York 62 SE3482
Sinderland Green Gt Man 47 SJ7389
Sindlesham Berks 22 SU7769
Singleton Lancs 53 SD3838
Singleton W Susx 11 SU8713
Singlewell Kent 14 TQ6570
Sinnarhard Gramp 94 NJ4713
Sinnington N York 63 SE7485
Sinton H & W 28 SO8160
Sinton Green H & W 28 SO8160
Sissinghurst Kent 14 TQ7937
Siston Avon 20 ST6875
Sithney Cnwll 2 SW6328
Sittingbourne Kent 14 TQ9063
Six Ashes Staffs 37 SO7988
Six Mile Bottom Cambs 31 TL5756
Six Rues Jersey 101 JS0000
Sixhills Lincs 50 TF1787
Sixpenny Handley Dorset 9 ST9917
Skaill Ork 103 HY5806
Skares Strath 74 NS5317
Skateraw Loth 76 NT7375
Skeabost Highld 90 NG4148
Skeeby N York 61 NZ1902
Skeffington Leics 40 SK7402
Skeffling Humb 57 TA3719
Skegby Notts 49 SK4961
Skegby Notts 50 SK7869
Skegness Lincs 51 TF5663
Skelbo Highld 97 NH7895
Skelbo Street Highld 97 NH7994
Skelbrooke S York 55 SE5012
Skeldyke Lincs 41 TF3337
Skellingthorpe Lincs 50 SK9272
Skelmanthorpe W York 55 SE2310
Skelmersdale Lancs 46 SD4606
Skelmorlie Strath 73 NS1967
Skelpick Highld 99 NC7256
Skelston D & G 66 NX8285
Skelton Cleve 62 NZ6618
Skelton Cumb 59 NY4335
Skelton Humb 56 SE7625
Skelton N York 55 SE3668
Skelton N York 56 SE5756
Skelwith Bridge Cumb 59 NY3403
Skendleby Lincs 51 TF4369
Skene House Gramp 95 NJ7610
Skenfrith Gwent 27 SO4520
Skerne Humb 57 TA0455
Skerray Highld 99 NC6563
Skerricha Highld 98 NC2350
Skerton Lancs 53 SD4763
Sketchley Leics 39 SP4292
Sketty W Glam 17 SS6292
Skewsby N York 56 SE6270
Skiall Highld 100 ND0267
Skidby Humb 56 TA0133
Skigersta W Isls 102 NB5461
Skilgate Somset 7 SS9827
Skillington Lincs 40 SK8925
Skinburness Cumb 67 NY1256
Skinflats Cent 82 NS9082
Skinidin Highld 90 NG2247
Skipness Strath 71 NR9057
Skipsea Humb 57 TA1654
Skipton N York 54 SD9851
Skipton-on-Swale N York 62 SE3679
Skipwith N York 56 SE6638
Skirlaugh Humb 57 TA1439
Skirling Border 75 NT0739
Skirmett Bucks 22 SU7790
Skirpenbeck Humb 56 SE7456
Skirwith Cumb 59 NY6132
Skirza Highld 100 ND3868
Skulamus Highld 85 NG6622
Skullomie Highld 99 NC6161
Skye Green Essex 24 TL8722
Skye of Curr Highld 93 NH9924
Slack W York 54 SD9728
Slacks of Cairnbanno Gramp 95 NJ8445
Slad Gloucs 28 SO8707
Slade Devon 6 SS5046
Slade Somset 7 SS8327

183

Slade Green Kent...... 23 TQ5276
Slade Hooton S York...... 49 SK5288
Slaggan Highld...... 91 NG8494
Slaggyford Nthumb...... 68 NY6752
Slaidburn Lancs...... 54 SD7152
Slaithwaite W York...... 55 SE0813
Slaley Nthumb...... 68 NY9657
Slamannan Cent...... 74 NS8572
Slapton Bucks...... 30 SP9320
Slapton Devon...... 5 SX8245
Slapton Nhants...... 29 SP6446
Slaugham W Susx...... 12 TQ2528
Slaughterford Wilts...... 20 ST8473
Slawston Leics...... 40 SP7894
Sleaford Hants...... 11 SU8038
Sleaford Lincs...... 50 TF0645
Sleagill Cumb...... 59 NY5919
Sleapford Shrops...... 37 SJ6315
Sleasdairidh Highld...... 97 NH6496
Sledmere Humb...... 56 SE9364
Sleightholme Dur...... 61 NY9510
Sleights N York...... 63 NZ8607
Slickly Highld...... 100 ND2966
Sliddery Strath...... 72 NR9323
Sligachan Highld...... 84 NG4829
Sligrachan Strath...... 80 NS1791
Slimbridge Gloucs...... 20 SO7303
Slindon Staffs...... 38 SJ8232
Slindon W Susx...... 12 SU9608
Slinfold W Susx...... 12 TQ1131
Slingsby N York...... 62 SE6974
Slip End Beds...... 30 TL0718
Slip End Herts...... 31 TL2837
Slipton Nhants...... 40 SP9579
Slitting Mill Staffs...... 38 SK0217
Slockavullin Strath...... 71 NR8297
Slogarie D & G...... 65 NX6568
Sloncombe Devon...... 5 SX7386
Sloothby Lincs...... 51 TF4970
Slough Berks...... 22 SU9879
Slough Green Somset...... 8 ST2719
Slumbay Highld...... 85 NG8938
Slyne Lancs...... 53 SD4765
Smailholm Border...... 76 NT6436
Small Dole W Susx...... 12 TQ2112
Small Heath W Mids...... 38 SP1085
Small Hythe Kent...... 14 TQ8930
Smallburgh Norfk...... 43 TG3324
Smalley Derbys...... 49 SK4044
Smallfield Surrey...... 12 TQ3143
Smallridge Devon...... 8 ST3001
Smallworth Norfk...... 32 TM0080
Smannell Hants...... 21 SU3749
Smarden Kent...... 14 TQ8742
Smarden Bell Kent...... 14 TQ8742
Smart's Hill Kent...... 13 TQ5242
Smearisary Highld...... 85 NM6476
Smeatharpe Devon...... 8 ST1910
Smeeth Kent...... 15 TR0739
Smeeton Westerby Leics...... 39 SP6892
Smerral Highld...... 100 ND1733
Smestow Staffs...... 38 SO8591
Smethwick W Mids...... 38 SP0287
Smisby Derbys...... 39 SK3418
Smith's Green Essex...... 32 TL6640
Smithfield Cumb...... 67 NY4465
Smithstown Highld...... 91 NG7977
Smithton Highld...... 93 NH7145
Smoo Highld...... 98 NC4167
Smythe's Green Essex...... 24 TL9218
Snade D & G...... 66 NX8485
Snailbeach Shrops...... 36 SJ3702
Snailwell Cambs...... 32 TL6467
Snainton N York...... 63 SE9282
Snaith Humb...... 56 SE6422
Snape N York...... 61 SE2684
Snape Suffk...... 33 TM3959
Snape Street Suffk...... 33 TM3958
Snaresbrook Gt Lon...... 23 TQ4089
Snarestone Leics...... 39 SK3409
Snarford Lincs...... 50 TF0482
Snargate Kent...... 15 TQ9928
Snave Kent...... 15 TR0129
Sneaton N York...... 63 NZ8907
Snelland Lincs...... 50 TF0780
Snelston Derbys...... 48 SK1543
Snetterton Norfk...... 32 TL1991
Snettisham Norfk...... 42 TF6834
Snig's End Gloucs...... 28 SO7828
Snitter Nthumb...... 68 NU0203
Snitterby Lincs...... 50 SK9894
Snitterfield Warwks...... 29 SP2159
Snitton Shrops...... 37 SO5575
Snodland Kent...... 14 TQ7061
Snow End Herts...... 31 TL4032
Snowshill Gloucs...... 28 SP0933
Soake Hants...... 11 SU6611
Soberton Hants...... 11 SU6116
Soberton Heath Hants...... 11 SU6014
Sockburn Nthumb...... 62 NZ3406
Soham Cambs...... 31 TL5973
Solas W Isls...... 102 NF8074
Soldridge Hants...... 11 SU6535
Sole Street Kent...... 14 TQ6567
Sole Street Kent...... 15 TR0949
Solihull W Mids...... 38 SP1679
Sollers Dilwyn H & W...... 27 SO4255
Sollers Hope H & W...... 27 SO6132
Solva Dyfed...... 16 SM8024
Solwaybank D & G...... 67 NY3077
Somerby Leics...... 40 SK7710
Somerby Lincs...... 57 TA0606
Somercotes Derbys...... 49 SK4253
Somerford Dorset...... 10 SZ1793
Somerford Keynes Gloucs...... 20 SU0195
Somerley W Susx...... 11 SZB198
Somerleyton Suffk...... 43 TM4897
Somersal Herbert Derbys...... 38 SK1335
Somersby Lincs...... 51 TF3472
Somersham Cambs...... 31 TL3678
Somersham Suffk...... 32 TM0848
Somerton Oxon...... 29 SP4928
Somerton Somset...... 8 ST4928
Somerton Suffk...... 32 TL8153
Sompting W Susx...... 12 TQ1505
Sonning Berks...... 22 SU7575
Sonning Common Oxon...... 22 SU7180
Sonning Eye Oxon...... 22 SU7476
Sopley Hants...... 10 SZ1596
Sopworth Wilts...... 20 ST8286
Sorbie D & G...... 64 NX4346
Sordale Highld...... 100 ND1462
Sorisdale Strath...... 78 NM2763
Sorn Strath...... 74 NS5526
Sortat Highld...... 100 ND2863
Sosgill Cumb...... 58 NY1024
Sotby Lincs...... 51 TF2078
Sots Hole Lincs...... 50 TF1264

Sotterly Suffk...... 33 TM4484
Sotwell Oxon...... 21 SU5890
Soughton Clwyd...... 46 SJ2466
Soulbury Bucks...... 30 SP8826
Soulby Cumb...... 60 NY7411
Souldern Oxon...... 29 SP5231
Souldrop Beds...... 30 SP9861
Sound Muir Gramp...... 94 NJ3652
Soundwell Avon...... 19 ST6575
Sourton Devon...... 5 SX5390
Soutergate Cumb...... 58 SD2281
South Acre Norfk...... 42 TF8114
South Alkham Kent...... 15 TR2441
South Allington Devon...... 5 SX7938
South Alloa Cent...... 82 NS8791
South Ambersham W Susx...... 11 SU9120
South Anston S York...... 49 SK5183
South Ashford Kent...... 15 TR0041
South Baddesley Hants...... 10 SZ3596
South Bank N York...... 56 SE5950
South Barrow Somset...... 9 ST6028
South Beddington Gt Lon...... 23 TQ2863
South Benfleet Essex...... 24 TQ7787
South Bersted W Susx...... 12 SU9300
South Bramwith S York...... 56 SE6211
South Brent Devon...... 5 SX6960
South Brewham Somset...... 20 ST7236
South Broomhill Nthumb...... 69 NZ2499
South Burlingham Norfk...... 43 TG3807
South Cadbury Somset...... 9 ST6325
South Carlton Lincs...... 50 SK6974
South Carlton Notts...... 49 SK5883
South Cave Humb...... 56 SE9230
South Cerney Gloucs...... 20 SU0497
South Charlton Nthumb...... 77 NU1620
South Cheriton Somset...... 9 ST6924
South Church Dur...... 61 NZ2128
South Cliffe Humb...... 56 SE8735
South Clifton Notts...... 50 SK8270
South Cockerington Lincs...... 51 TF3888
South Collingham Notts...... 50 SK8261
South Cornelly M Glam...... 18 SS8280
South Cove Suffk...... 33 TM4981
South Creake Norfk...... 42 TF8536
South Croxton Leics...... 39 SK6810
South Dalton Humb...... 56 SE9645
South Duffield N York...... 56 SE6833
South Elkington Lincs...... 51 TF2988
South Elmsall W York...... 55 SE4711
South Erradale Highld...... 91 NG7471
South Fambridge Essex...... 24 TQ8694
South Fawley Berks...... 21 SU3880
South Fernby Humb...... 56 SE9820
South Field Humb...... 56 TA0225
South Gorley Hants...... 10 SU1610
South Gosforth T & W...... 69 NZ2467
South Green Essex...... 24 TQ6893
South Green Kent...... 14 TQ8560
South Green Norfk...... 42 TG0510
South Gyle Loth...... 75 NT1871
South Hanningfield Essex...... 24 TQ7497
South Harting W Susx...... 11 SU7819
South Hayling Hants...... 11 SZ7299
South Heath Bucks...... 22 SP9101
South Hetton Dur...... 69 NZ3845
South Hiendley W York...... 55 SE3912
South Hill Cnwll...... 4 SX3272
South Hinksey Oxon...... 29 SP5104
South Holmwood Surrey...... 12 TQ1744
South Hornchurch Gt Lon...... 23 TQ5183
South Huish Devon...... 5 SX6941
South Hykeham Lincs...... 50 SK9364
South Hylton T & W...... 69 NZ3556
South Kelsey Lincs...... 50 TF0498
South Kessock Highld...... 93 NH6547
South Killingholme Humb...... 57 TA1416
South Kilvington N York...... 62 SE4284
South Kilworth Nhants...... 39 SP6081
South Kirkby W York...... 55 SE4410
South Kyme Lincs...... 50 TF1749
South Lawn Oxon...... 29 SP2814
South Leigh Oxon...... 29 SP3909
South Leverton Notts...... 50 SK7881
South Lopham Norfk...... 32 TM0481
South Luffenham Leics...... 40 SK9301
South Malling E Susx...... 13 TQ4210
South Marston Wilts...... 21 SU1987
South Milford N York...... 55 SE4931
South Milton Devon...... 5 SX7042
South Mimms Herts...... 23 TL2201
South Molton Devon...... 7 SS7125
South Moor Dur...... 69 NZ1951
South Moreton Oxon...... 21 SU5688
South Mundham W Susx...... 11 SU8700
South Newbald Humb...... 56 SE9035
South Newington Oxon...... 29 SP4033
South Newton Wilts...... 10 SU0834
South Normanton Derbys...... 49 SK4456
South Norwood Gt Lon...... 23 TQ3368
South Ockendon Essex...... 24 TQ5983
South Ormsby Lincs...... 51 TF3675
South Otterington N York...... 62 SE3787
South Owersby Lincs...... 50 TF0693
South Park Surrey...... 12 TQ2448
South Perrott Dorset...... 8 ST4706
South Petherton Somset...... 8 ST4316
South Petherwin Cnwll...... 4 SX3181
South Pickenham Norfk...... 42 TF8504
South Pill Cnwll...... 4 SX4259
South Pool Devon...... 5 SX7740
South Poorton Dorset...... 8 SY5297
South Queensferry Loth...... 82 NT1378
South Radworthy Devon...... 7 SS7432
South Rauceby Lincs...... 50 TF0245
South Raynham Norfk...... 42 TF8723
South Reston Lincs...... 51 TF4083
South Runcton Norfk...... 41 TF6308
South Scarle Notts...... 50 SK8463
South Shian Strath...... 79 NM9042
South Shields T & W...... 69 NZ3666
South Shore Lancs...... 53 SD3033
South Stainley N York...... 55 SE3063
South Stoke Avon...... 20 ST7461
South Stoke Oxon...... 21 SU5983
South Stoke W Susx...... 12 TQ0209
South Street E Susx...... 13 TQ3918
South Street Kent...... 15 TR0557
South Street Kent...... 15 TR1265
South Tarbrax Strath...... 75 NT0353
South Tawton Devon...... 7 SX6594
South Thoresby Lincs...... 51 TF4076
South Tidworth Wilts...... 21 SU2347
South Walsham Norfk...... 43 TG3613
South Warnborough Hants...... 22 SU7247
South Weald Essex...... 24 TQ5694
South Weston Oxon...... 22 SU7098
South Wheatley Cnwll...... 4 SX2492
South Widcombe Somset...... 19 ST5856

South Wigston Leics...... 39 SP5897
South Willesborough Kent...... 15 TR0240
South Willingham Lincs...... 50 TF1983
South Wingate Dur...... 62 NZ4134
South Wingfield Derbys...... 49 SK3855
South Witham Lincs...... 40 SK9219
South Woodham
Ferrers Essex...... 24 TQ8097
South Wootton Norfk...... 42 TF6422
South Wraxall Wilts...... 20 ST8364
South Zeal Devon...... 5 SX6593
Southall Gt Lon...... 22 TQ1279
Southam Gloucs...... 28 SO9725
Southam Warwks...... 29 SP4161
Southampton Hants...... 10 SU4112
Southborough Gt Lon...... 23 TQ4267
Southborough Kent...... 13 TQ5842
Southbourne Dorset...... 10 SZ1491
Southbourne W Susx...... 11 SU7705
Southburgh Norfk...... 42 TG0005
Southburn Humb...... 56 SE9854
Southchurch Essex...... 24 TQ9086
Southcott Cnwll...... 6 SX1995
Southcott Devon...... 6 SX5495
Southcott Devon...... 5 SX7580
Southcourt Bucks...... 30 SP8112
Southease E Susx...... 13 TQ4205
Southend Strath...... 72 NR6908
Southend-on-Sea Essex...... 24 TQ8885
Southerndown M Glam...... 18 SS8873
Southerness D & G...... 66 NX9022
Southerton Devon...... 8 SY0790
Southery Norfk...... 41 TL6194
Southfield Cent...... 74 NS8472
Southfleet Kent...... 14 TQ6171
Southgate Gt Lon...... 23 TQ2994
Southgate W Glam...... 17 SS5587
Southill Beds...... 30 TL1542
Southington Hants...... 21 SU5049
Southleigh Devon...... 8 SY2093
Southminster Essex...... 25 TQ9599
Southmoor Oxon...... 21 SU3998
Southmuir Tays...... 88 NO3852
Southoe Cambs...... 31 TL1864
Southolt Suffk...... 33 TM1968
Southorpe Cambs...... 40 TF0803
Southover Dorset...... 9 SY6294
Southowram W York...... 55 SE1123
Southport Mersyd...... 53 SD3317
Southrepps Norfk...... 43 TG2536
Southrey Lincs...... 50 TF1366
Southrop Gloucs...... 21 SP1903
Southrope Hants...... 22 SU6644
Southsea Hants...... 11 SZ6599
Southside Dur...... 61 NZ1026
Southtown Norfk...... 43 TG5106
Southwaite Cumb...... 67 NY4445
Southwark Gt Lon...... 23 TQ3279
Southwater W Susx...... 12 TQ1526
Southwell Notts...... 49 SK6953
Southwick Hants...... 11 SU6208
Southwick Nhants...... 40 TL0292
Southwick T & W...... 69 NZ3758
Southwick W Susx...... 12 TQ2405
Southwick Wilts...... 20 ST8355
Southwold Suffk...... 33 TM5076
Sowerby N York...... 62 SE4380
Sowerby Bridge W York...... 55 SE0523
Sowood W York...... 55 SE0818
Sowton Devon...... 4 SX5065
Sowton Devon...... 5 SX9792
Soyland Town W York...... 55 SE0320
Spain's End Essex...... 24 TL6637
Spalding Lincs...... 41 TF2422
Spaldington Humb...... 56 SE7633
Spaldwick Cambs...... 30 TL1372
Spalford Notts...... 50 SK8369
Spanby Lincs...... 40 TF0938
Sparham Norfk...... 42 TG0719
Spark Bridge Cumb...... 58 SD3084
Sparkford Somset...... 9 ST6025
Sparkhill W Mids...... 38 SP1083
Sparkwell Devon...... 5 SX5857
Sparrowpit Derbys...... 48 SK0880
Sparrows Green E Susx...... 13 TQ6332
Sparsholt Hants...... 10 SU4331
Sparsholt Oxon...... 21 SU3487
Spaunton N York...... 63 SE7289
Spaxton Somset...... 19 ST2237
Spean Bridge Highld...... 86 NN2081
Spearywell Hants...... 10 SU3127
Speen Berks...... 21 SU4567
Speen Bucks...... 22 SU8499
Speeton N York...... 63 TA1574
Speke Mersyd...... 46 SJ4383
Speldhurst Kent...... 13 TQ5541
Spellbrook Herts...... 31 TL4817
Spen Green Ches...... 47 SJ8160
Spencers Wood Berks...... 22 SU7166
Spennithorne N York...... 61 SE1388
Spennymoor Dur...... 61 NZ2533
Spetchley H & W...... 28 SO8953
Spettisbury Dorset...... 9 ST9102
Spexhall Suffk...... 33 TM3780
Spey Bay Gramp...... 94 NJ3565
Speybridge Highld...... 93 NJ0326
Speyview Gramp...... 94 NJ2541
Spilsby Lincs...... 51 TF4066
Spinkhill Derbys...... 49 SK4578
Spinningdale Highld...... 97 NH6789
Spital Berks...... 22 SU9675
Spital Hill S York...... 49 SK6193
Spital Dyfed...... 16 SM9723
Spittal Highld...... 100 ND1654
Spittal Loth...... 76 NT4677
Spittal Nthumb...... 77 NU0051
Spittal of Glenmuick Gramp...... 88 NO3085
Spittal of Glenshee Tays...... 88 NO1070
Spittal-on-Rule Border...... 76 NT5819
Spittalfield Tays...... 82 NO1040
Spixworth Norfk...... 43 TG2415
Splatt Devon...... 6 SS6605
Splayne's Green E Susx...... 13 TQ4224
Splottlands S Glam...... 19 ST2077
Spofforth N York...... 55 SE3651
Spondon Derbys...... 39 SK4036
Spooner Row Norfk...... 43 TM0997
Sporle Norfk...... 42 TF8411
Spott Loth...... 76 NT6775
Spottiswoode Border...... 76 NT6049
Spratton Nhants...... 30 SP7169
Spreakley Surrey...... 11 SU8341
Spreyton Devon...... 7 SX6996
Spriddlestone Devon...... 5 SX5351
Spridlington Lincs...... 50 TF0084
Springburn Strath...... 74 NS6068
Springfield D & G...... 67 NY3268
Springfield Essex...... 24 TL7208

Springfield Fife...... 83 NO3411
Springholm D & G...... 66 NX8070
Springkell D & G...... 67 NY2675
Springside Strath...... 73 NS3738
Springthorpe Lincs...... 50 SK8789
Springwell T & W...... 69 NZ2858
Sproatley Humb...... 57 TA1934
Sproston Green Ches...... 47 SJ7366
Sprotbrough S York...... 49 SE5301
Sproughton Suffk...... 33 TM1244
Sprouston Border...... 76 NT7535
Sprowston Norfk...... 43 TG2512
Sproxton Leics...... 40 SK8524
Sproxton N York...... 62 SE6181
Spurstow Ches...... 47 SJ5657
Spyway Dorset...... 9 SY5293
Squirrel's Heath Gt Lon...... 23 TQ5389
Stableford Shrops...... 37 SO7598
Stacey Bank Derbys...... 48 SK2890
Stackhouse N York...... 54 SD8165
Stackpole Dyfed...... 16 SR9896
Staddiscombe Devon...... 4 SX5151
Stadhampton Oxon...... 21 SU6098
Stadhlaigearraidh W Isls...... 102 NF7638
Staffield Cumb...... 59 NY5442
Staffin Highld...... 90 NG4967
Stafford Staffs...... 38 SJ9223
Stagsden Beds...... 30 SP9848
Stainburn Cumb...... 58 NY0129
Stainburn N York...... 55 SE2548
Stainby Lincs...... 40 SK9022
Staincross S York...... 55 SE3210
Staindrop Dur...... 61 NZ1220
Staines Surrey...... 22 TQ0371
Stainforth N York...... 54 SD8267
Stainforth S York...... 56 SE6411
Staining Lancs...... 53 SD3436
Stainland W York...... 55 SE0719
Stainsacre N York...... 63 NZ9108
Stainton Cleve...... 62 NZ4714
Stainton Cumb...... 59 NY4828
Stainton Cumb...... 59 SD5285
Stainton Dur...... 61 NZ0718
Stainton S York...... 49 SK5593
Stainton by Langworth Lincs...... 50 TF0677
Stainton le Vale Lincs...... 50 TF1794
Stainton with Adgarley Cumb...... 53 SD2472
Staintondale N York...... 63 SE9998
Stair Strath...... 73 NS4423
Stair Haven D & G...... 64 NX2153
Staithes N York...... 63 NZ7818
Stakeford Nthumb...... 69 NZ2685
Stakes Hants...... 11 SU6808
Stalbridge Dorset...... 9 ST7317
Stalbridge Weston Dorset...... 9 ST7116
Stalham Norfk...... 43 TG3725
Stalisfield Green Kent...... 14 TQ9552
Stallen Dorset...... 9 ST6016
Stallingborough Humb...... 57 TA1911
Stalmine Lancs...... 53 SD3745
Stalybridge Gt Man...... 48 SJ9698
Stambourne Essex...... 24 TL7238
Stambourne Green Essex...... 24 TL6938
Stamford Lincs...... 40 TF0307
Stamford Nthumb...... 77 NU2219
Stamford Bridge Ches...... 46 SJ4667
Stamford Bridge Humb...... 56 SE7155
Stamford Hill Gt Lon...... 23 TQ3387
Stamfordham Nthumb...... 68 NZ0771
Stamton Lees Derbys...... 48 SK2562
Stanbridge Beds...... 30 SP9624
Stanbury W York...... 54 SE0137
Stand Strath...... 74 NS7668
Standburn Cent...... 75 NS9274
Standeford Staffs...... 38 SJ9107
Standen Kent...... 14 TQ8540
Standerwick Somset...... 20 ST8150
Standford Hants...... 11 SU8134
Standingstone Cumb...... 58 NY0533
Standish Gt Man...... 53 SD5610
Standlake Oxon...... 21 SP3903
Standon Hants...... 10 SU4226
Standon Herts...... 31 TL3922
Standon Staffs...... 37 SJ8135
Stane Strath...... 74 NS8859
Stanfield Norfk...... 42 TF9320
Stanford Beds...... 31 TL1640
Stanford Kent...... 15 TR1238
Stanford Bishop H & W...... 28 SO6851
Stanford Bridge H & W...... 28 SO7265
Stanford Dingley Berks...... 21 SU5771
Stanford in the Vale Oxon...... 21 SU3493
Stanford le Hope Essex...... 24 TQ6882
Stanford on Avon Nhants...... 39 SP5978
Stanford on Soar Notts...... 39 SK5421
Stanford on Teme H & W...... 28 SO7065
Stanfree Derbys...... 49 SK4773
Stanghow Cleve...... 62 NZ6715
Stanground Cambs...... 41 TL2097
Stanhoe Norfk...... 42 TF8036
Stanhope Border...... 75 NT1229
Stanhope Dur...... 61 NY9939
Stanion Nhants...... 40 SP9186
Stanley Derbys...... 49 SK4140
Stanley Dur...... 69 NZ1953
Stanley Staffs...... 48 SJ9352
Stanley Tays...... 82 NO1033
Stanley Crook Dur...... 61 NZ1637
Stanley Pontlarge Gloucs...... 28 SP0030
Stanmer E Susx...... 12 TQ3309
Stanmore Gt Lon...... 23 TQ1692
Stanmore Hants...... 10 SU4628
Stannersburn Nthumb...... 68 NY7286
Stannington Nthumb...... 69 NZ2179
Stannington S York...... 49 SK2987
Stannington Station Nthumb...... 69 NZ2181
Stansbatch H & W...... 27 SO3461
Stansfield Suffk...... 32 TL7852
Stanstead Suffk...... 32 TL8449
Stanstead Abbots Herts...... 23 TL3811
Stanstead Street Suffk...... 32 TL8448
Stansted Kent...... 14 TQ6062
Stansted Mountfitchet Essex...... 31 TL5125
Stanton Gloucs...... 28 SP0634
Stanton Nthumb...... 69 NZ1390
Stanton Staffs...... 48 SK1245
Stanton Suffk...... 32 TL9673
Stanton by Bridge Derbys...... 39 SK3726
Stanton by Dale Derbys...... 49 SK4637
Stanton Drew Avon...... 19 ST5963
Stanton Fitzwarren Wilts...... 21 SU1790
Stanton Harcourt Oxon...... 29 SP4105
Stanton in Peak Derbys...... 48 SK2364
Stanton Lacy Shrops...... 37 SO4978
Stanton Long Shrops...... 37 SO5791
Stanton on the Wolds Notts...... 39 SK6330
Stanton Prior Avon...... 20 ST6762
Stanton St Bernard Wilts...... 20 SU0961

Stanton St John

Surlingham

Stanton St John *Oxon* **29** SP5709
Stanton St Quintin *Wilts* **20** ST9079
Stanton Street *Suffk* **32** TL9566
Stanton under Bardon *Leics* **39** SK4610
Stanton upon
Hine Heath *Shrops* **37** SJ5624
Stanton Wick *Avon* **19** ST6162
Stanway *Essex* **25** TL9424
Stanway *Gloucs* **28** SP0632
Stanwell *Surrey* **22** TQ0574
Stanwick *Nhants* **30** SP9771
Stanwix *Cumb* **67** NY4057
Staoinebrig *W Isls* **102** NF7532
Stape *N York* **63** SE7994
Stapeley *Ches* **47** SJ6749
Stapenhill *Staffs* **39** SK2521
Staple *Kent* **15** TR2756
Staple *Somset* **18** ST1141
Staple Cross *Devon* **7** ST0320
Staple Cross *E Susx* **14** TQ7822
Staple Fitzpaine *Somset* **8** ST2618
Staplefield *W Susx* **12** TQ2728
Stapleford *Cambs* **31** TL4751
Stapleford *Herts* **31** TL3117
Stapleford *Leics* **40** SK8018
Stapleford *Lincs* **50** SK8857
Stapleford *Notts* **49** SK4837
Stapleford *Wilts* **10** SU0737
Stapleford Abbotts *Essex* **23** TQ5194
Staplegrove *Somset* **8** ST2126
Staplehay *Somset* **8** ST2121
Staplehurst *Kent* **14** TQ7843
Staplestreet *Kent* **15** TR0660
Stapleton *H & W* **27** SO3265
Stapleton *Leics* **39** SP4398
Stapleton *N York* **61** NZ2612
Stapleton *Shrops* **37** SJ4704
Stapleton *Somset* **8** ST4621
Stapley *Somset* **8** ST1913
Staploe *Beds* **30** TL1560
Staplow *H & W* **28** SO6941
Star *Dyfed* **17** SN2434
Star *Fife* **83** NO3103
Star *Somset* **19** ST4358
Starbeck *N York* **55** SE3255
Starbotton *N York* **61** SD9574
Starcross *Devon* **5** SX9781
Stareton *Warwks* **39** SP3371
Starlings Green *Essex* **31** TL4631
Starston *Norfk* **33** TM2384
Startforth *Dur* **61** NZ0415
Startley *Wilts* **20** ST9482
Statenborough *Kent* **15** TR3155
Stathe *Somset* **8** ST3728
Stathern *Leics* **40** SK7731
Staughton Green *Cambs* **30** TL1365
Staughton Highway *Cambs* **30** TL1364
Staunton *Gloucs* **27** SO5512
Staunton *Gloucs* **28** SO7829
Staunton Green *H & W* **27** SO3661
Staunton on Arrow *H & W* **27** SO3660
Staunton on Wye *H & W* **27** SO3644
Staveley *Cumb* **59** SD3786
Staveley *Cumb* **59** SD4698
Staveley *Derbys* **49** SK4374
Staveley *N York* **55** SE3662
Staverton *Devon* **5** SX7964
Staverton *Gloucs* **28** SO8923
Staverton *Nhants* **29** SP5361
Staverton *Wilts* **20** ST8560
Stawell *Somset* **19** ST3738
Stawley *Somset* **7** ST0622
Staxigoe *Highld* **100** ND3852
Staxton *N York* **63** TA0179
Staynall *Lancs* **53** SD3643
Stean *N York* **61** SE0973
Steane *Nhants* **29** SP5538
Stearsby *N York* **56** SE6171
Steart *Somset* **19** ST2745
Stebbing *Essex* **24** TL6624
Stebbing Green *Essex* **24** TL6823
Stebbing Park *Essex* **24** TL6524
Stedham *W Susx* **11** SU8622
Steel *Nthumb* **68** NY9458
Steele Road *Border* **67** NY5293
Steen's Bridge *H & W* **27** SO5357
Steep *Hants* **11** SU7425
Steep Lane *W York* **55** SE0223
Steeple *Dorset* **9** SY9080
Steeple *Essex* **25** TL9303
Steeple Ashton *Wilts* **20** ST9056
Steeple Aston *Oxon* **29** SP4725
Steeple Bumpstead *Essex* **32** TL6841
Steeple Claydon *Bucks* **30** SP7026
Steeple Gidding *Cambs* **40** TL1381
Steeple Langford *Wilts* **10** SU0337
Steeple Morden *Cambs* **31** TL2842
Steeton *W York* **55** SE0344
Stein *Highld* **90** NG2656
Stelling Minnis *Kent* **15** TR1447
Stembridge *Somset* **8** ST4220
Stenalees *Cnwll* **3** SX0156
Stenhouse *D & G* **66** NX8093
Stenhousemuir *Cent* **82** NS8783
Stenscholl *Highld* **90** NG4767
Stenton *Loth* **76** NT6274
Steornabhagh *W Isls* **102** NB4232
Stepaside *Dyfed* **16** SN1407
Stepney *Gt Lon* **23** TQ3681
Steppingley *Beds* **30** TL0035
Stepps *Strath* **74** NS6568
Sternfield *Suffk* **33** TM3861
Stert *Wilts* **20** SU0259
Stetchworth *Cambs* **32** TL6459
Stevenage *Herts* **31** TL2325
Stevenston *Strath* **73** NS2742
Steventon *Hants* **21** SU5447
Steventon *Oxon* **21** SU4691
Steventon End *Essex* **31** TL5942
Stevington *Beds* **30** SP9853
Stewartby *Beds* **30** TL0142
Stewarton *Strath* **73** NS4245
Stewkley *Bucks* **30** SP8526
Stewley *Somset* **8** ST3118
Steyning *W Susx* **12** TQ1711
Steynton *Dyfed* **16** SM9107
Stibb *Cnwll* **6** SS2210
Stibb Cross *Devon* **6** SS4314
Stibb Green *Wilts* **21** SU2262
Stibbard *Norfk* **42** TF9828
Stibbington *Cambs* **40** TL0898
Stichill *Border* **76** NT7138
Sticker *Cnwll* **3** SW9750
Stickford *Lincs* **51** TF3560
Sticklepath *Devon* **7** SX6494
Stickling Green *Essex* **31** TL4732
Stickney *Lincs* **51** TF3457
Stiffkey *Norfk* **42** TF9742
Stilligarry *W Isls* **102** NF7638
Stillingfleet *N York* **56** SE5940
Stillington *Cleve* **62** NZ3723
Stillington *N York* **56** SE5867
Stilton *Cambs* **40** TL1689
Stinchcombe *Gloucs* **20** ST7298
Stinsford *Dorset* **9** SY7091
Stiperstones *Shrops* **36** SJ3600
Stirling *Cent* **81** NS7993
Stirling *Gramp* **95** NK1242
Stirtloe *Cambs* **31** TL1966
Stirton *N York* **54** SD9752
Stisted *Essex* **24** TL8024
Stithians *Cnwll* **2** SW7336
Stivichall *W Mids* **39** SP3376
Stixwould *Lincs* **50** TF1765
Stoak *Ches* **46** SJ4273
Stobo *Border* **75** NT1837
Stoborough *Dorset* **9** SY9286
Stoborough Green *Dorset* **9** SY9285
Stobs Castle *Border* **67** NT5008
Stobswood *Nthumb* **69** NZ2195
Stock *Avon* **19** ST4561
Stock *Essex* **24** TQ6998
Stock Green *H & W* **28** SO9859
Stock Wood *H & W* **28** SP0058
Stockbridge *Hants* **10** SU3535
Stockbriggs *Strath* **74** NS7936
Stockbury *Kent* **14** TQ8461
Stockcross *Berks* **21** SU4368
Stockerston *Leics* **40** SP8397
Stocking *H & W* **27** SO6230
Stocking Pelham *Herts* **31** TL4529
Stockingford *Warwks* **39** SP3391
Stockland *Devon* **8** ST2404
Stockland Bristol *Somset* **19** ST2443
Stockleigh English *Devon* **7** SS8506
Stockleigh Pomeroy *Devon* **7** SS8703
Stockley *Wilts* **20** ST9967
Stocklinch *Somset* **8** ST3817
Stockport *Gt Man* **48** SJ8990
Stocksbridge *S York* **49** SK2698
Stocksfield *Nthumb* **68** NZ0561
Stockton *H & W* **27** SO5261
Stockton *Norfk* **43** TM3894
Stockton *Shrops* **37** SJ7716
Stockton *Shrops* **37** SO7299
Stockton *Warwks* **29** SP4363
Stockton *Wilts* **20** ST9838
Stockton Heath *Ches* **47** SJ6185
Stockton on Teme *H & W* **28** SO7167
Stockton on the Forest *N York* **56** SE6556
Stockton-on-Tees *Cleve* **62** NZ4419
Stockwood *Avon* **19** ST6368
Stockwood *Dorset* **9** ST5906
Stodmarsh *Kent* **15** TR2260
Stody *Norfk* **42** TG0535
Stoer *Highld* **98** NC0328
Stoford *Somset* **9** ST5613
Stoford *Wilts* **10** SU0835
Stogumber *Somset* **18** ST0937
Stogursey *Somset* **19** ST2042
Stoke *Devon* **6** SS2324
Stoke *Hants* **21** SU4051
Stoke *Hants* **11** SU7202
Stoke *Kent* **14** TQ8274
Stoke *W Mids* **39** SP3778
Stoke Abbott *Dorset* **8** ST4500
Stoke Albany *Nhants* **40** SP8088
Stoke Ash *Suffk* **33** TM1170
Stoke Bardolph *Notts* **49** SK6441
Stoke Bliss *H & W* **27** SO6563
Stoke Bruerne *Nhants* **30** SP7449
Stoke by Clare *Suffk* **32** TL7443
Stoke Canon *Devon* **7** SX9398
Stoke Charity *Hants* **11** SU4839
Stoke Climsland *Cnwll* **4** SX3674
Stoke Cross *H & W* **27** SO6250
Stoke D'Abernon *Surrey* **22** TQ1258
Stoke Doyle *Nhants* **40** TL0286
Stoke Dry *Leics* **40** SP8596
Stoke Edith *H & W* **27** SO6040
Stoke Farthing *Wilts* **10** SU0525
Stoke Ferry *Norfk* **42** TF7000
Stoke Fleming *Devon* **5** SX8648
Stoke Gabriel *Devon* **5** SX8557
Stoke Gifford *Avon* **19** ST6279
Stoke Golding *Leics* **39** SP3997
Stoke Goldington *Bucks* **30** SP8348
Stoke Hammond *Bucks* **30** SP8829
Stoke Holy Cross *Norfk* **43** TG2301
Stoke Lacy *H & W* **27** SO6249
Stoke Lyne *Oxon* **29** SP5628
Stoke Mandeville *Bucks* **22** SP8310
Stoke Newington *Gt Lon* **23** TQ3386
Stoke Orchard *Gloucs* **28** SO9128
Stoke Poges *Bucks* **22** SU9783
Stoke Prior *H & W* **27** SO5256
Stoke Prior *H & W* **28** SO9467
Stoke Rivers *Devon* **7** SS6335
Stoke Rochford *Lincs* **40** SK9127
Stoke Row *Oxon* **22** SU6884
Stoke St Gregory *Somset* **8** ST3427
Stoke St Mary *Somset* **8** ST2622
Stoke St Michael *Somset* **20** ST6646
Stoke St Milborough *Shrops* **37** SO5682
Stoke sub Hamdon *Somset* **8** ST4717
Stoke Talmage *Oxon* **22** SU6799
Stoke Trister *Somset* **9** ST7428
Stoke upon Tern *Shrops* **37** SJ6328
Stoke Wake *Dorset* **9** ST7606
Stoke-by-Nayland *Suffk* **25** TL9836
Stoke-on-Trent (Hanley) *Staffs* **47** SJ8847
Stoke-upon-Trent *Staffs* **47** SJ8745
Stokeford *Dorset* **9** SY8687
Stokeham *Notts* **50** SK7876
Stokeinteignhead *Devon* **5** SX9170
Stokenchurch *Bucks* **22** SU7696
Stokenham *Devon* **5** SX8042
Stokesay *Shrops* **36** SO4381
Stokesby *Norfk* **43** TG4310
Stokesley *N York* **62** NZ5208
Stolford *Somset* **7** ST0332
Stolford *Somset* **19** ST2345
Ston Easton *Somset* **19** ST6253
Stondon Massey *Essex* **24** TL5800
Stone *Bucks* **30** SP7812
Stone *Gloucs* **20** ST6895
Stone *H & W* **38** SO8675
Stone *Kent* **14** TQ9427
Stone *S York* **49** SK5589
Stone *Staffs* **38** SJ9034
Stone Allerton *Somset* **19** ST3951
Stone Cross *Kent* **15** TR3257
Stone Street *Kent* **14** TQ5754
Stone Street *Suffk* **33** TM3882
Stonebridge *Avon* **19** ST3859
Stonebridge *W Mids* **39** SP2182
Stonebury *Herts* **31** TL3828
Stonechrubie *Highld* **96** NC2419
Stonecrouch *Kent* **14** TQ7033
Stoneferry *Humb* **57** TA1031
Stonefield Castle Hotel *Strath* **71** NR8671
Stonegate *E Susx* **14** TQ6628
Stonegrave *N York* **62** SE6577
Stonehall *H & W* **28** SO8848
Stonehaven *Gramp* **89** NO8786
Stonehouse *Ches* **46** SJ5070
Stonehouse *D & G* **66** NX8268
Stonehouse *Devon* **4** SX4654
Stonehouse *Gloucs* **28** SO8005
Stonehouse *Strath* **74** NS7546
Stoneleigh *Warwks* **39** SP3372
Stones Green *Essex* **25** TM1626
Stonesby *Leics* **40** SK8224
Stonesfield *Oxon* **29** SP3917
Stonewells *Gramp* **94** NJ2865
Stoney Middleton *Derbys* **48** SK2375
Stoney Stanton *Leics* **39** SP4994
Stoney Stoke *Somset* **9** ST7032
Stoney Stratton *Somset* **19** ST6539
Stoney Stretton *Shrops* **36** SJ3809
Stoneybridge *W Isls* **102** NF7532
Stoneyburn *Loth* **75** NS9862
Stoneygate *Leics* **39** SK6002
Stoneykirk *D & G* **64** NX0853
Stoneywood *Cent* **81** NS7982
Stoneywood *Gramp* **95** NJ8811
Stonham Aspal *Suffk* **33** TM1359
Stonnall *Staffs* **38** SK0603
Stonor *Oxon* **22** SU7388
Stonton Wyville *Leics* **40** SP7395
Stony Houghton *Derbys* **49** SK4966
Stony Stratford *Bucks* **30** SP7840
Stoodleigh *Devon* **7** SS6532
Stoodleigh *Devon* **7** SS9218
Stopham *W Susx* **12** TQ0219
Stopsley *Beds* **30** TL1023
Stormy Corner *Lancs* **46** SD4707
Stornoway *W Isls* **102** NB4232
Storrington *W Susx* **12** TQ0814
Storwood *Humb* **56** SE7144
Stotfield *Gramp* **94** NJ2270
Stotfold *Beds* **31** TL2136
Stottesdon *Shrops* **37** SO6782
Stoughton *Leics* **39** SK6402
Stoughton *Surrey* **12** SU9851
Stoughton *W Susx* **11** SU8011
Stoul *Highld* **85** NM7594
Stoulton *H & W* **28** SO9049
Stour Provost *Dorset* **9** ST7921
Stour Row *Dorset* **9** ST8221
Stourbridge *W Mids* **38** SO8983
Stourpaine *Dorset* **9** ST8609
Stourport-on-Severn *H & W* **37** SO8171
Stourton *Staffs* **38** SO8684
Stourton *Warwks* **29** SP2936
Stourton *Wilts* **9** ST7734
Stourton Caundle *Dorset* **9** ST7115
Stove *Shet* **103** HU4224
Stoven *Suffk* **33** TM4481
Stow *Border* **76** NT4544
Stow *Lincs* **50** SK8882
Stow Bardolph *Norfk* **41** TF6206
Stow Bedon *Norfk* **42** TL9596
Stow cum Quy *Cambs* **31** TL5260
Stow Longa *Cambs* **30** TL1070
Stow Maries *Essex* **24** TQ8399
Stow-on-the-Wold *Gloucs* **29** SP1925
Stowbridge *Norfk* **41** TF6007
Stowe *Shrops* **36** SO3173
Stowe by Chartley *Staffs* **38** SK0026
Stowell *Somset* **9** ST6822
Stowey *Somset* **19** ST5959
Stowford *Devon* **6** SX4398
Stowford *Devon* **7** SS6541
Stowford *Devon* **4** SX4387
Stowlangtoft *Suffk* **32** TL9568
Stowmarket *Suffk* **32** TM0458
Stowting *Kent* **15** TR1242
Stowting Common *Kent* **15** TR1243
Stowupland *Suffk* **32** TM0760
Straanruie *Highld* **93** NH9916
Strachan *Gramp* **89** NO6792
Strachur *Strath* **80** NN0901
Stradbroke *Suffk* **33** TM2373
Stradishall *Suffk* **32** TL7552
Stradsett *Norfk* **42** TF6605
Stragglethorpe *Lincs* **50** SK9152
Straiton *Loth* **75** NT2766
Straiton *Strath* **73** NS3804
Straloch *Gramp* **95** NJ8620
Straloch *Tays* **88** NO0463
Stramshall *Staffs* **38** SK0735
Strang *IOM* **52** SC3578
Strangford *H & W* **27** SO5827
Stranraer *D & G* **64** NX0560
Stratfield Mortimer *Berks* **22** SU6664
Stratfield Saye *Hants* **22** SU6861
Stratfield Turgis *Hants* **22** SU6959
Stratford *Gt Lon* **23** TQ3884
Stratford St Andrew *Suffk* **33** TM3560
Stratford St Mary *Suffk* **25** TM0434
Stratford Tony *Wilts* **10** SU0926
Stratford-upon-Avon *Warwks* **29** SP2055
Strath *Highld* **91** NG7978
Strathan *Highld* **98** NC0821
Strathan *Highld* **99** NC5764
Strathan *Highld* **85** NM9791
Strathaven *Strath* **74** NS7044
Strathblane *Cent* **81** NS5679
Strathcarron Sta *Highld* **91** NG9442
Strathcoil *Strath* **79** NM6830
Strathdon *Gramp* **94** NJ3512
Strathkanaird *Highld* **96** NC1501
Strathkinness *Fife* **83** NO4516
Strathmashie House *Tays* **87** NN5891
Strathmiglo *Fife* **82** NO2109
Strathpeffer *Highld* **92** NH4858
Strathtay *Tays* **87** NN9153
Strathwhillan *Strath* **72** NS0235
Strathy *Highld* **99** NC8464
Strathy Inn *Highld* **99** NC8365
Strathyre *Cent* **81** NN5617
Stratton *Cnwll* **6** SS2306
Stratton *Dorset* **9** SY6593
Stratton *Gloucs* **20** SP0103
Stratton Audley *Oxon* **29** SP6025
Stratton St Margaret *Wilts* **21** SU1786
Stratton St Michael *Norfk* **43** TM2093
Stratton Strawless *Norfk* **43** TG2220
Stratton-on-the-Fosse *Somset* **20** ST6650
Stravithie *Fife* **83** NO5313
Stream *Somset* **7** ST0639
Streat *E Susx* **12** TQ3515
Streatham *Gt Lon* **23** TQ3071
Streatley *Beds* **30** TL0728
Streatley *Berks* **21** SU5980
Street *Devon* **8** SY1888
Street *Somset* **19** ST4836
Street Ashton *Warwks* **39** SP4582
Street Dinas *Shrops* **36** SJ3338
Street End *Kent* **15** TR1453
Street End *W Susx* **11** SZ8599
Street Gate *T & W* **69** NZ2159
Street on the Fosse *Somset* **19** ST6239
Streethay *Staffs* **38** SK1410
Streetlam *N York* **61** SE3098
Streetly End *Cambs* **31** TL6148
Strelitz *Tays* **82** NO1836
Strelley *Notts* **49** SK5141
Strensall *N York* **56** SE6360
Strete *Devon* **5** SX8446
Stretford *Gt Man* **47** SJ7994
Strethall *Essex* **31** TL4839
Stretham *Cambs* **31** TL5174
Strettington *W Susx* **11** SU8907
Stretton *Ches* **47** SJ6282
Stretton *Derbys* **49** SK3961
Stretton *Leics* **40** SK9415
Stretton *Staffs* **38** SJ8811
Stretton *Staffs* **39** SK2526
Stretton Grandison *H & W* **27** SO6344
Stretton on Fosse *Warwks* **29** SP2238
Stretton Sugwas *H & W* **27** SO4642
Stretton under Fosse *Warwks* **39** SP4581
Stretton Westwood *Shrops* **37** SO5998
Stretton-on-
Dunsmore *Warwks* **39** SP4072
Strichen *Gramp* **95** NJ9455
Stringston *Somset* **19** ST1742
Strixton *Nhants* **30** SP9061
Stroat *Gloucs* **19** ST5797
Stromeferry *Highld* **85** NG8634
Stromness *Ork* **103** HY2508
Stronachlachar *Cent* **80** NN4010
Stronafian *Strath* **80** NS0281
Strone *Highld* **86** NN1481
Strone *Strath* **80** NS1980
Stronenaba *Highld* **86** NN2084
Stronmilchan *Strath* **80** NN1528
Strontian *Highld* **79** NM8161
Strood *Kent* **14** TQ7268
Stroud *Gloucs* **28** SO8505
Stroud *Hants* **11** SU7223
Stroud Green *Essex* **24** TQ8590
Stroud Green *Gloucs* **28** SO8007
Stroxton *Lincs* **40** SK9030
Struan *Highld* **84** NG3438
Struan *Tays* **87** NN8065
Strumpshaw *Norfk* **43** TG3407
Strutherhill *Strath* **74** NS7649
Struthers *Fife* **83** NO3709
Struy *Highld* **92** NH4040
Stuartfield *Gramp* **95** NJ9745
Stubbington *Hants* **11** SU5503
Stubbins *Gt Man* **54** SD7918
Stubton *Lincs* **50** SK8748
Stuckton *Hants* **10** SU1613
Studham *Beds* **30** TL0215
Studholme *Cumb* **67** NY2556
Studland *Dorset* **10** SZ0382
Studley *Warwks* **28** SP0764
Studley *Wilts* **20** ST9671
Studley Roger *N York* **55** SE2970
Studley Royal *N York* **55** SE2770
Stuntney *Cambs* **31** TL5578
Sturmer *Essex* **32** TL6943
Sturminster Common *Dorset* **9** ST7812
Sturminster Marshall *Dorset* **9** ST9500
Sturminster Newton *Dorset* **9** ST7814
Sturry *Kent* **15** TR1760
Sturton *Humb* **56** SE9604
Sturton by Stow *Lincs* **50** SK8980
Sturton le Steeple *Notts* **50** SK7883
Stuston *Suffk* **33** TM1377
Stutton *N York* **55** SE4841
Stutton *Suffk* **25** TM1534
Styal *Ches* **47** SJ8383
Stynie *Gramp* **94** NJ3360
Styrrup *Notts* **49** SK6090
Succoth *Strath* **80** NN2905
Suckley *H & W* **28** SO7251
Sudborough *Nhants* **40** SP9682
Sudbourne *Suffk* **33** TM4153
Sudbrook *Gwent* **19** ST5087
Sudbrook *Lincs* **50** SK9744
Sudbrooke *Lincs* **50** TF0376
Sudbury *Derbys* **38** SK1631
Sudbury *Gt Lon* **23** TQ1685
Sudbury *Suffk* **32** TL8741
Suddie *Highld* **93** NH6554
Suddington *H & W* **28** SO8463
Suffield *N York* **63** SE9890
Suffield *Norfk* **43** TG2232
Sugnall *Staffs* **37** SJ7931
Sugwas Pool *H & W* **27** SO4541
Suisnish *Highld* **84** NG5816
Sulby *IOM* **52** SC3894
Sulgrave *Nhants* **29** SP5544
Sulham *Berks* **21** SU6474
Sulhamstead *Berks* **21** SU6368
Sulhamstead Abbots *Berks* **21** SU6467
Sullom *Shet* **103** HU3573
Sullom Voe *Shet* **103** HU4075
Sully *S Glam* **19** ST1568
Summerbridge *N York* **55** SE2062
Summercourt *Cnwll* **3** SW8856
Summerfield *Norfk* **42** TF7538
Summerhouse *Dur* **61** NZ2019
Summersdale *W Susx* **11** SU8606
Summerseat *Gt Man* **54** SD7914
Summertown *Oxon* **29** SP5009
Sunbury *Surrey* **22** TQ1168
Sundaywell *D & G* **66** NX8284
Sunderland *Cumb* **58** NY1735
Sunderland *Lancs* **53** SD4255
Sunderland *Strath* **70** NR2464
Sunderland *T & W* **69** NZ3957
Sunderland Bridge *Dur* **61** NZ2637
Sundhope *Border* **75** NT3325
Sundridge *Kent* **23** TQ4855
Sunningdale *Berks* **22** SU9567
Sunninghill *Surrey* **22** SU9367
Sunningwell *Oxon* **21** SP4900
Sunniside *Dur* **61** NZ1438
Sunnyhill *Derbys* **39** SK3432
Sunnyhurst *Lancs* **54** SD6722
Sunnylaw *Cent* **81** NS7998
Sunnymead *Oxon* **29** SP5009
Sunwick *Border* **77** NT9052
Surbiton *Gt Lon* **23** TQ1867
Surfleet *Lincs* **41** TF2528
Surlingham *Norfk* **43** TG3106

Surrex Essex ... 24 TL8722
Sustead Norfk ... 43 TG1837
Susworth Lincs ... 50 SE8302
Sutcombe Devon ... 6 SS3411
Sutcombemill Devon ... 6 SS3411
Sutterby Lincs ... 51 TF3872
Sutterton Lincs ... 41 TF2835
Sutton Beds ... 31 TL2247
Sutton Cambs ... 40 TL0998
Sutton Cambs ... 41 TL4479
Sutton Devon ... 5 SX7042
Sutton E Susx ... 13 TV4999
Sutton Gt Lon ... 23 TQ2564
Sutton Kent ... 15 TR3349
Sutton N York ... 55 SE4925
Sutton Norfk ... 43 TG3823
Sutton Notts ... 49 SK6784
Sutton Notts ... 40 SK7637
Sutton Shrops ... 37 SO7386
Sutton Staffs ... 37 SJ7622
Sutton Suffk ... 33 TM3046
Sutton W Susx ... 12 SU9715
Sutton at Hone Kent ... 23 TQ5569
Sutton Bassett Nhants ... 40 SP7790
Sutton Benger Wilts ... 20 ST9478
Sutton Bonington Notts ... 39 SK5024
Sutton Bridge Lincs ... 41 TF4721
Sutton Cheney Leics ... 39 SK4100
Sutton Coldfield W Mids ... 38 SP1296
Sutton Courtenay Oxon ... 21 SU5094
Sutton Grange N York ... 61 SE2873
Sutton Green Surrey ... 22 TQ0054
Sutton Howgrave N York ... 62 SE3179
Sutton in Ashfield Notts ... 49 SK4958
Sutton Maddock Shrops ... 37 SJ7201
Sutton Mallet Somset ... 19 ST3736
Sutton Mandeville Wilts ... 9 ST9828
Sutton Montis Somset ... 9 ST6224
Sutton on Sea Lincs ... 51 TF5281
Sutton on the Hill Derbys ... 39 SK2333
Sutton on Trent Notts ... 50 SK7965
Sutton Scotney Hants ... 10 SU4639
Sutton St Edmund Lincs ... 41 TF3613
Sutton St James Lincs ... 41 TF3918
Sutton St Nicholas H & W ... 27 SO5245
Sutton upon Derwent Humb ... 56 SE7047
Sutton Valence Kent ... 14 TQ8149
Sutton Veny Wilts ... 20 ST9041
Sutton Waldron Dorset ... 9 ST8615
Sutton Weaver Ches ... 47 SJ5479
Sutton Wick Avon ... 19 ST5759
Sutton Wick Oxon ... 21 SU4894
Sutton-in-Craven N York ... 55 SE0043
Sutton-on-Hull Humb ... 57 TA1232
Sutton-on-the-Forest N York ... 56 SE5864
Sutton-under-Brailes Warwks ... 29 SP3037
Sutton-under-Whitestonecliffe N York ... 62 SE4882
Swaby Lincs ... 51 TF3877
Swadlincote Derbys ... 39 SK2919
Swaffham Norfk ... 42 TF8108
Swaffham Bulbeck Cambs ... 31 TL5562
Swaffham Prior Cambs ... 31 TL5764
Swafield Norfk ... 43 TG2832
Swainby N York ... 62 NZ4701
Swainsthorpe Norfk ... 43 TG2101
Swainswick Avon ... 20 ST7668
Swalcliffe Oxon ... 29 SP3737
Swalecliffe Kent ... 15 TR1367
Swallow Lincs ... 57 TA1703
Swallow Beck Lincs ... 50 SK9467
Swallowcliffe Wilts ... 9 ST9627
Swallowfield Berks ... 22 SU7264
Swan Green Ches ... 47 SJ7373
Swanage Dorset ... 10 SZ0378
Swanbourne Bucks ... 30 SP8026
Swanland Humb ... 56 SE9928
Swanley Kent ... 23 TQ5168
Swanley Village Kent ... 23 TQ5369
Swanmore Hants ... 11 SU5716
Swannington Leics ... 39 SK4116
Swannington Norfk ... 43 TG1319
Swanpool Garden Suberb Lincs ... 50 SK9569
Swanscombe Kent ... 14 TQ6074
Swansea W Glam ... 18 SS6592
Swanton Abbot Norfk ... 43 TG2625
Swanton Morley Norfk ... 42 TG0117
Swanton Novers Norfk ... 42 TG0231
Swanwick Derbys ... 49 SK4053
Swanwick Hants ... 11 SU5109
Swarby Lincs ... 50 TF0440
Swardeston Norfk ... 43 TG2002
Swarkestone Derbys ... 39 SK3728
Swarland Nthum ... 69 NU1602
Swarraton Hants ... 11 SU5636
Swarthmoor Cumb ... 58 SD2777
Swaton Lincs ... 40 TF1337
Swavesey Cambs ... 31 TL3668
Sway Hants ... 10 SZ2798
Swayfield Lincs ... 40 SK9922
Swaythling Hants ... 10 SU4416
Sweetham Devon ... 7 SX8899
Sweethaws E Susx ... 13 TQ5028
Sweets Cnwll ... 6 SX1595
Sweetshouse Cnwll ... 3 SX0861
Swefling Suffk ... 33 TM3463
Swepstone Leics ... 39 SK3610
Swerford Oxon ... 29 SP3731
Swettenham Ches ... 47 SJ8067
Swiftsden E Susx ... 14 TQ7328
Swilland Suffk ... 33 TM1852
Swillington W York ... 55 SE3830
Swimbridge Devon ... 6 SS6230
Swimbridge Newland Devon ... 6 SS6030
Swinbrook Oxon ... 29 SP2812
Swincliffe N York ... 55 SE2458
Swinderby Lincs ... 50 SK8663
Swindon Gloucs ... 28 SO9325
Swindon Staffs ... 38 SO8690
Swindon Wilts ... 20 SU1484
Swine Humb ... 57 TA1335
Swinefleet Humb ... 56 SE7621
Swineshead Beds ... 30 TL0565
Swineshead Lincs ... 51 TF2340
Swiney Highld ... 100 ND2335
Swinford Leics ... 39 SP5679
Swingfield Minnis Kent ... 15 TR2142
Swingfield Street Kent ... 15 TR2343
Swingleton Green Suffk ... 32 TL9647
Swinhill Strath ... 74 NS7748
Swinhoe Nthumb ... 77 NU2128
Swinithwaite N York ... 61 SE0489
Swinscoe Staffs ... 48 SK1247
Swinside Cumb ... 58 NY2421
Swinstead Lincs ... 40 TF0122
Swinton Border ... 77 NT8347
Swinton Gt Man ... 47 SD7701

Swinton N York ... 61 SE2179
Swinton N York ... 63 SE7573
Swinton S York ... 49 SK4599
Swithland Leics ... 39 SK5512
Swordale Highld ... 92 NH5765
Swordland Highld ... 85 NM7891
Swordly Highld ... 99 NC7463
Swynnerton Staffs ... 38 SJ8535
Swyre Dorset ... 8 SY5288
Sychtyn Powys ... 35 SH9907
Syde Gloucs ... 28 SO9511
Sydenham Gt Lon ... 23 TQ3671
Sydenham Oxon ... 22 SP7301
Sydenham Damerel Devon ... 4 SX4176
Syderstone Norfk ... 42 TF8332
Sydling St Nicholas Dorset ... 9 SY6399
Sydmonton Hants ... 21 SU4857
Syerston Notts ... 50 SK7447
Sykehouse S York ... 56 SE6316
Symbister Shet ... 103 HU5462
Symington Strath ... 73 NS3831
Symington Strath ... 75 NS9935
Symonds Yat H & W ... 27 SO5515
Symondsbury Dorset ... 8 SY4493
Syre Highld ... 99 NC6943
Syreford Gloucs ... 28 SP0220
Syresham Nhants ... 29 SP6241
Syston Leics ... 39 SK6211
Syston Lincs ... 50 SK9240
Sytchampton H & W ... 28 SO8466
Sywell Nhants ... 30 SP8267

T

Tackley Oxon ... 29 SP4719
Tacolneston Norfk ... 43 TM1495
Tadcaster N York ... 55 SE4843
Taddington Derbys ... 48 SK1471
Taddington Gloucs ... 28 SP0831
Tadley Hants ... 21 SU6061
Tadlow Cambs ... 31 TL2847
Tadmarton Oxon ... 29 SP3937
Tadworth Surrey ... 23 TQ2257
Taff's Well M Glam ... 18 ST1283
Taibach W Glam ... 18 SS7788
Tain Highld ... 100 ND2266
Tain Highld ... 97 NH7781
Tairbeart W Isls ... 102 NB1500
Takeley Essex ... 24 TL5621
Takeley Street Essex ... 24 TL5421
Tal-y-Bont Gwynd ... 45 SH7668
Tal-y-bont Gwynd ... 34 SH5921
Tal-y-bont Gwynd ... 44 SH6070
Tal-y-cafn Gwynd ... 45 SH7672
Tal-y-coed Gwent ... 27 SO4115
Tal-y-garn M Glam ... 18 ST0379
Talaton Devon ... 7 SY0699
Talbenny Dyfed ... 16 SM8411
Taleford Devon ... 8 SY0997
Talerddig Powys ... 35 SH9300
Talgarreg Dyfed ... 17 SN4251
Talgarth Powys ... 27 SO1533
Taliesin Dyfed ... 35 SN6591
Talisker Highld ... 84 NG3230
Talkin Cumb ... 67 NY5557
Talla Linnfoots Border ... 75 NT1320
Talladale Highld ... 91 NG9170
Tallaminnock Strath ... 64 NX4098
Tallam Green Clwyd ... 46 SJ4444
Tallentire Cumb ... 58 NY1035
Talley Dyfed ... 17 SN6332
Tallington Lincs ... 40 TF0908
Talmine Highld ... 99 NC5863
Talog Dyfed ... 17 SN3325
Talsarn Dyfed ... 34 SN5456
Talsarnau Gwynd ... 45 SH6135
Talskiddy Cnwll ... 3 SW9165
Talwrn Gwynd ... 44 SH4877
Talybont Dyfed ... 35 SN6589
Talybont-on-Usk Powys ... 26 SO1122
Talysarn Gwynd ... 44 SH4952
Tamerton Foliot Devon ... 4 SX4761
Tamworth Staffs ... 39 SK2003
Tan Office Green Suffk ... 32 TL7858
Tan-y-groes Dyfed ... 17 SN2849
Tandlemuir Strath ... 73 NS3361
Tandridge Surrey ... 13 TQ3750
Tanfield Dur ... 69 NZ1855
Tanfield Lea Dur ... 69 NZ1854
Tangley Hants ... 21 SU3252
Tangmere W Susx ... 11 SU9006
Tankerness Ork ... 103 HY5109
Tankersley S York ... 49 SK3499
Tankerton Kent ... 15 TR1166
Tannach Highld ... 100 ND3247
Tannachie Gramp ... 89 NO7884
Tannadice Tays ... 89 NO4758
Tanner Green H & W ... 38 SP0874
Tannington Suffk ... 33 TM2467
Tannochside Strath ... 74 NS7061
Tansley Derbys ... 49 SK3259
Tansor Nhants ... 40 TL0590
Tantobie Dur ... 69 NZ1754
Tanton N York ... 62 NZ5210
Tanworth in Arden Warwks ... 28 SP1170
Taobh Tuath W Isls ... 102 NF9989
Taplow Bucks ... 22 SU9182
Tarbert Strath ... 72 NR6551
Tarbert Strath ... 71 NR8668
Tarbert W Isls ... 102 NB1500
Tarbet Highld ... 98 NC1649
Tarbet Highld ... 85 NM7992
Tarbet Strath ... 80 NN3104
Tarbolton Strath ... 73 NS4327
Tarbrax Strath ... 75 NT0255
Tardebigge H & W ... 28 SO9669
Tarfside Tays ... 89 NO4879
Tarland Gramp ... 89 NJ4804
Tarleton Lancs ... 53 SD4520
Tarlton Gloucs ... 20 ST9599
Tarnock Somset ... 19 ST3752
Tarporley Ches ... 47 SJ5562
Tarr Somset ... 7 SS8632
Tarrant Somset ... 8 ST1030
Tarrant Crawford Dorset ... 9 ST9203
Tarrant Gunville Dorset ... 9 ST9213
Tarrant Hinton Dorset ... 9 ST9311
Tarrant Keynston Dorset ... 9 ST9204
Tarrant Launceston Dorset ... 9 ST9409
Tarrant Monkton Dorset ... 9 ST9408
Tarrant Rawston Dorset ... 9 ST9306
Tarrant Rushton Dorset ... 9 ST9305
Tarring Neville E Susx ... 13 TQ4403
Tarrington H & W ... 27 SO6140

Tarskavaig Highld ... 84 NG5810
Tarves Gramp ... 95 NJ8631
Tarvie Tays ... 88 NO0164
Tarvin Ches ... 46 SJ4966
Tasburgh Norfk ... 43 TM1996
Tatenhill Staffs ... 39 SK2021
Tathwell Lincs ... 51 TF3182
Tatsfield Surrey ... 23 TQ4156
Tattenhall Ches ... 46 SJ4858
Tatterford Norfk ... 42 TF8628
Tattersett Norfk ... 42 TF8429
Tattershall Lincs ... 51 TF2157
Tattershall Thorpe Lincs ... 51 TF2159
Tattingstone Suffk ... 25 TM1337
Tattingstone White Horse Suffk ... 25 TM1338
Tatworth Somset ... 8 ST3205
Tauchers Gramp ... 94 NJ3749
Taunton Somset ... 8 ST2224
Taverham Norfk ... 43 TG1613
Tavernspite Dyfed ... 17 SN1812
Tavistock Devon ... 4 SX4874
Taw green Devon ... 7 SX6597
Tawstock Devon ... 6 SS5529
Taxal Derbys ... 48 SK0079
Taychreggan Hotel Strath ... 80 NN0421
Tayinloan Strath ... 72 NR6946
Taynton Gloucs ... 28 SO7222
Taynton Oxon ... 29 SP2313
Taynuilt Strath ... 80 NN0031
Tayport Fife ... 83 NO4628
Tayvallich Strath ... 71 NR7487
Tealby Lincs ... 50 TF1590
Teangue Highld ... 85 NG6609
Teanord Highld ... 92 NH5964
Tebay Cumb ... 59 NY6104
Tebworth Beds ... 30 SP9926
Tedburn St Mary Devon ... 7 SX8194
Teddington Gloucs ... 28 SO9633
Teddington Gt Lon ... 22 TQ1670
Teddington Delamere H & W ... 28 SO6958
Tedstone Wafer H & W ... 28 SO6759
Teeton Nhants ... 30 SP6970
Teffont Evias Wilts ... 9 ST9931
Teffont Magna Wilts ... 9 ST9932
Tegryn Dyfed ... 17 SN2233
Teigh Leics ... 40 SK8615
Teigngrace Devon ... 5 SX8574
Teignmouth Devon ... 5 SX9473
Teindside Border ... 67 NT4408
Telford Shrops ... 37 SJ6908
Tellisford Somset ... 20 ST8055
Telscombe E Susx ... 13 TQ4003
Tempar Tays ... 87 NN6857
Templand D & G ... 66 NY0886
Temple Cnwll ... 3 SX1473
Temple Loth ... 75 NT3158
Temple Strath ... 74 NS5469
Temple Bar Dyfed ... 34 SN5354
Temple Cloud Avon ... 19 ST6257
Temple Ewell Kent ... 15 TR2844
Temple Grafton Warwks ... 28 SP1255
Temple Guiting Gloucs ... 28 SP0928
Temple Hirst N York ... 56 SE6024
Temple Normanton Derbys ... 49 SK4167
Temple Pier Highld ... 92 NH5330
Temple Sowerby Cumb ... 59 NY6127
Templecombe Somset ... 9 ST7022
Templeton Devon ... 7 SS8813
Templeton Dyfed ... 16 SN1111
Templetown Dur ... 68 NZ1050
Tempsford Beds ... 31 TL1653
Ten Mile Bank Norfk ... 41 TL5996
Tenbury Wells H & W ... 27 SO5968
Tenby Dyfed ... 16 SN1300
Tendring Essex ... 25 TM1424
Tendring Green Essex ... 25 TM1325
Tendring Heath Essex ... 25 TM1325
Tenterden Kent ... 14 TQ8833
Terling Essex ... 24 TL7715
Ternhill Shrops ... 37 SJ6332
Terregles D & G ... 66 NX9377
Terrington N York ... 56 SE6770
Terrington St Clement Norfk ... 41 TF5520
Terrington St John Norfk ... 41 TF5314
Teston Kent ... 14 TQ7053
Testwood Hants ... 10 SU3514
Tetbury Gloucs ... 20 ST8993
Tetchill Shrops ... 36 SJ3932
Tetcott Devon ... 6 SX3396
Tetford Lincs ... 51 TF3374
Tetney Lincs ... 51 TA3100
Tetsworth Oxon ... 22 SP6801
Tettenhall W Mids ... 38 SJ8800
Teversal Notts ... 49 SK4861
Teversham Cambs ... 31 TL6958
Teviothead Border ... 67 NT4005
Tewel Gramp ... 89 NO8085
Tewin Herts ... 31 TL2714
Tewkesbury Gloucs ... 28 SO8932
Teynham Kent ... 15 TQ9662
Thackley W York ... 55 SE1738
Thakeham W Susx ... 12 TQ1017
Thame Oxon ... 22 SP7005
Thames Ditton Surrey ... 22 TQ1567
Thamesmead Gt Lon ... 23 TQ4780
Thanington Kent ... 15 TR1356
Thankerton Strath ... 75 NS9738
Tharston Norfk ... 43 TM1894
Thatcham Berks ... 21 SU5167
Thaxted Essex ... 24 TL6131
The Beeches Gloucs ... 20 SO0302
The Braes Highld ... 84 NG5234
The Brunt Loth ... 76 NT6873
The Bungalow IOM ... 52 SC3986
The Butts Gloucs ... 28 SO8916
The City Bucks ... 22 SU7896
The Corner Shrops ... 36 SO4387
The Den Strath ... 73 NS3251
The Forstal Kent ... 14 TQ9846
The Forstal Kent ... 15 TR0438
The Green Cumb ... 58 SD1884
The Green Essex ... 24 TL7719
The Hill Cumb ... 58 SD1783
The Hirsel Border ... 77 NT8240
The Holt Berks ... 22 SU8078
The Lee Bucks ... 22 SP9004
The Lhen IOM ... 52 NX3801
The Lochs Gramp ... 94 NJ3062
The Moor Kent ... 14 TQ7529
The Mumbles W Glam ... 17 SS6187
The Mythe Gloucs ... 28 SO8934
The Neuk Gramp ... 89 NO7397
The Reddings Gloucs ... 28 SO9121
The Ross Tays ... 81 NN7621
The Stocks Kent ... 14 TQ9127
The Strand Wilts ... 20 ST9259
Theakston N York ... 61 SE3085

Thealby Humb ... 56 SE8917
Theale Berks ... 21 SU6471
Theale Somset ... 19 ST4645
Thearne Humb ... 57 TA0736
Theberton Suffk ... 33 TM4365
Theddingworth Leics ... 39 SP6685
Theddlethorpe All Saints Lincs ... 51 TF4688
Theddlethorpe St Helen Lincs ... 51 TF4788
Thelnetham Suffk ... 32 TM0178
Thelveton Norfk ... 33 TM1681
Thelwall Ches ... 47 SJ6587
Themelthorpe Norfk ... 42 TG0524
Thenford Nhants ... 29 SP5251
Therfield Herts ... 31 TL3337
Thetford Norfk ... 32 TL8783
Theydon Bois Essex ... 23 TQ4499
Thickwood Wilts ... 20 ST8272
Thimbleby Lincs ... 51 TF2470
Thimbleby N York ... 62 SE4495
Thingwall Mersyd ... 46 SJ2784
Thirkleby N York ... 62 SE4778
Thirlby N York ... 62 SE4883
Thirlestane Border ... 76 NT5647
Thirlspot Cumb ... 58 NY3118
Thirn N York ... 61 SE2185
Thirsk N York ... 62 SE4281
Thistleton Lancs ... 53 SD4037
Thistleton Leics ... 40 SK9118
Thistley Green Suffk ... 32 TL6676
Thixendale N York ... 56 SE8460
Thockrington Nthumb ... 68 NY9578
Tholomas Drove Cambs ... 41 TF4006
Tholthorpe N York ... 55 SE4766
Thomastown Gramp ... 94 NJ5736
Thompson Norfk ... 42 TL9296
Thong Kent ... 14 TQ6770
Thoralby N York ... 61 SE0086
Thoresway Lincs ... 50 TF1696
Thorganby Lincs ... 51 TF2097
Thorganby N York ... 56 SE6841
Thorgill N York ... 62 SE7096
Thorington Suffk ... 33 TM4174
Thorington Street Suffk ... 25 TM0035
Thorlby N York ... 54 SD9653
Thorley Herts ... 31 TL4718
Thorley Street IOW ... 10 SZ3788
Thormanby N York ... 62 SE4974
Thornaby-on-Tees Cleve ... 62 NZ4518
Thornage Norfk ... 42 TG0536
Thornborough Bucks ... 30 SP7433
Thornborough N York ... 61 SE2979
Thornbury Avon ... 19 ST6390
Thornbury Devon ... 6 SS4008
Thornbury H & W ... 27 SO6259
Thornbury W York ... 55 SE1933
Thornby Nhants ... 39 SP6775
Thorncliff Staffs ... 48 SK0158
Thorncombe Dorset ... 8 ST3703
Thorndon Suffk ... 33 TM1469
Thorndon Cross Devon ... 6 SX5394
Thorne S York ... 56 SE6812
Thorne Somset ... 8 ST5217
Thorne St Margaret Somset ... 8 ST1020
Thorner W York ... 55 SE3740
Thornes Staffs ... 38 SK0703
Thorney Cambs ... 41 TF2804
Thorney Notts ... 50 SK8572
Thorney Somset ... 8 ST4223
Thorney Hill Hants ... 10 SZ2099
Thornfalcon Somset ... 8 ST2823
Thornford Dorset ... 9 ST6012
Thorngrafton Nthumb ... 68 NY7865
Thorngumbald Humb ... 57 TA2026
Thornham Norfk ... 42 TF7343
Thornham Magna Suffk ... 33 TM1070
Thornham Parva Suffk ... 33 TM1072
Thornhaugh Cambs ... 40 TF0600
Thornhill Cent ... 81 NN6600
Thornhill D & G ... 66 NX8795
Thornhill Derbys ... 48 SK1983
Thornhill Hants ... 10 SU4612
Thornholme Humb ... 57 TA1164
Thornicombe Dorset ... 9 ST8703
Thornington Nthumb ... 77 NT8833
Thornley Dur ... 61 NZ1137
Thornley Dur ... 62 NZ3639
Thornliebank Strath ... 74 NS5559
Thorns Suffk ... 32 TL7455
Thornsett Derbys ... 48 SK0086
Thornthwaite Cumb ... 58 NY2225
Thornthwaite N York ... 55 SE1758
Thornton Bucks ... 30 SP7435
Thornton Cleve ... 62 NZ4713
Thornton Fife ... 83 NT2897
Thornton Humb ... 56 SE7645
Thornton Lancs ... 53 SD3342
Thornton Leics ... 39 SK4607
Thornton Lincs ... 51 TF2467
Thornton Nthumb ... 77 NT9547
Thornton Tays ... 88 NO3946
Thornton W York ... 55 SE0932
Thornton Curtis Humb ... 57 TA0817
Thornton Dale N York ... 63 SE8383
Thornton Heath Gt Lon ... 23 TQ3168
Thornton Hough Mersyd ... 46 SJ3080
Thornton in Lonsdale N York ... 60 SD6873
Thornton le Moor Lincs ... 50 TF0496
Thornton Rust N York ... 61 SD9689
Thornton Steward N York ... 61 SE1787
Thornton Watlass N York ... 61 SE2385
Thornton-in-Craven N York ... 54 SD9048
Thornton-le-Beans N York ... 62 SE3990
Thornton-le-Clay N York ... 56 SE6865
Thornton-le-Moor N York ... 62 SE3988
Thornton-le-Moors Ches ... 46 SJ4474
Thornton-le-Street N York ... 62 SE4186
Thorntonhall Strath ... 74 NS5955
Thorntonloch Loth ... 76 NT7574
Thornydykes Border ... 76 NT6148
Thornythwaite Cumb ... 59 NY3922
Thoroton Notts ... 50 SK7642
Thorp Arch W York ... 55 SE4345
Thorpe Derbys ... 48 SK1550
Thorpe Humb ... 56 SE9946
Thorpe N York ... 61 SE0161
Thorpe Notts ... 50 SK7649
Thorpe Surrey ... 22 TQ0186
Thorpe Abbotts Norfk ... 33 TM1979
Thorpe Arnold Leics ... 40 SK7720
Thorpe Audlin W York ... 55 SE4715
Thorpe Bassett N York ... 63 SE8673
Thorpe Bay Essex ... 24 TQ9185
Thorpe by Water Leics ... 40 SP8996
Thorpe Constantine Staffs ... 39 SK2508
Thorpe End Norfk ... 43 TG2810
Thorpe Green Essex ... 25 TM1623
Thorpe Green Suffk ... 32 TL9354
Thorpe Hesley S York ... 49 SK3796

Thorpe in Balne S York..........56 SE5910
Thorpe in the Fallows Lincs..........50 SK9180
Thorpe Langton Leics..........40 SP7492
Thorpe le Street Humb..........56 SE8343
Thorpe Lea Surrey..........22 TQ0170
Thorpe Malsor Nhants..........30 SP8378
Thorpe Mandeville Nhants..........29 SP5244
Thorpe Market Norfk..........43 TG2436
Thorpe Morieux Suffk..........32 TL9453
Thorpe on the Hill Lincs..........50 SK9065
Thorpe Salvin S York..........49 SK5281
Thorpe Satchville Leics..........40 SK7311
Thorpe St Andrew Norfk..........43 TG2508
Thorpe St Peter Lincs..........51 TF4860
Thorpe Thewles Cleve..........62 NZ3923
Thorpe Tilney Lincs..........50 TF1257
Thorpe Underwood N York..........55 SE4659
Thorpe Waterville Nhants..........40 TL0281
Thorpe Willoughby N York..........56 SE5731
Thorpe-le-Soken Essex..........25 TM1722
Thorpeness Suffk..........33 TM4759
Thorrington Essex..........25 TM0919
Thorverton Devon..........7 SS9202
Thrandeston Suffk..........33 TM1176
Thrapston Nhants..........30 SP9978
Threapwood Ches..........46 SJ4344
Threapwood Staffs..........48 SK0342
Threave Strath..........73 NS3306
Three Bridges W Susx..........12 TQ2837
Three Chimneys Kent..........14 TQ8238
Three Cocks Powys..........27 SO1737
Three Crosses W Glam..........17 SS5794
Three Cups Corner E Susx..........13 TQ6320
Three Leg Cross E Susx..........14 TQ6831
Three Legged Cross Dorset..........10 SU0805
Three Mile Cross Berks..........22 SU7167
Three Miletown Loth..........75 NT0675
Three Oaks E. Susx..........14 TQ8314
Threekingham Lincs..........40 TF0836
Threepwood Border..........76 NT5143
Threlkeld Cumb..........58 NY3125
Threshfield N York..........54 SD9863
Thrigby Norfk..........43 TG4612
Thringstone Leics..........39 SK4217
Thrintoft N York..........39 SE3192
Thriplow Cambs..........31 TL4346
Throcking Herts..........31 TL3330
Throckley T & W..........69 NZ1566
Throckmorton H & W..........28 SO9850
Throop Dorset..........9 SY8292
Throop Dorset..........10 SZ1195
Thropton Nthumb..........68 NU0202
Throsk Cent..........82 NS8591
Throughgate D & G..........66 NX8784
Throwleigh Devon..........5 SX6690
Throwley Forstal Kent..........15 TQ9854
Thrumpton Notts..........39 SK5031
Thrumster Highld..........100 ND3345
Thrunscoe Humb..........57 TA3107
Thrupp Gloucs..........20 SO8603
Thrushesbush Essex..........23 TL4909
Thrussington Leics..........39 SK6515
Thruxton H & W..........27 SO4334
Thruxton Hants..........21 SU2945
Thulston Derbys..........39 SK4031
Thundersley Essex..........24 TQ7988
Thurcaston Leics..........39 SK5610
Thurcroft S York..........49 SK4988
Thurgarton Norfk..........43 TG1834
Thurgarton Notts..........49 SK6949
Thurgoland S York..........49 SE2901
Thurlaston Leics..........39 SP5099
Thurlaston Warwks..........29 SP4670
Thurlbear Somset..........8 ST2621
Thurlby Lincs..........50 SK9061
Thurlby Lincs..........40 TF0916
Thurlby Lincs..........51 TF4776
Thurleigh Beds..........30 TL0558
Thurlestone Devon..........5 SX6742
Thurlow Suffk..........32 TL6750
Thurloxton Somset..........8 ST2730
Thurlstone S York..........55 SE2303
Thurlton Norfk..........43 TM4198
Thurmaston Leics..........39 SK6109
Thurnby Leics..........39 SK6403
Thurne Norfk..........43 TG4015
Thurnham Kent..........14 TQ8057
Thurning Nhants..........40 TL0882
Thurning Norfk..........42 TG0729
Thurnscoe S York..........55 SE4505
Thursby Cumb..........67 NY3250
Thursford Norfk..........42 TF9833
Thursley Surrey..........11 SU9039
Thurso Highld..........100 ND1168
Thurstaston Mersyd..........46 SJ2484
Thurston Suffk..........32 TL9265
Thurstonfield Cumb..........67 NY3156
Thurstonland W York..........55 SE1610
Thurton Norfk..........43 TG3200
Thurvaston Derbys..........48 SK2437
Thuxton Norfk..........42 TG0307
Thwaite N York..........60 SD8998
Thwaite Suffk..........33 TM1168
Thwaite Head Cumb..........59 SD3490
Thwaite St Mary Norfk..........43 TM3395
Thwing Humb..........57 TA0470
Tibbermore Tays..........82 NO0423
Tibbers D & G..........66 NX8696
Tibberton Gloucs..........28 SO7521
Tibberton H & W..........28 SO9057
Tibberton Shrops..........37 SJ6820
Tibbie Shiels Inn Border..........75 NT2420
Tibenham Norfk..........33 TM1389
Tibshelf Derbys..........49 SK4461
Tibthorpe Humb..........56 SE9555
Ticehurst E Susx..........14 TQ6830
Tichborne Hants..........11 SU5730
Tickencote Leics..........40 SK9009
Tickenham Avon..........19 ST4571
Tickhill S York..........49 SK5993
Ticklerton Shrops..........37 SO4890
Ticknall Derbys..........39 SK3523
Tickton Humb..........57 TA0541
Tidcombe Wilts..........21 SU2858
Tiddington Oxon..........29 SP6404
Tiddington Warwks..........29 SP2255
Tidebrook E Susx..........13 TQ6130
Tideford Cnwll..........4 SX3559
Tidenham Gloucs..........19 ST5595
Tideswell Derbys..........48 SK1575
Tidmarsh Berks..........21 SU6374
Tidmington Warwks..........29 SP2538
Tiers Cross Dyfed..........16 SM9010
Tiffield Nhants..........30 SP7051
Tigerton Tays..........89 NO5364
Tigh a Ghearraidh W Isls..........102 NF7172
Tigharry W Isls..........102 NF7172
Tighnabruaich Strath..........71 NR9873

Tigley Devon..........5 SX7660
Tilbrook Cambs..........30 TL0869
Tilbury Essex..........14 TQ6476
Tilbury Green Essex..........32 TL7441
Tile Hill W Mids..........39 SP2777
Tilehurst Berks..........22 SU6673
Tilford Surrey..........11 SU8743
Tilgate W Susx..........12 TQ2734
Tilham Street Somset..........9 ST5535
Tillicoultry Cent..........82 NS9197
Tillingham Essex..........25 TL9904
Tillington H & W..........27 SO4644
Tillington W Susx..........12 SU9621
Tillington Common H & W..........27 SO4545
Tillybirloch Gramp..........95 NJ6807
Tillycairn Gramp..........89 NO4697
Tillyfourie Gramp..........94 NJ6412
Tillygreig Gramp..........95 NJ8822
Tillyrie Tays..........82 NO1006
Tilmanstone Kent..........15 TR3051
Tilney All Saints Norfk..........41 TF5618
Tilney High End Norfk..........41 TF5617
Tilney St Lawrence Norfk..........41 TF5414
Tilshead Wilts..........20 SU0347
Tilstock Shrops..........37 SJ5437
Tilston Ches..........46 SJ4650
Tilstone Fearnall Ches..........47 SJ5660
Tilsworth Beds..........30 SP9824
Tilton on the Hill Leics..........40 SK7405
Tiltups End Gloucs..........20 ST8497
Timberland Lincs..........50 TF1258
Timberscombe Somset..........7 SS9542
Timble N York..........55 SE1853
Timpanheck D & G..........67 NY3274
Timperley Gt Man..........47 SJ7888
Timsbury Avon..........20 ST6758
Timsbury Hants..........11 SU3424
Timsgarry W Isls..........102 NB0534
Timsgearraidh W Isls..........102 NB0534
Timworth Suffk..........32 TL8669
Timworth Green Suffk..........32 TL8669
Tincleton Dorset..........9 SY7692
Tindale Cumb..........68 NY6159
Tindale Crescent Dur..........61 NZ1927
Tingewick Bucks..........29 SP6532
Tingley W York..........55 SE2826
Tingrith Beds..........30 TL0032
Tinhay Devon..........4 SX3985
Tinsley S York..........49 SK4090
Tinsley Green W Susx..........12 TQ2839
Tintagel Cnwll..........4 SX0588
Tintern Parva Gwent..........19 SO5200
Tintinhull Somset..........8 ST4919
Tintwistle Derbys..........48 SK0197
Tinwald D & G..........67 NY0081
Tinwell Leics..........40 TF0006
Tipp's End Norfk..........41 TL5095
Tippacott Devon..........18 SS7647
Tipton W Mids..........38 SO9492
Tipton St John Devon..........5 SY0991
Tiptree Essex..........24 TL8916
Tiptree Heath Essex..........24 TL8815
Tirabad Powys..........26 SN8741
Tiretigan Strath..........71 NR7162
Tirley Gloucs..........28 SO8328
Tirphil M Glam..........18 SO1303
Tirril Cumb..........59 NY5026
Tisbury Wilts..........9 ST9429
Tissington Derbys..........48 SK1752
Titchberry Devon..........6 SS2427
Titchfield Hants..........11 SU5405
Titchmarsh Nhants..........40 TL0279
Titchwell Norfk..........42 TF7643
Tithby Notts..........49 SK6937
Titley H & W..........27 SO3360
Titmore Green Herts..........31 TL2126
Titsey Surrey..........23 TQ4054
Tittensor Staffs..........38 SJ8738
Tittleshall Norfk..........42 TF8921
Titton H & W..........28 SO8370
Tiverton Ches..........47 SJ5560
Tiverton Devon..........7 SS9512
Tivetshall St Margaret Norfk..........33 TM1787
Tivetshall St Mary Norfk..........33 TM1686
Tivington Somset..........7 SS9345
Tixall Staffs..........38 SJ9722
Tixover Leics..........40 SK9700
Toab Shet..........103 HU3811
Toadmoor Derbys..........49 SK3451
Tobermory Strath..........79 NM5055
Toberonochy Strath..........79 NM7408
Tobha Mor W Isls..........102 NF7536
Tocher Gramp..........95 NJ6932
Tochieneal Gramp..........94 NJ5165
Tockenham Wilts..........20 SU0379
Tockington Avon..........19 ST6086
Tockwith N York..........55 SE4652
Todber Dorset..........9 ST7919
Todburn Nthumb..........69 NZ1295
Toddington Beds..........30 TL0128
Toddington Gloucs..........28 SP0333
Todds Green Herts..........31 TL2226
Todenham Gloucs..........29 SP2335
Todhills Cumb..........67 NY3762
Todhills Tays..........83 NO4239
Todmorden W York..........54 SD9324
Todwick S York..........49 SK4984
Toft Cambs..........31 TL3656
Toft Lincs..........40 TF0717
Toft Shet..........103 HU4376
Toft Hill Dur..........61 NZ1528
Toft Monks Norfk..........43 TM4294
Toft next Newton Lincs..........50 TF0386
Toftrees Norfk..........42 TF8927
Tofts Highld..........100 ND3668
Togston Nthumb..........69 NU2402
Tokavaig Highld..........84 NG6011
Tokers Green Oxon..........22 SU7077
Tolastadh W Isls..........102 NB5347
Toll Bar S York..........56 SE5507
Tolland Somset..........8 ST1032
Tollard Royal Wilts..........9 ST9417
Toller Fratrum Dorset..........9 SY5797
Toller Porcorum Dorset..........9 SY5698
Toller Whelme Dorset..........8 ST5101
Tollerton N York..........55 SE5164
Tollerton Notts..........39 SK6134
Tollesbury Essex..........25 TL9510
Tolleshunt D'Arcy Essex..........24 TL9211
Tolleshunt Knights Essex..........24 TL9114
Tolleshunt Major Essex..........24 TL9011
Tolpuddle Dorset..........9 SY7994
Tolsta W Isls..........102 NB5347
Tolworth Gt Lon..........23 TQ1966
Tomakneck Tays..........82 NN7521
Tomatin Highld..........93 NH8028
Tomchrasky Highld..........92 NH2512

Tomdoun Highld..........86 NH1500
Tomich Highld..........97 NC6005
Tomich Highld..........92 NH3027
Tomich Highld..........92 NH5348
Tomich Highld..........93 NH6971
Tomintoul Gramp..........94 NJ1619
Tomnacross Highld..........92 NH5143
Tomnavoulin Gramp..........94 NJ2126
Tonbridge Kent..........13 TQ5846
Tondu M Glam..........18 SS8984
Tonedale Somset..........8 ST1321
Tong Kent..........14 TQ9556
Tong Shrops..........37 SJ7907
Tong W York..........55 SE2230
Tong Norton Shrops..........37 SJ7908
Tong Street W York..........55 SE1930
Tonge Leics..........39 SK4223
Tongham Surrey..........22 SU8848
Tongland D & G..........65 NX6954
Tongue Highld..........99 NC5956
Tongwynlais S Glam..........18 ST1382
Tonna W Glam..........18 SS7798
Tonwell Herts..........31 TL3316
Tonypandy M Glam..........18 SS9991
Tonyrefail M Glam..........18 ST0188
Toot Baldon Oxon..........21 SP5600
Toot Hill Essex..........23 TL5102
Toothill Wilts..........20 SU1183
Tooting Gt Lon..........23 TQ2771
Tooting Bec Gt Lon..........23 TQ2872
Topcliffe N York..........62 SE3976
Topcroft Norfk..........43 TM2693
Topcroft Street Norfk..........33 TM2691
Toppesfield Essex..........24 TL7437
Toprow Norfk..........43 TM1698
Topsham Devon..........5 SX9688
Torbeg Strath..........72 NR8929
Torboll Highld..........97 NH7599
Torbreck Highld..........92 NH6441
Torbryan Devon..........5 SX8266
Torcastle Highld..........86 NN1378
Torcross Devon..........5 SX8241
Tore Highld..........92 NH6052
Torksey Lincs..........50 SK8378
Tormarton Avon..........20 ST7678
Tormitchell Strath..........64 NX2394
Tormore Strath..........72 NR8932
Tornagrain Highld..........93 NH7650
Tornaveen Gramp..........89 NJ6106
Torness Highld..........92 NH5826
Toronto Dur..........61 NZ1930
Torosay Castle Strath..........79 NM7335
Torpenhow Cumb..........58 NY2039
Torphichen Loth..........75 NS9672
Torphins Gramp..........89 NJ6202
Torpoint Cnwll..........4 SX4355
Torquay Devon..........5 SX9164
Torquhan Border..........76 NT4448
Torran Highld..........90 NG5949
Torrance Strath..........74 NS6173
Torranyard Strath..........73 NS3544
Torridon Highld..........91 NG9055
Torridon House Highld..........91 NG8657
Torrin Highld..........84 NG5721
Torrisdale Highld..........99 NC6761
Torrisdale Square Strath..........72 NR7936
Torrish Highld..........97 NC9718
Torrisholme Lancs..........53 SD4563
Torrobull Highld..........97 NC5904
Torry Gramp..........89 NJ9405
Torryburn Fife..........82 NT0286
Tortan H & W..........38 SO8472
Torteval Guern..........101 GN0000
Torthorwald D & G..........66 NY0378
Tortington W Susx..........20 TQ0004
Tortworth Avon..........20 ST7093
Torvaig Highld..........90 NG4944
Torver Cumb..........58 SD2894
Torwood Cent..........76 NS8385
Torwoodlee Border..........76 NT4738
Torworth Notts..........49 SK6586
Toscaig Highld..........85 NG7138
Toseland Cambs..........31 TL2462
Tosside Lancs..........54 SD7656
Tostock Suffk..........32 TL9563
Totaig Highld..........90 NG2050
Tote Highld..........90 NG4149
Tote Highld..........90 NG5160
Tote Hill W Susx..........11 SU8624
Totland IOW..........10 SZ3287
Totley S York..........49 SK3079
Totnes Devon..........5 SX8060
Toton Notts..........39 SK5034
Totronald Strath..........78 NM1656
Totscore Highld..........90 NG3866
Tottenham Gt Lon..........23 TQ3390
Tottenhill Norfk..........41 TF6411
Totteridge Gt Lon..........23 TQ2494
Totternhoe Beds..........30 SP9821
Tottington Gt Man..........54 SD7712
Totton Hants..........10 SU3613
Toulston Hants..........8 ST1931
Toulvaddie Highld..........97 NH8880
Tovil Kent..........14 TQ7554
Tow Law Dur..........61 NZ1138
Toward Strath..........73 NS1368
Toward Quay Strath..........73 NS1167
Towcester Nhants..........30 SP6948
Towednack Cnwll..........2 SW4838
Towersey Oxon..........22 SP7305
Towie Gramp..........94 NJ4312
Town End Cambs..........41 TL4195
Town Littleworth E Susx..........13 TQ4117
Town Street Suffk..........32 TL7785
Town Yetholm Border..........76 NT8128
Townend Strath..........81 NS3976
Townhead D & G..........66 NY0088
Townhead S York..........48 SE1602
Townhead of
    Greenlaw D & G..........65 NX7464
Townhill Loth..........82 NT1089
Towns End Hants..........21 SU5659
Townshend Cnwll..........2 SW5932
Towthorpe N York..........55 SE4839
Towton N York..........55 SE4839
Toxteth Mersyd..........46 SJ3588
Toy's Hill Kent..........13 TQ4651
Toynton All Saints Lincs..........51 TF3963
Trabboch Strath..........73 NS4421
Trabbochburn Strath..........73 NS4620
Traethsaith Dyfed..........16 SN2651
Trafford Park Gt Man..........47 SJ7896
Trallong Powys..........26 SN9529
Tranent Loth..........76 NT4072
Tranmere Mersyd..........46 SJ3187
Trantelbeg Highld..........99 NC8952
Trantlemore Highld..........99 NC8953

Trap Dyfed..........26 SN6518
Traquair Border..........75 NT3334
Traveller's Rest Devon..........5 SS6127
Trawden Lancs..........54 SD9138
Trawsfynydd Gwynd..........45 SH7035
Tre-groes Dyfed..........17 SN4044
Trealaw M Glam..........18 ST0092
Treales Lancs..........53 SD4332
Trearddur Bay Gwynd..........44 SH2579
Treaslane Highld..........90 NG3953
Trebarwith Cnwll..........4 SX0586
Trebetherick Cnwll..........3 SW9378
Treborough Somset..........7 ST0136
Trebullett Cnwll..........4 SX3278
Treburley Cnwll..........4 SX3577
Trecastle Powys..........26 SN8829
Trecwn Dyfed..........16 SM9632
Trecynon M Glam..........18 SN9903
Tredaule Cnwll..........4 SX2381
Tredegar Gwent..........18 SO1408
Tredington Gloucs..........28 SO9029
Tredington Warwks..........29 SP2543
Tredunhock Gwent..........19 ST3794
Treen Cnwll..........2 SW3923
Treeton S York..........49 SK4387
Trefacca Powys..........26 SO1431
Trefasser Dyfed..........16 SM8938
Trefeglwys Powys..........35 SN9690
Treffgarne Dyfed..........16 SM9523
Treffgarne Owen Dyfed..........16 SM8625
Trefforest M Glam..........18 ST0888
Trefilan Dyfed..........34 SN5456
Trefnant Clwyd..........45 SJ0570
Trefonen Shrops..........36 SJ2526
Trefrew Cnwll..........4 SX1084
Trefriw Gwynd..........45 SH7863
Tregadillett Cnwll..........4 SX2983
Tregare Gwent..........27 SO4110
Tregaron Dyfed..........26 SN6759
Tregarth Gwynd..........44 SH6067
Tregeare Cnwll..........4 SX2486
Tregeiriog Clwyd..........36 SJ1733
Tregele Gwynd..........44 SH3592
Tregidden Cnwll..........2 SW7523
Treglemais Dyfed..........16 SM8229
Tregole Cnwll..........6 SX1998
Tregonce Cnwll..........3 SW9373
Tregonetha Cnwll..........3 SW9563
Tregony Cnwll..........3 SW9244
Tregoyd Powys..........27 SO1937
Tregynon Powys..........36 SO0998
Trehafod M Glam..........18 ST0490
Trehan Cnwll..........4 SX4058
Treharris M Glam..........18 ST0996
Treherbert M Glam..........18 SS9498
Trekenner Cnwll..........4 SX3478
Treknow Cnwll..........4 SX0586
Trelawnyd Clwyd..........46 SJ0979
Trelech Dyfed..........17 SN2830
Treleddyd-fawr Dyfed..........16 SM7528
Trelewis M Glam..........18 ST1096
Trelights Cnwll..........3 SW9979
Trelill Cnwll..........3 SX0478
Trelleck Gwent..........27 SO5005
Trelogan Clwyd..........46 SJ1180
Trelow Cnwll..........3 SW9269
Tremadog Gwynd..........44 SH5640
Tremail Cnwll..........4 SX1686
Tremain Dyfed..........17 SN2047
Tremaine Cnwll..........4 SX2389
Tremar Cnwll..........4 SX2568
Trematon Cnwll..........4 SX3959
Tremeirchion Clwyd..........46 SJ0873
Trenance Cnwll..........3 SW8568
Trenance Cnwll..........3 SW9270
Trencreek Cnwll..........6 SX1896
Trenear Cnwll..........2 SW6731
Treneglos Cnwll..........4 SX2088
Trent Dorset..........9 ST5918
Trentishoe Devon..........18 SS6448
Treoes S Glam..........18 SS9478
Treorchy M Glam..........18 SS9597
Trequite Cnwll..........3 SX0377
Trerhyngyll S Glam..........18 ST0077
Trerulefoot Cnwll..........4 SX3358
Trescowe Cnwll..........2 SW5731
Tresean Cnwll..........2 SW7858
Tresham Gloucs..........20 ST7991
Tresillian Cnwll..........3 SW8646
Treskinnick Cross Cnwll..........6 SX2098
Tresmeer Cnwll..........4 SX2387
Tresparrett Cnwll..........4 SX1491
Tressait Tays..........87 NN8160
Tresta Shet..........103 HU3650
Tresta Shet..........103 HU6090
Treswell Notts..........50 SK7879
Trethevey Cnwll..........4 SX0789
Trethewey Cnwll..........2 SW3823
Trethurgy Cnwll..........3 SX0355
Tretire H & W..........27 SO5123
Tretower Powys..........27 SO1821
Treuddyn Clwyd..........46 SJ2557
Trevague Cnwll..........4 SX2379
Trevalga Cnwll..........4 SX0890
Trevalyn Clwyd..........46 SJ3856
Trevanson Cnwll..........3 SW9773
Trevarrian Cnwll..........3 SW8566
Treveal Cnwll..........2 SW7858
Treveighan Cnwll..........3 SX0779
Trevellas Downs Cnwll..........2 SW7452
Trevelmond Cnwll..........4 SX2063
Treverva Cnwll..........2 SW7531
Trevescan Cnwll..........2 SW3524
Trevine Dyfed..........16 SM8432
Treviscoe Cnwll..........3 SW9455
Trevone Cnwll..........3 SW8975
Trevor Clwyd..........36 SJ2742
Trewalder Cnwll..........3 SX0782
Trewarlett Cnwll..........4 SX3380
Trewarmett Cnwll..........4 SX0686
Treween Cnwll..........4 SX2182
Treween Cnwll..........4 SX2583
Trewen Cnwll..........3 SX0577
Trewen Cnwll..........4 SX2180
Trewint Cnwll..........3 SW8737
Trewithian Cnwll..........3 SW8737
Trewoon Cnwll..........3 SW9952
Treyford W Susx..........11 SU8218
Triangle W York..........55 SE0422
Trimdon Dur..........62 NZ3634
Trimdon Colliery Dur..........62 NZ3735
Trimdon Grange Dur..........62 NZ3635
Trimingham Norfk..........43 TG2838
Trimley Suffk..........25 TM2737
Trimley Heath Suffk..........25 TM2738
Trimsaran Dyfed..........17 SN4504
Trimstone Devon..........6 SS5043
Trinafour Tays..........87 NN7264

Tring Herts 22 SP9211
Trinity Jersey 101 JS0000
Trinity Tays 89 NO6061
Trinity Gask Tays 82 NN9718
Triscombe Somset 7 SS9237
Triscombe Somset 8 ST1535
Trislaig Highld 86 NN0874
Trispen Cnwll 3 SW8450
Tritlington Nthumb 69 NZ2092
Trochry Tays 82 NN9740
Troedrhiwfuwch M Glam 26 SO1204
Troedyraur Dyfed 17 SN3245
Troedyrhiw M Glam 18 SO0702
Trois Bois Jersey 101 JS0000
Troon Cnwll 2 SW6638
Troon Strath 73 NS3230
Troston Suffk 32 TL8972
Trotshill H & W 28 SO8855
Trottiscliffe Kent 14 TQ6460
Trotton W Susx 11 SU8322
Troughend Nthumb 68 NY8692
Troutbeck Cumb 59 NY4002
Troutbeck Bridge Cumb 59 NY4000
Troway Derbys 49 SK3879
Trowbridge Wilts 20 ST8558
Trowse Newton Norfk 43 TG2406
Trudoxhill Somset 20 ST7443
Trull Somset 8 ST2122
Trumpan Highld 90 NG2261
Trumpet H & W 27 SO6539
Trumpington Cambs 31 TL4454
Trunch Norfk 43 TG2834
Truro Cnwll 2 SW8244
Trusham Devon 5 SX8582
Trusley Derbys 39 SK2535
Trysull Staffs 38 SO8594
Tubney Oxon 21 SU4399
Tuckenhay Devon 5 SX8156
Tuckhill Shrops 37 SO7888
Tuckingmill Cnwll 2 SW6540
Tuckingmill Wilts 9 ST9329
Tuckton Dorset 10 SZ1492
Tuddenham Suffk 32 TL7371
Tuddenham Suffk 33 TM1948
Tudeley Kent 13 TQ6245
Tudhoe Dur 61 NZ2535
Tudweiliog Gwynd 44 SH2436
Tuffley Gloucs 28 SO8314
Tufton Dyfed 16 SN0428
Tufton Hants 21 SU4546
Tugby Leics 40 SK7601
Tugford Shrops 37 SO5587
Tughall Nthumb 77 NU2126
Tullibody Cent 82 NS8595
Tullich Highld 92 NH6328
Tullich Highld 97 NH8576
Tullich Strath 80 NN0815
Tulliemet Tays 88 NO0052
Tulloch Cent 81 NN5120
Tulloch Gramp 95 NJ8031
Tulloch Station Highld 86 NN3580
Tullochgorm Strath 71 NR9695
Tullybeagles Lodge Tays 82 NO0136
Tullynessle Gramp 94 NJ5519
Tulse Hill Gt Lon 23 TQ3172
Tumble Dyfed 17 SN5411
Tumby Lincs 51 TF2359
Tumby Woodside Lincs 51 TF2757
Tummel Bridge Tays 87 NN7659
Tunbridge Wells Kent 13 TQ5839
Tundergarth D & G 67 NY1780
Tunstall Humb 57 TA3031
Tunstall Kent 14 TQ8961
Tunstall Lancs 59 SD6073
Tunstall N York 61 SE2196
Tunstall Norfk 43 TG4107
Tunstall Staffs 37 SJ7727
Tunstall Staffs 37 SJ8651
Tunstall Suffk 33 TM3655
Tunstall T & W 69 NZ3953
Tunstead Derbys 48 SK1074
Tunstead Norfk 43 TG3022
Tunstead Milton Derbys 48 SK0180
Tunworth Hants 22 SU6748
Tur Langton Leics 40 SP7194
Turgis Green Hants 22 SU6959
Turkdean Gloucs 28 SP1017
Turleigh Wilts 20 ST8060
Turnastone H & W 27 SO3536
Turnberry Strath 73 NS2005
Turnditch Derbys 49 SK2946
Turner's Hill W Susx 12 TQ3435
Turners Puddle Dorset 9 SY8393
Turnhouse Loth 75 NT1674
Turnworth Dorset 9 ST8207
Turriff Gramp 95 NJ7250
Turton Bottoms Gt Man 54 SD7315
Turvey Beds 30 SP9452
Turville Bucks 22 SU7691
Turweston Bucks 29 SP6037
Tushingham cum
  Grindley Ches 46 SJ5246
Tutbury Staffs 39 SK2128
Tutshill Gloucs 19 ST5494
Tuttington Norfk 43 TG2227
Tuxford Notts 50 SK7471
Twatt Ork 103 HY2724
Twatt Shet 103 HU3253
Twechar Strath 74 NS6975
Tweedmouth Nthumb 77 NT9952
Tweedsmuir Border 75 NT1024
Twelve Oaks E Susx 14 TQ6820
Twelveheads Cnwll 2 SW7542
Twemlow Green Ches 47 SJ7868
Twenty Lincs 40 TF1520
Twerton Avon 20 ST7264
Twickenham Gt Lon 23 TQ1673
Twigworth Gloucs 28 SO8422
Twineham W Susx 12 TQ2519
Twinstead Essex 24 TL8636
Twitchen Devon 7 SS7930
Two Dales Derbys 49 SK2763
Twycross Leics 39 SK3304
Twyford Berks 22 SU7976
Twyford Bucks 30 SP6626
Twyford Hants 11 SU4824
Twyford Leics 40 SK7210
Twyford Norfk 42 TG0123
Twynholm D & G 65 NX6654
Twyning Gloucs 28 SO8936
Twyning Green Gloucs 28 SO9036
Twynllanan Dyfed 26 SN7524
Twywell Nhants 30 SP9578
Ty-n-dwr Clwyd 36 SJ2341
Ty'n-y-groes Gwynd 45 SH7771
Ty-croes Dyfed 17 SN6010
Ty-nant Clwyd 45 SH9944
Tyberton H & W 27 SO3839

Tycrwyn Powys 36 SJ1018
Tydd Gote Lincs 41 TF4518
Tydd St Giles Cambs 41 TF4216
Tydd St Mary Lincs 41 TF4418
Tye Green Essex 24 TL5424
Tye Green Essex 24 TL5935
Tyldesley Gt Man 47 SD6802
Tyler Hill Kent 15 TR1461
Tylorstown M Glam 18 ST0095
Tyn-y-nant M Glam 18 ST0685
Tyndrum Cent 80 NN3230
Tynemouth T & W 69 NZ3669
Tyningham Loth 83 NT6179
Tynron D & G 66 NX8093
Tynygraig Dyfed 35 SN6969
Tyringham Bucks 30 SP8547
Tythegston M Glam 18 SS8578
Tytherington Avon 20 ST6688
Tytherington Ches 48 SJ9175
Tytherington Wilts 20 ST9141
Tytherleigh Devon 8 ST3103
Tywardreath Cnwll 3 SX0854
Tywyn Gwynd 34 SH5800

U

Ubbeston Green Suffk 33 TM3271
Ubley Avon 19 ST5258
Uckerby N York 61 NZ2402
Uckfield E Susx 13 TQ4721
Uckinghall H & W 28 SO8637
Uckington Gloucs 28 SO9124
Uckington Shrops 37 SJ5709
Uddingston Strath 74 NS6960
Uddington Strath 74 NS8633
Udimore E Susx 14 TQ8719
Udny Green Gramp 95 NJ8726
Udny Station Gramp 95 NJ9024
Uffculme Devon 7 ST0612
Uffington Oxon 21 SU3089
Ufford Cambs 40 TF0903
Ufford Suffk 33 TM2952
Ufton Warwks 29 SP3762
Ufton Nervet Berks 21 SU6367
Ugadale Strath 72 NR7828
Ugborough Devon 5 SX6755
Uggeshall Suffk 33 TM4480
Ugglebarnby N York 63 NZ8707
Ughill Derbys 48 SK2590
Ugley Essex 31 TL5228
Ugley Green Essex 31 TL5227
Ugthorpe N York 63 NZ7911
Uig Highld 90 NG1952
Uig Highld 90 NG3963
Uig Strath 78 NM1654
Uig W Isls 102 NB0533
Uigshader Highld 90 NG4346
Uisken Strath 78 NM3919
Ulbster Highld 100 ND3241
Ulcat Row Cumb 59 NY4022
Ulceby Humb 57 TA1014
Ulceby Lincs 51 TF4272
Ulceby Skitter Humb 57 TA1215
Ulcombe Kent 14 TQ8448
Uldale Cumb 58 NY2437
Uley Gloucs 20 ST7898
Ulgham Nthumb 69 NZ2392
Ullapool Highld 96 NH1294
Ullenhall Warwks 28 SP1267
Ulleskelf N York 55 SE5239
Ullesthorpe Leics 39 SP5087
Ulley S York 49 SK4687
Ullingswick H & W 27 SO5949
Ullinish Lodge Hotel Highld 84 NG3237
Ullock Cumb 58 NY0724
Ulpha Cumb 58 SD1993
Ulrome Humb 57 TA1656
Ulsta Shet 103 HU4680
Ulverston Cumb 58 SD2878
Ulwell Dorset 10 SZ0280
Umachan Highld 90 NG6050
Umberleigh Devon 6 SS6023
Unapool Highld 98 NC2333
Under Burnmouth D & G 67 NY4783
Under River Kent 13 TQ5552
Underbarrow Cumb 59 SD4692
Undercliffe W York 55 SE1834
Underdale Shrops 37 SJ5013
Underwood Notts 49 SK4750
Undy Gwent 19 ST4386
Union Mills IOM 52 SC3577
Unstone Derbys 49 SK3777
Up Cerne Dorset 9 ST6502
Up Exe Devon 7 SS9402
Up Holland Lancs 46 SD5205
Up Marden W Susx 11 SU7913
Up Mudford Somset 9 ST5718
Up Nately Hants 22 SU6951
Up Somborne Hants 10 SU3932
Up Sydling Dorset 9 ST6201
Upavon Wilts 20 SU1354
Upchurch Kent 14 TQ8467
Upcott Devon 7 SS7529
Upcott Somset 7 SS9025
Upgate Norfk 43 TG1318
Uphall Dorset 9 ST5502
Uphall Loth 75 NT0671
Upham Devon 7 SS8808
Upham Hants 11 SU5320
Uphampton H & W 27 SO3963
Uphampton H & W 28 SO8364
Uphill Avon 19 ST3158
Uplawmoor Strath 73 NS4355
Upleadon Gloucs 28 SO7527
Upleatham Cleve 62 NZ6319
Uploders Dorset 8 SY5093
Uplowman Devon 7 ST0115
Uplyme Devon 8 SY3293
Upminster Gt Lon 24 TQ5686
Upottery Devon 8 ST2007
Upper Affcot Shrops 36 SO4486
Upper Ardchronie Highld 97 NH6188
Upper Arley H & W 37 SO7680
Upper Basildon Berks 21 SU5976
Upper Beeding W Susx 12 TQ1910
Upper Benefield Nhants 40 SP9789
Upper Bighouse Highld 99 NC8856
Upper Boddington Nhants 29 SP4852
Upper Brailes Warwks 29 SP3039
Upper Breakish Highld 85 NG6823
Upper Broadheath H & W 28 SO8056
Upper Broughton Notts 39 SK6826
Upper Bucklebury Berks 21 SU5468

Upper Burgate Hants 10 SU1516
Upper Caldecote Beds 31 TL1645
Upper Catesby Nhants 29 SP5259
Upper Chapel Powys 26 SO0040
Upper Chicksgrove Wilts 9 ST9529
Upper Chute Wilts 21 SU2953
Upper Clapton Gt Lon 23 TQ3487
Upper Clatford Hants 21 SU3543
Upper Coberley Gloucs 28 SO9816
Upper Cound Shrops 37 SJ5505
Upper Cumberworth W York 55 SE2008
Upper Dallachy Gramp 94 NJ3662
Upper Deal Kent 15 TR3651
Upper Dean Beds 30 TL0467
Upper Denby W York 55 SE2207
Upper Dicker E Susx 13 TQ5509
Upper Dounreay Highld 100 ND0065
Upper Dovercourt Essex 25 TM2330
Upper Drumbane Cent 81 NN6606
Upper Dunsforth N York 55 SE4463
Upper Eashing Surrey 12 SU9543
Upper Egleton H & W 27 SO6344
Upper Elkstone Staffs 48 SK0558
Upper Ellastone Staffs 48 SK1043
Upper Ethrie Highld 93 NH7662
Upper Farringdon Hants 11 SU7135
Upper Framilode Gloucs 28 SO7510
Upper Froyle Hants 11 SU7543
Upper Godney Somset 19 ST4842
Upper Gravenhurst Beds 30 TL1136
Upper Green Berks 21 SU3763
Upper Green Essex 24 TL5935
Upper Hale Surrey 22 SU8349
Upper Halliford Surrey 22 TQ0968
Upper Hambleton Leics 40 SK9007
Upper Harbledown Kent 15 TR1158
Upper Hartfield E Susx 13 TQ4634
Upper Hatherley Gloucs 28 SO9220
Upper Heaton W York 55 SE1719
Upper Helmsley N York 56 SE6956
Upper Hergest H & W 27 SO2654
Upper Heyford Nhants 30 SP6659
Upper Heyford Oxon 29 SP4925
Upper Hill H & W 27 SO4753
Upper Hopton W York 55 SE1918
Upper Hulme Staffs 48 SK0160
Upper Inglesham Wilts 21 SU2096
Upper Killay W Glam 17 SS5892
Upper Kinchrackine Strath 80 NN1627
Upper Lambourn Berks 21 SU3080
Upper Landywood Staffs 38 SJ9805
Upper Langford Avon 19 ST4659
Upper Langwith Derbys 49 SK5169
Upper Largo Fife 83 NO4203
Upper Leigh Staffs 38 SK0136
Upper Longdon Staffs 38 SK0614
Upper Lybster Highld 100 ND2537
Upper Lydbrook Gloucs 27 SO6015
Upper Lye H & W 27 SO3965
Upper Milton H & W 37 SO8072
Upper Minety Wilts 20 SU0091
Upper Moor H & W 28 SO9647
Upper Mulben Gramp 94 NJ3551
Upper Netchwood Shrops 37 SO6092
Upper Nobut Staffs 38 SK0335
Upper Norwood W Susx 12 SU9317
Upper Pond Street Essex 31 TL4636
Upper Poppleton N York 56 SE5553
Upper Quinton Warwks 29 SP1846
Upper Ratley Hants 10 SU3223
Upper Rochford H & W 27 SO6367
Upper Ruscoe D & G 65 NX5661
Upper Sapey H & W 28 SO6863
Upper Seagry Wilts 20 ST9480
Upper Shelton Beds 30 SP9843
Upper Sheringham Norfk 43 TG1441
Upper Skelmorlie Strath 73 NS2067
Upper Slaughter Gloucs 28 SP1523
Upper Soudley Gloucs 27 SO6510
Upper Standen Kent 15 TR2139
Upper Stepford D & G 66 NX8681
Upper Stoke Norfk 43 TG2502
Upper Stondon Beds 30 TL1435
Upper Stowe Nhants 29 SP6456
Upper Street Hants 10 SU1518
Upper Street Norfk 43 TG3217
Upper Street Norfk 43 TG3616
Upper Street Suffk 32 TL7851
Upper Street Suffk 33 TM1050
Upper Sundon Beds 30 TL0428
Upper Swell Gloucs 29 SP1726
Upper Tasburgh Norfk 43 TM1696
Upper Tean Staffs 48 SK0139
Upper Town Avon 19 ST5265
Upper Town Derbys 48 SK2361
Upper Town H & W 50 SO5848
Upper Town Suffk 32 TL9267
Upper Tysoe Warwks 29 SP3343
Upper Victoria Tays 83 NO5336
Upper Wardington Oxon 29 SP4945
Upper Weedon Nhants 29 SP6258
Upper Wellingham E Susx 13 TQ4313
Upper Weybread Suffk 33 TM2379
Upper Wield Hants 11 SU6238
Upper Winchendon Bucks 30 SP7414
Upper Woodford Wilts 10 SU1237
Upper Wraxall Wilts 20 ST8074
Upperby Cumb 67 NY4153
Upperglen Highld 90 NG3151
Uppermill Gt Man 54 SD9905
Upperthong W York 55 SE1208
Upperton W Susx 12 SU9522
Uppertown Highld 100 ND3576
Uppingham Leics 40 SP8699
Uppington Shrops 37 SJ5909
Upsall N York 62 SE4586
Upsettlington Border 77 NT8846
Upshire Essex 23 TL4101
Upstreet Kent 15 TR2263
Upton Berks 22 SU9779
Upton Bucks 22 SP7711
Upton Cambs 40 TF1000
Upton Cambs 31 TL1778
Upton Ches 46 SJ4069
Upton Cnwll 4 SX2772
Upton Devon 8 ST0902
Upton Devon 5 SX7043
Upton Dorset 9 SY9893
Upton Dorset 9 SY7893
Upton Hants 10 SU3716
Upton Hants 21 SU3555
Upton Lincs 39 SK8686
Upton Lincs 50 SK8686
Upton Mersyd 46 SJ2788
Upton Norfk 43 TG3912
Upton Notts 50 SK7354
Upton Notts 50 SK7476
Upton Oxon 21 SU5187

Upton Somset 7 SS9928
Upton Somset 8 ST4526
Upton W York 55 SE4713
Upton Wilts 9 ST8731
Upton Cheyney Avon 20 ST6970
Upton Cressett Shrops 37 SO6592
Upton Crews H & W 27 SO6527
Upton Cross Cnwll 4 SX2872
Upton Grey Hants 22 SU6948
Upton Hellions Devon 7 SS8403
Upton Lovell Wilts 20 ST9440
Upton Magna Shrops 37 SJ5512
Upton Noble Somset 20 ST7139
Upton Pyne Devon 7 SX9198
Upton Scudamore Wilts 20 ST8647
Upton Snodsbury H & W 28 SO9454
Upton St Leonards Gloucs 28 SO8615
Upton upon Severn H & W 28 SO8540
Upton Warren H & W 28 SO9267
Upwaltham W Susx 12 SU9413
Upwell Norfk 41 TF4902
Upwick Green Herts 31 TL4524
Upwood Cambs 41 TL2582
Urchfont Wilts 20 SU0357
Urmston Gt Man 47 SJ7694
Urquhart Gramp 94 NJ2862
Urra N York 62 NZ5601
Urray Highld 92 NH5052
Usan Tays 89 NO7254
Ushaw Moor Dur 61 NZ2242
Usk Gwent 19 SO3700
Usselby Lincs 50 TF0993
Usworth T & W 69 NZ3357
Utley W York 55 SE0542
Uton Devon 7 SX8298
Utterby Lincs 51 TF3093
Uttoxeter Staffs 38 SK0933
Uxbridge Gt Lon 22 TQ0584
Uyeasound Shet 103 HP5901
Uzmaston Dyfed 16 SM9714

V

Vale Guern 101 GN0000
Valley End Surrey 22 SU9564
Valtos Highld 90 NG5163
Valtos W Isls 102 NB0936
Vange Essex 24 TQ7186
Vatsetter Shet 103 HU5389
Vatten Highld 90 NG2843
Vaynor M Glam 26 SO0410
Velindre Powys 27 SO1836
Venn Ottery Devon 8 SY0891
Venngreen Devon 6 SS3711
Ventnor IOW 11 SZ5677
Venton Devon 5 SX5956
Vernham Dean Hants 21 SU3356
Vernham Street Hants 21 SU3457
Verwood Dorset 10 SU0809
Veryan Cnwll 3 SW9139
Vickerstown Cumb 53 SD1868
Victoria Cnwll 3 SW9861
Vidlin Shet 103 HU4765
Viewfield Gramp 94 NJ2864
Viewpark Strath 74 NS7061
Vigo Kent 14 TQ6361
Ville la Bas Jersey 101 JS0000
Villiaze Guern 101 GN0000
Vine's Cross E Susx 13 TQ5917
Virginia Water Surrey 22 TQ0067
Virginstow Devon 4 SX3792
Vobster Somset 20 ST7048
Voe Shet 103 HU4062
Vowchurch H & W 27 SO3636

W

Wackerfield Dur 61 NZ1522
Wacton Norfk 33 TM1791
Wadborough H & W 28 SO9047
Waddesdon Bucks 30 SP7416
Waddeton Devon 5 SX8756
Waddingham Lincs 50 SK9896
Waddington Lancs 54 SD7343
Waddington Lincs 50 SK9764
Waddon Dorset 9 SY6285
Wadebridge Cnwll 3 SW9972
Wadeford Somset 8 ST3110
Wadenhoe Nhants 40 TL0183
Wadesmill Herts 31 TL3617
Wadhurst E Susx 13 TQ6431
Wadshelf Derbys 49 SK3170
Wadworth S York 49 SK5696
Wainfleet All Saints Lincs 51 TF4959
Wainhouse Corner Cnwll 6 SX1895
Wainscott Kent 14 TQ7470
Wainstalls W York 55 SE0428
Waitby Cumb 60 NY7508
Waithe Lincs 51 TA2800
Wakefield W York 55 SE3320
Wakerley Nhants 40 SP9599
Wakes Colne Essex 24 TL8928
Walberswick Suffk 33 TM4974
Walberton W Susx 12 SU9705
Walbutt D & G 65 NX7468
Walcombe Somset 19 ST5546
Walcot Lincs 40 TF0635
Walcot Lincs 50 TF1356
Walcot Shrops 37 SJ5912
Walcot Wilts 20 SU1684
Walcot Green Norfk 33 TM1280
Walcote Leics 39 SP5683
Walcott Norfk 43 TG3532
Walden Stubbs N York 56 SE5516
Walderslade Kent 14 TQ7663
Walderton W Susx 11 SU7910
Walditch Dorset 8 SY4892
Waldridge Dur 69 NZ2549
Waldringfield Suffk 33 TM2845
Waldron E Susx 13 TQ5419
Wales S York 49 SK4882
Wales Somset 9 ST5824
Walesby Lincs 50 TF1392
Walesby Notts 49 SK6870
Walford H & W 36 SO3872
Walford H & W 27 SO5020
Walford Heath Shrops 36 SJ4419
Walgherton Ches 47 SJ6948
Walgrave Nhants 30 SP8071
Walk Mill Lancs 54 SD8729

Walkden
West Putford

Walkden Gt Man 47 SD7302
Walker T & W 69 NZ2864
Walker's Green H & W 27 SO5247
Walkerburn Border 76 NT3637
Walkeringham Notts 50 SK7792
Walkerith Notts 50 SK7892
Walkern Herts 31 TL2826
Walkerton Fife 83 NO2301
Walkhampton Devon 4 SX5369
Walkington Humb 56 SE9936
Walkley S York 49 SK3388
Walkwood H & W 28 SP0364
Wall Nthumb 68 NY9168
Wall Staffs 38 SK1006
Wallacetown Strath 73 NS2703
Wallacetown Strath 73 NS3422
Wallands Park E Susx 13 TQ4010
Wallasey Mersyd 46 SJ2992
Wallingford Oxon 21 SU6089
Wallington Gt Lon 23 TQ2864
Wallington Hants 11 SU5806
Wallington Herts 31 TL2933
Wallisdown Dorset 10 SZ0694
Walls Shet 103 HU2449
Wallsend T & W 69 NZ2966
Wallyford Loth 76 NT3671
Walmer Kent 15 TR3750
Walmer Bridge Lancs 53 SD4724
Walpole Suffk 33 TM3674
Walpole Cross Keys Norfk 41 TF5119
Walpole Highway Norfk 41 TF5114
Walpole St Andrew Norfk 41 TF5017
Walpole St Peter Norfk 41 TF5016
Walsall W Mids 38 SP0198
Walsden W York 54 SD9321
Walsham le Willows Suffk 32 TM0071
Walshaw W York 54 SD9731
Walshford N York 55 SE4153
Walsoken Norfk 41 TF4710
Walston Strath 75 NT0545
Walsworth Herts 31 TL1930
Waltham Humb 57 TA2603
Waltham Kent 15 TR1048
Waltham Abbey Essex 23 TL3800
Waltham Chase Hants 11 SU5614
Waltham Cross Herts 23 TL3600
Waltham on the Wolds Leics 40 SK8024
Waltham St Lawrence Berks 22 SU8276
Walthamstow Gt Lon 23 TQ3689
Walton Bucks 30 SP8936
Walton Cumb 67 NY5264
Walton Derbys 49 SK3568
Walton Leics 39 SP5987
Walton Powys 27 SO2559
Walton Shrops 37 SJ5818
Walton Somset 19 ST4636
Walton Suffk 25 TM2935
Walton W Susx 11 SU8104
Walton W York 55 SE3516
Walton W York 55 SE4447
Walton Cardiff Glouc 28 SO9032
Walton East Dyfed 16 SN0223
Walton Elm Dorset 9 ST7717
Walton Lower Street Suffk 25 TM2834
Walton on the Hill Surrey 23 TQ2255
Walton on the Naze Essex 25 TM2522
Walton on the Wolds Leics 39 SK5919
Walton Park Avon 19 ST4172
Walton West Dyfed 16 SM8612
Walton-in-Gordano Avon 19 ST4273
Walton-le-Dale Lancs 53 SD5628
Walton-on-Thames Surrey 22 TQ1066
Walton-on-the-Hill Staffs 38 SJ9520
Walton-on-Trent Derbys 39 SK2118
Walworth Dur 61 NZ2318
Walworth Gt Lon 23 TQ3277
Walwyn's Castle Dyfed 16 SM8711
Wambrook Somset 8 ST2907
Wanborough Surrey 12 SU9348
Wanborough Wilts 21 SU2082
Wandel Strath 75 NS9427
Wandsworth Gt Lon 23 TQ2574
Wangford Suffk 33 TM4679
Wanlip Leics 39 SK5910
Wanlockhead D & G 66 NS8712
Wannock E Susx 13 TQ5703
Wansford Cambs 40 TL0799
Wansford Humb 57 TA0656
Wanshurst Green Kent 14 TQ7645
Wanstead Gt Lon 23 TQ4088
Wanstrow Somset 20 ST7141
Wanswell Glouc 20 SO6801
Wantage Oxon 21 SU3988
Wapley Avon 20 ST7179
Wappenbury Warwks 29 SP3769
Wappenham Nhants 29 SP6245
Warbister Ork 103 HY3932
Warbleton E Susx 13 TQ6018
Warborough Oxon 21 SU5993
Warboys Cambs 41 TL3080
Warbreck Lancs 53 SD3238
Warbstow Cnwll 4 SX2090
Warburton Gt Man 47 SJ7089
Warcop Cumb 60 NY7415
Warden Nthumb 68 NY9166
Wardington Oxon 29 SP4846
Wardle Ches 47 SJ6156
Wardle Gt Man 54 SD9116
Wardley Leics 40 SK8300
Wardlow Derbys 48 SK1874
Wardy Hill Cambs 41 TL4782
Ware Herts 31 TL3514
Wareham Dorset 9 SY9287
Warehorne Kent 15 TQ9832
Warenford Nthumb 77 NU1328
Wareside Herts 31 TL3915
Waresley Cambs 31 TL2554
Warfield Berks 22 SU8872
Warfleet Devon 5 SX8750
Wargrave Berks 22 SU7978
Warham All Saints Norfk 42 TF9541
Warham St Mary Norfk 42 TF9441
Wark Nthumb 77 NT8238
Wark Nthumb 68 NY8577
Warkleigh Devon 7 SS6422
Warkton Nhants 40 SP8979
Warkworth Nhants 29 SP4840
Warkworth Nthumb 69 NU2406
Warlaby N York 62 SE3491
Warleggan Cnwll 3 SX1569
Warley Town W York 55 SE0524
Warlingham Surrey 23 TQ3658
Warmanbie D & G 67 NY1969
Warmfield W York 55 SE3720
Warmingham Ches 47 SJ7061
Warmington Nhants 40 TL0790
Warmington Warwks 29 SP4147
Warminster Wilts 20 ST8745
Warmley Avon 20 ST6673
Warmsworth S York 49 SE5400
Warmwell Dorset 9 SY7585
Warnford Hants 11 SU6223
Warnham W Susx 12 TQ1533
Warningcamp W Susx 12 TQ0307
Warninglid W Susx 12 TQ2426
Warren Ches 47 SJ8870
Warren Dyfed 16 SR9397
Warren Row Berks 22 SU8180
Warren Street Kent 14 TQ9252
Warrenhill Strath 75 NS9438
Warrington Bucks 30 SP8953
Warrington Ches 47 SJ6088
Warriston Loth 75 NT2575
Warsash Hants 11 SU4906
Warslow Staffs 48 SK0858
Warsop Notts 49 SK5667
Warter Humb 56 SE8750
Warthermaske N York 61 SE2078
Warthill N York 56 SE6755
Wartling E Susx 13 TQ6509
Wartnaby Leics 40 SK7123
Warton Lancs 53 SD4128
Warton Lancs 53 SD4972
Warton Warwks 39 SK2803
Warwick Cumb 67 NY4656
Warwick Warwks 29 SP2865
Wasdale Head Cumb 58 NY1808
Washaway Cnwll 3 SX0369
Washbourne Devon 5 SX7954
Washbrook Suffk 33 TM1142
Washfield Devon 7 SS9315
Washfold N York 61 NZ0502
Washford Somset 7 ST0541
Washford Pyne Devon 7 SS8111
Washingborough Lincs 50 TF0170
Washington T & W 69 NZ3155
Washington W Susx 12 TQ1112
Wasperton Warwks 29 SP2658
Wass N York 62 SE5579
Watchet Somset 18 ST0743
Watchfield Oxon 21 SU2490
Watchgate Cumb 59 SD5398
Water Devon 5 SX7580
Water Eaton Oxon 29 SP5112
Water End Essex 31 TL5840
Water End Herts 22 TL0310
Water End Humb 56 SE7938
Water Newton Cambs 40 TL1097
Water Orton Warwks 38 SP1790
Water Stratford Bucks 29 SP6534
Waterbeach Cambs 31 TL4965
Waterbeach W Susx 11 SU8908
Waterbeck D & G 67 NY2477
Watercombe Dorset 9 SY7585
Waterfall Staffs 48 SK0851
Waterfoot Strath 74 NS5655
Waterford Herts 31 TL3114
Watergate Cnwll 3 SX1181
Waterhead Strath 73 NS5411
Waterheads Border 75 NT2451
Waterhouses Staffs 48 SK0850
Wateringbury Kent 14 TQ6853
Waterloo Dyfed 16 SM9803
Waterloo Highld 85 NG6623
Waterloo Mersyd 46 SJ3298
Waterloo Strath 74 NS8154
Waterloo Tays 82 NO0537
Waterlooville Hants 11 SU6809
Watermillock Cumb 59 NY4422
Waterperry Oxon 29 SP6206
Waterrow Somset 7 ST0525
Waters Upton Shrops 37 SJ6319
Watersfield W Susx 12 TQ0115
Waterside Lancs 54 SD7123
Waterside Strath 73 NS4308
Waterside Strath 73 NS4843
Waterside Strath 74 NS6773
Waterstock Oxon 29 SP6305
Waterston Dyfed 16 SM9305
Watford Herts 22 TQ1196
Watford Nhants 29 SP6069
Wath N York 55 SE1467
Wath N York 62 SE3277
Wath upon Dearne S York 49 SE4300
Watlington Norfk 41 TF6111
Watlington Oxon 22 SU6894
Watten Highld 100 ND2454
Wattisfield Suffk 32 TM0074
Wattisham Suffk 32 TM0151
Watton Dorset 8 SY4591
Watton Humb 56 TA0150
Watton Norfk 42 TF9100
Watton-at-Stone Herts 31 TL3019
Wattsville Gwent 19 ST2091
Wauldby Humb 56 SE9629
Waulkmill Gramp 89 NO6492
Waunarlwydd W Glam 17 SS6095
Waunfawr Dyfed 34 SN6081
Waunfawr Gwynd 44 SH5259
Wavendon Bucks 30 SP9137
Waverbridge Cumb 67 NY2249
Waverton Ches 46 SJ4663
Waverton Cumb 67 NY2247
Wawne Humb 57 TA0936
Waxham Norfk 43 TG4426
Way Village Devon 7 SS8810
Wayford Somset 8 ST4006
Waytown Dorset 8 SY4797
Weacombe Somset 18 ST1140
Weald Oxon 21 SP3002
Wealdstone Gt Lon 22 TQ1589
Wear Head Dur 60 NY8539
Weardley W York 55 SE2944
Weare Somset 19 ST4152
Weare Giffard Devon 6 SS4721
Wearne Somset 8 ST4228
Weasenham All Saints Norfk 42 TF8421
Weasenham St Peter Norfk 42 TF8522
Weaste Gt Man 47 SJ8098
Weaverham Ches 47 SJ6174
Weaverthorpe N York 56 SE9670
Webheath H & W 28 SP0266
Wedderlairs Gramp 95 NJ8532
Weddington Warwks 39 SP3693
Wedhampton Wilts 20 SU0557
Wedmore Somset 19 ST4347
Wednesbury W Mids 38 SO9895
Wednesfield W Mids 38 SJ9400
Weedon Bucks 30 SP8118
Weedon Lois Nhants 29 SP6046
Weeford Staffs 38 SK1403
Week Somset 7 SS9133
Week St Mary Cnwll 6 SX2397
Weeke Hants 10 SU4630
Weekley Nhants 40 SP8881
Weel Humb 57 TA0639
Weeley Essex 25 TM1422
Weeley Heath Essex 25 TM1520
Weem Tays 87 NN8449
Weethley Hamlet Warwks 28 SP0555
Weeting Norfk 32 TL7788
Weeton Humb 57 TA3520
Weeton Lancs 53 SD3834
Weeton W York 55 SE2847
Weetwood W York 55 SE2737
Weir Lancs 54 SD8625
Weir Quay Devon 4 SX4365
Welborne Norfk 42 TG0610
Welbourn Lincs 50 SK9654
Welburn N York 56 SE7267
Welbury N York 62 NZ3902
Welby Lincs 40 SK9738
Welches Dam Cambs 41 TL4686
Welcombe Devon 6 SS2318
Welford Berks 21 SU4073
Welford Nhants 39 SP6480
Welford-on-Avon Warwks 28 SP1452
Welham Leics 40 SP7692
Welham Notts 49 SK7281
Welham Green Herts 23 TL2305
Well Hants 22 SU7646
Well Lincs 51 TF4473
Well N York 61 SE2681
Well Head Herts 31 TL1727
Welland H & W 28 SO7940
Wellbank Tays 83 NO4737
Wellbury Herts 30 TL1329
Wellesbourne Warwks 29 SP2855
Welling Gt Lon 23 TQ4675
Wellingborough Nhants 30 SP8967
Wellingham Norfk 42 TF8722
Wellingore Lincs 50 SK9856
Wellington Cumb 58 NY0704
Wellington H & W 27 SO4948
Wellington Shrops 37 SJ6511
Wellington Somset 8 ST1320
Wellington Heath H & W 28 SO7140
Wellow Avon 20 ST7458
Wellow IOW 10 SZ3888
Wellow Notts 49 SK6766
Wells Somset 19 ST5445
Wells-Next-The-Sea Norfk 42 TF9143
Wellstye Green Essex 24 TL6318
Welltree Tays 82 NN9622
Wellwood Fife 82 NT0988
Welney Norfk 41 TL5293
Welsh Frankton Shrops 36 SJ3533
Welsh Newton H & W 27 SO5017
Welsh St Donats S Glam 18 ST0276
Welshampton Shrops 36 SJ4335
Welshpool Powys 36 SJ2207
Welton Cumb 67 NY3544
Welton Humb 56 SE9627
Welton Lincs 50 TF0179
Welton Nhants 29 SP5865
Welton le Marsh Lincs 51 TF4768
Welton le Wold Lincs 51 TF2787
Welwick Humb 57 TA3421
Welwyn Herts 31 TL2316
Welwyn Garden City Herts 31 TL2312
Wem Shrops 37 SJ5128
Wembdon Somset 19 ST2837
Wembley Gt Lon 23 TQ1885
Wembury Devon 4 SX5248
Wembworthy Devon 7 SS6609
Wemyss Bay Strath 73 NS1969
Wendens Ambo Essex 31 TL5136
Wendlebury Oxon 29 SP5619
Wendling Norfk 42 TF9312
Wendover Bucks 22 SP8607
Wendron Cnwll 2 SW6731
Wendy Cambs 31 TL3247
Wenhaston Suffk 33 TM4275
Wennington Cambs 41 TL2379
Wennington Lancs 54 SD6170
Wensley Derbys 49 SK2661
Wensley N York 61 SE0989
Wentbridge W York 55 SE4817
Wentnor Shrops 36 SO3892
Wentworth Cambs 31 TL4878
Wentworth S York 49 SK3898
Wenvoe S Glam 18 ST1272
Weobley H & W 27 SO4051
Weobley Marsh H & W 27 SO4151
Wepham W Susx 12 TQ0408
Wereham Norfk 42 TF6801
Werrington Cambs 40 TF1603
Werrington Cnwll 4 SX3287
Wervin Ches 46 SJ4271
Wesham Lancs 53 SD4133
Wessington Derbys 49 SK3757
West Acre Norfk 42 TF7815
West Alvington Devon 5 SX7243
West Anstey Devon 7 SS8527
West Appleton N York 61 SE2294
West Ashby Lincs 51 TF2672
West Ashling W Susx 11 SU8107
West Ashton Wilts 20 ST8755
West Auckland Dur 61 NZ1826
West Ayton N York 63 SE9884
West Bagborough Somset 8 ST1733
West Bank Ches 46 SJ5183
West Barkwith Lincs 50 TF1580
West Barnby N York 63 NZ8212
West Barns Loth 83 NT6578
West Barsham Norfk 42 TF9033
West Bay Dorset 8 SY4690
West Beckham Norfk 43 TG1439
West Bedfont Surrey 22 TQ0674
West Bergholt Essex 25 TL9527
West Bexington Dorset 8 SY5386
West Bilney Norfk 42 TF7115
West Blatchington E Susx 12 TQ2707
West Boldon T & W 69 NZ3561
West Bowling W York 55 SE1630
West Brabourne Kent 15 TR0842
West Bradenham Norfk 42 TF9108
West Bradford Lancs 54 SD7444
West Bradley Somset 19 ST5536
West Bretton W York 55 SE2813
West Bridgford Notts 39 SK5836
West Bromwich W Mids 38 SP0091
West Buccleigh Hotel Border 67 NT3214
West Buckland Devon 7 SS6531
West Burton N York 61 SE0186
West Butterwick Humb 56 SE8305
West Byfleet Surrey 22 TQ0461
West Cairngaan D & G 64 NX1231
West Caister Norfk 43 TG5011
West Calder Loth 75 NT0163
West Camel Somset 9 ST5724
West Chaldon Dorset 9 SY7782
West Challow Oxon 21 SU3688
West Charleton Devon 5 SX7542
West Chelborough Dorset 8 ST5405
West Chevington Nthumb 69 NZ2297
West Chiltington W Susx 12 TQ0818
West Chinnock Somset 8 ST4613
West Clandon Surrey 12 TQ0452
West Cliffe Kent 15 TR3444
West Coker Somset 8 ST5113
West Compton Dorset 9 SY5694
West Compton Somset 19 ST5942
West Cottingwith N York 56 SE6942
West Cowick Humb 56 SE6421
West Cross W Glam 17 SS6189
West Curthwaite Cumb 67 NY3249
West Dean W Susx 11 SU8612
West Dean Wilts 10 SU2526
West Deeping Lincs 40 TF1008
West Derby Mersyd 46 SJ3993
West Dereham Norfk 42 TF6500
West Down Devon 6 SS5142
West Drayton Gt Lon 22 TQ0579
West Drayton Notts 49 SK7074
West Dunnet Highld 100 ND2171
West Ella Humb 56 TA0029
West End Avon 19 ST4569
West End Beds 30 SP9853
West End Berks 22 SU8275
West End Hants 10 SU4614
West End Herts 23 TL2608
West End Herts 23 TL3306
West End Norfk 43 TG5011
West End Surrey 22 SU9461
West End Surrey 22 TQ1263
West End Wilts 9 ST9824
West End Green Hants 22 SU6661
West Farleigh Kent 14 TQ7152
West Farndon Nhants 29 SP5251
West Felton Shrops 36 SJ3425
West Firle E Susx 13 TQ4707
West Grafton Wilts 21 SU2460
West Green Hants 22 SU7456
West Grimstead Wilts 10 SU2026
West Grinstead W Susx 12 TQ1720
West Haddlesey N York 56 SE5626
West Haddon Nhants 39 SP6371
West Hagbourne Oxon 21 SU5187
West Hagley H & W 38 SO9080
West Hallam Derbys 49 SK4341
West Halton Humb 56 SE9020
West Ham Gt Lon 23 TQ3983
West Handley Derbys 49 SK3977
West Hanney Oxon 21 SU4092
West Hanningfield Essex 24 TQ7399
West Harnham Wilts 10 SU1329
West Harptree Avon 19 ST5556
West Harting W Susx 11 SU7820
West Hatch Somset 8 ST2821
West Hatch Wilts 9 ST9227
West Haven Tays 83 NO5735
West Heath W Mids 38 SP0277
West Helmsdale Highld 97 ND0115
West Hendred Oxon 21 SU4488
West Heslerton N York 63 SE9176
West Hewish Avon 19 ST3963
West Hill Devon 8 SY0794
West Hoathly W Susx 12 TQ3632
West Holme Dorset 9 SY8885
West Horrington Somset 19 ST5747
West Horsley Surrey 12 TQ0752
West Hougham Kent 15 TR2640
West Howe Dorset 10 SZ0595
West Huntingtower Tays 82 NO0724
West Huntspill Somset 19 ST3044
West Hythe Kent 15 TR1234
West Ilsley Berks 21 SU4782
West Itchenor W Susx 11 SU7901
West Kennett Wilts 20 SU1168
West Kilbride Strath 73 NS2048
West Kingsdown Kent 14 TQ5763
West Kington Wilts 20 ST8077
West Kirby Mersyd 46 SJ2186
West Knapton N York 63 SE8775
West Knighton Dorset 9 SY7387
West Knoyle Wilts 9 ST8632
West Lambrook Somset 8 ST4118
West Langdon Kent 15 TR3247
West Laroch Highld 86 NN0758
West Lavington W Susx 11 SU8920
West Lavington Wilts 20 SU0052
West Layton N York 61 NZ1410
West Leake Notts 39 SK5226
West Leigh Devon 7 SS6805
West Leigh Devon 5 SX7557
West Leigh Somset 8 ST1230
West Lexham Norfk 42 TF8417
West Lilling N York 56 SE6465
West Linton Border 75 NT1551
West Littleton Avon 20 ST7675
West Lockinge Oxon 21 SU4187
West Lulworth Dorset 9 SY8280
West Lutton N York 56 SE9369
West Lydford Somset 9 ST5631
West Lyng Somset 8 ST3128
West Lynn Norfk 41 TF6120
West Malling Kent 14 TQ6757
West Malvern H & W 28 SO7646
West Marden W Susx 11 SU7713
West Markham Notts 49 SK7272
West Marsh Humb 57 TA2509
West Marton N York 54 SD8950
West Melbury Dorset 9 ST8720
West Meon Hants 11 SU6423
West Mersea Essex 25 TM0112
West Milton Dorset 8 SY5096
West Minster Kent 14 TQ9073
West Molesey Surrey 22 TQ1368
West Monkton Somset 8 ST2628
West Moors Dorset 10 SU0802
West Morden Dorset 9 SY9095
West Morriston Border 76 NT6040
West Mudford Somset 9 ST5620
West Ness N York 62 SE6879
West Newton Humb 57 TA2037
West Newton Norfk 42 TF6928
West Newton Somset 8 ST2829
West Norwood Gt Lon 23 TQ3171
West Ogwell Devon 5 SX8270
West Orchard Dorset 9 ST8216
West Overton Wilts 20 SU1267
West Parley Dorset 10 SZ0896
West Peckham Kent 13 TQ6452
West Pelton Dur 69 NZ2353
West Pennard Somset 19 ST5438
West Pentire Cnwll 2 SW7760
West Perry Cambs 30 TL1466
West Porlock Devon 18 SS8747
West Preston W Susx 12 TQ0602
West Pulham Dorset 9 ST7008
West Putford Devon 6 SS3616

West Quantoxhead *Somset* 18 ST1141
West Raddon *Devon* 7 SS8902
West Rainton *T & W* 69 NZ3246
West Rasen *Lincs* 50 TF0689
West Raynham *Norfk* 42 TF8725
West Rounton *N York* 62 NZ4103
West Row *Suffk* 32 TL6775
West Rudham *Norfk* 42 TF8127
West Runton *Norfk* 43 TG1842
West Saltoun *Loth* 76 NT4667
West Sandford *Devon* 7 SS8102
West Sandwick *Shet* 103 HU4588
West Scrafton *N York* 61 SE0783
West Stafford *Dorset* 9 SY7289
West Stockwith *Notts* 50 SK7895
West Stoke *W Susx* 11 SU8208
West Stour *Dorset* 9 ST7822
West Stourmouth *Kent* 15 TR2562
West Stow *Suffk* 32 TL8171
West Stowell *Wilts* 20 SU1361
West Street *Suffk* 32 TL9871
West Tanfield *N York* 61 SE2678
West Taphouse *Cnwll* 3 SX1463
West Tarbert *Strath* 71 NR8467
West Tarring *W Susx* 12 TQ1103
West Thorney *W Susx* 11 SU7602
West Thorpe *Notts* 39 SK6225
West Thurrock *Essex* 24 TQ5877
West Tilbury *Essex* 24 TQ6678
West Tisted *Hants* 11 SU6529
West Torrington *Lincs* 50 TF1381
West Town *Avon* 19 ST4868
West Town *Hants* 11 SZ7199
West Tytherley *Hants* 10 SU2729
West Tytherton *Wilts* 20 ST9474
West Walton *Norfk* 41 TF4613
West Walton Highway *Norfk* 41 TF4913
West Wellow *Hants* 10 SU2819
West Wembury *Devon* 4 SX5249
West Wemyss *Fife* 83 NT3294
West Wick *Avon* 19 ST3761
West Wickham *Cambs* 31 TL6149
West Wickham *Gt Lon* 23 TQ3766
West Williamston *Dyfed* 16 SN0305
West Winch *Norfk* 41 TF6316
West Winterslow *Wilts* 10 SU2331
West Wittering *W Susx* 11 SZ7898
West Witton *N York* 61 SE0588
West Woodburn *Nthumb* 68 NY8987
West Woodhay *Berks* 21 SU3963
West Worldham *Hants* 11 SU7436
West Worthing *W Susx* 12 TQ1302
West Wratting *Essex* 31 TL6052
West Youlstone *Cnwll* 6 SS2615
Westbere *Kent* 15 TR1961
Westborough *Lincs* 50 SK8544
Westbourne *W Susx* 11 SU7507
Westbrook *Berks* 21 SU4272
Westbrook *Kent* 15 TR3470
Westbury *Bucks* 29 SP6235
Westbury *Shrops* 36 SJ3509
Westbury *Wilts* 20 ST8751
Westbury Leigh *Wilts* 20 ST8649
Westbury on Severn *Gloucs* 28 SO7114
Westbury-on-Trym *Avon* 19 ST5777
Westbury-sub-Mendip *Somset* 19 ST5049
Westby *Lancs* 53 SD3831
Westcliff-on-Sea *Essex* 24 TQ8685
Westcombe *Somset* 20 ST6836
Westcote *Gloucs* 29 SP2120
Westcott *Bucks* 30 SP7116
Westcott *Devon* 7 ST0204
Westcott *Surrey* 12 TQ1448
Westcourt *Wilts* 21 SU2261
Westdean *E Susx* 13 TV5299
Westdowns *Cnwll* 3 SX0582
Wester Drumashie *Highld* 92 NH6032
Wester Essenside *Border* 76 NT4320
Wester Ochiltree *Loth* 75 NT0374
Wester Pitkierie *Fife* 83 NO5505
Westerdale *Highld* 100 ND1251
Westerdale *N York* 62 NZ6605
Westerfield *Suffk* 33 TM1747
Westergate *W Susx* 12 SU9305
Westerham *Kent* 23 TQ4454
Westerhope *T & W* 69 NZ1966
Westerland *Devon* 5 SX8662
Westerleigh *Avon* 19 ST6979
Westerton *Tays* 89 NO6754
Westfield *Avon* 20 ST6753
Westfield *Cumb* 58 NX9926
Westfield *E Susx* 14 TQ8115
Westfield *Loth* 75 NS9472
Westfield *Norfk* 42 TF9909
Westfield *Strath* 74 NS7273
Westfields of Rattray *Tays* 88 NO1746
Westgate *Dur* 60 NY9038
Westgate *Humb* 56 SE7707
Westgate on Sea *Kent* 15 TR3270
Westhall *Suffk* 33 TM4280
Westham *Dorset* 9 SY6679
Westham *E Susx* 13 TQ6404
Westham *Somset* 19 ST4046
Westhampnett *W Susx* 11 SU8806
Westhay *Somset* 19 ST4342
Westhide *H & W* 27 SO5843
Westhill *Gramp* 95 NJ8307
Westhope *H & W* 27 SO4651
Westhope *Shrops* 37 SO4786
Westhorpe *Lincs* 41 TF2231
Westhorpe *Suffk* 32 TM0468
Westhoughton *Gt Man* 47 SD6506
Westhouse *N York* 60 SD6773
Westhouses *Derbys* 49 SK4157
Westhumble *Surrey* 12 TQ1651
Westlake *Devon* 5 SX6253
Westleigh *Devon* 6 SS4728
Westleigh *Devon* 7 ST0617
Westleton *Suffk* 33 TM4369
Westley *Suffk* 32 TL8264
Westley Waterless *Cambs* 31 TL6156
Westlington *Bucks* 28 SP7610
Westlinton *Cumb* 67 NY3964
Westmarsh *Kent* 15 TR2761
Westmeston *E Susx* 12 TQ3313
Westmill *Herts* 31 TL3627
Westminster *Gt Lon* 23 TQ2979
Westmuir *Tays* 88 NO3652
Westnewton *Cumb* 67 NY1344
Westoe *T & W* 69 NZ3765
Weston *Avon* 20 ST7366
Weston *Berks* 21 SU3973
Weston *Ches* 47 SJ7352
Weston *Devon* 8 ST1400
Weston *Devon* 8 SY1688
Weston *Hants* 11 SU7221
Weston *Herts* 31 TL2530
Weston *Lincs* 41 TF2924
Weston *Nhants* 29 SP5846
Weston *Notts* 50 SK7767
Weston *Shrops* 37 SO6093
Weston *Shrops* 36 SJ2927
Weston *Shrops* 37 SJ5629
Weston *Staffs* 38 SJ9726
Weston *W York* 55 SE1747
Weston Beggard *H & W* 27 SO5841
Weston by Welland *Nhants* 40 SP7791
Weston Colley *Hants* 11 SU5039
Weston Colville *Cambs* 31 TL6153
Weston Corbett *Hants* 22 SU6846
Weston Coyney *Staffs* 48 SJ9343
Weston Favell *Nhants* 30 SP7962
Weston Green *Cambs* 32 TL6252
Weston Heath *Shrops* 37 SJ7713
Weston Jones *Staffs* 37 SJ7624
Weston Longville *Norfk* 43 TG1115
Weston Lullingfields *Shrops* 36 SJ4224
Weston Patrick *Hants* 22 SU6946
Weston Rhyn *Shrops* 36 SJ2835
Weston Subedge *Gloucs* 28 SP1241
Weston Turville *Bucks* 22 SP8510
Weston under Penyard *H & W* 27 SO6322
Weston under Wetherley *Warwks* 29 SP3669
Weston Underwood *Bucks* 30 SP8650
Weston Underwood *Derbys* 49 SK2942
Weston-in-Gordano *Avon* 19 ST4474
Weston-on-the-Green *Oxon* 29 SP5318
Weston-Super-Mare *Avon* 19 ST3260
Weston-under-Lizard *Staffs* 37 SJ8010
Weston-upon-Trent *Derbys* 39 SK4027
Westonbirt *Gloucs* 20 ST8589
Westoning *Beds* 30 TL0332
Westonzoyland *Somset* 8 ST3534
Westow *N York* 56 SE7565
Westport *Somset* 8 ST3820
Westquarter *Cent* 82 NS9178
Westridge Green *Berks* 21 SU5679
Westrigg *Loth* 74 NS9067
Westrop *Wilts* 21 SU2093
Westruther *Border* 76 NT6349
Westry *Cambs* 41 TL4098
Westward *Cumb* 67 NY2744
Westward Ho! *Devon* 6 SS4329
Westwell *Kent* 15 TQ9947
Westwell *Oxon* 29 SP2209
Westwell Leacon *Kent* 15 TQ9647
Westwick *Cambs* 31 TL4265
Westwood *Devon* 7 SY0199
Westwood *Kent* 15 TR3667
Westwood *Wilts* 20 ST8059
Westwoodside *Humb* 50 SE7400
Wetheral *Cumb* 67 NY4654
Wetherby *W York* 55 SE4048
Wetherden *Suffk* 32 TM0062
Wetheringsett *Suffk* 33 TM1266
Wethersfield *Essex* 24 TL7131
Wetherup Street *Suffk* 33 TM1464
Wetley Rocks *Staffs* 48 SJ9649
Wettenhall *Ches* 47 SJ6261
Wetton *Staffs* 48 SK1055
Wetwang *Humb* 56 SE9359
Wetwood *Staffs* 37 SJ7733
Wexcombe *Wilts* 21 SU2758
Weybourne *Norfk* 43 TG1142
Weybread *Suffk* 33 TM2480
Weybread Street *Suffk* 33 TM2479
Weybridge *Surrey* 22 TQ0764
Weycroft *Devon* 8 SY3099
Weydale *Highld* 100 ND1564
Weyhill *Hants* 21 SU3146
Weymouth *Dorset* 9 SY6779
Whaddon *Bucks* 30 SP8034
Whaddon *Cambs* 31 TL3546
Whaddon *Gloucs* 28 SO8313
Whaddon *Wilts* 20 ST8861
Whaddon *Wilts* 10 SU1926
Whaley *Derbys* 49 SK5171
Whaley Bridge *Derbys* 48 SK0180
Whaley Thorns *Derbys* 49 SK5271
Whaligoe *Highld* 100 ND3140
Whalley *Lancs* 54 SD7336
Whalton *Nthumb* 61 NZ1318
Whaplode *Lincs* 41 TF3224
Whaplode Drove *Lincs* 41 TF3213
Wharf *Warwks* 29 SP4352
Wharfe *N York* 54 SD7869
Wharles *Lancs* 53 SD4435
Wharncliffe Side *S York* 49 SK2994
Wharram-le-Street *N York* 56 SE8665
Wharton *H & W* 27 SO5055
Whashton *N York* 61 NZ1506
Whatcote *Warwks* 29 SP2944
Whateley *Warwks* 39 SP2299
Whatfield *Suffk* 32 TM0246
Whatley *Somset* 8 ST3607
Whatley *Somset* 20 ST7347
Whatlington *E Susx* 14 TQ7618
Whatsole Street *Kent* 15 TR1144
Whatstandwell *Derbys* 49 SK3354
Whatton *Notts* 40 SK7439
Whauphill *D & G* 64 NX4049
Wheatacre *Norfk* 43 TM4694
Wheathampstead *Herts* 31 TL1714
Wheathill *Shrops* 37 SO6282
Wheatley *Hants* 11 SU7840
Wheatley *Oxon* 29 SP5905
Wheatley Hill *Dur* 62 NZ3738
Wheatley Hills *S York* 56 SE5904
Wheaton Aston *Staffs* 38 SJ8512
Wheddon Cross *Somset* 7 SS9238
Wheelock *Ches* 47 SJ7559
Wheelton *Lancs* 54 SD6021
Wheldrake *N York* 56 SE6844
Whelford *Gloucs* 21 SU1699
Whelpley Hill *Bucks* 22 SP9904
Whempstead *Herts* 31 TL3221
Whenby *N York* 56 SE6369
Whepstead *Suffk* 32 TL8358
Wherstead *Suffk* 33 TM1540
Wherwell *Hants* 21 SU3841
Wheston *Derbys* 48 SK1376
Whetsted *Kent* 14 TQ6646
Whetstone *Leics* 39 SP5597
Whicham *Cumb* 58 SD1382
Whichford *Warwks* 29 SP3134
Whickham *T & W* 69 NZ2061
Whiddon Down *Devon* 5 SX6992
Whigstreet *Tays* 89 NO4844
Whilton *Nhants* 29 SP6364
Whimple *Devon* 7 SY0497
Whimpwell Green *Norfk* 43 TG3829
Whinburgh *Norfk* 42 TG0009
Whinnie Liggate *D & G* 65 NX7252
Whinnyfold *Gramp* 95 NK0733
Whippingham *IOW* 11 SZ5193
Whipsnade *Beds* 30 TL0117
Whipton *Devon* 5 SX9493
Whisby *Lincs* 50 SK9067
Whissendine *Leics* 40 SK8214
Whissonsett *Norfk* 42 TF9123
Whistlefield *Strath* 80 NS2393
Whistlefield Inn *Strath* 80 NS1492
Whistley Green *Berks* 22 SU7974
Whiston *Mersyd* 46 SJ4791
Whiston *Nhants* 30 SP8460
Whiston *S York* 49 SK4489
Whiston *Staffs* 38 SJ8914
Whiston *Staffs* 48 SK0347
Whitbeck *Cumb* 58 SD1184
Whitbourne *H & W* 28 SO7257
Whitburn *Loth* 75 NS9464
Whitburn *T & W* 69 NZ4062
Whitby *N York* 63 NZ8910
Whitchester *Border* 76 NT7159
Whitchurch *Avon* 19 ST6167
Whitchurch *Bucks* 30 SP8020
Whitchurch *Devon* 4 SX4972
Whitchurch *Dyfed* 16 SM8025
Whitchurch *H & W* 27 SO5517
Whitchurch *Hants* 21 SU4648
Whitchurch *Oxon* 21 SU6377
Whitchurch *S Glam* 19 ST1579
Whitchurch *Shrops* 37 SJ5341
Whitchurch Canonicorum *Dorset* 8 SY3995
Whitchurch Hill *Oxon* 21 SU6378
Whitcombe *Dorset* 9 SY7188
Whitcot *Shrops* 36 SO3791
Whitcott Keysett *Shrops* 36 SO2782
White Ball *Somset* 8 ST1019
White Chapel *Lancs* 53 SD5541
White Colne *Essex* 24 TL8729
White Cross *Cnwll* 2 SW6821
White End *H & W* 28 SO7834
White Lackington *Dorset* 8 SY7198
White Ladies Aston *H & W* 28 SO9252
White Notley *Essex* 24 TL7818
White Pit *Lincs* 51 TF3777
White Roding *Essex* 24 TL5613
White Stone *H & W* 27 SO5642
White Waltham *Berks* 22 SU8577
Whiteacre Heath *Warwks* 39 SP2292
Whitebridge *Highld* 92 NH4815
Whitebrook *Gwent* 27 SO5306
Whitecairns *Gramp* 95 NJ9238
Whitechapel *Gt Lon* 23 TQ3381
Whitecliffe *Gloucs* 27 SO5710
Whitecraig *Loth* 75 NT3470
Whitecrook *D & G* 64 NX1656
Whiteface *Highld* 97 NH7088
Whitefarland *Strath* 72 NR8642
Whitefaulds *Strath* 73 NS2909
Whitefield *Gt Man* 47 SD8006
Whitefield *Somset* 8 ST0729
Whiteford *Gramp* 95 NJ7126
Whitegate *Ches* 47 SJ6269
Whitehall *Ork* 103 HY6528
Whitehaven *Cumb* 58 NX9718
Whitehill *Hants* 11 SU7934
Whitehills *Gramp* 94 NJ6565
Whitehouse *Gramp* 94 NJ6114
Whitehouse *Strath* 71 NR8161
Whitekirk *Loth* 83 NT5981
Whitelackington *Somset* 8 ST3815
Whiteley Bank *IOW* 11 SZ5581
Whitemire *Gramp* 93 NH9854
Whitemoor *Cnwll* 3 SW9757
Whitemoor *Notts* 49 SK5441
Whiteness *Shet* 103 HU3844
Whiteparish *Wilts* 10 SU2423
Whiterashes *Gramp* 95 NJ8523
Whiterow *Gramp* 93 NJ0257
Whiterow *Highld* 100 NJ3648
Whiteshill *Gloucs* 28 SO8406
Whitesmith *E Susx* 13 TQ5213
Whitestaunton *Somset* 8 ST2810
Whitestone Cross *Devon* 5 SX8993
Whitewell *Lancs* 54 SD6646
Whitfield *Avon* 20 ST6791
Whitfield *Kent* 15 TR3045
Whitfield *Nhants* 29 SP6039
Whitfield *Nthumb* 68 NY7857
Whitford *Clwyd* 46 SJ1478
Whitford *Devon* 8 SY2595
Whitgift *Humb* 56 SE8122
Whitgreave *Staffs* 38 SJ9028
Whithorn *D & G* 64 NX4440
Whiting Bay *Strath* 72 NS0425
Whitington *Norfk* 42 TL7199
Whitkirk *W York* 55 SE3633
Whitland *Dyfed* 17 SN1916
Whitlaw *Border* 67 NT5012
Whitletts *Strath* 73 NS3623
Whitley *Berks* 22 SU7270
Whitley *N York* 56 SE5620
Whitley *S York* 49 SK3494
Whitley *Wilts* 20 ST8866
Whitley Bay *T & W* 69 NZ3571
Whitley Chapel *Nthumb* 68 NY9257
Whitley Lower *W York* 55 SE2217
Whitminster *Gloucs* 28 SO7908
Whitmore *Staffs* 37 SJ8140
Whitnage *Devon* 7 ST0215
Whitnash *Warwks* 29 SP3263
Whitney-on-Wye *H & W* 27 SO2747
Whitrigglees *Cumb* 67 NY2457
Whitsbury *Hants* 10 SU1219
Whitsome *Border* 77 NT8650
Whitson *Gwent* 19 ST3883
Whitstable *Kent* 15 TR1066
Whitstone *Cnwll* 6 SX2698
Whittingehame *Loth* 76 NT6073
Whittingham *Nthumb* 68 NU0611
Whittingslow *Shrops* 36 SO4388
Whittington *Derbys* 49 SK3875
Whittington *Gloucs* 28 SP0120
Whittington *H & W* 28 SO8753
Whittington *Lancs* 59 SD6075
Whittington *Shrops* 36 SJ3231
Whittington *Staffs* 38 SK1508
Whittington *Staffs* 38 SO8682
Whittington *Warwks* 39 SP2999
Whittle-le-Woods *Lancs* 54 SD5821
Whittlebury *Nhants* 30 SP6943
Whittlesey *Cambs* 41 TL2697
Whittlesford *Cambs* 31 TL4748
Whitton *Cleve* 62 NZ3822
Whitton *Humb* 56 SE9024
Whitton *Nthumb* 68 NU0501
Whitton *Powys* 36 SO2767
Whitton *Shrops* 37 SO5772
Whittonstall *Nthumb* 68 NZ0757
Whitway *Hants* 21 SU4559
Whitwell *Derbys* 49 SK5276
Whitwell *Herts* 31 TL1820
Whitwell *IOW* 11 SZ5277
Whitwell *Leics* 40 SK9208
Whitwell *N York* 61 SE2899
Whitwell Street *Norfk* 43 TG1022
Whitwell-on-the-Hill *N York* 56 SE7265
Whitwick *Leics* 39 SK4315
Whitworth *Lancs* 54 SD8818
Whixall *Shrops* 37 SJ5134
Whixley *N York* 55 SE4458
Whorlton *Dur* 61 NZ1014
Whorlton *N York* 62 NZ4802
Whyle *H & W* 27 SO5561
Whyteleafe *Surrey* 23 TQ3358
Wibdon *Gloucs* 19 ST5797
Wibsey *W York* 55 SE1430
Wibtoft *Warwks* 39 SP4887
Wichenford *H & W* 28 SO7860
Wichling *Kent* 14 TQ9256
Wick *Avon* 20 ST7072
Wick *Dorset* 10 SZ1591
Wick *H & W* 28 SO9645
Wick *Highld* 100 ND3650
Wick *M Glam* 18 SS9271
Wick *W Susx* 12 TQ0203
Wick St Lawrence *Avon* 19 ST3665
Wicken *Cambs* 31 TL5770
Wicken *Nhants* 30 SP7439
Wicken Bonhunt *Essex* 31 TL4933
Wickenby *Lincs* 50 TF0982
Wicker Street Green *Suffk* 32 TL9742
Wickersley *S York* 49 SK4791
Wickford *Essex* 24 TQ7493
Wickham *Berks* 21 SU3971
Wickham *Hants* 11 SU5711
Wickham Bishops *Essex* 24 TL8412
Wickham Green *Suffk* 33 TM0969
Wickham Market *Suffk* 33 TM3055
Wickham Skeith *Suffk* 33 TM0969
Wickham St Paul *Essex* 24 TL8336
Wickham Street *Suffk* 32 TM0869
Wickhambreaux *Kent* 15 TR2158
Wickhambrook *Suffk* 32 TL7554
Wickhamford *H & W* 28 SP0641
Wickhampton *Norfk* 43 TG4205
Wicklewood *Norfk* 42 TG0702
Wickmere *Norfk* 43 TG1733
Wickwar *Avon* 20 ST7288
Widdington *Essex* 31 TL5331
Widdrington *Nthumb* 69 NZ2595
Widdrington Station *T & W* 69 NZ2494
Widecombe in the Moor *Devon* 5 SX7176
Widegates *Cnwll* 4 SX2858
Widemouth Bay *Cnwll* 6 SS2002
Widford *Essex* 24 TL6904
Widford *Herts* 31 TL4216
Widmer End *Bucks* 22 SU8896
Widmerpool *Notts* 39 SK6327
Widmore *Gt Lon* 23 TQ4268
Widnes *Ches* 46 SJ5184
Widworthy *Devon* 8 SY2199
Wigan *Gt Man* 47 SD5805
Wigborough *Somset* 8 ST4415
Wiggaton *Devon* 8 SY1093
Wiggenhall St Germans *Norfk* 41 TF5914
Wiggenhall St Mary Magdalen *Norfk* 41 TF5911
Wiggenhall St Mary the Virgin *Norfk* 41 TF5813
Wiggens Green *Essex* 32 TL6642
Wigginton *Herts* 22 SP9310
Wigginton *N York* 56 SE6058
Wigginton *Oxon* 29 SP3833
Wigginton *Staffs* 39 SK2006
Wigglesworth *N York* 54 SD8156
Wiggold *Gloucs* 28 SP0404
Wiggonby *Cumb* 67 NY2952
Wighill *N York* 55 SE4746
Wighton *Norfk* 42 TF9439
Wigley *Hants* 10 SU3217
Wigmore *H & W* 27 SO4169
Wigmore *Kent* 14 TQ7964
Wigsley *Notts* 50 SK8570
Wigsthorpe *Nhants* 40 TL0482
Wigston *Leics* 39 SP6198
Wigston Parva *Leics* 39 SP4689
Wigthorpe *Notts* 49 SK5983
Wigtoft *Lincs* 41 TF2636
Wigton *Cumb* 67 NY2548
Wigtown *D & G* 64 NX4355
Wike *W York* 55 SE3342
Wilbarston *Nhants* 40 SP8188
Wilberfoss *Humb* 56 SE7350
Wilburton *Cambs* 31 TL4775
Wilby *Nhants* 30 SP8666
Wilby *Norfk* 32 TM0389
Wilby *Suffk* 33 TM2472
Wilcot *Wilts* 20 SU1360
Wildboarclough *Ches* 48 SJ9868
Wilden *Beds* 30 TL0955
Wilden *H & W* 38 SO8272
Wildmanbridge *Strath* 74 NS8253
Wildmoor *H & W* 38 SO9575
Wildsworth *Lincs* 50 SK8097
Wilkesley *Ches* 37 SJ6241
Wilkhaven *Highld* 97 NH9486
Wilkieston *Fife* 75 NT1268
Willand *Devon* 7 ST0310
Willaston *Ches* 46 SJ3377
Willaston *Ches* 47 SJ6852
Willcott *Shrops* 36 SJ3718
Willen *Bucks* 30 SP8740
Willenhall *W Mids* 38 SO9798
Willenhall *W Mids* 39 SP3676
Willerby *Humb* 56 TA0230
Willerby *N York* 63 TA0079
Willersey *Gloucs* 28 SP1039
Willersley *H & W* 27 SO3147
Willesborough *Kent* 15 TR0441
Willesborough Lees *Kent* 15 TR0342
Willesden *Gt Lon* 23 TQ2284
Willesley *Wilts* 20 ST8588
Willett *Somset* 8 ST1033
Willey *Shrops* 37 SO6799
Willey *Warwks* 39 SP4984
Willey Green *Surrey* 12 SU9351
Williamscot *Oxon* 29 SP4845
Willian *Herts* 31 TL2230
Willingale *Essex* 24 TL5907
Willingdon *E Susx* 13 TQ5902
Willingham *Cambs* 31 TL4070
Willingham *Lincs* 50 SK8784
Willingham Green *Cambs* 32 TL6254
Willington *Beds* 30 TL1150
Willington *Derbys* 39 SK2928

Place	Page	Grid Ref
Willington Dur	61	NZ1935
Willington Kent	14	TQ7853
Willington Warwks	29	SP2639
Willington Quay T & W	69	NZ3267
Willitoft Humb	56	SE7434
Williton Somset	18	ST0840
Willoughby Lincs	51	TF4771
Willoughby Warwks	29	SP5167
Willoughby Waterleys Leics	39	SP5792
Willoughby-on-the-Wolds Notts	39	SK6325
Willoughton Lincs	50	SK9293
Willows Green Essex	24	TL7219
Willtown Somset	8	ST3924
Wilmcote Warwks	28	SP1658
Wilmington Devon	8	SY2199
Wilmington E Susx	13	TQ5404
Wilmington Kent	23	TQ5372
Wilmslow Ches	47	SJ8481
Wilpshire Lancs	54	SD6832
Wilsden W York	55	SE0936
Wilsford Lincs	50	TF0042
Wilsford Wilts	20	SU1057
Wilsford Wilts	10	SU1339
Wilshaw W York	55	SE1109
Wilsill N York	55	SE1864
Wilson Leics	39	SK4024
Wilsontown Strath	75	NS9455
Wilstead Beds	30	TL0643
Wilsthorpe Lincs	40	TF0913
Wilstone Herts	30	SP9014
Wilton Cleve	62	NZ5819
Wilton H & W	27	SO5824
Wilton N York	63	SE8582
Wilton Wilts	10	SU0931
Wilton Wilts	21	SU2661
Wilton Dean Border	67	NT4914
Wimbish Essex	24	TL5936
Wimbish Green Essex	24	TL6035
Wimbledon Gt Lon	23	TQ2370
Wimblington Cambs	41	TL4192
Wimborne Minster Dorset	10	SZ0199
Wimborne St Giles Dorset	10	SU0311
Wimbotsham Norfk	41	TF6205
Wimpstone Warwks	29	SP2148
Wincanton Somset	9	ST7128
Winchburgh Loth	75	NT0975
Winchcombe Gloucs	28	SP0228
Winchelsea E Susx	14	TQ9017
Winchester Hants	11	SU4829
Winchet Hill Kent	14	TQ7340
Winchfield Hants	22	SU7654
Winchmore Hill Bucks	22	SU9395
Winchmore Hill Gt Lon	23	TQ3194
Wincle Ches	48	SJ9566
Wincobank S York	49	SK3891
Windermere Cumb	59	SD4098
Winderton Warwks	29	SP3240
Windhill Highld	92	NH5348
Windlesham Surrey	22	SU9364
Windmill Cnwll	3	SW8974
Windmill Hill E Susx	13	TQ6412
Windmill Hill Somset	8	ST3116
Windrush Gloucs	29	SP1513
Windsole Gramp	94	NJ5560
Windsor Berks	22	SU9576
Windsor Green Suffk	32	TL8954
Windsoredge Gloucs	28	SO8400
Windy Arbour Warwks	39	SP2971
Windygates Fife	83	NO3400
Wineham W Susx	12	TQ2320
Winestead Humb	57	TA2924
Winfarthing Norfk	33	TM1085
Winford Avon	19	ST5464
Winford IOW	11	SZ5584
Winforton H & W	27	SO2946
Winfrith Newburgh Dorset	9	SY8084
Wing Bucks	30	SP8822
Wing Leics	40	SK8903
Wingate Dur	62	NZ4036
Wingerworth Derbys	49	SK3867
Wingfield Beds	30	TL0026
Wingfield Suffk	33	TM2277
Wingfield Wilts	20	ST8256
Wingham Kent	15	TR2457
Wingmore Kent	15	TR1946
Wingrave Bucks	30	SP8719
Winkburn Notts	49	SK7058
Winkfield Berks	22	SU9072
Winkfield Row Berks	22	SU8971
Winkhill Staffs	48	SK0651
Winkleigh Devon	7	SS6308
Winksley N York	55	SE2571
Winlaton T & W	69	NZ1762
Winless Highld	100	ND3054
Winmarleigh Lancs	53	SD4647
Winnall Hants	11	SU4829
Winnersh Berks	22	SU7870
Winnington Ches	47	SJ6474
Winscombe Avon	19	ST4257
Winsford Ches	47	SJ6566
Winsford Somset	7	SS9034
Winsham Devon	6	SS5038
Winsham Somset	8	ST3706
Winshill Staffs	38	SK2623
Winshwen W Glam	18	SS6896
Winskill Cumb	59	NY5834
Winsley Wilts	20	ST7960
Winslow Bucks	30	SP7727
Winson Gloucs	28	SP0808
Winsor Hants	10	SU3114
Winster Cumb	59	SD4193
Winster Derbys	48	SK2460
Winston Dur	61	NZ1416
Winston Suffk	33	TM1861
Winstone Gloucs	28	SO9509
Winswell Devon	6	SS4913
Winterborne Came Dorset	9	SY7088
Winterborne Clenston Dorset	9	ST8303
Winterborne Herringston Dorset	9	SY6888
Winterborne Houghton Dorset	9	ST8204
Winterborne Kingston Dorset	9	SY8697
Winterborne Monkton Dorset	9	SY6787
Winterborne Stickland Dorset	9	ST8304
Winterborne Whitechurch Dorset	9	ST8300
Winterborne Zelston Dorset	9	SY8997
Winterbourne Avon	19	ST6480
Winterbourne Berks	21	SU4572
Winterbourne Abbas Dorset	9	SY6190
Winterbourne Bassett Wilts	20	SU0974
Winterbourne Dauntsey Wilts	10	SU1734
Winterbourne Earls Wilts	10	SU1734
Winterbourne Gunner Wilts	10	SU1735
Winterbourne Monkton Wilts	20	SU0971
Winterbourne Steepleton Dorset	9	SY6289
Winterbourne Stoke Wilts	20	SU0741
Winterburn N York	54	SD9358
Winteringham Humb	56	SE9221
Winterley Ches	47	SJ7457
Winterslow Wilts	10	SU2332
Winterton Humb	56	SE9218
Winterton-on-Sea Norfk	43	TG4919
Winthorpe Notts	50	SK8156
Winton Cumb	60	NY7810
Winton Dorset	10	SZ0893
Wintringham N York	63	SE8873
Winwick Cambs	40	TL1080
Winwick Ches	47	SJ6092
Winwick Nhants	39	SP6273
Wirksworth Derbys	49	SK2854
Wirswall Ches	47	SJ5444
Wisbech Cambs	41	TF4609
Wisbech St Mary Cambs	41	TF4208
Wisborough Green W Susx	12	TQ0525
Wiseman's Bridge Dyfed	16	SN1406
Wiseton Notts	49	SK7189
Wishaw Strath	74	NS7955
Wishaw Warwks	38	SP1794
Wisley Surrey	22	TQ0659
Wispington Lincs	51	TF2071
Wissett Suffk	33	TM3679
Wissington Suffk	25	TL9533
Wistanstow Shrops	36	SO4385
Wistanswick Shrops	37	SJ6629
Wistaston Ches	47	SJ6853
Wiston Dyfed	16	SN0218
Wiston Strath	75	NS9532
Wiston W Susx	12	TQ1512
Wistow Cambs	41	TL2780
Wistow N York	56	SE5935
Wiswell Lancs	54	SD7437
Witcham Cambs	41	TL4680
Witchampton Dorset	9	ST9806
Witchford Cambs	31	TL5078
Witcombe Somset	8	ST4721
Witham Essex	24	TL8214
Witham Friary Somset	20	ST7441
Witham on the Hill Lincs	40	TF0516
Withcall Lincs	51	TF2883
Withdean E Susx	12	TQ3007
Witherenden Hill E Susx	13	TQ6426
Witheridge Devon	7	SS8014
Witherley Leics	39	SP3297
Withern Lincs	51	TF4282
Withernsea Humb	57	TA3427
Withernwick Humb	57	TA1940
Withersdale Street Suffk	33	TM2680
Withersfield Essex	32	TL6548
Witherslack Cumb	59	SD4384
Witherslack Hall Cumb	59	SD4385
Withiel Cnwll	3	SW9965
Withiel Florey Somset	7	SS9833
Withington Ches	47	SJ8169
Withington Gloucs	28	SP0215
Withington Gt Man	47	SJ8492
Withington H & W	27	SO5643
Withington Shrops	37	SJ5713
Withington Staffs	38	SK0335
Withleigh Devon	7	SS9012
Withybed Green H & W	38	SP0172
Withybrook Warwks	39	SP4383
Withycombe Somset	7	ST0141
Withyham E Susx	13	TQ4935
Withypool Devon	7	SS8435
Withywood Avon	19	ST5667
Witley Surrey	12	SU9439
Witnesham Suffk	33	TM1751
Witney Oxon	29	SP3510
Wittering Cambs	40	TF0502
Wittersham Kent	14	TQ9027
Witton Norfk	43	TG3109
Witton Norfk	43	TG3331
Witton W Mids	38	SP0790
Witton Gilbert Dur	69	NZ2345
Witton le Wear Dur	61	NZ1431
Witton Park Dur	61	NZ1730
Wiveliscombe Somset	8	ST0827
Wivelrod Hants	11	SU6738
Wivelsfield E Susx	12	TQ3420
Wivelsfield Green E Susx	12	TQ3519
Wivenhoe Essex	25	TM0321
Wiveton Norfk	42	TG0442
Wix Essex	25	TM1628
Wixford Warwks	28	SP0854
Wixhill Shrops	37	SJ5528
Wixoe Essex	32	TL7143
Woburn Beds	30	SP9433
Woburn Sands Bucks	30	SP9235
Woking Surrey	22	TQ0058
Wokingham Berks	22	SU8168
Wold Newton Humb	63	TA0473
Wold Newton Humb	51	TF2496
Woldingham Surrey	23	TQ3755
Wolf Hills Nthumb	68	NY7258
Wolf's Castle Dyfed	16	SM9526
Wolfclyde Strath	75	NT0236
Wolferton Norfk	42	TF6528
Wolfhill Tays	82	NO1533
Wolfsdale Dyfed	16	SM9321
Wollaston Nhants	30	SP9062
Wollaston Shrops	36	SJ3212
Wollaton Notts	49	SK5239
Wollerton Shrops	37	SJ6130
Wollescote W Mids	38	SO9283
Wolseley Bridge Staffs	38	SK0220
Wolsingham Dur	61	NZ0737
Wolstanton Staffs	47	SJ8548
Wolston Warwks	39	SP4175
Wolvercote Oxon	29	SP4910
Wolverhampton W Mids	38	SO9198
Wolverley H & W	38	SO8379
Wolverton Bucks	30	SP8141
Wolverton Hants	21	SU5558
Wolverton Wilts	29	SP2062
Wolverton Wilts	9	ST7831
Wolvesnewton Gwent	19	ST4599
Wolvey Warwks	39	SP4387
Wolvey Heath Warwks	39	SP4388
Wolviston Cleve	62	NZ4525
Wombleton N York	62	SE6683
Wombourne Staffs	38	SO8793
Wombwell S York	49	SE4002
Womenswold Kent	15	TR2250
Womersley N York	56	SE5319
Wonersh Surrey	12	TQ0145
Wonford Devon	5	SX9491
Wonston Hants	11	SU4739
Wooburn Bucks	22	SU9087
Woobum Green Bucks	22	SU9188
Wood Bevington Warwks	28	SP0554
Wood Dalling Norfk	42	TG0827
Wood End Gt Lon	22	TQ1081
Wood End Herts	31	TL3225
Wood End Warwks	38	SP1171
Wood Enderby Lincs	51	TF2764
Wood Green Gt Lon	23	TQ3090
Wood Hayes W Mids	38	SJ9402
Wood Norton Norfk	42	TG0127
Wood Street Norfk	43	TG3722
Wood Street Surrey	12	SU9550
Wood Walton Cambs	41	TL2180
Wood's Corner E Susx	14	TQ6619
Wood's Green E Susx	13	TQ6333
Woodall S York	49	SK4880
Woodbastwick Norfk	43	TG3315
Woodborough Notts	49	SK6347
Woodborough Wilts	20	SU1159
Woodbridge Devon	8	SY1895
Woodbridge Suffk	33	TM2649
Woodbury Devon	5	SY0087
Woodbury Salterton Devon	5	SY0189
Woodchester Gloucs	20	SO8302
Woodchurch Kent	14	TQ9434
Woodcombe Somset	7	SS9546
Woodcote Gt Lon	23	TQ2962
Woodcote Oxon	21	SU6482
Woodcote Shrops	37	SJ7615
Woodcroft Gloucs	19	ST5495
Woodditton Cambs	32	TL6559
Woodeaton Oxon	29	SP5312
Woodend Highld	79	NM7861
Woodend Loth	75	NS9269
Woodend Nhants	29	SP6149
Woodend W Susx	11	SU8108
Woodend Green Essex	24	TL5528
Woodford Gloucs	20	ST6995
Woodford Gt Lon	23	TQ4191
Woodford Gt Man	47	SJ8882
Woodford Nhants	30	SP9676
Woodford Bridge Gt Lon	23	TQ4291
Woodford Halse Nhants	29	SP5452
Woodford Wells Gt Lon	23	TQ4093
Woodgate H & W	28	SO9666
Woodgate W Mids	38	SO9982
Woodgate W Susx	12	SU9304
Woodgreen Hants	10	SU1717
Woodhall N York	61	SD9790
Woodhall Spa Lincs	50	TF1963
Woodham Bucks	30	SP7018
Woodham Ferrers Essex	24	TQ7999
Woodham Mortimer Essex	24	TL8104
Woodham Walter Essex	24	TL8007
Woodhaven Fife	83	NO4126
Woodhead Gramp	95	NJ7838
Woodhill Somset	8	ST3527
Woodhorn Nthumb	69	NZ2988
Woodhouse Leics	39	SK5314
Woodhouse S York	49	SK4284
Woodhouse W York	55	SE2935
Woodhouse W York	55	SE3821
Woodhouse Eaves Leics	39	SK5214
Woodhouselee Loth	75	NT2364
Woodhouselees D & G	67	NY3975
Woodhouses Staffs	38	SK1518
Woodhurst Cambs	31	TL3176
Woodingdean E Susx	12	TQ3505
Woodkirk W York	55	SE2725
Woodland Devon	5	SX7968
Woodland Devon	5	SX6256
Woodland Dur	61	NZ0726
Woodland Gramp	95	NJ8723
Woodland Kent	15	TR1441
Woodland Strath	64	NX1795
Woodlands Dorset	10	SU0509
Woodlands Gramp	89	NO7895
Woodlands Hants	10	SU3211
Woodlands N York	55	SE3254
Woodlands S York	56	SE5308
Woodlands Somset	19	ST1640
Woodlands Park Berks	22	SU8678
Woodlands St Mary Berks	21	SU3375
Woodleigh Devon	5	SX7349
Woodley Berks	22	SU7773
Woodmancote Gloucs	28	SO9727
Woodmancote Gloucs	28	SP0008
Woodmancote Gloucs	20	ST7597
Woodmancote W Susx	11	SU7707
Woodmancote W Susx	12	TQ2314
Woodmancott Hants	21	SU5642
Woodmansey Humb	57	TA0538
Woodmansgreen W Susx	11	SU8627
Woodmansterne Surrey	23	TQ2759
Woodmanton Devon	5	SY0186
Woodnesborough Kent	15	TR3157
Woodnewton Nhants	40	TL0394
Woodplumpton Lancs	53	SD4934
Woodrising Norfk	42	TF9803
Woodrow H & W	38	SO8974
Woodseaves Staffs	37	SJ7925
Woodsetts S York	49	SK5483
Woodsford Dorset	9	SY7590
Woodside Berks	22	SU9371
Woodside Fife	83	NO4207
Woodside Gt Lon	23	TQ3467
Woodside Tays	82	NO2037
Woodstock Oxon	29	SP4416
Woodston Cambs	40	TL1897
Woodton Norfk	43	TM2994
Woodtown Devon	6	SS4123
Woofferton Shrops	37	SO5268
Wookey Somset	19	ST5145
Wookey Hole Somset	19	ST5347
Wool Dorset	9	SY8486
Woolacombe Devon	6	SS4643
Woolage Green Kent	15	TR2349
Woolaston Gloucs	19	ST5899
Woolaston Common Gloucs	19	SO5801
Woolavington Somset	19	ST3441
Woolbeding W Susx	11	SU8722
Woolbrook Devon	8	SY1289
Woolcotts Somset	7	SS9631
Wooler Nthumb	77	NT9927
Woolfardisworthy Devon	6	SS3321
Woolfardisworthy Devon	6	SS8208
Woolfords Strath	75	NT0056
Woolhampton Berks	21	SU5766
Woolhope H & W	27	SO6135
Woolland Dorset	9	ST7468
Woolley Avon	20	ST7468
Woolley Cambs	30	TL1574
Woolley W York	55	SE3212
Woolmer Green Herts	31	TL2518
Woolmere Green H & W	28	SO9663
Woolminstone Somset	8	ST4108
Woolpit Suffk	32	TL9762
Woolstaston Shrops	36	SO4598
Woolsthorpe Lincs	40	SK8333
Woolsthorpe Lincs	40	SK9224
Woolston Ches	47	SJ6489
Woolston Hants	10	SU4310
Woolston Shrops	36	SJ3224
Woolston Shrops	36	SO4287
Woolston Somset	18	ST0939
Woolston Somset	9	ST6527
Woolston Green Devon	5	SX7766
Woolstone Bucks	30	SP8738
Woolstone Gloucs	28	SO9630
Woolstone Oxon	21	SU2987
Woolton Mersyd	46	SJ4286
Woolton Hill Hants	21	SU4361
Woolverstone Suffk	25	TM1738
Woolverton Somset	20	ST7953
Woolwich Gt Lon	23	TQ4478
Woonton H & W	27	SO3552
Woore Shrops	37	SJ7342
Wootten Green Suffk	33	TM2372
Wootton Beds	30	TL0044
Wootton H & W	27	SO3252
Wootton Humb	57	TA0815
Wootton Kent	15	TR2246
Wootton Nhants	30	SP7656
Wootton Oxon	29	SP4419
Wootton Staffs	48	SK1044
Wootton Bassett Wilts	20	SU0682
Wootton Bridge IOW	11	SZ5492
Wootton Courtenay Somset	7	SS9343
Wootton Fitzpaine Dorset	8	SY3695
Wootton Rivers Wilts	21	SU1762
Wootton St Lawrence Hants	21	SU5953
Wootton Wawen Warwks	28	SP1563
Worcester H & W	28	SO8554
Worcester Park Gt Lon	23	TQ2165
Wordsley W Mids	38	SO8987
Worfield Shrops	37	SO7595
Workington Cumb	58	NY0028
Worksop Notts	49	SK5879
Worlaby Humb	56	TA0113
World's End Berks	21	SU4877
Worlds End Hants	11	SU6311
Worlds End W Susx	12	TQ3220
Worle Avon	19	ST3562
Worleston Ches	47	SJ6556
Worlingham Suffk	33	TM4489
Worlington Devon	7	SS7713
Worlington Suffk	32	TL6973
Worlingworth Suffk	33	TM2368
Wormald Green N York	55	SE3065
Wormbridge H & W	27	SO4230
Wormegay Norfk	42	TF6611
Wormelow Tump H & W	27	SO4930
Wormhill Derbys	48	SK1274
Wormingford Essex	25	TL9332
Worminghall Bucks	29	SP6308
Wormington Gloucs	28	SP0336
Wormiston Border	75	NT2345
Wormit Tays	83	NO4520
Wormleighton Warwks	29	SP4553
Wormley Herts	23	TL3605
Wormley Surrey	12	SU9438
Wormshill Kent	14	TQ8857
Wormsley H & W	27	SO4247
Worplesdon Surrey	12	SU9753
Worrall S York	49	SK3092
Worsbrough S York	49	SE3602
Worsbrough Bridge S York	55	SE3503
Worsbrough Dale S York	55	SE3604
Worsley Gt Man	47	SD7500
Worstead Norfk	43	TG3025
Worsthorne Lancs	54	SD8732
Worston Devon	5	SX5953
Worston Lancs	54	SD7742
Worth Kent	15	TR3355
Worth W Susx	12	TQ3036
Worth Abbey Surrey	12	TQ3134
Worth Matravers Dorset	9	SY9777
Wortham Suffk	32	TM0877
Worthen Shrops	36	SJ3204
Worthenbury Clwyd	46	SJ4146
Worthing Norfk	42	TF9919
Worthing W Susx	12	TQ1403
Worthington Leics	39	SK4020
Wortley S York	49	SK3099
Wortley W York	55	SE2732
Worton N York	61	SD9589
Worton Wilts	20	ST9757
Wortwell Norfk	33	TM2784
Wotton Surrey	12	TQ1247
Wotton Underwood Bucks	30	SP6815
Wotton-under-Edge Gloucs	20	ST7593
Woughton on the Green Bucks	30	SP8737
Wouldham Kent	14	TQ7164
Woundale Shrops	37	SO7793
Wrabness Essex	25	TM1731
Wrafton Devon	6	SS4935
Wragby Lincs	51	TF1378
Wragby W York	55	SE4116
Wrangaton Devon	5	SX6758
Wrangle Lincs	51	TF4250
Wrangway Somset	8	ST1218
Wrantage Somset	8	ST3022
Wrawby Humb	56	TA0108
Wraxall Avon	19	ST4971
Wraxall Somset	19	ST6036
Wray Lancs	54	SD6067
Wraysbury Berks	22	TQ0074
Wrayton Lancs	54	SD6172
Wrea Green Lancs	53	SD3931
Wreay Cumb	67	NY4348
Wrecclesham Surrey	22	SU8244
Wrekenton T & W	69	NZ2759
Wrelton N York	63	SE7686
Wrenbury Ches	47	SJ5947
Wreningham Norfk	43	TM1698
Wrentham Suffk	33	TM4982
Wrentnall Shrops	36	SJ4203
Wressle Humb	56	SE7131
Wressle Humb	56	SE9709
Wrestlingworth Beds	31	TL2547
Wretton Norfk	42	TF6900
Wrexham Clwyd	46	SJ3350
Wribbenhall H & W	37	SO7975
Wrinehill Staffs	47	SJ7547
Wrington Avon	19	ST4762
Writhlington Somset	20	ST6954
Wrockwardine Shrops	37	SJ6212
Wroot Humb	56	SE7103
Wrose W York	55	SE1636
Wrotham Kent	14	TQ6158
Wroughton Wilts	20	SU1480
Wroxall IOW	11	SZ5579
Wroxall Warwks	39	SP2271
Wroxeter Shrops	37	SJ5608
Wroxham Norfk	43	TG3017
Wroxton Oxon	29	SP4141
Wyaston Derbys	48	SK1842

Wyberton Lincs	51	TF3240
Wyboston Beds	31	TL1656
Wybunbury Ches	47	SJ6949
Wychbold H & W	28	SO9266
Wychnor Staffs	38	SK1715
Wyck Hants	11	SU7539
Wyck Rissington Gloucs	29	SP1821
Wycliffe Dur	61	NZ1114
Wycoller Lancs	54	SD9339
Wycomb Leics	40	SK7724
Wycombe Marsh Bucks	22	SU8892
Wyddial Herts	31	TL3731
Wye Kent	15	TR0546
Wyke Dorset	9	ST7926
Wyke W York	55	SE1526
Wyke Champflower Somset	9	ST6634
Wyke Regis Dorset	9	SY6677
Wykeham N York	63	SE9683
Wyken Shrops	37	SO7695
Wyken W Mids	39	SP3780
Wykey Shrops	36	SJ3824
Wylam Nthumb	69	NZ1164
Wylde Green W Mids	38	SP1294
Wylye Wilts	10	SU0037
Wymeswold Leics	39	SK6023
Wymington Beds	30	SP9564
Wymondham Leics	40	SK8418
Wymondham Norfk	43	TG1001
Wynford Eagle Dorset	9	SY5896
Wyre Piddle H & W	28	SO9647
Wysall Notts	39	SK6027
Wythall H & W	38	SP0774
Wytham Oxon	29	SP4708
Wythenshawe Gt Man	47	SJ8386
Wyton Cambs	31	TL2772
Wyton Humb	57	TA1733
Wyverstone Suffk	32	TM0468
Wyverstone Street Suffk	32	TM0367

Y

Y Felinheli Gwynd	44	SH5267
Y Ferwig Dyfed	17	SN1849

Y Ffor Gwynd	44	SH3939
Y Gyffylliog Clwyd	45	SJ0557
Y Maerdy Clwyd	45	SJ0144
Y Rhiw Gwynd	44	SH2227
Yaddlethorpe Humb	56	SE8806
Yafforth N York	62	SE3494
Yalberton Devon	5	SX8658
Yalding Kent	14	TQ6950
Yanwath Cumb	59	NY5127
Yanworth Gloucs	28	SP0713
Yapham Humb	56	SE7851
Yapton W Susx	12	SU9703
Yarborough Avon	19	ST3857
Yarburgh Lincs	51	TF3592
Yarcombe Devon	8	ST2408
Yard Devon	7	SS7721
Yardley W Mids	38	SP1386
Yardley Gobion Nhants	30	SP7644
Yardley Hastings Nhants	30	SP8657
Yardley Wood W Mids	38	SP1079
Yarkhill H & W	27	SO6042
Yarley Somset	19	ST5044
Yarlington Somset	9	ST6529
Yarm Cleve	62	NZ4112
Yarmouth IOW	10	SZ3589
Yarnbrook Wilts	20	ST8654
Yarnfield Staffs	38	SJ8632
Yarnscombe Devon	6	SS5623
Yarnton Oxon	29	SP4711
Yarpole H & W	27	SO4764
Yarrow Border	75	NT3528
Yarrow Feus Border	75	NT3325
Yarrowford Border	76	NT4030
Yarwell Nhants	40	TL0697
Yate Avon	20	ST7081
Yateley Hants	22	SU8161
Yatesbury Wilts	20	SU0671
Yattendon Berks	21	SU5574
Yatton Avon	19	ST4365
Yatton H & W	27	SO4366
Yatton H & W	27	SO6330
Yatton Keynell Wilts	20	ST8676
Yaverland IOW	11	SZ6185
Yaxham Norfk	42	TG0010
Yaxley Cambs	40	TL1891
Yaxley Suffk	33	TM1273
Yazor H & W	27	SO4046

Yeading Gt Lon	22	TQ1182
Yeadon W York	55	SE2041
Yealand Conyers Lancs	59	SD5074
Yealand Redmayne Lancs	59	SD4975
Yealmpton Devon	5	SX5851
Yearsley N York	62	SE5874
Yeaton Shrops	36	SJ4319
Yeaveley Derbys	48	SK1840
Yeavering Nthumb	77	NT9330
Yedingham N York	63	SE8979
Yelford Oxon	29	SP3604
Yelling Cambs	31	TL2662
Yelvertoft Nhants	39	SP5975
Yelverton Devon	4	SX5267
Yelverton Norfk	43	TG2902
Yenston Somset	9	ST7121
Yeoford Devon	7	SX7899
Yeolmbridge Cnwll	4	SX3187
Yeovil Somset	9	ST5515
Yeovil Marsh Somset	8	ST5418
Yeovilton Somset	8	ST5423
Yesnaby Ork	103	HY2215
Yetminster Dorset	9	ST5910
Yettington Devon	8	SY0585
Yetts o'Muckhart Cent	82	NO0001
Yielden Beds	30	TL0167
Yieldshields Strath	74	NS8750
Yiewsley Gt Lon	22	TQ0680
Ynysboeth M Glam	18	ST0695
Ynysddu Gwent	19	ST1792
Ynyshir M Glam	18	ST0292
Ynystawe W Glam	18	SN6800
Ynysybwl M Glam	18	ST0594
Yockleton Shrops	36	SJ3910
Yokefleet Humb	56	SE8124
Yoker Strath	74	NS5069
Yonder Bognie Gramp	94	NJ6046
York N York	56	SE6051
York Town Hants	22	SU8660
Yorkletts Kent	15	TR0963
Yorkley Gloucs	27	SO6307
Youlgreave Derbys	48	SK2064
Youlthorpe Humb	56	SE7655
Youlton N York	55	SE4963
Young's End Essex	24	TL7319
Yoxall Staffs	38	SK1418
Yoxford Suffk	33	TM3969

Ysbyty Ifan Gwynd	45	SH8448
Ysbyty Ystwyth Dyfed	35	SN7371
Ysceifiog Clwyd	46	SJ1571
Ystalyfera W Glam	26	SN7608
Ystrad M Glam	18	SS9895
Ystrad Aeron Dyfed	34	SN5256
Ystrad Meurig Dyfed	35	SN7067
Ystrad Mynach M Glam	18	ST1494
Ystradfellte Powys	26	SN9313
Ystradgynlais Powys	26	SN7910
Ystradowen S Glam	18	ST0077
Ythanbank Gramp	95	NJ9033
Ythanwells Gramp	94	NJ6338
Ythsie Gramp	95	NJ8830

Z

Zeal Monachorum Devon	7	SS7204
Zeals Wilts	9	ST7831
Zelah Cnwll	2	SW8151
Zennor Cnwll	2	SW4538
Zouch Notts	39	SK5023